Macroeconomics

Macroeconomics

FOURTH EDITION

Manfred Gärtner
University of St Gallen, Switzerland

PEARSON

Harlow, England • London • New York • Boston • San Francisco • Toronto • Sydney
Auckland • Singapore • Hong Kong • Tokyo • Seoul • Taipei • New Delhi
Cape Town • São Paulo • Mexico City • Madrid • Amsterdam • Munich • Paris • Milan

PEARSON EDUCATION LIMITED

Edinburgh Gate
Harlow CM20 2JE
United Kingdom
Tel: +44(0)1279 623623
Web: www.pearson.com/uk

First published as A Primer in European Macroeconomics 1997 (print)
Revised edition published as Macroeconomics 2003
Second edition Macroeconomics published 2006
Third edition Macroeconomics published 2009
Fourth edition published 2013 (print and electronic)

ISBN: 978-0-273-76995-8 (print)
       978-0-273-77004-6 (PDF)
       978-0-273-78083-0 (eText)

British Library Cataloguing-in-Publication Data
A catalogue record for the print edition is available from the British Library

Library of Congress Cataloging-in-Publication Data
Gärtner, Manfred.
  Macroeconomics / Manfred Gärtner, University of St. Gallen, Switzerland. —Fourth edition.
    pages cm
  ISBN 978-0-273-76995-8
  1. Macroeconomics. I. Title.
  HB172.5.G365 2013
  339—dc23

10 9 8 7 6 5 4 3 2 1
17 16 15 14 13

Cover: © Getty Images

Print edition typeset in Sabon LT Std 10/12 by 73
Print edition printed and bound in Great Britain by Ashford Colour Press Ltd, Gosport, Hampshire

NOTE THAT ANY PAGE CROSS–REFERENCES REFER TO THE PRINT EDITION

This edition is for

Juliana

the most amazing little girl I know

What are you doing step-bro ?!

BRIEF CONTENTS

CONTENTS

Companion Website

For open-access **student resources** specifically written
to complement this textbook and support your learning,
please visit **www.pearsoned.co.uk/gartner**

Lecturer Resources

For password-protected online resources tailored to support
the use of this textbook in teaching, please visit
www.pearsoned.co.uk/gartner

What to expect
Bullet points at the start of each chapter show what the reader can expect to learn, and highlight the core coverage.

> **What to expect**
>
> After working through this chapter, you will understand:
>
> 1 In more detail the meaning of potential income or output.
> 2 How wages and employment are determined in the labour market.
> 3 How regulations, trade unions, and other labour market characteristics, or demographic features, may give rise to involuntary unemployment which persists in the long run.
> 4 Why aggregate output produced by firms may temporarily exceed or fall short of the level of potential output produced in equilibrium (or the long run).
> 5 How unemployment may be decomposed into a temporary and a persistent component by means of the Beveridge curve.

Margin notes
Helpful tips and guidance appear in the margins, giving maths reminders, examples, rules, empirical notes and reality checks.

Key terms
Key terms and concepts in each chapter are highlighted in colour, with definitions in the margin.

> The aggregate supply curve shows the total quantity of goods and services supplied by all firms in the economy at different price levels.
>
> The extreme Keynesian aggregate supply curve is horizontal, stating that, at the current price, firms are ready to produce any output that is demanded. A refined Keynesian aggregate supply curve will be introduced later.

level of output was when we discussed money in the circular flow model in Chapter 1. There we considered two extreme cases of the aggregate supply (AS) curve, the line that indicates how much output firms produce at different price levels. For easy reference, Figure 6.1 replicates these two versions. The **horizontal aggregate supply curve** shown in panel (a) is the one we employed in Chapters 2–5 in the context of the Keynesian cross, the *IS-LM* model and the Mundell–Fleming model. It is usually referred to as the extreme Keynesian aggregate supply curve. It assumes there is slack and the presence of one or more production factors in abundance. Then how much firms produce depends only on demand. At the given price level, firms supply any level of output that is demanded. But then the price level never changes! How does this correspond with the real world where continuous price changes in the form of inflation are the rule rather than an exception? Quite obviously, a horizontal aggregate supply curve cannot be the whole story.

> Maths note. The two-period budget constraint states that since today's income is either consumed or saved, $Y_1 = C_1 + S_1$, and consumption next period is limited by the sum of period-2 income and period-1 saving plus interest, $C_2 = Y_2 + (1 + r)S_1$, the **present value** of consumption must equal the present value of income:
> $C_1 + \frac{C_2}{1 + r} = Y_1 + \frac{Y_2}{1 + r}$
> This is rewritten $C_2 = (1 + r)Y_1 + Y_2 - (1 + r)C_1$, which defines a straight line with slope $(1 + r)$. The **concept of present values** makes payments comparable that accrue at different points in time. For example, when the interest rate is 4% annually, €100,000 becomes €104,000 in a year. Then we may say that at an interest

To obtain an unobs... that each can be tak...

The consumption co... lyzed in a diagram t... and future consump... have already decide... comes that are thus ... immediately, in the ... point in the interter... **ment point**. In a lo... are identical. Then t... omy has been throw... from future income,...

In Figure 17.3 the ... Thus the endowmen... indicate the househo... produces nothing bu... to be consumed rig... riod in which it was...

Boxes
Boxes in each chapter present useful guidance to the reader and illustrate the concepts.

Case studies
Every chapter contains one or more case study that applies core concepts to recent experiences in Europe and in other parts of the world.

> **Box 17.1** A pocket guide to the history of macroeconomic thought
>
> Many bright minds have contributed to what macroeconomics is today. This box does not even try to do justice to the richness of ideas found in their writings. Instead, it settles for the modest goal of projecting the major **schools of macroeconomic thought** onto the *AD-AS* diagram and highlighting selected key contributions.
>
> **Classical economics**
> Long before the term macroeconomics had even been invented, classical economists (like Adam Smith, David Ricardo, David Hume and John Stuart Mill) believed that the flexibility of wages and prices ensured that markets very much cleared all the time. In the view of **classical macroeconomics** income remained so close to potential output that no policy intervention was warranted. Translated into the *AD-AS* diagram (which also had not been devised yet), the *AS* curve is vertical, and it moves slowly and smoothly as the labour force grows, the capital stock increases and technology improves. Shifts in the *AD-AS* curve cannot affect income. When nominal variables, such as the money supply, change, this affects only the price level but none of the real variables. This phenomenon is called the **classical dichotomy**. We actually have two separate, independent parts of the economy: one where real variables like the capital stock or productivity determine other real variables like income, employment or the real wage, and the other where nominal variables like the money supply or
>
> foreign prices determine other nominal variables like prices or the exchange rate.
>
> **Keynesianism**
> After a long reign well into the twentieth century, the experience of the Great Depression (1929–32) left the classical view in shambles. There was no way to rationalize a drop in industrial production of 47% within little more than three years, as had happened in the United States, or of 42%, as experienced in Germany, as a movement in potential income. British economist John Maynard Keynes came up with a new way to look at the economy. He argued that when there were high levels of unemployment, even at unchanged prices firms would produce any volume of output that was demanded. Under such circumstances *AS* is flat and the classical dichotomy breaks down. If an increase in government spending shifts *AD* to the right, this has real consequences in the form of a rise in income. While Keynes did not contest the possibility of a return of income to potential income in the long run, this was not the focus of his analysis. In fact, he shrugged it off with the famous remark: 'In the long run we are all dead.' With market forces considered too slow, Keynesians believed that during periods of lack of demand the government had to step in by means of fiscal and monetary policy.
>
> In the orthodox Keynesian scenario prices remain fairly constant, as postulated in our *IS-LM* and Mundell–Fleming models. Later, faced by the

Figure 17.14 Demand fluctuations do not affect income. Potential income evolves slowly. Classical dichotomy holds at all times.

Figure 17.15a Demand fluctuations affect income only. Classical dichotomy does not hold.

> **CASE STUDY 2.2** How to pay for the war: Great Britain in 1940
>
> Many of the tools we encounter in this and subsequent chapters are due to British economist John Maynard Keynes (1883–1946), who gave his name to such terms as Keynesian cross and Keynesianism (for an entire school).
>
> In 1940 Keynes published *How to Pay for the War*. One of the questions raised in this treatise is how Great Britain could meet the economic efforts required by the Second World War without generating inflation. In essence (after streamlining it in some inessential aspects), Keynes's argument runs as follows:
>
> 1 Income in 1938 (the latest available data) ran at £5,520 million. *Potential income* was estimated at £6,345 million. So income (output) could increase by $\Delta Y = 6,345 - 5,520 = £825$ million without risking inflation. (If demand were driven beyond potential income, he assumed, firms would start to raise prices.)
> 2 How far can government spending be raised without pushing income beyond potential income? The answer is certainly not £825 million! The permitted change of income and therefore the permitted change of government spending are related by the multiplier. We may take the one given in equation (2.14). Letting $m = 0$
>
> (private, income-sensitive imports would be controlled and low during the war), we obtain
>
> $$\Delta Y = \frac{1}{1 - c(1 - t)} \Delta G$$
>
> Knowing that $\Delta Y = 825$, all we need to know to calculate ΔG is c and t.
> 3 Assumptions. Proceeding from the 1938 data $Y = 5,520$, $C = 4,380$ and $T = 770$, a reasonable guess is to assume that marginal and average consumption and tax rates are the same, that is $c = C/Y = 4,380/5,520$ and $t = T/Y = 770/5,520$.
> 4 Result. Substituting the obtained rates $c = 0.79$ and $t = 0.14$ into the multiplier expression gives a multiplier of 3.15. Letting $\Delta Y = 825$ and solving the multiplier equation for ΔG finally yields $\Delta G = 262$. Therefore, government spending can be geared up by £262 million (in 1938 prices) without triggering inflation. (If that doesn't provide sufficient funds, tax rates may have to be raised (if politically feasible), which in turn reduces the multiplier and drives equilibrium income down.
>
> Keynes's assumptions, line of argument and results may also be presented graphically in the context of the Keynesian-cross diagram (see Figure 2.13).

Figure 2.13

CHAPTER SUMMARY

■ A country's income at a given point in time is determined by the steady-state level of income, the deviation of potential income from steady-state income, and the deviation of income from potential income. The latter is called the business cycle.

■ In the circular flow model there exists one equilibrium level of income at which actual spending is exactly as planned. What sets this level of income apart from all other feasible income levels is that firms will try to set production to this very level to avoid having to invest or disinvest involuntarily.

Key terms and concepts

actual expenditure *42*	Keynesian cross *47*
aggregate (planned) expenditure *42*	marginal income tax rate *51*
average income tax rate *51*	marginal propensity to consume *46*
boom *37*	multiplier *50*
business cycle *37*	net taxes *44*
capital costs *58*	permanent income *60*
consumption function *51*	potential income *37*
~~demand~~ side equilibrium *43*	rate of return *58*

Chapter summary
Each chapter ends with a bullet-point summary which highlights the material covered in the chapter and can be used as a quick reminder of the main issues.

Key terms and concepts
A list at the end of each chapter of all the key terms and concepts, for quick reference.

Recommended reading

The bible on issues of central bank independence is Alex Cukierman (1995) *Central Bank Strategy, Credibility, and Independence: Theory and Evidence*, Cambridge, MA and London: MIT Press.

The empirical evidence is gauged on a non-technical level in Alberto Alesina and Lawrence H. Summers (1992) 'Central bank independence and macroeconomic performance', *Journal of Money, Credit and Banking* 25: 151–62.

A survey of theoretical progress in political macroeconomics achieved in the 1990s is provided by Manfred Gärtner (2000) 'Political macroeconomics: a survey of recent developments', *Journal of Economic Surveys* 14: 527–61.

Sacrifice ratios are studied in Lawrence Ball (1994) 'What determines the sacrifice ratio?', in N. Gregory Mankiw (ed.) *Monetary Policy*, Chicago and London: University of Chicago Press.

A provoking view on inflation, central bank independence and monetary policy is offered in Paul Krugman (1996) 'Stable prices and fast growth: Just say no', *The Economist*, 31 August, pp. 17–20.

Several authors have forwarded proposals of how to integrate the kind of endogenous monetary policy discussed in this chapter into an *IS-LM* framework:

■ David Romer (2000) 'Keynesian macroeconomics without the *LM* curve', *Journal of Economic Perspectives* 14:149–69.
■ Carl Walsh (2002) 'Teaching inflation targeting: An analysis for intermediate macro', *Journal of Economic Education* 33: 333–46.

Recommended reading
Each chapter is supported by an annotated recommended reading section, directing the reader to additional printed and electronic sources in order to gain an alternative perspective, or to pursue a topic in more depth.

Exercises
Exercises at the end of each chapter are geared towards the chapter's central ideas and consolidate the acquired knowledge.

Applied problems
These optional problems show students how intermediate statistical skills may be applied to the study of macro-economics, and encourage them to try for themselves.

EXERCISES

2.1 Consider French real output between 1900 and 1991 as given in Figure 2.19. Add your guess of the paths of steady-state income and potential income to the graph.

Figure 2.19

2.2 Figure 2.20 displays the evolution of real GDP between 1978 and 2002 for the United States and France.
(a) Try to identify business cycles, marking peaks and troughs on the graphs.
(b) Identify the US position in 1991 in a diagram with prices on the vertical axis and income on the horizontal axis. Mark potential income, steady-state income and actual income.

Two US economists, Arthur F. Burns and Wesley C. Mitchell, claimed half a century ago that the typical business cycle lasts between six and thirty-two quarters.
(c) Does this agree with your findings?

2.3 Consider an economy with the following data (note that *I* is *planned* investment, which may not coincide with actual investment):

$C = 750$ $I = 500$ $T = 0$ $G = 250$
$NX = 250$ $Y = 1,000$

(a) Is this economy's circular flow in equilibrium in the sense that firms do not have to change inventories involuntarily?
(b) Translate the above data into a diagram with demand on the vertical axis and income on the horizontal axis.
Add the assumption $C = 0.75Y$.
(c) Draw the aggregate-expenditure and the actual-expenditure lines. Identify demand-determined income in equilibrium in your graph and analytically.
(d) What happens to equilibrium income if government expenditure increases by 500 units? Show your result in a graph and verify that it is supported by the multiplier formula of equation (2.9).
(e) Using a graph, show what happens if net exports fall from 250 to 100.

Figure 2.20

APPLIED PROBLEMS

EMPIRICAL RESEARCH

What explains sacrifice ratios?

Lawrence Ball ('What determines the sacrifice ratio?', in N. G. Mankiw (ed.) (1994) *Monetary Policy*, Chicago and London: University of Chicago Press) computes a sample of sacrifice ratios for different disinflation episodes in different countries. One question that he analyzes is whether the obtained sacrifice ratios depend on the SIZE of the disinflation (by how many percentage points is inflation reduced from the beginning to the end of the episode?) and by the LENGTH (how many quarters did the disinflation last?). The obtained estimation equation for twenty-eight disinflation episodes is (standard errors in parentheses):

Sacrifice ratio = $1.045 - 0.198$ SIZE $+ 0.120$ LENGTH
(0.325) (0.061) (0.034)
$$R^2_{adj} = 0.30$$

Larger disinflations come at lower disinflation costs: the coefficient for SIZE is negative and significant (t-statistic = 0.198/0.061 = 3.25). On the other hand, spreading the disinflation over a longer time appears to make it more costly: the coefficient for LENGTH is positive, with a t-statistic of 0.120/0.034 = 3.53). The coefficient of determination is only 0.30, however, meaning that only 30% of the differences of sacrifice ratios between disinflation episodes may be traced back to the size and the length of the disinflation.

WORKED PROBLEM

Does central bank independence ease disinflation pains?

Inflation can be reduced by moving down along the *SAS* curve. Then the slope of *SAS* determines the incurred sacrifices. Or the *SAS* curve may be shifted down by reducing inflation expectations. If this is accomplished, inflation may be reduced at no or at low cost. According to what we learned in this chapter, an independent central bank (which desires lower inflation than a dependent one) should be expected to be more successful in reducing inflation expectations. Hence, more CBI should come hand in hand with lower sacrifice ratios. Table 13.3 gives average sacrifice ratios for nine countries and CBI data.

To see whether there is a relationship we run a regression to obtain (standard errors in parentheses):

Sacrifice ratio = $-0.441 + 0.206$ CBI $R^2_{adj} = 0.59$
(0.553) (0.058)

The puzzling and unexpected result is that countries with more independent central banks have experienced higher sacrifice ratios. CBI explains some 59% of the differences in sacrifice ratios and the coefficient on CBI is highly significant (absolute t-statistic: 0.206/0.058 = 3.55). Similarly puzzling results have been reported in a number of research papers. Convincing explanations have not been advanced yet.

Table 13.3

Country	AUS	CDN	F	D	I	J	CH	GB	USA
Sacrifice ratio	1.00	1.50	0.75	3.10	1.29	0.70	1.57	0.68	2.11
CBI	9	11	7	13	5	6	12	6	12

Table 13.4

Country	A	B	CH	D	DK	E	F	GB	GR	I	IRL	NL	P
Hourly wages in $	25.5	27	29	32.1	24.82	12	19	14	8	16.5	13	24	5.33
CBI	9	7	12	13	8	5	7	6	4	5	7	10	3
Overvaluation in %	1.23	1.12	1.52	1.29	1.35	0.95	1.18	1.01	0.68	1.04	0.94	1.22	0.76

LIST OF CASE STUDIES AND BOXES

What makes this book unique?

This text reverses the usual priorities in undergraduate macroeconomics instruction. The ultimate goal is not simply to teach macroeconomic theories, models and concepts, with real-world applications thrown in for motivation and excitement; rather, students work through this book towards an understanding of the macroeconomic issues and challenges facing the global economy and individual countries. Macroeconomic concepts and models are taught only as they serve this end.

Content

The global financial crisis and the ensuing European sovereign debt crisis gave macroeconomics a rude awakening from a slumber of complacency. This poses challenges for research as well as teaching on all levels. Interestingly, though, many of the issues that dominated policy debates and concepts that proved useful during the crisis were taken from the undergraduate curriculum, not from cutting-edge research. Undergraduate teaching may, therefore, be less rattled by recent events than are graduate curriculums and research agendas. But the startling speed at which demand and employment receded, and the sheer magnitude at which incomes dropped, the stubbornness with which they resisted recovery, has tarnished belief in the self-healing powers of markets and the uniqueness of macroeconomic equilibria. This calls for a revitalized interest in what can go wrong in financial and goods markets, and when and how the government should step in to augment private demand when it is lacking.

Acknowledging this, the text's business cycle chapters use the events of 2008–2012 very much as a running theme that repeatedly features in Case Studies and Boxes. And the book places new emphasis on financial markets, on the possibility of instabilities and on multiple equilibria.

Chapters 1–9 are fairly conventional in content, amounting to a streamlined, no-frills introduction to the macroeconomic concepts that are useful for discussion of today's macroeconomic issues. Essential concepts are introduced in the context of the circular-flow-of-income model. Students are then led via the Keynesian cross, the *IS-LM* model, the Mundell–Fleming model and the aggregate demand-aggregate supply model to a fully dynamic aggregate demand-aggregate supply framework for analysing short- and medium-term macroeconomic issues. Chapters on the supply-side topics of unemployment and growth complete this predictable set of tools.

Chapters 10 and 11 extend the toolbox into areas that most intermediate macroeconomics textbooks barely mention in passing. The first one refines and extends the Solow growth model (introduced in Chapter 9) with discussions of human capital and poverty traps, and concludes with a first glimpse at endogenous growth. Under the heading 'Endogenous economic policy', Chapter 11 shows that politicians may steer economies along paths not considered desirable from society's point of view, and discusses how institutions should be structured to reduce this risk.

Chapters 12–15 explore issues at the heart of European and global economic integration. Chapters 12 and 13 look at monetary integration, with a focus on the challenges posed by and benefits offered by a single currency shared by many countries. Chapter 14 explores debt dynamics and takes a closer look at the market for government bonds. In Chapter 15 economic crises take centre stage. Standard models are expanded and refined to shed light on the consequences of oil price explosions, on the real estate and financial crisis, and on the sovereign debt crisis.

Chapters 16 and 17 offer a sneak preview of what macroeconomics courses at the Masters level have in store. They also make a serious effort to motivate students and explain why research had moved beyond the workhorse models of intermediate macroeconomics to study macroeconomic models with explicit microfoundations – of the real-business-cycle mould, or with sticky prices and information. To this end, students learn about the co-movement of macroeconomic variables, and why sticky prices or sticky information may perform better than sticky wages in explaining empirically observed patterns. They also grasp the intuition behind real-business-cycle dynamics, without the elaborate formal apparatus that usually comes with it.

What is new in the fourth edition?

Whenever possible, graphs, tables and information in general were updated. Many explanations have been improved, case studies brought up to date or replaced, and new exercises added.

Identifying equibria and exploring how these are affected by shocks and policy measures remains a key task of undergraduate macroeconomics. But recent crises triggered renewed interest in the conditions under which there may be different equilibria, good and bad ones, and in the factors that can cause prolonged deviations from existing equilibria. New topics and concepts that document this shifting emphasis are:

■ *The macroeconomics of financial and debt crises* This edition was prepared while there was still substantial fallout from this millennium's first global financial crisis, which had morphed into a sovereign debt crisis in most of Europe. In an effort to answer some of the key questions posed by these developments, coverage of the financial crisis has been increased and a closer look at debt crises is being offered. This is done with new case studies that make crisis economics a reoccurring theme throughout the book, and by adding new topics and putting greater emphasis on existing ones that have relevance for understanding the causes, mechanisms and policy options of major economic crises.
■ *Bubbles and self-fulfilling prophecy* These concepts help understand why prices, of assets and currencies in particular, may move even when this does not appear warranted by changes in fundamental market data.

- *Market psychology and risk premiums* These open the way for discussions of mood swings and panic in the financial industry and how this affects the economy.
- *Multiple equilibria* Their presence may cause shocks to trigger a permanent shift of economic conditions from some initial equilibrium to a new one.
- *Liquidity traps* These define conditions under which conventional monetary policy does not work and unorthodox policy measures or mixtures are needed.
- *Multiple interest rates* The distinction between short-run interest rates in the money market and long-run interest rates in the capital market is essential for understanding how quantitative easing works and fits into the workhorse models of undergraduate macroeconomics. Adding a third interest rate, for government bonds, permits discussions of debt crises and austerity packages.

Learning features

The book has a user-friendly design, featuring margin notes and definitions that emphasize important concepts. Exercises geared towards each chapter's central ideas consolidate the acquired knowledge. An extensive and innovative use of graphs facilitates access and enhances learning success. Every chapter contains one or more Case Studies that apply core concepts to recent or historic experiences in Europe and in other parts of the world. And all chapters feature links to elaborate online material that includes interactive graphical versions of the book's key models, guided exercises, an interactive road map, self-grading online tests, macroeconomic data, and much more. Suitable parts of the online material have been adapted for use on smart phones, with easy access provided by QR codes.

What courses does the book accommodate?

The organization of the book gives instructors various options:

- Primarily, the text is designed for courses in *undergraduate* or *intermediate macroeconomics* that on the one hand insist on providing a sound theoretical foundation, but on the other also want to make a point of emphasizing *applications* in the form of Case Studies or even, if so desired, elementary statistical work.
- The book's first half can also be used for a self-contained *short course in macroeconomics* whenever time does not permit working through a voluminous 600–900-page macroeconomics text which has become the standard.
- Also, the book readily accommodates courses in *Economic policy* and *Applied macroeconomics*. Such courses may be organized around an appropriate selection from the several dozen Case Studies and empirical applications. As deemed necessary, students can be referred to the required theory tools in the same textbook.
- Finally, the book accommodates *European studies* courses that can be organized around the applied topics discussed in Chapters 12–15. Here also, should it be necessary to freshen up or expand previously acquired theoretical knowledge, such material is readily available in the same textbook.

Prerequisites

Ideally, students should approach this book with a *Principles of economics* course under their belt. The mathematical requirements are mild: anything close to the most basic mathematics training in high school should do. Most of the formal manipulations are optional and either shown in margin notes or in separate sections that supplement graphical arguments.

I am confident, though, that the book can also be used successfully if a principles course is missing and algebraic manipulations are avoided altogether. Dozens of Case Studies, some brief, some elaborate, provide ample ammunition for keeping up motivation, and the big payoff waits in the later chapters of the book.

Finally, and though it may sound frivolous: I believe that the book is even suited for self-study. The acquired knowledge will definitely be more fragile and lack depth compared with what can be achieved under the guidance of an experienced instructor. But it should provide an up-to-date first foundation for informed discussion of today's national and global macroeconomic issues.

Acknowledgements

This brings me to the people I want to thank for their contributions to whatever merits this text may have. In the very first place, these are my students, who amaze me time and again. Most of all, teaching teaches the teacher. Students' questions and curiosity constantly force me to refine explanations, and in the process very often make me understand things better myself.

It has been a joy to work with the professionals at Pearson Education, to whom I owe a big 'thank you'. They helped and guided me, with unmatched skill and great patience, accommodating last-minute ideas of mine, in preparing this thoroughly extended fourth edition, and brought the book into its final shape: Anita Atkinson (senior editor), Kate Brewin (commissioning editor), Robert Chaundy (copy editor), Linda Dhondy (proofreader), Gemma Doel (assistant editor).

This text would not even be close to what it is without the talents and the enthusiasm of the people working with me at the University of St. Gallen's Institute of Economics. Larissa Zierow played a key role in the preparation of this new edition. She updated graphs, tables and other empirical information, and suggested numerous improvements. In the course of joint teaching ventures based on this textbook, Björn Griesbach and Giulia Mennillo offered criticism and many constructive suggestions that improved this edition. They also accepted the responsibility for proofreading along with Iskra Pavlova, Lennart Scherp and Anna Zimmermann. I am deeply indebted to all of them.

I have also benefitted from the reviews commissioned by Pearson Education. Both those that offered applause and encouragement, and those that were more reserved, helped shape the book into a better teaching tool.

The mere writing of a textbook may mostly happen at the desk. But the enthusiasm, the creativity and the discipline that are essential for such a project come from beyond office doors. In this respect I owe much more to my family than they can possibly know.

PUBLISHER'S ACKNOWLEDGEMENTS

We are grateful to the following for permission to reproduce copyright material:

Figure 1.1 from World Bank Key Statistics Online; Figure 9.6 from *Economics*, Prentice Hall Europe (Case, K., Fair, R., Gartner, M. and Heather, K. 1999); Figure 12.1 adapted from *Economics*, Prentice Hall Europe (Case, K., Fair, R., Gartner, M., and Heather, K. 1999); Figure 15.15 from European Central Bank.

In some instances we have been unable to trace the owners of copyright material, and we would appreciate any information that would enable us to do so.

Macroeconomic essentials

After working through this warm-up chapter, you will know:

1 What macroeconomics is all about, and how it relates to microeconomics.
2 All you need to know about national income accounting, including government budgets and the balance of payments.
3 What the circular flow model is, how to use it and what its limitations are.
4 How money fits into the macroeconomy.
5 Why economists need to use models, and why these simplified pictures of the real world are useful.
6 How to work with graphs.

1.1 The issues of macroeconomics

Economics is about how people use time and tools to produce what other people want to buy – and about the sometimes intricate choices that must be made and the things that can go wrong.

The two major subdisciplines of economics are microeconomics and macroeconomics. Microeconomics looks in great detail at how individuals make choices – as consumers, as employees, as entrepreneurs, as investors, or even as politicians. Macroeconomics looks at the big picture, at the way things are and how they develop after we add everything up, in the whole economy or in large segments or sectors of the economy. Of course, microeconomics and macroeconomics cannot lead separate lives. What happens in the macroeconomy must be the result of all the individual decisions analysed and explained in microeconomics. This is why the search for the *microfoundations of macroeconomics* ranks high on today's research agenda. However, to model all the choices of millions of different people and show how they interact to generate specific macroeconomic outcomes is simply not feasible. It probably never will be. Inevitably, at some point we have to resort to simplifications or abstractions: either by assuming, say, that all individuals are alike, which is what so-called *representative agents models* of the macroeconomy do; or by postulating relationships between macroeconomic variables which are *ad hoc* in the sense that they only *proxy* the outcomes of individual choices, but nevertheless seem to work well in many real-world situations.

> Microeconomics studies individual entities such as consumers or firms.
>
> Macroeconomics studies the whole economy from a bird's-eye perspective.

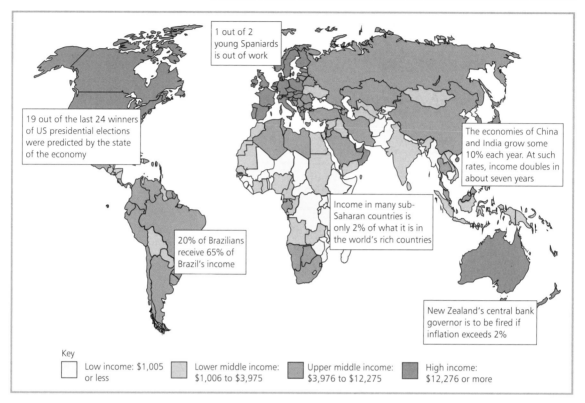

Figure 1.1 The map shows the huge differences that exist in the per capita incomes of the world's nations in 2015. Other important macroeconomic variables and issues are reported in boxes: economic growth, unemployment, inflation, the distribution of income and the close link between the economy and politics.

Source: World Bank Key Statistics Online.

Income is revenue derived from work and assets, such as wages, interest, dividends and profits.

The foremost single measure of how an economy performs is the aggregate level of income. Presenting the world at a glance, Figure 1.1 gives an overview of this variable by classifying countries according to income per capita, which is total income divided by population. Huge differences in per capita incomes exist. At the high end are the industrialized countries with annual incomes per head of $20,000 to $50,000. Lowest are a number of countries in sub-Saharan Africa with average annual per capita incomes of barely $100. To make matters worse, many of the world's poorest countries do not seem to be growing very much – if at all. In stark contrast, the Asian 'tigers' – Hong Kong, Singapore, South Korea and Taiwan – have been growing at or near double-digit percentage rates throughout the 1980s and much of the 1990s. Other Asian nations, China and India most notably, by far the world's most populous nations, are copying this miracle. At such growth rates, incomes double in less than ten years.

Rule of 72. As a rule of thumb, divide 72 by the annual income growth rate (in per cent) to learn in how many years income doubles. Example: 72/9 = 8.

Incomes given in Figure 1.1 are *nominal incomes*, i.e. incomes expressed in currency (here US dollars) at current prices. If you want to compare incomes between countries, nominal incomes may not be the best data to look at. Neither should we rely on nominal income as an indicator of how a country's income evolved over time.

Measuring income growth over time in a single country is the simpler problem. Note that nominal income is prices P times real income Y, that is $P \times Y$. Now consider that US nominal income per capita grew by 28% from $P_{2002} \times Y_{2002} = \$36{,}126$ in 2002 to $P_{2010} \times Y_{2010} = \$47{,}284$ in 2010. This does not necessarily mean that US citizens could buy 28% more goods and services in 2010 than they could in 2002. Possibly, the increase in nominal income might have been entirely due to a 28% rise in prices, with no real improvements in the purchasing power of US incomes at all. Of course, this has not really been the case. In fact, US prices rose by 20% from an index value of, say, 1 in 2002 to 1.20 in 2010. To obtain 2010 real income (expressed in 2002 prices), we need to divide 2010 nominal income by the 2010 price level and multiply by 2002 prices: $Y_{2010} = (P_{2010} \times Y_{2010})/P_{2010} \times P_{2010} = 47{,}284/1.20 \times 1 = \$39{,}403$. So while nominal income rose by 28%, real income grew by only 6.5%.

Similar issues, with one added complication, arise when comparing incomes between countries. Noting that per capita income in 2010 was \$47,284 in the United States but \$67,246 in Switzerland would only permit a meaningful comparison of purchasing power if one dollar bought the same in Switzerland as in the United States. Although \$11.13 buys three Big Macs at \$3.71 each in the United States, you need \$20.34 to buy the same (at \$6.78 each) in Switzerland. This price difference may have two causes: at 7.08 Swiss francs Big Macs may simply be expensive in local currency; or the dollar may be undervalued, meaning it takes too many dollars to buy a Swiss franc. Our current knowledge does not put us in a position to sort this out. All we know is that a dollar buys fewer Big Macs in Switzerland than in the United States, and that we need to take this into account when comparing Swiss income to US income.

Table 1.1 generalizes our Big Mac example. Column 2 shows that in 2010 nominal income per capita in Switzerland was almost \$20,000 higher than in the United States. In Poland it was less than a fifth of Switzerland's. Taking into account the level of prices relative to the United States, the picture changes substantially. In Switzerland, \$67,246 buys what only \$41,663 buys in the United States. So Switzerland's *real income* per capita is lower than America's. Prices in Poland are about a third lower than in the United States, and some 40% of what they are in Switzerland. Therefore, in terms of real income, Poland performs much better than it seems to perform in terms of nominal income.

Table 1.1 Nominal and real income in 2010. The second column shows *nominal income*. Because prices differ substantially between countries (third column), *real income*, the amount of goods that income can buy, turns out quite differently, as shown in the fourth column.

	Nominal income (per capita, in $) PY	Price level (relative to US price level) P	Real income (in US purchasing power) Y
Poland	12,300	0.65	18,936
Switzerland	67,246	1.61	41,663
United States	47,284	1	47,284

Source: IMF.

Empirical note. World-
wide the richest countries,
with 17% of the population,
make 71% of world income.
The poorest countries, with
47% of the population,
make 7% of world income.

A statistical *average*, which is what income per capita is, is one thing. The actual *distribution of income* may be quite another story. In Brazil, to give one example, the richest 20% of the population earn some 65% of the nation's aggregate income. The poorest 20% earn as little as 2.5%. In Europe, high average incomes conceal that almost one in ten of those who want to work do not find a job. Good unemployment insurance and social security have so far prevented high *unemployment* from showing up in a deteriorating distribution of income. But welfare states are struggling and are quickly scaling down the role of the government. This trend has been reinforced by Europe's soverign debt crisis, which put a number of countries on the brink of default.

In the United States the results of nineteen out of the twenty-four presidential elections could have been predicted simply by looking at how the economy was doing, as measured by key indicators such as income growth and inflation. This implies a close link between macroeconomic performance and all the other (and, you may argue, more important) things in life, not only because all these other things typically cost money, but because a precondition for being in power – and thus being able to realize one's dream, ideology or vision, in whatever field – is a satisfactory economic performance.

New Zealand's government made the headlines in the 1990s by putting a clause in the employment contract of its central bank governor that threatened him or her with the sack if inflation exceeded 2% annually. This reflects a serious concern for *inflation*, the rate at which prices grow. Many other nations share this concern, which points to inflation as a third important variable in the macroeconomic context.

The world abounds with economic challenges and puzzles. These differ from one part of the world to another, and they must be viewed in the context of different institutions, cultures and historical backgrounds. Despite this, a set of macroeconomic principles and concepts exists which can, applied wisely, be brought to bear on a variety of different issues. This book sets out to assemble such a basic macroeconomic tool-kit. While it focuses on and emphasizes what is needed to understand and discuss the experiences and prospects in one part of the world, the European Union and its neighbours, the perspective is global, as indicated by the range of issues, case studies and data.

The *European Union* grew out of economic and political integration efforts that started more than half a century ago. Today, it comprises the twenty-seven member states shown in blue in Figure 1.3. Figures 1.2 and 1.3 also provide some basic information on the member states' economies, the economies of Norway and Switzerland, whose governments had embarked on an integration path before voters rejected that option, plus a selection of other countries from around the globe.

While European countries appeared reasonably homogeneous in terms of per capita income from the world-wide perspective given in Figure 1.1, the more detailed information included in Figures 1.2 and 1.3 reveals some notable differences. These are not only the obvious differences in size and population, but also the differences in the standardized macroeconomic performance data mentioned earlier. Nominal per capita income, as measured

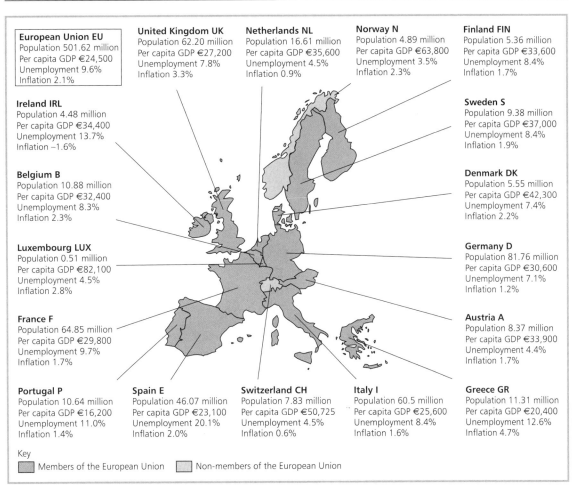

European Union EU
Population 501.62 million
Per capita GDP €24,500
Unemployment 9.6%
Inflation 2.1%

United Kingdom UK
Population 62.20 million
Per capita GDP €27,200
Unemployment 7.8%
Inflation 3.3%

Netherlands NL
Population 16.61 million
Per capita GDP €35,600
Unemployment 4.5%
Inflation 0.9%

Norway N
Population 4.89 million
Per capita GDP €63,800
Unemployment 3.5%
Inflation 2.3%

Finland FIN
Population 5.36 million
Per capita GDP €33,600
Unemployment 8.4%
Inflation 1.7%

Ireland IRL
Population 4.48 million
Per capita GDP €34,400
Unemployment 13.7%
Inflation −1.6%

Sweden S
Population 9.38 million
Per capita GDP €37,000
Unemployment 8.4%
Inflation 1.9%

Belgium B
Population 10.88 million
Per capita GDP €32,400
Unemployment 8.3%
Inflation 2.3%

Denmark DK
Population 5.55 million
Per capita GDP €42,300
Unemployment 7.4%
Inflation 2.2%

Luxembourg LUX
Population 0.51 million
Per capita GDP €82,100
Unemployment 4.5%
Inflation 2.8%

Germany D
Population 81.76 million
Per capita GDP €30,600
Unemployment 7.1%
Inflation 1.2%

France F
Population 64.85 million
Per capita GDP €29,800
Unemployment 9.7%
Inflation 1.7%

Austria A
Population 8.37 million
Per capita GDP €33,900
Unemployment 4.4%
Inflation 1.7%

Portugal P
Population 10.64 million
Per capita GDP €16,200
Unemployment 11.0%
Inflation 1.4%

Spain E
Population 46.07 million
Per capita GDP €23,100
Unemployment 20.1%
Inflation 2.0%

Switzerland CH
Population 7.83 million
Per capita GDP €50,725
Unemployment 4.5%
Inflation 0.6%

Italy I
Population 60.5 million
Per capita GDP €25,600
Unemployment 8.4%
Inflation 1.6%

Greece GR
Population 11.31 million
Per capita GDP €20,400
Unemployment 12.6%
Inflation 4.7%

Key
Members of the European Union   Non-members of the European Union

Figure 1.2 The map provides 2010 data on the countries of Western Europe that formed the European Union at the turn of the millennium, or that had completed negotiations before choosing not to join. GDP is a measure of a country's total income. Country names are followed by shorthand abbreviations that are used in the text.
Source: Eurostat.

by gross domestic product (GDP – see Box 1.1), in Luxembourg was more than twice as high as in Germany and five times that of Portugal; not to mention late entrants Bulgaria and Romania, where the ratio approached one to twenty. Unemployment ranged from a (by current standards) tolerable 4.4% in Austria to a more alarming 20.1% in Spain. Inflation peaked at 6.1% in Romania, but had ceased to be a major problem in the majority of EU member states, where it remained well below 3%. However, the European Central Bank's easier monetary policy in response to the financial crisis of 2007–09 along with its massive purchases of sovereign bonds from Eurozone countries that were hit severely by the 2010 debt crisis has created some fear that more inflation may be in the offing.

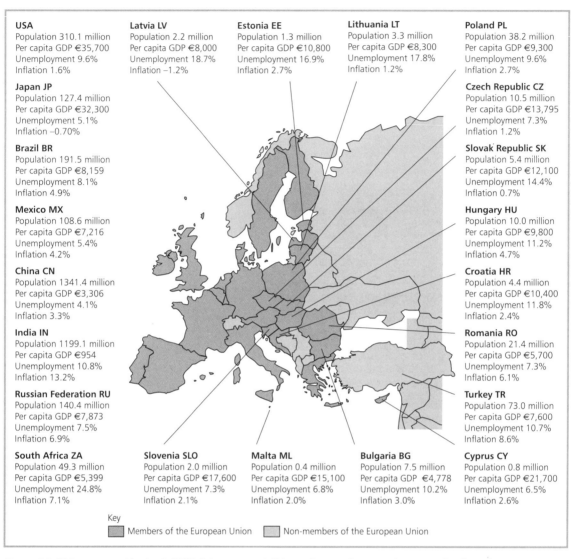

USA
Population 310.1 million
Per capita GDP €35,700
Unemployment 9.6%
Inflation 1.6%

Japan JP
Population 127.4 million
Per capita GDP €32,300
Unemployment 5.1%
Inflation −0.70%

Brazil BR
Population 191.5 million
Per capita GDP €8,159
Unemployment 8.1%
Inflation 4.9%

Mexico MX
Population 108.6 million
Per capita GDP €7,216
Unemployment 5.4%
Inflation 4.2%

China CN
Population 1341.4 million
Per capita GDP €3,306
Unemployment 4.1%
Inflation 3.3%

India IN
Population 1199.1 million
Per capita GDP €954
Unemployment 10.8%
Inflation 13.2%

Russian Federation RU
Population 140.4 million
Per capita GDP €7,873
Unemployment 7.5%
Inflation 6.9%

South Africa ZA
Population 49.3 million
Per capita GDP €5,399
Unemployment 24.8%
Inflation 7.1%

Latvia LV
Population 2.2 million
Per capita GDP €8,000
Unemployment 18.7%
Inflation −1.2%

Slovenia SLO
Population 2.0 million
Per capita GDP €17,600
Unemployment 7.3%
Inflation 2.1%

Estonia EE
Population 1.3 million
Per capita GDP €10,800
Unemployment 16.9%
Inflation 2.7%

Malta ML
Population 0.4 million
Per capita GDP €15,100
Unemployment 6.8%
Inflation 2.0%

Lithuania LT
Population 3.3 million
Per capita GDP €8,300
Unemployment 17.8%
Inflation 1.2%

Bulgaria BG
Population 7.5 million
Per capita GDP €4,778
Unemployment 10.2%
Inflation 3.0%

Poland PL
Population 38.2 million
Per capita GDP €9,300
Unemployment 9.6%
Inflation 2.7%

Czech Republic CZ
Population 10.5 million
Per capita GDP €13,795
Unemployment 7.3%
Inflation 1.2%

Slovak Republic SK
Population 5.4 million
Per capita GDP €12,100
Unemployment 14.4%
Inflation 0.7%

Hungary HU
Population 10.0 million
Per capita GDP €9,800
Unemployment 11.2%
Inflation 4.7%

Croatia HR
Population 4.4 million
Per capita GDP €10,400
Unemployment 11.8%
Inflation 2.4%

Romania RO
Population 21.4 million
Per capita GDP €5,700
Unemployment 7.3%
Inflation 6.1%

Turkey TR
Population 73.0 million
Per capita GDP €7,600
Unemployment 10.7%
Inflation 8.6%

Cyprus CY
Population 0.8 million
Per capita GDP €21,700
Unemployment 6.5%
Inflation 2.6%

Key
Members of the European Union   Non-members of the European Union

Figure 1.3 This map provides basic 2010 data on recent EU members and some other countries for reference.
Sources: Eurostat, IMF, World Bank.

1.2 Essentials of macroeconomic accounting

Factors of production are all resources used in the production of goods and services: labour, capital goods such as machines, and natural resources such as oil.

The focal point of macroeconomics is the level of income. Incomes are paid out to factors of production that are employed by firms to produce goods and services. This output is then put on the market for people to buy. The two major things that can go wrong in this process are as follows:

- Firms may not use all available production factors to produce output, thus leaving factors idle in the form of *unemployment* or slack.
- People may not want to buy all that is being produced, that is *demand may fall short of output.*

BOX 1.1 GDP as a measure of total output or income

How do modern economies measure total income (or output)? Usually it is done by means of a concept called gross domestic product (GDP). Nominal GDP evaluates all final goods and services produced in a country at current market prices. If 100 pizzas and 5 Alfas are produced in a given calendar year at prices of €10 and €30,000, respectively, GDP is 10 × 100 + 30,000 × 5 = €151,000. Important things to watch out for are the following:

- *Only count final products.* If Alfa Romeo buys tyres from an external supplier to put on its cars, you would not want to count tyres twice – once when Alfa Romeo buys them and again when consumers buy an Alfa, the price of which, of course, includes the cost of tyres. As indicated, one way to avoid double counting is by including *final products* only. Another way is to count only the *value added* at each stage during the production process.
- *Only count current production.* If the original Alfa owner resells her car next year, this obviously does not represent output and income generated during that period.

GDP increases, first, if more pizzas and/or Alfas are being produced, and second, if prices rise. Table 1.2 illustrates these two possibilities.

In 2012 nominal GDP is €151,000. *Real GDP* does not evaluate output in terms of current prices, but in prices in a given year. In terms of what nominal GDP buys in 2012, real GDP in 2012 of course is also €151,000. In 2013 nominal GDP has risen to €182,000. Since prices are the same as in 2012, real GDP has also risen to €182,000: the buying power of nominal GDP is at what €182,000 would have bought in 2012. Finally, in 2014 nominal GDP is at €244,000. But the increase is only due to price increases. Production quantities are the same as in 2013. This leaves real GDP unchanged at €182,000.

Sometimes total income is also measured as gross national product (GNP). The difference between the two concepts is that GDP refers to incomes generated within the geographical boundaries of a country, no matter by whom. Instead, GNP measures the incomes generated by the inhabitants of a country, no matter in what country. So if a Spaniard living in Barcelona owns Lufthansa stocks, the annual dividends she may receive are included in Germany's GDP, but in Spain's GNP. For most countries the difference between GDP and GNP is small (see case study 1.1). We will usually think of GDP when talking about total income or output.

Table 1.2 **An illustration of nominal and real GDP**

| Year | Pizzas | | Alfas | | Nominal GDP (in €) | Real GDP in prices of 2012 |
	Price	Quantity	Price	Quantity		
2012	10	100	30,000	5	151,000	151,000
2013	10	200	30,000	6	182,000	182,000
2014	20	200	40,000	6	244,000	182,000

Economists have analyzed economies very much in terms of these two failures: underutilization of production factors and/or insufficient (or excessive) demand. These will also be major themes in subsequent chapters of this book, as they lie at the heart of most prominent macroeconomic issues such as unemployment and inflation.

Before embarking on our task to assemble a set of macroeconomic tools and concepts for analysing these and other macroeconomic issues, we need to clarify some essential terminology and techniques.

The circular flow of income and spending

We start by looking at how economists measure income, and at how they divide it into useful components to facilitate subsequent efforts to understand what determines income and what makes it change. For this purpose we employ a preliminary stylized picture (or 'model') of the economy: the image of continuous circular flows. This model, which we begin to build in Figure 1.4, identifies the key actors (or sectors) of an economy, and then proceeds to describe and measure the interaction between them.

Suppose there are only two actors, *households* and *firms*. In an economy without money – economists call this a *barter economy* – households and firms interact through a continuous flow of real transactions. Households furnish firms with labour (and usually also capital goods like machines and buildings, or land). Firms use these factors of production, or *resources*, as they are also called, to produce goods (and services). These goods flow back to the households, constituting compensation for having supplied the factors of production.

It would not be very efficient if pizzerias were to compensate pizzaiolos with the Margaritas and Calzones they baked, and if Alfa Romeo were to pay employees with a brand new Giulietta every six months. In modern economies, firms pay households with money for using the factors of production. This relieves pizzaiolos of a tedious search for Alfa Romeo workers with just the right craving for pizza. Therefore, in the upper half of Figure 1.5, an appropriate amount of euros, pounds or kronas flows back to the households, completing this transaction. In the lower half, households spend their money incomes on the goods produced and put on the market by the firms. So in the end the counter-clockwise circular flow of real transactions between households and firms remains intact. It is now complemented by an outer circle flowing clockwise which records the payments streams that compensate for the goods received and for the labour provided.

The outer circle has an important advantage over the inner one: it is easier to measure, since all transactions are denominated in the same measuring units. This is not true for the inner circle. Typically, both the factors of production and the goods produced are very heterogeneous and cannot simply be added up. Economists therefore focus on the outer circle of income and spending to measure aggregate economic activity.

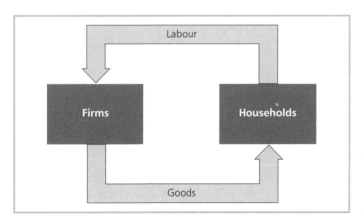

Figure 1.4 The circle shows that households furnish firms with production factors such as labour, and receive goods and services produced by firms in return. (Please excuse us for describing something that flows around four corners as a circle!)

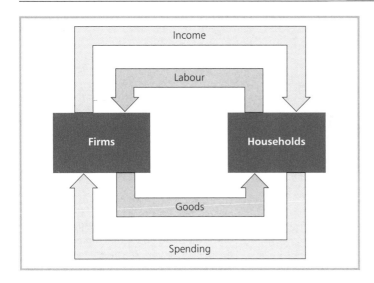

Figure 1.5 The outer circle shows that the inner real flow of labour and goods is financed by a monetary flow of income payments from firms to households and of households' spending on the firms' goods.

The *expenditure approach* measures aggregate output as the sum of all spending. The *income approach* adds up all incomes instead.

An important point to note is that one person's spending – flowing from right to left in the lower part of the outer circle – is another person's income, received after completion of the upper part of the outer circle. So all spending must add up to the same amount to which all incomes add up. Total production or aggregate output, the value of all goods and services produced by firms, may therefore be measured either by adding up all incomes, or by adding up all expenditures.

Figure 1.5 provided a very simple first picture, and there are a number of complicating factors. For example, consumers may not, and typically do not, spend all their income. As Figure 1.6 illustrates, if households save €20 out of an income of €100, only €80 arrives at the firms in demand for their goods. The €20 *leak* out of the circular flow system. On the other hand, the firms' products are not only bought by consumers. The pizza place may buy an Alfa and offer home deliveries. Such *investment demand* is typically not paid for out of current income (in fact, firms have no income) but is financed by borrowing money from banks. In this light, investments take the form of *injections* into the income circle.

Figure 1.6, with its focus on bringing savings and investment into the picture, illustrates how the basic circular flow model may be adapted to take into account complications that arise in reality. We now take a big step and introduce all those leakages and injections that will play prominent roles in the remainder of this book. First, income received by households may not arrive at the firms as demand for three main reasons:

1 *People save*. We have noted this point already. If people save part of their income, their consumption expenditures fall short of what they have produced and received as income. *Saving* may thus be viewed as a *leakage* of income out of the circular flow system.

2 *Governments levy taxes*. The taxes that governments levy on citizens are a part of income which is prevented from turning into demand – another leakage.

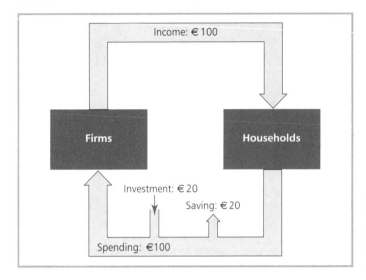

Figure 1.6 If households save part of the income that they receive from firms, income leaks out of the circular flow. If firms buy investment goods that are not directly being financed out of current income, spending is injected into the circular flow.

3 *People buy foreign goods*. Income earned at home which is used to buy goods produced in a foreign country constitute a third leakage of income from the domestic circular flow system.

But there is also more than one reason why demand from outside the circular flow may be directed towards domestic output. In fact, each of the leakages described above has a counterpart representing an *injection* into the circular flow:

1 *Firms invest*. As noted, firms build or buy new production facilities, new machines, distribution networks and so on. These investments are typically financed via credit from banks or credit markets in general.
2 *Government spending*. Government spending on such things as public consumption, infrastructure or transfers paid to households or firms represents an injection from the outside into the income circle.
3 *Foreigners buy our goods*. If residents of foreign countries decide to buy domestically produced goods, this represents a last injection of demand into the circular flow.

Figure 1.7 depicts the improved *circular flow of income* that allows for these six categories of *leakages* and *injections*. Note that we build on the outer, clockwise flow of income and spending introduced in Figure 1.5 and refined in Figure 1.6. For the sake of clarity we will now refrain from identifying firms and households in the circle. (To include them would complicate the picture since, for example, both firms and households buy imports which would entail separating out their respective imports.)

Leakages of spending are shown in the upper part of the 'circle', injections of spending in the lower part. Only if the sum of all leakages equals the sum of all injections does total expenditure (measured at the end of the lower leg of the circle) exactly match total income (measured at the outset of the upper leg). But wouldn't leakages match injections only by pure chance? The answer is *no*. Quite the contrary: in the end, when we add everything up, leakages and injections always match. Why is that?

Note. In economics the term **investment** describes purchases of capital goods. This differs from the popular use of the word which calls purchases of financial assets (say, stocks) out of savings '(financial) investments'.

Transfers are payments from governments to individuals or firms that do not involve goods or services, such as welfare payments or housing subsidies.

Figure 1.7 This diagram proceeds from the insight that all spending arrives somewhere else as income. In order for income to create an equivalent level of spending, all leakages out of the circular flow, given in the upper part of the circle, must be balanced by an equal amount of injections, given in the lower segment. Pairing leakages and injections in a meaningful way gives the circular flow identity $(T - G) + (S - I) + (IM - EX) = 0$, which always holds, except for measurement error. Data for Britain in 2002 are (in £billion): $T = 432.5$, $S = 175.7$, $IM = 440.8$, $EX = 421.2$, $I = 177.5$ and $G = 450.4$. Total income, the width of the stream, was 1,079.3.

Source: Eurostat.

Suppose that initially, with the amount of investment planned by firms, injections would fall short of leakages. Then spending tends to fall short of supplied output, and firms must add unsold output onto their existing stock of inventory. Whether they like it or not, they are forced to 'demand' that part of output themselves which they cannot sell. In the opposite case, if demand exceeds output, either firms must draw down their existing inventory, or, if that is not feasible, that part of demand which exceeds supply remains unsatisfied.

Now let investment not only be the purchase of machines, but also the addition to stocks of inventory (which are classified as capital goods). Then the forced changes of inventory described in the previous paragraph always render investment just high or low enough to make injections equal to leakages. So the bottom line is that, if investment is understood to include inventory changes, the leakages and injections always balance, and *the following equation holds at all times*:

$$(S - I) + (T - G) + (IM - EX) = 0 \tag{1.1}$$

Note. It is more common to call $EX - IM = NX$ net exports or, as an approximation, the *current account (CA)*.

Note that we have paired each leakage with an injection so as to yield a meaningful total, and to comply with Figure 1.7: $S - I$ is domestic private net savings; $T - G$ is public net savings (called the budget surplus), measuring

CASE STUDY 1.1

Measuring income: gross national income vs gross domestic product

Income is a key variable in any economy, both as proposed in our theoretical models, and as measured in reality. In our models we simply call it aggregate income, or output, and stick the label *Y* onto it. In reality, it can be measured in a number of ways. The two most important and most frequently used definitions are *gross domestic product* (GDP) and *gross national product* (GNP). Gross domestic product sums up what is being produced within the geographical borders of a country. Gross national product is the term for all income received by the inhabitants of a country, no matter whether it results from production at home or abroad. This is why it is often called **gross national income (GNI)** these days.

Which of these two measures of income is the proper one in a specific context depends on whether we are modeling economic activity in a geographic region or the material well-being of a group of people. In most models introduced in this book, the geographic region, say the UK, France, Europe or China, takes centre stage. Then the appropriate measure of income is GDP. In a few instances, though, such as when we talk about the effects and the motives behind globalization, we need to look at how people rather than regions are affected, and thus cast an eye on GNI.

In the real world, the distinction between GDP and GNI is not seriously relevant for most countries, as Figure 1.8 shows. In Europe, there is less than a handful of countries for which the difference between GDP and GNI is much larger than what may be attributed to measurement error. At one end, Ireland stands out, with a GNI that falls short of GDP by a whopping 19%. The reason is well known. By lowering taxes aggressively in competition with other European countries for foreign capital since the 1980s, Ireland succeeded in attracting foreign firms and capital investment from abroad at a breathtaking pace. As a consequence, a substantial part of the Irish capital stock – machines, buildings, computers, laboratories and more – belongs to foreigners, or has been bought with foreign capital. The earnings generated with this capital go to residents of foreign countries, and are thus included in Ireland's GDP, but not in its GNI.

The opposite applies to Switzerland. Here GNI exceeds GDP by 4%. This is because a substantial part of Switzerland's savings has been invested abroad, in countries such as Ireland. The capital

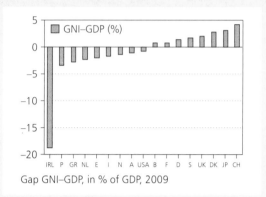

Gap GNI–GDP, in % of GDP, 2009

Figure 1.8
Source: World Bank.

GDP and GNI, 2009

Figure 1.9
Source: World Bank.

income generated by these investments – interest earnings, dividends, rents or profits – adds to Switzerland's GNI, but is not included in its GDP.

Figure 1.9 compares the absolute levels of GDP and GNI for the selected group of countries. The message is that for most countries the difference is barely visible, and we may not make a serious mistake by using one of the measures instead of the other: say, if the other is not available. Even for Switzerland and Ireland, the difference between the two income aggregates appears less dramatic in Figure 1.9 than it did in Figure 1.8.

the interactions between the domestic economy and the government sector; $IM - EX$ are net imports, the country's balance of trade in goods and services with the rest of the world.

As we shall see in subsequent chapters, the circular flow identity is an extremely effective gadget in any trained economist's tool-box. But it can also be very misleading if used in an uninformed way, that is without resolving the ambiguities in cause and effect that are often present in macroeconomics.

One example of such uninformed use would be to rearrange Equation (1.1) so as to yield

$$I = S + T - G + IM - EX \tag{1.2}$$

and then conclude that in order to raise what is perceived to be insufficient investment by 10 billion, all the government must do is raise taxes by 10 billion.

A look back at Figure 1.7 reveals that this recommendation naively assumes that increasing the tax leak leaves all other leakages and all injections except I unaffected, thus forcing investment to rise with taxes. Without an economic understanding of what determines the decisions of investors, consumers, exporters and importers, other equally valid (or invalid) interpretations would be the following:

- Raising taxes reduces savings by an equal amount (since equation (1.1) could be rearranged to yield $S = I - T + G - IM + EX$) but leaves investment unaffected.
- Raising taxes reduces imports (from $IM = I - S - T + G + EX$).
- Raising taxes raises exports (from $EX = S - I + T - G + IM$).

What sets these assertions apart is which variables are held fixed and which ones we allow to change after we changed T. Each version was arbitrary. Without an understanding of how investment, savings, import and export decisions are being made, there is no way of telling what will actually happen after a tax increase. It is possible that several of the other leaks and injections may change after T rises. To complicate things further, even the width of the circular flow stream, which measures the income level, may be affected by the tax increase.

So if it is to be used in the context of economic analysis, the circular flow equation needs to be combined with thorough economic reasoning. This will be enlarged upon in subsequent chapters. As it is, the circular flow identity only provides a glimpse at some key structural properties of a country's economy.

National income accounts report data for GDP and its components.

Actual numbers for the components of the leakages and injections combined in equation (1.1) and other related variables are assembled in the national income accounts of a country. Table 1.3 presents the sums involved, expressed as percentages of GDP. While country experiences differ, there are some common threads in the data:

- Most countries still run sizeable budget deficits. Governments spend more than they receive.
- In the majority of countries private savings exceed private investment. This is one way of financing the government budget deficit (or syphoning off the

net injections coming from the government sector). Instead of savings being passed on to firms for investment spending, they go to the government for financing the deficit.

■ About half of the countries shown here export less than they import. In those countries the net injection from the private and government sectors (the excess of $I + G$ over $S + T$) is neutralized by a net leakage of spending to other countries. Other countries may appear to refrain from buying our export goods with all the money they receive for our imports from them, but instead lend part of that money to our government and/or firms to finance the national deficit.

Countries run twin deficits if both the government budget and the current account are in deficit.

Discussion of the twin deficits that haunt the Greek economy offers ample real world examples of uninformed use of the circular flow identity, which the above stylized example attempted to discredit. To some, the Greek budget deficit, considered a result of excessive public spending and tax evasion, causes the current account deficit, and therefore it has to be removed (based on $EX - IM = S - I + T - G$). To others, the lacking competitiveness of Greece's economy along with German wage dumping causes the current account deficit, which in turn forces the Greek government budget into deficit (based on $T - G = I - S + EX - IM$). A third view is that neither is true. Rather, insufficient private savings in Greece drive the current account into deficit (based on $EX - IM = S - I + T - G$). Again, while there may be a grain of truth in all three explanations, no judgement is possible before we understand how the different actors in the economy make their choices.

Table 1.3 **The circular flow identity in numbers** (2010, as % of GDP). The data decompose the circular flow identity for a set of industrial countries. To permit comparability, aggregates are given in percentages of GDP. The data report similarities and differences between countries. Consider Greece and the United Kingdom, which run a similar government budget deficit. In the UK this is mostly financed by private domestic savings $S - I$. What sets the two cases apart is that the British government runs up its debt primarily against its own citizens, while Greece runs up debt against the rest of the world.

	$S - I$ in %	$T - G$ in %	$EX - IM$ (or $NX = CA$) in %
Belgium	5.3	−4.1	1.2
Denmark	7.7	−2.7	5.0
France	4.9	−7.0	−2.1
Germany	8.6	−3.3	5.3
Greece	0.1	−10.5	−10.4
Ireland	31.7	−32.4	−0.7
Italy	1.1	−4.6	−3.5
Netherlands	12.5	−5.4	7.1
Poland	4.6	−7.9	−3.3
Portugal	−0.8	−9.1	−9.9
Spain	4.7	−9.2	−4.5
United Kingdom	7.9	−10.4	−2.5
United States	7.4	−10.6	−3.2
China	7.8	−2.6	5.2
Japan	13.1	−9.5	3.6

Sources: Eurostat and IMF.

| CASE STUDY 1.2 | How circular flows link Germany and Greece |

The circular flow of income not only links the different sectors within an economy but also links economies across borders. A simple application may underscore that what happens in or is requested of one country is intrinsically tied to developments in other countries.

Suppose Germany's circular flow identity is

$$S - I + T - G = EX - IM \qquad (1)$$

and for Greece we write

$$S' - I' + T' - G' = EX' - IM' \qquad (2)$$

To simplify the argument, let the world consist of Germany and Greece only. Then Greek net exports are German net imports, and vice versa:

$$EX' - IM' = IM - EX \qquad (3)$$

Substituting (3) into (2) and equating the result with (1) gives

$$\underbrace{\underbrace{S - I}_{+} + \underbrace{T - G}_{0}}_{+} = \underbrace{G' - T' + I' - S'}_{+} \qquad (4)$$

Now, if thrifty Germans save more than is being invested in Germany, indicated by the plus sign underneath the term $S - I$, and if the German government balances its budget, as it did in 2007 and 2008, before the financial crisis called for government intervention, then the left-hand side of equation (4), representing Germany, is positive. Since this requires the right-hand side to be positive as well, Greek households must not be thrifty and/or their government must run a deficit. And Greece cannot reverse this unless German citizens or politicians spend more.

This result holds globally. The thriftiness of some countries like China, Germany, the Netherlands or Switzerland, which routinely feature trade surpluses between 5 and 10% of GDP, inevitably renders respective negative numbers of matching magnitude in other countries. Those countries accused of 'living beyond their means' cannot change their ways without the presumed 'good guys' changing theirs.

Money in the circular flow

Figure 1.5 featured a counter-clockwise flow of real factors such as labour and goods, and a compensating clockwise nominal flow of money income (evaluated at today's wages) and spending (evaluated at today's prices). We know that each flow is simply a mirror image of the other. It seems plausible that how labour is linked to income depends on the wage rate, and how goods relate to spending depends on prices. To sharpen our understanding of this we need to introduce **money** into the circular flow model. How does money fit in?

Money is anything that sellers generally accept as payment for goods and services.

Consider the example given in Figure 1.10. Firms only employ one factor of production – labour – to produce one good – cars. Assume this economy produces 6 cars annually, using 24,000 work-hours. Assume €30,000 float around in this economy, in notes and coins. To keep the argument simple, let there be no other money (such as bank accounts). Now if those €30,000 are being turned over (meaning that they flow from firms to households and back) 12 times a year, the firms' cash registers add up a total of €360,000. Since this sum represents the payments for 6 cars, the price of a car is obviously €60,000. On the other hand, over the course of a year €360,000 also arrive in the pockets of households as wage incomes, as compensation for 24,000 work-hours. So the hourly wage rate must be €15 per hour. *Nominal income* and spending equals €360,000, while *real income* and spending equals 6 cars.

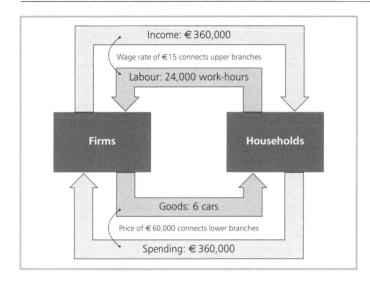

Figure 1.10 Looking at the inner circle first, we assume that firms use 24,000 hours of labour to produce 6 cars. If €30,000 circulates 12 times a year, annual income and annual spending must be €360,000. Hence the wage rate must be €15 per hour and the price of a car is €60,000. Thus, given all the other factors, the supply of money determines goods' prices and nominal wages.

The numerical example discussed here motivates the classical **quantity equation** $M \times V = P \times Y$. It states that the money supply M times the velocity of money circulation V equals nominal income PY (where P is the price level and Y denotes real income). In the example, M increases from €30,000 to €33,000, while we presume V constant at 12. In the first case, this raises P from €60,000 to €66,000, leaving Y unchanged. In the second case, Y rises from 6 to 6.6 at an unchanged price level. It should be obvious that both P and Y may rise, as long as $PY = $ €396,000.

Next, consider the following thought experiment – devised by an economist who later won the Nobel prize. Let a helicopter fly all over our imaginary country, and, little by little, scatter €3,000 in small notes. What are the consequences? If by now €33,000 continue to circulate at the speed of 12 turnovers a year, cash registers will count €396,000, as will wage earners. As regards prices, we consider two extreme cases.

One possibility is that the number of work-hours used in the production process remains at 24,000 hours. This could be because we are operating at the capacity limit, and this leaves output at 6 cars. Then €396,000 of income and spending must be compensation for 24,000 work-hours and payment for 6 cars. So the price of a car must have risen to €66,000, and the hourly wage rate to €16.50. Workers have to work 4,000 hours to earn enough money to buy a car, just as much as before the helicopter mission. Putting this differently, *nominal income*, income in terms of currency, grew by 10% from €360,000 to €396,000. **Real income**, income in terms of what it can buy, is unchanged at 6 cars.

As a second possibility, the increase of nominal spending to €396,000 may induce firms to increase output instead of raising prices. At the original price level, 6.6 cars can be sold. This requires 26,400 work-hours, which, at the going wage rate of €15, produces €396,000 of income. Workers still have to work 4,000 hours to make enough money to buy a car. This leaves the real wage rate, the purchasing power of one hour's work, unchanged at 0.00025 cars. Economy-wide **real income** has increased by 10% to 6.6 cars.

The quantity equation $M \times V = P \times Y$ becomes a theory of inflation, the quantity theory of money, by letting V be constant. Then the money supply determines nominal income: $P \times Y = \bar{V} \times M$.

The numerical example discussed here motivates the classical quantity equation

$$M \times V = P \times Y \qquad \text{Quantity equation}$$

It states that the money supply M times the velocity of money circulation V equals nominal income PY (where P is the price level and Y denotes real income).

In the above example, M increases from €30,000 to €33,000, while we presume V constant at 12. In the first case, when Y remains unchanged, this raises P from €60,000 to €66,000. In the second case, when P does not change, Y rises from 6 to 6.6. It should be obvious that both P and Y may rise, as long as $PY = $ €396,000.

The quantity equation, which can be traced back as far as Copernicus, merely states that the four variables involved are related in the proposed way.

CASE STUDY 1.3 Central banks and the subprime mortgage crisis of 2007–08

In 2007–08, repercussions from the US housing market gave the world economy quite a scare. Imprudent investments in US subprime mortgages generated losses for banks and other financial institutions that, according to IMF estimates, could tally up to 1 trillion US dollars around the globe. Such losses even drove bank heavyweights towards bankruptcy and into the arms of governments, which agreed to bail them out. Examples are *Northern Rock*, initially a British building society that evolved into a major bank, and *IndyMac*, a US mortgage bank. In September 2007 and July 2008, respectively, these two institutions suffered *bank runs*, the withdrawal of billions of deposits by panicking customers queuing outside branch offices, which current generations only knew from flickering silent movies and yellowed photographs.

Shared fears of severe national downturns and a global recession led major central banks, including the Bank of England, the European Central Bank and the US Federal Reserve System (called the Fed), the central bank of the United States of America, to cooperate and supply markets with hundreds of billions of euros worth of additional liquidity. A first answer as to why this was judged necessary is provided by the quantity equation introduced above.

The quantity equation, $M \times V = P \times Y$, says that M, the amount of money available in a country, multiplied by how often it circulates within a year, equals nominal income $P \times Y$. Now money M is a complex concept at which we look in more detail in Chapter 3. For now, let M be the total value of banknotes and coins in circulation.

People carry money for making their daily transactions – things such as purchasing groceries and the newspaper, paying the bus fare and buying lunch. If they had more money than they needed for all these transactions, they would bring this 'excess liquidity' to the bank, where it would

earn interest. Not doing so would cost in terms of interest earnings forgone, and would not be very rational – during normal times, that is.

There are times when this *transactions demand for money* is supplemented by a second motive, the proverbial fortunes kept under the mattress. Using money as a *store of value* becomes relevant when you lose trust in your bank. Then it may make sense to forgo the interest offered by the bank in order to eliminate the risk of losing your funds.

If we call L the transaction demand for money and L_s the part of wealth held in the form of money, we may write $M = L + L_s$. The amount of money supplied by the central bank, M, that is left for purchasing goods and services is then $L = M - L_s$. This part is relevant for the quantity equation, which generalizes to $(M - L_s) \times V = P \times Y$.

Table 1.4 provides a first macroeconomic perspective on the subprime crisis by means of a numerical illustration. Initially, €30,000 are in circulation, circulating 12 times a year, and money is not used for storing wealth. Then 6 cars are produced annually and sold at a price of €60,000. As the subprime crisis emerges and banks run into trouble, some people lose trust in their bank and withdraw all or part of their savings. Let the amount of wealth being held in the form of money rises, L_s, from 0 to €3,000. The amount of money available for transactions drops to €27,000. Thus, with the velocity of circulation unchanged at 12, all purchases conducted during one year total €27,000 × 12 = €324,000. The drop in sales revenue from €360,000 to €324,000 requires a drop in prices from €60,000 to €54,000, a drop in output from 6 to 5.4, or a mix of both. Since prices are not very flexible in real life, there is a risk that firms will reduce output, thus causing a recession. To prevent this, the central bank may inject liquidity into the economy by increasing the supply of money from €30,000 to €33,000.

Case study 1.3 continued

Table 1.4 Bank runs and the quantity equation: a numerical example

$(M - L_s) \times V$		$=$	$P \times Y$	Quantity equation
■ Situation before crisis				
$(30{,}000 - 0) \times 12$		$=$	€60,000 × 6.0	
■ Crisis unfolds: wealth held as money L_s rises to €3,000				
(€30,000 − €3,000) × 12		$=$	€60,000 × 5.4	→ income falls
	or		€54,000 × 6.0	→ price falls
	or		€57,000 × 5.7	→ price and income fall
■ Policy response: money supply M increased to €33,000				
(€33,000 − €3,000) × 12		$=$	€60,000 × 6.0	→ no change in price and/or income

It evolved into a theory, stating cause and effect, in the quantity theory of money formulated by US Nobel laureate Milton Friedman. He insisted, as we did in our numerical exercises above, that the velocity of money circulation V is constant. Then any changes in the money supply M affect nominal income PY. The price level remains constant only if the money supply grows at the same pace at which real income grows. If the money supply grows faster than real income, prices begin to increase. We end up having inflation.

Macroeconomists call a graphical picture of how much total or aggregate output is produced at different price levels an aggregate supply curve. The first case discussed above is tantamount to postulating a *vertical aggregate supply curve* (see Figure 1.11, panel (a)). Both at a price of €60,000 and at a price of €66,000, 6 cars are being produced. In the second case, producers are ready to produce different numbers of cars at one and the same price level. This is tantamount to postulating a *horizontal aggregate supply curve* (Figure 1.11,

> The aggregate supply curve indicates how much output firms are willing to produce at various price levels.

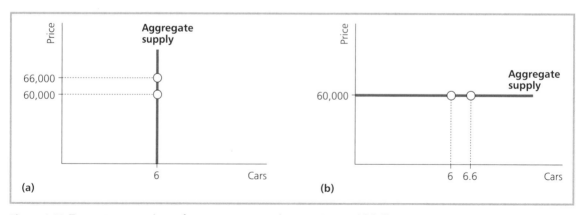

Figure 1.11 Two extreme versions of an aggregate supply curve. In panel (a), firms can or want to supply one specific amount of output only, no matter what the price level is. In panel (b), firms are ready to supply any amount of goods that the market demands at the given price level.

panel (b)). We will be looking at aggregate supply curves, their economic underpinning and slope, in some detail in later chapters. For now the simple but important lesson to be learned from this stylized example is that – with our extreme second case being an exception – the amount of money circulating in the economy directly bears on the price level. So if the supply of money changes, the price level changes. If this continues, we have inflation. Equipped with this tentative understanding we now turn to a brief look at the government budget and the balance of payments.

The government budget and the balance of payments

The government budget is primarily a planning instrument. In hindsight it breaks down government receipts and expenditures, and shows how deficits are being financed.

The balance of payments records a country's trade in goods, services and financial assets with other countries.

In addition to the national income accounts, which measure the circular flows with leakages and injections, there are two other accounts that macroeconomists need in their elementary tool-box. These are the government budget and the balance of payments. As Figure 1.7 shows, these two accounts simply trace the interactions between the domestic private sector and the government sector (characterized by the left-hand rectangle) on the one hand, and with other countries (characterized by the rectangle on the right) on the other hand. While the basic data on leakages from and injections into these sectors are already being supplied in the national income accounts, the government budget and the balance of payments break down these numbers in more detail. More importantly, though, they show how *budget deficits* in the first case, and *trade imbalances* in the second case, are being paid for.

The government budget has two main purposes: to break up the catch-all variables G and T into more detailed subcategories, and to show how a given budget deficit is being financed. Similarly, the balance of payments adds detail to the general notion of exports and imports. But, again, it also traces how a given imbalance between exports and imports is being financed.

The central bank is a government agency primarily responsible for supplying the economy with the right amount of money.

Let us start with a look at how governments can finance budget deficits. As is the case for you and me, governments can only spend more than they collect by running up debt (or running down wealth). Unlike private individuals, however, governments have the second option of running into debt with another public or government institution called the central bank. So if we denote government debt owed to the private sector by B_{PS} and government debt owed to the central bank (or, actually, to itself) by B_{CB}, a budget deficit must change either or both debt categories:

$$G - T = \Delta B_{PS} + \Delta B_{CB} \tag{1.3}$$

Here and in the remainder of the book the Greek letter Δ denotes the change of the attached variable over the preceding period.

A government budget deficit changes government bonds holdings either by private citizens or by the central bank.

The balance of payments records a country's international transactions. Usually these require the purchase or the sale of foreign currency (or foreign money). An exception to this rule is of course the euro area, where cross-border transactions are done in one currency. The balance of payments is subdivided into three major accounts: the current account CA, the capital account CP and the official reserve account OR. The official reserve account is sometimes displayed as a sub-category of a more broadly defined capital account. We list the two separately, however, because this enables us to keep private activities in the foreign exchange market, recorded in CP, apart from government intervention, recorded in OR. This distinction will prove useful when we talk about the virtues of different exchange rate systems in later chapters.

If we take the balance of payments of the euro area as an example, any transaction that involves the purchase of euros is recorded as a positive entry in one of the balance of payments accounts. Any transaction resulting in the sale of euros is entered as a negative number. Since any purchase of euros by one person requires the sale of euros by somebody else, any positive entry in one account gives rise to a negative entry of the same magnitude in the same or some other account. All entries must thus add up to zero. In other words, since purchases of currency must equal sales, the three accounts that make up the balance of payments must add up to zero:

$$\underbrace{CA}_{\text{Current account}} + \underbrace{CP}_{\text{Capital account}} + \underbrace{OR}_{\text{Official reserve account}} = 0 \qquad (1.4)$$

The current account records goods, services and transfers into and out of the country.

The current account records the flow of goods and services across borders that was represented as leakages from and injections into the 'rest of the world' box in Figure 1.7. More generally, it measures the net demand for domestic currency which results from the net sales of domestically produced goods and services to the world, plus cross-border income flows and transfer payments. For most of the book we will ignore income flows and transfers to obtain the convenient approximation $CA = EX - IM$. Now, if an American buys a Ferrari with a €180,000 price tag, this Italian export invokes the *purchase* of the appropriate amount of euros by the American customer in exchange for her dollars. It is recorded with a *positive sign*, as a credit item.

The capital account records the flow of financial assets into and out of the country.

The capital account records all purchases and sales of foreign assets, that is of such things as bonds, stocks or securities, that do not involve the central bank. It registers the net demand for the domestic currency which results from the net sales of domestic bonds and other assets to foreigners. If net foreign assets (defined as domestic holdings of foreign assets minus foreign holdings of domestic assets) are denoted by F, then the capital account measures the net fall in F that occurred during a given period, that is $CP = -\Delta F$. Let a Dutchman invest €50,000 in US government securities (Dutch F rises). Just as if he had bought an American car, he needs to purchase US dollars by selling euros in order to complete the transaction. Because euros are being *sold*, this transaction is being recorded with a *negative sign*, as a debit item.

The official reserve account records the purchases and sales of foreign currency by the central bank.

The official reserve account tracks the involvement of the central bank in the foreign exchange market. It measures the net demand for domestic currency which the purchase or sale of currency reserves held by the central bank constitutes. If RES denotes central bank foreign currency reserves, then OR measures the fall in RES: that is, $OR = -\Delta RES$. If the European Central Bank sells $1 million that it held in its vaults in exchange for euros, reserves fall by $1 million, and a $1 million net demand for domestic currency results. The equivalent amount of euros *purchased* is being recorded with a *positive sign*, as a credit item.

We will discuss balance of payments accounting in much more detail in Chapter 4.

Table 1.5 shows the composition of the balance of payments identity for some EU member states, Japan and the United States in 2010. In that year

Table 1.5 **The balance of payments accounts.** (2010, in millions of US dollars). Note that while in theory $CA + CP + OR = 0$, this does not hold in reality due to errors and omissions during data compilation.

	CA	CP	OR
Austria	11,949	−2,502	−1,435
Belgium	3,976	9,210	−6,968
Denmark	15,550	12,367	−4,279
Finland	5,602	20,209	−2,516
France	−53,052	25,040	−7,790
Germany	176,084	−170,570	−2,130
Greece	−35,961	36,308	−1,213
Ireland	−1,477	17,521	42
Italy	−71,986	120,467	−1,338
Japan	194,754	−86,620	−43,850
Netherlands	55,832	−21,876	−181
Portugal	−22,637	23,343	−1,271
Spain	−63,258	59,768	−1,061
Sweden	29,615	−43,612	1,077
United Kingdom	−56,016	57,930	−10,010
United States	−470,244	238,910	−1,820

Source: IMF.

many central banks participated heavily in the foreign exchange market, accumulating or running down foreign currency reserves.

Using the definitions given in the last three sections we may rewrite the balance of payments definition (equation (1.4)) in a way that reveals how the home country finances trade imbalances with the rest of the world:

$$EX - IM = \Delta F + \Delta RES \tag{1.5}$$

If exports exceed imports, this means that traders exercise an excess demand for domestic currency (which they need to buy our exports). This can be balanced either by us accepting – i.e. buying – foreign debt titles (which raises F), or the central bank can supply the required domestic currency, thus running up foreign currency reserves RES.

The similarity between the interpretation of the government budget and of the balance of payments should be evident. Both show how an asymmetry between leakages and injections can be financed, regarding the government sector in the first case, and the rest of the world in the second case. And in both cases two options are available: one involving the market alone, and one involving the central bank.

In real life the central bank does not use helicopters to 'pump' money M into the economy. What really happens may be illustrated by means of a simplified balance sheet, which includes just three items that are essential here (see Table 1.6). The central bank's one liability is the currency it puts into circulation. For our present purposes this is equal to the money supply. Note that bank notes printed in the central bank's basement are not part of the money supply, and not effective economically, as long as the central bank does not put them into circulation.

Assets equal liabilities and are of two kinds: first, government securities – i.e. the amount of government debt held by the central bank B_{CB}; second, currency

Table 1.6 The central bank balance sheet

Assets		Liabilities	
Government securities	B_{CB}	Currency in circulation (money)	M
Currency reserves	RES		

reserves – i.e. the amount of dollars, yen and other foreign currencies in the central bank's vaults.

Now B_{CB}, RES and M are obviously closely related. In fact, $M = B_{CB} + RES$. So the two ways to increase the money supply are to buy either government bonds or foreign exchange:

$$\Delta M = \Delta B_{CB} + \Delta RES \qquad (1.6)$$

Or, put the other way: if a government budget deficit (unmatched leakages into and injections from the left-hand rectangle in Figure 1.7) is being financed by the central bank buying up government debt, or if the central bank at any time buys government bonds previously held by households, B_{CB} rises and the money supply increases. Also, if the central bank buys foreign currency, be it to finance a current account surplus or for other reasons, RES rises and the money supply increases as well. Our numerical example discussed above indicates that such money supply increases may either raise prices or raise output, or a combination of both. But these issues will be examined in more detail in later chapters.

1.3 Beyond accounting

National income accounts, government budgets and the balance of payments provide indispensable information about the current state of the economy. The macroeconomist's foremost task is to move beyond pure measurement towards a logically coherent understanding of how the variables listed in the previous sections, and other variables not mentioned yet, influence each other. Only then may we hope to link undesirable developments documented in the data, such as a current account deficit, a recession, unemployment or rising inflation, to an underlying cause and then to propose remedies.

The art of simplifying and model-building

A model is a simplified, logically coherent story that links economic variables like consumption and taxes to each other.

When addressing this task, economists draw simplified pictures of the real world. These they call models. Simplifications are necessary, since anything close to a perfect account of the real world would be too complicated for any one to understand. On the other hand, the economist's way of making assumptions in order to simplify some problem at hand remains one of the biggest obstacles to a constructive dialogue between economists and non-economists; not so much because these models may often seem complicated, but because they are considered unrealistic, that is, of little relevance for real-world problems. This prejudice against economic theorizing is widespread. We therefore pause briefly here to consider the purpose of simplifying and model-building. Consider the following analogy.

A tourist wonders how to get from Sète to Bocuse-sur-Mer. She is unlikely to launch into space to obtain an unobstructed, realistic view of the world, before setting out to tackle her problem. Even if she did, this would be of little help, since neither town could be seen from up there. What she might do is use a high-performance telescope and focus on southern France. But even this would distort her perspective from reality, as the rest of the world would slip out of sight.

It is more likely that she will obtain a road map of southern France – a cheap and easy-to-use but extremely unrealistic device: it misses many important parts of the world like the Sahara or the Shetland Islands, it shows neither trees nor bushes, ignores the true colours of the Mediterranean Sea and pastures, and its smell is a far cry from the fragrance of *Herbes de Provence*. Yet despite these drawbacks, people seem to find maps – these naive, unrealistic pictures (or, we could say, models) of the world – very useful and buy them by the million every year. Of course, some maps are better than others, and you could get the wrong one for your purpose: a map of the London underground system would be of little help for our traveller, as would be an aerial navigation map or a hiker's map of southern France. But the reason that these maps are useless is not because they are unrealistic, but because they focus on the wrong things for the purposes of our traveller.

For very much the same reason it is perfectly acceptable and even mandatory for economists to build models of the economy that are unrealistic. Under no circumstances should the goal be to include as many features of the real world as possible, that is, to make them as realistic as possible – just as no publisher would cram all the real-world features onto a road map. So in the end no models are too unrealistic or abstract. But there may be models that focus on the wrong features for the problem at hand.

Mathematical models

A mathematical model tells its simplified, logically coherent story by means of algebraic equations.

Macroeconomic models come in all shapes and sizes. Some are written in prose. Some are presented in diagrams. Most frequently they are cast in a set of mathematical equations which forces rigour into economists' reasoning. It may seem unnecessarily awkward to express a simple statement like 'the number of tickets for a ferry trip across the English Channel which people want to buy per month falls as the fare increases' by

$$D = a - bP$$

where D = demand for ferry tickets, P = price of a ticket, and a and b are parameters, stand-ins for some positive numbers which we do not exactly know. However, a linear equation like this tells us exactly by how much D falls if P increases. Sometimes we may want to be less specific and write the more general equation

$$D = f(P)$$

where f states that D is a function of P. Dealing with such general functions and stating their properties requires calculus, though we will avoid that unless it is absolutely necessary.

Even models that consist of mathematical equations can be made more transparent and more accessible by transferring them into diagrams. We will do so frequently throughout this text and use purely mathematical reasoning as sparingly as possible.

Empirical tests

Just as the effectiveness of road maps is judged by the ease with which they guide their users to unfamiliar destinations, the quality of an economic model is judged by its potential to help us understand what happens in the real world. Such confrontation of models with reality is attempted in a variety of ways, using both a historical perspective and sophisticated statistical techniques. Most empirical tests address either of two questions:

■ Can the model provide a specific macroeconomic event with a coherent explanation? Examples of such events are the oil price explosions of the 1970s and what they did to unemployment and inflation, German unification and the subsequent crises in the European Monetary System, or the Asian crisis of 1998.
■ Are the building blocks, the equations, used in the construction of the model, or the conclusions offered by the model, supported by real-world data?

Statistical techniques for this purpose are provided by the discipline of *econometrics*. A first glimpse at the underlying concepts is offered at the end of the book in the appendix 'A primer in econometrics'. This material is optional. The book can be studied without using it and the empirical end-of-chapter exercises that illustrate the use of econometrics and provide the opportunity for first hands-on experience. If time permits, however, I strongly encourage you to give them a try.

While the first part of this book emphasizes the development of the concepts and *tools of macroeconomics* and only occasionally looks at empirical questions, the balance shifts increasingly towards the *issues of macroeconomics* as we progress from chapter to chapter.

Institutions

Model-building is an art. Good models ignore those features of the real world that are not relevant for the issue under consideration and focus on the important ones. Economists have become increasingly aware that individuals, whose behaviour they want to explain, are very sensitive to the institutional environment in which they operate. They therefore show a heightened sensitivity to whether the models they want to apply to a specific set of issues take proper account of the relevant institutional background. Because institutions differ – to give one example – labour economists have been using quite different models when studying European labour markets than when looking at the United States. In the United States, with trade unions being very weak, it may be a reasonable approximation to ignore their role and focus on individual behaviour in the wage bargaining process. In Europe, trade unions have traditionally been much stronger, and for many countries it may be severely misleading to ignore their role in the centralized bargaining process that has been established.

Empirical tests are confrontations of hypotheses (statements) derived from models (or theories) with real-world data or events. They serve to gauge whether a model is useful or not.

Institutions are economic, political or legal structures within which individuals operate. Examples are formal organizations, written law, or informal customs and norms.

BOX 1.2   Working with graphs (part I)

Graphs are an indispensable tool in economics. Economists use the technique frequently to provide illustrative examples, in dealing with non-economists, and also in teaching, as we will do abundantly in this book.

Lines in a diagram illustrate the relationship between two variables displayed on the axes of the graph, either as it results from behaviour, in equilibrium or by definition. The demand function shown in the text, $D = a - bP$, is one such example. It shows the negative relationship between the demand for ferry passages and the price. The vertical intercept of this line is a. The slope is $-b$, meaning that increasing the price by one unit reduces demand by b units (see Figure 1.12, panel (a)).

An example of a positive relationship between two variables is the supply function, $S = c + dP$, indicating that the supply of ferry transport rises when the price moves up (panel (b)). The equilibrium condition $S = D$ requires supply to equal demand. In the graph this obtains where both curves intersect (panel (c)). The price equilibrium is $\bar{P}$. Demand and supply are $\bar{D}$ and $\bar{S}$, respectively.

What do we do if our equation proposes a relationship between more than two variables? Suppose the demand function is $D = a - bP + fT$, where T is the price for transport through the Eurotunnel. For these three variables we could draw a three-dimensional (3D) graph, showing the dependence of the demand for ferry transport on the price for ferry transport and, positively, on the price for transport through the Eurotunnel. A 3D graph is often useful to give a visual image of a relationship in the form of a plane, but it is rarely

used for analytical purposes. The reason is that as more relationships (planes) are added to such a graph, it tends to become confusing. Also, the technique obviously breaks down as we deal with more than three variables. What is done then is to hold one (or more) variable(s) constant, and only focus on the relationship between the two remaining variables that are permitted to change in a 2D graph. In the Channel passage example we may fix Eurotunnel transport fares at some (arbitrary) level and only trace how demand changes with the price for ferry transport. (Alternatively, we may fix the ferry price at some arbitrary level and then draw a graph of how demand responds to tunnel fares.)

As long as we keep T constant and only vary P, we are moving along the curve. But we may also ask what happens if T changes. This will generate a shift of the curve: at any P demand is different from what it was before, because T is different (see Figure 1.13). The failure to distinguish between *movements along a curve* and *shifts of a curve* is a frequent source of confusion for those new to using graphical models in economics.

Using unspecified position and slope parameters in the equations and in the graphs reflects that we either do not know any exact values of a, b, c and d, or that we would like our result to be robust to changes in those parameters, as long as these remain positive.

Sometimes we may not even know whether the relationship is linear, i.e. a straight line as in panel (a) in Figure 1.14, or non-linear, i.e. a curve as in panel (b). The latter is probably the more general case. Very often, however, working with more

(a)

(b)

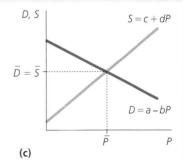

(c)

Figure 1.12

Box 1.2 continued

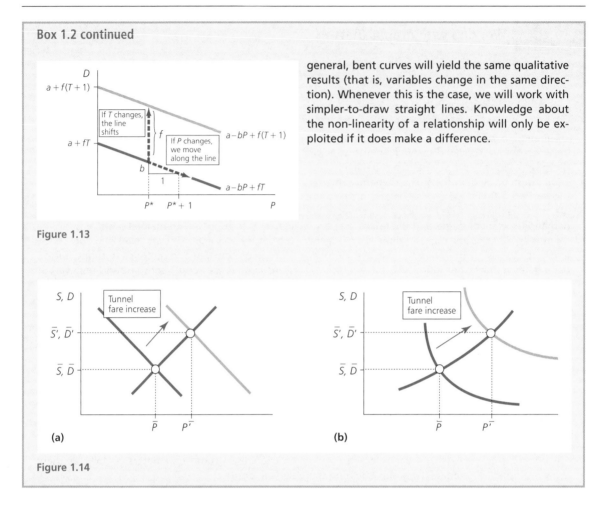

general, bent curves will yield the same qualitative results (that is, variables change in the same direction). Whenever this is the case, we will work with simpler-to-draw straight lines. Knowledge about the non-linearity of a relationship will only be exploited if it does make a difference.

Figure 1.13

Figure 1.14

Other institutional features that are being closely scrutinized are the following:

- *The (international) monetary system.* Are exchange rates flexible, determined in the market, or set by the government and the central bank? Are groups of countries sharing a common currency, or does each country retain its own national currency?
- *Central bank independence.* Does the central bank act on government orders, or can it take its own independent decisions on monetary policy? The importance of this issue is easily seen by looking back at equation (1.3), which showed that one way to pay for excessive public spending that results in a government budget deficit is by making the central bank buy government securities and thus increase the money supply. Or is monetary policy even delegated to some supranational authority such as the European Central Bank?
- *International capital markets.* Borrowing and lending, the investment of financial wealth, has quickly moved beyond national borders onto the global stage. The extent to which a country participates in this process, to which financial assets move freely across borders or meet obstacles,

encouraging or deterring potential investors, has an increasingly important role for a nation's economic prospects.

■ *International trade relations as regulated in the World Trade Organization (WTO)*. Does the presence of this institution and its particular design bear on the issues of whether it is good or bad for a country to protect its industries by using tariffs or non-tariff barriers to trade, or on who benefits and who loses?

While many of these institutions have evolved historically, European integration requires redesigns and another look at old motives.

After these preliminaries we are now ready to assemble a basic set of macroeconomic models. This will eventually carry us a long way towards understanding not only Europe's recent experience, current challenges and ongoing debates of macroeconomic issues, but those in other countries and continents and on a global scale as well.

CHAPTER SUMMARY

This chapter has introduced essential concepts and insights:

■ Macroeconomics looks at the big picture, at what things like income, spending, unemployment or inflation look like after we add everything up.

■ The circular flow model shows the real and monetary flows between households and firms. It can be enhanced to account for interactions with the government sector and other countries. Leakages out of and injections into this circle always balance. At the core of this 'model' is the identity between income and output on the one hand, and between spending and output on the other.

■ Output, income and spending all measure the same thing. Depending on whether we define a country by its geographic boundaries or by its residents, the empirical counterpart of these concepts is gross domestic product (GDP) or gross national income (GNI). The latter used to be called gross national product (GNP).

■ The central bank is the arm of the government responsible for monetary policy. If the central bank provides the economy with more money, this raises nominal income, which is defined as the price level times real income. Only economic analysis (to be provided in later chapters) will reveal under what circumstances it is more likely for the price level to rise or for real income to rise.

■ The national income accounts reveal who buys aggregate output and how aggregate income is spent.

■ The government budget records the interaction between the private sector and the government sector. It also reveals how the government finances budget surpluses or deficits.

■ The balance of payments records the interaction with the rest of the world. It also reveals how imbalances in the trade of goods and services are being financed.

■ Economists work with simplified pictures of the world, which they call models. Models are instrumental in understanding the key economic issues in today's world.

Key terms and concepts

aggregate output 9	institutions 24
aggregate supply curve 18	macroeconomics 1
balance of payments 19	mathematical model 23
capital account 20	microeconomics 1
central bank 19	model 22
circular flow model 8	money 15
current account 20	national income accounts 13
empirical tests 24	official reserve account 20
factors of production 6	quantity equation 16
government budget 19	quantity theory of money 18
gross domestic product (GDP) 7	real income 16
gross national income (GNI) 12	transfers 10
gross national product (GNP) 7	twin deficits 14
income 2	

EXERCISES

1.1 Table 1.7 gives real and nominal per capita incomes in US dollars.
  (a) What is your country's price level relative to the United States price level of 1? (If your country is not included, choose any country.)
  (b) Rank your country and any two other countries according to their price levels.

1.2 Which of the following transactions constitute leakages, and which ones injections?
  (a) The home country receives aid from the International Monetary Fund.
  (b) Immigrant workers transfer their salaries to their home countries.
  (c) Domestic firms invest in foreign countries.
  (d) The government raises taxes and uses the proceeds to buy computers abroad.

1.3 Table 1.8 contains data for the Netherlands, Germany and Spain in 2009. All numbers are in billions of euros. Fill in the missing numbers, following the logic of the circular flow model.

Table 1.7 Nominal and real per capita incomes, expressed in US dollars, 2010

Country	Nominal	Real
Austria A	44,986.58	39,634.13
Belgium B	42,630.11	36,100.23
Switzerland CH	67,246.00	41,663.05
Germany D	40,631.24	36,033.28
Denmark DK	56,147.14	36,449.55
Spain E	30,639.30	29,741.73
France F	41,018.60	34,077.04
United Kingdom UK	36,119.85	34,919.51
Greece GR	27,301.54	28,433.86
Italy I	34,058.72	29,392.40
Ireland IRL	45,688.76	38,549.80
Luxembourg LUX	108,831.70	81,383.26
Norway N	84,443.63	52,012.51
Netherlands NL	47,172.14	40,764.55
Portugal P	21,558.78	23,222.78
Sweden S	48,874.61	38,031.48

Source: International Monetary Fund, World Economic Outlook Database, April 2011.

Table 1.8

	Saving	Investment	Taxes	Government expenditure	Budget deficit	Imports	Exports	Current account
Netherlands	249			226	−44	459	518	
Germany		549	400	656		1,212	1,377	165
Spain		358	131		−178		347	−27

Source: World Bank.

1.4 You head your country's central bank and must determine the amount of money to circulate next year. You know that every euro circulates four times a year. The statistical office forecasts that production will remain unchanged at 1,000 barrels of whisky (the only good produced in your country) next year.

(a) What is the slope of the aggregate supply curve if the production of whisky remains constant as forecasted?

(b) Compute the price of one barrel of whisky if you fix the money supply at €4,000.

(c) What would be the price of one barrel of whisky if the velocity of money circulation rose to 5 while the money supply remained at €4,000?

(d) Given the rising velocity of money circulation from (c) and constant production of whisky, how would you fix the money supply if your targeted price level was €5 per barrel of whisky?

(e) What is the price of whisky if output rises to 1,600 barrels in the following year while the money supply remains at €4,000 and money circulates four times a year?

1.5 Some time after an increase in the money supply from 50 billion to 100 billion units, the government of country A learns that the price level has increased from 100 to 150 while the velocity of money circulation has remained constant. What does that tell you about the slope of the aggregate supply curve?

1.6 The government of country B plans to spend €10,000 next year. Due to political constraints, taxes cannot exceed €5,000. Eighty per cent of the budget deficit will be financed by issuing government bonds to the private sector, the rest by issuing bonds to the central bank in exchange for money.

(a) Compute the anticipated change in the money supply if neither international trade nor international capital movements take place.

(b) What will be the effect on the price level if real output stays constant at $Y = 10,000$ and V at 4?

(c) Compute the anticipated change in the money supply if international trade in goods takes place, but international capital movements are still forbidden. The statistical office forecasts a current account deficit of €3,000.

(d) Can you think of arguments that render the assumption of a constant level of real production (employed above) implausible?

1.7. A country's net foreign assets stand at 500. Next year's exports are expected to be 30, expected imports are 20. The central bank will not intervene in the foreign exchange market. What are the country's net foreign assets by the end of next year?

1.8 Consider Figure 1.15. The graph shows a stylized demand curve for DVD recorders.

(a) What are the endogenous variables in this model?

(b) The price of a DVD recorder is 1,500 Swiss francs. What is the quantity demanded?

(c) If the price fell to only one-third of its previous level, what would market demand be?

(d) The supply curve can be described by the following equation:

$$P = 500 + 0.000025 \times \text{Quantity}$$

Draw the curve into the diagram in the figure.

(e) Determine the equilibrium price level and the quantity sold graphically.

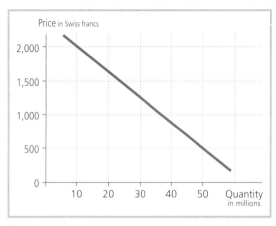

Figure 1.15

(f) It becomes unfashionable to waste time in front of the TV. Show how this change of preferences affects market demand. What will be the effect on the equilibrium price level and quantity?

(g) Due to a new technology it becomes cheaper to produce DVD recorders. How will that affect the diagram?

(h) The government introduces a tax on DVDs. How will that affect the diagram? What happens if the government introduces a tax on visits to the cinema but does not levy a tax on DVDs?

Online resources

Interactive circular flow applet www.eurmacro.eu/tutor/circularflow_applet.html

Circular flow video www.eurmacro.eu/tutor/circularflow_movie.html

X-ercise on circular flow www.eurmacro.eu/xercises/circularflow.html

Self quiz

www.eurmacro.eu/selfquiz/sq-ch01.html

Recommended reading

Data

For macroeconomic data including national income accounts, government budgets and the balance of payments, a good source to start searching are international organizations. The broadest set of countries is covered by the IMF (International Monetary Fund) publications *International Financial Statistics* and *Government Financial Statistics* (Washington DC).

A very good and inexpensive first source and overview on most countries of the world is provided by the World Bank in *The World Bank Atlas* (Washington DC). Standardized data on its twenty-three members are provided by the OECD (Organization for Economic Cooperation and Development) in *Economic Outlook* and *Historical Statistics* (Paris).

Relatively short series on EU member states are published by the European Commission in *European Union* and *Eurostat* (Brussels).

If you do not find what you are looking for in these international publications, you may have to go to national sources. All governments have statistical offices. But beware: definitions and compilation procedures may vary between countries, so data may not be directly comparable.

An excellent discussion of the obstacles encountered when trying to measure income, the key variable in macroeconomics, in the real world is provided by S. Landefeld, E. Seskin and B. Fraumeni (2008) 'Taking the pulse of the economy: Measuring GDP', *Journal of Economic Perspectives* 22: 193–216.

Economics

If the repetition of concepts in this chapter was too dense on occasion, you may want to go back to a principal text such as David Begg, Stanley Fischer and Rudiger Dornbusch (2008) *Economics*, 9th edn, London: McGraw-Hill; Paul Krugman and Robin Wells (2009) *Economics*, 2nd edn, New York: Palgrave Macmillan; or Gregory N. Mankiw (2011) *Principles of Economics*, 4th edn, Mason, OH: Southwestern College Publishing.

A now dated but still excellent history of economic thought in a nutshell that you may want to read here, and again after Chapter 10, is given in 'Schools brief: Paradigm lost', *The Economist*, 3 November 1990, pp. 82–3.

Economy

International periodicals that keep you on top of economic developments are *The Economist*, *The Financial Times* and *The Wall Street Journal Europe*. *The Economist* is particularly renowned for high-standard analyses of current economic issues. Also, do not forget the section on the economy in your favourite national newspaper.

Mathematics

If you would like to read up on the few maths tools that I use in this book, the didactically superb classic to be recommended is A. Chiang and K. Wainwright (2005) *Fundamental Methods of Mathematical Economics*, 4th edn, Singapore: McGraw-Hill. There you will find it all – and more.

APPENDIX ## Logarithms, growth rates and logarithmic scales

Logarithms

Taking the logarithm of a number or of a variable is nothing mysterious. Just as taking the square root of 9 amounts to picking 3, since $3^2 = 3 \times 3 = 9$, taking the logarithm of 1 to base 5 is zero, since $5^0 = 1$. Economists find it convenient to use Euler's number $e \equiv 2.71828\ldots$ as the base. Logarithms to the base of e are called natural logarithms and are referred to by the shorthand symbol ln. Then, in general terms: the natural logarithm of some number or variable a is the power to which e must be raised to yield a, that is $e^{\ln a} = a$.

Logarithms possess some properties that assist with model-building and the visual display of models and data in graphs. Since we are not interested in the higher mathematics of logarithms, we skip proofs and illustrate the concepts needed by means of numerical examples.

Consider a country's nominal income PY, which is the product of the price level P and real income Y. If $P = 100$ and $Y = 200$, then $PY = 20,000$. Now take your pocket calculator, key in 100 for the price level, and press the ln button. This should give you the natural logarithm of 100, that is ln $100 = 4.605$. For real income you get ln $200 = 5.298$. Now type in nominal income and your calculator gives you ln $(100 \times 200) = $ ln $20,000 = 9.903$. What is noteworthy about this result is that obviously ln $(100 \times 200) = $ ln $100 + $ ln 200, since $9.903 = 4.605 + 5.298$. That is, the logarithm of the product PY is the sum of the logarithms of its two components. This result

$$\ln PY = \ln P + \ln Y \qquad \qquad \text{Property 1}$$

holds generally, as you may check by entering other numbers for P and Y. You may use the above or other numbers to convince yourself that

$$\ln (P/Y) = \ln P - \ln Y \qquad \qquad \text{Property 2}$$

that is, the logarithm of the fraction P/Y equals the difference between the logarithms of the numerator and the denominator.

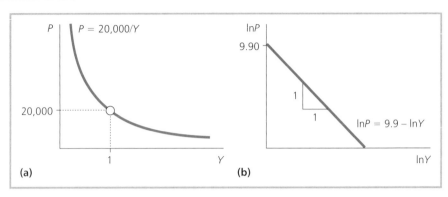

Figure 1.16

A third useful property is

$$\ln X^n = n \ln X \qquad\qquad \textbf{Property 3}$$

You may again convince yourself by entering some numbers into your pocket calculator, or you may derive this third property directly from property 1. For n being an integer, X^n may be written as

$$X^n = \underbrace{X \times X \times X \times \ldots \times X}_{n \text{ times}}$$

With the above rules for products, taking the logarithm of this gives

$$\ln X^n = \underbrace{\ln X + \ln X + \ln X + \ldots + \ln X}_{n \text{ times}} = n \ln X$$

What is so great about these results? Assume that you want to know what combinations of P and Y multiply into a given nominal income of 20,000. After writing $PY = 20,000$ you may solve for P to obtain $P = 20,000/Y$. The graph of this relationship is curved (called a hyperbola) as shown in panel (a) in Figure 1.16. Drawing it is not easy, since the slope is different for each value of Y. Working with it is not easy either: increasing nominal income from 20,000 to, say, 22,000 shifts and turns the line at the same time.

Now take the logarithm on both sides of $P = 20,000/Y$ and you obtain $\ln P = \ln 20,000 - \ln Y$. This new equation is additive and linear (see panel (b)). It intersects the vertical axis at $\ln 20,000 = 9.90$ and has a slope of -1 all over. Working with such a linear graph or model is much more convenient than manipulating a hyperbola.

Growth rates

The growth rate of Y over its previous value Y_{-1} is computed as $(Y - Y_{-1})/Y_{-1}$. Logarithms come in handy when we discuss such growth rates. Let inflation be 10%, or 0.1. As the P column in Table 1.9 illustrates, this means that the

Table 1.9

Time	P	$\Delta P = P - P_{-1}$	$(P - P_{-1})/P_{-1}$	$\ln P$	$\Delta \ln P = \ln P - \ln P_{-1}$
1	100			4.605	
2	110	10	0.1	4.700	$0.0953 \sim 0.1$
3	121	11	0.1	4.7957	$0.0953 \sim 0.1$
4	133.1	12.1	0.1	4.8911	$0.0953 \sim 0.1$
5	146.41	13.31	0.1	4.9864	$0.0953 \sim 0.1$
6	161.05	14.64	0.1	5.0817	$0.0953 \sim 0.1$

price level rises in larger and larger increments: after a change in the price level of 10 units in period 2, the change in period 6 is already 14.64. If P is plotted against the time axis, P turns out to follow a non-linear, accelerating path. This acceleration is not very visible for such short time horizons, but it becomes more and more pronounced as time passes.

Now look at the sixth column in Table 1.9, which gives $\Delta \ln P$. The period-to-period changes in the logarithm of P are obviously constant at 0.0953 – and they closely approximate the growth rate of P which is 0.1. The useful property of logarithms suggested by these numbers is that if a variable grows at a constant rate, and thus the variable moves up at an accelerating pace as time progresses (see panel (a) in Figure 1.17), the logarithm of this variable moves up at a constant pace. Thus as time progresses, the logarithm of this variable follows a straight line. The slope of this line closely approximates the growth rate of the variable.

The approximation becomes better as the growth rates become smaller: $(P - P_{-1})/P_{-1} = 0.05$ is approximated by $\ln P - \ln P_{-1} = 0.04879$; at $(P - P_{-1})/P_{-1} = 0.01$ the logarithmic approximation is $\ln P - \ln P_{-1} = 0.00995$. With high precision it only holds for very small growth rates. As a rule of thumb, however, for practical purposes *growth rates smaller than 0.2 may be*

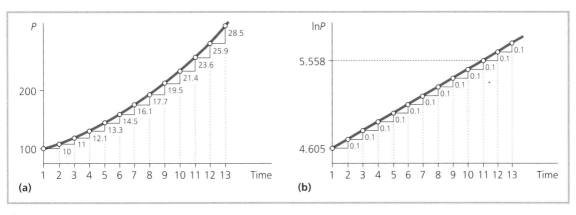

(a)   (b)

Figure 1.17

approximated by the change in the logarithm of the variable under consideration:

$$\frac{Y - Y_{-1}}{Y_{-1}} \cong \ln Y - \ln Y_{-1} = \Delta \ln Y$$

Growth rates along a given path as depicted in Figure 1.17 also turn smaller, and the approximation becomes better, if we make time units shorter. When the time unit becomes very small, infinitesimally small, we enter the world of differential calculus. We would have to write $P(t)$ to indicate that P is a function of time, but we omit this for convenience. Now the derivative of the logarithm of a variable with respect to time equals the instantaneous growth rate of this variable:

$$\frac{d \ln P}{dt} = g_P \qquad\qquad \text{Property 4}$$

with g_P denoting the growth rate of P. Combined with properties 1 and 2 stated above, this new property of logarithms makes it easy to determine the growth rates of composite variables such as nominal income $P \times Y$ or the real money supply M/P.

Examples: Taking the logarithm of nominal income and differentiating with respect to time yields

$$\ln(PY) = \ln P + \ln Y$$

$$\frac{d \ln (PY)}{dt} = \frac{d \ln P}{dt} + \frac{d \ln Y}{dt} \Longrightarrow g_{PY} = g_P + g_Y$$

So the growth rate of nominal income PY is the sum of the growth rates of its two components. Similarly, when we look at a fraction, such as the real money supply M/P, we obtain

$$\ln (M/P) = \ln M - \ln P$$

$$\frac{d \ln(M/P)}{dt} = \frac{d \ln M}{dt} - \frac{d \ln P}{dt} \Longrightarrow g_{M/P} = g_M - g_P$$

which shows that the growth rate of a fraction M/P equals the difference between the growth rates of the numerator M and the denominator P.

Logarithmic scales

The one major drawback that arises when the logarithm of a variable is measured along the axis instead of the variable itself is that the units of measurement do not have a direct interpretation. To overcome this we may retain the logarithm as the unit of measurement that determines the equidistant tick marks on the vertical axis, but after that translate the logarithms back into original values. This is called **logarithmic scaling**. Figure 1.18 illustrates the procedure. The vertical axis on the left measures the logarithm of P. The distance between two tick marks equals 0.0953 units of $\ln P$. The vertical axis

Figure 1.18

on the right translates each value of ln P back into the corresponding value for P. What happens then, and this is important, is that now one tick mark on the ordinate represents ever larger changes of P as we move up. In fact, equal distances on this vertical axis represent equal percentage increases of 10%. So the distance between 100 and 110 is the same as the distances between 200 and 220 or between 1,000 and 1,100.

Booms and recessions (I): the Keynesian cross

What to expect

After working through this chapter, you will understand:

1 The difference between steady-state income, potential income and actual income and what booms and recessions are.

2 How aggregate (planned) expenditure determines output and income in the short run.

3 How additional government spending may trigger additional private spending via the multiplier.

4 That economic decisions are often made on the basis of what people expect to happen in the future rather than on what they observe today.

At the very least, a macroeconomic model should explain why an economy produces a specific volume of goods and services and no other. In terms of the circular flow of income (Chapter 1), this amounts to explaining why the stream of income is exactly as wide as it is. This question is not trivial:

■ As Figure 2.1 illustrates, income per capita differs by a factor of more than 50 between the richest and the poorest countries in the world. Even within the (by world standards) rich set of EU member states, per capita income in the four richest economies is about three times as high as in the four poorest ones.

■ Figure 2.2 looks at how income develops in the very long run. In the sample of European and other industrialized countries incomes have typically increased tenfold or more since the beginning of the 20th century. In Japan income was 56 times as high in 2010 as it was in 1900.

So, *the most important goal of macroeconomics is to develop an understanding of what makes incomes differ between countries, and what makes them grow or fluctuate over time*. One way of simplifying this task is by slicing up the current volume of income or output into components that are conveniently analyzed separately, because they are determined by different factors. Rather than talking about this in the abstract, consider the development of British GDP since the turn of the 20th century (Figure 2.3).

Visual inspection of the graph suggests a separation of the path of real income into three components:

1 There is a long-run or *secular trend* that connects the pre-First World War path with the path on which Britain has moved since about 1970. On the

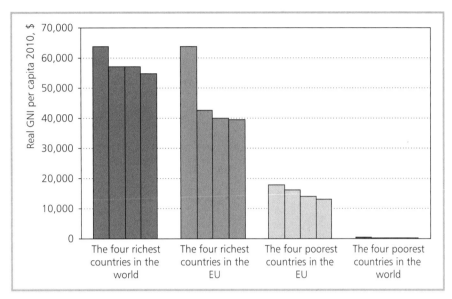

Figure 2.1 This figure shows, along with Figure 2.2, why economists are so eager to understand why countries produce the output and generate the income that they do. Incomes (here for 2010) between countries may vary by a factor of 50 or more. Figure 2.2 shows that industrialized countries have tripled incomes over the past four decades.
Source: World Bank, *World Development Indicators,* 2011.

The **steady-state income** results when all variables, including the capital stock, have adjusted to their desired or equilibrium levels.

secular-trend line, income is in a steady state. Steady-state income is the level of income that is generated:

(a) if all factors of production are being used at normal rates, and

(b) if the economy's capital stock is at its long-run equilibrium level (or growth path).

2 Displacements from the steady-state income path may occur. Evidently, major displacements strike in the wake of wars. Through a destruction of the private capital stock and public infrastructure, income can fall dramatically below pre-war and steady-state levels. Rebuilding the capital stock may take decades. Consequently, it also takes decades to bring potential income, based on currently *available* capital, back towards steady-state income. The two light grey lines illustrate this convergence of potential income back to steady-state income after the First and Second World Wars. As inferred by the data, these lines postulate linear convergence within some forty years.

Potential income is the income that can be produced with current labour and capital. The capital stock may or may not have reached its equilibrium level.

The **business cycle** refers to recurring fluctuations of income relative to potential income. A **boom** (or expansion) describes rising income (relative to potential income) which culminates in a peak. A **recession** describes declining income (relative to potential income) which bottoms out at a trough.

3 Even during periods for which it appears safe to believe that potential income evolved smoothly, income does fluctuate. These short-run ups and downs are what we mean by the term business cycle. From the bird's-eye perspective employed in Figure 2.3 the business cycle is dwarfed by long-run growth and by the shocks to potential output due to the two world wars. Figure 2.4 expands the part of the graph that shows the development of real income during the last twenty years. This demonstrates that economies operate substantially above normal capacity levels during booms (which culminate in a *peak*) and below potential income during recessions (which bottom out in a *trough*) (see Figure 2.4).

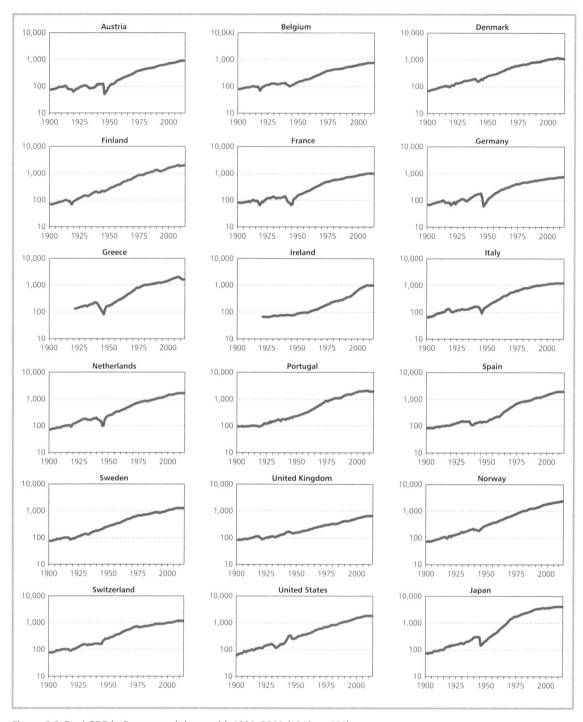

Figure 2.2 Real GDP in Europe and the world, 1900–2009 (1913 = 100).

Sources: IMF; A. Maddison (1995) *Monitoring the World Economy, 1820–1992*, Paris: OECD.

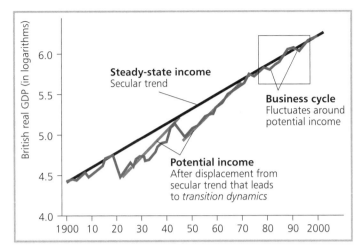

Figure 2.3 By using British real GDP the graph shows that **actual income** may be divided into **steady-state income**, **potential income** (which may deviate from steady-state income) and the **business cycle** (which is the deviation of actual income from potential income).

Sources: A. Maddison (1989), *The World Economy in the 20th Century*, Paris: OECD; IMF: *International Financial Statistics*.

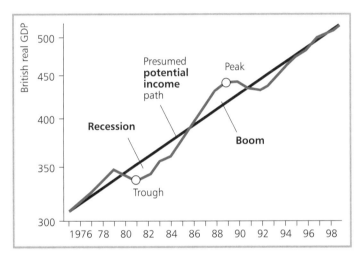

Figure 2.4 **Business cycles** describe movements of income around potential income. During a **recession** actual income falls below potential income. A **boom** drives actual income above potential income. Extreme values relative to potential income are called **peaks** and **troughs**. Operational definitions of when exactly a recession starts or ends may differ between organizations or countries.

Source: IMF, *International Financial Statistics*.

But why does annual GDP data not reflect the smoothness suggested by the concept of potential income? Why do we observe business cycles when the section of the population eligible for work and the stock of capital goods used in the generation of income change slowly and smoothly? The answer is that in the short run, temporarily, firms freely employ more or less of available capital or labour. Firms operate temporarily below capacity levels, or even beyond normal capacity levels. Why would they do that? Because they experience a drop in the demand for their products and do not want to build up stocks, or because demand is booming above normal levels and they would like to cash in.

So if we want to understand how output and income move in the short run, during **booms** and **recessions**, the key word is **demand**. The production possibilities laid out by the production function under normal use of production factors do not strictly limit output in the short run. Firms do have a certain flexibility to adjust the volume of goods and services produced to the demand that they experience. In this chapter we will take an extreme view. We assume that, at current prices, firms produce exactly the amount of output that is demanded. The short-run *AS* curve is therefore horizontal.

In the long run, however, labour and capital utilization will have to return to normal levels and put a lid on the output that can be produced, no matter what the price level is. This makes the long-run *AS* curve vertical, as we shall see in Chapter 6.

BOX 2.1 **Actual income, potential income and steady-state income: Great Britain in 1933**

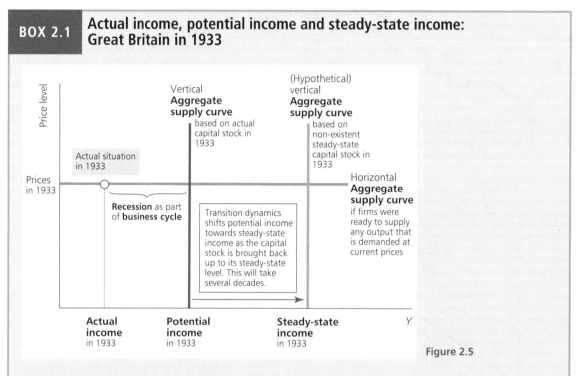

Figure 2.5

The year 1933 in Great Britain provides a good opportunity to elaborate on the concepts of steady-state income, potential income and actual income. Figure 2.5 recasts this macroeconomic situation, taken from Figure 2.3, in terms of a price–income diagram. We have already used such a diagram to introduce the concept of aggregate supply curves in the context of the circular flow economy (which produced cars only) in Chapter 1.

Actual income can be taken from Figure 2.3. Combining this with 1933 prices identifies the actual situation in 1933. Britain, like the rest of the world, experienced a severe recession at that time. Hence, actual income is substantially below potential income that might have been produced. Figure 2.5 features a vertical aggregate supply curve over potential income, postulating that what a country can potentially produce is independent of the price level. The capital stock had not fully recovered from First World War destruction. Hence steady-state income (the income that could have been produced had the First World War not occurred

and had the capital stock grown smoothly since then) exceeds potential income. The light blue vertical line marking steady-state income at all price levels marks a reference point or very long-run centre of gravity for the British economy. (We will discuss in Chapter 9, in the context of economic growth, which mechanisms tend to drive an economy, very slowly, towards the steady state.)

The actual situation observed in 1933 demonstrates that firms deviate from potential income, at least temporarily. One way to interpret this is to concede that the vertical aggregate supply curve over potential income does not properly describe aggregate supply in the short and medium run. In the short run, firms respond along a horizontal aggregate supply curve, following demand.

Chapters 2 to 8 focus on the deviations of income from potential income, the analysis of the ups and downs of the business cycle. The discussion of the medium- and long-run reference path, potential income and steady-state income, is left for Chapters 6, 9 and 10.

2.1   The circular flow model revisited: terminology and overview

We begin by building up some terminology and clarifying key concepts. For that purpose we revisit the circular flow diagram from Chapter 1 (see Figure 2.6).

In an attempt to develop an expression for the total spending (or total demand) which comes back to domestic firms, note that households receive **gross income** Y (top left-hand corner). Payment of taxes reduces this to **disposable income** $Y - T$. After removing savings from the loop we obtain what is left for consumption, i.e. $C = Y - T - S$. Because of the third leakage we have to subtract from this **imports** IM from abroad. Therefore, what remains at the end of the upper segment and what comes around the right-hand-side curve to the lower segment of the income circle is $C - IM$. Adding to this the three demand injections shown in the lower part of the circle gives total spending on domestically produced goods:

$$\text{Total expenditure} = C + I + G + EX - IM (= \text{total income})$$

The equality between expenditure (or demand) and income is always guaranteed because investment may include an undesired component. To illustrate this crucial point once more, let the rest of the world start to boycott our

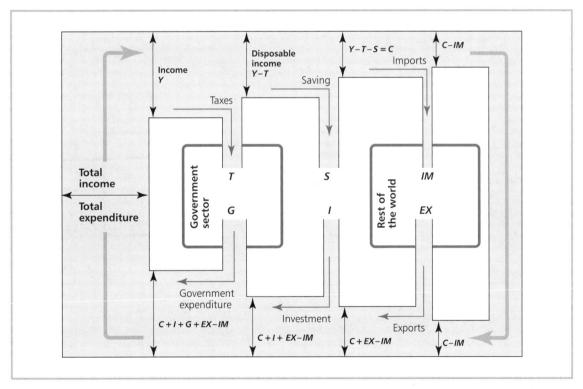

Figure 2.6 The circle begins with income Y on the left. Taxes reduce this to disposable income $Y - T$, and savings to consumption $C \equiv Y - T - S$. Taking away imports leaves $C - IM$. Addition of exports, investment and government expenditure in the circle's lower segment gives total expenditure as $C + I + G + EX - IM$.

country, eliminating exports. If other spending plans and taxes remain unchanged we are left with a gap between output and planned expenditure exactly the same size as the former exports. Firms are being forced to close that gap by unplanned investment spending in the form of involuntary inventory build-up (see Figure 2.7).

Henceforth, the variable I always stands for *planned* investment. *Unplanned* investment is denoted by I^u. The sum of all planned demand is called aggregate expenditure. For contrast we call the sum of all demand, planned and unplanned, actual expenditure.

So far the circular flow model gives us only a vague understanding of where the level of income might be at any point in time. Even if we knew that desired demand was at 100, income might be at 200 with 100 units of undesired investment, or at 95 with -5 units of undesired investment. Anything can happen.

In this situation firms can be expected to go to great lengths to avoid having to undertake investments they had not planned and do not want to make. In order to achieve this, they must set output exactly to the level they expect others plan to buy, that is to aggregate expenditure. At this point the economy is in **equilibrium**. Plans work out and do not need to be revised.

> **Aggregate expenditure** is the sum of all planned or voluntary spending on domestically produced goods and services.
>
> **Actual expenditure** is the sum of all categories of demand, including unplanned investment.

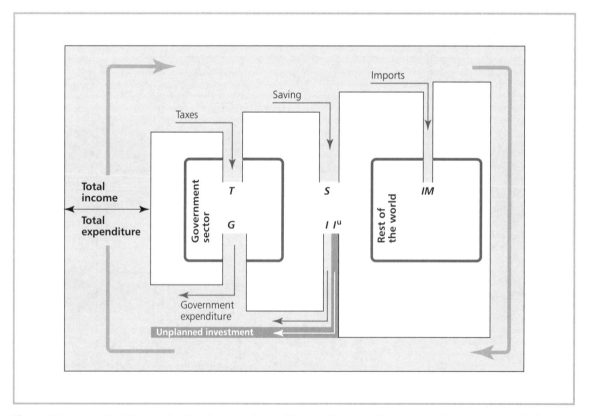

Figure 2.7 Assume that the circular flow has been in equilibrium. If exports drop to zero, income exceeds desired spending by the amount represented by the blue injection. This exactly equals the former level of exports, and must now be demanded *involuntarily* by firms which are being forced to stock up inventory.

Note. The equilibrium concept employed here is a demand-side equilibrium. Note that we do not consider where this demand-side equilibrium is relative to potential income or steady-state income. Later on in this book we will do so.

Having a firm grasp of the concepts of actual expenditure, output, income and aggregate expenditure is essential for much of what will be discussed below. For easy reference and for control, Figure 2.8 shows these concepts and how they interrelate. The grey area in Figure 2.8 defines actual expenditure. Because it comprises all components of demand, even those that are not planned, it always equals income (or output). The blue column defines *planned expenditure*, which henceforth we call aggregate expenditure, as

$$AE \equiv C + I + G + EX - IM \qquad \textbf{Aggregate expenditure} \qquad (2.1)$$

It only equals income if firms succeed in setting output to a level that does not require them to undertake any unplanned investment in the form of undesired inventory changes. They will do everything they can to succeed in this effort. Income, therefore, is much more likely to be at the level marked by aggregate expenditure than at any other level. It is therefore crucial to understand what determines the different components of aggregate expenditure. To the right of each expenditure category you find references to where this variable is discussed in this book.

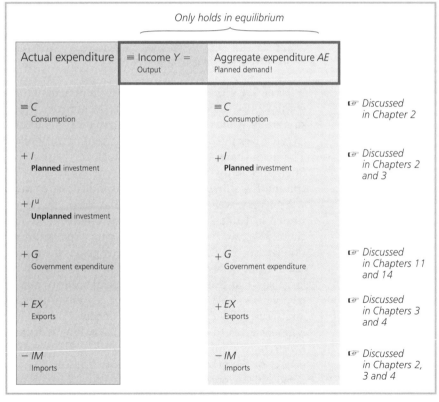

Figure 2.8 The diagram shows how income relates to expenditure. **Income always equals actual expenditure**: this is because if nobody wanted to buy the firms' production (which equals income) voluntarily, the firms would be forced to buy it themselves, having to undertake unplanned investment (first column). **Income equals aggregate (desired) expenditure in equilibrium**, that is, if all spending is as planned, then firms need not change inventories in an undesired way (third column).

Table 2.1 **Demand categories in the circular flow model** (2009, as % of GDP). Consumption is the dominating category of aggregate expenditure. Investment and government spending follow with shares of about 20% each. The small balance is filled by net exports. This conceals that exports can be sizeable, ranging from 11% in the United States to 88.5% in Ireland.

Country	C	G	I	EX-IM	EX
Austria	54.2	19.9	21.3	4.5	50.5
Belgium	52.4	24.7	20.2	2.7	73.0
Denmark	49.2	29.9	17.1	3.8	47.8
Finland	54.1	25.1	18.3	2.5	37.4
France	58.3	24.6	19.0	−1.9	23.0
Germany	58.9	19.7	16.5	4.9	40.8
Greece	75.3	19.1	16.2	−10.6	18.6
Ireland	52.3	19.0	13.7	14.9	88.5
Italy	59.9	21.6	18.9	−0.4	24.0
Netherlands	45.7	28.5	18.5	7.3	69.4
Portugal	66.8	21.1	19.8	−7.7	28.0
Spain	56.5	21.2	24.5	−2.2	23.4
Sweden	48.8	27.8	16.6	6.9	48.5
United Kingdom	65.3	23.5	13.6	−2.4	27.7
Japan	59.6	19.7	20.4	0.3	12.5
United States	71.4	17.2	14.2	−2.7	11.2
Average	58.0	22.7	18.1	1.2	39.0

Source: World Bank, *World Development Indicators*, 2011.

Table 2.1 gives real data for the components of aggregate expenditure that we have just encountered. For most countries the lion's share goes to consumption. It averages 58% of aggregate expenditure. The rest is divided between government spending, investment (with similar shares) and net exports. The small shares of net exports, which can be negative, camouflage the intense international involvement of those economies shown. To remedy this, the last column *EX* shows export shares as indicators of the openness of economies.

You may well be puzzled by the small shares of the government sector shown in Table 2.1. Isn't everybody complaining about big governments that claim 35%, 40% or 50% of aggregate expenditure? This apparent contradiction is resolved after noting that only government purchases are injections into the circular flow of income. In addition to those purchases, governments pay large sums in transfers, such as social security and unemployment insurance payments. These payments do not represent government demand for goods and services. They are best seen as negative taxes, as something that the government gives to citizens rather than taking it from them. On the aggregate, *transfers paid for by taxes cancel out*: the government takes taxes out of one pocket of the private sector and puts transfers back into the other. Aggregate disposable income is therefore unaffected. For this reason, when we talk about taxes *T* we mean net taxes (gross taxes minus transfers), and *G* only represents government purchases of goods and services. It excludes all transfer payments and interest payments on government debt.

Taxes *T* in our models are net taxes, the difference between all taxes and transfers. Government spending *G* in our models are government purchases of goods and services. It does not include transfers.

The remaining part of this chapter shows that under reasonable assumptions only one equilibrium level of income exists. The next section introduces some basic concepts by means of a stylized example.

CASE STUDY 2.1 | Income vs leisure time in France and the USA

In 2005 GNP in the United States of America stood at $12,449 billion while GNP in France was $2,138 billion. This is a preliminary, raw comparison of incomes, however, which does not take into account a number of factors.

One very important factor is that one US dollar does not buy the same amount of goods in all countries – its purchasing power is not the same. Adjusting for differences in purchasing power, on a common measure French GNP is worth only $1,952 billion. This means that when French people spend $2,138 billion in France (and on imports into France), it buys them only what $1,952 billion would have bought them in the USA. The reason is that prices, expressed in dollars, are some 10% higher in France than in the USA.

A second factor we need to take into account is population sizes. With populations of 296.4 million in the USA and 60.9 million in France, per capita GNP was $42,000 in the USA, but only $32,070 in France.

Next consider that a smaller share of the population work in France than in the USA, either because they are not active (meaning they are too young or too old), because they do not want to work, or because they cannot find work. In 2005 employment in France was 24.9 million and in the USA it was 141.7 million. This puts output per worker at $87,838 in the USA and $78,340 in France.

To push the argument one step further, note that in France workers work an average of 1,546 hours per year, while in America they work 1,804 hours. Thus GNP per hour worked is $50.67 in France, compared with $48.69 worth of output produced in the USA during one work-hour.

What is the message in this? We started by noting that US per capita GNP exceeds per capita GNP in France. Thus a standardized 'family' comprising,

say, two adults and two children, earns more dollars in the USA than in France. However, fewer persons in the French family work. And those who work do work fewer hours than their US counterparts. So who is better off? The US family, having higher income but little time to spend it? Or the French family, with ample leisure time but less money to spend? It is your decision: since there is an obvious trade-off between income and leisure, it is your preferences that must determine what is right for you or for your country. The point is that comparing the welfare of French and Americans by looking at per capita GNP alone may be just as misleading as comparing it by looking at leisure time alone.

Table 2.2 Population, employment, work-hours and GNP

	France	USA
Total GNP (2005)		
in million dollars	2,137,573	12,449,237
in million international $	1,952,197	12,449,237
Population (2005)	60,873,000	296,410,404
GNP per capita		
in dollars	35,115	42,000
in international $	32,070	42,000
Employment (2005)	24,919,400	141,730,000
GNP per worker		
in dollars	85,779	87,838
in international $	78,340	87,838
Annual work-hours per worker	1,546	1,804
GNP per work-hour (2005)		
in dollars	55.48	48.69
in international $	50.67	48.69

Sources: World Bank Atlas; OECD; ILO.

2.2 | Income determination: a first look

Human behaviour in the circular flow

In a state of equilibrium, desired and actual expenditure must be equal. In order to understand what individuals do desire to spend, we first look at the four components that constitute aggregate expenditure. Let all but one of the expenditure categories be autonomous, that is independent of income or other variables. We may even keep these autonomous spending variables fixed:

$$G = \text{constant} \tag{2.2}$$

$$I = \text{constant} \tag{2.3}$$

$$NX(\approx CA) = EX - IM = \text{constant} \tag{2.4}$$

Equation (2.4) defines net exports $EX - IM$ as NX. As a reminder we state that net exports are a good first approximation for the current account CA in the balance of payments.

For consumption C we assume that individuals always want to spend a constant fraction c of their income Y (taxes T are assumed to be zero for now); c is the marginal propensity to consume and should be taken to be around 0.8:

The marginal propensity to consume says by how much consumption rises if income rises by one unit.

$$C = cY \qquad\qquad \textbf{Consumption function} \tag{2.5}$$

Note. Since we assume that $T = 0$ here, income is either consumed or saved, $Y = C + S$. Hence, equation (2.5) implies the savings function $S = (1 - c)Y$.

Substituting equation (2.5) for C in equation (2.1) gives

$$AE = cY + I + G + NX$$

It shows that aggregate spending is not independent of income, but increases as Y rises. The aggregate expenditure line in Figure 2.9 shows how AE relates to Y and also breaks up aggregate expenditure into its four components.

Equilibrium income

The graphical representation of aggregate expenditure can now be used to determine **equilibrium income**.

Figure 2.10 replicates the aggregate-expenditure line from Figure 2.9. This line has a positive intercept, depicting those components that are immune to income changes. Its slope is positive but smaller than 1, since individuals do

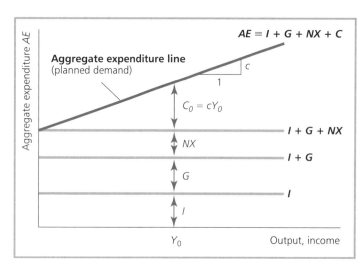

Figure 2.9 Aggregate (or planned or desired) expenditure varies with income. The graph stacks four demand categories. It starts with I, G, and NX, which are all considered independent of income. That makes these lines horizontal. Consumption spending increases with income, with a marginal rate of consumption of c. This gives the aggregate-expenditure line slope c. The line meets the vertical axis at the level of autonomous expenditure.

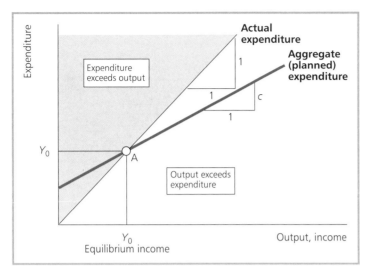

Figure 2.10 The **Keynesian cross** contains two lines. The 45° line measures **actual expenditure** which always equals income. At points above this line, desired demand exceeds output; at points below, the opposite is true. The **aggregate-expenditure** line indicates the sum of all spending plans. Both lines cross in A, meaning that here spending plans are perfectly compatible with income.

The Keynesian cross is a diagram which plots *planned* expenditure against income and *actual* expenditure against income. Equilibrium income obtains where both lines cross.

not want to consume their entire income, but wish to save a small fraction of it. By contrast, the actual-expenditure line passes through the origin and has slope 1. This is because actual spending always equals income. The two lines intersect at point A, which marks that level of income Y_0 at which actual expenditure is exactly as planned. At higher income levels, actual spending exceeds planned expenditures. At lower income levels, planned spending exceeds actual spending. This type of graph is known as the Keynesian cross.

Since we are currently assuming that firms produce any amount of goods that is demanded, the kind of equilibrium determined by the Keynesian cross is called a **demand-side equilibrium.**

We should note here that if income is initially at the wrong level, i.e. out of equilibrium, it tends to move back towards equilibrium. If Y exceeds Y_0, firms cannot sell all the output they produce. A reasonable reaction would be to reduce output, moving it closer to Y_0. If Y falls short of Y_0, firms realize that they could sell more than they are currently producing, and so increase production.

What if spending plans change?

The derived unique equilibrium income depends on planned spending. An important question to follow from this is, how does equilibrium income change if one of the actors involved revises spending plans?

Assume that the government raises expenditure by ΔG. Then income obviously also rises by ΔG. But this cannot be the end of the story. Households will want to spend part of this additional income: this added consumer spending again adds to income, which raises consumer spending even further, and so on. This process is complicated and worth looking at in more detail with the help of Figure 2.11 and Table 2.3.

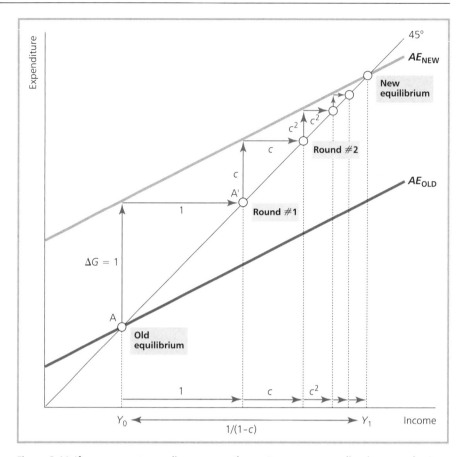

Figure 2.11 If government spending or any other autonomous spending increases by 1, the AE line shifts up by 1. Income rises by $\Delta Y > 1$ due to the multiplier effect. The reasoning behind this is that the government's spending increase of 1 not only raises income by 1, leading to point A'. It also induces added consumption of c, adding c to income. This raises consumption and income by another c^2, and so on. All these effects add up to the **multiplier** $\Delta Y = 1/(1 - c)$.

Table 2.3 Income effects of an increase of government expenditure. The table traces the income gains generated by a one-unit increase in government spending. In round #1, income only rises by 1 as output follows demand. In round #2, individuals want to consume a fraction c out of their income increase experienced in round #1. This raises output and income by c as well, bringing the total effect to $1 + c$ (fifth column). This process continues. The initial demand increase multiplies into more and more additions to demand in subsequent rounds. Note, however, that these additions become smaller and smaller.

Round	ΔG	ΔC	ΔY (this round only)	ΔY (summed over all rounds)
#1	1	0	1	1
#2	0	c	c	$1 + c$
#3	0	c^2	c^2	$1 + c + c^2$
#4	0	c^3	c^3	$1 + c + c^2 + c^3$
⋮	⋮	⋮	⋮	⋮
#237	0	c^{236}	c^{236}	$1 + c + c^2 + c^3 + \cdots + c^{236}$
⋮	⋮	⋮	⋮	⋮

Let the economy initially be in equilibrium at the point labelled A. Now the government increases expenditure per period by one unit ($\Delta G = 1$). We will trace the consequences of this spending increase through a series of fictitious rounds, in order to finally arrive at the cumulative total effect. These rounds may have a time dimension – say, months, because consumers respond to income increases with a lag of one month. Or we may consider the division of the total effect into a number of rounds as simply a conceptional tool to guide the analysis, and the total effect may actually accrue instantaneously thanks to the foresight of firms.

In round #1, one additional unit of government expenditure shifts the aggregate-expenditure line upwards by one unit. This constitutes an increase of aggregate spending at the old income level Y_0 by one unit, and also raises income by one unit to $Y_0 + 1$. In round #2, consumers plan to spend the fraction c of their first-round income increase, also raising income by c. By now the total income increase adds up to $1 + c$, and already exceeds the increase in government spending which triggered this process. The process continues, however. In round #3, consumers add a fraction c of their second-round income increase of c to their old level of spending, meaning that they increase consumption by $c \cdot c = c^2$. Income increases by c^2 as well. By analogous reasoning, consumption and income increase by c^3 in round #4, by c^4 in round #5 and so on.

Does this process ever end? Yes and no. With respect to time or rounds, it does go on forever, but the income increases that accrue in each new round will eventually peter out. This is because the marginal propensity to consume c is between zero and one. Raising c to the power of a higher and higher number yields smaller and smaller results. If the second-round effect was $c = 0.8$, the effect in round #11 is already reduced to $c^{10} = 0.107$. This guarantees that the total effect of a one-unit increase of government spending does not grow infinitely large, despite the fact that an algebraic expression for this comprises infinitely many terms:

$$1 + c + c^2 + c^3 + c^4 + \cdots + c^\infty \qquad (2.6)$$

But then how large is the total effect on income? One way to figure this out is by noting that in equilibrium

income Y = aggregate expenditure AE

$$Y = C + I + G + NX \qquad \text{Equilibrium condition}$$

Substituting the consumption function (2.5) for C gives

$$Y = cY + I + G + NX$$

Subtracting cY from both sides and dividing by $1 - c$ yields an expression for equilibrium income as a function of all autonomous expenditure:

At equilibrium income all spending is planned spending (or income equals aggregate expenditure).

$$Y = \frac{1}{1 - c}(G + I + NX) \qquad \text{Equilibrium income} \qquad (2.7)$$

Income only changes if either G, I or NX changes:

$$\Delta Y = \frac{1}{1 - c}(\Delta G + \Delta I + \Delta NX) \qquad (2.8)$$

Maths note. We have hit upon a rule that has many uses in economics: for any parameter $-1 < x < 1$ the series $x^0 + x^1 + x^2 + \ldots$ converges to $1/(1 - x)$ as the exponent grows to infinity. Or, more precisely,

$$\sum_{i=0}^{\infty} x^i = \frac{1}{1 - x}.$$

As $c^0 = 1$ and $c^1 = c$, the effects listed in equation (2.6) and in Table 2.3 constitute such a series.

The multiplier measures the income change resulting from a one-unit increase in autonomous expenditure.

In our present example we have $\Delta I = \Delta NX = 0$. Substituting this into equation (2.8) and dividing by ΔG gives us

$$\frac{\Delta Y}{\Delta G} = \frac{1}{1 - c} \qquad \text{Multiplier} \quad (2.9)$$

An increase of government expenditure (or investment, or net exports) by 1 *multiplies* into an income increase by $1/(1 - c)$. This is why the expression given on the right-hand side is called the multiplier. Its numerical value depends on the value of c. For $c = 0.8$ the multiplier is 5. For $c = 0.9$ the multiplier is 10. The verbal explanation is that additional government spending initially makes firms produce just that much more. To be able to do that, they need to employ more labour and pay for it and so income rises. Part of this income returns to the firms as consumption demand. So more labour must be hired and income rises further. When this process comes to a halt, income has risen by the multiplier times the initial increase in government spending.

Additional insight into the economics behind the multiplier is obtained by giving it a circular-flow-of-income interpretation. We recall that some initial, exogenous increase in demand, such as a rise in government spending, not only generates an increase in output and income to match. Rather, this generated increase in income gives rise to even higher demand and, hence, even higher income, and thus larger demand still, and so on. In terms of the circular flow of income, the multiplier exists only to the extent that at least a fraction of income eventually returns to firms in the form of demand for domestically produced goods and services. The larger this fraction is, the larger is the multiplier. How does this correspond to our multiplier formula $1/(1 - c)$?

Note that by making use of the identity $1 - c = s$, the multiplier formula rewrites $1/s$. The number 1 in the numerator is the presumed increase in government spending – an injection of €1 into the income circle. The denominator, s, is the fraction of the injected demand that leaks out of the income circle. So if the entire injection leaks out of the income circle, that is if $s = 1$, the multiplier is down to 1. Hence, the rise in government spending does not trigger any additional spending at all. (In this case the aggregate-expenditure line in Figure 2.10 would be horizontal.) At the other extreme, if none of the added government spending leaks from the income circle, because s drops to zero, the multiplier approaches infinity. (Now the *AE* line would have a slope of 1.) This leads to the general rule that the multiplier becomes smaller when the leakages out of the income circle generated by any income gain become larger. This rule will prove useful when we look at the multiplier in the context of a more refined model.

Rule. The multiplier is small when a large part of any increase in income leaks out of the circular flow.

What has fascinated previous generations of economists (and politicians) about the multiplier is that by raising spending, governments can induce income increases far greater than the initial spending increase. Before we get too excited about this result, however, let me caution that many of the refinements to be discussed in the remaining sections of this chapter and in subsequent chapters will gradually erode the *quantitative* importance of the multiplier.

2.3 Income determination: a second look

Now that we understand the basic concepts of **equilibrium income** and the **multiplier** we move on to a more realistic scenario. This perspective includes more plausible behavioural and institutional features, and then introduces expectations. We begin by deriving a refined but traditional version of the multiplier.

The previous analysis has ignored taxes T. When individuals pay taxes, this reduces gross income Y to disposable income $Y - T$. Individuals are free only to decide how to split disposable income between consumption and savings. Hence

> Disposable income is that part of income left to households after the payment of taxes.

$$C = c(Y - T) \qquad \text{Consumption function} \quad (2.10)$$

In the simplest case, taxes can be thought of as being proportional to income,

$$T = tY \qquad \text{Tax equation} \quad (2.11)$$

where t is the marginal and average income tax rate.

> The marginal income tax rate says by how much taxes rise if income rises by one unit. The average income tax rate gives the share of taxes on income on average, that is T/Y. In equation (2.11) the marginal and the average income tax rate are the same.

For a first look at imports IM, which we shall refine later, let these also be proportional to income.

$$IM = mY \qquad \text{Import function} \quad (2.12)$$

where m denotes the marginal propensity to import. We continue to consider the remaining components of demand, I, G and EX, exogenous.

This refined model of aggregate demand yields a much flatter AE line than the previous model, as Figure 2.12 illustrates. An equation for the AE line is obtained by substituting equations (2.10), (2.11) and (2.12) into (2.1). After collecting terms this gives

$$AE = [c(1 - t) - m]Y + I + G + EX \qquad \text{Aggregate expenditure} \quad (2.13)$$

The slope $c(1 - t) - m$ of the flatter AE line is due to two effects. First, income-dependent taxes reduce disposable income to $(1 - t)Y$ even before

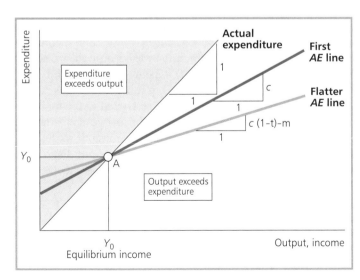

Figure 2.12 If taxes and imports rise with income, the leaks out of the circular flow increase as income rises. Hence, aggregate expenditure does not increase with income as fast as it did in Figure 2.10. This is represented by the flatter AE line, which now has slope $c(1 - t) - m$. A flatter AE line signals a smaller multiplier effect. (Note that the flatter line is drawn for higher autonomous spending. Otherwise both lines would intersect on the vertical axis, not at A.)

individuals decide whether to save or consume. Consumption out of each unit of income then is only $c(1 - t)$. Second, m out of each unit of income leaks abroad in payment for imports, so only $c(1 - t) - m$ out of each additional unit of income is used to buy domestically produced goods.

An algebraic expression for equilibrium income in the refined model is obtained by requiring aggregate spending (as shown in equation (2.13)) to equal income. After solving for Y this yields

$$Y = \frac{1}{1 - c(1 - t) + m} (G + I + EX) \qquad \text{Equilibrium income}$$

The new multiplier is obtained by taking first differences, letting $\Delta I = \Delta EX = 0$ and dividing by ΔG:

$$\frac{\Delta Y}{\Delta G} = \frac{1}{1 - c(1 - t) + m} \qquad\qquad \text{Multiplier} \quad (2.14)$$

Empirical note. Empirical estimates of multipliers for industrial countries range between values of 1.5 and 3.

Substituting some plausible numbers into the multiplier equations (2.9) and (2.14) illustrates that the achieved refinement has important quantitative consequences. With a marginal propensity to consume of $c = 0.9$, the simple multiplier given in equation (2.9) stands at a value of 10. Now substitute the same value for c into the refined multiplier given in equation (2.14), assume a modest tax rate of $t = 0.2$, let the marginal propensity to import be about one-fifth ($m = 0.22$), and you will arrive at a multiplier of 2.

Why has the multiplier shrunk? Remember our rule: the multiplier becomes smaller when the leakages out of the income circle that result from a given income hike do grow. More precisely and in general terms: the multiplier is the initial increase in demand, the injection, divided by the added leakages. By making taxes and imports dependent on income we have added two more channels through which the initial increase in income, triggered by the government spending hike, leaks out of the income circle. This becomes visible if we make use of the identity $c = 1 - s$ to rewrite the refined multiplier from (2.14) as

$$\frac{\Delta Y}{\Delta G} = \frac{1}{s(1 - t) + t + m}$$

Each term in the denominator refers to one particular leakage. Starting from the right, when government spending rises by €1, raising output and income by €1 as well (the number in the numerator), a fraction m leaks abroad, a fraction t goes to the government, and a fraction $s(1 - t)$ is being saved, which is that part of income left to the disposal of households, $1 - t$, times the savings rate, s.

Equation (2.14) also shows that fiscal policy is not restricted to the manipulation of government spending. A second instrument of fiscal policy is the tax rate, which it can change independently of government spending, if so desired. If the government decreases the marginal rate of income taxation, disposable income increases, the multiplier increases and the AE line becomes steeper (see Figure 2.14, overleaf). Equilibrium income rises from Y_0 to Y_1.

We conclude this chapter by discussing consumption and investment demand from a more modern *intertemporal perspective*. The payoff will be a first encounter with expectations, which play a prominent role in modern economic analysis, and a first insight into when it is safe to work with the multiplier model, and when not to.

CASE STUDY 2.2 **How to pay for the war: Great Britain in 1940**

Many of the tools we encounter in this and subsequent chapters are due to British economist **John Maynard Keynes** (1883–1946), who gave his name to such terms as Keynesian cross and Keynesianism (for an entire school).

In 1940 Keynes published *How to Pay for the War*. One of the questions raised in this treatise is how Great Britain could meet the economic efforts required by the Second World War without generating inflation. In essence (after streamlining it in some inessential aspects), Keynes's argument runs as follows:

1 Income in 1938 (the latest available data) ran at £5,520 million. *Potential income* was estimated at £6,345 million. So income (output) could increase by $\Delta Y = 6{,}345 - 5{,}520 = £825$ million without risking inflation. (If demand were driven beyond potential income, he assumed, firms would start to raise prices.)

2 How far can government spending be raised without pushing income beyond potential income? The answer is certainly not £825 million! The permitted change of income and therefore the permitted change of government spending are related by the multiplier. We may take the one given in equation (2.14). Letting $m = 0$

(private, income-sensitive imports would be controlled and low during the war), we obtain

$$\Delta Y = \frac{1}{1 - c(1 - t)} \Delta G$$

Knowing that $\Delta Y = 825$, all we need to know to calculate ΔG is c and t.

3 *Assumptions.* Proceeding from the 1938 data $Y = 5{,}520$, $C = 4{,}380$ and $T = 770$, a reasonable guess is to assume that marginal and average consumption and tax rates are the same, that is $c = C/Y = 4{,}380/5{,}520$ and $t = T/Y = 770/5{,}520$.

4 *Result.* Substituting the obtained rates $c = 0.79$ and $t = 0.14$ into the multiplier expression gives a multiplier of 3.15. Letting $\Delta Y = 825$ and solving the multiplier equation for ΔG finally yields $\Delta G = 262$. Therefore, government spending can be geared up by £262 million (in 1938 prices) without triggering inflation. If that doesn't provide sufficient funds, tax rates may have to be raised (if politically feasible), which in turn reduces the multiplier and drives equilibrium income down.

Keynes's assumptions, line of argument and results may also be presented graphically in the context of the Keynesian-cross diagram (see Figure 2.13).

Figure 2.13

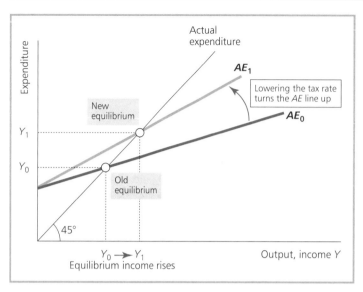

Figure 2.14 If the marginal tax rate is lowered, households retain more disposable income at any level of gross income. Since households spend a constant fraction of disposable income, they spend more at any given level of income. The upward shift of this spending is shown by turning the aggregate expenditure curve from AE_0 into AE_1. With more spending out of given income, equilibrium income is higher.

2.4   An intertemporal view of consumption and investment

A second look at consumption

Relationships such as the consumption function $C = cY$ used above are necessarily simplifications, i.e. abstractions of reality. Today's economists agree that individuals make consumption decisions in the context of a rather intricate optimization problem. The approach taken here is that such precise, micro-based consumption behaviour is overly complicated and therefore not practical for many applications. So we will continue to work with simplifications, while trying to foster an understanding of those circumstances under which they break down.

Lifetime patterns of income and consumption
Why is $C = cY$ a simplification? First, people evidently do not consume, say, 80% of their income on their weekly or monthly payday. They realize that the pay covers a given period of work and so spread consumption possibilities more or less evenly over that period. But if people are intelligent enough to realize and do that, wouldn't they apply the same principle if they inherited €1,000,000 at age 21? Assume that you inherited that sum under the condition that you refrained from any other paid work for the rest of your life. What would your consumption spending plan look like? You would probably try to spread consumption possibilities deriving from the inherited fortune over your expected lifetime. Your consumption during the first year after your twenty-first birthday would be only a very small fraction of the inherited million.

These ideas can be generalized. Utility-maximizing individuals will not adjust current consumption to every kink in the development of their income. In much the same way as they do over the course of a month, individuals would like to obtain a smooth consumption path over their lifetime. The restriction is, of course, that they usually cannot spend more than they earn. But because of the possibility of obtaining loans and to save, this need not apply for each period of time, but only over the total lifetime.

Figure 2.15 shows a stylized but fairly typical income pattern over an individual's lifetime (light blue lines). As a rule, income rises during the early stages of a career as the person becomes more productive and experienced. Income then levels out during the later years of the person's career. On retirement, income drops to some fraction of previous income levels, depending on the retirement plan and the amount of private savings.

Ideally, individuals would like to keep consumption fairly constant along a path like the light grey lines in Figure 2.15. However, this may not always be possible, particularly because of the reluctance of banks to extend loans to young people on the mere expectation of higher future income. But it is what individuals would prefer. So to simplify the argument, if we ignore bequests, rule out that individuals die in debt, and ignore interest payments on savings, total (planned) lifetime consumption equals total (expected) lifetime earnings. Consumption per period equals expected lifetime income divided by expected remaining lifetime n:

$$C = \frac{1}{n}Y + \frac{1}{n}(Y^{e}_{+1} + Y^{e}_{+2} + Y^{e}_{+3} + \cdots + Y^{e}_{+n-1})$$

The superscripts e on each Y in parentheses indicate that individuals do not know this value yet, but have to form an **expectation** of it. Y^{e}_{+1} is the income expected one period from today in the future. Note that while the series given in parentheses may represent a complicated time profile of income, it is simply all income expected from tomorrow until we die. For the sake of notational convenience, we may denote this sum of all expected future income by Y^{e}_{+} to obtain the more compact consumption function:

$$C = \frac{1}{n}Y + \frac{1}{n}Y^{e}_{+} \tag{2.15}$$

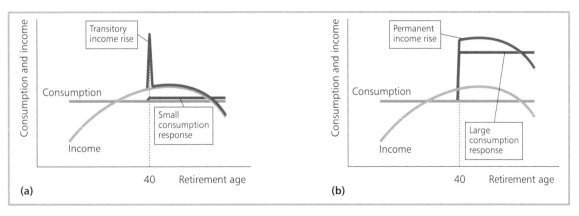

(a) ... 40   Retirement age   **(b)** ... 40   Retirement age

Figure 2.15 Lifetime patterns of income exhibit rising and falling sections as illustrated by the light-blue line. The grey line is the attached consumption plan. A perceived transitory income rise (panel (a)) increases consumption by very little. A perceived permanent income rise (panel (b)) results in a large consumption response.

Now let individuals enjoy an income increase in period 40. The first question to ask is whether or not this was expected. If the experienced income rise is part of the expected lifetime income pattern, there is absolutely no need to revise the lifetime consumption plan, and consumption will not respond at all.

Things are different if income increased unexpectedly, way beyond what the lifetime pattern prescribed (blue lines in Figure 2.15). Then a second crucial question must be asked: will the individual be able to sustain this added stream of income in the future? Or is it purely temporary, windfall income that will not have an impact on expected future income streams?

Panel (a) in Figure 2.15 illustrates the case in which the unexpected income bonus is considered to be purely *temporary*. Then expected lifetime income only increases by a very small percentage and the consumption of this period's income bonus is spread out over all the remaining periods of one's life. This is reflected in a very small upwards shift of the consumption path in period 40.

In panel (b), the increase in income is considered to be *permanent*. This shifts the entire pattern of income upward by the observed change of income and the impact on expected lifetime income is very large. The response to this increase is to consume roughly the full amount of the income increase during this period.

The lesson to be learned from this is that *exceptional* (or *transitory*) income, i.e. not expected to accrue regularly, period after period, produces consumption reactions quite different from those to *regular* (or *permanent*) income. Thus, when we apply our models, it is advisable to ask whether individuals consider an experienced income change permanent or transitory. Only in the first case may we expect to observe a substantial increase in consumption demand via multiplier effects.

The above discussion provides a first opportunity to appreciate that economic decisions are made on the basis of what people expect to happen in the future (will income stay up permanently?) rather than what they observe today. This **pivotal role of expectations** will be a recurring theme throughout this book, and is a general characteristic of modern economics.

Stocks and other assets

While individuals save during the early years of their professional careers, they accumulate wealth. Wealth may be held in the form of money, but this appears relevant only in times of crisis and war (see Box 2.2). Normally, savings are placed into interest-bearing bank accounts, government bonds, corporate stocks or real estate. Individuals expect to draw on these assets and the generated returns later on in their lives, when salaries and wage payments dry up. If the value of acquired assets changes, this mandates an adjustment of consumption plans.

Suppose again that you are lucky as an heiress or heir. This time, though, you inherit €1,000,000 worth of corporate stocks. While you are still partying and to your utter dismay, the stock market plunges by 22.6% on a single day, just as Wall Street did on 19 October 1987. So your inherited million is down to €774,000, and the initial lifetime consumption plan you drew up after you had learned the good news is no longer viable. After you recover from the shocking news, you implement a more modest consumption plan,

Empirical note. Empirical studies indicate that the marginal propensity to consume out of permanent income increases is close to 1, say 0.9. Out of transitory income increases, individuals consume much less, between 0.2 and 0.4. This is much more, however, than our theoretical arguments would suggest.

BOX 2.2   Big stock market crashes

A *stock market crash* is a sudden plunge of stock prices across a large segment of the market, similar to, but also different from *bear markets*, which are periods of declining stock prices that may extend over years. In an interaction between bad news, herd behaviour and market psychology, many investors try to flee the market at the same time. This culminates in panic selling during which the total value of the stock market drops, which affects other markets and, eventually, the economy at large. Crashes in the stock market often lead to major recessions or even depression, as this chapter's analysis insinuates: (i) because they drain the economy of liquidity, and (ii) because they destroy wealth in a serious way, making people respond by cutting back spending. Stock market crashes are not frequent. But when they occur they can be severe. Here are some of the most severe stock market crashes on record.

The Wall Street crash of 1929
A string of terrible days led to a more than 40% drop in the US stock market from the beginning of September 1929 to the end of October 1929. The market continued to decline until July 1932 when it bottomed out, down nearly 90% from its 1929 highs. At the same time, the real economy experienced one of the most serious downturns in modern times, known as the Great Depression, which spread around the world. In the USA, GDP dropped by 27% between 1929 and 1933, accompanied by deflation, i.e. a drop in prices, of some 25%. Industrial production in Canada fell by 42% within three years. Australia's unemployment rate rose to 32% in 1932. The effect on European countries was less severe, but German unemployment rose to over 16%.

The stock market crash of 1987
On 19 October 1987 the Dow Jones Industrial Average stock market index dropped 22.6% in a single day, the largest one-day drop recorded in stock market history. Having started in Hong Kong, the crash spread west to Europe and finally hit the USA. By the end of October, stock markets had fallen by 45.8% in Hong Kong, 41.8% in Australia, 60% in New Zealand, 31% in Spain and 26.4% in the UK. The crash of 1987 was very short-lived compared to the crash of 1929, and most indices managed to end positive for the year. Repercussions on

the real economy were minor, not least because central banks responded by immediately pumping liquidity into the market.

The New Economy crash of 2000
Similar to the crash of 1929, and different from the crash of 1987, the New Economy crash, sometimes referred to as the 'bursting of the dotcom bubble', was more of a dragged-out slide of stock prices that began in March 2000 and ended two and a half years later in October 2002. During that time the NASDAQ Composite index lost 78% of its value of 11 March 2000. Effects on the real economy have been kept modest.

The crash of 2008
The crash (or panic) of 2008 was embedded into a global financial crisis, which grew out of the subprime mortgage crisis originating in the US real estate market. Its main feature was not so much record-breaking single-day drops, but a relentless decline that began in 2007 in most countries and showed no reliable sign of having bottomed out as 2008 ended. The first markets to start their decline were the Nikkei 225 index in Japan and Switzerland's SMI (Figure 2.16). Both reached all-time highs around the middle of 2007 and began their descent immediately after. By the time they bottomed out, the SMI had lost 57% of its value, the Nikkei as much as 62%. Stock markets in Germany, the UK and the USA peaked later, but experienced similar drops. Germany's DAX remained near its all-time high right until the end of 2007 before it began to recede, shedding 55% of its peak value. The Dow lost 54% of its value and the FTSE in London about 49%.

The combined repercussions of the crash of 2008 and the financial crisis were deep recessions in most industrialized countries and, as many argue, the European sovereign debt crisis which started in late 2009.

The crash of 2011
When the European sovereign debt crisis peaked (so we hope) during the second half of 2011, the fear of country defaults, of contagion and a looming Eurozone recession or even global depression triggered a rapid drop in stock indexes. The DAX, for example, shed 25% of its value between 27 July and 10 August. After that the pace slowed,

Box 2.2 continued

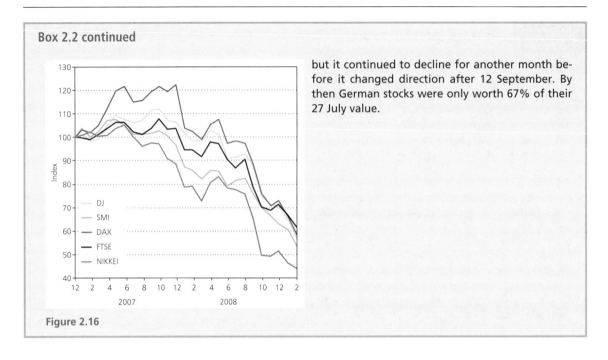

but it continued to decline for another month before it changed direction after 12 September. By then German stocks were only worth 67% of their 27 July value.

Figure 2.16

along with all other households whose wealth took a beating from the stock market crash.

This example adds to last section's discussion of intertemporal aspects of consumption spending. Households' consumption decisions take into account not only the lifetime patterns of labour income, but also changes that result from price movements in asset markets. Thus, major asset markets, such as the stock market or the real estate market, may at times be the origin of major shocks to the economy. During such moments they assume significance beyond the passive role they play during normal times, when their role in our macroeconomic model may be safely ignored.

The practical relevance of this theoretical insight rests on whether the drop in asset prices is substantial, whether it is considered permanent, and whether stocks are in the hands of a large proportion of the population or owned by the richest households only. Since such conditions are being met infrequently, we do not lose much by not making the stock and other asset markets explicit features of our model. True to our pragmatic approach, we keep the model as transparent as possible. We note, however, that exceptional events in the world's asset markets may generate exogenous shifts in the simple consumption function through their effect on household wealth.

When do firms invest?

Capital costs are the costs of financing the purchase of capital goods. They equal the interest payment for a loan, or the interest forgone because money was invested and not lent out.

The motive behind investment is to make profits. Profits accrue as the difference between the gross returns generated by a project relative to the invested funds and the capital costs, i.e. the costs of financing the acquired capital goods. Figure 2.17 illustrates this basic principle and demonstrates how this cost-benefit calculation by firms determines the volume of investment during a given period.

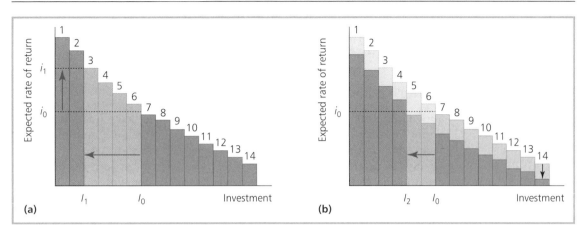

Figure 2.17 Both panels rank investment projects by their expected internal rate of return. Only those projects are realized whose rates of return exceed the interest rate. Panel (a) shows that a rising interest rate reduces investment. Panel (b) shows that falling expected rates of return, due to lower expected future income, reduce investment.

The internal rate of return is the revenue generated by a project as a percentage of the invested funds.

At any point in time a very large number of potential investment projects exists. Each project has its own (expected) internal rate of return. Both panels in Figure 2.17 rank all projects according to their respective internal rates of return. Each project is represented by a column. The height marks the rate of return expected from this project. The width indicates the project's investment volume to be assigned to the current period.

The internal rate of return represents expected gross profits generated by the project. Only if these exceed capital costs, or the returns from capital had it been put to other uses, will the firm go ahead with the investment project. So for each project the rate of return must be compared with the interest rate at which the firm could borrow or lend (we simplify by assuming that both rates are the same). At an interest rate i_0 only the first six projects have a higher rate of return and will therefore be implemented. All the other projects remain on the drawing board. Total investment at an interest rate i_0 is I_0.

What happens if the interest rate changes? Let i increase to i_1 (panel (a)). Now projects #3, #4, #5 and #6 become unprofitable and will be dropped. Total investment falls to I_1. This holds generally. If capital costs in the economy, as measured by the interest rate, increase, while all other things remain unchanged, investment falls. We may thus assume a negative relationship between investment and the interest rate.

The second factor we identified as a determinant of investment demand is the internal rate of return. Anything that changes this rate affects today's investment. The rate of return to be expected from a project crucially depends on the demand expected during the lifetime of the project. Since we know that demand varies positively with income, if the firm expects aggregate income to be lower in the future, it can expect a lower internal rate of return. Panel (b) illustrates the economy-wide effect. If expected income falls, this decreases the expected internal rates of return of all investment projects. At a given interest rate i_0, formerly feasible projects #5 and #6 now become unprofitable and total investment falls from I_0 to I_2.

Generalization of these arguments gives the investment function

$$I = aY^e_+ - bi$$

which states that investment is a function of all expected future income and of the current rate of interest. Current income is not included because it is safe to assume that it takes at least one period for the project to generate any sales.

The Keynesian cross with income expectations

So what are the implications of this for our previous determination of equilibrium income in the circular flow and for the expenditure multiplier? The first result, that a unique equilibrium income level exists and that a neat first attempt to determine it is at the point of intersection between the aggregate demand line and the 45° line in the Keynesian cross, remains intact. The multiplier, however, has lost some of its pervasiveness and must be handled with much more care.

Figure 2.18 draws a distinction between the *AE* line resulting from perceived **permanent income** increases and from perceived temporary or **transitory income** increases. In the first case the line is fairly steep, not only because *c* may be reasonably large, as in previous sections, but because the higher expected future income may also raise investment. An increase in autonomous expenditure (such as government expenditure or exports) then raises income via a significant multiplier. With a perceived transitory income increase, the line is rather flat, particularly if the economy is also very open, with a substantial share of consumption leaking abroad. Then the multiplier effect can be very small, or virtually absent. We must keep these insights in mind when we extend and refine our model in subsequent chapters.

This chapter's analysis has an important **bottom line**: small changes in autonomous expenditure may cause large changes in income. Thus booms and recessions can be triggered by the government changing spending levels, by booms and recessions abroad that affect our exports, or by changes in consumption or investment spending. At the root of the last two effects may be changes in the income tax rate, expectations of income changes in the future or changes in the interest rate.

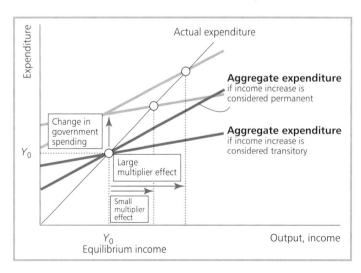

Figure 2.18 For changes of income that are regarded as permanent, the aggregate-expenditure line is very steep. Accordingly, multiplier effects are fairly large. If an income increase is considered transitory, both the slope of the aggregate-expenditure line and the multiplier effect are small.

CHAPTER SUMMARY

- A country's income at a given point in time is determined by the steady-state level of income, the deviation of potential income from steady-state income, and the deviation of income from potential income. The latter is called the business cycle.

- In the circular flow model there exists one equilibrium level of income at which actual spending is exactly as planned. What sets this level of income apart from all other feasible income levels is that firms will try to set production to this very level to avoid having to invest or disinvest involuntarily.

- An increase in autonomous expenditure, such as government purchases, generates an income increase that may vastly exceed the original stimulus. This multiplier effect occurs because the exogenous spending increase raises income and thus induces consumers to spend more and raise income even higher.

- When the multiplier is large, small changes in government expenditure or other autonomous injections or leakages may cause sizeable booms or recessions.

- Factors that reduce the size of the multiplier are high marginal income tax rates and a high marginal propensity to import.

- Consumption does not depend on current income only, but, more importantly, on expected future income.

- Multiplier effects apply fully only if consumers consider observed income changes to be permanent.

- The multiplier becomes much smaller if observed income changes are considered transitory.

- Investment rises when expected future income rises and/or when the interest rate falls.

Key terms and concepts

actual expenditure *42*

aggregate (planned) expenditure *42*

average income tax rate *51*

boom *37*

business cycle *37*

capital costs *58*

consumption function *51*

demand-side equilibrium *43*

disposable income *51*

equilibrium income *49*

government purchases *44*

import function *51*

Keynesian cross *47*

marginal income tax rate *51*

marginal propensity to consume *46*

multiplier *50*

net taxes *44*

permanent income *60*

potential income *37*

rate of return *59*

recession *37*

steady-state income *37*

transitory income *60*

EXERCISES

2.1 Consider French real output between 1900 and 1991 as given in Figure 2.19.
Add your guess of the paths of steady-state income and potential income to the graph.

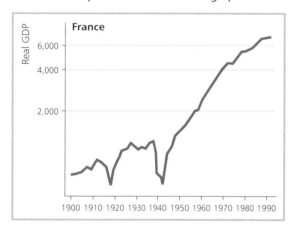

Figure 2.19

2.2 Figure 2.20 displays the evolution of real GDP between 1978 and 2002 for the United States and France.
  (a) Try to identify business cycles, marking peaks and troughs on the graphs.
  (b) Identify the US position in 1991 in a diagram with prices on the vertical axis and income on the horizontal axis. Mark potential income, steady-state income and actual income.

Two US economists, Arthur F. Burns and Wesley C. Mitchell, claimed half a century ago that the typical business cycle lasts between six and thirty-two quarters.
  (c) Does this agree with your findings?

2.3 Consider an economy with the following data (note that *I* is *planned* investment, which may not coincide with actual investment):

$$C = 750 \quad I = 500 \quad T = 0 \quad G = 250$$
$$NX = 250 \quad Y = 1{,}000$$

  (a) Is this economy's circular flow in equilibrium in the sense that firms do not have to change inventories involuntarily?
  (b) Translate the above data into a diagram with demand on the vertical axis and income on the horizontal axis.
Add the assumption $C = 0.75Y$.
  (c) Draw the aggregate-expenditure and the actual-expenditure lines. Identify demand-determined income in equilibrium in your graph and analytically.
  (d) What happens to equilibrium income if government expenditure increases by 500 units? Show your result in a graph and verify that it is supported by the multiplier formula of equation (2.9).
  (e) Using a graph, show what happens if net exports fall from 250 to 100.

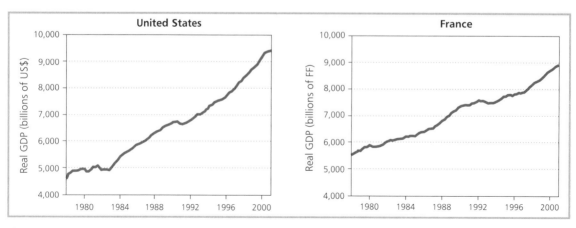

Figure 2.20

(f) Using a graph, show what happens if the marginal propensity to consume rises from 0.75 to 0.8.

2.4 One effect of German unification was a rise in demand for most Western countries' exports. However, the impact differed considerably among countries, depending on the multipliers that transform an exogenous change in demand into a change in income.

Consider the Netherlands and the United Kingdom. The share of imports in Dutch GDP is 52%, the share of imports in British GDP is 27%. Assume that these average import propensities are also the marginal propensities to import. Assume, further, that for both countries the marginal propensity to consume is 80% and the average tax rate is 30%.

(a) Calculate the equilibrium effect of an exogenous increase of export demand by 100 units on Dutch and British GDP.

(b) Employ the successive-rounds interpretation of the multiplier. By how much has income increased after round #3 in total?

2.5 In the summer of 1991 the German parliament imposed a surcharge of 7.5% on personal and corporate income tax (the so-called *Solidaritätszuschlag*), promising that this tax surcharge would be removed after one year. However, following a decision in March 1993 the solidarity surcharge was reintroduced in January 1995 and was still in effect in 1996. What would you expect aggregate consumption to look like, starting at the first announcement of the solidarity surcharge? Does it make any difference whether individuals believed the government's pledge that the surcharge would be removed after one year?

2.6 Figure 2.21 shows quarterly data for nominal GDP and nominal consumption in France. (Both time series are deviations from a non-linear trend.) What is your interpretation of these time series in the light of the hypothesis that consumption only responds to permanent changes of income?

2.7 Consider an economy characterized by $C = cY$, with $c = 0.75$, $T = 0$, $G = 250$, $NX = 250$, and $I = \bar{I} - bi$, with $\bar{I} = 500$ and $b = 5{,}000$. Note that investment depends on the interest rate.

Figure 2.21

(a) Assume that, due to the increasingly pessimistic expectations of investors, autonomous investment decreases from 500 to 300. The interest rate and all other exogenous variables stay constant. Calculate the resulting change in equilibrium income.

(b) At the same time the interest rate decreases from 0.06 to 0.05. Calculate the effect on equilibrium income.

2.8 Consider the economy of exercise 2.7, except that consumption now depends on disposable income: $C = c(Y - T)$. The government increases expenditure from 250 to 750 (i.e. $\Delta G = 500$). This additional expenditure is financed partly by taxes, which account for 50% of government revenue, and partly by issuing bonds. This sudden appearance of huge quantities of government bonds on the capital market drives up interest rates from 0.05 to 0.06. What is the effect of all these changes on equilibrium income? Would it have been better to finance the expenditure entirely by taxes (then $\Delta G = \Delta T = 500$ and $\Delta i = 0$)?

2.9 Investment decisions not only depend on the interest rate but also on expectations of the future overall economic situation, represented by future GDP.

(a) Through what channels might Y enter the investment decision?

(b) Assume that, to form their expectations about future GDP, investors simply extrapolate today's GDP, that is: $Y_{+}^{e} = Y$. Moreover, assume that these expectations enter the investment function in the following form (note that we neglect the influence of the interest rate):

$$I = \alpha Y$$

(i) How will this modification affect the multiplier?

(ii) Derive the multiplier for this case, in which Y influences investment.

2.10 An open economy exhibits the following aggregate expenditure function:

$$AE = C + I + G + NX$$

where $C = c(Y - T)$ and $T = tY$. I, G and NX are exogenous variables.

(a) The country enters a war, which boosts government expenditure G. Show the effect on income Y in the Keynesian cross.

(b) You recognize that the actual increase in Y is smaller than the one you found in question (a). What factors may be responsible for this 'too small' multiplier? Specify the variants that go with the given aggregate expenditure function and illustrate them in the Keynesian cross.

Online resources

Interactive Keynesian cross applet www.eurmacro.eu/tutor/keynesiancross.html

X-ercise on paradox of thrift www.eurmacro.eu/xercises/paradoxofthrift.html

Self quiz

www.eurmacro.eu/SelfQuiz/sq-ch02.html

Recommended reading

While much of the discussion in this and the next chapter derive from John Maynard Keynes's thinking, his writing is very heavy-going and reading it at this stage may confuse rather than enlighten. The graphical apparatus on which we rely has been introduced by John Hicks (1937) 'Mr. Keynes and the "Classics": A suggested interpretation', *Econometrica* 5: 147–59. Concepts such as the Keynesian cross and the multiplier are discussed extensively in almost every macroeconomics textbook. If you desire a more extended or alternative discussion, consult any introductory or intermediate macroeconomics text or the general introductory texts listed at the end of Chapter 1.

APPLIED PROBLEMS

EMPIRICAL RESEARCH

Consumption out of permanent and transitory income

One important issue in the context of the simple macroeconomic model discussed in Chapter 2 is whether consumption does respond to all income changes, whether or not individuals consider them transitory or permanent. Addressing this very issue, Michael R. Darby, in 'The permanent income theory of consumption – a restatement' (1974, *Quarterly Journal of Economics* 88: 228–50), looks at the relationship between personal consumption expenditures C, and the permanent component Y^P and the transitory component Y^T of disposable income in the United States. Employing the statistical method of ordinary least squares (OLS) described in the Appendix to this book, he arrives at the following equation (the numbers in parentheses are absolute *t*-statistics):

$$C = -1.35 + 0.93\,Y^P + 0.57\,Y^T \qquad R^2 = 0.999$$
$$(0.49)\ (121.6)\quad\ (3.40)$$

The obtained coefficients suggest that if permanent income increases by one dollar, consumption rises by 93 cents. If the income increase is considered transitory, consumption rises by only 57 cents. According to our rule of thumb that coefficients are significantly different from zero only if they carry absolute t-statistics larger than 2, the constant term is not significant, but the other two coefficients are.

The coefficient of determination called R^2 is high. At 0.999 it suggests that the estimated equation explains US consumption spending very well.

WORKED PROBLEM

Pizza e pasta – consuming in Italy

Table 2.4 contains data on consumption spending C and on disposable income $(Y - T)$ in billion lire for Italy.

As a first step, we want to find out how well these data comply with the simple consumption function $C = c_0 + c_1 (Y - T)$. The OLS method yields

$$C = -3,764.9 + 0.71(Y - T)$$
$$(5.11) \qquad (486.5)$$
$$R^2 = 0.999 \quad \text{Annual data 1961–91}$$

As in the above example from published research, this even simpler equation explains Italian consumption almost perfectly. The marginal propensity to consume is found to be 0.71. The t-statistic of 486.5 renders this coefficient highly significant.

It can be argued that parts of consumption spending cannot be adjusted to changing income immediately: your summer vacation that has been booked since the previous autumn; high car maintenance costs that can only be reduced by selling the car at a loss; your second daughter who insists on taking

ballet lessons just like her older sister, and so on. To allow for such adjustment lags we may suppose that only desired consumption C^* is related to income, that is $C^* = c_0 + c_1 (Y - T)$. If desired consumption drifts away from actual consumption, the response of actual consumption only closes a fraction a of this gap. Formally we may write $C - C_{-1} = \alpha(C^* - C_{-1})$. Substituting the above explanation of desired consumption for C^* in the partial adjustment equation yields $C = \alpha c_0 + (1 - \alpha)C_{-1} + \alpha c_1 (Y - T)$. Estimating this equation yields

$$C = -1,830.6 + 0.22C_{-1} + 0.57(Y - T)$$
$$(3.07) \qquad (6.31) \qquad (25.10)$$
$$R^2 = 0.999 \quad \text{Annual data 1961–91}$$

The autoregressive coefficient (the one in front of C_{-1}) $0.22 = 1 - \alpha$ carries a t-statistic of 6.31, rendering it highly significant. The coefficient of disposable income is also significant, but smaller than in our first estimate above. Note, however, that it represents the product αc_1. Since α is estimated at 0.78, we may compute $c_1 = 0.57/0.78 = 0.73$, which barely differs from the previous estimate. So while the long-run marginal propensity to consume is the same as estimated above, the short-run effect is smaller. If disposable income increases by 100,000L, consumption immediately goes up by 57,000L. This is not the end, however. One period later, consumption goes up by another $0.22 \times 57,000 = 12,540$L, one period later by another $0.22 \times 0.22 \times 57,000 = 2,758.8$L, and so on. So while the partial adjustment version of the consumption function estimates the same overall response of consumption as the simple version, it suggests that the response is spread over a longer span of time.

Table 2.4

Year	C	Y − T	Year	C	Y − T	Year	C	Y − T
1960	14,561	22,520	1971	43,660	65,960	1982	335,448	475,205
1961	15,919	25,151	1972	47,951	72,136	1983	387,170	553,129
1962	17,967	28,215	1973	58,484	86,914	1984	443,268	634,682
1963	21,017	32,109	1974	73,637	108,296	1985	498,048	706,280
1964	22,784	34,988	1975	85,972	120,875	1986	551,868	782,365
1965	24,366	37,708	1976	106,383	153,198	1987	606,889	858,348
1966	26,873	40,973	1977	129,209	187,982	1988	670,883	953,439
1967	29,767	45,192	1978	150,848	222,825	1989	740,267	1,037,647
1968	31,762	49,082	1979	185,051	275,473	1990	806,593	1,137,230
1969	34,838	54,302	1980	236,603	344,912	1991	881,171	1,231,558
1970	39,992	60,652	1981	284,030	406,106			

Consumption function in first differences

One thing to note in the above study of Italian consumption functions is that both consumption and disposable income show a clear upward trend during the thirty-one years considered here. This can be a problem. Regressing two heavily trended variables on each other may give a statistically significant result, although the two have nothing to do with each other (a classic example is the negative correlation between the number of telephones and the number of storks during the first half of the 20th century). In an attempt to alleviate this problem we may compute first differences on both sides of the consumption function to obtain $\Delta C = c_1 \Delta(Y - T)$. Please check whether this formulation is supported by the data.

Money, interest rates and the global economy

What to expect

After working through this chapter, you will understand:

1 Why it is useful to divide the economy into a goods market, a money market and a foreign exchange market.

2 How money supply rules, interest rules and other monetary policy rules are related, and how they affect the economy.

3 Which variables determine and are influenced by the interest rate.

4 Under what conditions the goods market and the money market are in equilibrium – separately and simultaneously.

5 How fiscal and monetary policy affect income in the global economy.

6 More about how to work with graphs.

With Athens leading the way by coining silver around 700 years BC, Europe has a long tradition of making economic transactions by using money. The discussion of equilibrium income and the multiplier in Chapter 2 did not really need money. Just as in our first look at the circular flow model in Chapter 1, it was possible to exchange the real thing: labour, goods and services. This analysis yielded important first insights, but was also bound to leave loose ends.

For instance, we found that a crucial determinant of investment is the interest rate. Yet we have no idea what determines the interest rate. It certainly does not move about arbitrarily. In fact, it is what we forfeit if we decide to retain money – coins and notes – in our pockets instead of putting it in an interest-bearing bank account. So understanding the interest rate seems impossible without considering **money**.

Also, the discussion of exports and imports in Chapter 2 remained silent about the exchange rate. This facilitated a first look at equilibrium income and the multiplier. But it needs to be remedied as we move on to a more comprehensive view of the economy. The exchange rate is the price of one country's money in terms of another country's money. So again, we need to bring money into the picture in order to understand exchange rates.

The exchange rate is the price of one unit of foreign currency in terms of domestic currency.

This and the next chapter pick up these loose ends and tie them together. Step by step we will arrive at a richer picture of the economy which will eventually enable us to discuss many important new questions that Chapter 2's simple multiplier model cannot handle. The knowledge acquired in Chapter 2 will find its way into this extended model, however. In addition to the goods market, which is all Chapter 2's economy consists of, we will look at the domestic money market in this chapter and at the foreign exchange market in Chapter 4.

3.1 The money market, the interest rate and the *LM* curve

The notion of a money market, in which supply and demand interact, may sound odd. It appears plausible that central banks control the money supply by printing and issuing bank notes and coins. But it seems less straightforward indeed to envisage a well-defined demand for money. Don't people always want more money? So how can there ever be equilibrium in a market with a finite supply and unlimited demand?

Such reservations are rooted in a mix-up between *money* and *wealth* resulting from how the term 'money' is being used in everyday language. When people portray Bill Gates as having 'a lot of money' they do not literally suggest that he is carrying a lot of cash in his wallet, or has billions sitting in his bank account. What they mean is that when all his possessions are added up, we end up with a very big number. Economists call this Bill Gates's wealth. Money may be a part of it, albeit a very small one. So money is a form of holding wealth. But it must not be confused with wealth.

Of course, to combine the value of all other assets, things as different as bonds and houses, stocks and pieces of art, airplanes and real estate, into a single number we need a yardstick. Incidentally, this is one of the important functions of money – being a **unit of account**, a convenient measuring rod that helps gauge and compare things that are entirely different in nature.

There is no need actually to hold money in order to use it as a unit of account. We may estimate Bill Gates's material wealth at $56 billion, suggest that the Aldi family's fortune made from their discount stores is around €33 billion, or that Richard Branson's net worth is £2.6 billion, without actually holding dollars, euros or pounds. Therefore, the reason why individuals choose to demand money must derive from other functions of money from which we only benefit if we actually do hold money. We now take a look at these.

The demand for money

A comprehensive, systematic view of why people demand money, and of the factors that affect this demand for money, evolves from looking at the essential *functions* of money. Apart from being a *unit of account*, a measuring rod that helps gauge and compare quite different things such as a haircut and a pair of Italian shoes, money serves as a **medium of exchange**, enabling us to carry out purchases and sales swiftly and easily, and as a **store of value**, permitting us to save buying power that we do not want to exercise today for future use.

Money as a medium of exchange
Recall that in Chapter 1 money was defined as anything that sellers generally accept as payment for goods and services. So if individuals hold money, one reason is because they need it for transactions in the goods market. Instead of looking at this transactions demand for money in the abstract, consider the following illustration.

Assume that there are only two assets. One is *savings accounts*, which pay a fixed rate of interest *i*. The other one is *money*, which yields no interest payment and which, for simplicity, we limit to cash holdings for now. Consider

Transactions demand for money is money held to cover routine expenditures.

a consumer who receives income Y_0 at the beginning of each month, does not pay any taxes, does not save, and thus consumes the amount $C_0 = Y_0$ over the course of each month.

A flow variable is measured over a *period* of time. Examples are income, consumption and exports.

Consumption is a flow variable, measured from the beginning to the end of a month. Money, by contrast, is a stock variable, measured at a specific moment in time. Our consumer's money holdings cannot remain constant over the course of a month, as money is being held for the very purpose of getting rid of it in exchange for goods and services. So if we ask how much money the consumer holds, we are talking about *average* holdings during the entire month.

A stock variable is measured at a *point* in time. Examples are the money supply, the number of workers and the capital stock.

Our consumer's average money holdings, her **demand for money,** depend on two factors. First, it depends on her level of consumption. Since purchases of goods and services typically involve an exchange of money, a higher level of consumption spending requires more money to conduct the purchases involved. Since planned consumption increases with the level of income, as suggested by the consumption function $C = cY$, we may note that *the demand for money goes up when income goes up*.

Secondly, it depends on how often she refills her purse in the course of a month. Here our consumer has a large set of options. One extreme case is shown in panel (a) of Figure 3.1. If our consumer decides to go to the bank only once a month, she must obtain the amount of money that matches one month's consumption spending and income Y_0. Otherwise she could not carry out her consumption plan. If purchases are spread evenly over the month, her money holdings decline linearly day by day and hit bottom on the evening before the next pay day. The *average* holding of money, or her demand for money, is obviously $Y_0/2$. This comes at a cost, however. By holding this amount of money, she forgoes interest payments totalling $iY_0/2$.

Panel (b) in Figure 3.1 displays a second option. On receiving her salary at the start of the month, the consumer may opt for cash withdrawal of half her monthly pay only, depositing the other half in a savings account. In this case she runs out of cash by the middle of the month, being forced to take an additional trip to the bank and withdraw the second half of her salary from the savings account to refill her empty purse. The additional visit to the bank reduces average money holdings to $Y_0/4$ and forgone interest payments to $iY_0/4$.

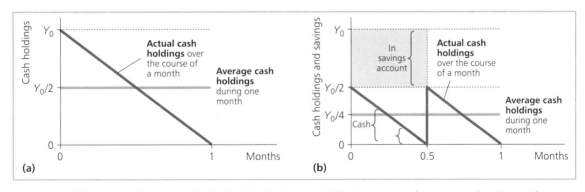

Figure 3.1 With one monthly trip to the bank, all cash (or money) that buys a month's consumption Y_0 must be picked up. Cash linearly declines from Y_0 to 0 during one month (panel (a)). With two monthly trips to the bank only, cash worth $Y_0/2$ must be picked up each time. It declines to 0 in half a month (panel (b)). Average cash holdings equal $Y_0/2$ in the first case and $Y_0/4$ in the second.

Maths note. Total costs $TC = an + iY/(2n)$ of holding liquidity to pay for one month's consumption $C = Y$ comprise shoe leather costs $a \times n$ and forgone interest $iY/(2n)$. Both depend on the number of trips to the bank, n. The first-order condition for a minimum, $dTC/dn = a - iY/(2n^2) = 0$, implies $n = [iY/(2a)]^{0.5}$. Substituting this into average money holdings $L = Y/(2n)$ shows that money demand $L = [aY/(2i)]^{0.5}$ rises with income Y and falls with the interest rate i.

Maths note. Solve (3.1) for i to obtain $i = kY/h - L/h$, which defines a surface the height of which is measured in i. Holding Y constant leaves a negative relationship between i and L. Holding i constant leaves a positive relationship between Y and L. The figure below shows vertical slices cut parallel to the L axis.

The average demand for money and the interest earnings lost can be reduced still further by going to the bank weekly or even every day. General expressions for average money demand and forgone interest earnings are then $Y_0/(2n)$ and $iY_0/(2n)$, respectively, where n denotes the number of trips to the bank per month.

The reduction in forgone interest income that is achieved this way is not free. Each trip to the bank costs time, possibly parking fees, transaction fees, etc. Economists conveniently sum all these items up as *shoe leather costs*. Consumers are more likely to take an additional trip to the bank and incur the attached cost when this trip generates a lot of added interest income. And this is the case when the interest rate is high. So higher interest rates generate more frequent visits to the bank and, thus, lower average money holdings. Hence, *the demand for money goes down when the interest rate goes up.*

We may combine these insights into a simple money demand equation:

$$L = kY - hi \qquad \text{Money demand function} \quad (3.1)$$

L denotes the demand for money (or liquidity). The first term on the right-hand side of the equation captures the insight that money holdings are positively related to income. The more income Y is received at the beginning of a month, the higher is consumption spending and, thus, the volume of planned transactions – and the more money must therefore be held for a given number of trips to the bank. The second term states that the demand for money falls as the interest rate i rises. A higher interest rate makes holding money more costly, induces more frequent trips to the bank, and thus causes a lower average demand for money at any given level of income.

Panel (a) in Figure 3.2 illustrates one version of the money demand function. The line is drawn while holding income constant. The negative slope indicates that the demand for money rises as the interest rate falls. An increase of income shifts the curve to the right: if the interest rate is fixed at, say, i_0, which fixes the number of trips to the bank, average money holdings needed for transaction purposes increases when income rises.

This section has looked at how households manage the liquidity needed for conducting their regular purchases. We now turn to other motives for holding money that derive from money being a *store of value.*

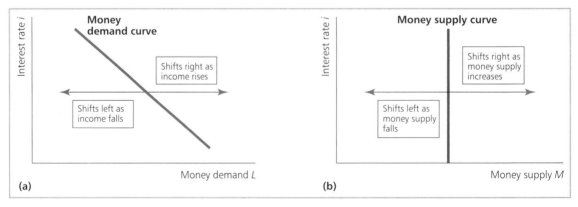

(a) Money demand curve — Shifts right as income rises — Shifts left as income falls — Money demand L

(b) Money supply curve — Shifts right as money supply increases — Shifts left as money supply falls — Money supply M

Figure 3.2 Rising interest rates raise the opportunity costs of holding money. Therefore they drive down the demand for money at given income levels (panel (a)). Rising income raises transactions and shifts the money demand curve to the right. The money supply curve is vertical. Changing supply shifts the curve left or right (panel (b)).

Money as a store of value

In order to extend the above discussion, consider a second consumer who possesses a substantial amount of material wealth. Suppose his transactions demand for money is taken care of in the way described in the preceding section. The additional decision he needs to take is what kind of assets to invest his wealth in. The options are many, ranging from savings accounts via the money market, government bonds and corporate stocks to real estate. As mentioned earlier, money as a financial asset is inferior to other assets because it does not generate any return: no interest earnings, no dividends, no rent being collected. And since monthly routine purchases are already taken care of by the transactions demand for money, there is no reason to hold wealth in the form of money. Then why do households typically hold more than 10% of wealth in the form of money?

Here the uncertainties of life come into play. Things do not always go as planned. While the transactions demand for money covers planned consumption, there's always the risk of unexpected spending needs deriving from things that break or wear out prematurely, including mishaps, accidents or natural disasters, and life's surprises in general: repair or replacement bills, a car accident or an opportunity for a bargain that we do not want to miss. To be prepared for such needs, emergencies or opportunities, individuals prefer to keep a significant fraction of their accumulated wealth liquid, in the form of money. This part of the demand for money is called the precautionary demand for money.

Technically, this precautionary demand for money, the amount of wealth held as money, increases when either the cake itself becomes bigger, or money claims a bigger share of it. During normal times, a country's wealth, the size of the cake, changes only slowly. And wealth usually reflects income levels. Households that generate higher incomes are usually more wealthy. So we may expect the precautionary demand for money to be positively related to income, just as the transactions demand for money is. Also, rational households cut down on the share of wealth devoted to precautionary money holdings when these become more expensive. We know from our discussion of the transactions demand for money that these opportunity costs of holding money rise when interest rates go up. So the precautionary demand for money is also inversely related to the interest rate. Both of these channels are being accounted for by equation (3.1) as explained above.

You may have noted the qualification 'during normal times' in the preceding paragraph. It cautions that there may be times when wealth does not grow smoothly, but drops in leaps. Examples of events that have a dramatic impact on (actual or perceived) household wealth and, thus, on precautionary money holdings, are stock market crashes and the bursting of a real estate bubble. When such financial catastrophes hit, the demand for money may drop in ways that equation (3.1) cannot explain.

But this is only one channel through which markets for other assets may affect the money market. While assets other than money have the advantage of offering a return, they also have the disadvantage of being more risky. During times when these risks become excessive, households may decide to drop out of such financial investments altogether. Bank runs, experienced as side-effects of the global financial crisis of 2007–08, are but

Precautionary demand for money is wealth held in the form of money for the purpose of covering unexpected expenditures.

BOX 3.1 **Money and monetary policy**

What is money?

There is no simple answer to this question. Norwegian kroner will certainly do the trick in Oslo or Trondheim (and maybe even in Copenhagen, but probably not in Florence). A Eurocheque or a Visa card are other options. Both draw on your bank account, and will fail in certain instances. Stocks will only be accepted on rare occasions. Your car, your house? Probably not.

So there is obviously no strict way of telling what is money and what is not. Central bank statistics therefore offer a number of different data series on money, and economists use these as considered appropriate for the problem at hand. The most narrow aggregate includes all coins and bills in circulation plus those that private banks are required to hold as reserves in the central bank's vaults. This aggregate is called the **monetary base**, or **high-powered money**, or simply **M0**. It has the advantage of being under the direct and perfect control of the central bank. Its disadvantage is that it is clearly an incomplete measure of liquidity. Demand deposits (wealth held in bank accounts that can be withdrawn on demand, that is, without prior notice) on which cheques can be written or credit cards used can serve as a means of payment in all but the most trivial or rare situations. **M1** replaces current reserves by demand deposits. **M2** and **M3** widen the spectrum by including assets with successively lower degrees of liquidity.

- **M0** (monetary base, high-powered money): comprises currency in circulation CU (coins and bills) plus the currency reserves $CRES$ which private banks hold at the central bank, that is

$$M0 = CU + CRES \tag{1}$$

- **M1**: comprises currency plus demand deposits DEP that the public holds in private banks, that is

$$M1 = CU + DEP \tag{2}$$

- **M2**: M1 plus demand deposits with unrestricted access plus small-denomination time deposits.
- **M3**: M2 plus large-denomination time deposits.

As mentioned above, only M0 is under direct control of the central bank and, hence, classifies as a policy instrument. As soon as we move to wider monetary aggregates, which are the relevant ones from a macroeconomic perspective, these include components that are eventually determined in the market. For example, the money supply M1 includes demand deposits, the size of which is determined by the behaviour of both private banks and households. So with what justification can we then speak of a monetary policy? The key assumption is that there is a stable, or at least a predictable, relationship between the controlled policy instrument, say M0, and the targeted aggregate, say M1.

The money multiplier

To obtain a formal relationship between the monetary base M0 and M1, divide both sides of (1) and (2) by deposits DEP. This yields

$$\frac{M1}{DEP} = \frac{CU}{DEP} + \frac{DEP}{DEP} \tag{3}$$

$$\frac{M0}{DEP} + \frac{CU}{DEP} + \frac{CRES}{DEP} \tag{4}$$

Dividing (3) by (4) gives us the ratio between M1 and M0:

$$\frac{M1}{M0} = \frac{\dfrac{CU}{DEP} + 1}{\dfrac{CU}{DEP} + \dfrac{CRES}{DEP}} \tag{5}$$

This ratio depends on the two fractions CU/DEP and $CRES/DEP$. The first one is the ratio of currency to demand deposits, which we may call $cdr \equiv CU/DEP$. It is a behavioural relationship, indicating which way households wish to split their money demand between currency and bank deposits. In the euro area this ratio is about $1/6$. The second fraction is the ratio of reserves of the banking system to bank deposits, which we call the **reserve ratio** $rdr \equiv CRES/DEP$. This ratio is a policy variable, imposed by the central bank, which requires banks to hold part of their deposits with the central bank. In Euroland it runs at a magnitude of 0.02. Making use of these definitions, we may rewrite equation (5) as

$$M1 \equiv \frac{cdr + 1}{cdr + rdr} M0 \tag{6}$$

The coefficient of M0 is called the **money multiplier**. It tells us that the monetary base, controlled by the central bank, multiplies into a much higher money supply. In the euro area M1 is more than six times as high as the monetary base. Thus, the monetary

Box 3.1 continued

base of €1,034.9 billion in August 2011 generated a money supply M1 of €4,779.5 billion. This includes €209.5 billion of reserves that banks held with the European Central Bank (ECB), out of which €207 billion were required reserves, and €2.5 billion were excess reserves which banks did not have to hold.

The instruments of monetary policy

We may draw on equation (6) for a discussion of how monetary policy is conducted – in general, and by the ECB in particular. Central banks typically control three instruments that target one or both of the parameters *rdr* and M0:

- **Open-market operations**
  This is the most direct instrument of monetary policy. The central bank participates in the open market for bonds (or other assets it sees fit) to pump currency into the economy or to withdraw currency from it. When the central bank purchases 1 million euros worth of government bonds, it pays with euros and therefore increases the currency part of the monetary base and, via the money multiplier, the money supply. If the central bank sells some of the government bonds it holds, it gets paid in euros, which are thus taken out of the hands of the public. Both the monetary base and the money supply shrink.
- **Quantitative easing**
  This new monetary policy tool is a special case of open-market operations. It consists of purchases of long-term government or commercial bonds in an effort to bring down long-term interest rates when short-term rates are stuck near zero.
- **Reserve requirements**
  Central banks require commercial banks to keep some of the funds they have received from customers as reserves. These required reserves are some percentage of the demand deposits which banks owe to customers. If this (required) **reserve ratio** was 10%, banks would have to keep 10% of their demand deposits in the form of cash or in accounts they have at the central bank. Only the remaining 90% could be passed on as loans to other customers, and thus create more money. By raising the reserve ratio the central bank affects the money supply indirectly, via the money multiplier: the multiplier shrinks, which reduces the money supply. The monetary base may appear to be affected as well, since it includes currency

reserves. But since M0 is simply the sum of currency in circulation and currency reserves, only a reshuffle occurs, moving currency out of circulation into reserves, leaving M0 largely unaffected.
- **The discount rate**
  The discount rate is the interest rate that central banks charge on loans they extend to commercial banks. Banks borrow from the central bank when they have insufficient reserves to meet reserve requirements. The higher the discount rate, the more costly it is to borrow reserves, the less banks borrow at the central bank's lending facility, and the larger is the part of required reserves they take out of their demand deposits. Hence, an increase in the discount rate lowers the monetary base and the money supply.

How the ECB conducts monetary policy

All central banks have their own idiosyncratic ways of using the monetary policy instruments just described, and so does the ECB.

The ECB's most important group of operations is **open market operations**. Within this group, the key instrument is **reverse transactions**, which are being used for the provision of liquidity. Reverse transactions refer to operations where the Eurosystem, the ECB and the national central banks of countries that have adopted the euro, buys or sells eligible assets under repurchase agreements. Other available open-market instruments are **outright transactions** and **foreign exchange swaps**. The use of both is being confined to fine-tuning operations.

The ECB requires commercial banks to hold compulsory deposits on accounts with euro area national central banks. The required reserve ratio that determines these deposits was set to 2% when the euro was introduced, and has not been changed since. Thus **required reserves** are not being used as an active instrument of monetary policy, but they are a prerequisite for the effective use of the discount rate.

The Eurosystem offers two **standing facilities** which banks can use for overnight loans or overnight deposits. While the ECB does not use the label **discount rate** in this context, the interest rate on the marginal lending facility is basically just that. By setting the two interest rates on overnight loans and deposits, the ECB determines the corridor within which the overnight money market rate, a key interest rate, may fluctuate.

one extreme example. If I see a chance of one in twenty that my bank will go bankrupt during the next twelve months, 3% interest on my savings account will not keep me from withdrawing my savings – either to deposit these funds with some other bank which I trust, or to hang on to cash until the sky clears and the banking industry as a whole has regained my trust. Another example are stock market crashes. Again, even the promise of substantial dividends may not keep me in the stock market if I fear a (continuing) slide in stock prices. Instead, I may prefer to keep my assets liquid and be prepared to re-enter the stock market the moment prospects improve. Money held in order to sidestep temporarily excessive risks or uncertainty in return-generating assets is called the speculative demand for money. This part of the demand for money may be safely ignored during normal times, but it can move to centre stage in times of crisis in financial markets and the economy at large.

> Speculative demand for money is wealth held as money at times when other assets are considered excessively risky.

To sum this up: our discussion of *money as a store of value* revealed additional channels through which income and interest rates affect the demand for money, which leaves the relationship provided by equation (3.1) intact. In addition, we found that the demand for money is also affected by developments in other asset markets, such as the stock market or the market for real estate. During normal times, when asset prices move predictably or smoothly, this influence is muted and there is not much harm done by keeping the money demand equation simple, and parsimonious, as formalized in equation (3.1) and depicted in Figure 3.2. In times of crisis, however, when risk spins out of control, the speculative demand for money adopts a leading role and developments in the money market can only be understood by augmenting the standard view of the demand for money with speculative money holdings that may culminate in bank runs, with risk premia or with the possibility of a liquidity trap. Case study 3.1 exemplifies this in the context of the subprime crisis that started in 2007.

> The risk premium is the difference between the risk-free interest rate and the expected return on an alternative, risky asset.

The money supply

No market is complete without supply. Supply in the money market is determined by the central bank. As we discussed in Chapter 1, the central bank is a monopolist which determines how much currency circulates in the economy, but also controls wider monetary aggregates, by sales or purchases of treasury bills (either directly from the government, or from the private sector) or by buying or selling foreign exchange. When faced with a downward-sloping money demand schedule, the central bank's situation is like that of any monopolist facing a downward-sloping demand curve for its product: it can either set the quantity on offer, and accept the price at which the market is willing to buy it; or it may set the price, and live with whatever quantity the market is prepared to acquire.

In the money market, the good being traded is money. The price for holding one unit of money for a given period of time is the applicable interest rate. So monetary policy, the control of an economy's liquidity by the central bank, may be conducted either by manipulating the money supply M or by setting the interest rate i – or a combination of both.

Manipulating the money supply

Discretionary control of the money supply has been the traditional way of conducting monetary policy. Alternative paradigms have gained prominence in recent years, under which central banks use interest rates as policy instruments or follow a more general monetary policy rule. While these alternatives will also be discussed and fitted into our general framework below, our main focus is on manipulating the money supply. This has the pedagogical advantage of describing the interaction of supply and demand in the money market in a fashion that is already familiar from other markets. It also provides the most general basis for understanding monetary policy, even in situations when bank runs, risk premia and liquidity traps come into play.

We start by graphing the money supply curve in the same diagram that features the money demand curve. Under money supply targeting, the central bank has the discretion to set the supply of money to its preferred value:

$$M = \overline{M} \qquad\qquad \text{Exogenous money supply}$$

Since this value does not depend on the interest rate, panel (b) in Figure 3.2 shows the money supply curve as a vertical line positioned at $M = \overline{M}$. Monetary policy shifts this vertical line to the left or to the right by lowering or raising the money supply.

Are L and M nominal or real variables? Well, when individuals demand money they want to have a certain buying power in their wallet, depending on their real income Y, and on i. So L must be a demand for real money. The money supply M controlled by the central bank is a nominal variable. It loses value if the price level rises. In equilibrium, the real money demand must equal the real supply of money, $L = M/P$. For the moment, we are assuming the price level to be fixed. For the sake of convenience we may also suppose prices to be fixed at $P = 1$. Then M also represents the real money supply in this chapter and $L = M$ in equilibrium.

Figure 3.3 merges the money supply and the money demand curves and shows how they interact. The figure shows how equilibrium is obtained. Only one interest rate i_0 exists at which individuals want to hold the exact volume of money that the central bank has decided to provide. If the interest rate is higher than i_0, individuals economize on their money holdings, and supply exceeds demand. At an interest rate below i_0 an excess demand for money exists.

The interest rate i_0 clears the money market only if income equals Y_0. If Y rises to Y_1, desired money holdings increase at any given interest rate. The demand curve shifts to the right, reflecting an excess demand at the old interest rate i_0. A rise in the interest rate is required to offset the demand increase caused by the income rise. Only as the interest rate reaches the higher level i_1 is the money market back in equilibrium (see Figure 3.4, panel (a)).

The *LM* curve representing money market equilibria

Panel (a) in Figure 3.4 teaches us that money demand can equal a given supply at many different interest rates, provided they are paired with the right

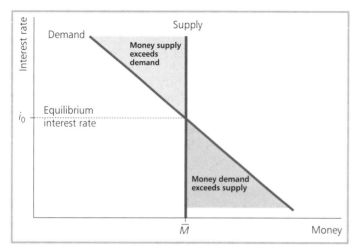

Figure 3.3 Money demand and supply are equal at one interest rate i_0. At higher interest rates there is an excess supply. A lower interest rate generates an excess demand.

income level. If the interest rate rises from i_0 to i_1, thus pushing demand down, income needs to rise from Y_0 to Y_1 to make up for this loss and stimulate demand by the exact amount needed. The equilibrium points A and B can be transferred onto a diagram with i and Y on the axes (panel (b)). All other equilibrium combinations are to be found on a line through A and B. This line is called the *LM curve* because it combines all points at which money demand L equals a given money supply M. An important point to keep in mind is that the money supply is always the same as we move along a given *LM* curve. Or, in other words, *any LM curve is drawn for a given supply of money.*

The *LM* curve identifies combinations of income and the interest rate for which the demand for money equals the money supply.

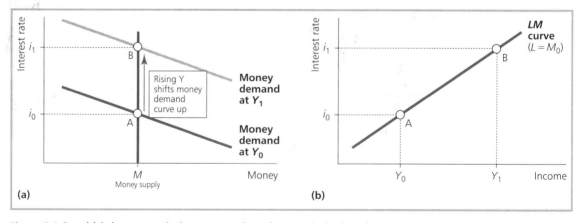

Figure 3.4 Panel (a) shows a vertical money supply and a negatively sloped money-demand curve. Rising income raises money demand at any interest rate, shifting the money-demand curve right. To retain equilibrium, the interest rate must rise to contain money demand at its old level. Transferring points A and B into panel (b) gives two points on the *LM* curve, the money-market equilibrium line.

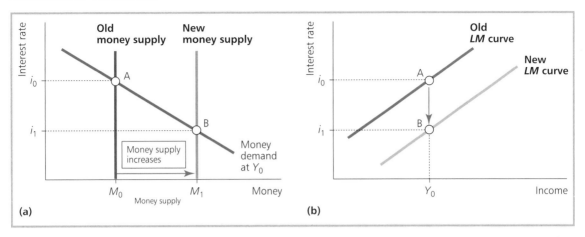

Figure 3.5 In panel (a) the money supply increase shifts the vertical money-supply curve to the right. To retain equilibrium, money demand must be spurred by lowering the interest rate from i_0 to i_1. Transferring points A and B to panel (b) gives two money-market equilibrium points on two different *LM* curves, each one drawn for a different money supply.

An algebraic expression for the *LM* curve is obtained by substituting the equilibrium condition $L = M$ into equation (3.1) along with the supply equation $M = \overline{M}$, and solving for i to obtain

$$i = \frac{k}{h}\, Y - \frac{1}{h}\, \overline{M} \qquad\qquad \textit{LM} \text{ curve} \quad (3.2)$$

Figure 3.5, panel (a), looks at the demand and supply diagram again and shows what an increase in the money supply does to the *LM* curve. A money supply increase shifts the vertical supply curve to the right, forcing the market-clearing interest rate down at all given income levels. The result is a shift of the *LM* curve to the right. What actually happens to income and the interest rate still remains unclear and, as we will see, is eventually determined in interaction with other markets.

Targeting the interest rate

News in the media often speculates on whether the Bank of England or the European Central Bank will reduce interest rates at some forthcoming board meeting. This may seem at odds with the previous view that central banks influence the economy by controlling the money supply. This section will show that there is no fundamental conflict between these two views. Both are based on the same perspective of how supply and demand interact in the money market, but they differ in operational aspects.

Panel (a) in Figure 3.6 shows money demand functions for two levels of income again. When, instead of targeting the money supply, the central bank targets the interest rate at

$$i = \bar{i} \qquad\qquad \text{Exogenous interest rate}$$

this implies a horizontal money supply curve instead of a vertical one. The central bank is prepared to supply the market with any amount of money required to bring the interest rate to the desired level. For instance, when income

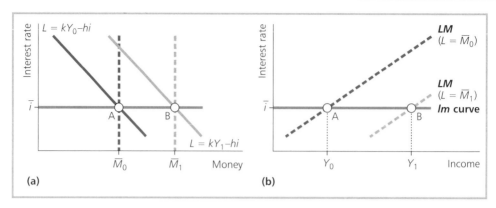

Figure 3.6 In order to keep the interest rate at $\bar{i}$, the central bank must accommodate an increase in the demand for money, caused by a rise in income from Y_0 to Y_1, by raising the money supply from $\overline{M}_0$ to $\overline{M}_1$ (panel (a)). Transferring equilibrium points A and B to panel (b) gives two money-market equilibrium points on two different *LM* curves, each one drawn for a different money supply. Both points sit on one *lm* curve, however, drawn for a given interest rate target.

is Y_0, the supply of money required for bringing the interest rate to $\bar{i}$ is $\overline{M}_0$. This entails moving the money supply curve, shown as dashed vertical lines, into the appropriate position. If income rises to Y_1, the central bank responds by raising the money supply to $\overline{M}_1$ in order to keep the interest rate on target.

Panel (b) notes that one combination that generates a money market equilibrium is an interest rate of $\bar{i}$ and income Y_0. It also shows, however, that the same interest rate could just as well be combined with a higher level of income Y_1 and still render a money market equilibrium. How this is possible is shown in panel (a). When income rises to Y_1, shifting the money demand curve to the right and raising demand at the initial interest rate $\bar{i}$, the central bank responds by raising the supply of money to $\overline{M}_1$ in order to prevent the interest rate from rising. This means, however, that the supply of money does not remain constant as we move along the horizontal money market equilibrium line in panel (b). It is obviously higher at point B than at A. The horizontal money market equilibrium line through these two points also has the property $L = M$, of course. To differentiate it from the conventional *LM* curve derived in the previous section, which is drawn for a fixed money supply, we call this horizontal equilibrium line an *lm* **curve**. Monetary policy can move the *lm* curve up or down by changing the targeted interest rate.

Monetary policy rules

The suggestion that central banks set the money supply or the interest rate at their discretion is a simple, albeit one-dimensional first take at monetary policy. In practice, many major central banks have adopted **monetary policy rules** for guidance. The **Taylor rule** or **inflation rules** are well known examples. Compared with our previous discussions of the discretionary control of the money supply or the interest rate, monetary policy rules are more complex. Typically, a rule specifies how a policy instrument should respond to one or more macroeconomic variables, such as the interest rate, the exchange rate, inflation or income. To some extent, this makes monetary policy an endogenous part of the economy. Related issues, including the rationale for specific monetary policy rules, will be discussed in considerable depth in Chapters 11 and 13. As a first encounter with this topic, suppose the central bank steers the money supply according to the monetary policy rule:

$$M = \overline{M} + a(i - \overline{i})$$ **Monetary policy rule** (3.3)

The rule states that the central bank has targets for both the money supply and the interest rate. When the interest rate is where it should be, at $\overline{i}$, the money supply remains at its normal level $\overline{M}$. If the interest rate rises above target, the central bank leans against this trend by supplying more money. When the interest rate becomes too low, the money supply shrinks. The parameter a measures how strongly the money supply responds to movements of the interest rate.

Here also, the money market is in equilibrium when supply equals demand: that is, when $L = M$. Substituting equations (3.1) and (3.3) into this equilibrium condition and solving for the interest rate gives

$$i = \frac{k}{a+h}Y - \frac{\overline{M}}{a+h} + \frac{a}{a+h}\overline{i}$$ *lm* **curve under monetary policy rule**   (3.4)

which is the *lm* curve resulting from this particular monetary policy rule. As an important *reminder*: we call this the *lm* curve in order to distinguish it from the conventional *LM* curve. Both curves show i/Y combinations that generate equilibria in the money market. But only as we move along a conventional *LM* curve does the supply of money remain constant. As we move along an *lm* curve, the money supply changes.

It is interesting to note that the *lm* curve under the monetary policy rule (3.3) comprises the money market equilibrium lines derived for money supply targeting and interest rate targeting as special cases (see Figure 3.7). Eliminating the response to interest rate movements by setting the reaction parameter $a = 0$, we obtain the conventional *LM* curve given in equation (3.2). Letting a go towards infinity, meaning that the smallest deviation of the interest rate from target triggers an enormous response of the money supply, the policy rule simplifies to $i = \overline{i}$, and so does the *lm* curve.

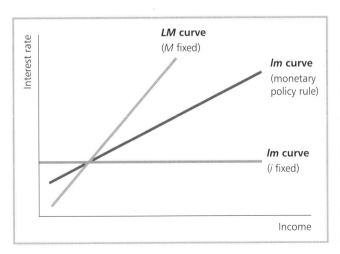

LM curve
(*M* fixed)

Interest rate

lm curve
(monetary policy rule)

lm curve
(*i* fixed)

Income

Figure 3.7 The dark blue line shows a money market equilibrium line, an *lm* curve, derived from a monetary policy rule such as (3.3) in which both the money supply and the interest rate feature as targets. When only the money supply is targeted ($a = 0$), the equilibrium line turns into the steeper, light blue *LM* curve. When only the interest rate is targeted ($a \to \infty$), the money market equilibrium line becomes horizontal.

To sum up, as Figure 3.7 shows, only in the extreme case of pure interest rate targeting is the money market equilibrium line horizontal. For finite non-negative values this line has a positive slope, with the standard *LM* curve obtained for $a = 0$ providing the upper limit. This is important because it means that the very same qualitative insights that we will derive under the assumption of money supply targeting and the simple *LM* curve are still valid under a wider range of monetary policy rules. Only under the somewhat unrealistic assumption of pure interest rate targeting will results differ somewhat. For an extensive understanding of how the money market works and how it interacts with the goods market, this chapter focuses on money supply targeting, which may also be considered a stand-in for other monetary policy rules, but it also looks at interest rate targeting for completeness.

3.2   Aggregate expenditure, the interest rate and the exchange rate: the *IS* curve

We return to the goods market, which was at the centre of the discussion in Chapter 2. We review the components of aggregate expenditure, introduce the exchange rate and state a **generalized equilibrium condition for the goods market** in a form that will eventually allow us to tie up loose ends with the two other markets. This generalized equilibrium condition will be called the *IS* curve.

Reminder. Y_+^e is a stand-in for all income expected to accrue during future periods. Period incomes may be weighted to reflect time discounting. Then Y_+^e would be a present value.

Consumption and investment

The earlier discussion of consumption taught us that consumption spending depends on current income and on expected future income:

$$C = c_1 Y + c_2 Y_+^e \qquad \textbf{Consumption function} \quad (3.5')$$

where c_1 may be thought to be relatively small, say about 0.3. The sum of both coefficients, $c_1 + c_2$, is close to 1, say 0.9. So a one-unit increase of current income ($\Delta Y = 1$) that does *not* affect expectations of future income ($\Delta Y_+^e = 0$) increases consumption by 0.3. The same one-unit increase of current income expected to *last* into the future ($\Delta Y_+^e = 1$) raises consumption by 0.9.

Investment spending was found to depend on two major factors – expected future income and the interest rate:

$$I = b_1 Y_+^e - b_2 i \qquad \textbf{Investment function} \quad (3.6')$$

For pragmatic reasons, in a continuing effort to keep the analysis transparent, for most of the time we will work with the simpler consumption and investment functions

$$C = cY \qquad \textbf{Simple consumption function} \quad (3.5)$$

and

$$I = \bar{I} - bi \qquad \textbf{Simple investment function} \quad (3.6)$$

BOX 3.2   Working with graphs (part II)

I do not recommend learning the slopes of equilibrium curves like *LM* by heart. Neither do I advise memorizing which factor shifts the graph which way. As long as the economic reasoning behind some market equilibrium is understood, slopes and shifts of curves can, in most cases, be worked out by simple thought experiments. Algebra or calculus is not necessary.

For example, take the *LM* curve to demonstrate the nature of the thought process. Suppose you forgot how the graph slopes in the *i*/*Y* diagram and how it shifts when the money supply increases. Here is a way out.

The slope of a curve

1 Pick an arbitrary point A in the *i*/*Y* plane. Assume that A is an equilibrium, i.e. a point on *LM*. (You may safely do that as, without any further information, you are free to position the *LM* curve anywhere in the diagram.) See Figure 3.8.

2 Move horizontally from A to B. With *i* being the same at A and B, but *Y* being larger at B, the demand for money at B is obviously higher than at A. Thus, as we are holding the money supply constant, B features an excess demand for money. In other words, B is not on *LM*!

3 Starting from B, work out in which direction *i* has to move in order to restore equilibrium. As

demand is too high in B, *i* must change so as to reduce money demand via higher opportunity costs, i.e. it must rise. At some point such as C it will have risen just enough to re-establish equilibrium.

4 Now that we have two points A and C on the *LM* curve, we have identified the curve's slope. In fact, we may draw the curve right through A and C.

How does the curve shift?

1 As before, pick an arbitrary point A in the *i*/*Y* plane. Assume that it is an equilibrium point, i.e. it lies on *LM*. See Figure 3.9.

2 Assume that the money supply has been increased. Since the old money supply equalled demand at A, A must now feature an excess supply of money.

3 Holding *i* constant, work out whether *Y* has to rise or to fall in order to raise money demand and thus re-establish equilibrium. Here the answer is, obviously, that *Y* has to rise. So the new equilibrium point is found east of A – say, at B.

4 As we could have started from any other point on the old *LM* curve and obtained the same qualitative result, we may now conclude that the entire *LM* curve has shifted to the right into the position of the new *LM* curve.

Figure 3.8

Figure 3.9

The consumption function (3.5) is compatible with (3.5') if we keep in mind that c is small, i.e. around 0.3 if an observed income change is considered *transitory*, and around 0.9 if income is believed to have changed *permanently*.

Expected future income may be suppressed in the investment function with the argument that its influence on demand is (implicitly) already taken care of in the consumption function, and that the additional effect on aggregate demand via investment is likely to be small.

Exports and imports

When car buyers consider buying either a Peugeot or a Renault, they consider the quality and characteristics of the product, look at the price tag and then make a choice. If one of the two cars becomes cheaper, other things remaining unchanged, demand for this model will increase.

This also applies in the open economy, at the international level. British imports from France tend to fall when the price of French products expressed in pounds increases. For the same reason exports from the United Kingdom to France will increase. The price of French cars expressed in British pounds changes whenever the exchange rate changes, even if French car manufacturers keep the euro price constant. Therefore the exchange rate must be a major determinant of the exports and imports of a country.

If the real exchange rate of the euro falls below purchasing power parity, it is cheaper to buy imported goods: French people will buy Jaguars or Minis rather than Citroëns, enjoy cheddar and cheshire over roquefort and brie, and eventually, although the exchange rate would have to be very low, they may even switch to drinking British wine. Considering all of these factors means that French imports from Britain rise as the exchange rate falls. The opposite occurs if the real exchange rate goes up. Domestic goods gain a price advantage and domestic residents purchase fewer and fewer imported goods and services. These arguments generalize the import function to

$$IM = m_1 Y - m_2 R \qquad \text{Import function} \quad (3.7)$$

making imports not only more dependent on income as stated above, but also on the relative price of domestic and foreign goods as measured by the real exchange rate R.

The export function must be a mirror image of the import function, since our exports are simply the imports of the rest of the world from us. The two determinants of our exports would thus be *world income* and the real exchange rate:

$$EX = x_1 Y^{\text{World}} + x_2 R \qquad \text{Export function} \quad (3.8)$$

The exchange rate affects our exports with a positive coefficient. If our currency *depreciates* against other currencies, other currencies *appreciate* against our currency. This makes our exports cheaper for foreigners and they will want to buy more of them.

The algebra of the *IS* curve

An equation for the *IS* curve is obtained by substituting equations (3.5), (3.6), (3.7) and (3.8) into the goods market equilibrium condition

The real exchange rate R is the ratio between the price of a (bundle of) good(s) abroad and at home: $R \equiv EP^{\text{World}}/P$.

Purchasing power parity denotes the exchange rate E^{PPP} that equates prices abroad and at home in domestic currency: $E^{\text{PPP}} \times P^{\text{World}} = P$.

The *IS* curve shows those combinations of income and the interest rate for which aggregate expenditure equals income (or output). Its name derives from the fact that in an economy with no government (then $T - G = 0$) and no trade with other countries (then $IM - EX = 0$) the required balancing of leakages and injections $[(S - I) + (T - G) + (IM - EX) = 0]$ obtains if $I = S$.

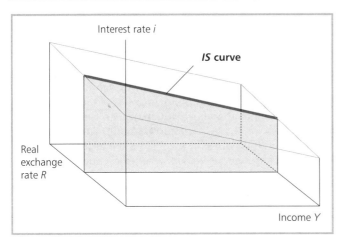

Figure 3.10 All goods market equilibria form a plane in *R-i-Y* space. It slopes up as we move towards the rear (depreciation generates excess demand; to reverse this, the interest rate must rise). The plane slopes down as we move to the right (rising income leads to an excess supply; to eliminate this, the interest rate must fall). Placing a vertical cut parallel to the income axis carves out an equilibrium line (*IS* curve) for a given real exchange rate.

$Y = C + I + G + EX - IM$. Since we would like to obtain an equilibrium condition which can be shown on the *i–Y* surface along with the *LM* curve obtained above, we solve the equilibrium condition for *i*. This yields

$$i = -\frac{1 - c + m_1}{b}Y + \frac{x_2 + m_2}{b}R + \frac{\dot{I} + G + x_1 Y^{\text{World}}}{b} \qquad IS \text{ curve} \quad (3.9)$$

The negative coefficient in front of *Y* shows that the curve slopes down. This simply reflects Chapter 2's result that a rise in the interest rate reduces investment and thus lowers equilibrium income. The positive coefficient in front of *R* signals that a real depreciation stimulates net exports and thus raises equilibrium income. Finally, the coefficients in front of the autonomous expenditures indicate that an increase shifts the curve up, and by how much it does so. Equation (3.9) can actually be graphed as an *IS plane*, with the two endogenous variables *i* and *R* on the horizontal axis (see Figure 3.10). The 2D equilibrium line in *i–Y* space, the *IS* curve, is obtained by placing a vertical cut through the *IS* plane parallel to the income axis (Figure 3.11).

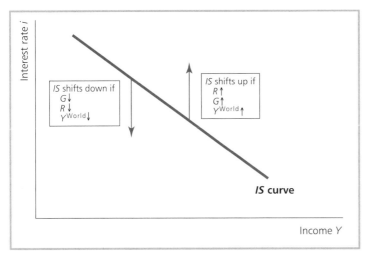

Figure 3.11 The *IS* curve shows all combinations of interest rates and income that make aggregate spending equal to output. It is drawn for given government expenditures, world income and a given exchange rate. As these variables rise, the *IS* curve moves up (or to the right).

BOX 3.3 Exchange rates

The **nominal exchange rate**, or, for short, the exchange rate, E is the price of one unit of foreign currency in terms of domestic currency:

$$\text{Exchange rate: } E = \frac{\text{Swiss francs}}{\text{Swedish kronor}}$$

If the Swiss francs/Swedish kronor exchange rate is 0.125, this means that one Swedish krona costs 0.125 Swiss francs. This commonly used definition has a *counter-intuitive implication* which may cause confusion for students new to international economics: if Switzerland's exchange rate goes up, the Swiss franc loses value – it *depreciates*. The Swiss need more francs to obtain a given number of Swedish kronor. A falling exchange rate means that the domestic currency is getting stronger – it *appreciates*.

Formally, we have

$$\text{Rate of depreciation: } \varepsilon = \frac{E - E_{-1}}{E_{-1}}$$
$$\approx \ln E - \ln E_{-1}$$

The rate of depreciation may be positive, in which case the currency *depreciates,* or it may be negative, in which case the currency actually *appreciates*. The right-hand part of the equation draws on the insight provided in the appendix to Chapter 1 that the percentage change in a variable can be approximated by the change in the natural logarithm of this variable over time.

We speak of *appreciation* and *depreciation* only if the exchange rate is moved by market forces. If governments decide to move the franc up to 0.2 against the krona in a system of fixed exchange rates, the franc is *devalued*. In the opposite case it is *revalued*.

On its own, the nominal exchange rate does not provide any information about the actual buying power of a given amount of money in different countries. It can only do this in combination with information about individual prices or the general price level. If the Volvo S60 sells for 50,000 francs in Switzerland and for 300,000 kronor in Sweden, where is it cheaper? A measure of the relative price level in two countries is the **real exchange rate**:

Real exchange rate:
$$R = \frac{E \times P^{\text{World}}}{P}$$
$$= \frac{\dfrac{\text{Swiss francs}}{\text{Swedish kronor}} \times \text{Swedish price}}{\text{Swiss price}}$$

In the above example, to purchase an S60 costs 50,000 francs in Switzerland, but only $0.125 \times 300,000 = 37,500$ francs in Sweden. This also follows from substituting prices and the exchange rate into the above equation. The real exchange rate of $0.125 \times 300,000/50,000 = 0.75$ means that the Swiss only pay 75% of what the S60 costs in their home market when they buy the car in Sweden.

In this case, or whenever the real exchange rate is below 1, the Swiss franc is said to be **overvalued**. If the real exchange rate is higher than 1, and Swiss franc prices abroad exceed home prices, the franc is **undervalued**.

When the real exchange rate changes we speak of *real depreciation* and *real appreciation*.

The exchange rate that exactly equalizes the domestic and the international purchasing power of a currency is called **absolute purchasing power parity**. It is the nominal exchange rate which sets the real exchange rate to a value of 1:

$$\text{Purchasing power parity: } E^{\text{PPP}} = \frac{P}{P^{\text{World}}}$$
$$= \frac{\text{Swiss price}}{\text{Swedish price}}$$

In the present example the purchasing-power-parity exchange rate turns out to be $50,000/300,000 = 1/6$.

Macroeconomists do not usually look at prices for individual goods but at economy-wide price indexes which constitute a representative basket of goods and services.

There is still a second, weaker version of purchasing power parity, called **relative purchasing power parity**. It predicts that the real exchange rate remains constant, which requires the rate of depreciation, ε, to be determined by the difference between the rate of inflation at home, π, and the rate of inflation abroad, π^{World}:

Relative purchasing power parity:
$$\varepsilon^{\text{PPP}} = \pi - \pi^{\text{World}}$$
$$= \text{Swiss inflation} - \text{Swedish inflation}$$

Relative purchasing power parity does not predict goods to cost the same abroad as at home, as absolute purchasing power parity does. What it predicts is that any price difference that exists remains the same over time.

Note. We may also draw on the Keynesian cross to derive the negatively sloped *IS* curve:

The *IS* curve depicts the equilibrium income levels from Chapter 2 at different interest rates. While drawing the curve, autonomous expenditures and the real exchange rate are kept constant. Raising either of these moves *IS* up and raises equilibrium income at any given interest rate.

The slope of the *IS* curve depends on the marginal propensity to consume (and to import) (equation (3.9)). The larger c is, the smaller is the numerator in the fraction preceding Y, and the flatter is the line. So when an income increase is considered permanent, meaning that c is large, the *IS* curve looks comparatively flat. For an income increase that consumers classify as transitory, the *IS* curve looks rather steep. The reasoning behind this is that in the latter case an interest rate reduction does stimulate investment and income in the first round, but there will be few of the second- and third-round effects described by the multiplier, since consumers adjust their consumption by only a small amount.

To strengthen understanding of the *IS* curve we may look at it from a different angle by referring back to the circular flow. Figure 3.12 shows this flow again and includes what we know by now about the factors that influence leakages and injections.

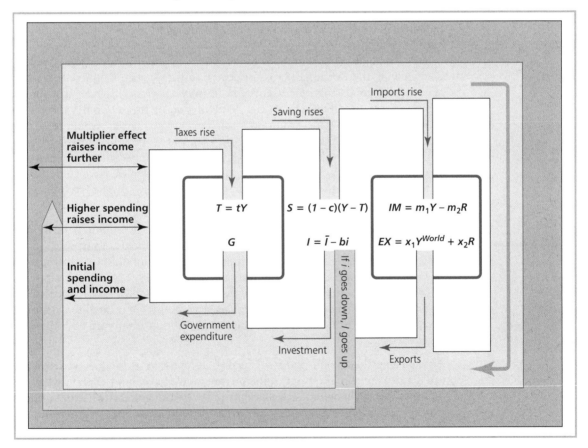

Figure 3.12 This shows how what we learned in this chapter fits into the circular flow diagram. If *i* falls, *I* goes up. *I* increases by the grey segment of the investment injection. This demand rise adds to income. Since this stimulates consumption, second-round effects set in. The fact that leakages also get larger (not shown in graph) ensures that income does not continue to rise forever. Eventually, the stream of income settles into a new width determined by the multiplier. Note that changes of world income, the exchange rate or taxes affect the circular flow in a similar way.

Now suppose the interest rate falls. This boosts investment injected into the flow. To maintain equilibrium, i.e. equality between aggregate expenditure and income, income must rise. So when i goes down, Y must go up to keep the circular flow (the goods market) in equilibrium. This is reflected in the negative slope of the IS curve.

Next, suppose the exchange rate depreciates (rises), with i remaining unchanged. Then exports rise (do you remember why?) and imports fall, increasing injections and lowering leakages, respectively. To maintain equilibrium, income must rise. Thus a rise in R shifts the IS curve to the right (or up).

Similar arguments reveal how changes in G, T or world income affect the position of IS.

3.3 The *IS-LM* or the global-economy model

The loose end left over after the discussion of the goods market in section 3.2 is the exchange rate. The exchange rate is determined in yet another market, the foreign exchange market. We postpone the introduction of the foreign exchange market until the next chapter. The reason for this is mainly didactic, but not entirely so.

Recall that our first macroeconomic model of the determination of aggregate income, the Keynesian cross discussed in Chapter 2, comprises only *one* market: the goods market. Eventually, however, we will arrive at a model composed of *three* markets on the demand side of the economy: the goods market, the money market and the foreign exchange market. Going from one market to three interacting markets will turn out to be a huge step, perhaps too big a step to be taken in one stride. For this reason we will pause here and assemble a macroeconomic model from the two markets we have come across so far, the goods market and the money market. Doing so yields two kinds of benefits:

- It shows us how to handle two markets that operate simultaneously and interact with each other, and thus serves a methodological purpose.
- It generates a model that, while it still has clear limitations, constitutes a substantial improvement over the Keynesian cross. Since the limitations concern international macroeconomic aspects, the model is best understood as a picture of the global economy, as if viewed from a satellite camera in outer space, or of a national economy that does not interact with the outside world.

Regarding the second point we need to accept that as long as we leave the foreign exchange market out of the picture, and thus cannot explain what determines the exchange rate, we cannot properly understand what determines exports and imports. This does not matter as long as we consider an economy with no foreign trade, which would obviously be the case for the world, or the global economy. So whatever we learn in the remaining pages of this chapter will have relevance for income determination on a global scale, on a scale that ignores what happens in individual, national economies. Our insights would also be applicable to isolationist countries that choose not to trade with the rest of the world. But not many such countries exist anymore. Our insights also give us a first, while incomplete and, therefore, imprecise, glimpse of how income is determined in large countries that export only a rather small fraction of their output.

The goods market equilibrium condition for the global economy reduces to $Y = C + I + G$, since $EX = IM = NX = 0$. On substituting the consumption function (3.5) and the investment function (3.6) we obtain a new, global *IS* curve:

$$i = -\frac{1-c}{b} Y + \frac{\bar{I} + G}{b}$$

Global-economy *IS* curve   (3.10)

Comparing this to the national-economy *IS* curve given in equation (3.9) shows the following:

- The global-economy *IS* curve is much simpler. The reason is that there are fewer leaks and injections. So everything that determines imports and exports, that is the exchange rate, foreign income, and the marginal propensity to import, drops out of the picture.
- The global-economy *IS* curve has a negative slope, just as the national-economy *IS* curve. The reason for this negative slope is investment behaviour, which is the same in both the global-economy and the national-economy version of the curve.
- The global-economy *IS* curve is flatter. This is a consequence of less income leaking out of the circular flow because there are no imports. Hence, the multiplier is larger. If a falling interest rate now raises investment by a given amount, this translates into a larger rise in equilibrium income than it does with the national-economy *IS* curve.

The graphical *IS-LM* model

Both the *IS* and the *LM* curves show combinations of interest rates and income levels that render the market under consideration in equilibrium. It is thus straightforward to merge the two curves onto one graph to obtain a model of the global economy thought to comprise a goods and a money market. Figure 3.13 does just that.

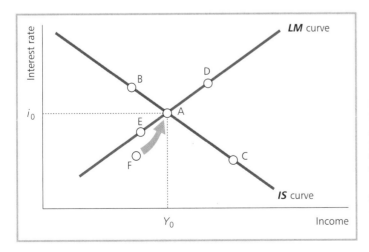

Figure 3.13 While points A, B and C indicate goods market equilibria and A, D and E mark money market equilibria, only point A is an economy-wide equilibrium with both markets being in equilibrium at the same time. At F there is disequilibrium in both markets. The arrow indicates how such a disequilibrium might be removed. Our *IS-LM* model does not really cover this. It only tells where the equilibrium is, not how we get there.

There are many points in this graph (on the *IS* curve) that render a goods market in equilibrium, such as points A, B and C. And there are also many points (on the *LM* curve) that equalize supply and demand in the money market, such as points A, D and E. But there is only one point, A, at which both markets are in equilibrium at the same time and, hence, the entire global economy is in equilibrium.

At B the goods market alone is in equilibrium. At this level of income, though, the interest rate is much too high to clear the money market. Hence, the demand for money is too low, and we have an excess supply of money. This tends to drive down the price for holding money, which we know is the interest rate.

At D the money market is in equilibrium. But at this interest rate income is much too high to permit a goods market equilibrium. Firms are producing more than consumers, investors and the government want to buy. Responding to this signal of insufficient demand, firms cut down production, making income fall.

At a point such as F we have disequilibrium in both markets. Demand exceeds supply in the goods market as well as in the money market. As a result, there will be upward pressure on the interest rate and rising income. This moves the economy towards and eventually into global macroeconomic equilibrium point A as depicted by the arrow. Note, though, that this adjustment path is not the only one that could result from our verbal sketch of disequilibrium dynamics. In fact, quite complicated paths are conceivable. We do not go deeper into these, focusing instead on the economy's point of gravity, its equilibrium, and how this can be influenced by policy measures. We should keep in mind, however, that the equilibrium we are looking at is just that, a gravity point, from which the economy may deviate temporarily. It is a highly useful indicator of the direction in which the economy moves, but does not necessarily indicate the economy's exact position at each point in time.

Monetary policy

Monetary policy manipulates the money supply (or the interest rate) to achieve policy goals (such as a rise in income).

By adding the money market to our model we introduced a second policy option for governments and central banks – monetary policy. Monetary policy comprises central bank action geared towards steering the money supply. This can happen directly, by purchasing or selling bonds or foreign currency. It can also happen indirectly, by setting interest rates and inducing the market to hold liquidity in the desired amount. Here we use monetary policy as a synonym for direct control of the money supply.

Now suppose the central bank decides to increase the money supply. As we learned from Figure 3.5, this shifts the *LM* curve to the right. The reason is that at any point on the old *LM* curve, such as at A (Figure 3.14), we would now have an excess supply of money in the amount by which the money supply was raised. In order to drive money demand up to the same level, either income must go up or the interest rate must fall, or a combination of the two.

Now, while there are many new $i-Y$ combinations that would render the money market in equilibrium – all points on LM_1 – only the combination i_1-Y_1 at the same time renders a goods market equilibrium. The motor

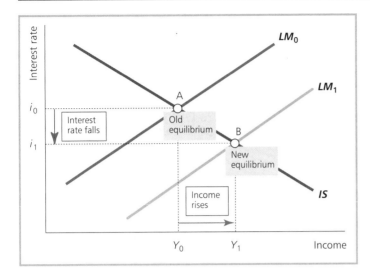

Figure 3.14 When the money supply increases, the *LM* curve shifts to the right, indicating that we need higher income or lower interest rates (or some combination of these effects) to induce people to increase money demand. The slope of the *IS* curve causes the macroeconomic equilibrium to move from A to B. Only the indicated fall in the interest rate and the indicated rise in income will keep the goods market in equilibrium while restoring money market equilibrium after the money supply increase.

moving the economy from A to B is that once the money supply has increased, shifting the *LM* curve to the right, there is excess supply of money at A. At their current level of income Y_0 individuals do not want to hold the amount of money supplied by the central bank. This drives down the price of holding money, the interest rate. Now the declining interest rate makes investment projects cheaper, so planned investment increases. At the initial level of income Y_0 and an interest rate below i_0 firms perceive an excess demand for their goods and services, thus step up production, raising income. This process continues until a new overall equilibrium obtains at a lower interest rate and higher income.

The potency of monetary policy depends, of course, on the quantitative effects at each link in the reaction sequence. The leverage of monetary policy is greater, the more a given money supply increase drives down the interest rate and the more a given fall in the interest rate stimulates investment. The latter condition refers to the slope of the *IS* curve. As you may easily convince yourself, the steeper the *IS* curve, the smaller is the income increase resulting from a given downward shift of the *LM* curve. If investment was unresponsive to the interest rate, the *IS* curve would be vertical, and monetary policy would not have an impact on income at all.

Fiscal policy in the *IS-LM* model

Fiscal policy manipulates government spending and taxes to achieve policy goals (such as a rise in income).

We are now equipped to refine our understanding of fiscal policy as set out in Chapter 2. Fiscal policy comprises all policy measures related to the government budget. At the aggregate level this amounts to government spending and raising government revenue by levying taxes.

As we saw when we discussed the goods market in section 3.2, the *IS* curve moves to the right (or up) when the government increases spending. (The same thing happens when the government reduces taxes.) The reason is that at any point on the old *IS* curve, at a given interest rate and given income, the additional demand exercised by the government creates an excess demand for

BOX 3.4 Money supply vs interest control in a changing world

In section 3.1 we concluded that it does not really matter whether the central bank uses the money supply or the interest rate as a policy instrument. This is true in a world that does not change. A second look at this issue is required, however, in a world of change and uncertainty.

Suppose the central bank has two options: announce a money supply target at the beginning of the year, and stick with it, no matter what happens, or, announce an interest rate target and stick with it. Further, suppose the world is stochastic, meaning that the *LM* curve or the *IS* curve may shift due to shocks. This can happen either because people change their behaviour, which would affect the coefficients of the *LM* or *IS* equations. Or it can happen because there are other factors determining money or goods demand, which our streamlined, simplified equations omitted. The two left-hand panels in Figure 3.15 look at the situation in which

the *IS* curve is subject to change and uncertainty. While it is in the bold position at the beginning of the year, it may end up anywhere in the shaded area bounded by the thin blue lines. The two panels on the right consider change and uncertainty in the money market.

Consider first the policy option of announcing and implementing a specific money supply, as depicted in the two upper panels. On the left, with no uncertainty in the money market, the *LM* curve stays put. As the *IS* curve fluctuates, the economy moves up or down the black segment of the *LM* curve, making income fluctuate modestly within the extremes marked by the vertical dotted lines. On the right, with no change in the goods market, *IS* stays put. Changing behaviour on the money market's demand side keeps shifting *LM*. Being focused on keeping $\overline{M}$ as planned, the central bank does not do anything about it. The economy moves

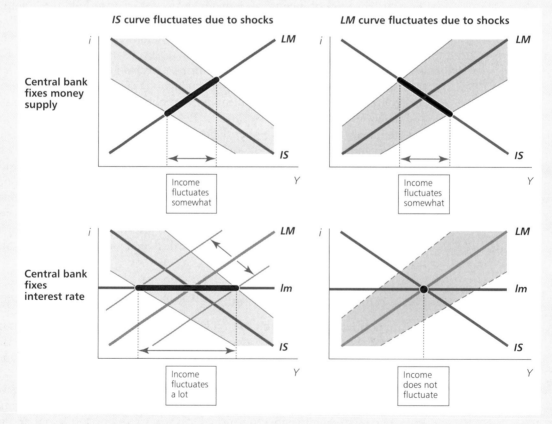

IS curve fluctuates due to shocks

LM curve fluctuates due to shocks

Central bank fixes money supply

Income fluctuates somewhat

Income fluctuates somewhat

Central bank fixes interest rate

Income fluctuates a lot

Income does not fluctuate

Figure 3.15

goods. To restore equilibrium in the goods market, either the interest rate must rise to drive down investment demand and thus make room for higher government purchases, or firms must produce more, raising Y. So the new equilibrium must be above and/or to the right of the old one, on a new *IS* curve that has shifted upward, as shown in Figure 3.16.

The new macroeconomic equilibrium is, of course, at point C, where *LM* and the new *IS* curve intersect. But how do we get there? Recall that the *IS* curve is an equilibrium condition. It lists all possible interest rate/income combinations that equate goods supply with goods demand. So as a first step, after G has been raised, while the economy is still in Y, firms experience an increased demand for their products which they cannot meet. So they decide to increase production, which raises income. The economy moves from A to the right. Now in a second step, because of their higher incomes people want to hold more money than banks can supply at the current interest rate. This excess demand in the money market drives the interest rate up. Both movements – the increase in income and the rise in the interest rate – drive the economy towards and into its new equilibrium at C.

We may deepen our understanding of the effect of fiscal policy in the *IS-LM* model by comparing it with the effect derived in the context of the Keynesian cross in Chapter 2. The lower panel in Figure 3.16 depicts the effect of fiscal policy in the Keynesian cross. The story we told there was that an increase in government purchases G creates excess demand in the goods market. As production expands to meet this new demand and income rises, so does consumption, creating excess demand again. This continues until income has increased by the full multiplier effect which is much larger than the initial rise in G. Investment has not changed, because the interest rate, an exogenous variable in the Keynesian cross, has not changed. At the current interest rate, income rises from Y_0 to Y_1^{Kcross}.

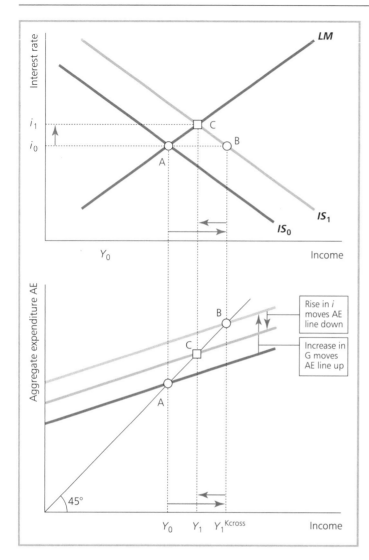

Figure 3.16 The *IS-LM* model rests on the Keynesian cross, but extends this. In the Keynesian cross, an increase in government spending moves the aggregate expenditure line up, moving the economy from A to B. In the *IS-LM* diagram the *IS* curve moves to the right. The same macroeconomic equilibrium B would only obtain if the interest rate did not change. Since money market equilibrium requires the interest rate to rise, investment is driven down and the new equilibrium is in C, where *LM* and the new *IS* curve intersect. In the Keynesian cross this rise in *i* and fall in *I* moves the *AE* line down and the new equilibrium is also at C.

How does this effect relate to our analysis of the *IS-LM* model in the upper panel of Figure 3.16? Well, it is a hypothetical effect in this context. It is the income increase needed to restore goods market equilibrium if the interest rate was not permitted to change. This hypothetical equilibrium is given by point B. It again reflects the full multiplier effect of the postulated rise in *G* on income. Now when the established excess demand in the money market drives the interest rate up, it drives down investment – and equilibrium income – until we arrive at C. In the lower panel the effect of a rising interest rate and falling investment is reflected in a downward shift of the aggregate expenditure line which moves the economy from B back to C.

The term crowding out refers to the phenomenon that an increase in one category of demand goes at the expense of a reduction in some other component of demand. Here *G* rises at the expense of a drop in *I*.

The fall in income while the economy moves from B to C is called crowding out. This expression refers to the fact that when we add the money market

CASE STUDY 3.1   Policy options during the financial crisis of 2007–09

The subprime crisis of 2007–09 forced governments to use the full arsenal of policy instruments at their disposal. The US experience is particularly instructive from the perspective of this chapter, because it comes closest to the ideal of a closed economy. We may, therefore, use the *IS-LM* model to acquire a deeper understanding of how the crisis unfolded and how the US central bank (the Fed) and the government responded.

Some additional tools

In order to succeed, we need to introduce three extensions to this chapter's basic version of the *IS-LM* model. All concern the demand for money and, thus, the *LM* curve.

1 The demand for money comprises both regular transactions demand *L* and speculative demand for money L_s. Thus the equilibrium condition for the money market becomes $M = L + L_s$.

2 If households consider holding money the safer option compared to holding money in a bank, then the interest rate paid by the bank is not the expected opportunity cost of holding money any longer. Rather, the opportunity cost of holding money equals the risk-free interest rate $i - RP$, which is the market interest rate *i* minus a percentage *RP* deducted (called a risk premium) for keeping money in a bank they cannot fully trust.

   Adding these two features renders the money market equilibrium condition $M = L + L_s = kY - h(i - RP) + L_s$, which solves for *i* to yield the *LM* curve:

$$i = \frac{k}{h}Y + \frac{L_s - M}{h} + RP$$

Thus the *LM* curve shifts up when households increase speculative money holdings and/or when the required risk premium for keeping money in savings accounts and similar assets increases.

3 In this textbook most relationships are drawn as straight lines that can be based on linear equations. In most cases this is a good enough approximation of reality, but in extreme situations this may not be so. Recall that *LM* slopes upwards because, when interest rates go down and bonds lose part of their advantages as a store of value, individuals hold larger shares of their wealth in the form of money. Since bonds lose their dominance as a store of value completely once the interest rate is at (or near) zero,

the *LM* curve cannot extend into the region of negative interest rates. To avoid this, *LM* must become flatter as *i* falls and becomes horizontal at or just above a zero interest rate. The existence of such a horizontal segment of the *LM* curve does not really matter as long as the *IS* curve intersects *LM* on the upward-sloping section. This is the configuration we have in mind throughout this textbook. In the unlikely case that *IS* intersects *LM* where it is flat, we have a problem. Then the economy is in a *liquidity trap*. A general *LM* curve that comprises both a horizontal and a positively sloped section must be represented by a more general equation such as

$$i = F_1(Y) + F_2(L_s - M) + RP$$

where F_1 and F_2 denote mathematical functions with appropriate properties.

The crisis unfolds

We now have all the extensions needed to tell the story of the repercussions of the financial crisis of 2008 on the real economy and of the policy options in *IS-LM* guise (see Figure 3.17).

Initially, the economy is in the pre-crisis equilibrium A. When home prices cease to rise and even start to fall, four things happen:

1 Banks with bad mortgages and mortgage-backed derivatives run into trouble. Along with a few isolated bank runs (e.g. Northern Rock), increases in speculative and precautionary money demand shift *LM* left.

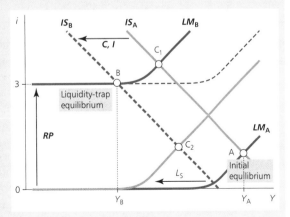

Figure 3.17

---

2 At the same time, millions of home owners default on their mortgages. Wealth deteriorates, reinforced by deteriorating stock markets. *IS* shifts left, reinforced by liquidity-strapped banks becoming more reluctant to extend loans to firms with investment projects. The economy moves to point C_2.

3 With a recession in the offing, central banks supply liquidity on a grand scale to shift *LM* back to the right. The US government provides a first, modest fiscal stimulus package totalling some $150 billion. This shifts *IS* a little bit to the right, but the economy does not return to A, as intended.

4 Customers do not trust their banks any more. So they start to require a risk premium to keep money in savings accounts or other assets. *LM* moves up by the required risk premium – say 3%. This pushes the economy further into recession at point B, with income still lower and interest rates around 3%. Since the risk-adjusted interest rate is near zero, the economy sits in a liquidity trap in B, even though market interest rates are well above zero.

Policy options and responses

The injection of more liquidity into the market, which pushes *LM* east into the dashed position, does not affect income. What is needed in order to pull the economy out of the liquidity trap in either:

- A substantial fiscal policy effort that moves *IS* a lot to the right. In Figure 3.17 this would move the economy towards C_1. The negative side effect would be still higher interest rates with negative repercussions on investment.
- Measures that reduce the risk premium by enhancing confidence in banks again. Taken alone, such measures would move the economy towards C_2.

A combination of both could move the economy back into its original positions in A.

Both types of measure suggested by our generalized *IS-LM* model were discussed or implemented by many countries around the globe in 2009, when the financial crisis was at its peak.

---

to our model economy, an increase in government spending squeezes some investment out of the picture. The effect is a smaller increase in income and, hence, a smaller multiplier. The extent by which government purchases crowd out private investment depends on the slope of the *IS* curve, of course. The steeper the *IS* curve, the less sensitive investment demand is to changes in the interest rate, the smaller is the crowding out effect. Only if the *IS* curve was vertical would there be no crowding out at all and we could enjoy the full multiplier effect.

Government spending also does not crowd out investment demand when monetary policy targets the interest rate (see Figure 3.18). In this case the shifting *IS* curve moves equilibrium, identified by the point of intersection between the *IS* and *lm* curves, horizontally to the right. Crowding out is not permitted because of the dedication of the central bank to keep the interest rate on target. In doing so, it responds to the increasing demand for money, caused by the rise in income, by letting the money supply increase by the same amount. This results in an endogenous shift of the *LM* curve to the right, to where it passes through point B, where IS_1 and *lm* already intersect. This shows that the conduct of monetary policy affects the potency of fiscal policy. When monetary policy adopts an interest rate target rather than a money supply target, it is forced to support fiscal policy by letting the supply of money rise or fall along with increases or reductions in government spending.

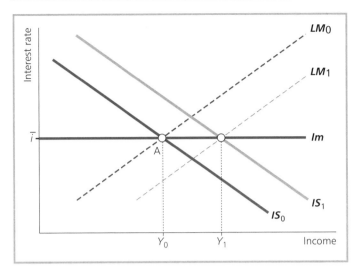

Figure 3.18 An increase in government spending shifts the *IS* curve to the right. If the money supply was kept unchanged, this would move the economy up from A along LM_0, raising the interest rate and crowding out some private investment. When the central bank wants to keep the interest rate unchanged at $\bar{i}$ instead, it must increase the money supply appropriately and shift *LM* into LM_1, moving the economy into point B. Expansionary fiscal policy has a bigger income effect when the central bank fixes the interest rate. Crowding out is prevented because the central bank is forced to respond to an increase in government spending by expanding the money supply.

The algebra of the *IS-LM* model

The *IS-LM* model consists of two markets, the equilibrium lines of which we found out to be

$$i = \frac{k}{h} Y - \frac{1}{h} M \qquad\qquad \text{*LM* curve} \quad (3.2)$$

$$i = -\frac{1 - c}{b} Y + \frac{\bar{I} + G}{b} \qquad\qquad \text{Global-economy *IS* curve} \quad (3.10)$$

The two endogenous variables, i and Y, are determined simultaneously in both markets. Substituting (3.10) for the interest rate in (3.2) and solving for Y yields

$$Y = \frac{1}{1 - c + bk/h} \left(\bar{I} + G + \frac{b}{h} M \right) \qquad \text{Equilibrium income} \quad (3.11)$$

which says that income goes up either if the government raises spending (or firms increase autonomous investment) or if the central bank expands the money supply. Via

$$\frac{\Delta Y}{\Delta G} = \frac{1}{1 - c + bk/h} \qquad \text{*IS-LM* government spending multiplier}$$

we can also see that the government spending multiplier is smaller than it was in the Keynesian cross. The reason becomes clear if we substitute (3.11) into (3.2) to obtain the equilibrium interest rate as

$$i = \frac{k}{(1 - c)h + bk}(\bar{I} + G) - \frac{1 - c}{(1 - c)h + bk}M \qquad \text{Equilibrium interest rate}$$
$$(3.12)$$

Equation (3.12) reveals that an increase in G not only raises income, but also the interest rate, which exerts a negative effect on investment.

BOX 3.5   **Loanable funds: an alternative theory of interest rate determination**

In order to keep models transparent, economists routinely speak of *the* interest rate, sidestepping the fact that there are many different interest rates: money market rates, but also interest rates for government bonds, for commercial bonds, for mortgages, and many more. As long as these rates move up and down together, separated by a more or less constant mark up, as they do during normal times, little harm is done by postulating a single interest rate only.

Figure 3.19

But since the monetary sector extends beyond the money market, on which we focused so far, we may ask what links the different interest rates. Figure 3.19 splits the monetary sector into two financial markets: the money market and the capital market. It reveals that banks act as intermediaries between households and firms.

Section 3.1 showed how the interaction between the demand for and supply of money determines the interest rate in the money market (see Figure 3.20, panel (a)). Section 3.2 then assumed that firms pay this very same rate when they take out loans to finance investment projects. This allowed us to ignore the capital market.

Alternatively, the **loanable funds theory** explains the interest rate in the capital market through the interaction between the supply of and the demand for loans. Figure 3.20 shows this in panel (c).

In an economy without government, the *supply of loans* is given by household saving $S = (1 - c)Y$, which is independent of the interest rate and drawn as a vertical line. The *demand for loans* equals investment $I = \bar{I} - bi$, shown as the negatively sloped line. The pale blue curves show an initial scenario in which money and the capital market, linked via the *IS-LM* diagram in panel (b), are all in equilibrium at points A at the same interest rates.

Now suppose the central bank expands the money supply to M_2 in order to bring down the money market interest rate. As long as income remains at its initial level Y_A this drives the money market towards C and lowers its interest rate to i_C. The capital market still clears at the interest rate i_A (panel (c)). And there is an excess demand in the goods market (panel (b)). Firms respond to this by increasing output. This shifts the money demand curve to the right in panel (a), raising the money market interest rate, and shifts the loanable-funds supply curve to the right in panel (c), lowering the capital market interest rate. This process is accompanied by an upward movement along the new *LM* curve from C towards D in panel (b), and it continues until both interest rates are the same again.

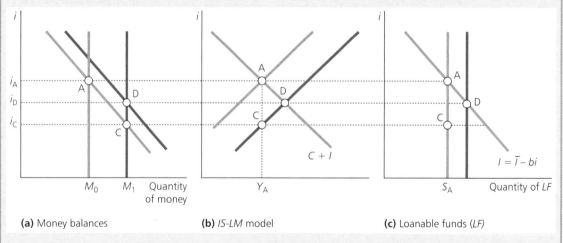

(a) Money balances   **(b)** *IS-LM* model   **(c)** Loanable funds (*LF*)

Figure 3.20

Bottom line

This chapter has refined the discussion of equilibrium income (in the Keynesian cross or in the circular flow model) presented in Chapter 2. The important result is that a unique income level exists at which income equals aggregate expenditure. The introduction of the interest rate into the picture links this equilibrium income level to the money market. This adds monetary policy, which may attempt to steer the money supply or the interest rate, to the arsenal available to policy makers.

An endogenous interest rate deprives the second policy instrument, fiscal policy, of some of its power, when the central bank targets the money supply. Then fiscal policy crowds out investment spending, which leads to a smaller multiplier. Crowding out does not occur when the central bank targets the interest rate.

It is important to keep in mind that this chapter's *IS-LM* model assumes an economy with no international trade. This is why the *IS-LM* model may also be called the global economy model.

CHAPTER SUMMARY

- The domestic money market is in equilibrium if income and the interest rate assume values that make individuals' demand exactly equal to the amount of money supplied by the central bank.

- Rising income increases the transaction volume per period and, hence, the demand for money. A rising interest rate makes holding money more costly. Hence, it reduces the demand for money.

- The central bank may conduct monetary policy by using the money supply or the interest rate as instruments. When it sets its policy instrument according to a set of macroeconomic variables, it is said to follow a monetary policy rule.

- The goods market is in equilibrium if income and the interest rate take on values that make aggregate demand equal to output produced.

- Aggregate expenditure rises with income (through consumption) and falls as the interest rate rises (through investment).

- The *IS-LM* model is a model of the global economy. If the global money supply rises, interest rates fall and income rises.

- If government spending rises, income increases. When the central bank keeps the money supply fixed, interest rates go up, there is some crowding out of private investment and, hence, a reduced multiplier. When it keeps the interest rate fixed, the full multiplier effect obtains.

- Only one macroeconomic equilibrium (defined as simultaneous equilibrium in both markets) exists: income and the interest rate assume one specific value each.

crowding out 92
exchange rate 67
fiscal policy 89
flow variable 69
global economy *IS* curve 87
IS curve 82
IS-LM model 87
LM curve 76
lm curve 78
monetary base (high-powered
  money) 72
monetary policy 88

monetary policy rule 78
money demand function 70
money market 68
precautionary demand for
  money 71
purchasing power parity 82
real exchange rate 82
risk premium 74
speculative demand for money 74
stock variable 69
transactions demand for money 68

EXERCISES

3.1 Which of the following variables are flow variables, and which are stock variables?
(a) A nation's GDP.
(b) A firm's cars and machines.
(c) The gold reserves in the vaults of your country's central bank.
(d) Ferrari Testarossa sales between 1987 and 2010.
(e) Aggregate investment.
(f) British lager consumption per capita in 2011.
(g) The number of Rioja bottles in your cellar.
(h) The profits of your country's central bank in 2012.
(i) The number of all Skoda models registered in Warsaw.

3.2 Recall the quantity equation from Chapter 1: $M \times V = P \times Y$. In that chapter the velocity of money circulation was assumed to be constant. Is this assumption reasonable in the light of the model of money demand? How would you expect V to change with an increase in the interest rate? Assume that the interest rate remains at its new higher level, with M and Y unchanged. How does this affect the price level?

3.3 (a) In recent years a number of institutional and technical innovations such as cash machines have made it less expensive to obtain cash. Explain the consequences of this development by using the model of money demand in the text. If this trend continues, will average cash holdings decrease or increase?
(b) How do decreasing transaction costs affect the *LM* curve? (Hint: Start with the money demand equation and show how transaction costs determine the slope of the money demand function. Look at two different interest rates, including $i = 0$. Then work your way through to Figure 3.14 and decide if – with lower transaction costs – a given increase in money supply leads to a larger or to a smaller shift of the *LM* curve.)

3.4 Consider Table 3.1, which shows end-of-month exchange rates for the British pound (GBP), the US dollar (USD) and the Chinese yuan (CNY) versus the euro (EUR) during the first half of 2011. Which month recorded the largest appreciation of the euro versus the dollar? How many yuan did one dollar cost in May? In which months did the yuan appreciate against the pound?

Table 3.1

	January	February	March	April	May	June
GBP/EUR	0.8458	0.8463	0.8665	0.8829	0.8779	0.8874
USD/EUR	1.3365	1.3645	1.3999	1.4448	1.4349	1.4388
CNY/EUR	8.8178	8.9734	9.1902	9.4316	9.3198	9.3161

3.5 In Table 3.2 prices for an Italian mid-range car and a man's haircut for both St Gallen (Switzerland) and Stuttgart (Germany) are listed, as well as the Swiss franc/euro exchange rate. Focus on one of the two goods to decide whether the Swiss franc is over- or undervalued. What might explain the apparent difference?

Table 3.2

Average exchange rate in 2012: €1 = 1.2 SFR	Price in Stuttgart (Germany)	Price in St Gallen (Switzerland)
Italian car	€15,500	SFR 23,500
Haircut	€20	SFR 48

3.6 You are a Swiss girl visiting Barcelona in the summer of 2012. On a shopping tour you buy a black winter coat at Zara for €140. You saw exactly the same coat at a Zara store located in Zürich, where it cost 220 Swiss francs. When you exchanged your Swiss francs for euros, you paid 1.2 Swiss francs for €1. Assuming the winter coat is a representative basket of goods, calculate the real exchange rate and interpret your result.

3.7 *The Economist* regularly publishes its Big Mac Index. Data on the cost of a Big Mac is gathered in several countries and these prices are then translated into the US dollar price equivalent to produce the index. What are the advantages and disadvantages of using such an index for the purpose of making comparisons?

3.8 (a) What would happen to the slope of the *IS* curve if trade was completely abolished?
(b) What happens to the slope of the *IS* curve if investment does not depend on the interest rate?

3.9 How do the following changes of exogenous variables shift the *LM* and the *IS* curves? (Note: apply the thought experiment suggested in

Box 3.2. Make sure you understand the economic reasoning.)
(a) An increase in money supply.
(b) A decrease in government expenditure.
(c) A decrease in foreign income.
(d) An increase in the foreign price level.

3.10 Suppose the demand-for-money function for three different levels of income looks as shown in Figure 3.21.
(a) What does the *LM* curve look like? It may help to identify points A–D in your new diagram.
(b) What happens to Y and i if income initially is 80, the interest rate is i_0 and the real money supply expands?

3.11 Suppose the central bank and the government cannot agree on the direction of economic policy, so that the government raises spending while the central bank contracts the money supply. Trace in a diagram what happens to income and the interest rate.

3.12 Assume the central bank sets an interest rate target range between 2 and 3%, meaning that it allows the interest rate to be determined by

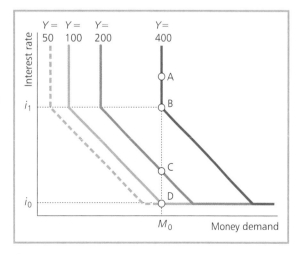

Figure 3.21

market forces within this range, but does not permit it to move above 3 or below 2%.

(a) How does income fluctuate when the goods market is subject to occasional shocks?

(b) How does income fluctuate when there are stochastic shocks to the demand for money? Draw diagrams similar to those used in Box 3.4. Compare your results with those obtained when the central bank targets the money supply and when it targets the interest rate.

3.13 Suppose country A's central bank follows the monetary policy rule $M = \overline{M} + a(\overline{Y} - Y)$ while country B's monetary policy is determined by $i = \bar{i} - b(\overline{Y} - Y)$.

(a) First compute the equations for both countries' *Im* curves.

(b) Compare each of these two *Im* curves with a conventional *LM* curve. Discuss any observed differences.

(c) Which monetary policy rule would you recommend for a country that is subject to occasional demand shocks in the money market and wants to stabilize income?

(d) Consider another country that is subject to occasional demand shocks in the goods market and wants to adopt country B's policy rule. Identify parameter values for *b* that would make this policy rule superior to what happens under a conventional *LM* curve.

3.14 The text does not distinguish between the interest rate that banks pay on savings accounts and the interest rate they charge firms for loans (which would make it difficult for banks to earn any profits). More realistically, suppose that while banks pay an interest rate *i* on savings accounts, they charge firms an interest rate that is two percentage points higher for extended loans.

(a) How does that affect the *IS* curve? Compute the equation for the global-economy *IS* curve.

(b) Draw a diagram with *i* and *Y* on the axes, featuring your modified *IS-LM* model. Does monetary and fiscal policy work in ways similar to or different from the discussion in the text?

(c) Suppose reduced competition in the banking sector permits banks to increase the mark-up on interest rate for loans to three percentage points over *i*. How does this affect income?

Online resources

Interactive applet on *IS-LM* model www.eurmacro.eu/tutor/islm.html

X-ercise on liquidity trap www.eurmacro.eu/xercises/liquiditytrap.html

X-ercise on risk premiums and liquidity trap www.eurmacro.eu/xercises/liquiditytrap2.html

Self quiz

www.eurmacro.eu/SelfQuiz/sq-ch03.html

Recommended reading

Half a dozen leading macroeconomists discuss how the concepts on which we built in this chapter fit into current research in 'Symposium: Keynesian economics today', *Journal of Economic Perspectives* 7 (1993).

Jordi Gali (1992) 'How well does the *IS-LM* model fit the postwar US data?', *Quarterly Journal of Economics* 107: 709–38, demonstrates the empirical relevance of the *IS-LM*.

An interactive learning module on the interaction between money and capital markets, with a special focus on times of crisis, can be found at www. eurmacro.eu/xercises/crisis.html.

APPLIED PROBLEMS

EMPIRICAL RESEARCH

Money demand in the United States

This chapter postulated that the real demand for money L depends on two factors: income Y and the nominal interest rate i. R. W. Hafer and S. Hein ('The shift in money demand: What really happened?', Federal Reserve Bank of St Louis, *Review*, February 1982) assume that income and two interest rates i_C (commercial paper rate) and i_B (bank deposit rate) affect desired real money holdings L^*: $L^* = c_0 + c_1 Y + c_2 i_C + c_3 i_B$. If we assume again that actual money holdings gradually adjust to desired money holdings, $L - L_{-1} = a(L^* - L_{-1})$, we may substitute the above equation to obtain $L = ac_0 + (1 - a)L_{-1} + ac_1 Y + ac_2 i_C + ac_3 i_B$. Estimating this with quarterly data (all measured in logarithms) for the United States gives

$$L = -0.61 + 0.778L_{-1} + 0.125Y - 0.016i_C - 0.32i_B$$
$$\quad (2.8) \quad (6.0) \qquad (2.7) \qquad (3.0) \qquad (2.1)$$
$$R^2_{adj} = 0.976$$

quarterly data 1960I to 1973IV

The absolute t-statistics given in parentheses show that all the coefficients are significant and have the expected sign. In particular, when income grows or interest rates fall, the demand for money rises. The demand for money seems to respond differently to the two interest rates considered here. As measured by the coefficient of determination of 0.976, the equation's fit is quite high. From $(1 - a) = 0.778$ for the coefficient on $L - 1$ we get $a = 0.222$. Since the coefficient on Y is $ac_1 = 0.125$ this gives $c_1 = 0.56$. So if income grows by 1%, desired money holdings grow by about 0.56%.

WORKED PROBLEM

Investment, interest rates and oil prices in Norway

This chapter showed that investment depends on expected future income and the interest rate: $I = aY_+^e - bi$. In reality this relationship may not be instantaneous but implies lags, say between the decision to undertake the project to its eventual

implementation. We might assume, for example, that this lag is one period, so that this year's investment depends on last year's interest rate and income (assuming that expected income follows actual income). Estimating such an equation for Norway on the basis of annual data for 1979–2000, given in Table 3.3, yields

$$I = 109.83 - 3.76r_{-1} + 0.14Y_{-1} \quad R^2_{adj} = 0.43$$
$$\quad (3.73) \qquad (2.20) \qquad (3.88) \qquad \text{(parentheses}$$
$$\qquad\qquad\qquad\qquad\qquad\qquad\qquad\text{contain absolute}$$
$$\qquad\qquad\qquad\qquad\qquad\qquad\qquad t\text{-statistics)}$$

where r is the real interest rate (nominal interest rate minus inflation). The equation supports the hypotheses that higher interest rates drive investment down, while higher income (leading individuals to expect higher income in the future) spurs investment.

When considering how this equation may still be improved or augmented, we may note that the structure of investment spending in Norway is unusual, with some 20% going into North Sea oil fields. The profitability of oil field varies directly with the price at which crude oil can be sold. While, again, investment decisions will be based on expected future oil prices, we may assume that the latter will be positively influenced by the price of oil observed in the recent past. The following equations test this idea by adding the price of oil OIL, observed at various lags, to the above equation.

$$I = 81.97 - 2.99r_{-1} + 0.15Y_{-1} + 0.04OIL_{-1} \; R^2_{adj} = 0.42$$
$$\quad (1.88) \quad (1.55) \qquad (3.73) \qquad (0.87)$$

$$I = 51.00 - 3.08r_{-1} + 0.18Y_{-1} + 0.08OIL_{-2} \; R^2_{adj} = 0.52$$
$$\quad (1.32) \quad (1.94) \qquad (4.72) \qquad (2.15)$$

$$I = 32.39 - 4.19r_{-1} + 0.20Y_{-1} + 0.12OIL_{-3} \; R^2_{adj} = 0.66$$
$$\quad (1.05) \quad (3.17) \qquad (6.24) \qquad (3.73)$$

The results indicate that if oil prices influence investment at all, they do so slowly. Only at lags of two or three years is this influence significant, as measured by the t-statistic of 2.15 and 3.73, respectively, and the coefficient of determination is significantly improved. One would have to look into the decision processes behind North Sea oil investment to find out whether such lags are realistic.

Table 3.3

Year	Interest rate i	Income Y	Investment I	Oil price OIL
1977	–	–	–	223.9
1978	–	–	–	201.3
1979	–	–	–	251.2
1980	−0.63	735.3	198.1	417.1
1981	−1.33	735.9	199.2	455.1
1982	1.83	730.9	199.3	405.5
1983	4.45	747.4	208.2	380.1
1984	5.88	791.5	208.9	384.6
1985	6.91	829.5	205.4	363.2
1986	6.28	794.2	220.7	156.8
1987	4.83	796.4	223.1	161.3
1988	6.27	782.9	222.1	120.0
1989	6.28	799.0	205.0	146.4
1990	6.61	812.9	175.7	172.4
1991	6.45	829.8	171.1	145.9
1992	7.44	834.1	166.1	129.8
1993	4.25	855.3	174.7	113.8
1994	5.73	888.9	183.8	120.4
1995	4.36	928.7	192.5	107.7
1996	4.68	1003.5	213.4	147.1
1997	2.55	1055.0	242.6	128.3
1998	3.09	1044.6	260.8	79.6
1999	3.05	1097.4	244.0	173.1
2000	3.29	1252.7	242.5	–

*All variables in real terms.
Sources: IMF-IFS and Statistics Norway.

YOUR TURN

Swiss money demand

Table 3.4 gives annual data on the real money supply, real income and nominal interest rates for Switzerland, 1970–93.

(a) Check if the data support a money demand function of the form $\log(M/P) = \alpha + \beta \log Y - \gamma i$. Since both M/P and Y exhibit heavy trends (check the plots), you may want to rewrite the equation in terms of changes of the variables and estimate $\Delta \log(M/P) = \alpha + \beta\Delta \log Y - \gamma\Delta i$.

(b) Which hypothesis gives a better fit – the hypothesis that the logarithm of real money demand depends linearly on the interest rate, or that the relationship is non-linear? (Hint: Compare the fit obtained for the above equation with the fit of equations of the form $\Delta \log(M/P) = \alpha + \beta\Delta \log Y - \gamma\Delta i^z$, where you raise interest rates to the powers of, say, $z = 2$, $z = 0.5$ or $z = 0.1$.)

Table 3.4

Year	M/P	Y	i
1970	49.45	148.53	5.72
1971	52.84	154.88	5.27
1972	56.69	160.24	4.96
1973	53.62	165.30	5.59
1974	50.06	167.25	7.13
1975	48.92	156.02	6.44
1976	51.60	154.71	4.98
1977	53.81	158.36	4.05
1978	60.43	159.30	3.33
1979	63.91	163.18	3.45
1980	57.07	170.33	4.77
1981	51.69	172.78	5.57
1982	50.10	171.18	4.59
1983	52.20	172.90	4.18
1984	52.10	175.96	4.55
1985	50.61	182.49	4.70
1986	51.12	187.72	4.24
1987	53.65	191.53	4.04
1988	59.82	197.08	4.02
1989	54.29	204.69	5.19
1990	49.18	209.40	6.44
1991	47.21	209.34	6.23
1992	45.98	208.70	6.41
1993	49.21	206.92	4.55

Exchange rates and the balance of payments

What to expect

After working through this chapter, you will understand:

1 What globalization is and what it means in the context of macroeconomics.

2 What the balance of payments is and why it is a mirror image of the foreign exchange market.

3 How the mobility of international capital affects the nature of foreign exchange market equilibria.

4 How the goods market, the money market and the foreign exchange market are put together to form an open-economy model of the national economy called the *IS-LM-FE* model or the Mundell–Fleming model.

5 How default risk and the resulting risk premium affects financial investors and the spread between domestic and foreign interest rates.

Chapter 3's *IS-LM* or global-economy model provides an understanding of the world economy as if viewed from a satellite camera in outer space. Looking at the globe from that vantage point, international borders and national detail disappear and can, therefore, be ignored. In this chapter we start to move in closer, zooming in on the individual country and its national economy, as it interacts with the rest of the world. The degree of a country's interaction with the rest of the world determines to what extent Chapter 3's global-economy model may serve as a first approximation for how a national economy works. If a country's international involvement is relatively moderate, the approximation can be quite good. If the involvement is intense, the approximation may become poor, if not useless.

Following dramatic developments known as **globalization**, the world's national economies now interact more intensively than ever before. This makes it mandatory to refine and augment the picture set out in Chapter 3, but we don't need to start from scratch. Our knowledge of the *IS-LM* model continues to be useful for two reasons. First, it explains what goes on in the world that surrounds and influences the individual country; second, it remains an integral part of the national-economy model to be developed in this and the next chapter.

To begin this chapter's discussion we first look at quantitative dimensions of globalization. We then proceed to look at international transactions. Not only how they are being recorded and structured in the balance of payments, but also at their key determinant, the exchange rate, and how it is determined in the foreign exchange market. The *IS-LM* model is then augmented by the foreign exchange market to form a complete model of the national economy.

4.1   Globalization

A closed economy is an economy that does not trade or interact financially with other countries. The global economy is a closed economy.

An open economy trades (goods or assets) with other countries. Most national economies are open economies.

Empirical fact. The US was the world export champion in 2009, selling €1,578 billion worth of output abroad. In second place was Germany (€1,360 billion) and China came third (€1,333 billion). Total exports from the euro area amounted to €4,555 billion.

Example. A country imports €10 billion worth of produce, prepares oven-ready meals employing €5 billion worth of labour and exports 50% of the meals for €7.5 billion. Then GDP is €5 billion, the import share is 200% and the export share 150%.

The global economy discussed in Chapter 3, section 3.3, is often referred to as a closed economy. It neither exports nor imports. By contrast, an economy that trades a lot with other countries is an open economy. These days most countries have open economies. Therefore, the national-economy model to be developed and analyzed in this and the next chapter is an open-economy model.

A country's openness may have many dimensions. The most frequently used measure of the openness of an economy is the ratio of exports (or imports) to income. Table 4.1 gives export and import shares for the world's largest economies and the euro area.

Interestingly, if you look at two of the world's largest economies, Japan and the United States, exports or imports amount to only some 15% of national income. This is still sizeable, but it also means that if we were using Chapter 3's closed-economy model to study these countries, results should not be completely off. This may serve as a justification for using the *IS-LM* model in Case study 3.1 on the liquidity trap in the United States. Note, though, that openness is already 50% higher for the euro area, still higher or much higher for many individual countries, and increasing worldwide. Figure 4.1 illustrates the latter two points by comparing export ratios for EU members and several other countries in 2010 with what they were five decades earlier.

The most striking message in the picture given in Figure 4.1 is the almost universal trend towards more openness. All countries have experienced often dramatic increases in their export shares. Many countries have more than doubled their export shares. Almost all European countries shown have export shares exceeding 20%. Belgium and the Netherlands are approaching 100%, which Luxembourg had already exceeded a while ago. Such high export shares are only possible if a country serves as a trading hub, by importing goods, then adding value by refining or modifying them, and then exporting them again.

Globalization trends do not only show up in the trade of goods and services. Another, possibly more comprehensive measure of how intensively national economies interact nowadays, is the volume of transactions

Table 4.1 **Openness indicators**, 2010

	Euro area	Japan	United States
Exports as % of GDP	22.6	15.9	12.5
Imports as % of GDP	22.0	14.6	15.9

Source: ECB, *Statistics Pocket Book*.

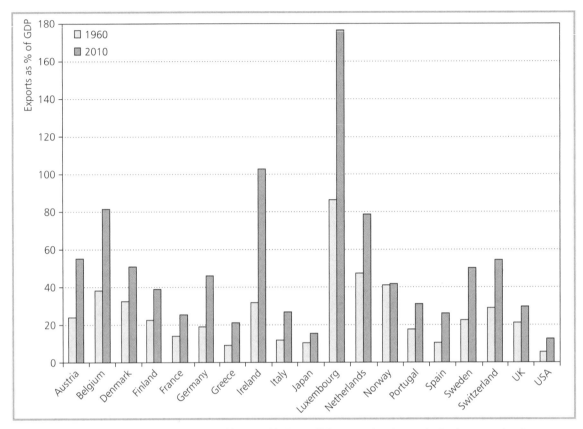

Figure 4.1 The last 50 years are characterized by steadily intensifying cross-border trade. In the countries shown here, exports as a share of income roughly doubled over a period of 50 years. The only exception is Norway, where the export share stagnated. The least open countries in this sample, by the measure employed here, are the USA and, perhaps surprisingly, Japan.

Sources: OECD, *Historical Statistics;* Eurostat.

in the foreign exchange markets. In 2010 the equivalent of about $3,981,000,000,000 (yes, that is $3.98 trillion) changed hands in the foreign exchange markets around the world on any average trading *day*. This is 50 times higher than it was in 1980. And to put the number in perspective: world GDP generated in 2010 was about $63 trillion. So one year's worth of world income was spent in the foreign exchange markets in much less than a month. This is an important insight we should keep in mind because it will prove useful later on.

Motivated by the growing openness of modern economies demonstrated by these statistics, we now turn to the task of tying up the second loose end left over from Chapter 3. We will do so in two steps. In section 4.2 we first look at the foreign exchange market and the balance of payments, where international transactions take place and are recorded. In this chapter's remaining two sections we will then *model* the foreign exchange market on a level of abstraction similar to the one we worked on when we modelled the goods market and the money market, and then add it to the *IS-LM* model to complete our first macroeconomic model of the national economy.

4.2 The exchange rate and the balance of payments

From the beginning of this book we have repeatedly noted that a country's macroeconomic performance depends on, among other things, exports and imports. We saw this when we spelled out the circular flow of income, when we discussed the Keynesian cross, and also when we looked into the goods market and the *IS* curve in Chapter 3. We also noted that a crucial determinant of exports and imports is the exchange rate, since it affects the relative price of goods at home and abroad. While this is an interesting insight, it is of little use as long as we do not know what determines the exchange rate. In principle, the answer is simple. It is supply and demand in the foreign exchange market. We deliberately refrained from adding this market to our model in Chapter 3 so as not to take too big a step at that time. Now, however, the time has come to take a look at the foreign exchange market.

A market brings together potential buyers and sellers of a specific good. A functioning market generates a price that balances supply and demand, thus clearing the market. The commodity traded in the foreign exchange market is foreign currency, or rather, foreign currencies. There are, in fact, dozens of currencies traded around the clock in the world's currency markets, and each pair of currencies has its market. One that trades euros against yen, one that trades pounds sterling against dollars, one that trades dollars against euros, and so on. We will sidestep the complications arising from this by lumping all foreign currencies – dollars, roubles, shekels, yen and so forth – under the heading foreign exchange. Foreign exchange is, then, simply all currencies other than the domestic currency.

Now when we start thinking about why individuals may want to purchase or sell foreign currency, we need not start from scratch. Luckily, countries began many years ago to record all their international transactions. This record is called the balance of payments. Since any international transaction between countries with their own national currencies requires the purchase and sale of foreign exchange, the balance of payments is at the same time a meticulous record of foreign exchange market transactions. The balance of payments is therefore a mirror image of the foreign exchange market. And the conditions for a balance-of-payments equilibrium are at the same time the conditions for equilibrium in the foreign exchange market. Since this chapter's main aim is to develop an understanding of the foreign exchange market and how it determines the exchange rate, it is worthwhile pausing here and taking a closer look at the balance of payments.

This is not the place to go into the intricate details of balance of payments accounting. After all, we are assembling a macroeconomic model with a high level of abstraction. However, an understanding of the basic mechanisms linking the various balance of payments accounts will be very helpful.

Balance of payments basics

Any transaction that requires a purchase of domestic currency is a credit (positive) item in that country's balance of payments. Any transaction that requires a sale of domestic currency is a debit (negative) item. Since domestic currency can only be purchased if someone else is prepared to sell, the sum of all credit items (of all purchases of domestic currency) must equal the sum of all debit items (sales). This means that the demand for domestic currency always equals the supply of domestic currency, and that the foreign exchange market always clears. This is why the conditions that equalize the balance of payments also equalize the foreign exchange market.

Traditionally, the balance of payments is broken into three subaccounts, as we saw in Chapter 1. The **current account** CA which mainly records cross-border transactions in goods and services, the **capital account** CP which records private financial transactions, and the **official reserves account** OR which records changes in the central bank's foreign exchange reserves.

$$BP = CA + CP + OR = 0 \tag{4.1}$$

The balance of payments is always zero because of double-entry bookkeeping, as stated above. Therefore, any entry in one of the accounts must be accompanied by an equivalent entry of opposite sign in the same account or one of the other two accounts. Let us look at what this means in practical terms. To do so consider a stylized world with only two countries, Britain and Sweden. Suppose Britain wants to import one Volvo S60 vehicle from Sweden that costs 300,000 kronor. To obtain the 300,000 kronor requested by the Swedish car maker, the UK customer must supply £30,000 at the current exchange rate. In reality, the UK buyer only sees and settles the £30,000 price tag. But since Volvo insists on receiving payment in kronor to pay for Swedish labour and steel, someone must be willing to offer £30,000 in exchange for 300,000 kronor. According to the balance-of-payments identity, this can happen in three distinct ways.

Consider Figure 4.2. Following the rule stated above, the Volvo import shows up as a debit item (that is, with a minus) in Britain's current account. Now who sold 300,000 kronor in exchange for £30,000?

First, there can be another, balancing transaction in the current account (Figure 4.2, left-hand column). Sweden may import 2,000 Duffy CDs costing £15 apiece. To pay the British record company, the Swedish importer must acquire £30,000 in exchange for 300,000 kronor. Since this is exactly the amount the UK Volvo importer needs, both transactions, the import and the export, go through as planned. In this case the current account balances. Exports equal imports, i.e. net exports are zero.

A second option shown in Figure 4.2's middle column is that there is a balancing transaction in the capital account. Suppose Swedes want no Duffy CDs. Then Britain as a whole is unable to pay Volvo in kronor. The only way to import the S60 would be if Volvo did not insist on immediate payment, accepting instead the promise of payment some time in the future. Britain goes into debt to Sweden.

In reality it will not be the UK importer who is in debt to Volvo. Instead, some British institution would go into debt to some Swedish institution or individual. The middle column in Figure 4.2 assumes that a wealthy Swede buys £30,000 worth of UK Treasury bills. Because payment is required in pounds sterling, she offers 300,000 kronor in the foreign exchange market to acquire £30,000. Since this is the exact amount the Volvo importer needs, both transactions go through. In this case the item balancing the car import is recorded

Reality check. Of course, UK importers do not look for UK exporters (or Swedish importers) to buy kronor from, but go to a bank that serves as a middleman. Ignoring this does not affect the substance of the issues.

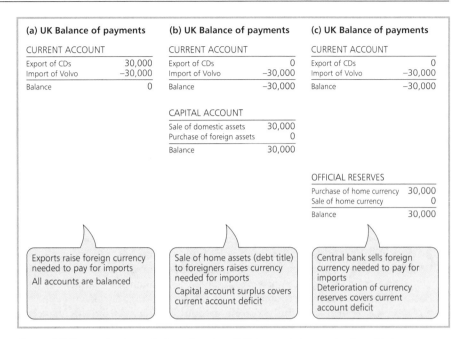

Figure 4.2 To pay for imports from Sweden, Britain needs to acquire Swedish kronor. There are three ways to do so: (a) it can export and accept payment in kronor; (b) it can ask Swedes to lend the required amount of kronor and hand over debt titles instead; (c) it can persuade the Bank of England (or the Sveriges Riksbank) to sell kronor for pounds.

in the capital account. The current account records a deficit, but the capital account shows a surplus of equal magnitude.

As a third option, which is actually a variant of the second option, the Bank of England could sell 300,000 kronor worth of currency reserves it may hold in exchange for £30,000. In this case, as shown in the right-hand column of Figure 4.2, the current account records a £30,000 deficit, the capital account is balanced, and the official reserves account records a £30,000 surplus.

The advantage of recording private capital flows and the change in official net foreign assets (mostly covering central bank currency reserves) separately is that it reveals at a glance whether foreign exchange market transactions were due to market forces alone, or whether they included the central bank as a buyer or seller. This is important for two reasons.

First, it gives meaning to the notion of balance of payments imbalances, which is actually self-contradictory. How can you speak of a country having a balance of payments surplus when according to equation (4.1) double-entry bookkeeping ensures that the balance of payments is always zero? This is indeed rather unfortunate terminology. What is actually meant by a balance of payments surplus is that the balance of payments, hypothetically, would have been in surplus had the central bank not participated in the foreign exchange market. So according to the numbers given in Box 4.1 on balance of payments terminology, the euro area ran a balance of payments *surplus* in the year 2010. Because if the European Central Bank (ECB) had not bought €10.2 billion

The balance of payments surplus ($BP^{surplus}$) is defined as $BP^{surplus} = -OR$.

worth of foreign assets, the supply of euros would have fallen short of its demand in the foreign exchange market. So the balance of payments surplus is actually defined as the balance generated by private, non-official involvement in the foreign exchange market. It is equal to the official reserves account with a negative sign.

BOX 4.1   Traditional vs new balance of payments terminology

Due to the initiative of international institutions like the IMF and the OECD, economists have to get used to some new, unfamiliar balance-of-payments terminology. Table 4.2 uses the euro area's balance of payments with regard to the rest of the world to describe the major differences between the traditional and the new classification. On the left are the old terms and on the right the new ones that have been implemented by many countries.

There is a slight change in the **current account** definition. While the current account traditionally included transfers not made out of current income, so-called wealth transfers, these will now be recorded in a separate account called the **capital account**. The intention is to clearly separate current income from changes in the stock of assets. Note that this new capital account has nothing to do with the capital account in its traditional definition!

What was formerly called the capital account now obviously needs a new name. It will be called the **financial account**. It includes all the items traditionally recorded in the capital account plus the official reserves balance. Hence, the official reserves account disappears, and there is no longer a distinction between private and non-private financial transactions on this level of aggregation. This information, of course, can still be retrieved from the financial account.

In traditional terminology, the euro area recorded a current account deficit (the sum of all credit items less the sum of all debit items in the current account) of €28.9 billion. The capital account was in surplus by €44.5 billion. The fact that the difference was not entirely offset by the official reserves account deficit of €10.2 billion must be due to recording errors and omissions amounting to a statistical discrepancy of €5.4 billion.

Table 4.2 **Balance of payments of the euro area in 2010 (billions of euros)**

Traditional classification		Credit	Debit	New classification
Current account: −28.9	Exports of goods	1,564.3		**Current account: −36.6**
	Imports of goods		1,543.6	
	Export of services	515.1		
	Import of services		474.0	
	Income received on investments	426.3		
	Income paid on investments		424.5	
	Transfer payments from abroad	87.7		
	Transfer payments to abroad		187.9	
	Net wealth transfers	7.7		**Capital account: +7.7**
Capital account: 44.5	Direct investment		78.6	**Financial account: 34.3**
	Portfolio investment	143.2		
	Financial derivatives	8.0		
	Other investment		28.1	
Official reserves account: −10.2	Official reserves balance		10.2	
Statistical discrepancy: 5.4			5.4	**Statistical discrepancy**

Source: ECB, Statistical Data Warehouse.

Note. Under flexible exchange rates $OR = 0$ and the balance of payments reduces to $BP = CA + CP = 0$ or $CA = -CP$.

The second reason why it is useful to know the extent of central bank involvement in the foreign exchange market is that it tells you to what extent the price in this market, the exchange rate, was left to market forces alone. If more individuals want to sell euros than are prepared to buy euros, and the central bank jumps in to purchase this incipient excess supply, the resulting exchange rate is obviously a distorted price. A true, undistorted market price only results if the central bank abstains from the foreign exchange market. Thus under an ideal system of flexible exchange rates the central bank does not intervene in the foreign exchanges and the official reserves account is zero.

Real-world current accounts and capital accounts

When the central bank refrains from foreign exchange market involvement ($OR = 0$), the capital account is a mirror image of the current account ($CA = -CP$). This property serves as a test of how close a country's actual experience was to an ideal system of flexible exchange rates determined by private market forces.

Note. Errors and omissions are sometimes quite sizeable and may cause CA to not exactly match $-CP$ despite OR being zero.

Figure 4.3 shows current account and capital account balances for 15 countries from 1975 to 2010. If one balance is a perfect reflection of the other, the central bank abstained from the foreign exchanges. This is indeed the case for most countries. A positive current account goes with a negative capital account, meaning that we lend to foreign countries to buy our exports. In the opposite case we borrow from their private citizens so that we can pay for our high level of imports. The less perfectly the capital account mirrors the current account, the stronger must be central bank involvement in the foreign exchange market. This was obviously the case in Switzerland around 1980 and in 2009 and 2010, in some European Monetary System member countries such as Italy in the 1990s, or in Japan at the turn of the millennium.

4.3 Back to *IS-LM*: enter the *FE* curve

The loose end remaining after the discussion of the goods market in Chapter 3 (section 3.2) is the exchange rate. Left to market forces in a system of flexible exchange rates, currency prices tend to move about quite a bit – more than any other macroeconomic variable. While there may be market psychology and speculation involved, a number of strings attach the exchange rate to the set of variables we are focusing on in macroeconomics. This section identifies and formalizes these relationships.

Being the price of one currency in terms of another, the exchange rate, like any price, is determined by supply and demand. Section 4.2 taught us that, being a comprehensive record of a country's residents' international transactions and a mirror image of the foreign exchange market, the balance of payments is an excellent way of identifying and structuring the determinants of currency supply and demand. From the balance of payments identity $BP = CA + CP + OR = 0$ and the insight that under flexible exchange rates, when $OR = 0$, the non-official components of BP do balance, we obtain $CA + CP = 0$ as a condition for foreign exchange market equilibrium. We now analyze this condition by first taking isolated looks at each of the two involved accounts, and then putting them together.

In the foreign exchange market different currencies are traded for one another.

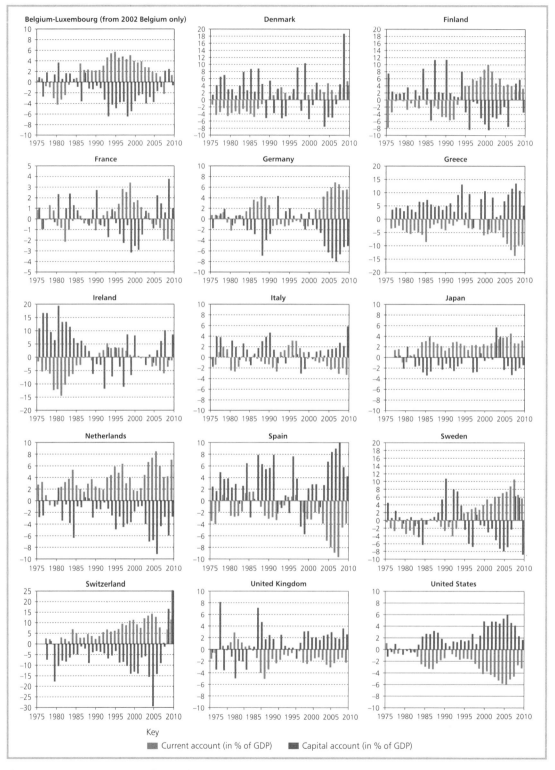

Figure 4.3 Current account and capital account in 15 industrialized countries, 1975–2010.

Source: IMF, *IFS* and Eurostat.

Note. Economists rarely work with 3D graphs. They are used here and below to show where the 2D graphs on the right of Figure 4.4 come from. If you have no problem understanding the 2D graph you can ignore the 3D version.

Maths note. One euro invested at home grows to $(1 + i)$ euro after one period. If invested abroad it grows to $(1 + i^{\text{World}})(1 + (E^e_{+1} - E)/E)$. Setting this equal to $(1 + i)$ and subtracting 1 from both sides gives interest parity as

$$i = i^{\text{World}} + \frac{E^e_{+1} - E}{E}$$
$$+ i^{\text{World}}\frac{E^e_{+1} - E}{E}$$

Equation (4.4) simplifies this by ignoring the involved exchange rate gain on the interest payment, which is small under normal circumstances.

The **current account** tracks net exports of goods and services. These we already know from the above analysis of the goods market.

$$CA \equiv NX = EX - IM = x_1 Y^{\text{World}} + x_2 R - m_1 Y + m_2 R \qquad (4.2)$$

Figure 4.4, panel (a), shows the current account as a function of income and the interest rate. While the interest rate has no impact on the current account (i is missing from equation (4.2)), CA deteriorates with a factor m_1 as income rises.

For given world income and real exchange rate, only one income level exists which balances the current account. An algebraic expression for this is obtained by letting $CA = 0$ in equation (4.2) and solving for Y. This yields

$$Y = \frac{x_1}{m_1}Y^{\text{World}} + \frac{x_2 + m_2}{m_1}R \qquad \text{\textbf{Current account equilibrium}} \quad (4.3)$$

All points that balance the current account lie on a vertical line in the $i{-}Y$ plane, as shown in Figure 4.4, panel (b). As indicated in the graph, this $CA = 0$ line shifts as its positioning parameters change. For example, if the real exchange rate goes up, meaning that the home currency depreciates, exports rise and imports fall. At the initial level of income, i.e. on the old $CA = 0$ line, where there was $EX = IM$ by definition, we now face the disequilibrium situation $EX > IM$. Imports, which are too small at this new real exchange rate and the initial level of income, can only rise up to the now higher exports if domestic income increases. So what we need is a movement to the right to find a new current account equilibrium: after a real depreciation a new equilibrium with $CA = EX - IM = 0$ can only be found to the right of the initial $CA = 0$ line. Therefore, a real depreciation moves the $CA = 0$ line to the right. By analogous arguments we find that an increase in world income moves $CA = 0$ to the right as well. The text in the white boxes summarizes these results.

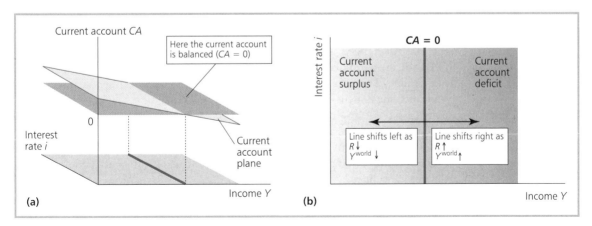

Figure 4.4 The current account worsens as rising income raises imports. The interest rate does not affect CA. The current account equilibrium line, therefore, projects as a vertical line onto the $i{-}Y$ plane. An exchange rate depreciation or a rise in world income moves the CA plane up, shifting the $CA = 0$ line to the right.

CASE STUDY 4.1 · Italy's current account before and after the 1992 EMS crisis

In open-economy models of the macroeconomy the exchange rate provides the key link between the monetary sector and the goods market. Changes in policy variables, such as the money supply or the interest rate, affect the exchange rate which, in turn, affects, imports and exports and, hence, income.

Whether the assumed effect of the (real) exchange rate on imports, exports and, hence, the current account does indeed have an impact in the real world is often difficult to judge and may require the use of sophisticated statistical techniques. The reason is that imports are not only driven by the exchange rate, but also by domestic income. And exports are not only influenced by the exchange rate, but also by world income. Usually, all these determinants of the current account change all the time, and the movement of one may offset the effects resulting from the movement of another.

A graphic example is provided occasionally when one determinant of the current account changes so dramatically that its effects dominate any effects that may stem from concomitant small changes in the other determinants. This happened after the 1992 crisis in the European Monetary System, when Italy suspended membership in the system and the lira depreciated fast and substantially, relative to the currencies of Italy's trading partners.

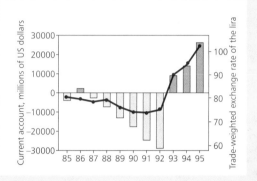

Figure 4.5

Figure 4.5 shows a trade-weighted exchange rate index for the lira between 1985 and 1995, adjusted for inflation differences. The lira appreciated steadily from 1985 through to 1992, making Italy's exports gradually more expensive for foreigners and imports more affordable for Italians. As a result, the current account, which was roughly balanced in the mid-1980s, moved into greater deficit each year – just as the textbook says it should. After 1992 the exchange rate changed its course, depreciating by more than 25% within a short period of time. The turnaround in the current account followed immediately. Within three years the current account deficit of 30 billion dollars (or 40,000 billion lire) in 1992 had become a current account surplus of almost equal size.

A second and separate question is what happens to the current account if, hypothetically, as a thought experiment, we wander off a given $CA = 0$ line. Then the real exchange rate, which positions the $CA = 0$ line, as we just saw, remains unchanged. Letting domestic income rise moves us to the right of the $CA = 0$ line. Imports increase, but exports remain unchanged, since R does not change. This is why, to the right of any given $CA = 0$ line, we have a current account deficit, $IM > EX$. By analogous reasoning, the current account is in surplus at any point to the left of the $CA = 0$ line. Here income is too low to keep imports as high as exports. These results are visualized by the grey shading, which turns darker as we move from left to right, indicating that the current account deteriorates and switches from surplus into deficit as we cross the $CA = 0$ line.

The **capital account** records how capital flows across borders in search of the highest returns. Just as a Londoner's purchase of a Ferrari calls for the purchase of euros, the purchase of bonds issued by the Italian government calls for buying euros as well. So the next question to be addressed is what determines international financial investment decisions.

Investing one unit of capital in the home country gives an annual return equal to the interest rate i. Investing the same amount abroad yields the foreign interest rate plus the percentage change of the exchange rate. If investors are risk neutral, they are only then indifferent between having domestic or foreign governments' bonds in their portfolio if

An individual is risk neutral if he is indifferent between a guaranteed payment of €500, and playing a free lottery in which he can win either €0 or €1,000 with a probability of 50% each.

$$i = i^{\text{World}} + \frac{E^e_{+1} - E}{E} \qquad \text{Capital account equilibrium} \qquad (4.4)$$
$$\text{(Uncovered interest parity)}$$

This equation is called the open or **uncovered interest parity** condition. It is uncovered because the return on the right-hand side is not guaranteed, but only an expectation. To keep things simple here, assume that financial investors expect the exchange rate to remain where it is today. Then $E^e_{+1} - E = 0$ and (4.4) simplifies to $i = i^{\text{World}}$. If $i > i^{\text{World}}$, investors want to move their wealth into domestic bonds, moving the capital account into surplus. An interest rate deficit, $i < i^{\text{World}}$, moves the capital account into deficit. Thus the capital account is determined by the interest differential:

$$CP = \kappa(i - i^{\text{World}}) \qquad (4.5)$$

Figure 4.6, panel (a), shows the capital account as a function of income and the interest rate. Here income has no impact, as it does not feature in equation (4.5). But CP deteriorates as the interest rate falls.

In the $i-Y$ plane the line that balances domestic and international returns is obviously horizontal at the world interest rate (Figure 4.6 panel (b)). On this line financial investors do not care whether they hold wealth in domestic or foreign bonds and leave their portfolio the way it is. At higher domestic interest rates capital flows in, moving CP into surplus. At lower domestic interest rates capital flows out.

The balance of payments or foreign exchange market equilibrium is determined by the interaction of the current account and the capital account. If we

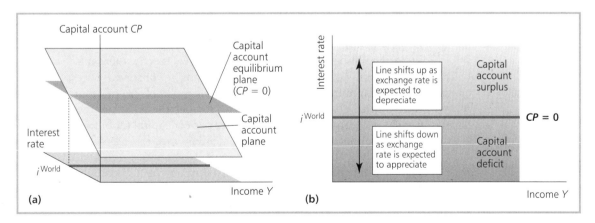

Figure 4.6 The capital account improves as a rising interest rate makes domestic bonds more attractive. Income does not impact on *CP*. The capital account equilibrium line, therefore, projects as a horizontal line onto the *i–Y* plane. An expected depreciation would make domestic bonds less attractive, thus shifting the *CP* = 0 line upwards. Unless stated otherwise, we assume expected depreciation to be zero.

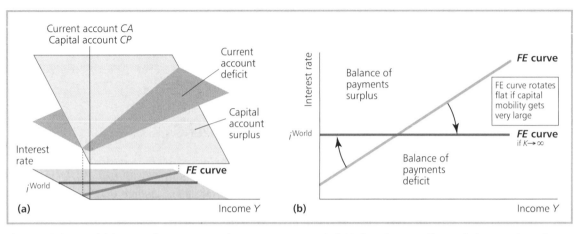

Figure 4.7 In panel (a) one surface measures the current account *deficit*, the other one the capital account *surplus*. When both are equal, the balance of payments and, hence, the foreign exchange market are in equilibrium. The line of intersection between both surfaces projects as a positively sloped line onto the $i-Y$ surface. If capital mobility increases, the *CP* plane becomes steeper, and the *FE* curve rotates to be flatter.

merge both planes in one diagram, foreign exchange market equilibrium may obtain when the capital account surplus (deficit) exactly matches the current account deficit (surplus) $(-CA = CP)$. Panel (a) in Figure 4.7 depicts the capital account surplus against the current account deficit. It turns out that projecting the line of intersection down onto the $i-Y$ plane produces a positively sloped line. This line is repeated in panel (b). The thinking behind its positive slope is that an increase of income stimulates imports, which deteriorates the current account. To match this, we need to export more interest-bearing assets. This is only achieved if a higher interest rate makes those more attractive.

There is no question that in today's highly integrated financial markets investors set the pace. Purchases and sales of foreign exchange deriving from the export or import of goods and services amount to some 1.5% of the transaction volume in the foreign exchange markets. Small differences between domestic and foreign returns lead to a huge reshuffling of international capital which easily dwarfs any existing trade imbalances.

Translating this into our model, the coefficient κ in the capital account equation, which measures investors' reactions to observed excess returns, must be very large. In terms of the *CP* planes in panels (a) of Figures 4.6 and 4.7, these must be very, very steep. The steeper the *CP* plane becomes, the flatter is the accompanying *FE* line. Under perfect capital mobility it is reasonable to assume that it is horizontal, coinciding with the $CP = 0$ line shown previously.

There is a very important difference between the $CP = 0$ line and the nearly horizontal *FE* curve. On the $CP = 0$ line the capital account would be in equilibrium. On the *FE* curve the capital account can only be in equilibrium if the current account is also in equilibrium. If the current account is in surplus or deficit on *FE*, the capital account must feature a deficit or surplus of equal size. How is that possible? Again the reason is that the smallest interest differential would trigger enormous flows of capital across borders.

Empirical note. In 2010 world trade amounted to the equivalent of $14.8 trillion. But $3.98 trillion worth of foreign exchange changed hands every single day.

BOX 4.2   **Forecasting the US dollar in 2004: an exercise in predicting exchange rates**

In 2004 many analysts expected the US dollar to continue its slide. Obstfeld and Rogoff (2004) predicted that the dollar might lose another 20–40% of its end-of-2004 value of 1.30 to the euro. How do economists arrive at such numbers?

Exchange rates are very difficult to forecast – in the short run. It is a bit like a layman forecasting tomorrow's temperature. Without help from weather satellites we probably have to concede that tomorrow being a warmer day is just as likely as tomorrow being colder. So *we usually expect tomorrow's temperature to be about the same as today's*. With a longer horizon, however, we would probably be prepared to bet on any day in December that the first Sunday of May will be warmer.

With exchange rates it is similar. It is nearly impossible to say what the exchange rate will do tomorrow or next month. This is why the assumption made in the text, that the exchange rate is not expected to change next year, is quite reasonable. But there are long-run anchors that give us some guidance as to what the exchange rate may do in a few years from now. Such gravity values can be provided in the simplest, static case by purchasing power parity (PPP). PPP postulates that the exchange rate will eventually return to a value that equates goods prices across countries. To make this operational, we need to look at one or more specific goods, such as a McDonald's Big Mac, which renders the concept rather arbitrary. Also, PPP focuses on one balance-of-payments (BOP) account only, the current account (*CA*). It thus ignores the role of financial flows in exchange rate determination. More refined analyses include the capital account (*CP*) as well.

To show how such a view may generate a forecast for the value of the US dollar, consider the circular flow identity, along with rounded US data for 2004 (in $ billion):

$$S - I + T - G = EX - IM(\approx CA)$$
$$-100 - 500 = -600$$

which features the budget deficit and the *CA* deficit (referred to as the twin deficits). The facts that the government spends $500 billion in excess of revenues and the private sector does not even save enough to finance private investment must be mirrored in a *CA* deficit of equivalent size.

The BOP provides the interpretation that any *CA* deficit is reflected in a *CP* surplus of equal size (we ignore the official reserves account):

$$CA + CP = 0$$
$$-600 + 600 = 0$$

This provides a static view of the BOP. In order to uncover BOP *dynamics*, we note two things:

1 The current account includes more transactions than net exports $NX \equiv EX - IM$. One important additional item is cross-border factor incomes. This includes wages for workers working in one country and living in another. It also records interest payments on investment abroad. We focus on these here. Denoting net foreign assets by *F*, the generalized current account reads $CA = NX + i^W F$, where the second term measures interest income from net foreign assets.
2 Whenever foreign assets are bought or sold, this is recorded in the capital account. So the capital account measures the net fall in foreign assets, denoted by $-\Delta F$.

With this refinement and notational change we may rewrite the BOP as

$$CA + CP = 0$$
$$NX + i^W F - \Delta F = 0$$
$$-600 + 600 = 0$$

In a final step, note that there is probably some limit to how far a country's international debt may rise. Eventually, other countries will consider it too risky to extend credit lines still further. In such a long-run equilibrium, when $\Delta F = 0$, the BOP simplifies to

$$NX = -i^W F$$

This long-run BOP restriction says that eventually, when the rest of the world is not prepared to grant any more credit to the US, the current account will be forced to balance. Then net exports must equal the interest payment on the accumulated foreign debt (if net foreign assets are negative). In 2004 net foreign debt amounted to 25% of US GDP. Forecasts say that by 2010 it may have passed 40% of GDP and by 2020 exceed 60%.

Now suppose foreigners refuse to continue lending to the US around the year 2010. At 40% of $16,000 billion, the US GDP expected for

---

Box 4.2 continued

2010, foreign debt amounts to $6,400 billion by then. At an interest rate of, say, 3%, total interest payments to the rest of the world equal $i^{WF} = -0.03 \times (-\$6,400\text{ billion}) = \$192\text{ billion}$. To match this, exports (which fell short of imports by $496 billion in 2003) must then exceed imports by $192 billion. This could only be achieved at much more competitive prices than today, and hence with a much cheaper dollar.

All this suggests that the dollar will eventually have to depreciate substantially. The open and related questions are *when* and by *how much?* In 2006, by 10%? In 2010, by 25%? Or in 2020, by 45%? Here our circular-flow and BOP identities remain silent, and we would need more refined theories such as the ones employed by Obstfeld and Rogoff (2004).

Further reading: Checking the depth gauge, *The Economist*, 13 November 2004, p. 88; Obstfeld, M. and K. Rogoff, The unsustainable US current account position revisited, *Proceedings, Federal Reserve Bank of San Francisco*, February 2005.

So even if we had a sizeable current account deficit, the domestic interest rate would only need to rise by an infinitesimally small amount over the world interest rate, and investors would be willing to supply all the capital needed to finance the *CA* deficit. This means, of course, that the *FE* curve is not completely identical to the *CP* = 0 line. But for practical purposes it is a useful approximation to assume that the *FE* is horizontal when capital is perfectly mobile.

The algebra of the *FE* curve

The discussion of the foreign exchange market equilibrium line may well be one instance where a little algebra says more than six graphs. The foreign exchange market is in equilibrium when the supply of and the demand for currency balance without central bank intervention, that is when

$$BP = CA + CP = 0 \qquad (4.6)$$

Substituting (4.2) and (4.5) into (4.6) gives

$$x_1 Y^{\text{World}} + x_2 R - m_1 Y + m_2 R + \kappa(i - i^{\text{World}}) = 0$$

Solving for the interest rate and collecting terms gives the foreign exchange market equilibrium line

$$i = i^{\text{World}} + \frac{m_1}{\kappa} Y - \frac{x_1}{\kappa} Y^{\text{World}} - \frac{m_2 + x_2}{\kappa} R \qquad \text{General } \textit{FE} \text{ curve} \quad (4.7)$$

The *FE* curve identifies combinations of income and the interest rate for which the foreign exchange market is in equilibrium.

The position of the *FE* curve always shifts one to one with the world interest rate. If κ is very large, meaning that capital flows respond very strongly to opening interest differentials, the other coefficients become very small. Thus the slope of the curve becomes very small and neither world income nor the real exchange

---

BOX 4.3	Interest rates, default risk and the risk premium

The main text assumes that creditors can always be sure that interest payments will be made and loans will be paid off at maturity. So we are talking about bonds with *no default risk*. In such a situation all that financial investors need to do when investing in international bonds is compare interest rates (assuming they do not expect the exchange rate to change, or countries share the same currency, as in the eurozone).

While this is a reasonable first assumption when talking about government bonds in many industrial countries, governments do occasionally default on international loans or interest payments as Europe's sovereign debt crisis reminded us. In the presence of such **default risk** the equilibrium condition for the international capital market changes and thus needs to be reconsidered.

Assume there is no default risk in Germany. Then one euro invested there grows to

$$1 + i^D \qquad (1)$$

after one period. A euro invested in Greece, where default risk is DR, can be expected to grow to

$$(1 + i^{GR})(1 - DR) \qquad (2)$$

since we need to take into account the possibility of default. Risk-neutral investors are indifferent between investing in Germany or Greece if these two expressions are the same. Setting (1) equal to (2) and expanding terms this yields

$$i^D = i^{GR} - DR - i^{GR}DR$$

If we ignore the last term on the right-hand side, which is small under normal circumstances, this simplifies to

$$i^D = i^{GR} - DR$$

So default risk may drive a wedge between domestic and foreign interest rates. Investors require a higher interest rate (or, more generally, a higher expected return) on Greek assets; a **risk premium** RP, which is equal to the default risk in our case. Generally, the risk premium on international investments, RP^{World}, drives a wedge between domestic and foreign interest rates:

$$i = i^{World} - RP^{World}$$

While we only looked at default risk here, many other things may give rise to a risk premium in financial markets, such as expropriation risk or risk aversion.

---

rate has a relevant impact on the position of the *FE* line. Letting $\kappa \rightarrow \infty$, as we assume henceforth, (4.7) simplifies to

$$i = i^{World} \qquad\qquad FE \text{ curve} \quad (4.8)$$

4.4 Equilibrium in all three markets

Equilibrium with graphs

We now know how to draw equilibrium lines for the money market, the goods market and the foreign exchange market in the $i-Y$ plane. Each line yields interesting insights into a particular sector of the economy. But these are not yet sufficient to pin down a unique macroeconomic equilibrium – which is what we are primarily interested in and set out to identify.

If the isolated discussion of individual markets only carried us so far, perhaps we can achieve progress by merging them. Let us construct the macroeconomic equilibrium step by step (Figure 4.8).

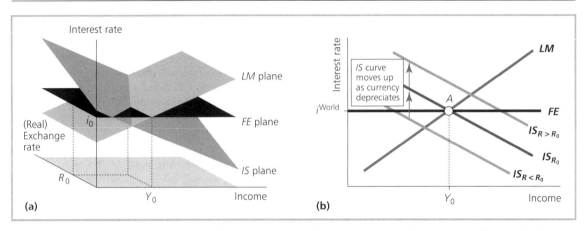

Figure 4.8 Panel (a) shows in 3D that there is only one triplet of endogenous variables, R_0, i_0 and Y_0 that yields an overall equilibrium in all three markets. Panel (b) derives the same result in 2D. The intersection of *FE* and *LM* (both curves are independent of R) identifies $i_0 = i^{World}$ and Y_0. *IS* must also pass through this point. This requirement determines R.

Note. We are still assuming that prices are fixed. Then the real exchange rate R (see Box 3.3) moves one to one with the nominal exchange E. In fact, if we let $P = P^{World} = 1$ we may use E and R interchangeably.

Note that our model contains three endogenous variables that need to be determined: the interest rate i, the exchange rate R and income Y. A good starting point is the *FE* curve. It notes that the only way for the foreign exchange market to be in equilibrium is if the domestic interest rate equals the world interest rate. Next add the *LM* curve. Once the equilibrium interest rate has been determined in the foreign exchange market, the money market equilibrium tells us exactly where equilibrium income Y_0 must be. In Figure 4.8 Y_0 is determined by the point of intersection between the *FE* and the *LM* curve.

What might be puzzling here is that we have determined equilibrium income without even looking at the goods market. How can we be sure that the *IS* curve, the equilibrium condition for the goods market, passes through A? And how can we be sure that the equilibrium conditions stated by *IS* are compatible with the already predetermined levels of i and Y?

The answer is that there is a whole series of *IS* curves, each for a different exchange rate, and there is always one *IS* curve that passes through A. The underlying exchange rate is the equilibrium exchange rate R_0. But what if the *IS* curve is at $IS_{R > R_0}$ because the exchange rate is too high at $R > R_0$, while the interest rate and income are determined by point A? At the given exchange rate, A represents an excess demand for domestic goods, which puts upward pressure on income and upward pressure on the interest rate which eventually drives down the exchange rate and, hence, the *IS* curve. This goes on until *IS* passes through A. But this question will be dealt with in much more detail in the next chapter where the focus will be the interaction between the three markets we have just learned to understand.

The algebra of *IS-LM-FE* equilibrium

The three markets discussed in this chapter constitute the *IS-LM-FE* model. Algebraically, the model consists of three equilibrium conditions for three markets:

$$R = \frac{1 - c + m_1}{m_2 + x_2}Y - \frac{\bar{I} + G + x_1 Y^{World}}{m_2 + x_2} + \frac{b}{m_2 + x_2}i \qquad \text{IS curve} \quad (4.9)$$

$$Y = \frac{M}{k} + \frac{b}{k}i \qquad\qquad\qquad\qquad\qquad\qquad \text{LM curve} \quad (4.10)$$

$$i = i^{World} \qquad\qquad\qquad\qquad\qquad\qquad\qquad \text{FE curve} \quad (4.11)$$

These are the *IS*, *LM* and *FE* curves already discussed. If they look unfamiliar, it is because equations (3.2) and (3.9) have been rearranged so as to show, along with (4.8), the three endogenous variables of the model on the left-hand side. The equilibrium values of *R*, *Y* and *i* are relatively easy to obtain because the model is recursive, meaning that equilibrium values are obtained step by step. We start at the bottom.

1 *The interest rate.* The equilibrium interest rate is determined directly by equation (4.11):

$$i = i^{World} \qquad\qquad\qquad\qquad\qquad \text{Equilibrium interest rate}$$

2 *Equilibrium income.* Substitute the equilibrium interest rate into equation (4.10) to obtain equilibrium income as

$$Y = \frac{M}{k} + \frac{b}{k}i^{World} \qquad\qquad\qquad \text{Equilibrium income}$$

3 *Equilibrium exchange rate.* Now substitute equilibrium income and the equilibrium interest rate into (4.9) to finally obtain the equilibrium exchange rate:

$$R = \frac{1 - c + m_1}{m_2 + x_2}\left(\frac{M}{k} + \frac{b}{k}i^{World}\right) - \frac{\bar{I} + G + x_1 Y^{World}}{m_2 + x_2} + \frac{b}{m_2 + x_2}i^{World}$$

Equilibrium exchange rate

Bottom line

This chapter has refined the discussion of equilibrium income by a further step. The one important result still obtaining is that a unique income level exists at which income equals aggregate demand. Bringing the foreign exchange market into the picture modifies the link between equilibrium income and the money supply and links this income to the world interest rate. Chapter 5 will look at how equilibrium income in the *IS-LM-FE* model is influenced by policy and other factors.

To this end we will need to consider the interaction between the three markets analyzed here. Before moving to this rather demanding task, make sure that you have a clear understanding of the isolated money market (*LM* curve), goods market (*IS* curve) and foreign exchange market (*FE* curve).

BOX 4.4   The *IS-LM-FE* model in a different dress

The *IS-LM-FE* model comprises three markets which determine three endogenous variables. Under flexible exchange rates these are *i*, *E* and *Y*. When we reduced the 3D graph of this model shown in Figure 4.8 to two dimensions we chose to show *i* and *Y* on the two axes, thus relegating *E* to an invisible role in the background. While this is the traditional choice, we may just as well have chosen to show *i* and *E* on the two axes, or *E* and *Y*. You often find the latter display in current textbooks, with the valid argument that when the interest rate cannot move under perfect capital mobility, why waste an axis on *i*? To see what the *IS-LM-FE* model looks like in an *E-Y* diagram, let us restate the algebraic expressions for the three market equilibrium lines. Letting $P = P^{World} = 1$, so that $R = E$, equations (4.9–4.11) can be rewritten as

$$E = \frac{1 - c + m_1}{m_2 + x_2}Y - \frac{\bar{I} + G + x_1 Y^{World}}{m_2 + x_2}$$

$$+ \frac{b}{m_2 + x_2}i \qquad \textbf{\textit{IS}} \textbf{ curve} \quad (1)$$

$$Y = \frac{M}{k} + \frac{h}{k}i \qquad \textbf{\textit{LM}} \textbf{ curve} \quad (2)$$

$$i = i^{World} \qquad \textbf{\textit{FE}} \textbf{ curve} \quad (3)$$

The positive coefficient of *Y* in equation (1) indicates that the *IS* curve is a positively sloped line in an *E-Y* diagram (see Figure 4.9). The logical reason is that a depreciating exchange rate raises net exports. So firms need to raise output in order to keep the goods market in equilibrium.

Since the exchange rate plays no role in the money market, the *LM* curve is a vertical line in

an *E-Y* diagram. It shifts to the right if the money supply or the interest rate increases.

Equation (3) evidently cannot be displayed in an *E-Y* diagram since it contains neither *E* nor *Y*. In order not to lose the valuable information conveyed by the *FE* curve, equation (3) may be substituted into equations (1) and (2). We then obtain what we may call an *IS** curve and an *LM** curve, goods market and money market equilibrium lines conditional on a simultaneous equilibrium in the foreign exchange market. *IS** and *LM** move up and to the right, respectively, if the world interest rate increases.

It is important to note that the *E-Y* diagram is only a different way of displaying and manipulating the *IS-LM-FE* model. It is still the same model with the same properties. You may want to check that, and deepen your grasp of the *IS-LM-FE* model at the same time, by taking the results that Chapter 5 derives in the context of the *i-Y* diagram and replicating them in an *E-Y* diagram.

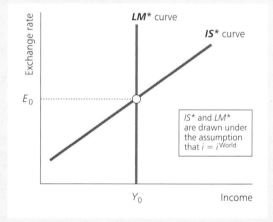

Figure 4.9

BOX 4.5   Endogenous and exogenous variables

The *IS-LM-FE* model provides a good opportunity to illustrate and re-emphasize the distinction between endogenous and exogenous variables, and to show how institutional arrangements change the nature of a variable.

A model always comprises

■ *exogenous variables* – their values are determined outside the model, and

■ *endogenous variables* – to describe their behaviour is the very purpose of the model.

A model may have an arbitrary number of exogenous variables. But it can only explain as many endogenous variables as it has (independent) equations.

The *IS-LM-FE* model has been reduced to three equations – which take the form of market equilibrium conditions – to explain three

Box 4.5 continued

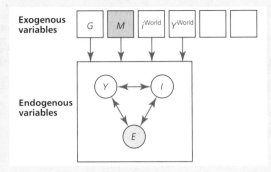

Figure 4.10 Flexible exchange rates

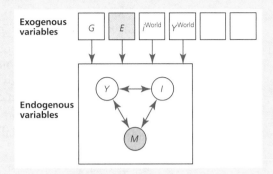

Figure 4.11 Fixed exchange rates

endogenous variables. Figure 4.10 sketches how the exogenous variables have an impact on the three endogenous variables, and how the latter interact.

We must remember here, however, that our initial larger model, with equations explaining other endogenous variables such as consumption, investment, exports, imports and more, has been reduced to three equations by repeatedly substituting equations into each other and thus eliminating these variables. Thus, for example, consumption does not appear any more. But it can be considered a hidden endogenous variable whose equilibrium value is retrieved by substituting equilibrium income into the consumption function.

Institutions and the endogeneity of variables

The above interpretation implicitly assumes that the exchange rate is flexible, determined by market forces. This makes the money supply M exogenous, and puts it under the control of the policy-maker.

The roles of the exchange rate and of the money supply are reversed if we move to a system of *fixed exchange rates*. Then the exchange rate becomes exogenous, is set by policy-makers, and the money supply adjusts endogenously. This modifies the model's structure to that shown in Figure 4.11.

In terms of the representations of market equilibria in the i-Y plane, the two institutional scenarios work as shown in panels (a) and (b) of Figure 4.12.

Under *flexible exchange rates* the positions of FE and LM are set exogenously. The exchange rate determines the position of IS, and endogenously adjusts so as to let IS pass through the given point of intersection between FE and LM (panel (a)).

Under *fixed exchange rates* the positions of FE and IS are set exogenously. The money supply, which determines the position of LM, endogenously adjusts so as to let LM pass through the given point of intersection between FE and IS (panel (b)).

(a) Flexible exchange rates

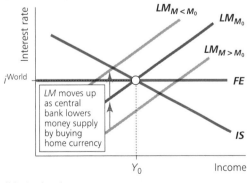

(b) Fixed exchange rates

Figure 4.12

CHAPTER SUMMARY

- Globalization has led to large increases in most countries' exports (relative to income) and in the volumes traded in the world's foreign exchange market.

- The balance of payments is a meticulous record of a country's inhabitants' cross-border transactions. It is useful for macroeconomic purposes as a mirror image of the foreign exchange market. Viewed this way, it helps identify the main motives behind the demand for foreign currency.

- The goods market is in equilibrium if income, the interest rate and the exchange rate assume values that make aggregate demand equal to output produced.

- Aggregate demand rises with income (through consumption), falls as the interest rate rises (through investment), and rises with the exchange rate (through net exports).

- The foreign exchange market is dominated by financial investors. The demand exercised by importers and exporters is negligible in relative volume.

- Equilibrium in the foreign exchange market obtains if domestic assets and foreign assets yield identical returns. If individuals have stationary exchange rate expectations this means that the domestic interest rate must equal the world interest rate.

- Using interest rate parity as the equilibrium condition for the foreign exchange market does not imply that the capital account is balanced. It means that investors are indifferent between holding domestic or foreign assets. Hence, they are ready to finance any current account disequilibrium that might occur.

- Only one macroeconomic equilibrium (defined as simultaneous equilibrium in all three markets) exists. Income, the interest rate and the exchange rate assume one specific value each.

Key terms and concepts

balance of payments
surplus *110*
capital account *114*
closed economy *105*
current account *110*
FE curve *118*
flexible exchange rates *111*

foreign exchange market *111*
globalization *105*
IS-LM model *111*
official reserves account *108*
open economy *105*
risk neutral *115*
risk premium *119*

EXERCISES

4.1 How open is your country's economy at present
  (a) as measured by the export ratio?
  (b) as measured by the import ratio?

Use data from *Eurostat*, the IMF, the OECD or national sources to address this question.

4.2 Suppose an artificial country called Spain recorded the cross-border transactions listed below:

500 Seat Toledos sold to Ireland	€7,500,000
10,000 Duffy CDs sold in Spain	€150,000
Sergio Garcia flies Air France to New York 10 times, using the A380 from Paris	€70,000
Franz Beckenbauer spends several golf holidays in Marbella	€40,000
Ruud van Nistelrooy sends cheques home to mum in Holland	€200,000
Julio Iglesias earns dividend on Microsoft stocks	€1,900,000
Spain's government contributes to EU budget	€1,000,000
Ford acquires office building in Barcelona	€10,000,000
Real Madrid invests in Eurosport TV stocks	€5,000,000
Government pays interest on Spanish government bonds held abroad	€2,800,000

Assemble Spain's balance of payments. Assume there are no statistical discrepancies. What is the current account balance? What are net exports? What is the capital account balance? Is the balance of payments in surplus or deficit?

4.3 Consider a small open economy that faces the macroeconomic situation as shown in Figure 4.13.

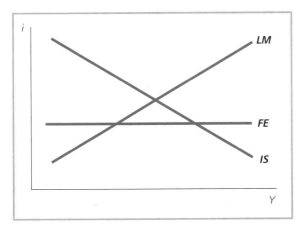

Figure 4.13

Describe the mechanisms that bring about a macroeconomic equilibrium in which all three-market equilibrium lines intersect
(a) under flexible exchange rates
(b) under fixed exchange rates.

4.4 Suppose investment is independent of the interest rate and the *FE* curve is horizontal. Sketch the macroeconomic equilibrium under fixed and flexible exchange rates and describe the mechanisms that help achieve it.

4.5 Consider an economy that is characterized by constant prices, flexible exchange rates and perfect capital mobility, and where the *IS* and *LM* curves can be written as follows:

(*LM*) $M = 0.25Y - 10i$
(*IS*) $i = 0.1(\bar{I} + G + 0.1Y^{World} - 0.4Y + 40R)$

Initially, the exogenous variables take the following values:

$M = 500$
$i^{World} = 5$
$Y^{World} = 5,000$
$\bar{I} = 160$
$G = 200$

(a) Draw the equilibrium curves for the money market, the foreign exchange market and the goods market into an *i–Y* diagram.
(b) Compute the equilibrium levels of the interest rate, income and the foreign exchange rate.

4.6 Consider an economy with fixed exchange rates and perfect capital mobility. It is characterized as follows:

(*LM*) $M = 0.25Y - 5i$
(*IS*) $i = 0.1(\bar{I} + G + 0.2Y^{World} - 0.2Y + 50R)$
(*FE*) $i = i^{World}$

Use the following initial values of the exogenous variables:

$\bar{I} = 100$
$G = 100$
$Y^{World} = 500$
$i^{World} = 5$

(a) Suppose the exchange rate is fixed at 1. What is the resulting equilibrium level of income and the resulting money supply?
(b) To what level does the world interest rate have to move in order to obtain an income level of 1,600? What is the corresponding money supply?

4.7 Usually, we assume the simplified *FE* curve represented by equation $i = i^{World}$. We now introduce taxes on interest earnings.
Analyze Switzerland (a small country with bank secrecy law) and the rest of the world using the graphical apparatus of the Mundell–Fleming model. Suppose that foreigners pay taxes on their interest earnings at home at the rate z^{World}, and the Swiss pay taxes at the rate $z^{CH} < z^{World}$.

Distinguish between scenarios (a) and (b):

(a) The governments of both countries are perfectly informed about interest earnings of their inhabitants. Investors have to pay taxes in their country of residence independent of where their returns are generated. What is the equilibrium condition on the international capital market (*FE* curve)?

(b) Suppose that foreigners do not report their returns realized in Switzerland to their revenue authorities. This is possible because of the bank secrecy law in Switzerland. They prefer to pay the withholding tax which is set to z^{CH} for simplicity. What is the equilibrium condition on the capital market?

Suppose the *FE* curve is characterized by the situation described in (b).

(c) What happens to the Swiss economy if the bank secrecy law is abolished? Does your answer depend on whether the exchange rate is flexible or fixed?

APPLIED PROBLEMS

EMPIRICAL RESEARCH

Testing uncovered interest parity

Uncovered interest parity introduced in equation (4.4) states that the difference between the domestic interest rate i and the foreign interest rate $i*$ equals the expected depreciation of the home currency ε^e: $\varepsilon^e = i - i*$. If depreciation expectations are rational (for more on this see Chapter 8), they should be correct on average: $\varepsilon = \varepsilon^e + \nu$ where ν denotes expectations errors which on average are zero. Substituting the first into the second equation gives $\varepsilon = i - i* + \nu$. M. Chinn and G. Meredith ('Testing uncovered interest parity at short and long horizons', University of California Santa Cruz, *Working Paper* 2000–01) test this equation by regressing depreciation rates on interest differentials, that is they estimate the coefficients of the equation $\varepsilon = \alpha + \beta(i - i*)$

If open interest parity holds together with rational expectations, the estimate of α should be 0 and the estimate of β should equal 1. Selected estimation results based on quarterly data for the sample period 1983:I–2000:I are

German mark

$$\varepsilon = 0.006 + 0.851(i - i^*) \qquad R^2 = 0.40$$
$$\quad (0.003) \ (0.180)$$

Japanese yen

$$\varepsilon = 0.038 + 0.388(i - i^*) \qquad R^2 = 0.10$$
$$\quad (0.005) \ (0.144)$$

British pound

$$\varepsilon = -0.003 + 0.562(i - i^*) \qquad R^2 = 0.43$$
$$\quad (0.004) \ (0.106)$$

where standard errors are shown in parentheses. While there is a statistically significant relationship between the interest differential and the rate of depreciation, important differences remain:

- A much larger share of variations in the rate of depreciation can be attributed to variations in the interest differential for the mark and the pound than for the yen. Respective coefficients of determination are 0.40, 0.43 and 0.10.
- The equations estimated for Germany and Japan have significant constant terms, meaning that there is a depreciation tendency unrelated to the interest differential.
- The null hypothesis $\beta = 1$ is rejected for the yen and the pound, but not for the mark. (Example: Testing $\beta = 1$ for the pound yields the t-statistic $(1 - 0.562)/0.106 = 4.13$. Therefore the null hypothesis must be rejected.)

All in all the results are mixed. To the extent that coefficients are not as expected, it remains open to question whether this is due to expectations not being rational or because uncovered interest parity does not hold.

WORKED PROBLEM

Amadeus by the dollar

A country's exports depend on the real exchange rate (as a measure of relative prices) and on the level of income in the destination country. This should also hold for each category of exports. If Austria welcomes American tourists, it exports. Tourists pay for the privilege of enjoying Vienna and the Alps, just as the British pay for Spanish exports of sherry to the

Table 4.3

	NIGHTS (thousands)	SHPER$	USGDP in '87 (billions)
1971	1,774.172	19.18385	2,955.9
1972	1,838.577	17.24196	3,107.1
1973	1,569.763	14.44078	3,268.6
1974	1,339.987	13.99124	3,248.1
1975	1,230.936	13.09453	3,221.7
1976	1,378.784	13.30245	3,380.8
1977	1,428.656	12.36859	3,533.3
1978	1,272.219	11.28735	3,703.5
1979	1,090.836	11.15924	3,796.8
1980	1,332.572	11.53090	3,776.3
1981	1,170.124	14.66295	3,843.1
1982	1,438.524	15.81757	3,760.3
1983	1,740.612	16.61142	3,906.6
1984	2,203.027	18.28409	4,148.5
1985	2,376.876	18.98412	4,279.8
1986	1,408.803	14.01424	4,404.5
1987	1,719.816	11.87747	4,539.9
1988	1,591.663	11.83786	4,718.6
1989	1,697.928	12.97130	4,838.0
1990	2,139.202	11.37000	4,897.3
1991	1,191.496	11.77773	4,867.6
1992	1,526.478	10.97878	4,979.3
1993	1,371.261	11.54847	5,134.5
1994	1,393.102	11.29254	5,342.3

United Kingdom. Now consider the data in Table 4.3 on nights spent by US visitors to Austria (NIGHTS), the real exchange rate of schilling versus dollar (SHPER$) and US real GDP (USGDP).

To check whether our export equation explains US tourism to Austria we regress NIGHTS on SHPER$ and USGDP. The result is

$$\text{NIGHTS} = -842.7 + 104.3 \ \text{SHPER\$} + 0.236 \ \text{USGDP}$$
$$\qquad\quad (1.60) \qquad (4.92) \qquad\qquad (3.02)$$

24 annual observations 1971–94; $R^2_{adj} = 0.50$

Both coefficients are positive as expected, and are significantly different from 0, as the t-values of 4.92 and 3.02 indicate. If the schilling depreciates by one schilling per dollar (at 1987 prices), US tourists spend 104,300 more nights in Austria. If American GDP rises by one billion dollars (at 1987 prices), 236 more nights are being spent in Austria. The coefficient of determination is 0.50, saying that half of the variance in the number of nights spent by US tourists per year is accounted for by changes in the real exchange rate and in US income.

YOUR TURN

Are international interest rates equal?

A key ingredient of the Mundell–Fleming model (to be discussed in the next chapter) is the interest parity condition, stating that interest rates may only differ between countries to the extent by which the exchange rate is expected to change. If the exchange rate is expected to remain where it is currently, the domestic interest rate should equal the world interest rate. To check whether this assumption is a well-guided first guess, consider the money market interest rates for Germany and the

Table 4.4

Year	i_D	i_{NL}	Year	i_D	i_{NL}
1980	9.06	10.13	1988	4.01	4.48
1981	11.26	11.01	1989	6.59	6.99
1982	8.67	8.06	1990	7.92	8.29
1983	5.36	5.28	1991	8.84	9.01
1984	5.54	5.78	1992	9.42	9.27
1985	5.19	6.30	1993	7.49	7.10
1986	4.57	5.83	1994	5.35	5.14
1987	3.72	5.16			

Netherlands (annual data) in Table 4.4. Let Holland be the home country and assume that the German interest rate approximates the world interest rate. Check whether the hypothesis $i_{NL} = i_D$ is supported by the data.

Booms and recessions (II): the national economy

After working through this chapter, you will understand:

1 What the national-economy Mundell–Fleming model is, and how it differs from the global-economy model.

2 How fiscal policy affects equilibrium income in the Mundell–Fleming model.

3 How monetary policy affects equilibrium income in the Mundell–Fleming model.

4 How demand shocks in general, including those originating from abroad, affect equilibrium income.

5 The difference between comparative statics and adjustment dynamics.

6 How things alter if prices are permitted to change.

7 The meaning of speculative bubbles and what risks they generate for the macroeconomy.

The Mundell–Fleming model is a tool for analyzing macroeconomic issues. It comprises the goods market (*IS*), the money market (*LM*) and the foreign exchange market (*FE*). Its simplicity has made it a tool often used in communications between professional and academic economists. Employed wisely, with an informed sense of its limits, the Mundell–Fleming model can be a very powerful tool for understanding the role of aggregate demand in the business cycle.

Chapter 3 and 4 made us look beyond the circular-flow and Keynesian-cross representations of the macroeconomy. We saw that proper treatment of monetary and financial aspects, which feature prominently in modern industrial economies, recommends breaking down the open, national economy into three markets: the **goods market**, the **money market** and the **foreign exchange market**. By now we have a clear understanding under what conditions each of these markets is in equilibrium. It also makes perfect sense that a macroeconomic equilibrium is only possible when each individual market is in equilibrium. The national-economy model built in Chapter 3 and 4 is called the *IS-LM-FE* **model,** with obvious reference to its constituent markets. A better known name for it is the Mundell–Fleming model after British economist J. Marcus Fleming and Canadian Nobel prize winner Robert Mundell who laid its foundations.

What Chapter 4 and 5 do with the Mundell–Fleming model echoes the questions that Chapter 2 raised in the context of the Keynesian cross and Chapter 3 within the *IS-LM* framework. In both cases we first determined equilibrium income. Then we showed how equilibrium income responded to changes in autonomous demand or policy instruments via the multiplier. These same two questions, which could be dealt with within a single chapter in the simple models underlying the Keynesian cross and the *IS-LM* model, require one chapter each for the more refined Mundell–Fleming model. Chapter 4 determined the unique equilibrium of the Mundell–Fleming model. Chapter 5 takes this equilibrium as a starting point. We proceed to ask whether and how equilibrium can be influenced by fiscal and monetary policy, and how one country's equilibrium income may be linked to that of others.

This chapter is designed to sharpen our understanding of the *IS-LM-FE* or Mundell–Fleming model. We will do so

- by reconsidering the effects of **government expenditures**, and of fiscal policy in general, and
- by taking a first look at **monetary policy**.

Along the way we will learn to appreciate the important role of the **exchange rate system**. As a recurrent theme we will also discuss the role of **expectations**.

5.1 Fiscal policy in the Mundell–Fleming model

Fiscal policy manipulates government spending and taxes to achieve policy goals (such as a rise in income).

Fiscal policy comprises all policy measures related to the government budget. On the aggregate level this amounts to government spending and raising government revenue by levying taxes.

In terms of the Mundell–Fleming model, if the government increases expenditures the *IS* curve shifts to the right. The size of this shift is given by the multiplier derived in Chapter 2 (times ΔG). There the interest rate was (implicitly) considered constant, and the multiplier indicated by how much equilibrium income rises after a one-unit increase of government expenditure. As this holds at all interest rates, the *IS* curve shifts exactly by the size of the original multiplier to the right (see Figure 5.1).

If the interest rate actually remains at the level of the world interest rate, and the foreign exchange market equilibrium condition says it must, equilibrium moves from A to B. B is not a money market equilibrium, however. With the interest rate unchanged and higher income than at A, individuals wish to hold more money at B than is being supplied. This excess demand for money puts upward pressure on the interest rate. If we could ignore the *FE* curve, this

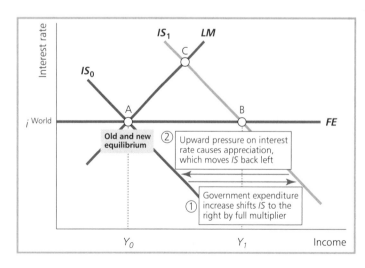

Figure 5.1 (Flexible exchange rates.) A rise in government spending shifts *IS* to the right. Now there is an excess demand for goods in A. As this starts to make income rise, moving along *LM* from A towards C pushes the domestic interest rate beyond the world interest rate. This increases the demand for domestic interest-bearing assets and appreciates the domestic currency. This, in turn, makes domestic goods more expensive, reducing net exports, driving *IS* back towards the left. This continues until *IS* is back at IS_0 and the economy is back at A.

would drive up the interest rate along IS_1 until it reached equilibrium in the money market at C.

But point C is not a foreign exchange market equilibrium. So we will not really move up to C. At the slightest increase of the domestic interest rate, financial investors will want to shift wealth into domestic bonds. For this they need to acquire domestic currency. The result is an *incipient* excess demand for domestic currency. What are the macroeconomic consequences of this? Well, this depends on how the foreign exchange market is organized. Is the exchange rate flexible, left to be determined by the market? Or have governments agreed to set a specific exchange rate (called parity rate) and buy or sell any amount of currency the market wants at that price? We will consider each option separately.

Flexible exchange rates

We speak of a system of flexible exchange rates when governments (or central banks) allow the exchange rate to be determined by market forces alone.

Under a system of flexible exchange rates the central bank simply ignores the excess demand for domestic currency and leaves things up to the market. So the currency price must change in order to match supply and demand. If financial investors cannot obtain domestic currency at the current price, which is the reciprocal value of the exchange rate, they offer more. This drives *up* the price per unit of domestic currency, and it drives the exchange rate *down*. The domestic currency appreciates. As we know, this has repercussions in the goods market. Domestic goods become more expensive relative to foreign goods and net exports fall. The *IS* curve shifts to the left. During this process C gradually slides down the *LM* curve towards A. This slide cannot come to a halt before A has been reached. Otherwise the domestic interest rate would still exceed the world interest rate, causing the excess demand for domestic currency to continue. Only as *IS* returns to its original position and the economy returns to A are all three markets in equilibrium.

Crowding out occurs when an increase in government spending reduces private spending (such as net exports or investment).

This yields an important insight: under a system of flexible exchange rates and when capital is perfectly mobile across borders, fiscal policy does not give the government leverage over aggregate income. As long as the central bank holds the money supply constant, there will be complete crowding out. The exchange rate will be forced to appreciate just enough to reduce net exports by as much as government expenditures increased, leaving aggregate demand unchanged. This means that after G is raised, the composition of demand at point A in Figure 5.1 is different from what it was before. This is also easy to see by looking at the circular flow identity from Chapter 1:

$$(S - I) + (T - G) + (IM - EX) = 0$$
$$0 \quad 0 \quad\ \ 0 \qquad\ + \qquad\ + \qquad -$$

The line under the identity shows whether a particular variable has increased (+), fallen (−) or remained unchanged (0). Savings has remained the same since it only depends on income, which remains unchanged. Investment is the same because it depends on the interest rate, which remains unchanged. Taxes depend on income and, thus, remain unchanged. Government outlays have increased, which deteriorates the government budget. To compensate for this, the current account must deteriorate as well. At current income and an appreciated currency, imports are higher. Exports are lower because of the appreciation.

Fixed exchange rates

We speak of a system of fixed exchange rates when governments (or central banks) announce an exchange rate (the parity rate) at which they are prepared to buy or sell any amount of domestic currency.

In a system of fixed exchange rates the exchange rate is set to a particular value by unilateral decision or multilateral agreement on the political level. At this exchange rate the central bank must buy or sell any amount of domestic currency that the market offers or demands. This is tantamount to taking control of the money supply out of the central bank's hands. Figure 5.2 shows what an increase in government expenditures does to income under these conditions.

Again, higher government expenditures shift the *IS* curve to the right, and again the resulting income increase tends to push up the interest rate beyond the world interest rate. Now, however, the resulting excess demand for domestic currency cannot and need not be eliminated by appreciation. Instead, the central bank is obliged to supply just that amount of additional money that would-be buyers cannot find in the market. So two things happen, which did not happen under flexible exchange rates:

1 The exchange rate cannot appreciate, meaning that the *IS* curve cannot shift back. It remains in its new position IS_1.
2 The domestic money supply increases due to the mandatory foreign exchange market intervention of the central bank, shifting the *LM* curve to the right.

The *LM* curve must continue to shift until it intersects IS_1 at B. It cannot come to a halt earlier because this would leave an incipient advantage for the domestic interest rate, creating excess demand for domestic money.

Moving from flexible to fixed exchange rates reverses the roles of fiscal and monetary policy. Under flexible exchange rates monetary policy sets the limit and can enforce a complete crowding out of government expenditure. Under fixed exchange rates fiscal policy is in the driver's seat. The exchange rate regime forces monetary policy to accommodate any government expenditure increase so as to yield the full multiplier effect.

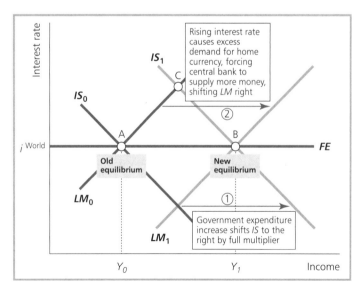

Figure 5.2 (Fixed exchange rates.) The initial rise in government expenditure shifts *IS* to the right. Along with income the demand for money increases, pushing the interest rate up. This makes domestic bonds more attractive, thus raising the demand for domestic currency. The central bank is obliged to supply the requested domestic currency for foreign currency, thus shifting *LM* to the right too. Income rises from Y_0 to Y_1.

BOX 5.1 The Mundell–Fleming model under capital controls

In this book we assume that capital moves unhindered across borders. This describes the current situation quite well in industrial and many other countries. But there are still some countries, mostly in the developing world, that do not permit free movements of capital in and out. In Tanzania, for example, citizens need to submit proof of an import contract and obtain a permit if they want to acquire foreign currency. The purchase or sale of currency is usually not permitted for financial investments. As a consequence the capital account cannot really respond to interest rate differentials. In algebraic terms $\kappa = 0$ in equation (4.5). What does that do to the FE curve? This is best seen after solving the general FE curve, equation (4.7), for Y to obtain

$$Y = \frac{\kappa}{m_1}(i - i^{\text{World}}) + \frac{m_2 + x_2}{m_1}R + \frac{x_1}{m_1}Y^{\text{World}} \quad (1)$$

Letting $\kappa = 0$ to signal that capital is not permitted to respond to changes in interest rates, the interest differential drops out of the equation and equation (1) simplifies to

$$Y = \frac{m_2 + x_2}{m_1}R + \frac{x_1}{m_1}Y^{\text{World}} \quad \begin{array}{c}\textbf{\textit{FE} curve under}\\ \textbf{capital controls}\end{array} \quad (2)$$

This equation restates the current account equilibrium (equation (4.3)) we derived in Chapter 4. Obviously, when there are no capital flows and, thus, $CP = 0$, the foreign exchange market can only be in equilibrium if the current account is in equilibrium: $CA = EX - IM = 0$.

The FE curve under strict capital controls is a vertical line, just as is the $CA = 0$ line in Chapter 4, the position of which is determined by the real exchange rate and world income. The reasons for this are exactly the same as those given for why the position of the $CA = 0$ line depends on R and Y^{World}. See Figure 4.4 and the explanations given there. The general macroeconomic equilibrium is as depicted in Figure 5.3.

- Can you explain why FE moves right when the real exchange rate depreciates?
- Can this country stimulate income by raising government spending when the exchange rate is fixed?

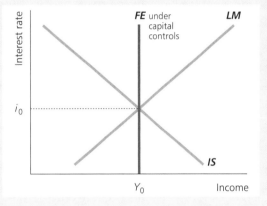

Figure 5.3

Government expenditure is one autonomous demand factor. Similar results to those derived for government expenditure increases obtain for other variables that affect autonomous demand: taxes, world income, or the autonomous components of consumption, investment, imports or exports.

We now look at the flip side of the coin and check whether the results obtained for government expenditures are confirmed if we analyze the effects of monetary policy directly.

5.2 Monetary policy in the Mundell–Fleming model

Monetary policy manipulates the money supply (or the interest rate) to achieve policy goals (such as a rise in income).

Monetary policy comprises central bank action geared towards steering the supply of money. This can happen directly, by purchasing or selling bonds or foreign currency. It can also happen indirectly, as we saw in Chapter 3, by setting interest rates and inducing the market to hold liquidity in the desired amount. Here we use monetary policy as a synonym for direct control of the money supply.

As above, it will prove useful to consider different exchange rate regimes separately.

Flexible exchange rates

An increase of the money supply shifts LM to the right. If we could ignore the foreign exchange market equilibrium line, this shift of LM would drive the interest rate down, stimulate investment demand and bring the economy to point D. D is not really feasible, however, as it violates the foreign exchange market equilibrium. As soon as domestic interest rates begin to move below the world interest rate, international investors start to move out of domestic bonds. In the wake of this, they try to get rid of domestic currency. The incipient excess supply of domestic currency leads to a depreciation. This makes domestic goods and services cheaper and stimulates net exports. The IS curve shifts to the right. This process must go on until IS_1 intersects LM_1 at B (see Figure 5.4).

So our previous result is indeed confirmed. Under flexible exchange rates monetary policy sets the pace. Not only is fiscal policy completely ineffective if used in isolation against the course of monetary policy, but monetary policy is extremely effective at stimulating aggregate demand and income, even if it does not get any help from fiscal policy.

Fixed exchange rates

Under fixed exchange rates the first step is the same. If the money supply is increased via the purchase of domestic bonds by the central bank, the LM curve shifts to the right. And again, the increased liquidity tends to drive the interest rate down. As investors get rid of domestic bonds and throw domestic currency on the market, the exchange rate cannot respond. Instead, the central bank is called upon as the 'buyer of last resort'. It is required to take any

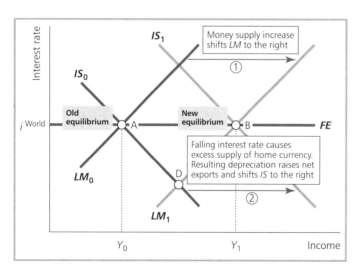

Figure 5.4 (Flexible exchange rates.) A money-supply increase shifts LM to the right. This tends to drive down the interest rate along IS_0 towards D. As soon as the interest rate moves below the world interest rate, investors will start to withdraw funds from domestic assets. The exchange rate depreciates, spurring net exports andshifting IS to the right. As IS reaches IS_1 a new equilibrium obtains in B.

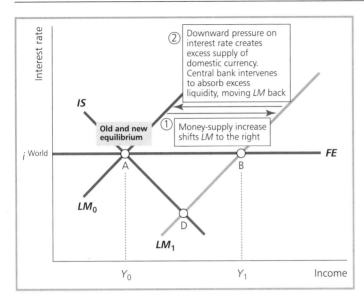

Figure 5.5 (Fixed exchange rates.) A money-supply increase shifts *LM* right. As this tends to push interest rates down, investors withdraw funds from domestic assets. Wanting to move into foreign assets, they sell domestic currency for foreign currency. Under fixed exchange rates the central bank is obliged to sell the requested foreign currency. Since it receives domestic currency as payment, the domestic money supply is reduced, shifting *LM* back left. Eventually we are back at A.

excess liquidity out of the market which the market does not want to hold. This reduces the money supply, and continues until the money supply is back at its original level. Then the *LM* curve is back in its original position LM_0 and nothing has changed: neither aggregate income or demand, nor the composition of aggregate demand (see Figure 5.5).

This completes our discussion of fiscal and monetary policy under fixed and flexible exchange rates, and fits right in with the results obtained above. Fiscal policy affects output when exchange rates are fixed. Monetary policy fails because mandatory intervention in the foreign exchange market forces the central bank to sterilize (that means *undo*) any money supply change brought about previously. Under flexible exchange rates, monetary policy can influence income quite effectively. Fiscal policy does not work. The demand added by the government is nullified by complete crowding out via the exchange rate (see Table 5.1).

Table 5.1 **Does a policy instrument affect output?** Which instrument affects output depends on the exchange rate system. Fiscal policy works when exchange rates are fixed. If they are flexible, full crowding out of net exports occurs via exchange rate appreciation. Monetary policy works when exchange rates are flexible. Under fixed exchange rates, monetary policy is not really available. The obligation to intervene takes money-supply control out of the hands of the central bank.

	Exchange rates system	
Policy instrument	Fixed exchange rates	Flexible exchange rates
Fiscal policy	Yes	No (full crowding out via exchange rate)
Monetary policy	No (forced sterilization through intervention)	Yes

Note: International capital is assumed to be perfectly mobile.

CASE STUDY 5.1   The 1998 Asia crisis

In late 1997 and 1998 many Asian economies suffered a dramatic economic downturn. Figure 5.6 documents this for four of the largest South-east Asian countries: Indonesia, Malaysia, the Philippines and Thailand. After stunning growth until the mid-1990s, in 1998 incomes contracted by between 5% in the Philippines and 13% in Indonesia.

Industrial countries worried that falling incomes in Asia would reduce demand for their own exports, dragging them into recessions too. Policy-makers, therefore, were urged to ease monetary policy to fend off such dangers.

The Mundell–Fleming model helps understand some key features of the Asia crisis. Take the perspective of an industrial country, say France. France's economy before the crisis is at point A in Figure 5.7. For simplicity, suppose the world consists of France and South-east Asia only. Then i^W is South-east Asia's interest rate and Y^W is Asia's income.

As the crisis hits Asia and Asia's incomes fall, the demand for French exports falls. This shifts France's *IS* curve to the left, which pushes the interest rate and income towards point B. As the French interest rate moves below the world interest rate, however, international investors want to move their wealth out of French assets. This creates an excess supply of French francs. If the exchange rate is flexible, the French franc depreciates relative to Asian currencies. This makes French products more affordable for Asians, so French exports rise again. This shifts the *IS* curve back right, and it continues to do so until

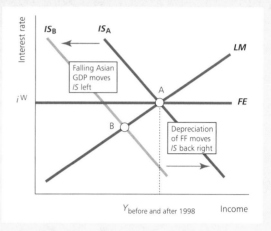

Figure 5.7

IS has returned to its original position. French income remains entirely unaffected by the depression in Asia.

Are you happy with this story? Probably not. Two things are particularly unsatisfactory:

■ First, if a depreciation of the exchange rate so easily protects us from the fall in Asian incomes, why were the industrial countries so worried in 1998, and why did some even start to ease monetary policy?

■ Second, the model says that the French franc *depreciates* and, hence, Asian currencies *appreciate*. In fact, exactly the opposite happened. As Figure 5.8 shows, all major Asian currencies depreciated substantially in 1997 and 1998: Indonesia's rupiah by more than 500%, but others too, like the Thai baht, the Philippine peso and Malaysia's ringgit, by as much as 60%.

So this cannot be the whole story. Let us refine it by looking at the situation more closely.

An important aspect to note is that Asia's crisis not only affected trade but also the international asset markets. Before the crisis, Asia's impressive growth performance had attracted international investment on a grand scale, and, as we can tell with the benefit of hindsight, made investors virtually blind with regard to the underlying risk. This changed rather abruptly in late 1997 and 1998. The dramatic worsening in Asia's overall economic performance, plunging stock markets, political

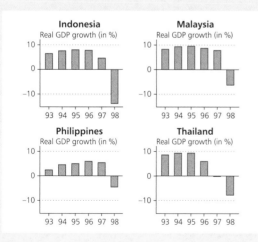

Figure 5.6

Case study 5.1 continued

Figure 5.8

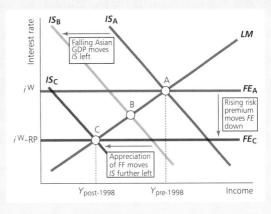

Figure 5.9

scandals and crises suddenly made investors aware of the high risk involved.

In terms of our model, investors were only willing to hold on to Asian assets if the interest rate (or expected return) exceeded the French interest rate by a risk premium RP^W. If investors see different default risks at home and abroad the international capital market equilibrium condition modifies to $i = i^W - RP^W$. If French investors are prepared to accept the higher risk perceived in Asian assets only if the expected return is, say, 5% higher than at home, then Asia's interest rate must exceed France's interest rate by 5%. Hence, $i = i^W - 5$. The two interest rates, which were about the same before the crisis, drift apart.

The percentage of non-performing loans (i.e. loans that ended in default) is one indicator of riskiness. As seen in Table 5.2, this percentage was substantially higher in 1998 than it had been in 1997 for all four countries. In the Philippines the increase is only 25%. In the other three countries it is much higher, with Malaysia suffering from a 100% jump

upwards. Taking note of this, investors respond by requiring a (higher) risk premium for holding bonds, stocks and other assets in these countries.

How does that fit into the Mundell–Fleming model? Consider Figure 5.9, in which again we let France's pre-1998 equilibrium be disturbed by the downward shift of the IS curve due to falling incomes in and exports to Asia. Now the FE curve moves down as well, however, because investors suddenly require a risk premium for holding Asian assets. As long as French interest rates exceed $i^W - RP^W$, funds flow out of Asia, making Asian currencies depreciate. This shifts the IS curve still further to the left, until a new equilibrium obtains in point C at income $Y_{\text{post-1998}}$.

Bottom line

From the perspective of other parts of the world, the real danger from the 1998 crisis in Asia did not come from the fall in Asian incomes. A flexible exchange rate would have taken care of most of this. Much more dangerous was the loss of trust in Asian assets which made Asian currencies depreciate and put exports to Asia in real jeopardy.

Data sources
GDP data are from the Asian development bank. Exchange rates and the price indexes needed to compute real exchange rates are from the IMF. Data on non-performing loans are from G. Corsetti, P. Pesenti and N. Roubini (1997), *What Caused the Asian Currency and Financial Crisis?* Part I: *A macroeconomic overview.* NBER Working Paper 6833, Table 22.

Table 5.2 **Default risk in South-east Asian countries.** Non-performing loans as % of banks' assets

	Indonesia	Malaysia	Philippines	Thailand
1997	11	7.5	5.5	15
1998	20	15	7	25

5.3 The algebra of monetary and fiscal policy in the Mundell–Fleming model

A little algebra illustrates the policy options more clearly.

Flexible exchange rates

The determinants of equilibrium income under flexible exchange rates have already been derived in Chapter 4. Combining the *FE* curve and the *LM* curve we obtained

$$Y = \frac{M}{k} + \frac{b}{k} i^{\text{World}} \qquad\qquad \textbf{Equilibrium income}$$

So there are only two variables that can stimulate output. That is the money supply, which transmits into output changes according to

$$\Delta Y = \frac{1}{k} \Delta M$$

and the world interest rate. Changes in the world interest rate increase output by

$$\Delta Y = \frac{b}{k} \Delta i^{\text{World}}$$

Fiscal policy or other components of autonomous demand do not affect equilibrium income. Any increases in $G, \bar{I}$ or Y^{World} are completely crowded out by exchange rate appreciation. The exchange rate effect can be seen by looking at

$$R = \frac{1 - c + m_1}{m_2 + x_2}\left(\frac{M}{k} + \frac{b}{k} i^{\text{World}}\right) - \frac{\bar{I} + G + x_1 Y^{\text{World}}}{m_2 + x_2} + \frac{b i^{\text{World}}}{m_2 + x_2}$$

Equilibrium exchange rate

which is replicated from Chapter 4, section 4.4.

Fixed exchange rates

Under fixed exchange rates, equilibrium income is obtained by substituting the *FE* curve ($i = i^{\text{World}}$) into (4.9) and solving for Y:

$$Y = \frac{m_2 + x_2}{1 - c + m_1} R - \frac{b}{1 - c + m_1} i^{\text{World}} + \frac{1}{1 - c + m_1}(G + \bar{I})$$

$$+ \frac{x_1}{1 - c + m_1} Y^{\text{World}}$$

R is now a policy variable controlled by the government. It can raise output via the multiplier

$$\Delta Y = \frac{m_2 + x_2}{1 - c + m_1} \Delta R$$

The money supply is endogenous: that is, outside government or central bank control. Fiscal policy is effective and raises output via the multiplier

$$\Delta Y = \frac{1}{1 - c + m_1} \Delta G$$

which corresponds to the one we had obtained in Chapter 2.3 (letting taxes be independent of income ($t = 0$)). Finally, both interest and income changes in the rest of the world spill over into the domestic economy via the multipliers

$$\Delta Y = \frac{-b}{1 - c + m_1} \Delta i^{\text{World}}$$

$$\Delta Y = \frac{x_1}{1 - c + m_1} \Delta Y^{\text{World}}$$

5.4   Comparative statics versus adjustment dynamics

Comparative static analysis looks at how equilibrium positions change after policy changes. It says nothing about whether and how the economy gets there.

If an equilibrium is stable, the economy moves towards this equilibrium from all disequilibrium situations.

Dynamic analysis looks at whether an equilibrium is stable, and traces the transition from one equilibrium to another.

The purpose of the Mundell–Fleming model is to show how equilibrium is affected by policy instruments or other factors which are exogenous to the model. It *compares* equilibria, situations in which the economy has come to rest, in which variables do not change any more and become static. This kind of reasoning is called comparative static analysis.

Comparative static analysis does not say anything about how long it takes to reach the new equilibrium. Nor does it describe how the endogenous variables evolve as we move from the old equilibrium to the new one. In fact, comparative static analysis does not even indicate whether the new equilibrium will ever be reached, that is whether the equilibrium is stable. These are all aspects of the dynamic analysis of a model. A thorough treatment of these dynamic aspects calls for the explicit introduction of a time dimension into the model which recognizes that not all reactions take place instantaneously.

We will not make stability an issue here, as this can be shown to apply in the Mundell–Fleming model under reasonable dynamic specifications. Also, we will not spell out an explicit dynamic version of the model, although we will do so in the context of more developed models in Chapters 7 and 8. What we will try to do is develop an intuitive understanding of what transition paths look like.

The first thing to realize is that *some variables are slow while others are fast*. Hence some markets may clear quickly when pushed out of equilibrium and others may take quite some time to adjust.

Empirical note. Multiplier effects take up to two years to materialize fully.

A good rule of thumb is that *prices in financial markets adjust instantaneously*. Examples are the interest rate and the exchange rate. This keeps the money market and the foreign exchange market, where the interest rate and the exchange rate play key roles in equating supply and demand, in equilibrium at all times. In the goods market *output adjusts slowly*. If firms observe an increase or a fall in sales, they need time to gear up or scale down production. Changing production, and, hence, income, may take time to affect consumption. All this adds up to quite a time lag for the multiplier effect to materialize. In a similar vein, following an exchange rate change importers and exporters may need time to get out of existing contracts or business relationships, to find new suppliers or enter new markets.

The crux is that we may expect to be *on* the *LM* curve and *on* the *FE* curve all the time, even while moving from one overall equilibrium to another. We may well be *off* the *IS* curve for extended periods of time, however. If the economy is to the left of *IS*, firms register an excess demand for goods and services and gradually increase output. To the right of *IS*, firms experience insufficient demand and reduce output.

What does this mean in the cases discussed above? Consider the increase of government expenditure under fixed exchange rates. The expenditure increase shifts *IS* out to IS_1 immediately. As long as income does not respond yet, the money market and the foreign exchange market can remain in equilibrium at A, and the goods market registers an excess demand. As income grows a little bit, the demand for money grows a little bit, and the central bank must engineer a corresponding money-supply increase by intervening in the foreign exchange market. This shifts *LM* somewhat to the right, but not into its eventual equilibrium position LM_1 yet. As income continues to grow, it keeps pulling *LM* to the right until all markets finally settle into the new equilibrium point B (see Figure 5.10).

Figure 5.11 contrasts the comparative static with the dynamic effect of a government expenditure increase by plotting both effects along the time axis. The comparative static effect states *where* equilibrium goes. The dynamic adjustment path states *when* output is where, at each point in time.

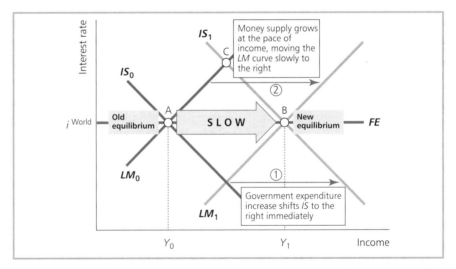

Figure 5.10 (Fixed exchange rates.) Comparative static analysis says that an increase of government spending shifts the economy's equilibrium point from A to B if exchange rates are fixed. Since output (and income) is a slow variable, however, the adjustment from A to B may be slow as well. Temporarily, while firms take measures to gear up production, the goods market remains to the left of IS_1 (the equilibrium line) in disequilibrium.

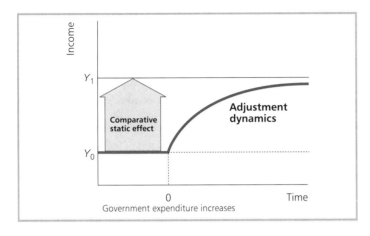

Figure 5.11 (Fixed exchange rates.) This graph shows the time profile of output, after government spending increased. The black line shows the full comparative-static effect, the increase in equilibrium income. Adjustment dynamics is slower, and only gradually approaches the new equilibrium.

5.5   Adjustment dynamics with expected depreciation

Things become trickier if we consider a money-supply increase under flexible exchange rates. Initially, the money-supply increase shifts LM to the right into LM_1 (see Figure 5.13). This means that the new long-run equilibrium moves to B, but also the short-run or temporary equilibrium determined by the intersection between FE and LM. This requires income to rise. Since this takes time, the economy cannot move out to B immediately. No short-run equilibrium appears feasible!

The solution to this puzzle is hidden in the foreign exchange market equilibrium. When deriving it in Chapter 4 we simplified the uncovered interest parity condition to $i = i^{\text{World}}$ by assuming that individuals expect no depreciation. This is a useful assumption in comparative static analysis, which describes situations where the exchange rate has settled to a constant value. In the context of dynamic adjustment from one equilibrium to another, it is less appropriate. As the exchange rate may move towards a new value, international investors must be allowed to take that into account when allocating portfolios. So equilibrium in the foreign exchange market is given by the equation

$$i = i^{\text{World}} + \frac{E^e_{+1} - E}{E} \qquad \text{Uncovered interest parity} \quad (5.1)$$

As we have already noted, the second term on the right-hand side, expected depreciation, moves the horizontal FE curve up or down. Since expectations exercise this pivotal role during dynamic adjustment, we need to take a closer look at how expectations of future exchange rates are being formed.

Exchange rate expectations

A useful way of thinking about exchange rate expectations is in terms of some exchange rate equilibrium E^* and deviations from it. It facilitates the discussion if the exchange rate and the equilibrium exchange rate are expressed in logarithms as e and e^*, respectively. The advantage of this is that the linear difference $e^* - e$ simply proxies the percentage deviation of the exchange rate from equilibrium. If individuals harbour the picture of an inherent tendency for the exchange rate to move towards its equilibrium, depreciation expectations may be formed according to

$$\frac{E^e_{+1} - E}{E} = d(e^* - e) \qquad\qquad \text{Expected depreciation} \qquad (5.2)$$

The parameter d measures the speed at which the exchange rate is expected to regress to e^*. If $e^* = 10$, $e = 9.9$ and $d = 0.5$, expected depreciation is 0.05 or 5%. Upon substituting equation (5.2) into (5.1) the foreign exchange market equilibrium condition becomes

$$i = i^{\text{World}} + d(e^* - e) \qquad\qquad\qquad\qquad (5.3)$$

Equation (5.3) can be drawn as a straight line with slope $-d$ in an i-e diagram. Its position is determined by the world interest rate and the equilibrium exchange rate (Figure 5.12, panel (a)). The message of this line is that the foreign exchange market may be in equilibrium for many different interest rates, if only the interest rate is combined with the right exchange rate. If i falls short of i^{World} this must be made up by an expected appreciation. For this to happen, the exchange rate first has to rise above its equilibrium value. Then investors expect it to appreciate (fall) back towards its equilibrium value.

Panel (b) in Figure 5.12 shows what this implies in the current context of a money-supply increase under flexible exchange rates (compare also Figure 5.13). First, note that at the new static equilibrium point B, the *IS* curve has shifted to the right due to real depreciation. Hence the money supply increase raises the equilibrium exchange rate from e^*_0 to e^*_1. This moves the foreign exchange market equilibrium line in Figure 5.12, panel (b), to the right into FE_1, so that it passes through the point marked by the world interest rate and the new equilibrium exchange rate (B).

In Figure 5.13 the *LM* curve has shifted to LM_1. Output is stuck at Y_0 in the very short run. At this income level the money market only clears if the

(a)

(b)

Figure 5.12 (Flexible exchange rates.) If investors expect the exchange rate to regress back towards equilibrium e^*, foreign exchange market equilibrium may obtain at different interest rates, depending on where the exchange rate is relative to e^* (panel (a)). If a money-supply increase raises Y under flexible exchange rates, the equilibrium exchange rate rises, shifting the generalized *FE* curve to the right (panel (b)).

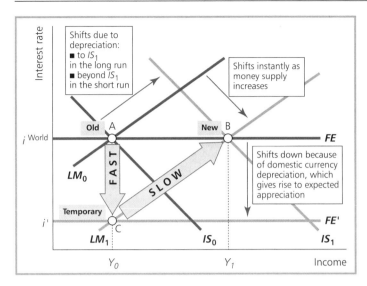

Figure 5.13 (Flexible exchange rates.) A money-supply increase shifts *LM* to the right. Only *i* and *e* can respond quickly. *Y* remains stuck at Y_0. Two things happen. The interest rate falls to *i'*, since only this equilibrates the money market. Since this drives investors out, the exchange rate depreciates. To restore open interest parity $i = i^{World} + d(e_1^* - e)$, *e* needs to rise above e_1^* (see also panel (b), Figure 5.14). This shifts *IS* right, even beyond IS_1. Gradually, as *Y* rises, the economy moves along LM_1 towards B while the exchange rate eases back towards e_1^*.

interest rate drops to *i'*. At this rate nobody wants domestic bonds. The exchange rate depreciates. As it rises above the new equilibrium exchange rate, prospects of future appreciation of the domestic currency emerge. As soon as the exchange rate has depreciated to *e'*, appreciation expectations have grown large enough to compensate for the interest rate deficit. Investors are again indifferent between holding domestic or foreign bonds. The foreign exchange market is in equilibrium.

Depreciation has shifted *IS* to the right – even beyond IS_1, as at *e'* the exchange rate is higher than e_1^*, the new equilibrium rate which determines the position of IS_1. This creates excess demand for goods and services, and income begins to rise. This raises the demand for money, the interest rate begins to rise, and the exchange rate inches back towards e_1^*. Appreciation expectations become smaller. The *FE* curve starts to move up. This process continues, and the point of intersection between the *FE* and the *LM* curves gradually moves up LM_1 until it reaches point B.

Exchange rate overshooting

Almost in passing we have hit upon a very important insight. Take a look at the adjustment dynamics triggered by a money-supply increase under flexible exchange rates (see Figure 5.14). Panel (a) plots output. Output dynamics is unexciting, the normal thing. Output must rise in the long run, but it needs time to achieve this.

Panel (b) in Figure 5.14 shows the exchange rate, where something puzzling is happening. The exchange rate needs to depreciate in the long run (comparative static effect), from e_0^* to e_1^*. The immediate, short-run response of the exchange rate is to move beyond where it must go in the long run. After that the exchange rate gradually adjusts to its long-run level, apparently from the wrong side. This immediate, short-run overreaction of the exchange rate has become famous under the term exchange rate overshooting. It is considered a key characteristic of flexible exchange rates and will play an important role in later chapters.

Exchange rate overshooting occurs if the immediate response of the exchange rate to a disturbance (such as a money-supply increase) exceeds the response that is needed in the long run.

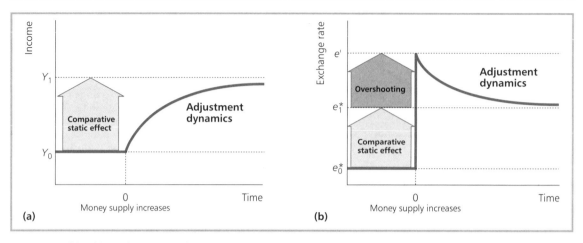

(a)

(b)

Figure 5.14 (Flexible exchange rates.) The Mundell–Fleming model suggests that the comparative static effects of a money-supply increase are higher income and a higher (depreciated) exchange rate. The exchange rate's response is quick and could bring about the required adjustment immediately. Output adjustment is slow. Output cannot respond immediately. In the short run, the exchange rate must also bear the output's burden of adjustment and overshoot its long-run response.

CASE STUDY 5.2 | **Switzerland and the eurozone**

Flexible exchange rates often shield countries from negative developments abroad. But this is not always so, as the Swiss experience during Europe's sovereign debt crisis shows.

Figure 5.15 puts Switzerland's pre-crisis equilibrium at point A.

Before the financial crisis broke, international investors did not attribute any particular risk to government bonds or other investments in Eurozone countries. Also, there was no relevant trend in

the Swiss franc/euro exchange rate, as shown in Figure 5.16, panel (a).

So the equilibrium condition for the international capital market, Switzerland's *FE* curve, may have read

$$i = i^{€} \tag{1}$$

When investors became itchy after 2009, initially about Greece's solvency, as documented by

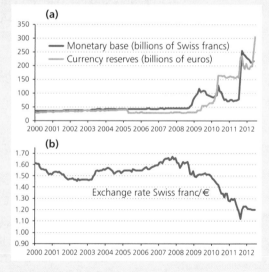

Figure 5.15

Figure 5.16

Case study 5.2 continued

skyrocketing insurance premiums (so-called credit default swaps or CDSs) for Greek government bonds and massive credit rating downgrades, but subsequently about the solvency of further Eurozone members and about the stability and the survival of the euro at large, they looked for safe havens outside the Eurozone. A preferred refuge in times of crisis is the Swiss franc. The ensuing massive influx of financial investments into Switzerland put massive appreciation pressure on the Swiss franc. Panel (a) in Figure 5.16 shows this downward trend, which started in 2008, but accelerated in 2010 when the financial crisis morphed into a debt crisis. This, in turn lured even more investors and speculators into the Swiss franc, hoping to profit from a further strengthening of Switzerland's currency. In terms of Figure 5.15, expected appreciation of the Swiss franc and a much lower risk in Switzerland as compared to the Eurozone drove a significant wedge between Eurozone interest rates and Swiss interest rates. This shifted Switzerland's FE curve down into the position

$$i = i^{\text{€}} - RP^{\text{€}} + \varepsilon_{+1}^{e} \qquad (2)$$

with $RP^{\text{€}}$ being the risk premium for assets denominated in euros and $\varepsilon_{+1}^{e} < 0$ denoting expected future depreciation against the euro. Left to market forces, this development threatened Swiss exports

and to drive the economy into a deep recession at point B in Figure 5.15. Alarmed by this, and under pressure from exporters and trade unions, the Swiss National Bank (SNB) began to intervene in the foreign exchange market by purchasing dollars and euros. This shows both in the increase of foreign reserves and in the rise of the money supply (Figure 5.16, panel (b)). But since this could only slow but not halt the appreciation trend, the SNB published a media release on 6 September 2011, stating: *The SNB is aiming for a substantial and sustained weakening of the Swiss franc. (I)t will no longer tolerate a EUR/CHF exchange rate below CHF 1.20. (It) will enforce this minimum rate with the utmost determination and is prepared to buy foreign currency in unlimited quantities.*

This strong, public statement of intent essentially aimed at breaking appreciation expectations, shifting the FE curve back up again and thus actually relieving the pressure on the exchange rate. In the ideal case this could halt the appreciation trend and discourage speculators without really requiring further interventions. And it actually worked – for a while. In May 2012 new massive interventions were needed again to defend the minimum exchange rate, signalling that this game between the SNB and global investors may not be over yet.

5.6 # When prices move

Remember our first encounter with money in the circular flow model in Chapter 1? By means of a numerical illustration we saw that endowing people with more money can lead to either more output (at given prices) or higher prices (for given output). The standard version of the Mundell–Fleming model considered so far focuses on the first option: at the current price level, firms are prepared to produce any volume of goods and services that aggregate demand desires. This assumption may be a useful approximation when there is slack in the economy. However, it is misleading when the economy operates at full capacity. This section gives a first flavour of this. A more general treatment of the interaction between aggregate supply and demand will be postponed until Chapters 7 and 8.

Consider an economy that operates at full capacity or potential income Y^*, employing all factors of production. It is reasonable to assume that if equilibrium income as determined by the fixed-price Mundell–Fleming model exceeds Y^*, firms raise prices. If aggregate demand falls short of Y^*, prices fall. We look at those policy measures that previously were found to affect equilibrium output: fiscal policy under fixed exchange rates, and monetary policy under flexible exchange rates.

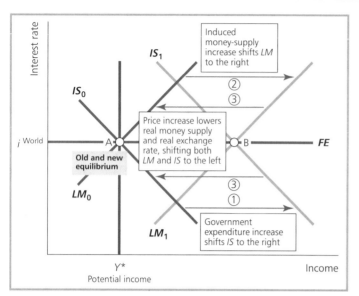

Figure 5.17 (Fixed exchange rates.) Raising government spending under fixed exchange rates leads from A to B. Since B is above potential income Y^*, firms start to raise prices. Rising prices make the real exchange rate EP^{World}/P appreciate, shifting IS back to the left. The real money supply M/P is also reduced, moving LM back to the left. The economy returns to A. Income and real money circulation are the same as before. Since government spending has fully crowded out net exports, the real exchange rate is now lower.

Let the economy be at equilibrium point A in Figure 5.17. Let the government increase spending and the exchange rate be fixed. In a by-now familiar fashion, as G increases, IS shifts out to IS_1. The economy moves to B if output may temporarily be raised beyond Y^*. Income at B exceeds potential income. So prices move up. This affects the goods market, since it makes the real exchange rate EP^{World}/P appreciate, which shifts IS back to the left. But it also affects the real money supply. We pause here to see why.

Remember that the main purpose for holding money is to facilitate transactions. Transactions are purchases of real things, such as shoes, wine, bread or haircuts. To be able to buy the same basket of goods again and again the money balances held must have a constant buying power. In other words, the demand for money shown again in Figure 5.18 is a demand for real money balances. If the price level doubles, the nominal demand for money also doubles.

On the other hand, the central bank controls the *nominal* supply of money M. Previously we did not explicitly distinguish between the nominal money supply M and the real money supply M/P, since the price level was considered fixed. With the price level, which is an index anyway, being set to 1, which we may do without changing the argument, nominal and real money were even identical.

If the price level can change, it can affect the real money supply. If prices rise, the real money supply M/P obviously falls, even if the central bank keeps M unchanged. The vertical money supply line then shifts to the left. Individuals are willing to make do with lower cash balances only at a higher interest rate. So the new money market equilibrium now obtains at the same level of income, but at a higher interest rate. Hence, if the price level rises with M remaining constant, the LM curve shifts to the left – just as it does when the nominal money supply is reduced at a constant price level.

So, returning to Figure 5.17, the price increase originating from the goods market shifts both the IS curve and the LM curve to the left. This process can only come to a halt when both curves are back in their original positions and the economy is back in the original equilibrium point A.

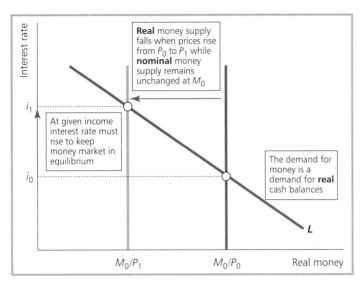

Figure 5.18 At any interest rate the private sector exercises a demand for real money L, as given by the negatively sloped line. The money supply M is nominal and fixed at M_0. A price increase from P_0 to P_1 shifts the vertical money-supply line to the left. The real money demand is only reduced to this lower level if the interest rate rises.

This has two interesting implications: since the position of the LM curve is determined by the real money supply, LM being back in its old position means that the real money supply is unchanged. Hence the nominal money supply and the price level must have increased by the same percentage. The position of the IS curve is determined by government expenditures and the real exchange rate. Since government expenditures have increased, net exports must be lower. Hence the real exchange rate must have appreciated. This was brought about by a price increase in the face of a constant exchange rate and foreign price level.

Consider next a money-supply increase under flexible exchange rates. The argument is very similar to the previous one (see Figure 5.19). The money-supply increase shifts LM to the right. As this tends to push the interest rate

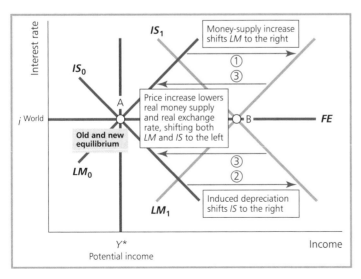

Figure 5.19 Under flexible exchange rates, a money-supply increase leads from A to B. Since B is above potential income Y^*, prices rise. This reduces the real money supply, shifting LM back to the left. The real exchange rate is also reduced, moving IS back to the left and the economy back to A. Income, real money circulation and the real exchange rate are the same as before.

down, the home currency depreciates. This stimulates net exports, shifting the *IS* curve to the right. At point B output exceeds full capacity output Y^* and prices begin to rise. Rising prices reduce the real money supply, shifting *LM* to the left. Rising prices also make domestic goods more expensive compared with foreign goods. The real exchange rate falls (appreciates), which reduces net exports and shifts *IS* to the left. This process continues until both the money market and the goods market equilibrium curves are back in their original positions and the economy is at point A again. That means that the real money supply is the same as before the central bank increased the nominal money supply. So prices rose by just as much as the nominal money supply. It also means that the real exchange rate is unchanged. So the exchange rate depreciated by just as much as the price level rose.

5.7   Today's exchange rate and the future

Interesting insights into the behaviour of exchange rates are obtained by writing out full employment equilibria such as A in terms of algebraic equations.

Let us be more general than we were in Figure 5.19. There we assumed that financial investors do not expect the exchange rate to change, so that $i = i^{World}$ was the foreign exchange market equilibrium condition. In general, if for whatever reason the exchange rate is expected to depreciate, open interest parity in the general form given in equation (5.1) above holds. Introducing some shorthand, this foreign exchange market equilibrium condition can be written as

$$i = i^{World} + \varepsilon^e_{+1} \qquad \text{Open interest parity or } FE \text{ curve} \qquad (5.4)$$

where $\varepsilon^e_{+1} \equiv (E^e_{+1} - E)/E$ is the expected rate of depreciation from today until next period. As long as expected depreciation remains the same, the economy's full employment equilibrium is at point C (Figure 5.20).

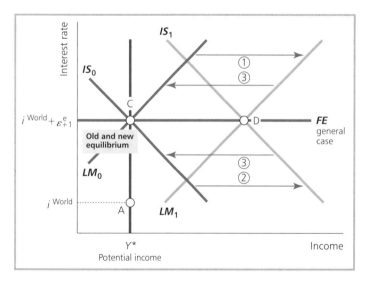

Figure 5.20 (Flexible exchange rates.) Expected depreciation drives a wedge between the domestic and the world interest rate. *FE* is in the blue position and the new long-run equilibrium is in C. Just as described in Figure 5.19 for the case of zero depreciation expectations, attempts to stimulate income by increasing the money supply are sooner or later nullified by price increases of equal magnitude.

Point C, or other equilibria on the vertical line over Y^* that would result if the world interest rate or expected depreciation changed, may be thought to obtain either in the long run, after prices have had enough time to adjust, or even in the short run, if prices are very quick to adjust.

At equilibrium point C the interest rate and income remain unchanged. In order to keep the *IS* curve in the position that passes through C, the real exchange rate EP^{World}/P must remain unchanged. Suppose the real exchange rate required to make *IS* pass through C is 1, so that $EP^{World} = P$, or, taking logarithms (denoted by lower-case letters)

$$e + p^{World} = p \hspace{2cm} \text{Long-run } \textit{IS} \text{ curve} \hspace{1cm} (5.5)$$

At C the money market is also in equilibrium. Suppose the money demand function is semi-logarithmic (that means, the logarithm of real money demand depends on Y and i):

$$m - p = kY^* - hi \hspace{2cm} \text{Semi-logarithmic } \textit{LM} \text{ curve} \hspace{1cm} (5.6)$$

Now let $Y^* = 0$, $p^{World} = 0$ and $i^{World} = 0$ (we can do this, since these exogenous variables may be at any arbitrary value anyway). Then substitute equation (5.5) into (5.6) for p and (5.4) into (5.6) for i to obtain $m - e = -h\varepsilon^e_{+1}$. Solving this equation for e gives

$$e = m + h\varepsilon^e_{+1} \hspace{6cm} (5.7)$$

The present exchange rate responds one-to-one to changes in the money supply, but it also reflects depreciation expected to occur tomorrow. This can be brought out in a slightly different form if we note that $\varepsilon^e_{+1} = e^e_{+1} - e$, which means that the expected rate of depreciation equals the difference between the logarithm of tomorrow's expected exchange rate and the logarithm of the current exchange rate. Substituting this into equation (5.7) and solving for e gives

$$e = \alpha m + (1 - \alpha)e^e_{+1} \hspace{5cm} (5.8)$$

where $\alpha = 1/(1 + h)$. The equation makes the important statement that today's exchange rate is a weighted average of today's money supply and the exchange rate expected to prevail tomorrow. So whatever the market expects to happen to the exchange rate in the future (an appreciation or a depreciation) in an almost self-fulfilling fashion already happens today.

Using this equation, the 2002 exchange rate depends on the concurrent money supply and on the exchange rate expected for 2013:

$$e_{2012} = \alpha m_{2012} + (1 - \alpha)e^e_{2013} \hspace{4cm} (5.9)$$

Does this mean that the investors' time horizon ends in 2013? No, for if we know that one year's exchange rate always depends on next year's exchange rate and the current money supply, we should anticipate that equation (5.8) also links the 2013 exchange rate to the exchange rate expected for 2014:

$$e^e_{2013} = \alpha m^e_{2013} + (1 - \alpha)e^e_{2014} \hspace{4cm} (5.10)$$

Taken together, equations (5.9) and (5.10) provide a link between 2014 and the exchange rate in 2012. Equation (5.10) leaves it open, though, how e^e_{2011} is being determined. This is not difficult to find out, however. Since equation (5.10) links any two periods in time, we can move it one year ahead to see that e^e_{2014} depends on e^e_{2015}, and two years ahead to see that e^e_{2015} depends on e^e_{2016}. Actually, we can do this as often as we want. By doing it ten more times, we notice that the 2012 exchange rate depends on the exchange rate expected for the year 2026. And this once again depends on what we expect for 2027. The important lesson to be learned from this exercise is that today's exchange rate is linked to all expected future developments. If we come to expect the exchange rate to depreciate two years from now, this will make the exchange rate depreciate today.

But while we used the Mundell–Fleming model and focused on the exchange rate to arrive at this important result, other examples where prices depend on expected future price are frequent in economics. These examples are not limited to financial markets. In addition to stock prices being influenced by expected future stock prices, real estate prices may be driven by expected future price movements, and so may prices for precious metals, or even for tulips. This can trigger waves of speculation and create enormous risks for entire economies. Although this insight is not new, the financial and debt crises that haunt the global economy since 2007 alerted economists that these risks may be far greater than previously believed. The next section takes a first look at these risks.

5.8 Speculative bubbles

Looking at equation (5.8) we may ask whether there is a time path for the exchange rate along which whatever investors expect for next period does actually come true. In formal terms: what would a time path look like along which $e^e_{+1} = e_{+1}$? In order to find an answer, we may substitute this into equation (5.8) which then becomes $e = \alpha m + (1 - \alpha)e_{+1}$. This equation links exchange rates observed at different points in time. Such an equation is called a *first-order linear difference equation* (see Box 5.2). If we show the usually omitted time subscript t and keep the money supply constant at $m_t = \overline{m}$, the equation may be rewritten as:

$$e_{t+1} - \frac{1}{1 - \alpha} e_t = -\frac{\alpha}{1 - \alpha} \overline{m} \tag{5.11}$$

BOX 5.2 First-order linear difference equations: solution recipes

Dynamic equations link values of a variable observed at different points in time. The simplest example of a dynamic equation is a *first-order linear difference equation*. The general form of such an equation is

$$x_{t+1} + ax_t = b$$

The variable x is observed at times t and $t + 1$, while $a \neq -1$ and b are parameters. The equilibrium value x' at which x does not change $(x' = x_{t+1} = x_t)$ is given by

$$x' = \frac{b}{1 + a} \tag{2}$$

The solution recipe for equation (1) is (for a proof see any maths textbook):

$$x_t = x' + (x_0 - x')(-a)^t$$

This means that at any time t the variable x is at its equilibrium value x' plus a term that accounts for the deviation from this equilibrium. This deviation is determined by the initial deviation from x' at time $t = 0$, multiplied by some current weight. Whether this weight $(-a)^t$ increases or decreases over time depends on the absolute value of a. If $a < -1$ the weight increases monotonically. If $a > 1$ the weight grows in an oscillating fashion. If $-1 < a < 1$ the weight decreases either in an oscillating or monotonic fashion. Then the process is stable and x converges towards its equilibrium value x'.

Fundamentals and bubbles

The stationary equilibrium e', the equilibrium at which the exchange rate does not change any more, is obtained by postulating $e' = e_t = e_{t+1}$ and substituting this into equation (5.11). Solving for e' yields

$$e' = \overline{m} \tag{5.12}$$

This equilibrium is determined by the relevant exogenous variables of the model, the so-called fundamentals. Here only the money supply shows up, because we assumed other fundamentals to be zero.

Fundamentals are exogenous variables that determine the equilibrium of an economy or a market.

The general solution to equation (5.11) is a bit more complex. But we may follow the recipe provided in Box 5.2 and make use of equation (5.12) to obtain

$$e_t = \overline{m} + (e_0 - \overline{m})\left(\frac{1}{1 - \alpha}\right)^t \tag{5.13}$$

This equation says that at any point in time the exchange rate is determined by two factors:

(i) by its equilibrium value, which is determined by the fundamental variables, which here is the exogenous money supply $\overline{m}$;
(ii) by the deviation from its equilibrium value, described by the second term in equation (5.13).

This second term in equation (5.13) has a peculiar and potentially worrisome property. Note that since $1/(1 - \alpha) > 1$, which follows from $0 < \alpha \equiv 1/(1 + h) < 1$, the weight $(1/(1 - \alpha))^t$ keeps growing over time. Therefore, any initial deviation from its stationary equilibrium grows bigger and bigger. Figure 5.21 illustrates this.

If at time 0 the exchange rate is at its equilibrium value $\overline{m}$ the second term on the right-hand side of equation (5.12) vanishes and the exchange rate develops along the horizontal line, the path numbered 3 in the diagram. Any deviation from the equilibrium value at time 0, no matter whether it is negative or positive, becomes bigger and bigger over time. The exchange rate

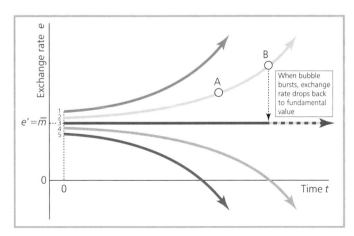

Figure 5.21 The graphs show five examples of time paths along which the exchange rate moves as expected. Along the horizontal path, the exchange rate is not expected to and does not change. This is called the fundamental equilibrium. Along the other paths the exchange rate moves further and further away from its fundamental value, simply because it is expected to move away. Such diverging paths driven by expectations are called bubbles. When bubbles burst, as in point B, the exchange rate returns to its fundamental value.

In a speculative bubble investors pay a price that exceeds the fundamental value of an asset because they anticipate the price to be even higher tomorrow.

follows an explosive path that leads further and further away from the equilibrium value. Examples are the paths numbered 1, 2, 4 and 5. This development occurs despite the fact that the fundamental variable, the money supply, remains unchanged.

The paths that lead further and further away from the stationary equilibrium, the equilibrium determined by fundamental variables, are called speculative bubbles, or just bubbles. When such a bubble is under way, investors typically do not purchase the involved asset or good because they want to own and use or keep it, but because they want to profit from expected future price increases. Such speculators do not care whether the price of an asset is justified by its fundamental value, as long as they expect the price to be sufficiently higher tomorrow.

Since in our example investors base their expectations on the underlying model, the Mundell–Fleming model with flexible prices, the described bubbles may be called *rational* speculative bubbles. Along all bubble paths shown in Figure 5.21 no errors are being made and the involved three markets are in equilibrium:

1 *Goods market*: since prices are assumed to be flexible, they always move to equate supply and demand in the goods market, so that $Y = Y^*$. This implies that prices exactly follow the exchange rate to keep the real exchange rate unchanged, that is $e = p$ (with $p^{\text{World}} = 0$).
2 *Money market*: since, say in the case of bubble #2, prices rise at an accelerating pace while the nominal money supply and income remain constant at $\bar{m}$ and Y^*, respectively, the real money supply falls and the interest rate increases period after period (see equation (5.6)).
3 *Foreign exchange market*: in the foreign exchange market the equilibrium condition $i = i^{\text{World}} + e^e_{+1} - e$ holds. In a point such as A in Figure 5.21 financial investors are indifferent between assets at home or abroad because the steadily increasing interest rate on domestic assets is counterbalanced by the expectation of a matching depreciation of the domestic currency.

When bubbles collapse

Economic history provides many examples of speculative bubbles. Notable examples on record are the Dutch Tulip Bubble (1634–38), the South Sea Bubble (1720), the Stock Market Bubble of the Roaring Twenties (1924–29), the Dot-com Bubble (1995–2000) and the recent real estate bubbles. What they all have in common is that they had finite lives. Important questions to ask are, therefore: how do bubbles end? And what are the consequences of the collapse of a bubble?

Suppose an economy is at point B in Figure 5.21. Suppose that by now the domestic interest rate is 10 percentage points higher than the world interest rate. Nevertheless, investors see no need to reshuffle their asset portfolio as long as they expect the domestic currency to depreciate by 10% next period. This is, as we know from equation (5.4), the equilibrium condition for the international capital market and equalizes expected returns at home and abroad. But what happens if financial investors, for whatever reason, suddenly expect no further depreciations but, instead, figure that the exchange rate will now remain where it currently is? Could the economy then simply remain in point B?

No, it could not. Not for a moment. As soon as investors expect no further depreciation, a stampede-like movement towards domestic assets sets in, for two reasons. First, at the moment, expected returns on domestic assets exceed those on foreign ones by 10 percentage points. This alone entices financial investors in search of the highest returns to shift much of their wealth into domestic assets. Second, because demand for domestic currency rockets and the domestic currency appreciates, the exchange rate e falls. The anticipation of this and, possibly, the expectation that this appreciation may continue in the future, adds to the appeal of domestic assets and increases the speed at which the exchange rate bubble collapses. A new and simultaneous equilibrium in all three markets is reached only when the exchange rate is at its stationary equilibrium level e'. Then prices have fallen by the same percentage as the exchange rate, and the real money supply has risen just enough to bring the domestic interest rate down to the level of the world interest rate.

In our simple model the bursting of the bubble has no real consequences. This is because all prices are flexible, which permits income to always remain at potential income. Reality is not like this. If, more realistically, prices are too slow to follow the crashing *nominal* exchange rate, the consequence is a substantial appreciation of the *real* exchange rate. Exports become way too expensive to compete on the world markets. They, therefore, contract quickly and the domestic economy is driven into a severe recession.

As mentioned above, speculative bubbles of the kind we just encountered in an economy wide, macroeconomic context may also be and often are at work in specific sectors of an economy. For example, the bursting of the real estate bubbles that had developed in the United States and several European countries including Britain, Greece, Ireland and Spain is often considered a key trigger of the financial crisis that erupted in 2007. We will return to this topic in Chapter 15.

Bottom line

This chapter's second look at booms and recessions leaves much of Chapter 2's and Chapter 3's **bottom lines** intact. Small changes in autonomous spending may cause large changes in income, and thus may be a cause of as well as a potential remedy for business cycle fluctuations. A refined picture has emerged, however. First, large income responses may not only be triggered by direct changes in autonomous spending. Indirect stimulation of spending via an expansion of the money supply may serve the same purpose. While we had already seen this result in Chapter 3, monetary policy works via the exchange rate in the open economy rather than directly via the interest rate. Second, which policy measures work and which do not crucially depends on the exchange rate system. The government spending multiplier of Chapter 2 only then reappears in the Mundell–Fleming model if exchange rates are fixed. Under flexible exchange rates government spending is completely crowded out by a fall in exports. Then monetary policy takes its place as an effective means of stimulating demand and income. Third, if the economy already operates at potential income, rising prices sooner or later nullify efforts to stimulate income, no matter which instrument is being used.

Finally, we encountered a first example of how speculation in financial markets may destabilize economies and put employment and real income at risk. While we took a first look at such speculative bubbles in a macroeconomic context, embedded into a version of the Mundell–Fleming model with flexible prices, we should keep in mind that similar bubbles may occur in other financial markets or even in goods markets.

CHAPTER SUMMARY

- The Mundell–Fleming model explains demand-side equilibria in the open economy as an interaction between the goods market, the money market and the foreign exchange market.

- Fiscal policy (that is, a change in government spending or a tax change) affects income when exchange rates are fixed. Under flexible exchange rates there is complete crowding out.

- Monetary policy affects output when exchange rates are flexible. When exchange rates are fixed, monetary policy is ineffective. The central bank is forced to sterilize (neutralize) any attempted money-supply increase immediately through foreign exchange market intervention.

- During the transition from one equilibrium to another, individuals may expect the exchange rate to change. Depreciation expectations affect the *FE* curve and, hence, the specifics of the adjustment process.

- Because after a disturbance the foreign exchange market and the money market adjust faster than the goods market, the exchange rate may be forced to overreact, that is, it overshoots its long-run equilibrium level.

- If the economy operates at potential output, there is full crowding out via price increases. In the case of a money-supply increase, the price increase drives the real money supply back to its original level. In the case of a government expenditure increase, the price increase makes the real exchange rate appreciate just enough to drive down net exports by as much as government expenditures increased.

- Speculative bubbles in the foreign exchange market can drive exchange rates far away from where they should be according to fundamentals. This may create significant risks for the real economy, in particular at the time when bubbles collapse.

Key terms and concepts

comparative static analysis *139*	fundamentals *151*
crowding out *131*	monetary policy *133*
dynamic analysis *139*	Mundell–Fleming model *129*
exchange rate overshooting *143*	risk premium *145*
fiscal policy *130*	speculative bubble *152*
fixed exchange rates *132*	stable equilibrium *139*
flexible exchange rates *131*	

EXERCISES

5.1 Suppose the government raises the income tax rate. What are the effects on income, the interest rate and the exchange rate
(a) with a flexible exchange rate?
(b) with a fixed exchange rate?
(Derive your results graphically, assuming perfect international capital mobility.)

5.2 The central bank reduces the money supply. What are the consequences for income, the interest rate and the exchange rate
(a) with a flexible exchange rate?
(b) with a fixed exchange rate?
(Derive your results graphically, assuming perfect international capital mobility.)

5.3 Analyze the consequences of an increase of the world interest rate. Assume fixed exchange rates and perfect international capital mobility. What might be the reason for the increasing foreign interest rate? What does the result tell you about problems of international policy coordination?

5.4 How does a devaluation of the domestic currency in a system with fixed exchange rates and perfect capital mobility affect the domestic interest rate and output?

5.5 Your country is exposed to a positive demand shock (say, foreign demand for domestic goods increases) and you are in charge of monetary and fiscal policy. Formally, your country maintains a regime of flexible exchange rates with all trading partners, but for some reason you wish to keep the exchange rate where it was before the shock. What can you do? Use the graphical apparatus of the Mundell–Fleming model to explain your answer.

5.6 Suppose that investors suddenly lose confidence in the domestic currency and expect it to depreciate by 5% every period from now on. Trace the consequences in the Mundell–Fleming model. What does the result tell you about 'self-fulfilling prophecies'? Will the induced changes in income and the (flexible) exchange rate last? (Hint: Work with the general equilibrium condition $i = i^W + \varepsilon^e_{+1}$.)

5.7 Consider Figure 5.22, which depicts returns to US and German government bonds since 1960. What do these time series tell us about investors' expectations concerning the Deutschmark/dollar exchange rate?

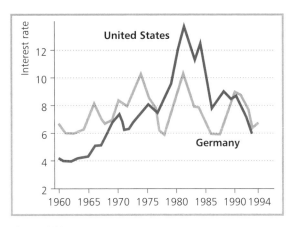

Figure 5.22

5.8 Consider the macroeconomic situation shown in Figure 5.23 in which the FE curve is vertical.
(a) Discuss the conditions under which the FE curve might be vertical.
(b) Describe the mechanisms that bring about a macroeconomic equilibrium in which all three lines intersect under flexible exchange rates, and under fixed exchange rates.
(c) Analyze the effect of expansionary monetary and fiscal policy in a system of flexible exchange rates with perfect capital immobility.

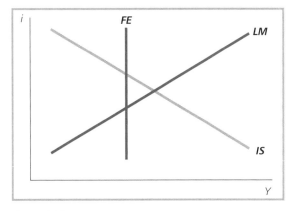

Figure 5.23

5.9 Suppose investment is independent of the interest rate and the FE curve is vertical. Sketch the macroeconomic equilibrium under fixed and flexible exchange rates and describe the mechanisms that help achieve it.

Online resources

Interactive applet on Mundell–Fleming model: basic version www.eurmacro.eu/tutor/mundellfleming.html

Interactive applet on Mundell–Fleming model: advanced version www.eurmacro.eu/tutor/advanced-mundell-fleming.html

Interactive learning module on macroeconomics of financial crises www.eurmacro.eu/xercises/crisis.html

X-ercise on 'perfect trap' www.eurmacro.eu/xercises/perfecttrap.html

Self quiz

www.eurmacro.eu/SelfQuiz/sq-ch05.html

Recommended reading

The original sources for the Mundell–Fleming model are the following:

- J. Marcus Fleming (1962) 'Domestic financial policies under fixed and floating exchange rates', IMF *Staff Papers* 9: 369–79.
- Robert A. Mundell (1962) 'Capital mobility and stabilization policy under fixed and flexible exchange rates', *Canadian Journal of Economic and Political Science* 29: 475–85.

A more recent view on the flexible vs fixed exchange rates controversy is offered by Stanley Fischer (2001) 'Exchange rate regimes: is the bipolar view correct', *Journal of Economic Perspectives* 15: 3–24.
An excellent example of how flexible the Mundell–Fleming apparatus is in terms of permitting the incorporation of new research results is Luis Céspedes, Roberto Chang and Andrés Velasco (2003) 'IS-LM-BP in the Pampas', IMF *Staff Papers* 50, Special issue: 143–56.

APPLIED PROBLEMS

EMPIRICAL RESEARCH

Explaining exchange rates

If flexible prices keep the economy at potential income at all times, the exchange rate is determined by $e = m + h\varepsilon^e_{+1}$. The equation is this compact only because, in order to demonstrate the role of monetary policy in the clearest way possible, we held other variables, including foreign ones, constant and normalized them to zero. In reality other countries do not stand still. While we change our money supply, they change theirs. Taking this into account, the exchange rate measured against that of some other country is not only determined by our money supply, but, with a negative sign, by the other country's as well. Further, in reality potential income is not zero and even changes over time. So the difference between the two countries' income levels should also feature in the exchange rate equation. In this spirit Jeffrey

Frankel (1979, 'On the mark: a theory of floating exchange rates based on real interest differences', *American Economic Review* 69: 610–22) estimates the following equation for the Deutschmark/dollar exchange rate (monthly data July 1974 to February 1978; standard errors in parentheses):

$$e = 1.33 + 0.87(m - m^*) - 0.72(y - y^*)$$
$$(0.10) \quad (0.17) \qquad (0.22)$$
$$+ 28.65(\pi^e - \pi^{*e})_{+1} \qquad R^2 = 0.80$$
$$(2.70)$$

where e, m and y are the logarithms of the exchange rate, the money supply and real income, respectively; π^e denotes expected inflation. US variables carry an asterisk.

The first coefficient after the constant is not significantly different from 1 (the t-statistic for the null hypothesis that the coefficient is 1 is $(1 - 0.87)/0.17 = 0.73$). So if the German money supply rises by 1%

relative to the US money supply, the Deutschmark depreciates by about 1%. The next coefficient states that if German income grows 1% over US income, the Deutschmark appreciates by 0.72%. The last coefficient measures the influence of the difference in inflation expectations. This difference is used as a proxy for expected depreciation: if the real exchange rate is to remain constant, then depreciation must reflect the inflation differential: $\varepsilon = \pi - \pi^*$. Then expected depreciation should equal the difference in expected inflation rates. The positive coefficient of 28.65 states that the more depreciation the market expects, the more the exchange rate depreciates today. The equation explains 80% of the variance of this exchange rate during the sample period.

Note: Frankel's equation also includes the difference in interest rates. Its coefficient is not significant and is not shown here.

WORKED PROBLEM

In and out of the United States

Net exports as a building block of the Mundell–Fleming model have been specified in equation (4.2) (Chapter 4) as (after rearranging)

$$NX = (x_2 + m_2)R + x_1 Y^{World} - m_1 Y \qquad (5.14)$$

This type of equation should explain all net exports, the current account, or certain categories of net exports. Table 5.3 gives data for US net travel and transportation receipts (TRAVEL), the effective exchange rate of the currencies of major trading partners versus the dollar (R), US GDP (Y^{USA}) and OECD GDP (Y^{OECD}). Attempting to estimate equation (5.4) from these data gives

$$\text{TRAVEL} = -6,102.1 - 273.80R + 12.35Y^{USA}$$
$$\qquad (0.36) \qquad (2.68) \qquad (0.79)$$
$$\qquad -205.71Y^{OECD}$$
$$\qquad (0.24)$$

$R^2_{adj} = 0.56$; 22 annual observations 1973–94

The equation does not perform quite as expected. While the real exchange rate index has the expected negative sign (since this index is the reciprocal of the dollar exchange rate versus other currencies), and with a t-value of 2.68 is also significant, income levels in the United States and in the OECD countries do not seem to exert the expected influence on net travel receipts. And even if the coefficients were significant, they would have the wrong sign. What may have caused this is that net travel expenditures

Table 5.3

	TRAVEL in $m	R (March 1973 = 100)	Y^{USA} in 1987 $	Y^{OECD}*
1973	−3,158	98.9	3,268.6	69.4
1974	−3,184	99.4	3,248.1	69.1
1975	−2,812	94.0	3,221.7	63.6
1976	−2,558	97.6	3,380.8	68.8
1977	−3,565	93.4	3,533.3	72.0
1978	−3,573	84.4	3,703.5	74.9
1979	−2,935	83.2	3,796.8	78.5
1980	−997	84.9	3,776.3	78.9
1981	144	101.0	3,843.1	79.3
1982	−992	111.8	3,760.3	77.3
1983	−4,227	117.4	3,906.6	78.8
1984	−8,438	128.9	4,148.5	83.8
1985	−9,798	132.5	4,279.8	86.3
1986	−7,382	103.7	4,404.5	87.2
1987	−6,481	90.9	4,539.9	90.3
1988	−1,511	88.2	4,718.6	95.3
1989	5,071	94.4	4,838.0	98.4
1990	8,978	86.0	4,897.3	100.0
1991	17,957	86.5	4,867.6	99.7
1992	20,885	83.5	4,979.3	99.4
1993	20,840	90.0	5,134.5	99.1
1994	18,000	88.6	5,342.3	103.6

*Index of industrial production (1990 = 100)

cannot adjust immediately to changes in income levels or the real exchange rate. One way to check this is to assume that the above equation only models desired net exports NX^*. Actual net exports NX only adjust by a fraction of the change in desired travel expenditures each period:

$$NX - NX_{-1} = \alpha(NX^* - NX_{-1}) \qquad (5.15)$$

Substituting equation (5.14) for NX^* into equation (5.15) and solving for NX gives

$$NX = (1 - \alpha)NX_{-1} + \alpha(x_2 + m_2)R$$
$$\qquad + \alpha x_1 Y^{World} - \alpha m_1 Y \qquad (5.16)$$

So if adjustment is slow, net exports not only depend on the current real exchange rate and domestic and foreign incomes, but also on last year's net exports. Estimating this equation with our travel data yields

$$\text{TRAVEL} = -3053.1 + 0.88 \text{ TRAVEL}_{-1} - 117.36R$$
$$\qquad (0.57) \quad (12.71) \qquad\qquad (3.38)$$
$$\qquad -12.11Y^{USA} + 782.32Y^{OECD}$$
$$\qquad (2.27) \qquad\qquad (2.79)$$

$R^2_{adj} = 0.96$; 22 annual observations 1973–94

All coefficients are now as expected and, except for the constant term, significantly different from zero. Since the estimate for the autoregressive coefficient (in front of $TRAVEL_{-1}$) is $1 - a = 0.88$, we have $a = 0.12$. This means that, within a year, travel expenditures only adjust by a fraction of 0.12 to a change in desired travel expenditures, which makes for a very slow adjustment.

YOUR TURN

Business cycle links under different exchange rate regimes

A very important result from this chapter is that domestic income is affected by income developments abroad depending on whether exchange rates are flexible or fixed. Under flexible exchange rates there is no link between domestic and foreign income. If the rest of the world falls into a recession, the exchange rate works as a buffer, making sure domestic exports and income are not affected. Under fixed exchange rates no such buffer exists and domestic income will be dragged down by falling world income.

The income data for Austria (A), Germany (D) and Norway (N) given in Table 5.4 provide an opportunity to explore this implication of the Mundell–Fleming model. For both Austria and Norway, Germany is an important trading partner. The difference between the two countries relevant for our purposes is that Austria had a more or less fixed exchange rate versus the German mark before both countries adopted the euro, while Norway's exchange rate was flexible. Hence, there should be a significant influence from German income on Austrian income, but not on Norwegian income. To test this, you may want to run a linear regression of the form $Y^A = c_0 + c_1 Y^D$ for Austria–Germany and a similar one for Norway–Germany.

As we noted in the your-turn section at the end of Chapter 2, regressing two heavily trended variables on each other may give a statistically significant result even though the two have nothing to do with

each other. This problem can be alleviated by taking first differences or growth rates of the variables involved. So you may want to run a regression of the form $\Delta Y^A / Y^A = c_0 + c_1 \Delta Y^D / Y^D$ and see whether the effect is there still for Austria but not for Norway.

Table 5.4

Year	Y^A	Y^D	Y^N
1975	54.3	52.6	44.6
1976	56.8	55.1	47.6
1977	59.4	56.8	49.4
1978	59.4	58.5	51.7
1979	62.3	61.0	53.9
1980	64.1	61.7	56.6
1981	64.0	61.8	57.2
1982	65.2	61.1	57.3
1983	67.1	62.1	59.3
1984	67.3	63.9	62.8
1985	68.8	65.3	66.0
1986	70.4	66.9	68.4
1987	71.6	67.8	69.8
1988	73.9	70.2	69.7
1989	77.0	72.8	70.4
1990	80.5	77.0	71.8
1991	83.3	85.3	74.4
1992	84.4	89.1	76.4
1993	84.8	88.1	78.5
1994	86.8	90.2	82.8
1995	88.3	91.8	86.0
1996	90.1	92.5	90.7
1997	91.3	93.8	93.8
1998	94.2	95.8	95.7
1999	96.9	97.0	96.6
2000	100.0	100.0	100.0

Enter aggregate supply

What to expect

After working through this chapter, you will understand:

1 In more detail the meaning of potential income or output.

2 How wages and employment are determined in the labour market.

3 How regulations, trade unions, and other labour market characteristics, or demographic features, may give rise to involuntary unemployment which persists in the long run.

4 Why aggregate output produced by firms may temporarily exceed or fall short of the level of potential output produced in equilibrium (or the long run).

5 How unemployment may be decomposed into a temporary and a persistent component by means of the Beveridge curve.

The aggregate supply curve shows the total quantity of goods and services supplied by all firms in the economy at different price levels.

The extreme Keynesian aggregate supply curve is horizontal, stating that, at the current price, firms are ready to produce any output that is demanded. A refined Keynesian aggregate supply curve will be introduced later.

The classical aggregate supply curve is vertical, stating that firms produce only one output Y^*, no matter how high prices are.

By now we have a good understanding of aggregate demand: that is, of what happens on the economy's demand side. This contrasts with our understanding of aggregate supply, the treatment of which so far has been, well, rather simplistic. The only time we have explicitly touched upon the issue of firms' level of output was when we discussed money in the circular flow model in Chapter 1. There we considered two extreme cases of the aggregate supply (AS) curve, the line that indicates how much output firms produce at different price levels. For easy reference, Figure 6.1 replicates these two versions. The **horizontal aggregate supply curve** shown in panel (a) is the one we employed in Chapters 2–5 in the context of the Keynesian cross, the *IS-LM* model and the Mundell–Fleming model. It is usually referred to as the extreme Keynesian aggregate supply curve. It assumes there is slack and the presence of one or more production factors in abundance. Then how much firms produce depends only on demand. At the given price level, firms supply any level of output that is demanded. But then the price level never changes! How does this correspond with the real world where continuous price changes in the form of inflation are the rule rather than an exception? Quite obviously, a horizontal aggregate supply curve cannot be the whole story.

Panel (b) in Figure 6.1 shows a **vertical aggregate supply curve**. Firms supply potential output Y^* no matter what the price level is. This curve is generally referred to as the classical aggregate supply curve, for reasons that will become evident in a moment. The drawback here is that, unless we assume that the AS curve shifts backwards and forwards all the time, only prices change, but never income. This is clearly at odds with real-world observations

Figure 6.1 The panels repeat two extreme views of an aggregate supply curve employed so far. In panel (a), firms supply any volume of goods which the market demands at the given price level. In panel (b), firms supply one specific volume of output only, no matter what the price level is.

of business cycles, evidence of which was presented in Chapter 2. Again, a vertical aggregate supply curve cannot be the whole story either.

It is time to take a closer look at the economy's supply side. This chapter will do so by addressing three questions:

1 What exactly is potential output? How is this mysterious variable Y^* really determined?
2 How is it possible that in macroeconomic equilibrium, when income and output are at the potential level Y^*, involuntary unemployment exists and persists?
3 What can induce firms to supply output levels that deviate from potential output?

6.1 Potential income and the labour market

Potential output or equilibrium output is what an economy produces if it leaves no available factors of production idle. What are these factors? It is easy to draw up a long list of what contributes to the production potential of a country: the number of factories, the number of workers, their qualifications, the area and quality of land, the climate, natural resources, property rights, the political and legal system, and so on. These factors can be grouped into two main categories: capital K and labour L. So output Y at any point in time is a function F of these two factors:

Maths note. Formally, we assume for first and second derivatives F_K, $F_L > 0$ and F_{KK}, $F_{LL} < 0$.

$$Y = F(K, L) \qquad\qquad \text{Production function} \quad (6.1)$$

The **production function** is the key to the economy's supply side. Figure 6.2 illustrates a production function and highlights two assumptions which economists usually make about its shape:

■ Output increases as either factor increases.
■ If one factor remains fixed, increases of the other factor yield smaller and smaller output gains.

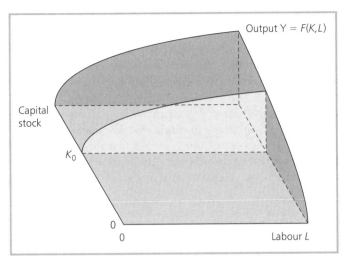

Figure 6.2 The full-scale **3D production function** shows how, for a given production technology, output rises as greater and greater quantities of capital and/or labour are being employed.

This second assumption refers to partial production functions, obtained by placing a vertical cut through the production function parallel to the axis measuring the factor that varies. Figure 6.3 shows such a partial production function, obtained in this case by fixing the capital stock at K_0.

The **partial production function** is drawn for given technology and stock of capital. The function itself tells us how much output is produced with a given labour input. For example, according to the partial production function drawn for a capital stock of K_0 in Figure 6.3, L_1 units of labour produce Y_1 units of output. The slope of the production function indicates (as an approximation) by how much output increases if we add one unit of labour. The output gain accomplished relative to a small increase in L – which is called the **marginal product of labour** – is measured by the slope of the production function. As the given capital stock is being combined with more and more labour,

Note. Strictly, the marginal product of labour is output gained by an infinitesimally small increase in labour. Our text and graph magnifies this by looking at a one-unit increase in labour.

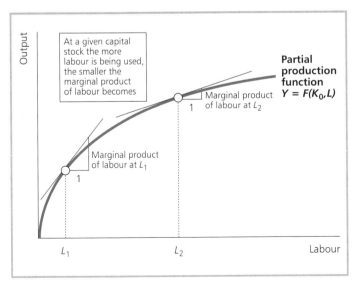

Figure 6.3 This partial production function shows how output increases as more labour is employed, while the capital stock remains fixed at K_0. The slope of $F(K_0, L)$ measures how much output is gained by a small increase of labour. The two tangent lines measure this marginal product of labour at L_1 and L_2 and indicate that it decreases as L rises.

each additional unit of labour has to make do with less and less capital. Therefore, one-unit increases of L yield smaller and smaller output increases. The
two tangent lines measure this diminishing marginal product of labour. By
similar reasoning, the marginal product of capital is also decreasing. It can be
dealt with in the same kind of diagram, and we shall do this when discussing
economic growth in Chapter 9.

So, knowing what income levels firms will generate with a particular amount
of labour, **how much labour are firms going to employ?** As we shall see straight-
away, this is just as much a matter of how much labour firms *want to employ*
as it is of how much labour workers *want to offer*. The market where the supply of and the demand for labour interact is known as the labour market.

The classical labour market

In the classical view the **labour market** is seen as being just like any other
market. The good being traded on this particular market is labour (measured
in work hours). It is supplied by (potential) workers, and demanded by firms.
The price for one unit of this good, the hourly wage, adjusts so as to balance
supply and demand.

Labour demand

Let us look at the demand for labour first. Firms demand another unit of labour whenever they think it will raise more revenue than it costs. We know
that how much (real) revenue another unit of labour produces (or how much
more output it produces) can be directly read off the partial production function. This point is repeated in the top panel of Figure 6.4.

If we measure the slope of the partial production function at all labour
input levels and transfer all these marginal products onto a separate graph
in the centre panel, the result is the downward-sloping marginal product of
labour schedule. The nice thing about this schedule is that at the same time it
is a labour-demand curve.

To see this, let the real wage, $w \equiv (W/P)$, which can be measured along the
ordinate in units of real output, be w_1. Then as long as employment falls short
of L_1 the marginal product of labour always exceeds w_1, the marginal cost
of labour, and it raises profits to increase employment. At employment levels
above L_1 the marginal cost of labour exceeds its marginal product. Hence,
given w_1, firms maximize profits by demanding exactly L_1 units of labour.
This result is re-emphasized in the bottom panel of Figure 6.4 by showcasing
the relationship between firms' (real) profits and the level of employment explicitly, as given by the equation

$$\Pi = Y(K_0, L) - w \times L \tag{6.2}$$
$$\text{Profits} = \text{Output} - \text{Wage costs}$$

Equation (6.2) defines profits as the difference between output (which equals
the firm's revenue) and wage costs. Note that the **profit curve** shown is drawn
for a given wage rate w_1. Hence, employment L_1 maximizes profits only for
this wage rate. However, the exercise may be repeated for other real wage rates,
with different results for profit-maximizing employment, of course. It turns
out that the marginal product of labour curve indicates profit-maximizing

The marginal product of
labour schedule indicates the
additional output produced by
one more unit of labour that
obtains at various levels of
employment.

The (aggregate) labour
demand curve shows the
(aggregate) quantity of labour
that firms demand at different
real wage rates.

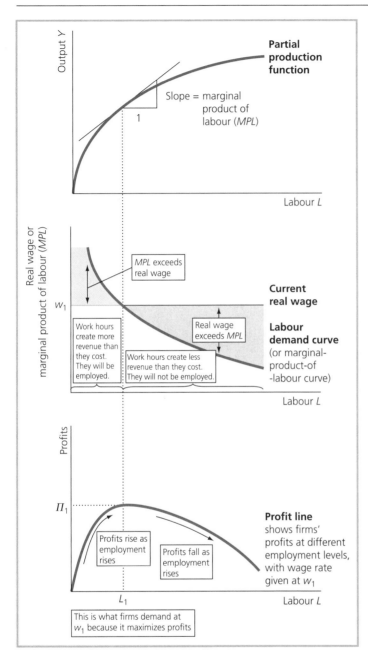

Figure 6.4 The top panel repeats a partial production function. With a fixed capital stock, output increases as labour input increases. The centre panel depicts the marginal product of labour (MPL) as a function of labour. This marginal product of labour becomes smaller as the amount of labour already used increases. The **marginal product of labour** measures how much one more unit of labour is worth to the firm. Hence, at a real wage such as w_1 the firm keeps demanding more and more labour until the marginal product of labour falls below the real wage. This happens when labour input exceeds L_1. The bottom panel visualizes the profit-maximizing nature of L_1, the level of employment suggested by the labour demand curve. Profits rise as L rises, until they peak at L_1. Further increases in employment drive profits down again.

employment and, hence, the employment that firms demand at different real wages, and thus is also the labour-demand curve.

Figure 6.5 looks at the relationship between profits, employment and the wage rate in more detail, and introduces the concept of **iso-profit lines** that will come in handy later on in this chapter. We do so in a new diagram in order not to overcrowd the previous one.

We start with point A which says that when the wage rate is w_1, employment L_1 maximizes profits at Π_1. Of course, the firm's profits increase when

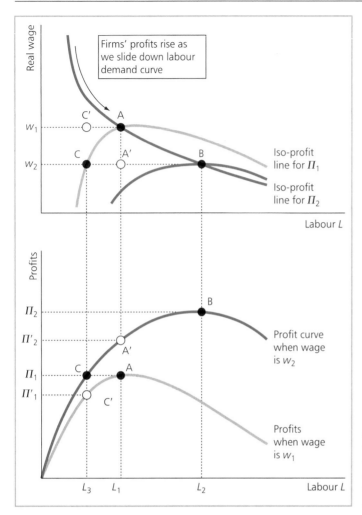

Figure 6.5 Firms' iso-profit lines have an inverted U-shape (upper panel). Iso-profit lines positioned further down are associated with higher profits. When facing a given wage demand, firms extend employment to the point where they reach the lowest possible iso-profit line. This is what makes iso-profit lines always peak where they intersect the labour demand curve. When faced with a low wage claim w_2, firms respond with high employment L_2 and enjoy high profits Π_2. A more aggressive wage demand w_1 drives down employment and the profits of firms as well.

the wage rate falls, say to w_2, even if employment remains at L_1. This is because output and revenues remain unchanged while production costs become lower. In the upper panel we move off the labour demand curve into point A'. In the lower panel we move off the initial profit curve into A', which sits on a new profit curve. Profits increase from Π_1 to Π'_2. Now this is not the highest profit the firm can generate when the wage rate is w_2. Since labour has become cheaper, additional labour generates revenue that exceeds its cost. By increasing employment to L_2, profits rise to a maximum of Π_2, as indicated by point B in the lower panel. In the upper panel this corresponds to a movement to the right onto the labour demand curve. All this generates the insight that a firm's profits increase when we move down vertically in the labour market diagram (reflected in an upward movement in the profit diagram), and profits also increase as we slide down the labour demand curve, as exemplified by points A and B.

The two inverted U-shaped curves in the upper panel are iso-profit lines. An iso-profit line combines all wage/employment combinations that generate a given level of profits. The iso-profit line for Π_1 would obviously have to pass through point A, because the combination of w_1 and L_1 generates profits Π_1. But other wage/employment combinations could generate the same level of profits. For instance, suppose firms would reduce employment to L_3. This would make profits shrink to Π'_1, of course, at unchanged wages (point C'). But a fall in the wage rate to w_2 could compensate for this and keep profits unchanged (point C). So the Π_1 iso-profit line would pass through points A and C. Similarly, if employment was raised above L_1 with the wage rate remaining at w_1, profits would drop. Again, this drop in profits could be compensated by a reduction in the wage rate. This means that the Π_1 iso-profit line bends down to the right of point A (but it always remains above the labour demand curve! Why?). Similar iso-profit lines with the shape of an inverted U, open from below, can be drawn for other profit levels. The one passing through point B represents the higher profit level Π_2. In general terms, behind the labour demand curve there is an infinite number of iso-profit lines. They all have the shape of an inverted U, and each one peaks exactly where it passes through the labour demand curve. And the lower the iso-profit line sits, the higher is the associated level of profits. Profit-maximizing firms, therefore, always want to end up as far down to the right on their labour demand curve as possible.

Labour supply

Next we need to identify the supply of labour. To avoid confusion in this chapter and further down the road, let's lay down some terminology first.

The basic element to start with when thinking about employment is the **population**. The labour market diagram in Figure 6.6 marks this with a vertical grey line. Part of the population is inactive from an employment perspective. According to OECD definitions (also used by the EU) these are all persons younger than 15 or older than 64. Subtracting the number of those that are too young or too old from the total population gives us what we may call the **active population** N. However, not all of those who could potentially be active may choose to work. Subtracting those who voluntarily stay out of employment from the active population gives us the **labour force**. Unlike the population and the active population, which simply reflect demographics at any point in time, the labour force is not a fixed number. As Figure 6.6 illustrates, it is a curve that reflects how the willingness of people to work depends on how much it pays to work. The sketch assumes that if the real wage exceeds w_2 everybody who is eligible for work also wants to work. Thus in this segment the active population and the labour force are the same. As the real wage moves below w_2, however, more and more people withdraw from the labour force, giving the labour-force curve a positive slope in this segment. At the lower end nobody is prepared to work for less than w_0. So here the labour force is zero.

Put another way, the labour force is that part of the population that can and wants to offer themselves for work. Therefore, we may also refer to the labour force as the **labour supply**. The upward-sloping labour supply curve reflects the assumption that more labour is being supplied as working becomes more attractive through higher pay. Figure 6.7 combines a labour supply curve with a labour demand schedule, both in linear form. Under perfect conditions the market clears at employment L^* and the real wage w^*.

Empirical note. In 2011 the EU population was 503 (millions). The active population (age 15 to 64 according to OECD definitions) was 343, while the labour force was 237. Out of those, 216 were working and 21 were looking for work.

The aggregate labour supply curve shows the (aggregate) quantity of labour supplied by workers at different real wage rates.

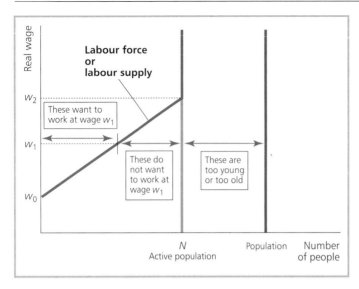

Figure 6.6 The **labour force** is obtained by subtracting from the total **population** those who are too young or too old to work, and those who do not want to work. Since the labour force thus counts all those who offer their labour, successfully or not, we may also call it the **labour supply.**

Note that employers' demand for and workers' supply of labour depends on the real wage $w \equiv W/P$, which is the money wage divided by the price level. Under the ideal conditions assumed here, changes in the price level do not impact on the labour market equilibrium. For example, if workers initially supplied the market-clearing amount of labour L^* at a money wage of €20 per hour, with the price level being at €10, $(W/P)^*$ equalled 2. After prices doubled to €20 workers only continue to supply L^* if money wages rise to €40 in order to keep the real wage, the buying power of labour income, unchanged at 2. For similar reasons, firms only keep demanding L^* if money wages respond to price changes so as to hold the real wage at 2. The crux of this argument is that with perfectly flexible money wages, the price level does not affect the

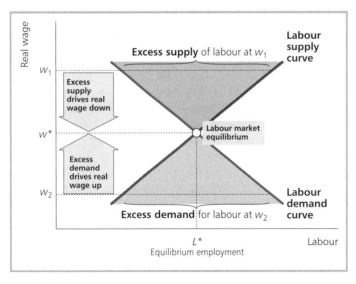

Figure 6.7 At a real wage such as w_1 workers supply more labour than firms want. Those who cannot find work bid down the wage until it is at w^*. If the wage is at w_2 firms want to employ more labour than workers are ready to supply. Competition among firms for scarce labour bids up the real wage until it is at w^*. Only at the real wage w^* does demand equal supply at L^*, and the labour market comes to rest in equilibrium.

market-clearing real wage and employment. But then, neither can it affect output. Therefore, the classical labour market discussed here implies a vertical aggregate supply curve as depicted in Figure 6.1, panel (b).

Figure 6.8 shows the steps that lead from a labour market equilibrium that is independent of the price level to a vertical aggregate supply curve. In the lower left-hand panel equilibrium employment L^* is determined. The partial production function in the panel above shows the equilibrium output that results from this employment. The 45° line brings this potential output around to the diagram in the lower right-hand panel. Here, no matter where the price level is, the economy's output is always at Y^*. We call the level of output that results when the labour market is in equilibrium **potential output**.

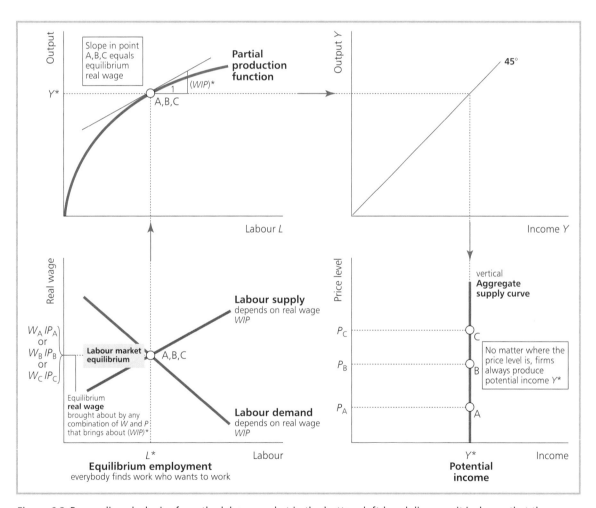

Figure 6.8 Proceeding clockwise from the labour market in the bottom left-hand diagram, it is shown that the classical view of the labour market implies a vertical aggregate supply curve. The reason is that the labour market clears only at one real wage *(W/P)** and at one level of employment L^*. *(W/P)** may be brought about by an infinite number of combinations of *W* and *P*. If *P* rises, *W* only needs to rise by the same percentage. So no matter how high prices are, as long as the real wage clears the market, employment is L^* and output is Y^*.

6.2   Why is there unemployment in equilibrium?

In the classical view the real wage adjusts instantly so as to clear the labour market at all times. Everyone who wants to sell labour at that real wage can do so. Everyone who wants to buy labour can do so too. In this benchmark scenario not all people work. But those who want to work at the current wage do find a job. Involuntary unemployment does not exist.

This conclusion conflicts with the reality of quite substantial average unemployment rates most industrial countries have to cope with for half a century. As Figure 6.9 documents, unemployment in Europe and beyond is not a phenomenon that occurs because of short-lived, temporary displacements of the labour market from equilibrium. Such displacements do occur (and we will look at them in section 6.3). If anyone needs reminding, take a look at what the financial and debt crises have done to unemployment rates in Greece, Ireland, Portugal and Spain.

What hits the eye is the upward trend in unemployment in many countries. This is important because the causes of such trend-like increases or persistence of unemployment at high levels are very different from what makes unemployment rise during recessions – and so are the remedies. Cyclical unemployment eventually takes care of itself. If 'eventually' lasts too long, the government may speed up the adjustment process with the help of fiscal or monetary policy. Equilibrium unemployment reflects the institutional characteristics of the labour market and the economy at large. We need to understand how these affect employment and unemployment before we think about remedies.

Having developed a benchmark view of the labour market in the preceding section, we now ask how reality differs from this ideal, or *classical view*. Conditions in the real world are not perfect, as suggested by last section's model. Many factors may keep the labour market from reaching an equilibrium such as at A, B, C in Figure 6.8, in which no involuntary unemployment exists. The introduction of real-world features into the labour market will give us a number of clues as to the possible causes of today's unemployment problem. We now discuss some of these features.

Cyclical unemployment is unemployment that arises temporarily during the downswing of the business cycle.

The economy returns to **equilibrium unemployment** after a boom or a recession. Equilibrium unemployment reflects the institutional characteristics of the labour market.

Minimum wages

In most industrial countries, governments feel compelled to restrict or guide market forces in the labour market by implementing some sort of minimum wage legislation. The noble intentions of such legislation are undisputed. But a look at our labour market diagram reveals unintended side effects (Figure 6.10). Of course, as long as law-makers fix the minimum wage below w^*, it remains ineffective. Employers will voluntarily raise wages to w^* and expand employment to L^*, as in the classical case. As legal minimum wage rates are raised beyond w^*, say to w_{min}, two things happen. First, employers, facing higher unit labour costs, *reduce* their demand for labour to L_D. Second, workers *expand* their supply of labour to L_S. With the wage being prevented by law from falling, in order to equalize supply and demand, labour in the amount of $L_S - L_D$ remains involuntarily unemployed.

Unit labour costs are the wage costs per unit of output. *Marginal unit labour costs* (what are the wage costs of one more unit of output?) are higher than average unit labour costs ($W \times L/Y$) when the marginal product of labour falls.

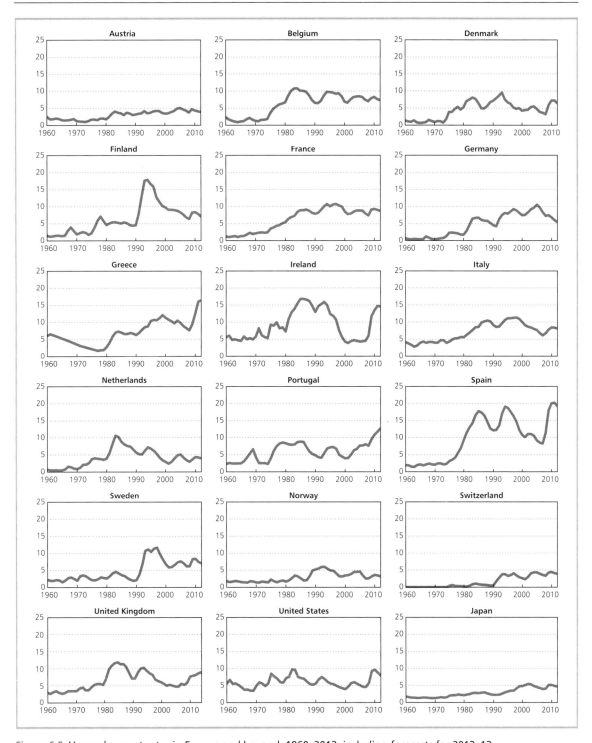

Figure 6.9 Unemployment rates in Europe and beyond, 1960–2013, including forecasts for 2012–13.

Source: OECD, *Economic Outlook*.

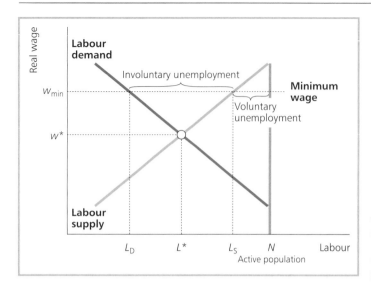

Figure 6.10 If regulations prevent the wage from falling below w_{min} the labour market cannot clear. At w_{min} L_S units of labour are offered and L_D units are demanded. This produces involuntary unemployment at the magnitude $L_S - L_D$.

Involuntary unemployment needs to be distinguished from **voluntary unemployment**. If N is the total labour force, unemployment statistics typically include both involuntary unemployment $L_S - L_D$ and voluntary unemployment, which may be as large as $N - L_S$. These people do not really want to work at the wage w_{min}, but may be tempted to take advantage of unemployment benefits nevertheless.

Minimum wages come in many forms: as an economy-wide wage floor enacted and periodically adjusted by the government; in the form of industry-wide wages negotiated periodically by trade unions and employers, declared binding by the government. Even legal action primarily motivated by concerns for justice and equality, such as outlawing wage discrimination for reasons of sex, religion, age, and so on, may have an impact on the segment of the labour force involved in a similar way to that resulting from direct minimum wage legislation.

A second possible cause of unemployment, also under the government's control, is the tax wedge. This is where taxes (and similar things, such as social security contributions) drive a wedge between the labour costs of firms and the pay that workers actually take home. Figure 6.11 illustrates how the tax wedge affects employment.

The tax wedge is the difference between the labour costs of firms and the wage that workers take home.

Suppose there is no tax initially, so that negotiated wages reflect the labour costs of firms and the net pay of workers. The market clears at the wage rate w_0^* (not shown) and employment is L_0^*. Now the government introduces two kinds of tax. First, a tax is levied on workers' incomes. This drives the take-home wage below the negotiated wage, making workers less eager to work at each negotiated wage rate. The labour supply curve shifts left and employment falls. Second, firms are subjected to a payroll tax. This raises employers' labour costs above the negotiated wage rate and reduces the number of workers that can be profitably employed at each negotiated wage. The labour demand curve shifts left and employment moves further down to L_1^*.

To sum this up, higher taxes and social security contributions drive employment down. Thus, the number of those who cannot be employed rises. Note,

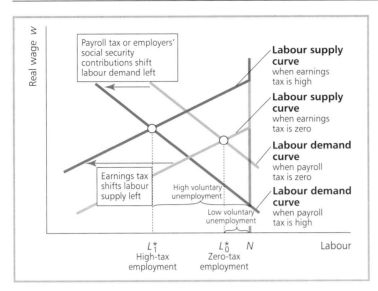

Figure 6.11 An earnings tax shifts the labour supply curve left and drives down employment. A tax on the firms' payroll shifts the labour demand curve left and also drives down employment. Both taxes drive down employment further below available employment and may raise the voluntary unemployment included in official unemployment rates.

however, that all who drop out of employment do so *voluntarily*. Therefore, **involuntary unemployment is not caused by the tax wedge.** But some of those who voluntarily drop out may exploit the unemployment insurance system and drive up official unemployment statistics.

Monopolistic trade unions

Another institutional feature which causes labour markets in many industrial countries – and particularly in a host of European economies – to deviate from the ideal classical scenario, is the prominent role of **trade unions** in the wage negotiating process. Wages are set in a collective negotiating process between a trade union and one large employer or an association of employers. These negotiated wage rates then serve as minimum wages for individual shops or industries throughout regions or entire countries. In many economies, such as Germany's, negotiated wages represent minimum wages and are also binding for workers who are not members of the trade union.

Like any monopolist in a traditional goods market, trade unions do not possess the power to set both wages *and* employment levels. What they can do is set wages at their discretion. After that, employers are free to decide on how much labour to demand at the given wage rate. This choice, as has been shown above, is always the respective point on the labour demand curve. Trade unions anticipate that they will eventually end up on the labour demand curve. So they will choose a wage rate that predetermines that point from all the options offered by the labour demand curve which best serves trade union interests.

What are the interests of the trade union? One simple but reasonable assumption is that trade unions care about both employment L and high wages by maximizing the *wage sum S*:

$$S = L \times w$$

Wage sum   (6.3)

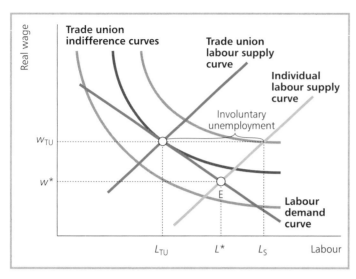

Figure 6.12 Monopolistic trade unions that care about wages and employment bargain for real wages determined by the point of tangency between one of their grey indifference curves and the labour demand curve. The resulting wage w_{TU} typically exceeds the wage $w*$ obtained in a competitive labour market. As a result, involuntary unemployment is at $L_S - L_{TU}$.

Maths note. If you are unfamiliar with hyperbolas, suppose $w = 5/L$. Use a pocket calculator to compute the real wages for all L from 1 to 10. Plot these values in a $w - L$ diagram and you have a **hyperbola**.

Trade union **indifference curves**, which depict those combinations of L and w that produce some given wage sum S' (that is why the union is indifferent between them), are given by

$$w = \frac{S'}{L} \qquad \qquad \text{Union indifference curve} \quad (6.4)$$

The indifference curves have the shape of hyperbolas, as Figure 6.12 shows. The wage sum increases as we move northeast. So, given that possibilities are restricted by the menu offered by the labour-demand schedule, the trade union maximizes the wage sum at the point of tangency between the labour demand schedule and an indifference curve.

This tangent point might lie on that part of the labour-demand curve southeast of E. This point would not be a feasible outcome, however, since in this situation individuals would not be willing to supply the amount of labour demanded by firms. The best that trade unions could do in this situation would be to settle for $w*$ and the concomitant employment level $L*$. It is not particularly logical that trade union preferences would lead them to go for exactly the same bargaining result that the market generates without them. If trade unions are to make any difference and thus justify their role in the collective bargaining process, they will go for a wage rate that is higher than the wage rate that would clear a perfect market.

A real wage rigidity is a market imperfection that keeps the real wage from falling to the level that eliminates involuntary unemployment.

If the real wage does not fall despite the existence of involuntary unemployment, we speak of a real wage rigidity. We now turn to other explanations of why real wages may be rigid.

Insiders and outsiders

As before, let workers be represented by a monopolistic trade union. Let the economy be in the same equilibrium that we identified in the preceding section. Now, however, assume that the trade union only cares about

Insiders are all currently employed workers. Outsiders are those currently out of employment who are seeking employment.

employed members, the insiders. Union members who are out of employment, be it voluntarily or not, are outsiders. In many countries, only employed trade union members can exercise active membership rights, such as voting about whether to accept a bargaining settlement between union leaders and employers.

If the interests of outsiders are being ignored in collective bargaining, this means that whether these people find employment or not is irrelevant. So the indifference curves of the trade union must have a kink at the current employment level. Here the indifference curves all turn horizontal, since employment gains beyond the current level accrue to outsiders and therefore do not yield utility to the union. Thus, additional employment of outsiders could not possibly compensate the trade union (members) for wage concessions.

Next, let the economy be hit by an adverse supply shock which shifts the labour demand curve to the left. The two oil price explosions of the 1970s are usually considered to have had such an effect. Wages and employment after the shock are determined by the point of tangency between an unkinked union indifference curve and the new labour demand curve. Once employment has been reduced to L_1 all union indifference curves become horizontal at this level (see Figure 6.13).

This alone does not create new or additional unemployment. But it may do so if the shock is reversed. Assume that the oil price shock was temporary and the labour demand curve moves back into the original position. Now unions maximize utility by negotiating the highest possible real wage for the current insiders, L_1, which is obtained where one of the new kinked indifference curves touches the labour demand curve. Employment stays at L_1, but the wage rises to w_2. This creates *collective voluntary unemployment* in the amount $L_2^s - L_1$ and raises *individual involuntary unemployment* way above the level that would exist at the trade union monopoly bargaining point without insider–outsider effects.

In addition to the trade union version of the insider–outsider theory there is a second version which does not rely on the existence of a union. It argues that, because of specific knowhow that can only be acquired within the firm and because of turnover (hiring and firing) costs, insiders can extract a premium over the wage for which outsiders are willing to work. Again, the result is involuntary unemployment.

Efficiency wages

Efficiency wage theory argues that raising the real wage may lower costs per unit of output by raising labour productivity.

So far we have assumed that labour productivity depends only on the amount of capital with which labour is combined, but not on the received wage. Efficiency wage theory questions this assumption. Various arguments are advanced as to why the work *effort*, or efficiency, as it is called in the context of these theories, and hence (given a specific amount of capital) labour productivity may increase with the real wage. These are as follows:

■ *Nutrition.* This basic idea has played a major role in development theory. It is argued that as farmers raise wages above the subsistence level, farm workers become stronger and healthier and, consequently, more productive. While there are, sadly enough, still too many countries in the world for

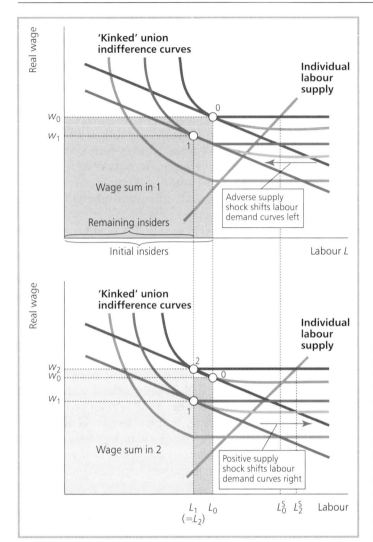

Figure 6.13 Initially collective wage bargaining brings the labour market to point 0, where the highest possible union indifference curve just touches the grey labour demand curve. Union indifference curves are horizontal to the right of L_0 since the union is not concerned with the employment of these outsiders. Next, an adverse supply shock shifts labour demand down to the blue position, moving the economy to point 1. After the supply shock is reversed in period 2, only L_1 insiders are kept employed. Real wages rise to w_2 and unemployment is higher at $L_2^S - L_1$ than it was before the shock.

which such arguments are highly relevant, the relationship between nutrition and efficiency does not describe a feature of today's industrialized countries.

■ *Adverse selection*. Here the basic idea is that workers are heterogeneous, being equipped with different individual skills and productivities. When hiring workers, firms find it difficult to sort out those workers with high productivity. Workers know their own skill levels much better. Since they expect firms to learn their true productivity sooner or later, better workers are more likely to apply for jobs endowed with a high salary or wage than bad ones. Thus, the higher the wage, the more qualified and productive the firm's workforce must be expected to be.

■ *Shirking*. Firms may find it difficult to monitor continuously the work efforts of their workers. A worker caught shirking during a spot check will be fired, however. As long as the firm pays the market wage only, this is not really a punishment, since a worker can always get an equivalent job with the same pay elsewhere. To provide an incentive to reduce shirking, the firm must raise the wage rate above the market clearing wage. Will that do any good, since it must be expected that all firms in the industry pay efficiency wages (wages that are above the market clearing wage)? Yes, because if all firms pay an 'excessive' real wage we end up with involuntary unemployment. If a worker is caught shirking now, he or she can indeed expect to receive the same real wage at any other firm, but may not find a job. So as long as unemployment benefits are below wages, workers caught shirking must expect their real income to drop. This provides an incentive to reduce shirking and increase efficiency.

- *Turnover costs*. Labour turnover is costly to firms. Costly hiring and firing activities include advertising and other search activities, screening candidates, contract negotiations and legal fees. Additional indirect costs may be related to on-the-job training for new workers and the time it takes for them to find their best place in the firm's structure. If a worker's probability to quit is negatively related to the real wage, a firm may profit from paying higher wages than other firms by enjoying lower turnover costs.

- *Fairness*. This explanation augments the economic view of the labour market with sociological elements. It focuses on the simple observation that there is a distinctively positive relationship between the morale of people and their perception of whether they are being fairly treated. While this notion is intuitively appealing, it has also been substantiated by empirical research, such as laboratory experiments, to show that subjectively perceived fairness affects work quality or productivity.

Before we look at how efficiency wage considerations impact on the labour market, Figure 6.14 illustrates the classical case with which we have worked so far. Panel (a) shows that labour productivity or efficiency or effort, which we use as synonyms in this context, is at x' for all wage levels. **Unit labour costs**, the real wage costs of one unit of output produced, w/x', are simply marked by the slope of a ray through the origin which intersects the vertical efficiency line at a given real wage. Since efficiency is constant, unit labour costs obviously double as wages rise from 1 to 2. Panel (b) shows the general relationship between unit labour costs and the wage rate to be a positively sloped straight line through the origin. Employers who want to minimize unit labour costs thus will try to pay the lowest wage they can.

Next, Figure 6.15 contrasts this orthodox view with the efficiency–wage argument. The innovation in panel (a) is highlighted by comparing it with panel (a) of Figure 6.14: work effort is positively related to the wage rate. It is zero if the wage is zero. As long as pay is low, effort rises faster than the wage rate. Beyond some threshold w_x saturation sets in, and additional wage increases yield smaller and smaller efficiency gains. The consequence of this relationship between effort and wage rates for unit labour costs can be traced again by following the slope of a ray from the origin to the effort curve (see Figure 6.15, panel (a)). Initially, since for low pay levels effort rises faster than the wage rate, the slope of this ray becomes smaller as firms raise wages. Beyond the wage rate w_x, however, unit labour costs rise. Panel (b) illustrates how this translates into a C-shaped relationship between unit labour costs and

Labour productivity or **efficiency** *or* **effort** *x* can be measured as output produced per work hour, $x = Y/L$. **Unit labour costs** *ULC* are wage costs per unit of output. The manipulations $ULC \equiv wL/Y = w/(Y/L) = w/x$ show that *ULC* can also be expressed as the real wage divided by labour productivity, w/x.

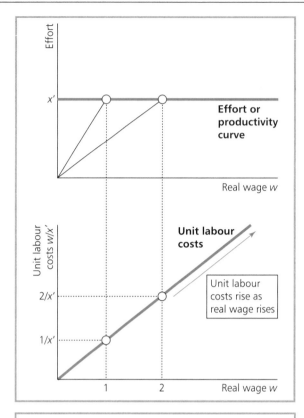

Figure 6.14 Panel (a) illustrates the assumption employed so far, that work effort measured, say, as pieces produced per hour, is at x', independent of pay. Unit labour costs are w/x', and thus vary with the wage. They are represented by the slope of a ray from the origin to the point of intersection between the vertical line over x' and the horizontal line at the current wage. Panel (b) illustrates that unit labour costs increase linearly with the real wage w.

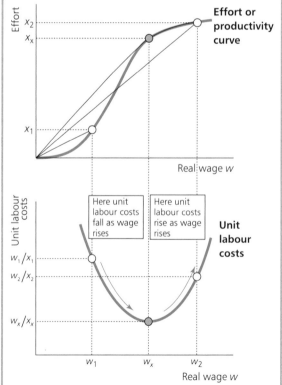

Figure 6.15 Panel (a) proposes that work effort (that is, productivity) may be related to the real wage. As the wage increases, productivity first increases at an accelerating and then at a decelerating pace. Unit labour costs, w/x, vary with the wage. They are represented by the slope of a ray from the origin to the point of intersection between the horizontal line at the current wage and the effort curve. Panel (b) illustrates that unit labour costs initially fall as firms raise wages, but increase again as wages move beyond w_x, yielding a U-shaped unit labour costs curve.

The efficiency wage is the wage that minimizes unit labour costs.

the wage rate. The wage rate w_x that minimizes unit labour costs is called the efficiency wage.

A simple model

A simple model may illustrate how the efficiency wage considerations introduced above fit into our previously developed picture of the labour market, and how they account for the existence of involuntary unemployment in equilibrium.

Let output Y depend on physical labour input L and on work effort or efficiency x (which depends on the real wage w):

$$Y = Y[x(w)L] \qquad \text{Partial production function} \qquad (6.5)$$

Then the firms' profits Π are given by the difference between output (which equals the firms' revenue) and wage costs.

$$\Pi = Y[x(w)L] - wL \qquad \text{Profits} \qquad (6.6)$$

Profits = Output − Wage costs

This innocent-looking modification of the production function can have dramatic consequences for a firm's behaviour in the labour market. This is the case if work effort responds strongly to a change in the wage rate, meaning that its elasticity is very high. Suppose work effort increases by 2% if the real wage rises by 1%. Then currently employed labour becomes 1% more expensive, but it produces 2% more. Costs go up by 1%, but revenue rises by 2%. So profits increase. Figure 6.16 shows how this affects iso-profit lines and the labour demand of firms.

Elasticity measures by how many percentage points one variable responds if some other variable changes by 1%.

What remains unchanged is that for each wage rate there is an optimal, profit-maximizing level of employment, just as explained in our discussion of the conventional classical labour demand curve in Figures 6.4 and 6.5. If the wage rate is w_1, employment L_1 maximizes profits, as identified by point A. The iso-profit line for the corresponding level of profits Π_1 passes through A. Of course, profits fall if we move to the left of A, say into A′, or to the right of A, into A″, for reasons already discussed earlier in this chapter. But this time, a drop in the wage rate does not help to restore profits to Π_1. The reason is that while a lower wage rate indeed reduces costs, it reduces labour efficiency and, hence, output and revenues even further. Thus profits actually drop even further when wages go down. The logical conclusion is that wages actually have to move in the opposite direction to restore profits. When, starting in A′(A″), the wage rate rises to w_3 (w_2), output and revenue rise more than wage costs, and profits go up. At point C (B) profits are back at the level Π_1. This is why the corresponding iso-profit line passes through points C, A and B.

Work effort is elastic with respect to wages when its wage elasticity exceeds 1 in absolute size.

So when work effort is elastic with respect to the real wage, iso-profit curves are U-shaped, and the labour market diagram is actually filled with an infinite number of such U-shaped indifference curves. And, since profits rise when the wage rate goes up, the further up an iso-profit line sits, the higher is the associated level of profits. This has the important implication that firms would like to end up as far *up* on their 'labour demand curve' as they possibly can. In other words, they would constantly beg their workers to accept higher and higher wages! Is this realistic? Of course not.

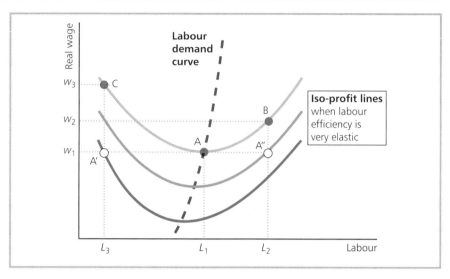

Figure 6.16 This shows the non-standard case, when labour efficiency (or productivity, or effort) depends positively on the real wage, and its real-wage elasticity exceeds 1. Then efficiency rises faster than wages, and unit labour costs, the wage cost of one unit of output, actually fall as wages go up. This makes iso-profit lines U-shaped (compare with the standard case shown in Figure 6.5). Iso-profit lines positioned further up are associated with higher profits. When facing a given wage demand, say w_1 or w_2, firms extend employment to the point where they reach the highest iso-profit line possible. This puts the bottom of each iso-profit line at the point where it intersects the 'labour demand curve'. However, this labour demand curve existed only if firms were prohibited from paying higher wages than trade unions demand. If wages are free to rise, they begin to drift upwards until labour efficiency can no longer increase faster than real wages, and this segment of the labour demand curve vanishes.

The reason why we ended up with a somewhat unconvincing result is that we postulated that rising wages could increase labour efficiency without limits. This is not feasible. Realistically, as postulated in Figure 6.15, the wage elasticity of labour efficiency may be very high indeed as long as wages are low. At such wage levels iso-profit lines are really U-shaped as depicted in Figure 6.16. But beyond some threshold w_x saturation takes over and efficiency gains cannot keep up with wage increases any longer. Work effort becomes inelastic. The iso-profit lines change their shape to an inverted U, the conventional case covered in Figure 6.5. When we merge cases onto a single diagram, iso-profit lines become concentric, looking like squeezed circles or ellipses, with a clearly defined maximum in the centre (Figure 6.17). In the region above w_x the wage elasticity of labour efficiency is smaller than 1. Below w_x it exceeds 1. In striving for the highest profits, firms want to move down their labour demand curve to the point of maximum profits when wages exceed w_x, but move up their (dashed, fictional) labour demand curve when wages are below w_x.

Firms maximize profits by voluntarily paying the efficiency wage w_x and setting the employment to L_x. Firms do not want to employ more labour, since at the level of labour productivity determined by w_x additional labour would cost more than it produces. Also, while firms could obtain L_x labour

Work effort is inelastic with respect to wages when its wage elasticity is smaller than 1 in absolute size.

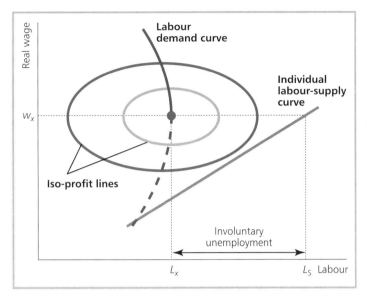

Figure 6.17 If work effort increases with the real wage, unit labour costs are minimized (and profits are maximized) by paying w_x and employing L_x. Moving away from w_x or L_x in either direction reduces profits. Hence iso-profit lines are concentric around the profit maximum marked by the blue dot. Workers who do not find employment at w_x cannot bid down wages since firms voluntarily pay w_x in order to minimize costs. As a result, involuntary unemployment in the amount $L_S - L_x$ persists.

input at a lower wage rate, they refrain from doing so. The reason is that if wages drop below w_x, productivity falls faster than the wage.

The unintended side effect of the firms' profit-maximizing behaviour is that we end up with involuntary unemployment in the amount $L_S - L_x$.

Mismatch

The concept of the classical labour market rests on various simplifying assumptions. The more important ones are as follows:

- All transactions are done in one place. There is **no geographic dimension**.
- **Labour is homogeneous.** There are no particular skills, experiences or talents needed to fill a specific job opening. Hence, any unemployed worker can be hired by any firm with a job vacancy.
- All participants in the labour market possess **perfect information**. Firms know where to find unemployed workers, and workers are always aware of job openings.

Figure 6.18 shows how the labour market is affected if we give up these assumptions. The two light blue lines give the gross employment supplied and demanded at various wage levels. As the real wage differs from w^* supply and demand are not equal. Employment is now determined by whichever of the two is smaller. For $w > w^*$ this is demand, for $w < w^*$ it is supply.

Now assume that because of geographical or vocational mismatch, or because of imperfect information, at any wage level a certain fraction of supply and demand remains ineffective. Then effective supply and demand curves are given by the dark blue lines. These are obtained by subtracting that part from gross demand (supply) which is not seen by employers (workers), or which is of no use because of geographical mismatch or misfit skills.

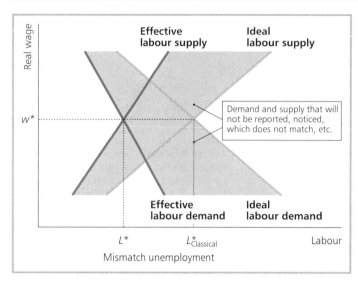

Figure 6.18 In a labour market with mismatch and information problems, labour demand and supply are not given by their respective ideal curves (light blue lines), but by their respective effective schedules indicated by the dark blue lines. As a result, involuntary unemployment results and coexists with unfilled vacancies.

Mismatch unemployment occurs when the skills or geographic location of jobseekers do not fit the patterns of job vacancies.

Structural unemployment is unemployment that does not go away in equilibrium, due to institutions or habits.

Frictional unemployment exists because it takes time to find existing jobs, to relocate or to retrain.

As a consequence, labour market 'equilibrium' obtains at lower employment L^*. Equilibrium carries unfilled vacancies and involuntary unemployment. The latter is measured by the horizontal distance between the effective and the gross labour supply curve at the equilibrium wage w^*. It is generally referred to as **equilibrium unemployment**. Other terms that refer to unemployment (or components thereof) in equilibrium are mismatch unemployment, structural unemployment and frictional unemployment.

Equilibrium unemployment versus cyclical unemployment

Since unemployment statistics say nothing about what share of unemployment reflects equilibrium and what share reflects the business cycle, economists have developed a battery of approaches to identify equilibrium unemployment. One such concept is the **Beveridge curve**. This curve directly derives from the introduction of imperfections into the labour market diagram that we just discussed.

Figure 6.19, panel (a) provides a slightly different illustration of the view that in real-world labour markets, informational imperfections or mismatch are responsible for some parts of supply and demand remaining ineffective. So even if the real wage is at its market-clearing level w^*, U^* people are still looking for jobs while firms have the same number of vacancies, V^*, unfilled. Let us take U^* and V^* and identify this combination by point A in panel (b), where vacancies are measured along the vertical axis and unemployment is measured along the horizontal axis.

Now suppose the real wage exceeds its market-clearing level. At w_1 unemployment is at U_1. Vacancies have fallen but, standing at V_1, have not vanished. Take the pair of new unemployment/vacancy observations and mark it in panel (b). This gives point B. To obtain a third point, let the real wage be too low, at w_2. This drives unemployment down to U_2, but boosts vacancies to V_2. Transposing it into panel (b) gives point C. We could perform the same exercise

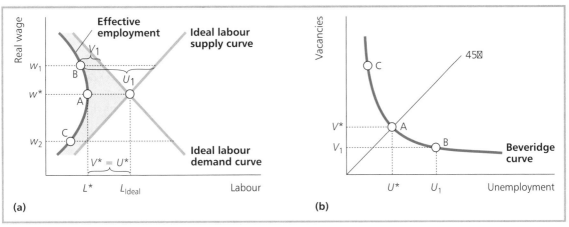

Figure 6.19 Job vacancies and unemployment coexist because of mismatch, friction and information problems. The Beveridge curve shows the ratio between vacancies and unemployment at different wages.

CASE STUDY 6.1 Ford's focus: an experiment in efficiency wages

Something bizarre happened at the world's first car plant in Dearborn, Michigan, in 1913. Henry Ford really caught his workers off guard by telling them that from 14 January 1914, they would not only have to work less but would earn more as well. What qualifies this step as one of the best known experiments in efficiency wages is its magnitude. As shown in columns 2 and 3 of Table 6.1, the length of a workday was reduced by more than 10% from 9 to 8 hours. A day's pay more than doubled from $2.34 to $5. Both changes combined made the hourly wage rise by 138% from 26 cents to 62 cents.

Did this dramatic increase in labour costs really pay off? Not directly so, it appears. While productivity did increase from 1913 to 1914 by some estimated 30% to 50%, as efficiency wage theory proposes, this gain falls way short of the increase in labour costs.

Changes in unit labour costs may be too narrow a measure, however. Some other side effects of the huge wage increase may provide a broader, more complete picture. As column 5 shows, in 1913 production at Ford suffered from a very high fluctuation rate. This rate standing at 370% means that Ford on average had to replace each worker it started with at the beginning of the year 3.7 times! This must have caused enormous costs in areas such as training, administration including bookkeeping, recruitment and so on. As the numbers for 1914 and 1915 show, Henry Ford's wage increase brought down fluctuation rates substantially.

Other measures show similar trends. The firing rate, for example, came down from 62% in 1913 to 0.1% in 1915. Further, while in 1913 some 10% of Ford's workforce was absent on an average workday, this rate was brought down to 2.5% within one year. All these factors must have contributed to the fact that Ford enjoyed a sizeable increase in profits between 1913 and 1914, despite higher unit labour costs.

The numbers presented here cannot possibly give a complete account of why Ford's profits rose. We also cannot be sure what motivated Ford's exceptional step. Nor is it clear whether the implemented wage increase was of optimal size from the perspective of efficiency wage theory, or perhaps too large. What the numbers do demonstrate, however, is that wages may have quite sizeable effects on productivity and turnover costs, as emphasized by efficiency wage theory.

Table 6.1 Wages, work hours and turnover costs at Ford's Dearborn plant

Year	Daily wage $	Daily work hours	Implied hourly wage $	Fluctuation rate %	Firing rate %	Absence rate %
1913	2.34	9	0.26	370	62	10
1914	5.00	8	0.62	54	7	2.5
1915	5.00	8	0.62	16	0.1	

Source: D. Raff and L. Summers (1987) 'Did Henry Ford pay efficiency wages?', *Journal of Labor Economics*, October.

The **Beveridge curve** is a negatively sloped line, depicting an inverse relationship between the vacancy rate and the unemployment rate. A boom represents a movement up this line, a recession a slide down the line.

for any other real wage. Lining up the obtained levels of unemployment and vacancies in panel (b) gives the blue line. This line is called the Beveridge curve, named after the British economist who first drew attention to it.

In theory, all we need to do now is add the 45° line to the Beveridge curve diagram, and where it cuts the Beveridge curve (at point A) unemployment is in equilibrium U^* – equilibrium in the sense that in the aggregate the number of jobs matches the number of workers. Outside this equilibrium, say during a recession, real wages rise, as does unemployment, and vacancies become less. Thus we slide down the Beveridge curve to the right. Cyclical unemployment is measured as the difference between U and U^*. Similarly, the economy slides up the Beveridge curve during a boom.

Real wage rigidities and the aggregate supply curve

When discussing the classical view of the labour market we noted that both firms and workers base decisions on the real wage, that is on the buying power of wages. Price movements would not change that real wage which equated labour demand with supply, and, hence, would not change employment and output. This makes the aggregate supply curve a vertical line over potential output or income denoted by $Y^*_{Classical}$ in Figure 6.20.

Most imperfections discussed in this section push and keep the real wage above the market clearing real wage. They are therefore called **real wage rigidities**. This reduces actual employment below market clearing employment, and, via the production function, output below the level of output produced in the classical scenario. Since trade union monopoly wages or unit-labour-cost-reducing efficiency wages are also cast in real terms, a changing price level does not affect the established unemployment equilibria. Hence, all that an imperfection such as a monopolistic trade union or some other real wage rigidity does is to move the vertical aggregate supply curve to the left towards a lower output level Y^* that is associated with individually involuntary equilibrium unemployment.

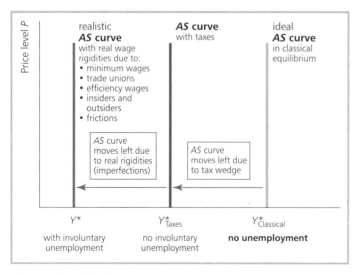

Figure 6.20 When nominal wages are fully flexible, as we assumed throughout the first part of this chapter, the AS curve is vertical. If the labour market is classical, all who are willing to work do work and produce output $Y^*_{Classical}$. Taxes move AS to the left due to a *voluntary* reduction of employment. If real rigidities exist, however, output is still lower at Y^*, and some workers remain *involuntarily* unemployed.

6.3 Why may actual output deviate from potential output?

The final question to be addressed in this chapter is what induces firms to supply output levels that differ from potential output. By drawing an *AS* curve for the short and medium run which is horizontal or positively sloped, we imply that the adjustment of wages and/or prices, which makes the long-run *AS* curve vertical, takes time. This needs explanation and, as trivial as it may seem to laypeople, is giving economists a very hard time!

Rather than giving a superficial summary of the many pertinent approaches that economists have discussed in recent years, we focus on one approach which economists are employing frequently in applied work. This **New Keynesian theory of aggregate supply** exploits the institutional feature that wages are not negotiated day by day, as the classical model of the labour market implies, but are laid down in contracts for a fixed period of time.

Sticky money wages due to long-term contracts

About 80% of wage contracts negotiated by trade unions in the United States are three years in length! This is extreme by European standards. But even in Europe typical contracts last a minimum of one year. Figure 6.21 shows how this institutional characteristic influences wages, employment and, by the same token, aggregate supply.

We assume a simple but reasonably realistic structure.

■ Negotiations fix the money or nominal wage rate for the length of the contract. This rate is binding, no matter what happens later on to the price level and, hence, to the real wage.
■ Firms can then employ any number of available workers at the negotiated nominal wage.

The familiar-looking bottom left-hand diagram in Figure 6.21 permits us to trace the wage setting and employment decisions. First we consider *wage setting*. When the wage contract is signed, neither employers nor workers know the price level that will apply during the time for which the nominal wage is set. Hence, bargaining is based on *expectations* of real wages and the outcome is where the *expected* labour supply curve cuts the expected labour demand curve. This yields an *expected* real wage that, given price level expectations P^e, determines the nominal wage W_0 to be written into the contract.

Second, we consider *employment*. The negotiated nominal wage W_0 will clear the labour market if prices are as expected. Then the real wage is as expected and employment is L^*. Frequently, however, prices will not be as expected. Consider the case $P_A < P^e$, where prices turn out to be lower than anticipated. Then the real wage is higher than anticipated. Labour is more expensive than expected during negotiations. According to their demand schedule, firms reduce employment to L_A. Since, in addition, the higher real wage increases the labour supply, a substantial amount of unemployment occurs.

Next, consider the opposite case $P_C > P^e$. Now, the opposite reaction is observed. Labour is cheaper than anticipated, and firms increase demand to L_C. Here the similarity to the previous case breaks down, however. Firms cannot generally find the desired number of workers at such a low real wage. And

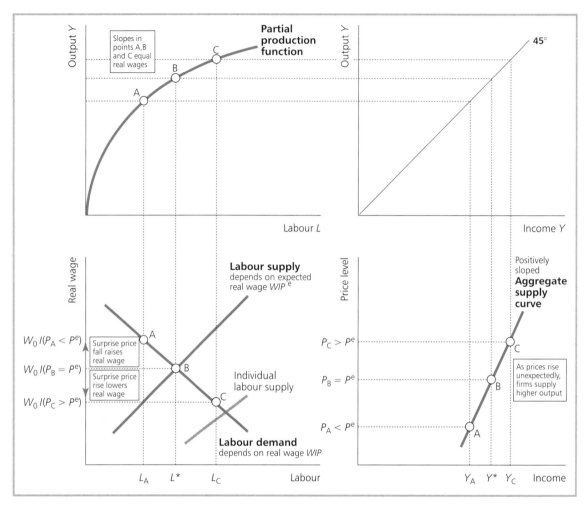

Figure 6.21 Labour market participants commit themselves to a long-term nominal wage contract at which they expect the market to clear. Employment is L^* and output equals potential output Y^*. If prices are then lower than expected, the real wage is higher than planned. Employment falls below L^* to L_A. Output falls below potential output to Y_A. The opposite occurs if the price level is higher than expected. The firms' higher demand for labour leads then to higher employment if enough involuntary unemployment is available.

nobody can force workers to work at a wage at which they would rather not. So does that mean that employment falls if prices rise unexpectedly and drive down real wages? Probably not, as firms will only then not find workers if the expected labour market equilibrium L^* was a full-employment equilibrium without individually involuntary unemployment, as derived from the classical labour market. In the presence of real wage rigidities, as discussed in the previous section, firms searching for workers may still be successful.

Suppose contracts were negotiated by a monopolistic trade union. Then nominal wages and expected equilibrium employment reflect the collective trade union labour supply curve derived previously, which lies northwest of the individual labour supply curve, shown as a grey line in Figure 6.21. Even though the real wage falls below the real wage targeted by the trade union, firms can (up to a certain threshold) obtain additional workers out of the pool of involuntarily unemployed workers. In the graph employment rises to L_C.

The result of this discussion is that, in the presence of contractually fixed money wages, employment moves up or down with the price level (relative to P^e). The production function (top left-hand diagram in Figure 6.21) translates employment into output. Bringing output levels down into the lower right-hand diagram in Figure 6.21 shows that income increases when prices increase.

The important point to note about this positively sloped *AS* curve is that if prices are as expected, no matter how high or low, firms supply potential output Y^*. So it is obviously not the absolute price level that matters for aggregate supply. Only unexpected increases of the price level raise output beyond Y^*, and unexpected decreases of the price level drive output below Y^*. A linear formal approximation of this positively sloped aggregate supply curve is $Y = Y^* + 1/\lambda(P - P^e)$, or, solving for P

$$P = P^e + \lambda(Y - Y^*) \qquad \text{Aggregate supply curve} \qquad (6.7)$$

This equation also reveals the link to the vertical aggregate supply curve derived in section 6.1. If the price level is as expected, no matter how high or low, actual supply is at potential output. This follows from letting $P = P^e$ in equation (6.7) which yields $Y = Y^*$.

In concluding this chapter, Figure 6.22 shows the two aggregate supply curves we have derived. In an economy with long-run wage contracts, the vertical aggregate supply curve (which is likely to be to the left of the classical *AS* curve) is where we are if the price expectations held during wage negotiations turn out to be correct afterwards. If prices move up or down unexpectedly, the positively sloped *AS* curve indicates how aggregate supply responds.

The effect of an unexpected change in prices on the real wage and on income is temporary, lasting only as long as the wage contract prevents the nominal wage from adjusting to the new price level and thus re-establishing

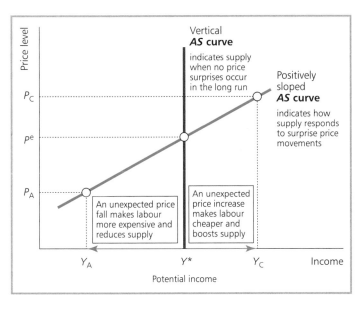

Figure 6.22 In the long run, or if prices move as expected, the *AS* curve is vertical. Firms produce Y^* independently of prices. Unexpected movements of the price level push supply above or below Y^*.

the targeted real wage. Once a new contract is negotiated that takes the new price level into account, the nominal wage is set so as to return the real wage to its targeted level. Such a nominal wage, which takes time to respond, is called a sticky nominal wage.

A sticky nominal wage needs time to respond to new information.

Before we can determine on which one of the two *AS* curves and where on that curve the economy is at a particular point in time, we need to answer two questions: where is the price level, and what price level did the market expect? The price level is obviously determined by supply and demand. To answer the question, therefore, we need to look at the interaction between aggregate demand and aggregate supply. To know which price level people expect, we must look at how expectations are being formed. Both these issues will be addressed in the next chapter.

CHAPTER SUMMARY

- Potential output is produced with all employment that the labour market yields in equilibrium.

- In the *classical view* perfectly flexible real wages keep the labour market in permanent equilibrium. No involuntary unemployment occurs.

- Taxes reduce the equilibrium level of employment. They do not cause involuntary unemployment.

- New Keynesian theories challenge this classical result on two grounds. First, it is argued, real wage rigidities may give rise to labour market equilibria with involuntary unemployment. Second, nominal wage stickiness may permit temporary displacements from equilibrium.

- Real rigidities prevent the real wage from moving down until the market clears. Sources of real wage rigidities are minimum wage legislation, monopolistic trade unions, efficiency wages and insider–outsider effects.

- Nominal stickiness in the labour market prevents the nominal wage from bringing about the real wage adjustment required after a price change. One important institutional feature making nominal wages sticky is the existence of long-term wage contracts. Nominal wage stickiness gives rise to a positively sloped *AS* curve in the short run.

- The Beveridge curve is an empirical relationship between unemployment and vacancy rates. It can be used to break recorded unemployment into a structural and a temporary component.

Key terms and concepts

aggregate supply curve *159*

Beveridge curve *182*

classical aggregate supply
   curve *159*

classical labour market *162*

cyclical unemployment *168*

efficiency wage *177*

efficiency wage theory *173*

elastic *177*

elasticity *177*

equilibrium unemployment *168*

extreme Keynesian aggregate
   supply curve *159*

frictional unemployment *180*

EXERCISES

6.1 Suppose that, due to a technological innovation, labour productivity increases significantly. How does this affect the partial production function? How does it affect the labour demand curve?

6.2 Suppose that the nominal wage rate rises from £11 to £13.22, while the index of the price level increases from 241 to 296. Does this increase or decrease the real wage rate?

6.3 Explain why both labour demand and labour supply depend on the real wage rate instead of the nominal wage rate.

6.4 What happens to potential output if workers attribute a higher value to leisure than before, which makes them supply less labour at any given real wage rate? Trace the consequences step by step, using the diagram of Figure 6.8.

6.5 Suppose that the government levies a proportional tax on labour income.
  (a) The government uses the tax revenue for government consumption. What are the effects on potential output?
  (b) Suppose that the government uses the tax revenue for public investment, improving the infrastructure and thus labour's productivity. What happens to the result you derived in (a)? Derive your results using Figure 6.8.

6.6 Measuring unemployment is trickier than it may seem at first glance. Find out how it is measured in

(a) the United States
(b) Germany
(c) the United Kingdom.
Which procedure comes closest to measuring the concept of 'involuntary unemployment' suggested by theory? If you are not living in one of these countries, how does the definition employed in your country fit in?

6.7 The argument in this chapter (illustrated in Figure 6.10) seems to make a compelling case against minimum wages. Can you think of arguments in favour of minimum wages?

6.8 Figure 6.23 depicts average rates of unionization and unemployment from 1985 to 1995 for 13 European countries.

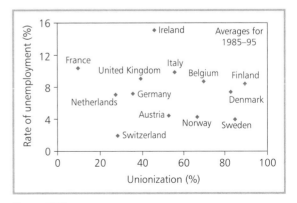

Figure 6.23

(a) Do these data support the link between monopoly power of trade unions and the rate of unemployment suggested by the theory?

(b) Is the rate of unionization a good measure to reflect the degree of monopoly power on the supply side of the labour market?

6.9 In past decades one of the dominant ideas was that there was a fairly constant 'natural rate' of unemployment in equilibrium, not affected by transititory business cycle fluctuations. Use the insider–outsider model to explain why reality seems to contradict this idea.

6.10 Use the logic of the efficiency-wage model to determine the effects of rising unemployment benefits on the optimal real wage rate. (Hint: How do unemployment benefits influence the effort curve in Figure 6.15?)

6.11 Your country's Beveridge curve is $v = 4/u$, where v is the vacancy rate.
(a) The current rate of unemployment is 6(%). Your task is to reduce unemployment to 2. Propose appropriate measures. Assume that both v and u have the same 'visibility' meaning that statistical data cover all unemployment and all vacancies.
(b) How is your proposal affected if you know that v only has one-fourth of the 'visibility' of u (meaning that there are four times as many vacancies as the official vacancy rate suggests)?

6.12 Let the labour market be characterized by the following demand and supply curves:

$$L^s = -10{,}000 + 5{,}000 \cdot w$$
$$L^d = 40{,}000 - 5{,}000 \cdot w$$

For five points in time you have data on the real wage and employment.

Observation	1	2	3	4	5
Real wage w	5	7	4	3	6
Employment L	10,000	2,500	7,500	2,500	7,500

Draw the economy's Beveridge curve.

6.13 What happens to the *AS* curve
(a) if the government improves the flow of information between enterprises with vacant positions and potential employees?
(b) if administrative prescriptions prevent workers from moving across regions?
(c) if programmes to change professional qualifications are increasingly supported by the government?

6.14 Let the production function be $Y = AK^\alpha L^{1-\alpha}$, and suppose the government installs a value-added tax of vat per cent on all sales in the economy.
(a) Derive the labour demand curve that results under profit maximization.
(b) Show graphically how the introduction of this tax affects equilibrium in the labour market. What happens to unemployment? Do nominal wages respond fully to this new tax?

6.15 Suppose that the labour market is dominated by binding long-term contracts, giving rise to an *AS* curve that is positively sloped in the short run. How does an increase in the productivity of labour affect this *AS* curve?

Online resources

Interactive applet on the labour market www.eurmacro.eu/tutor/labourmarket-applet.html
X-ercise on prices and employment www.eurmacro.eu/xercises/employment.html

Self quiz
www.eurmacro.eu/SelfQuiz/sq-ch06.html

Recommended reading

While a 672-page monograph must be intimidating, the first chapter of Richard Layard, Stephen Nickell Richard Jackman (2005) *Unemployment: Macroeconomic Performance and the Labour Market*, 2nd edn, Oxford: Oxford University Press, provides an excellent and highly readable overview of the facts to be explained and of what we know.

APPLIED PROBLEMS

EMPIRICAL RESEARCH

Why do unemployment rates differ between countries?

To explain the differences in unemployment between twenty countries, Richard Layard, Stephen Nickell and Richard Jackman (*Unemployment: Macroeconomic Performance and the Labour Market,* Oxford: Oxford University Press, 1991) estimate the following cross-sectional equation (absolute *t*-statistics in brackets):

Unemployment rate (%, average 1983–88)
= 0.24 (0.1)
+0.92 (2.9) benefit duration (years)
+0.17 (7.1) replacement ratio (%)
−0.13 (2.3) active labour market spending (%)
+2.45 (2.4) coverage of collective bargaining
−1.42 (2.0) union coordination
−4.28 (2.9) employer coordination
−0.35 (2.8) change in inflation (% points)
$R^2_{adj} = 0.91$

The equation accounts for over 90% of the differences in unemployment rates. The first six variables measure institutional characteristics of the labour market. The first two refer to how well workers are protected in case of unemployment. Both the duration of benefits and, even more so, their level are important. If the replacement ratio (the percentage of unemployment benefits as a share of the last wage income received) rises from, say, 50% to 60%, unemployment moves up by 1.7 percentage points. Active labour market spending (on things like placement, counselling, training, recruitment subsidies) appears to succeed in reducing unemployment. The more people who are covered by collective bargaining agreements, the higher the unemployment rate. It helps, however, if union or employers coordinate wage bargaining. The final coefficient on the change of inflation shows how monetary policy can influence unemployment. A country that raised inflation by 10 percentage points between 1983 and 1988 would have ended up with an unemployment rate 3.5 percentage points lower.

WORKED PROBLEM

Dutch Beveridge curves

Table 6.2 gives Dutch unemployment and vacancy rates.

A linear approximation of the Beveridge curve introduced in the text gives the estimation equation

$$v = 2.29 - 0.19u \qquad R^2 = 0.84$$
   (19.40)   (10.86)

While the coefficients are highly significant and the fit of the equation looks OK, the result is not

Table 6.2

	Unemployment in %	Vacancy rate in %
1964	0.5	2.9
1965	0.6	2.8
1966	0.8	2.5
1967	1.7	1.4
1968	1.5	1.6
1969	1.1	2.2
1970	1.0	2.6
1971	1.3	2.2
1972	2.3	1.3
1973	2.4	1.4
1974	2.9	1.4
1975	5.5	0.9
1976	5.8	0.9
1977	5.6	1.1
1978	5.6	1.2
1979	5.7	1.3
1980	6.4	1.0
1981	8.9	0.4
1982	11.9	0.2
1983	12.1	0.2
1984	11.6	0.3
1985	10.5	0.4
1986	10.2	0.5
1987	10.0	0.4
1988	9.3	0.4

quite satisfactory: the graphical derivation of the Beveridge curve in Figure 6.19 and the data shown in figure 6.20 suggests that the Beveridge curve is curved and not a straight line. Forcing a straight line through these data points must lead to the result that data points do not deviate randomly from the line. Instead, in the upper left section most points will be way above the line, in the middle section most points will be below the line, and in the lower right section most points will be above the line again. So a straight line systematically misrepresents the data in certain sections. (Technically speaking, the residuals are *autocorrelated*. But we do not address this issue here.)

To obtain a better representation of the data we may want to fit a non-linear curve. How can that work when all equations considered so far were linear and additive? What we can do is transform u, say to $1/u$, and then assume that v is linearly related to $1/u$. The resulting estimate is

$$v = 0.56 + 1.48(1/u) \qquad R^2 = 0.82$$
$$\quad (5.87) \quad (10.89)$$

Note that now the coefficient of $1/u$ is positive. This is still as expected, for if u grows, its reciprocal value $1/u$ falls and v falls by $1.48 \times (1/u)$. Note, however, that the fit of the equation is rather worse than the one obtained above.

Since our model only suggests that the Beveridge curve is bent, but does not give a specific functional form, by using $1/u$ we may be 'overbending' the curve. Since we are free to experiment with other functions, let's try a combination of the two above specifications. This gives

$$v = 1.45 + 0.84\,(1/u) \;-\; 0.11u \qquad R^2 = 0.95$$
$$\quad (11.03) \quad (7.41) \qquad\quad (7.39)$$

This combined specification seems to match the data much better, boosting R^2 to 0.95. All coefficients are significant, meaning that when unemployment rises, this bears on vacancies via a linear channel $-0.11u$ and via a non-linear channel $0.84/u$. Non-linear relationships are quite a common phenomenon in economics.

YOUR TURN

Unemployment and the black economy

By definition, unofficial economic activity in what is called the black economy escapes being recorded in a country's GDP. While no official data on the size of the unofficial economy exist, informed estimates range from around 5% up to some 25% of GDP (see Table 6.3).

It is conceivable that official and unofficial employment are substitutes: if one goes up, the other goes down. Then the size of the black economy should go up if unemployment rises. Use the international data provided in Table 6.3 to check whether they support this proposition.

Table 6.3

	B	CH	D	E	F	I	J	NL	S	UK	US
BLACK unofficial economy as % of GDP	13	4	9	25	8	20	4	7	13	7	7
u unemployment rate	10	5	9	23	12	11.5	3	7	8	9.5	6.5

Booms and recessions (III): aggregate supply and demand

What to expect

After working through this chapter, you will understand:

1 How to draw the aggregate supply curve in price–income space.
2 How to derive the aggregate demand curve and draw it in price–income space.
3 The concept of adaptive expectations.
4 How to use the *AD–AS* model to trace how an economy moves in price–income space.
5 That the policy options offered by the model depend on whether we have fixed or flexible exchange rates.

This chapter brings together what we have learned so far and consolidates it into a coherent explanation of macroeconomic fluctuations around potential income. The two isolated results that we want to merge are what we learned about aggregate supply (the firms' production decisions) in the last chapter, and what we learned about aggregate demand (the spending decisions) in Chapters 2–5.

The Mundell–Fleming model focused on aggregate demand. Aggregate supply only enters this model hypothetically, by asking what equilibrium income would be if, at the current price level, firms were ready to produce all goods and services that are demanded. This assumption is only reasonable when the economy operates well below capacity, with a substantial share of production facilities being idle.

Chapter 6 made a point of demonstrating that under normal conditions firms are only willing to supply one specific level of output at a given price level. This level is indicated by the *AS* curve. If the Mundell–Fleming model's demand-side equilibrium differs from this level, that is from aggregate supply, we end up with excess demand or excess supply in the goods market. In such situations prices are likely to change and to restore equilibrium.

This chapter follows the lead given in Chapter 5, where we briefly touched upon this issue of the confrontation of aggregate demand with aggregate supply that is fixed at potential income Y^*. Now, however, we include the more realistic positively sloped aggregate supply curve derived in section 6.3 of Chapter 6.

7.1   The short-run aggregate supply curve

In Chapter 6, section 6.3, we acquired a qualitative understanding of the aggregate supply (AS) curve. When prices rise unexpectedly, firms extend production beyond its normal level, causing the AS curve to feature as a positively sloped line in a price–income diagram. The economic reasoning behind it is that once nominal wages are fixed by collective contracts, higher prices mean lower real wages W/P. And the lower the real wage, the more workers will firms seek to employ and the more output will be produced. This relationship was summed up in the equation

$$P = P^e + \lambda(Y - Y^*) \tag{7.1}$$

We already noted during its introduction in Chapter 6 that this linear relationship between prices and income was only an *approximation* of the AS curve in the neighbourhood of its current level of prices. The further we move away from this level, the more imprecise this approximation becomes. You may see that by noting that according to equation (7.1) an increase in prices from 1 to 2 raises aggregate output just as much as an increase from 100 to 101. This does not make sense economically, because in the first case real wages (with nominal wages fixed) are cut in half, and in the second case they fall by a meagre 1%. To make economic sense, the same percentage drop in the real wage should always trigger the same output response, no matter whether the price level is 1,100 or 1,000,000. But this means that at a higher price level you need a larger price increase to prompt the same change in output. This calls for a *non-linear AS* curve as drawn in Figure 7.1, panel (a).

A drawback of this refined perspective of the AS curve is that non-linear curves are a bit more cumbersome to handle graphically and very awkward to manipulate mathematically. Fortunately, the kind of non-linearity

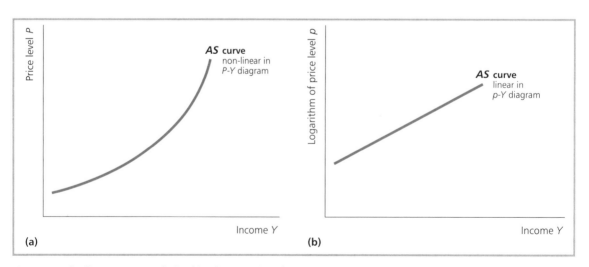

Figure 7.1 The linear AS curve derived in Chapter 6 is only an approximation. By developing the argument more accurately, we find the AS curve to be a curved line in a price–income diagram as shown in panel (a). Conveniently, when this precise AS curve is redrawn in a diagram that uses a logarithmic scale, or that measures the logarithm of the price level on the vertical axis, it turns out to be a straight line as depicted in panel (b).

encountered here is a specific; one we can take care of by assuming that the natural logarithm of the price level $\ln P$ is linearly related to income, that is $\ln P = \ln P^e + \lambda(Y - Y^*)$ or, after defining $\ln P \equiv p$,

$$p = p^e + \lambda(Y - Y^*) \qquad\qquad \text{AS curve} \quad (7.2)$$

As you may remember if you worked through the appendix on logarithms in Chapter 1, a given change in p (the logarithm of P) always indicates the same percentage change in P, no matter how high p and P are. So a linear relationship between p and Y, as given in equation (7.2) and shown in Figure 7.1, panel (b), reflects the economic mechanisms of the labour market correctly and is in substance equivalent to displaying the AS curve as in panel (a). The bonus is that we may continue to work with a linear equation.

The positively sloped AS curve shows what firms are willing to produce at different price levels. They will do so only if sufficient demand is there. Therefore, the supply-side decisions reflected in the AS curve must be augmented by information about the economy's demand side.

7.2 The aggregate demand curve

The natural counterpart to the labour market, which stands behind the AS curve, is the Mundell–Fleming model. The labour market and AS curves show output supplied, assuming that all output produced will also be demanded. The Mundell–Fleming model focuses on the demand side of the economy. It assumes that whatever is demanded will eventually, in equilibrium, be supplied. So if we arrive at an equilibrium of $Y^* = 100$, this means that 100 units will be demanded, provided firms produce them. The Mundell–Fleming model *assumes* that they are being produced. Our previous discussion of aggregate supply, however, says they may not. For this reason, from now on we will refer to the Mundell–Fleming equilibrium as demand-side equilibrium. The issue to be addressed in this section is how demand-side equilibrium is affected by the price level. The reason we need to know this is that we found aggregate supply to depend on the price level according to equation $Y = Y^* + \frac{1}{\lambda}(p - p^e)$. For given price expectations this aggregate supply curve is a positively sloped line in a p-Y diagram. If we want to represent the economy's demand side, as represented by the Mundell–Fleming model, in the same diagram and analyze its interaction with aggregate supply, we first need to find out how demand-side equilibrium income is affected by the price level.

The term demand-side equilibrium refers to the income level at which the economy would be in equilibrium, provided that firms supply all goods and services that are being demanded.

We noted earlier that the assumption of a permanently fixed price level, which underlies the standard Mundell–Fleming model, is acceptable only in situations of severe capacity underutilization or in the very short run. We also showed, however, that the effect of price increases on output can be traced in the Mundell–Fleming model. The usual presentation is awkward to work with. First, neither the price level nor inflation can be read directly off the axes. Second, it is difficult to analyze the interaction between the Mundell–Fleming model and the supply side of the economy, which was shown to depend on actual and expected prices.

What we would like to have is a graphical representation of supply decisions and of demand-side equilibria in a common diagram, with the price level on one axis and income on the other. This will prove useful in analyzing today's foremost macroeconomic problems – inflation and unemployment – in graphical terms.

Equilibrium income and the price level: the *AD* curve

How does an increase in the price level affect equilibrium in the Mundell–Fleming model? Since the argument focuses on different transmission channels under different exchange rate regimes, we must answer this question separately for flexible and fixed exchange rates.

The first step is to derive the aggregate demand (*AD*) curve in a price–income diagram. In a second step, to be taken in Chapter 8, we move on to a representation in an inflation–income diagram by means of dynamic aggregate demand (*DAD*) curves. The algebra of *AD* and *DAD* curves is not difficult, but it is cumbersome. Therefore, it is relegated to appendices. The main text develops the *AD* curve by means of graphs and discussion.

Flexible exchange rates

Figure 7.2 shows the economy initially in equilibrium at Y_0 with a price level of P_0. Recall that under flexible exchange rates income is determined by the equilibrium conditions in the money market, the *LM* curve, and in the foreign exchange market, the *FE* curve, alone. This was shown in Chapter 5. The real exchange rate changes endogenously so as to make *IS* go through the point where *LM* and *FE* intersect. If we leave all other exogenous variables that affect *LM* and *FE* (including the nominal money supply) unchanged, an increase in the price level reduces the real money supply and thus shifts *LM* up. This moves the point of intersection between *FE* and *LM* to the left, thus lowering equilibrium income to Y_1. An accompanying real appreciation drives down net exports, moving *IS* to the left as well.

The lower graph in Figure 7.2 projects the result onto a *P-Y* surface. When prices were low at P_0, income was high at Y_0. This fixes one demand-side equilibrium point. When prices rose to P_1, income fell to Y_1: a second equilibrium point. This generalizes into a negative relationship between income and prices. We may approximate this relationship linearly by writing

$$P = a - bY + \text{other factors} \qquad\qquad \textit{AD curve} \quad (7.3)$$

What are the 'other factors' that determine the position of the *AD* curve? These must definitely be all those factors that were previously found to affect equilibrium income in the Mundell–Fleming model at a given price level. Since, under flexible exchange rates, income is determined by the point of intersection between the *FE* curve and the *LM* curve, the *IS* curve is redundant. The real exchange rate simply adjusts to make *IS* pass through the point where *FE* and *LM* cross. Hence, under flexible exchange rates, *the 'other factors' are those that affect the positions of FE and LM.*

The *LM* curve only shifts due to changes in the real money supply *M/P*. Changes of *P* have already been discussed. They move the economy along the *AD* curve. Increases in *M* shift *LM* to the right, raising income at any given price level. Hence if *M* rises, the *AD* curve shifts to the right.

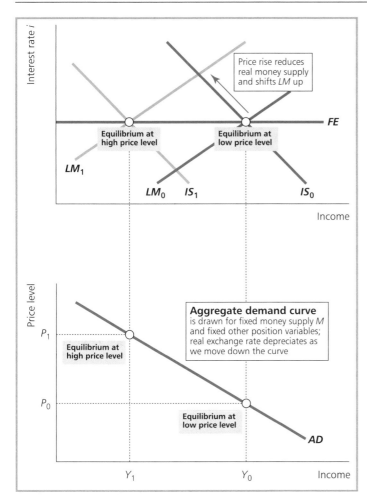

Figure 7.2 (Flexible exchange rates.) Prices are low at P_0, LM is at LM_0 and output at Y_0. Now a price rise to P_1 reduces the real money supply M/P, moving LM up to LM_1. The new equilibrium at the price level P_1 obtains where LM_1 and FE intersect. Output has dropped to Y_1. Since IS shifts into IS_1 endogenously, the real exchange rate appreciates. The line in the lower graph generalizes this negative relationship between P and Y. It is called the aggregate demand curve (AD).

The position of the FE curve is determined by two factors: the world interest rate, now given as i^W, and expected depreciation ε^e. Both shift the foreign exchange market equilibrium line up. Figure 7.3 shows that this moves macroeconomic equilibrium up and to the right along the LM curve, raising income. As this leaves the price level unchanged, the lower panel shows the implied shift of the AD curve to the right.

With these arguments a preliminary way to write the complete AD curve under flexible exchange rates is

$$P = a - bY + \text{other factors } [M(+), i^W(+), \varepsilon^e(+)] \qquad \begin{array}{c} AD \text{ curve} \\ \text{flexible exchange rates} \end{array} \qquad (7.4)$$

Fixed exchange rates

Under fixed exchange rates the IS curve and the LM curve switch roles. Income is determined by the intersection between the FE curve and the IS curve. Now the LM curve becomes technically redundant because the money supply must adjust so as to make LM pass through the point where FE and IS cross.

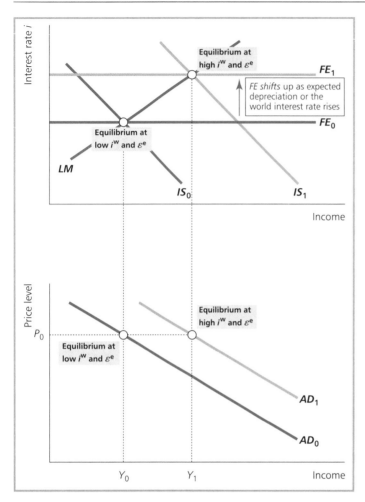

Figure 7.3 (Flexible exchange rates.) Initially prices are at P_0 and income is Y_0. Now the world interest rate or depreciation expectations rise, shifting FE up into FE_1. If the money supply and prices are unchanged the LM curve stays put. The new equilibrium obtains where LM and FE_1 intersect. (IS moves endogenously into IS_1 via a real depreciation.) The lower graph notes that, with unchanged prices, a rise in i^W or ε^e raises income. Since this would apply at any initial price level, the whole AD curve shifts to the right.

Following the above line of argument, Figure 7.4 starts from an initial demand-side equilibrium in the Mundell–Fleming model at a low price level. As the price rises, the real exchange rate $R = EP^W/P$ appreciates (i.e. *falls*), depressing net exports and shifting IS to the left. Equilibrium income falls from Y_0 to Y_1. Again, the lower panel shows that this implies a negatively sloped aggregate demand curve in the P-Y plane.

Evidently, the AD curve looks the same under flexible and under fixed exchange rates. Again, we may tentatively write

$$P = a - bY + \text{other factors} \qquad\qquad AD \text{ curve} \qquad (7.5)$$

What differs is the transmission channel from price changes to income changes. (Note also that the slope parameter b is different under the two exchange rate systems. See the appendix to this chapter.) Under flexible exchange rates the starting point is the exogenous reduction in the real money supply caused by the price increase. This makes the real exchange rate appreciate endogenously. Under fixed exchange rates the starting point is an exogenous reduction in the real exchange rate caused by the price increase. This obliges the real money supply to decline endogenously.

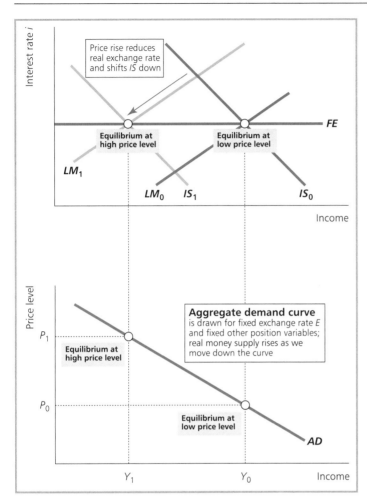

Figure 7.4 (Fixed exchange rates.) Prices are low at P_0, LM is at LM_0 and output at Y_0. Now a price rise to P_1 reduces the real exchange rate EP^W/P, moving IS to IS_1. The new equilibrium obtains where IS_1 and FE intersect. Income has dropped to Y_1. LM shifts into LM_1 endogenously due to a reduction of the real money supply. The line in the lower graph generalizes this negative relationship between P and Y. It is the aggregate demand curve (AD) under fixed exchange rates.

This has one important implication when we draw AD. Under flexible exchange rates AD is drawn for a given nominal money supply M. As we move along the curve, the real exchange rate changes. Under fixed exchange rates AD is drawn for a given nominal exchange rate. As we move along the curve, the real money supply changes. Common to both exchange rate systems is that the real money supply and the real exchange rate rise as we move down AD.

When exchange rates are fixed the 'other factors' are those that affect FE or IS. The IS curve only shifts due to changes in all factors that affect the demand for goods and services: government expenditures, world income, the exchange rate and the world price level. As taxes fall or any of the other variables rises, the IS curve shifts to the right, raising income. Since this happens at a given price level, the AD curve shifts to the right.

As mentioned above, the position of the FE curve is determined by the world interest rate i^W and expected depreciation ε^e. Both shift the foreign exchange market equilibrium line up. Since under fixed exchange rates the equilibrium moves along the IS curve, income falls. Figure 7.5 shows this and the resulting shift of the AD curve to the left.

With these arguments the complete *AD* curve under fixed exchange rates now reads

$$P = a - bY + \text{other factors } [E(+), P^{W}(+), G(+), Y^{W}(+), i^{W}(-), \varepsilon^{e}(-)] \quad (7.6)$$

AD curve
fixed exchange rates

We now have a good qualitative understanding of the aggregate demand curves under flexible and fixed exchange rates. Both are negatively sloped lines in a *P-Y* diagram. The point to note here, again, is that the *linear* relationships between *P* and *Y* proposed in equations (7.3)–(7.6) are only *approximations* of the *AD* curve in the neighbourhood of its current price level. As we move away from this level, this approximation becomes less and less precise. The reason for this echoes the discussion of the functional form of the *AS* curve we had in section 7.1.

Consider flexible exchange rates. According to equation (7.4) an increase of the price level from 1 to 2 lowers aggregate demand just as much as an increase from 100 to 101. This does not fit the economic reasoning behind the Mundell–Fleming model and the *AD* curve. Note that under flexible exchange rates prices

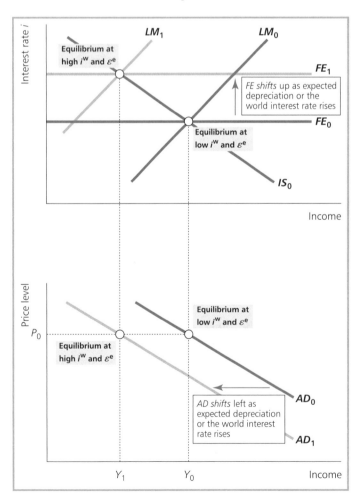

Figure 7.5 Initially prices are at P_0 and income is Y_0. Now the world interest rate or devaluation expectations rise, shifting *FE* up into FE_1. If the nominal exchange rate and prices are unchanged the *IS* curve stays put. The new equilibrium obtains where *IS* and FE_1 intersect. (*LM* moves endogenously into LM_1 via a forced reduction of the money supply.) The lower graph notes that, with unchanged prices, a rise in i^{W} or ε^{e} reduces income. Since this would apply at any initial price level, the whole *AD* curve shifts to the left.

affect aggregate demand because they affect the *real* money supply M/P. Now a price rise from 1 to 2 cuts the real money supply in half while a price rise from 100 to 101 cuts the real money supply by only 1%. In order to suit our economic line of reasoning, the same percentage change in the real money supply should always trigger the same output response, no matter what the initial price level is. This means that at a higher initial price level you need a higher price increase to prompt the same change in aggregate demand. This calls for a non-linear AD curve as drawn in Figure 7.6, panel (a). Again, the unwelcome mathematical side effect that arises from this can be avoided if we repeat what we did with the AS curve in section 7.1, that is postulate a linear relationship between the logarithm of P and income (and the other variables). Ignoring the constant term, the tentative AD curve under flexible exchange rates can now be spelled out explicitly as

$$p = m - bY + h(i^{\mathrm{W}} + \varepsilon^{\mathrm{e}})$$

AD curve   (7.7)
flexible exchange rates

So the position of the AD curve in p-Y space depends on the (logarithm of the) money supply, the world interest rate and expected depreciation. Note that it is crucial to include $m \equiv \ln M$ on the right-hand side and not M. Only by writing the logarithm of the money supply in this equation can we ensure that a change in the real money supply is required in order to move the curve.

Similar arguments apply under fixed exchange rates. Equation (7.6) states that a price increase from 1 to 2 reduces aggregate demand just as much as an increase from 100 to 101. This does not fit well with the economic reasoning behind the Mundell–Fleming model and the AD curve. When exchange rates are fixed, prices affect aggregate demand because they affect the *real* exchange rate $R \equiv EP^{\mathrm{W}}/P$. Now an increase of P from 1 to 2 cuts the real exchange rate in half. An increase from 100 to 101 reduces it by only 1%. To mend this inaccuracy of equation (7.6), the same percentage change in the real exchange rate should always trigger the same response in aggregate demand,

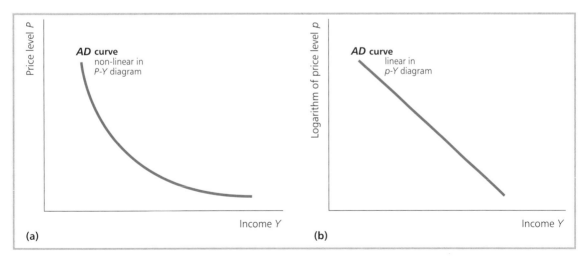

(a)   (b)

Figure 7.6 The straight *AD* curve derived and shown in Figures 7.2–7.5 is only an approximation. By developing the argument more accurately, we find the *AD* curve to be non-linear in a price–income diagram as shown in panel (a). Conveniently, when this precise *AD* curve is redrawn in a diagram that uses a logarithmic scale, or that measures the logarithm of the price level on the vertical axis, it turns out to be a straight line as shown in panel (b).

independently of the initial price level. This calls for a non-linear AD curve as it was depicted in panel (a) of Figure 7.6. This non-linear relationship between P and Y is equivalent in content to a linear relationship between p and Y as shown in panel (b) and as expressed by the equation

$$p = e + p^W - bY + \gamma Y^W + \delta G - f(i^W + \varepsilon^e) \qquad \begin{array}{c} \textbf{\textit{AD}} \text{ curve} \\ \text{fixed exchange rates} \end{array} \qquad (7.8)$$

So the position of the AD curve in p-Y depends (under fixed exchange rates) on the (logarithm of the) exchange rate, (the logarithm of) world prices, world income, government spending, the world interest rate and expected depreciation. The exchange rate and world prices need to be entered as logarithms, because this ensures that the same percentage change of the real exchange rate always has the same effect on aggregate demand.

Time to pause – we have come a long way

The AD curve, the graphical image of demand-side macroeconomic equilibria, is an admittedly complex concept with a deep foundation that stretches over several chapters. Before we proceed to combine the AD curve with the AS curve to obtain the most sophisticated model of booms and recessions discussed in this book, let us pause, step back and recall what we achieved so far. Figure 7.7 reminds us of the main concepts and how they fit together.

We had chosen two kinds of perspectives. Initially, because it was the simpler perspective to start with, we considered the global (or closed) economy. It is composed of the goods market, which we analyzed in terms of the Keynesian cross and the IS curve in Chapters 2 and 3, and of the money market, which was also discussed in Chapter 3 in terms of the LM curve. Still in the same chapter, both markets were merged into the IS-LM or global-economy model that permitted the analysis of monetary and, in refined form, fiscal policy.

The second more demanding but more relevant perspective adopted was that of a national economy with international ties. The national-economy perspective embraces the IS-LM model as a starting block and adds trade in goods, services and international assets and the foreign exchange market. This is done in Chapter 4 and the completed model, the IS-LM-FE or Mundell–Fleming model is analyzed in Chapter 5.

Assuming fixed prices, the IS-LM-FE model is designed for the study of short-run effects. To explain why and how prices move in the medium and long run, we need to study the interaction between the economy's supply and demand sides. After aggregate supply had been given a somewhat shabby treatment in earlier chapters, Chapter 6 mends this by introducing the labour market. The labour market determines employment and, via the production function, output produced. The visual image of output supplied at different price levels is the AS curve. The visual image of demand-side equilibria as spelled out by the IS-LM-FE model is the AD curve. Merging both curves into one diagram permits us to analyze how aggregate supply and demand interact and drive income and prices. It is this AD-AS model, standing on the shoulders of the models discussed in earlier chapters, to which we now turn our attention.

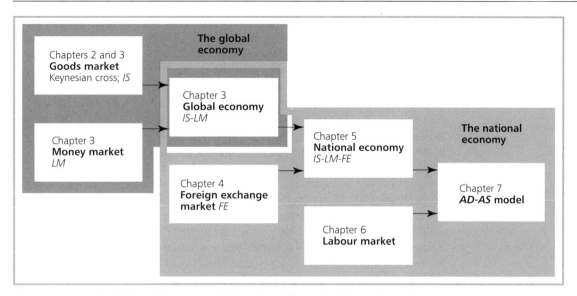

Figure 7.7 Note the building blocks assembled so far and how they fit together. The *IS-LM* model, our first model of the aggregate global economy, comprises the money market and the goods market (which is tantamount to the Keynesian cross). By adding the foreign exchange market to the *IS-LM* model (thereby introducing trade in goods and financial assets) we arrive at the basic model of the national economy. We call this the Mundell–Fleming or *IS-LM-FE* model. Chapter 6 refined this view of the national economy by adding the labour market, thus digging deeper on the supply side. Adding the labour market to the Mundell–Fleming model yields the aggregate-demand/aggregate-supply model, our workhorse for analyzing booms and recessions. (We might also go back and add the labour market to the *IS-LM* model to obtain a refined model of the global economy, but refrain from doing so.)

7.3 The *AD-AS* model: basics

Before we put the *AD-AS* model to work by analyzing economic policy options, let us summarize what we know so far and identify the model's short-run and long-run equilibria. Keeping an eye on the time horizon is called for because the *AD-AS* model is our first model with an explicitly dynamic structure (that is, it has its roots in the labour market, the market behind the *AS* curve). Unlike previous, comparative static models that identify equilibria but say nothing about how we move from one equilibrium to another, the *AD-AS* describes such dynamic processes.

The *AD-AS* model is also our first macroeconomic model in which the demand side and the supply side show up as equals. The model is captured by two equations which vary somewhat depending on the exchange rate system. Under flexible exchange rates the *AD-AS* model reads

$$p = m - bY + h(i^{\mathrm{W}} + \varepsilon^{\mathrm{e}}) \qquad\qquad \text{AD curve} \quad (7.7)$$
$$\text{flexible exchange rates}$$

$$p = p^{\mathrm{e}} + \lambda(Y - Y^*) \qquad\qquad \text{AS curve} \quad (7.2)$$

Panel (a) in Figure 7.8 sums up what we know about the positively sloped *AS* curve. First, it moves up as the expected price level rises, because this would make trade unions demand higher money wages and induce firms to produce less output at any given price level. Second, as we move up on a given *AS* curve, drawn for given nominal wages and price expectations, the real wage declines. This makes labour cheaper and coaxes firms into hiring more labour and producing more output.

Panel (b) in Figure 7.8 enumerates our understanding of the negatively sloped *AD* curve. Under the system of flexible exchange rates assumed here, it moves up (or to the right) if either the money supply expands or if the domestic interest rate is driven up by rising world interest rates or an increase in expected depreciation. Both stimulate demand for domestic products. The first directly, because consumers buy more of our exports with their increased incomes. The second indirectly, by making our currency depreciate and our exports cheaper. Note that the identified shift variables are exactly those which affect income in the Mundell–Fleming model under flexible exchange rates. As we slide down a given *AD* curve, the real money supply increases and the exchange rate depreciates. The higher real exchange rate is needed to stimulate net exports and raise demand-side equilibrium income.

Under fixed exchange rates the *AS* curve is unchanged, but the *AD* curve is different:

$$p = e + p^{\text{W}} - bY + \gamma Y^{\text{W}} + \delta G - f(i^{\text{W}} + \varepsilon^{\text{e}}) \qquad \begin{array}{l} AD \text{ curve} \\ \text{fixed exchange rates} \end{array} \quad (7.8)$$

$$p = p^{\text{e}} + \lambda(Y - Y^*) \qquad\qquad\qquad\qquad AS \text{ curve} \quad (7.2)$$

While the *AD* curve has a negative slope under both exchange rate systems, this is where the similarity ends. First, the slope is not the same under fixed and flexible exchange rates, though we are using the same parameter $-b$

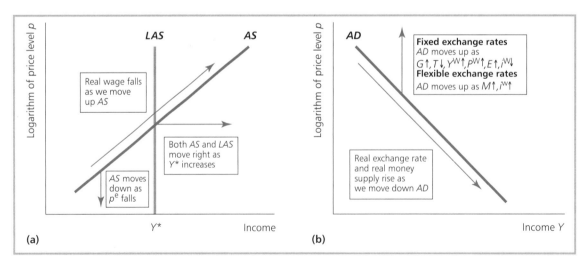

(a)   (b)

Figure 7.8 Panel (a) sums up what we know about the *AS* curves. Both *LAS* and *AS* move to the right if potential income increases, say due to technological improvements or a growing labour force. *AS* moves up if price expectations go up. Then unions request higher money wages which makes firms demand fewer work hours at any given price level. As we move up the *AS* curve the real wage declines. Only this can make firms hire more workers and generate more output. The *AD* curve shown in panel (b) moves up if the indicated variables change in direction of the attached arrows. These shift variables are those which affect income in the Mundell–Fleming model under flexible or fixed exchange rates. As we slide down the *AD* curve, falling prices increase the real money supply and make the real exchange rate depreciate.

(see also the appendix to this chapter). Second, the position of the *AD* curve is affected by a different set of variables, or if by the same variables, then in different directions. The *AD* curve moves up if the exchange rate, world prices, world income or government spending increases, or if interest rates are driven down by falling world interest rates or a reduction in expected depreciation. Again, the link to the Mundell–Fleming model is that these are the very variables that affect income under fixed exchange rates. The real money supply and the real exchange rate both rise as we slide down the *AD* curve.

Short-run and long-run *AS* curves

In Chapter 6 we realized that there were two kinds of aggregate supply curves. One describes the short-run response of aggregate supply to an unexpected increase in prices. This is equation (7.2), which was repeated for convenience in the preceding sections. As we move up or down this curve, we take expected prices p^e (and, implicitly, the nominal wage) as given. This is a situation which cannot prevail in the long run, of course. Suppose prices and expected prices equal 1, initially. Now prices rise by 50% to 1.5. If prices stay at that level for good, an expected price level of 1 underestimates actual prices by 1/3 period after period. This is costly and will obviously not go on for ever. Eventually actors will learn and raise expected prices closer towards actual prices. But this moves the *AS* curve up and thus affects income.

We will take a closer look at how people form expectations in the next chapter. It is sufficient for now to contend that in the long run, if individuals are capable of some rudimentary learning, expected and actual prices must be the same. Setting $p = p^e$ in equation (7.2) and solving for *Y* yields the long-run *AS* curve

$$Y = Y^* \hspace{4cm} \text{Long-run } AS \text{ curve}$$

which is a vertical line in *p-Y* space. Figure 7.9 combines the long-run *AS* curve (*LAS*) with the arbitrarily drawn *AD* and short-run *AS* curves.

The equilibrium price level

The *AD* curve identifies the level of aggregate demand obtaining at different price levels. Yet if we do not know prices, we cannot determine the level of aggregate demand. The *AS* curve identifies aggregate supply at different price levels. Again: we cannot identify aggregate supply until we know the price level. What helps here is that in equilibrium aggregate demand must equal aggregate supply. Graphically, therefore, the equilibrium price level is where the *AD* curve and the *AS* curve intersect. But which *AS* curve? Didn't we just state that we have two – a short-run *AS* curve and a long-run *AS* curve? And these two *AS* curves do not necessarily intersect the *AD* curve at the same point. Do we then have two equilibrium price levels? Exactly so: one that applies in the long run and one that applies in the short run, just as we have one *AS* curve for each time horizon.

Point A, where the *AD* and the long-run *AS* curves intersect, identifies the **long-run equilibrium** price level p^{LR}. Remember: each point on the *AD* curve corresponds to a simultaneous equilibrium in the goods market, the money market and the foreign exchange market. Each point on the long-run *AS* curve

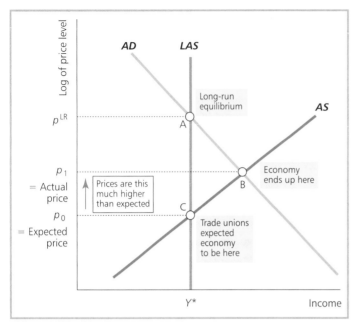

Figure 7.9 This graph emphasizes key points in the *AD-AS* diagram. C is the point trade unions have been aiming for. They must do so on the basis of expectations, since money wages cannot be renegotiated for a while after they are fixed in a contract. Obviously unions expected *AD* to pass through C and prices to equal p_0. Actually, the *AD* curve turned out to be positioned much further up, rendering prices unexpectedly high and real wages lower than planned. Firms employ an unusually large number of workers and the economy ends up in B. B cannot last, because it resulted from unions committing expectational errors. Once these are corrected, the economy will settle into its long-run equilibrium in A.

corresponds to a long-run equilibrium in the labour market in the sense that the plans and expectations of both employers and trade unions have worked out. Neither party wants to revise wages and thus move away from this point as long as there is no change in monetary, fiscal or exchange rate policy, or in the economic conditions in the rest of the world. Thus point A qualifies as a long-run equilibrium in which all four markets clear and prices are as expected at $p = p^e = p^{LR}$ and income is at its potential level Y^*.

B, the point of intersection between the *AD* curve and the short-run *AS* curve, is a **short-run equilibrium**. Since B is also on the *AD* curve, all three markets on the demand side of our model economy are in equilibrium. With B being *on* the short-run *AS* curve but *off* the long-run *AS* curve, it corresponds to a short-run, temporary equilibrium in the labour market only. In this equilibrium the employers' plans work out, because they employ all the labour they want at the current real wage, but not the trade unions' plans. Here B is to the right of the long-run *AS* curve. So real wages are lower than what trade unions had aimed for (because prices are higher than expected). Unions are stuck with this (in their view less than ideal) situation as long as current wage contracts last. When these expire, unions will renegotiate the money wage rate, which changes the current equilibrium.

C is the point the trade unions had been aiming for. By basing their wage negotiations on an expected price level of p_0 they made the *AS* curve pass through C. Had prices turned out as expected, income would have equalled potential income and trade unions' utility would have been at a maximum (subject to the restriction provided by the labour demand curve).

The link between the temporary, short-run equilibrium at B and the long-run equilibrium at A is provided by the ability of trade unions to learn from and correct expectational errors. Since prices at B are higher than expected, for whatever reason, a rational response by trade unions will be to expect higher prices when entering next year's wage negotiations than they expected last time. But higher expected prices position the *AS* curve further up, moving the point of intersection with the *AD* curve northwest. This process continues until the economy eventually ends up at A. We will look at such dynamic processes in more detail below and particularly in Chapter 8.

7.4   Policy and shocks in the *AD-AS* model

Let us now put the *AD-AS* model to work. First, by looking at the effects of fiscal and monetary policy, then by analyzing how the national economy is affected by economic changes in the world around us.

Fiscal policy

Fiscal policy – that is, the use of government spending or taxes as a means of influencing the course of the economy – has already been analyzed in the context of the Mundell–Fleming model in Chapter 5. There we learned that fiscal policy is only effective when exchange rates are fixed. Under flexible exchange rates an increase in government spending only crowds out net exports by making the exchange rate appreciate. In the context of the *AD-AS* model this means that under flexible exchange rates an increase in government spending cannot shift the *AD* curve. So there is no change in aggregate income or the price level. What a look at the *AD-AS* diagram conceals, however, are the changes going on underneath the highest level of aggregation. As already indicated, even though Y does not change when G increases, the *composition* of aggregate demand changes. This is easily revealed by considering the circular flow identity introduced in this book's introductory chapters. From the requirement that leaks out of and injections into the circular flow of income must balance we obtained the useful identity

$$(S - I) + (T - G) + (IM - EX) = 0 \qquad \textbf{Circulate flow identity}$$
$$\underbrace{0 \quad 0}_{\textstyle 0} \quad \underbrace{0 \quad +}_{\textstyle -} \quad \underbrace{+ \quad -}_{\textstyle +} \qquad \text{Directions of change}$$

The row beneath the variables indicates in which direction each variable changes after the increase in G. S and T do not change because they depend on income, and income does not change, so we have zeros there. I is also unchanged because the interest rate, on which investment depends, does not change. Drawing these insights together, we note that $S - I$ remains unchanged, but the government budget surplus deteriorates. With $T - G$ going down and $S - I$ unchanged, $IM - EX$ must rise in order to keep the identity. Since income is unchanged, net imports can only rise if the exchange rate appreciates. This raises imports and reduces exports, permitting us to fill in the $+$ and $-$ sign beneath IM and EX. This small exercise is an illustration of the potential of the circular flow identity (while not being a real model in its own right) to provide useful information when combined with insights from models like the *AD-AS* model.

Let us turn next to fixed exchange rates, the scenario in which fiscal policy can affect aggregate income. Figure 7.10 assumes that the economy is in a long-run equilibrium in A_0 and shows the corresponding AD_0 and AS_0 curves.

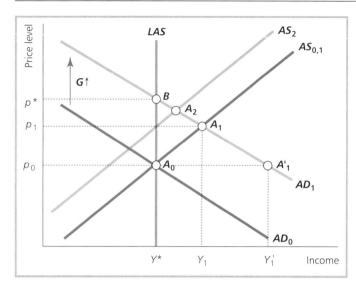

Figure 7.10 When the government raises spending, aggregate demand goes up at all price levels. Consequently, the AD curve shifts to the right. If the AS curve were horizontal, as implicitly assumed in the Keynesian cross, the IS-LM and the Mundell–Fleming model, income would rise to Y_1'. When AS is positively sloped, however, firms increase production only if prices go up and lower the real wage. Rising prices at the same time reduce aggregate demand. With supply sliding up the AS curve and demand up AD, supply finally equals demand when prices reach p_1 and income is Y_1. A_1 is only a temporary equilibrium based on faulty expectations, however. After expectational errors have been corrected, the economy settles into B.

Income is $Y_0 = Y^*$ and prices are p_0. Since the economy has been in this situation for a while, expected prices equal actual prices. Now suppose in period 1 the government decides to increase spending, which had not been anticipated when the currently binding wage contracts were negotiated at the end of period 0. Thus the AS curve, the position of which reflects the current money wage W_1, stays put while the rise in G moves the AD curve up into position AD_1. Let us first focus on what happens in period 1 and compare the effects with those derived in previous, simpler models.

The increase in government spending has increased aggregate demand at all price levels. If the price level was fixed at p_0, aggregate demand would rise to Y_1'. This is identical to the income response that would result in the Keynesian cross and in the Mundell–Fleming model. There we assumed that the aggregate supply curve was of an extreme Keynesian nature, namely horizontal, meaning that firms were prepared to meet any level of demand at the current price level. AD_1 would indeed intersect such a horizontal AS curve in point A_1'.

Our refined AS curve indicates a different story. At the current price level firms would not profit from producing more than Y^*. Hence, they will not do so. This means that demand exceeds supply at the price level p_0. In the face of excess demand for goods, prices will begin to rise. This has consequences both on the supply side of the economy and on the demand side. On the supply side, where the nominal wage is fixed, real wages fall and firms begin to hire more workers who produce more output. As we start to move northeast along $AS_{0,1}$ aggregate supply increases. On the demand side, where the exchange rate is fixed, rising prices reduce the real exchange rate. Domestically produced goods become more expensive compared to foreign goods. Demand for our products falls as we move up on AD_1 in a northwesterly direction. With rising prices causing the supply of goods to increase and the demand for goods to fall, excess demand will eventually be eliminated after prices have risen to p_1 and the economy has settled into a new, temporary equilibrium at A_1.

Point A_1 only represents a temporary equilibrium, as explained above. Prices have moved higher than trade unions had anticipated, eroding real wages. When at the end of period 1 new wages will be negotiated for period 2, unions will do so on the basis of expected higher prices. To make matters simple, suppose trade unions always expect prices to remain for the next period where they are now. This is a special case of adaptive expectations (to be discussed in more detail in Chapter 8) and reads

$$p_t^e = p_{t-1}$$

Applied to the current situation this means that prices expected for period 2 equal prices observed in period 1: $p_2^e = p_1$. This moves AS_2 into a position where it passes through the point where a horizontal line through A_1 intersects the long-run *AS* curve. Since this shows that supply is reduced at all price levels, there is now excess demand at p_1. Using the same arguments advanced above, this will cause prices to rise again until we find a new, temporary equilibrium in A_2. Since period 2 prices were again higher than expected by trade unions, expectations will be revised upwards again, shifting the *AS* curve up in period 3. The entire process continues until the economy finally settles into its new long-run equilibrium at point *B*. This new long-run equilibrium is characterized by the same level of income generated at *A*, before government spending was increased, and by higher prices. So if an economy operates at near full capacity (which we call potential income) an expansionary fiscal policy only has a temporary effect on income. Temporary may well mean a number of years, however. Beyond that, in the long run only prices are affected.

> Adaptive expectations are formed on the basis of the recent history of the variable under consideration alone. Expectations adapt to what the variable did in the past. Adaptive expectations are driven by the general equation $p^e = p_{-1}^e + a(p_{-1} - p_{-1}^e)$ How quickly expected prices adapt to actual prices is measured by the coefficient *a*.

Monetary policy

Let us now look at the effects of monetary policy in the *AD-AS* model. Since we learned in Chapter 5 that the central bank has no control over the money supply when exchange rates are fixed, we only look at flexible exchange rates. Figure 7.12 does more than trace the consequences of a money supply increase on income and prices, however, paying tribute to our claim that the six frames assembled piled upon each other trace the events observed in the *AD-AS* model back to what happens in the Keynesian cross, the Mundell–Fleming model and the labour market. The Keynesian cross and the Mundell–Fleming model are shown in panels (a) and (b). Panel (c) features the *AD* curve. The final panel depicts the labour market, though slightly modified compared with Chapter 5. In order to be able to use the same measurement on the horizontal axis as the other five panels, the demand for labour exercised by firms is translated into output units using the production function. The same is done for the labour supply. Panel (e) shows the *AS* curve, and panel (d) finally features the *AD-AS* model.

Initially, in period 0, the economy is in the long-run equilibrium identified by the dark blue lines and dots in all six panels. In period 1 the central bank expands the money supply, shifting the *LM* curve in the Mundell–Fleming frame to the right into the light blue position. Nothing has happened yet to the *AD* curve, in the Keynesian cross, and on the economy's supply side. Only after the incipient downward pressure on the interest rate in the Mundell–Fleming diagram makes the exchange rate depreciate does the aggregate expenditure line in the Keynesian cross move up and the *AD* line shift to the right into their respective light blue positions. So these curves are not directly affected by

CASE STUDY 7.1   International evidence on the quantity equation and the *AD* curve

You may have wondered how the quantity equation $PY = VM$ introduced in Chapter 1 relates to the *AD* curve discussed in this chapter. Well, you simply solve this equation for *P* to obtain $P = VM/Y$, which is a negatively sloped line in a price–income diagram. So the quantity equation can be seen as some rudimentary *AD* curve. It also moves up when the money supply increases. But it is rudimentary in the sense that it does not rest on any detailed study of demand-side markets. For example, it does not explain when *V*, the velocity of circulation changes, and what factors might ignite such changes. The *AD* curve is more explicit in this respect, attributing this role to the interest rate, and identifying the factors that might influence the interest rate.

The quantity equation and the *AD* curve have in common that they are incomplete explanations of income and prices without an aggregate supply curve. Without an *AS* curve both curves only offer a menu of possibilities: when the money supply increases and *V* remains constant, either prices go up, or income goes up, or both grow a little bit.

The quantity equation is usually used to make statements about the long-run behaviour of prices. In this and the previous chapter we argued that the long-run *AS* curve is vertical, meaning that income is constant at Y^*. In this case, there is a one-to-one relationship between *P* and *M* for any time horizon. For the year 2000 we have $P_{2000} = VM_{2000}/Y^*$. For 1969 we have $P_{1969} = VM_{1969}/Y^*$. Subtracting the second equation from the first and dividing the obtained difference by the second equation we obtain

$$\frac{P_{2000} - P_{1969}}{P_{1969}} = \frac{M_{2000} - M_{1969}}{M_{1969}} \quad (1)$$

which proposes that the price increases can be traced back to money supply increases to their full extent. Panel (a) in Figure 7.11 shows that this implication of the quantity equation (and of the *AD* curve) receives some empirical support from the displayed group of countries, since all countries are roughly positioned along a straight line through the origin with slope 1.

Equation (1) is not precise in the sense that potential output Y^* is not really constant. We assume

so for convenience when analyzing business cycles, but as Figure 2.2 underscored, such short-run fluctuations occur against the background of long-run income growth due to population growth and technological progress. Since money supply increases administered to accommodate higher income levels need not lead to higher prices, a more general (approximate) version of equation (1) is

$$\frac{P_{2000} - P_{1969}}{P_{1969}} = \frac{M_{2000} - M_{1969}}{M_{1969}} - \frac{Y_{2000} - Y_{1969}}{Y_{1969}} \quad (2)$$

The right-hand part shows the evidence based on this refined equation. There are minor, though barely visible improvements in the closeness of data points to the 45° line. Remaining deviations must be attributed to changes in the velocity of circulation over time.

(a)

(b)

Figure 7.11

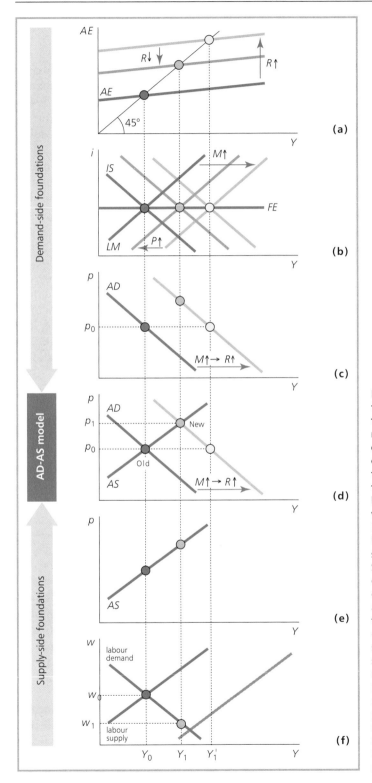

Figure 7.12 This figure emphasizes the foundations of the *AD-AS* model. When the money supply increases, the *LM* curve moves right in the Mundell–Fleming diagram (panel (b)). This drives up the exchange rate and shifts *IS* to the right too. The impact of exchange rate depreciation on aggregate expenditure can also be seen in the Keynesian cross (panel (a)) where equilibrium income rises to Y_1' as in the Mundell–Fleming model. Since this happens at unchanged prices, it means a shift of *AD* to the right (panels (c) and (d)). Since supply has remained at Y_0 so far, demand exceeds supply. Excess demand drives prices up. On the supply side, as documented in panels (d), (e) and (f), this drives down the real wage, raising employment and output. On the demand side, rising prices lower the real money supply and the exchange rate, shifting the aggregate expenditure line down in the Keynesian cross and demand-side equilibrium income left in the Mundell–Fleming panel (b). In panels (c) and (d) we witness an upward move along *AD*. Prices rise to make supply increase and demand fall until at p_1 excess demand in the goods market is eliminated and income is Y_1.

the money supply, but indirectly via the money supply's effect on the exchange rate. The *AE* line sums up all planned spending, including exports. So as the exchange rate depreciates and exports rise, the *AE* line moves up, causing income to rise via the multiplier effect. Regarding the *AD* curve we see that if it moves to the right after a money supply increase it is because the exchange rate depreciates and demand-side equilibrium income is higher at any given price level. Note that the rightward shift of the *AD* curve is equal to the increase in income observed in the Keynesian cross and the Mundell–Fleming model, because the price level is assumed constant in these models.

The light blue dots identify the new equilibrium obtained in the Mundell–Fleming model and show where this equilibrium is positioned in the other diagrams. Since prices and real wages have not changed yet, this new demand-side equilibrium sits horizontally to the right of the initial dark blue dots in panels (c) and (d). The important point to note is that the money supply increase has driven a wedge between supply and demand. The exchange rate depreciation induced by the money supply increase has raised aggregate demand but not aggregate supply (see panel (c)). This excess demand at the current level of prices triggers price increases that affect both aggregate demand and aggregate supply.

On the demand side, because rising prices reduce the real money supply and therefore the real exchange rate, exports fall. This moves the *AE* line down in the Keynesian cross and the *IS* curve (along with the *LM* curve) left in the Mundell–Fleming diagram. On the *AD* curve this fall in income shows a movement up in a northwesterly direction.

On the supply side, rising prices reduce real wages. This increases the demand for labour and employment (since we assume involuntary unemployment to exist at potential income), resulting in an upward move on the *AS* curve. The goods market only clears after prices have increased to p_1. This is when the dampening effect of price increases on demand and the stimulating effect on supply combined are large enough to remove the excess demand that the money supply increase had generated at the initial price level p_0.

Bottom line

This chapter has merged our, by now, quite sophisticated understanding of the economy's demand side, developed in Chapters 1–5, with the insights into the supply side obtained in Chapter 6. The interaction between supply and demand explains the macroeconomic role of prices. Comparing this chapter's analyses of fiscal and monetary policy with pertinent analyses within the Mundell–Fleming model (see Chapter 5), we note that both instruments lose some of their potency. In the *AD-AS* model the price increases generated by expansionary policies dampen their effects on income even in the short run. They turn out to be smaller than they were in the Mundell–Fleming model. In the long run, prices even rise so much that no effect on income remains.

The *AD-AS* model is a very powerful tool for understanding the temporary ups and downs in modern economies. However, as presented in this chapter, it has one severe practical disadvantage that becomes obvious when we consider the history of price movements documented for 15 countries in Figure 7.13. None of these countries experienced a period of stable prices between 1960 and 2011. The *AD-AS* model in *p-Y* space assumes that in

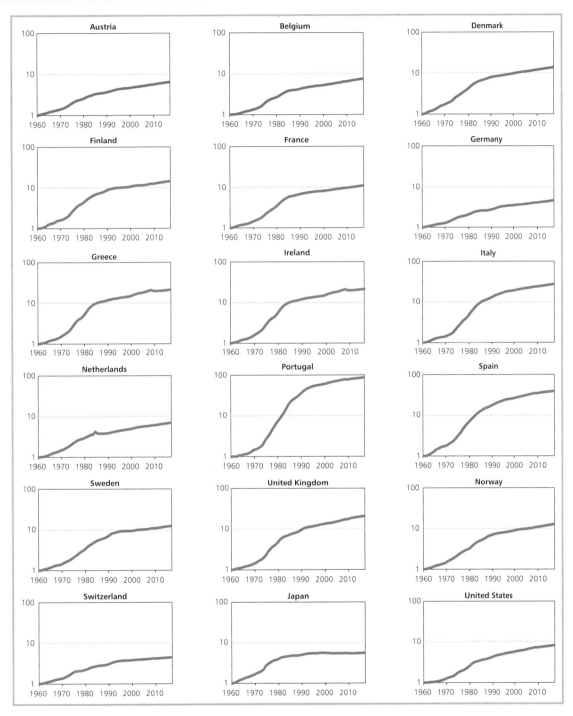

Figure 7.13 Price levels in Europe and the world, 1960–2010, and forecasts until 2016.

Source: IMF, *International Financial Statistics*, 2011.

long-run equilibrium prices are stable. Prices only move temporarily, during phases of excess demand. This does not seem to fit the empirical picture where there appears to be permanent inflation, even in equilibrium. Inflationary equilibria can occur in the *AD-AS* model, but it is impractical to display and analyze them in a price–income diagram. The reason is simply that such an equilibrium would move up the long-run *AS* curve and, sooner or later, out of view.

Because of this practical limitation we consider the graphical form of the aggregate demand–aggregate supply model introduced in this chapter as only a stepping stone on the way to a more refined presentation that suits the discussion of inflation much better. This form of the *AD-AS* model will be derived and discussed in more detail in the next chapter.

CASE STUDY 7.2   *AD-AS* in crises

Case study 3.1 argued that liquidity-trapped money markets were a major cause of the severe macroeconomic repercussions of the global economic crisis that started in 2007–08. They explain why the aggressively expansionary policies of central banks had no visible effect on aggregate demand. After this chapter's discussion of aggregate demand one may wonder, however, why a simple price drop does not close the gap between aggregate demand and potential output.

Liquidity traps: from *IS-LM* to *AD*
Figure 7.14(a) shows the *IS-LM* model with a general *LM* curve that turns horizontal when the interest rate approaches zero. All *LM* curves have such a horizontal section. But this is usually not displayed because during normal times *IS* and *LM* intersect on *LM*'s upward-sloping segment, in a point such as A. Since *LM* curves are drawn for a given nominal money supply and a given price level, point A maps onto a *p–Y* diagram (Figure 7.14(b)). When prices fall, say to p_B, *LM* moves to the right, raising equilibrium income. This is why the *AD* curve slopes downward.

When prices drop further still, say to p_C, *LM* shifts further to the right, but there is no more effect on income. Income stays where it was when prices were at p_B, implying that the *AD* curve is vertical. This connects to what we said above: just as all *LM* curves have a *horizontal* segment, all *AD*

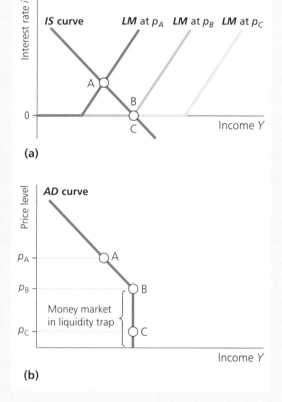

(a)

(b)

Figure 7.14

Case study 7.2 continued

Figure 7.15

curves have a *vertical* segment. One is the mirror image of the other. We usually do not bother to display this segment either, because during normal times *AS* curves intersect *AD* on the downward-sloping segment.

Crises and deflation

Figure 7.15 displays such a normal equilibrium that applied before the world economy fell into recession. Now, when the subprime crisis hit the financial markets, two things happened:

1 Households started to mistrust banks and, in particular, the financial products they sold. As a consequence, households wanted a risk premium on their interest-bearing deposits. In terms of Figure 7.14(a) and as discussed in Case study 3.1, this moves the *LM* curve up and lowers equilibrium income.

2 Banks started to mistrust other banks, but also firms, since it was unclear who would survive the unfolding meltdown. Therefore, they requested a significant risk premium from firms who wanted financing for their investment projects. In terms of Figure 7.14(a) this shifts *IS* left and reduces equilibrium income also.

Both effects reduce equilibrium income at any given price level and thus shift *AD* left. If this combined effect, which was supported by the negative effect of the deteriorating stock markets on wealth

and the business climate, and, thus, on consumption and investment, is strong enough, the *AD* curve shifts so much left that it loses contact with the equilibrium aggregate supply curve. This means that there is no more equilibrium between aggregate demand and supply that market forces may bring about. Without any government interference, there is a risk of deflation, of falling prices, that market forces alone will not be able to stop.

There is reason to fear deflation. It played a key role during the Great Depression, when prices in the US fell by almost 30 per cent between 1926 and 1933. Persistent deflation between 1999 and 2006 also characterized Japan's recent 'lost decade'. And first signs of receding wholesale prices in major economies were witnessed in the summer of 2008. In the US wholesale prices fell be 6.5 per cent from July to November 2008. In December Mervyn King, the governor of the Bank of England, warned that 'Britain would flirt with deflation [in 2009]'.

Policy options

To prevent deflation from starting (or accelerating), policy-makers must shift *AD* back to the right quickly, far enough to bring a point of intersection between *AD* and *EAS* back onto the radar and thus re-establish a macroeconomic equilibrium toward which market forces could move. The factors that generated insufficient demand in the first place are the key to the solution. If a liquidity trap prevents monetary policy from stimulating demand, the government may stimulate demand directly, bypassing the money market – by putting money directly into the hands of households and firms, or extending its own spending aggressively. Such *expansionary fiscal policy measures* need to be accompanied by *measures that remove the uncertainty and mistrust* between the economy's key players, thus reducing the risk premiums that paralyze markets and foster the return to normal conditions. In addition, new forms of monetary policy have been used, called *quantitative easing*. We will discuss these in Chapter 15.

Food for thought: Why are politicians so afraid of deflation? How would a deflation of 1% per year affect the *IS-LM* equilibrium and the liquidity trap, in particular? What would be the effect of a 10% deflation? *Hint*: Case study 8.1 provides some answers to these questions.

CHAPTER SUMMARY

- An economy's supply side can be represented in price–income space by means of a vertical long-run aggregate supply curve (LAS) and a positively sloped short-run aggregate supply curve (AS).

- The demand side can be represented in price–income space by means of a negatively sloped aggregate demand curve (AD).

- Under flexible exchange rates the aggregate demand curve has a negative slope for the following reason. A price increase reduces the real money supply. Since the domestic interest rate cannot deviate from the world interest rate, the demand for money must be reduced by a decline in income.

- Under fixed exchange rates the aggregate demand curve has a negative slope for the following reason. A price increase reduces the real exchange rate. This appreciation creates an excess supply of domestic goods at the old level of income. Since the interest rate is fixed to the world interest rate, the supply of goods can only equal the demand for goods at a lower level of income.

- All policy measures and changes in the economic environment that affected demand-side equilibrium income in the Mundell–Fleming model, shift the AD curve.

- All income responses identified in the Mundell–Fleming model also show up in the AD-AS model. However, these effects disappear in the long run. In the short run the effects are smaller than they were in the Mundell–Fleming model because there is some crowding out via price increases.

Key terms and concepts

EXERCISES

7.1 When deriving the AS curve in Chapter 6 we assumed that real rigidities (say, in the form of monopolistic trade unions) cause involuntary unemployment at normal employment levels. Now consider an economy in which no such real rigidities exist. Normal employment is determined by the point of intersection between the individual labour supply and the labour demand curves. What does the AS curve look like in such an environment? Does it make a difference whether individuals enter longer-term wage contracts or whether wages can be renegotiated any time?

7.2 This chapter derives the *AD* curve for the national economy from the Mundell–Fleming model. Derive the global-economy *AD* curve graphically from the *IS-LM* model.

7.3 Figure 7.2 and 7.4 derive the *AD* curve for the national economy under flexible and fixed exchange rates. Find out, by means of graphical analysis, under which exchange rate system the *AD* curve is steeper.

7.4 Suppose world interest rates go up, driving the world into a recession (that is, world income falls). Use the *AD-AS* model to analyze how this affects prices and income in our national economy. Do your results depend on whether exchange rates are fixed or flexible?

7.5 What happens to the *AD* curve with flexible exchange rates and perfect international capital mobility if
(a) the money supply increases?
(b) the world interest rate decreases?
(c) the government reduces spending?

7.6 Why does an increase in the world interest rate shift the *AD* curve *up* under flexible exchange rates, but *down* under fixed exchange rates?

7.7 Why does a change in world income shift the *AD* curve under fixed exchange rates but not when exchange rates are flexible? Start with the Mundell–Fleming model to determine which curves shift (and which do not) as foreign income increases. Does that mean that changes in foreign income do not change anything if exchange rates are flexible?

7.8 We examine a small open economy with fixed exchange rates. In period 0, the country is in its long-run equilibrium. The government carries out a one-time revaluation of the currency in period 1. Trace the effects of such a revaluation in the *AD-AS* model for periods 1 and 2. Where is the new long-run equilibrium? Assume that price expectations are formed adaptively ($p^e = p_{-1}$).

7.9 Suppose a country's potential income Y^* increases because lawmakers reduce trade union monopoly power. What will be the short-, medium- and long-run effects on prices and income in the *AD-AS* model? Let price expectation be formed according to $p^e = p_{-1}$.

7.10 Suppose the economy's demand side can be described by the Keynesian cross with the equilibrium condition

$$Y = AE = 0.4Y + 1000$$

(a) What is the level of income?
(b) Suppose government spending rises by 100. What is the new demand-side equilibrium income?
(c) If the income level computed under (a) was equal to potential income and the short-run *AS* curve was positively sloped, what is the excess demand generated by the increase of government spending by 100 at the initial price level?

7.11 Box 5.1 demonstrated that the *FE* curve is vertical when a country controls cross-border capital flows. Derive the *AD* curve graphically for this case of controlled capital flows.
(a) Consider flexible exchange rates first. Which policy variables and exogenous variables shift the *AD* curve?
(b) Now derive the *AD* curve for fixed exchange rates. Which variables determine the position of the *AD* curve?

Online resources

Interactive applet on *AD-AS* model www.eurmacro.eu/tutor/adas.html
X-ercise on monetary policy rules www.eurmacro.eu/xercises/adas.html
Interactive road map www.eurmacro.eu/tutor/map.html

Self quiz

www.eurmacro.eu/SelfQuiz/sq-ch07.html

Recommended reading

For an alternative to the *IS-LM-FE* model that replaces the money market (*LM* curve) with the assumption that the central bank follows a simple interest rate rule, see David Romer (2000) 'Keynesian macroeconomics without the *LM* curve', *Journal of Economic Perspectives* 14: 149–69.

An accessible general perspective on the future of macroeconomics by a Nobel prize winner is given in Robert M. Solow (2000) 'Toward a macroeconomics of the medium run', *Journal of Economic Perspective* 14: 151–8.

A critical discussion of the aggregate-supply/ aggregate-demand apparatus as a teaching device is given in David Colander (1995) 'The stories we tell: A reconsideration of AS/AD analysis', *Journal of Economic Perspectives* 9: 169–88. I hesitate to recommend reading it at this stage, however, as it may throw you off balance. While a number of the issues raised are well worth thinking about, others attack presumed blunders in the presentation of *AS* and *AD* which we avoid, as do most other textbooks.

APPENDIX   The algebra of the *AD* curve

The algebra of the *AD* curve is straightforward, though tedious. Two assumptions make it easier on us, without affecting the substance of the results:

1 In two behavioural functions we propose a linear relationship between a variable and the *logarithm* of some variable. The economic justification for this has been given in the text.

2 We let investment be exogenous, independent of the interest rate (which makes *IS* vertical). We thus focus on one transmission channel between the monetary sector (money market plus foreign exchange market) and the goods market only. Again, as the main text illustrates, this does not affect the qualitative results.

The goods market equilibrium condition serves as a point of departure:

$$Y = C + I + G + NX \tag{A7.1}$$

Letting $C = cY$, $I = 0$ and $NX = x_1 Y^{\mathrm{W}} + x_2(e + p^{\mathrm{W}} - p) - m_1 Y + m_2(e + p^{\mathrm{W}} - p)$ and solving for Y yields

$$Y = \frac{x_2 + m_2}{1 - c + m_1}(e + p^{\mathrm{W}} - p) + \frac{x_1}{1 - c + m_1}Y^{\mathrm{W}} + \frac{1}{1 - c + m_1}G \tag{A7.2}$$

The *logarithm* of the real money supply $m - p$ (which equals money demand at all times) depends on income and the interest rate

$$m - p = Y - hi \tag{A7.3}$$

Postulating semi-logarithmic relationships in equations (A7.2) and (A7.3) renders the benefit of keeping all equations encountered below additive.

Flexible exchange rates

Under flexible exchange rates the foreign exchange market equilibrium condition reads

$$i = i^{\mathrm{W}} + \theta(\bar{e} - e) + \bar{\varepsilon}^{\mathrm{e}} \tag{A7.4}$$

The last two terms describe expected depreciation. First, the exchange rate is expected to regress towards its equilibrium value (indicated here by a bar) according to $\theta(\bar{e} - e)$, as we had assumed previously. In an inflationary equilibrium we need to add a second term $\bar{\varepsilon}^e$. This ensures that even if the exchange rate is in equilibrium, investors expect the exchange rate to change if they expect the equilibrium exchange rate to depreciate.

Under flexible exchange rates, aggregate demand is determined by the intersection between *LM* and *FE*. Substituting equation (A7.4) into (A7.3) yields

$$m - p = Y - hi^W - h\theta\bar{e} + h\theta e - h\bar{\varepsilon}^e \tag{A7.5}$$

This equation still contains two endogenous variables, e and $\bar{e}$. To eliminate e, we solve equation (A7.2) for e to obtain

$$e = p - p^W + \frac{1 - c + m_1}{x_2 + m_2} Y - \frac{1}{x_2 + m_2} G - \frac{x_1}{x_2 + m_2} Y^W \tag{A7.6}$$

To obtain $\bar{e}$ we write the goods market equilibrium (A7.2) and the monetary sector equilibrium (*LM* plus *FE*), equation (A7.5), in terms of equilibrium values:

$$\bar{Y} = \frac{x_2 + m_2}{1 - c + m_1} (\bar{e} + p^W - \bar{p}) + \frac{x_1}{1 - c + m_1} Y^W + \frac{1}{1 - c + m_1} G \tag{A7.7}$$

$$m - \bar{p} = \bar{Y} - h(i^W + \bar{\varepsilon}^e) \tag{A7.8}$$

Substituting equation (A7.8) for $\bar{p}$ in (A7.7) and solving for $\bar{e}$ gives

$$\bar{e} = m - p^W - \left(1 - \frac{1 - c + m_1}{x_2 + m_2}\right)\bar{Y} + h(i^W + \bar{\varepsilon}^e) - \frac{x_1}{x_2 + m_2} Y^W - \frac{1}{x_2 + m_2} G \tag{A7.9}$$

Now substitute equations (A7.6) and (A7.9) for e and $\bar{e}$ in (A7.5) and solve for p to obtain the **AD curve under flexible exchange rates**:

$$p = m - \frac{x_2 + m_2 + h\theta(1 - c + m_1)}{(1 + h\theta)(x_2 + m_2)} Y + h(i^W + \bar{\varepsilon}^e)$$

$$+ \frac{(1 - c - x_2 + m_1 - m_2)}{(1 + h\theta)(x_2 + m_2)} h\theta\bar{Y} \tag{A7.10}$$

Compare equation (A7.10) with (7.7). The influence of m, Y, and i^W is the same in both equations, denoting the first fraction in equation (A7.10) by b. The role of depreciation expectations differs slightly since ε^e is considered exogenous in the text, but endogenous in this appendix.

Fixed exchange rates

Under fixed exchange rates the demand-side equilibrium obtains directly from the goods market. The monetary sector simply follows what happens in the goods market.

Solving equation (A7.2) for prices yields the *AD* **curve under fixed exchange rates:**

$$p = e + p^W - \frac{1 - c + m_1}{x_2 + m_2} Y + \frac{x_1}{x_2 + m_2} Y^W + \frac{1}{x_2 + m_2} G \quad (A7.11)$$

Compare equation (A7.11) to (7.8). The influence of e, p^W, Y, Y^W and G is the same, denoting the three fractions by b, γ and δ. The positioning variables of *FE*, i^W and ε^e do not show up here because we let *IS* be vertical.

Booms and recessions (IV): dynamic aggregate supply and demand

What to expect

After working through this chapter, you will understand:

1 How to draw the aggregate supply curve in inflation–income space.

2 How to draw the aggregate demand curve in inflation–income space.

3 The concepts of adaptive and rational expectations, and how individuals choose to form expectations.

4 How to use the *DAD-SAS* model to trace how an economy moves in inflation–income space.

5 That the policy options offered by the *DAD-SAS* (and the *AD-AS*) model depend on whether we have fixed or flexible exchange rates.

6 That the economy's responses to monetary and fiscal policy depend on how individuals form expectations.

In Chapter 7 we assembled a complete macroeconomic model of the business cycle in which four markets interact and prices are endogenous. This is the model we were driving at from the beginning of this text. The form in which the aggregate demand–aggregate supply model is presented and handled graphically and algebraically has one major drawback, however: it does not permit a direct analysis of inflation. Of course, inflation is nothing but a steady increase in prices. So when we analyze prices we implicitly analyze inflation as well. From a practical viewpoint, however, it would be desirable to make inflation more explicit. After all, real-world economies rarely feature full price stability, as the long-run equilibrium in the *AD-AS* diagram would imply. In fact, only a minority of economists would even recommend striving for complete price stability. Monetary policy discussions these days centre on whether central banks should aim at an inflation target, not at a price level target, and if they should, whether the inflation target should be 2, 3 or 4%. When monetary policy becomes restrictive, the inflation rate falls, but rarely the level of prices. Disinflation, a reduction of the inflation rate, is something completely different from deflation, a reduction of the price level.

For the reasons stated, this chapter recasts the *AD-AS* model in a form that permits its graphical analysis in an inflation–income diagram. We will call this the *DAD-SAS* model, though it should be emphasized, however, that the

DAD-SAS model is not really a new model, but simply the *AD-AS* model in new, more practical clothing.

A second main theme of this chapter is the formation of expectations. While expected prices already played a role in Chapter 7's *AD-AS* model, we were content with a rather elementary treatment. In this chapter we look at expectations formation in much more detail, discussing the whole spectrum of possibilities from adaptive via rational expectations to perfect foresight.

Equipped with a refined understanding of expectations we take a second look at fiscal and monetary policy. The key insight will be that what policy-makers can achieve depends crucially on the way the public forms expectations.

8.1 The aggregate supply curve in an inflation–income diagram

In Chapter 7 we drew the *AS* curve in a diagram with the (logarithm of the) price level on the vertical axis, as a straight line. The underlying formula is

$$p = p^e + \lambda(Y - Y^*) \qquad\qquad \text{AS curve} \quad (8.1)$$

To obtain a formulation that can be drawn in an inflation–income diagram is no magic. Simply subtract (the logarithm of) last period's price level p_{-1} from both sides of (8.1) to obtain $p - p_{-1} = p^e - p_{-1} + \lambda(Y - Y^*)$. The difference $p - p_{-1}$ is the change in the logarithm of the price level. This approximates the percentage rate of change of the price level (see appendix to Chapter 1), which is the rate of *inflation* π. The other difference $p^e - p_{-1}$ is expected inflation π^e. So we may rewrite equation (8.1) as

$$\pi = \pi^e + \lambda(Y - Y^*) \qquad\qquad \text{SAS curve} \quad (8.2)$$

This is simply a new way of writing the aggregate supply curve. Written like this, it states that the level of output firms are willing to supply depends on normal output Y^* and on unexpected or surprise inflation. We call this curve the *SAS* curve, where the first *S* stands for *surprise*.

The *SAS* curve indicates the aggregate output that firms are willing to produce at different inflation rates.

Of course, equations (8.1) and (8.2) state the same thing. Equation (8.2) is more convenient to work with in an inflationary environment and yields a basis for viewing aggregate supply in an inflation–income diagram (see Figure 8.1).

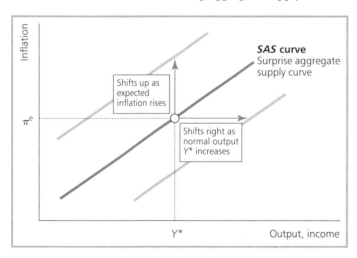

Figure 8.1 The *SAS* curve has a positive slope. If inflation is as expected, potential output Y^* is produced. If inflation is higher than expected, real wages are too low and firms hire more labour and produce more than normal. The *SAS* curve shifts up as π^e rises and moves to the right as Y^* increases.

This positively sloped *SAS* curve shows what firms are willing to produce at different inflation rates. They will do so only if demand is there. Therefore, as in the context of last chapter's *AD-AS* model, the supply side represented by the *SAS* curve must be augmented by information about the demand side.

8.2 Equilibrium income and inflation: the *DAD* curve

It would be nice to have the aggregate demand curve in a form that permits us to draw demand-side equilibria in the same diagram as the *SAS* curve. To obtain such a representation in inflation–income space, recall that in Chapter 7 we found the *AD* curve to read

$$p = m - bY + h(i^{\mathrm{W}} + \varepsilon^{\mathrm{e}}) \qquad\qquad \text{AD curve} \quad (8.3)$$
$$\text{flexible exchange rates}$$

under flexible exchange rates and

$$p = e + p^{\mathrm{W}} - bY + \gamma Y^{\mathrm{W}} + \delta G - f(i^{\mathrm{W}} + \varepsilon^{\mathrm{e}}) \qquad \text{AD curve} \quad (8.4)$$
$$\text{fixed exchange rates}$$

in a system of fixed exchange rates.

Looking at flexible exchange rates first, we can derive a dynamic representation of the aggregate-demand curve for inflation–income space, a **DAD curve**, by manipulating equation (8.3). Copying what we did in section 8.1 when we rewrote the *AS* curve, take first differences on both sides of equation (8.3) (which means that we deduct last period's values), remembering $\pi = p - p_{-1}$ and defining the money growth rate $\mu = m - m_{-1}$, to obtain:

$$\pi = \mu - bY + bY_{-1} + h(\Delta i^{\mathrm{W}} + \Delta \varepsilon^{\mathrm{e}}) \qquad \text{DAD curve} \quad (8.5)$$
$$\text{flexible exchange rates}$$

Among the last two factors in this equation, the presence of Δi^{W} takes care of the dependence on the world economy. The presence of $\Delta \varepsilon^{\mathrm{e}}$, which we treat as an exogenous variable here, may reflect the impact of market psychology.

Why does money growth μ enter with a coefficient of exactly 1? Recall from previous discussions of the Mundell–Fleming model that when all factors affecting equilibrium remain constant, income does not change. One factor that needs to remain constant under flexible exchange rates is the real money supply. So if all other factors remain unchanged as well ($\Delta i^{\mathrm{W}} = \Delta \varepsilon^{\mathrm{e}} = 0$), nominal money needs to grow at the rate of inflation in order to keep real money constant and to keep income where it was one period ago ($Y = Y_{-1}$).

Under fixed exchange rates with possible devaluations the *DAD* curve is derived by taking first differences on both sides of equation (8.4):

$$\pi = \varepsilon + \pi^{\mathrm{W}} - bY + bY_{-1} + \gamma \Delta Y^{\mathrm{W}} + \delta \Delta G - f(\Delta i^{\mathrm{W}} + \Delta \varepsilon^{\mathrm{e}})$$
$$\text{DAD curve} \quad (8.6)$$
$$\text{fixed exchange rates}$$

Here the rates of devaluation and world inflation enter with a coefficient of 1. The reason is that for unchanged other factors (that is $\Delta Y^{\mathrm{W}} = \Delta G = \Delta i^{\mathrm{W}} = \Delta \varepsilon^{\mathrm{e}} = 0$) the real exchange rate must remain constant to keep (demand-side) equilibrium income where it was last period. The real exchange

Note. The first appendix to this chapter derives very much the same *DAD* curve with more plausible *endogenous* depreciation expectations. Considering $\Delta \varepsilon^{\mathrm{e}}$ exogenous in the main text's graphical discussion provides a handle for analyzing the role of market psychology, that is, what happens if investors lose confidence in a currency for no obvious reason.

Note. Under fixed exchange rates with occasional realignments the **expected devaluation** is the probability of a realignment times the expected size of the realignment. Example: $\varepsilon^{\mathrm{e}} = 0.2 \times 10 = 2$. If the probability of a 10% realignment rises from 0.2 to 0.5, the expected devaluation becomes 5 (%). Hence devaluation expectations have changed by $\Delta \varepsilon^{\mathrm{e}} = 5 - 2 = 3$.

Figure 8.2 The *DAD* curve has a negative slope. As we move down *DAD* the real exchange rate rises, and so does aggregate demand. Panel (a) demonstrates that under flexible exchange rates the position of *DAD* is mainly determined by money growth, μ, but also by changes in the world interest rate and changes in expected depreciation. The curve moves up as any of those factors increases. Panel (b) shows that under fixed exchange rates the position of *DAD* is mainly determined by world inflation π^{w}, but also by changes in world income, government spending, the world interest rate, and expected devaluation. As any of those factors increases, *DAD* moves. It moves up with the first three factors and down with the last two.

rate EP^{W}/P remains unchanged if domestic inflation equals the sum of devaluation and world inflation. Our knowledge of the *DAD* curve is summarized in Figure 8.2.

8.3   The *DAD-SAS* model

Our macroeconomic model is now complete. It boils down to two equations, or curves, which can be analyzed in a simple π-Y diagram. The equations comprising the *DAD-SAS* model under flexible exchange rates read

$$\pi = \mu - bY + bY_{-1} + h(\Delta i^{W} + \Delta \varepsilon^{e})$$

DAD curve
flexible exchange rates

$$\pi = \pi^{e} + \lambda(Y - Y^{*})$$

SAS curve

The *DAD-SAS* model under fully fixed exchange rates $(\varepsilon = \Delta \varepsilon^{e} = 0)$ reads

$$\pi = \pi^{W} - bY + bY_{-1} + \delta \Delta G + \gamma \Delta Y^{W} - f \Delta i^{W}$$

DAD curve
fixed exchange rates

$$\pi = \pi^{e} + \lambda(Y - Y^{*})$$

SAS curve

Do not let the unpretentious elegance of this model deceive you. The *DAD* curve is nothing but a new way of stating the insights obtained during our discussions of the Mundell–Fleming model. If we want to know what is going on behind the curve, say in the money market or the balance of payments, we must go back to the Mundell–Fleming model and its constituent markets. But note again: the Mundell–Fleming model and the *DAD* curve are merely two different ways of stating the same thing. Therefore, the Mundell–Fleming model and the *DAD* curve (taken alone) cannot give different answers to the same question.

The *SAS* curve combines, and to some extent hides, all the insights already gained or to be gained in our discussions of the economy's supply side: the labour market (in Chapter 6), the capital stock and economic growth (in Chapters 9 and 10). The curve says that firms are ready to supply output in excess of full-capacity or potential output only if inflation turns out to be higher than anticipated. In the absence of unanticipated inflation, output rests at its normal level Y^*. We treat Y^* as a fixed number during graphical discussions of the model. In reality, as will be discussed in Chapter 9, potential output grows over time, due to improvements in technology, a growing labour force and accumulation of human and physical capital. Potential output also goes hand in hand with unemployment, a substantial part of which may be involuntary.

With these important reminders we now proceed to analyze how the economy's supply and demand sides interact.

Equilibrium in the *DAD-SAS* model

The *DAD-SAS* model is dynamic. It describes the development of income, inflation and (behind a veil) the interest rate, the exchange rate and the composition of aggregate demand over time. Two factors make the model inherently dynamic. First, the *DAD* curve moves over time as income changes, since its position is endogenously determined by last period's income. Second, the position of *SAS* depends on expected inflation. Inflation expectations may be wrong, may change over time in response to actual inflation, and hence shift the position of the *SAS* curve. Before we trace the dynamic interaction between the economy's demand and supply sides in subsequent sections, we pause here to identify long-run results – the equilibrium.

In the **long run**, or **in equilibrium** if you like, all adjustment processes have petered out and individuals make no more mistakes. In the context of our model, this means that individuals anticipate the rate of inflation correctly. If this is the case, we may substitute $\pi = \pi^e$ into the *SAS* curve equation to obtain the equilibrium aggregate supply (*EAS*) curve

$$Y = Y^* \qquad\qquad \textit{EAS} \text{ curve}$$

Thus, in equilibrium, the aggregate supply curve is simply a vertical line through normal output Y^* (just as the vertical classical *AS* curve) (see Figure 8.3), a fact we already know and that applies independently of the current exchange rate regime.

This has a straightforward implication for the equilibrium aggregate demand curve. Since, in equilibrium, aggregate supply cannot change, we may let $Y - Y_{-1} = 0$ in the *DAD* curve. Under *flexible exchange rates* we thus obtain the equilibrium aggregate demand (*EAD*) curve (letting $\Delta i^W = \Delta \varepsilon^e = 0$)

$$\pi = \mu \qquad\qquad \textit{EAD} \text{ curve}$$
$$\text{flexible exchange rates}$$

Note. In Chapter 7 we called the vertical line denoted by $Y = Y^*$ the long-run aggregate supply curve (*LAS*), because under adaptive price expectations adjustment towards it takes time. We now switch terminology, calling $Y = Y^*$ the equilibrium aggregate supply curve (*EAS*). This is more general and accommodates the situation when under other inflation expectations schemes, analyzed below, adjustment is immediate.

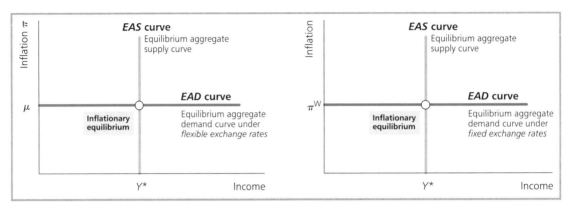

Figure 8.3 In equilibrium the labour market clears and income remains at Y^*, no matter where inflation is. So *EAS* is vertical. For the demand-side equilibrium (as given by the *AD* curve) to remain unchanged, the real money supply must stay constant under flexible exchange rates (hence $\pi = \mu$ in panel (a)), or the real exchange rate must remain the same under fixed exchange rates (hence $\pi = \pi^W$ in panel (b)).

This *EAD* is a horizontal line where inflation equals the money supply growth rate. The intersection between *EAD* and *EAS* determines the inflationary equilibrium in which money growth determines inflation and output is at Y^*.

Under *fixed exchange rates* (letting $\Delta G = \Delta Y^W = \Delta i^W = 0$) the *EAD* curve turns out to be

$$\pi = \pi^W$$

EAD curve
fixed exchange rates

Thus, equilibrium inflation is given by world inflation. Next we would like to learn how to analyze the consequences of *permanent shocks*, which define a new equilibrium, and *transitory shocks*, which displace the economy from equilibrium. Let us begin by going through the mechanics of how to determine the positions of *DAD* and *SAS* curves at specific points in time.

How to draw and trace *DAD* and *SAS* curves

To position the *SAS* or *DAD* curve, all we need to do is identify one point on the curve and then draw the curve with a positive or negative slope, respectively, right through it.

- *Positioning SAS.* We know from equation (8.2) that if inflation were exactly as expected ($\pi = \pi^e$), output would be at its normal level ($Y = Y^*$). Therefore *mark expected inflation on the vertical axis. Then go horizontally to the right until you hit the vertical line over Y^*.* This is a point on the current *SAS* curve! Now simply draw the curve with positive slope through this point.
- *Positioning DAD.* Under flexible exchange rates, if income remained where it was last period, inflation would equal the growth rate of the money supply (since $\pi - \mu = -b(Y - Y_{-1})$). Under fixed exchange rates, if income remained where it was last period, inflation would equal world inflation (since $\pi - \pi^W = -b(Y - Y_{-1})$, holding the other factors constant). Therefore *mark last period's income on the horizontal axis. Move vertically up until you hit either the horizontal line (EAD curve) at the money growth rate*

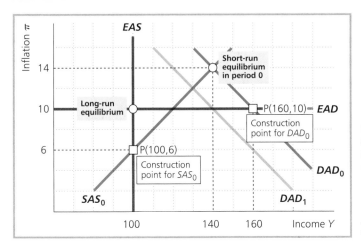

Figure 8.4 To position SAS_0: inflation expectations are 6; if inflation was also 6 (hypothetically!), income would be equal to potential income, which is 100. To position DAD_0: last period's income is 160; for income to remain there, inflation would have to equal money growth, which is 10. Actual inflation and income are obtained where DAD_0 and SAS_0 intersect.

when exchange rates are flexible, or the horizontal line at world inflation plus devaluation when exchange rates are fixed. This gives you a point on the current *DAD* curve! Draw the curve through this point.

Since this may sound a bit abstract, consider the following numerical flexible exchange rates example (see Figure 8.4). Let $Y^* = 100$, $\mu = 10\%$, $\pi^e = 6\%$, $Y_{-1} = 160$, and suppose $\lambda = b = 0.2$. To determine *SAS*, move up to a value of 6 on the vertical axis. Then move horizontally to the right to the vertical line at $Y^* = 100$. The point P(100, 6) pins down the current-period *SAS* curve at SAS_0. To determine *DAD*, start at 160 on the horizontal axis. Move straight up to the horizontal line at $\mu = 10$. The point P(160, 10) pins down the current-period *DAD* curve at DAD_0.

Note that P(100, 6) and P(160, 10) are just easily determined points that help locate DAD_0 and SAS_0. The actual macroeconomic outcome is determined by the point of intersection of the two curves. It turns out to be at P(140, 14).

It is this outcome that triggers the dynamics to move both curves into new positions next period. The position of DAD_1 is now determined by the fact that income during the preceding period had fallen to 140. Thus, the *DAD* curve moves down to the left. The position of SAS_1 is determined by new inflation expectations. Since period 0's inflation stood at 14% while only 6% had been expected, it is likely that inflation expectations will have been revised upwards. This moves the *SAS* curve up. But how far? There is no way of telling unless we know precisely how inflation expectations are being formed and revised. It is time to address this topic.

8.4 Inflation expectations

Expectations play a pivotal role in economics. Besides our current concern with inflation expectations, recall previous discussions of whether consumers and investors expect income to change permanently or not. This issue crucially affected the multiplier derived in the Keynesian cross in Chapter 2, and continues to determine by how much the *DAD* curve shifts. Also recall the discussion of expected depreciation in the context of transition dynamics in the Mundell–Fleming model in Chapter 5 and, of course, the role of expected prices in Chapters 6 and 7.

In stark contrast to the fact that almost everything in economics depends on expectations, no simple, easy-to-use hypothesis is accepted of how individuals form expectations. We will discuss why, and show what the consequences are in the *DAD-SAS* model.

Adaptive expectations are being formed on the basis of what the variable actually did in the past. Adaptive inflation expectations are driven by the equation $\pi^e = \pi^e_{-1} + a(\pi_{-1} - \pi^e_{-1})$. How quickly expectations adapt to actual inflation is measured by the adjustment coefficient a.

A seasoned workhorse in economics is the assumption of adaptive expectations. The general idea is that if previous expectations were wrong, individuals move them closer to what actually happened.

Adaptive expectations have one big advantage: they are simple and easy to compute. Their simplest form (letting $a = 1$ in the margin note) is

$$\pi^e = \pi_{-1}$$

which, in many situations will give you a reasonable first shot. What will be tomorrow's weather? The same as today's. Who will be the world's best golfer one year from now? The same person who holds this title now. What will be Europe's best-selling car next year? The same as this year. Panel (a) in Figure 8.5 generalizes these examples. It illustrates that whenever we are dealing with a variable that changes infrequently, adaptive expectations do a reasonable job and lead to low average forecast errors. As well as being simple, adaptive expectations can also be quite accurate if the variable to be forecast does not change very often or only in small steps. Panel (b) shows a variable that changes more often, i.e. every period. In this case adaptive expectations constantly lag behind and forecast errors are sizeable on average.

The stylized patterns given in Figure 8.5 are also encountered in real-world macroeconomic time series. Figure 8.6 shows inflation rates in France and India for the 1990s. Adaptive expectations would have performed quite satisfactorily during this decade for France, with an average absolute forecast error of only 0.37 percentage points. Performance in India would have been comparatively poor, with an average forecast error of almost 4 percentage points.

If adaptive expectations perform poorly *and* if errors are costly, individuals will look for ways to improve forecasts. In this attempt they process all

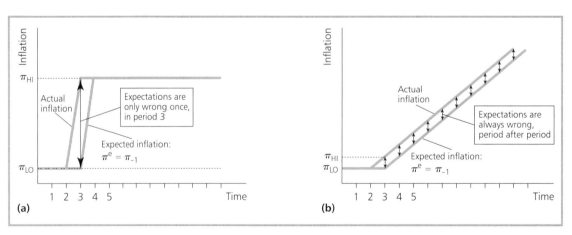

Figure 8.5 Adaptive expectations (here $\pi^e = \pi_{-1}$) perform well if inflation changes infrequently (panel (a)). If inflation changes constantly, such expectations would prove erroneous period after period (panel (b)).

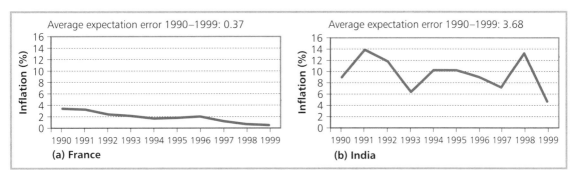

Figure 8.6 Large changes in French inflation were infrequent between 1990 and 1999. Adaptive expectations ($\pi^e = \pi_{-1}$) worked well, missing actual inflation by only 0.37 percentage points on average. India experienced constantly changing inflation rates. Adaptive expectations would have been wrong by 3.68 percentage points on average.

Source: IMF, *IFS*.

Rational expectations draw on all available information. This may include a wide set of other variables, or even knowledge of a macroeconomic model such as *DAD-SAS*.

information that is available to them. Such expectations have been coined rational expectations.

The crucial question in the context of rational expectations is: what information is available? An established benchmark case in macroeconomics is to assume that individuals know just as much as the economists who built the model, namely the model itself. For instance, if we want to determine rational inflation expectations in the context of the *DAD-SAS* model, as we shall do shortly, we must assume that individuals *know* how this model relates inflation to other endogenous and exogenous variables.

To give a simpler example, assume that our model stated that inflation always equals last period's money growth rate, $\pi = \mu_{-1}$. Rational expectations make use of this knowledge and expect inflation to follow money growth with a one-period lag: $\pi^e = \mu_{-1}$. All that individuals need to do is observe money growth and transform it into a perfect forecast.

This recipe does not work, however, if the variable to be forecast is related to other variables that are also not yet known, say $\pi = \mu$. Then the task of forecasting inflation simply becomes the task of forecasting money growth. But conventional macroeconomic models do not explain policy changes. Policy changes usually come as surprises even for individuals who form rational

Perfect foresight is never wrong. It assumes that individuals know and foresee everything, taking the concept of rational expectations to the extreme.

expectations. If even policy changes are foreseen, we will speak of perfect foresight, implying that there is no uncertainty left, no surprises possible. Perfect forsight permits us to trace the effects of policy measures that are *anticipated*.

Rational expectations are an important benchmark case. But the label's implication that all other expectations formation schemes are not rational is misleading. As has been stressed above, other expectations formation schemes, such as adaptive expectations, have the advantage of being simpler and cheaper – cheaper in terms of the time and attention that we need to pay to the issue, and in terms of other resources. A rational individual weighs the costs that she needs to incur in order to improve expectations performance against the benefits expected to accrue. The result is economically rational expectations. What these are may vary over time and space, from market to market.

Economically rational expectations suppose that individuals collect information and increase the sophistication of their forecasts only to the point where the costs begin to exceed the expected benefits.

In some cases economically rational expectations may indeed be *rational* or *perfect foresight* in the above narrow sense, but often they may be adaptive in a rather crude way. To cover the entire spectrum we shall analyze policy measures under all three expectations formation schemes introduced here.

8.5 The *DAD-SAS* model at work

We are finally in a position to put the *DAD-SAS* model to work. This section looks at monetary policy to show the effects of a permanent change in the context of the model, and at fiscal policy, which is used to represent a transitory change.

Monetary policy

Since we want to focus on the role of money growth, all other exogenous factors previously found to affect the position of the *DAD* curve are assumed to remain constant. This is tantamount to letting their first differences be zero, and yields a compact representation of the *DAD-SAS* model:

$$\pi = \mu - bY + bY_{-1} \qquad\qquad \text{DAD curve}$$
$$\text{flexible exchange rates}$$

$$\pi = \pi^e + \lambda(Y - Y^*) \qquad\qquad \text{SAS curve}$$

The permanent policy change considered here is an increase of the money growth rate from μ_{LO} to μ_{HI}. The economy's response to this change depends critically on how individuals form inflation expectations.

Adaptive expectations
In Figure 8.7, let the economy be in the inflationary equilibrium point at μ_{LO} and Y^*. In period 1 the central bank raises the growth rate of the nominal money supply to μ_{HI}. As money grows faster than prices, the real money supply increases, shifting the original *DAD* curve to the right into DAD_1. To pin down the position of DAD_1, follow the method given above: hypothetically,

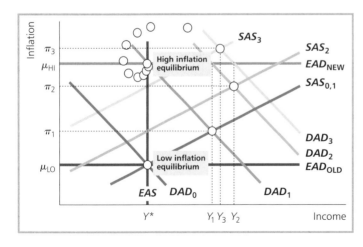

Figure 8.7 The economy is in a low inflation equilibrium with DAD_0 and SAS_0. An unexpected increase in money growth to μ_{HI} shifts DAD into DAD_1, raising income along SAS_1 to Y_1 and inflation to π_1. This process continues along a path sketched by white circles until the economy settles into the high inflation equilibrium at $\pi = \mu_{HI}$ and $Y = Y^*$.

if inflation rose to μ_{HI} simultaneously with money growth, the real money supply would not change, and demand-side equilibrium income could remain at Y^*. Hence the *DAD* curve shifts up by $\Delta\mu = \mu_{HI} - \mu_{LO}$.

Inflation does not follow money growth instantaneously. Nominal wages for period 1 were set before we entered period 1, based on adaptively formed inflation expectations $\pi_1^e = \pi_0$. SAS_0 tells how firms respond to a perceived increase in demand, given the current nominal wage. Any perceived demand increase makes firms move up SAS_0, raising both prices and output. Equilibrium in period 1 is given at π_1 and Y_1, the point of intersection between DAD_1 and SAS_0 (which also happens to be SAS_1).

Now labour market participants revise plans. They expect inflation to be at π_1 in period 2, raising the nominal wage by that rate. This moves the aggregate supply curve to SAS_2. The *DAD* curve does not remain in its period-1 position either. If the real money supply remained unchanged, income could remain at Y_1. This moves the curve into position DAD_2. Equilibrium in period 2 is at inflation π_2 and income Y_2.

The development in periods 3, 4, 5 and so on, can be tracked in a similar fashion. Figure 8.7 doesn't show demand and supply curves beyond period 3 as the graph is crowded enough already. The details of the later phase of the adjustment process should not be overemphasized. They are sensitive to specific parameter constellations and are quantitatively unimportant. There is a general lesson, however, that we should keep in mind: if inflation expectations adjust slowly, a permanent increase in money growth raises income for some time above its normal level. As inflation catches up with money growth, and temporarily exceeds it, income eases back towards its normal level.

This result also applies if reasons other than the adaptive formation of inflation expectations prevent nominal wages or prices from adjusting quickly. These may be adjustment costs or uncertainty about the nature of an observed increase in demand.

DAD-SAS and Mundell–Fleming: a look behind the scene

Let us pause to look at what is going on beneath the surface of the *DAD-SAS* model as displayed in the π-Y diagram. The purpose of this interlude is to emphasize that whatever happens in the *DAD-SAS* model can be traced back to the Mundell–Fleming model, and vice versa. We look at the immediate response to an increase in money growth first, which moves the economy up along SAS_1.

The short-run response in DAD-SAS and IS-LM-FE representation In Figure 8.8 the economy is in equilibrium at point A. The upper panel shows this in the *DAD-SAS* model. The lower panel depicts it in the Mundell–Fleming model.

For convenience, suppose the initial equilibrium is non-inflationary: that is, $\pi_0 = \mu_0 = 0$. In period 1 the money supply growth rate increases from 0 to 10%, so that the *nominal* money supply rises by 10%. In the Mundell–Fleming model, where prices are considered fixed, the *real* money supply also increases by 10%. This shifts *LM* to the right into the broken blue position. If the price level really did not respond, the exchange rate would depreciate just enough to shift *IS* right into the broken blue position, raising income to Y_C. In the upper panel, income would also have risen to Y_C if inflation had stayed at 0. However, this would have required the *SAS* curve to be horizontal.

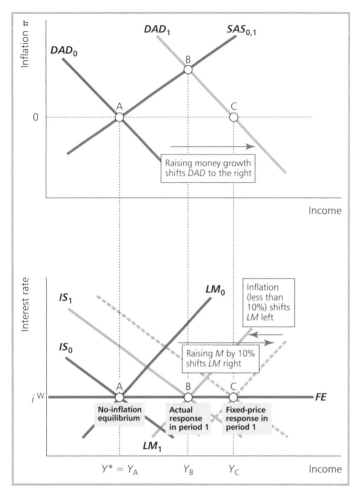

Figure 8.8 (Flexible exchange rates.) An acceleration of money growth shifts *DAD* to the right. In the Mundell–Fleming model this shifts *LM* and, through endogenous depreciation, *IS* to the right into the broken blue positions. Since insufficient supply at the old price level triggers inflation, the economy moves from C to B along DAD_1 in the upper panel. In the lower panel the rising price level reduces the real money supply and the real exchange rate. *LM* and *IS* move back into the solid light blue position. Income has increased from Y^* to Y_B, and not to Y_C as it would have if the *SAS* curve was horizontal.

Now *SAS* is not horizontal, but positively sloped. This means that the labour market is not prepared to supply output Y_C at unchanged prices. Only as prices rise (or inflation goes up) and real wages fall, will output increase along SAS_1. Given DAD_1, period 1 equilibrium in the upper panel is at B. How does this translate into the lower panel? Well, the increase of inflation from 0 to π_1 nibbles away at the real money supply increase. As a result, *LM* shifts back left into the light blue position, bringing the economy to point B. At the same time, inflation reduces the real exchange rate, shifting *IS* back left into the light blue position.

So, after taking into account the price changes required to bring aggregate supply up to meet aggregate demand, the Mundell–Fleming model gives the same income response to the money supply increase as the *DAD-SAS* model. The drawback of the Mundell–Fleming model is that it does not tell us what price changes do indeed occur as we move from one equilibrium to another.

The long-run response in DAD-SAS and IS-LM-FE representation Let us now look at how the *long-run adjustment* from A to A′ is reflected in the Mundell–Fleming diagram (Figure 8.9). First, note some properties of A′. In the new

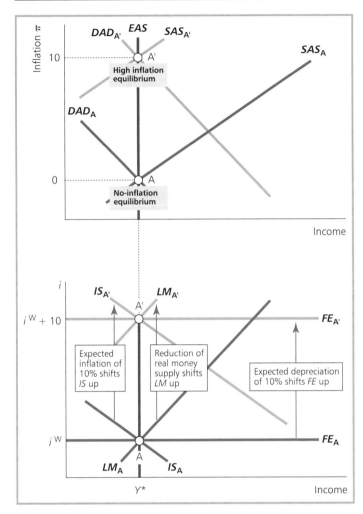

Figure 8.9 (Flexible exchange rates.) After inflation has adjusted, *DAD* and *SAS* are in the light blue positions and the economy has moved from A to A' (upper panel). Inflation is at 10% permanently, and e also is 10%. In equilibrium this depreciation must be expected. This shifts the *FE* curve up by ten percentage points in the lower panel. The intersection between this new *FE* line and the vertical line over potential income marks A'. To shift *LM* up to pass through A', the real money supply must have fallen. *IS* shifts up because it must go up by ten percentage points to keep the real interest rate unchanged.

equilibrium, the movements of *LM* and *IS* that occurred during the transition from A to A' have ended. So the real money supply, which determines the position of *LM*, remains constant, meaning that money and prices grow at the same rates: $\pi = \mu$. The real exchange rate, which determines the position of *IS*, must be constant as well, meaning that depreciation equals inflation (supposing world inflation is 0): $\varepsilon = \pi$. So π, μ and ε are all 10%. If our currency depreciates by 10% period after period, the market sooner or later expects this. Financial investors are then only prepared to hold domestic bonds if these carry interest rates 10% higher than the world interest rate – as compensation for the anticipated loss in value through depreciation. So the new position of *FE* is at $i^W + 10$, which identifies the new long-run equilibrium A' in the lower panel of Figure 8.9. The fact that both *LM* and *IS* pass through A' offers two new insights:

1 Since *LM* has shifted up compared with where it was when the equilibrium was A, the real money supply has fallen. Do not confuse this with the fact that once we are at A', inflation equals money growth and *M/P* remains constant. During the *transition* from A to A′ the sum of all price changes must have been larger than the sum of all changes in the money supply. The resulting reduction of the real money supply is needed, since individuals want to hold less (real) money when interest rates are at 10% (as at A′) than at interest rates of 0% (that applied at A).

2   It is tempting, but wrong, to think that for similar reasons the real exchange rate must have depreciated to shift *IS* out and make it go through A′. To see why this is wrong, we now need to stress the distinction between the nominal interest rate i and the real interest rate $r \equiv i - \pi$ that results after we deduct inflation from the nominal interest rate. This distinction was not important in earlier chapters in which the price level was considered fixed. There i was both the nominal and the real interest rate. Now, with inflation brought into the picture, we need to recognize that the interest rate that determines investment decisions of firms is the real interest rate.

Suppose a bank lends £100 for one year to a firm that wants to invest. At a 5% interest rate the bank will have £105 at the end of the year. If prices have remained the same, the purchasing power of the £100 lent out has increased by 5%. Therefore, the real return, or the real interest rate, is 5%. Now assume that same scenario, except that prices rose by 5%. Then the £105 which the bank has at the end of the year only buys what the £100 would have bought at the beginning of the year. Everything costs 5% more. The bank has not received any real compensation for lending the money. The real interest rate is 0. To receive the same real compensation that the bank received when there was no inflation, the nominal interest rate would have to be 10%. Then the real interest rate would be $r = 10\% - 5\% = 5\%$. With the same argument, the firm that borrows the money also knows that, in the face of inflation, the pounds it gives back to repay the loan will be worth less than the pounds it received. Thus, what is relevant for firms deciding how much to borrow and which investment projects to undertake is the real interest rate which takes account of inflation.

Rewriting the investment schedules as $I = \bar{I} - b(i - \pi)$, the *IS* curve shifts up one by one if inflation goes up. The increase of inflation from 0 to 10% shifts the *IS* curve up into A′, since the nominal interest rate needs to be 10 percentage points higher to make firms undertake the same level of investment as at A. No change in the real exchange rate is needed.

The decomposition of the nominal interest rate into the real interest rate and inflation is known as the Fisher equation. Augmented with the assumption of an approximately constant normal real interest rate $\bar{r}$, it constitutes a theory of the behaviour of nominal interest rates:

$$i = \bar{r} + \pi \qquad\qquad \text{Fisher equation} \quad (8.7)$$

Keep in mind, however, that this version of the Fisher equation only holds in equilibrium, on *EAS*. During booms the interest rate falls below what equation (8.7) says; during recessions it rises above what equation (8.7) says. The key reason for this is that firms and banks do not know inflation when they agree on the interest rate for a loan, but need to base decisions on inflation *expectations*. Equation (8.7) does not qualify as a short-run relationship because inflation may differ from expected inflation, and because income may be above or below normal levels for a while.

The real interest rate is the nominal interest rate (as observed in the market) minus the inflation rate. It deducts from nominal interest payments the purchasing power lost due to price increases.

Maths note. Repeating the derivation of the *IS* curve in Chapter 5 with the new investment function $I = \bar{I} - b(i - \pi)$ gives the new *IS* curve for an inflationary environment

$$i = \pi - \frac{1 - c + m_1}{b}Y + \frac{x_2 + m_2}{b}R + \frac{\bar{I} + G + x_1 Y^W}{b}.$$

Since $di/d\pi = 1$, a one percentage point rise in π shifts *IS* up by 1 percentage point.

The Fisher equation (named after the American economist irving Fisher, 1867–1947) says that interest rates change if either the real interest rate or inflation changes. The implication that a one percentage point increase in inflation raises the nominal interest rate by one percentage point is called the **Fisher effect**.

CASE STUDY 8.1 Deflation: inflation's uglier sister

This chapter taught us that an acceleration in money supply growth that increases inflation has a positive effect on income. We also learned that this does not last. Even when inflation expectations are not rational, they eventually catch up with the actual inflation rate. Sooner or later income retreats to potential income. This independence of aggregate income from money and prices is known as the *neutrality of money*. Most economists agree that this neutrality applies in the longer run.

While **inflation** appears to be a widespread accessory of modern economies, **deflation** – a continuing fall of the price level – is rare. But when it does occur, as it did during the Great Depression of 1929–32, during which US consumer prices fell at an annual rate of 10%, or when it is seen looming on the horizon, as during the financial crisis of 2008, it gives markets and politicians quite a scare. It is not straightforward to see why this is so, because we just learned that markets can cope with and digest inflation. And deflation is nothing but inflation with a negative sign. Therefore, shouldn't we expect this chapter's results to hold no matter whether the rate of inflation is 10, 6, 2, −1 or −5%? The answer depends on how rapidly prices fall.

Figure 8.10 shows a closed economy with a history of stable prices. Keeping the economy closed permits us to develop the argument within the simplest framework, the *IS-LM* model combined with a vertical *AS* curve. This way we don't have to keep an eye on exchange rate systems, capital mobility or other complications. The grey lines identify the initial equilibrium at potential income that obtains at stable prices: that is, under zero inflation. Now the country slides into a deflation of 2% annually.

In the long run, after all adjustments have taken place, or in the short run, if nominal wage rates and prices are fully flexible, the 2% deflation equilibrium depicted by the blue lines obtains.

The *IS* and *LM* curves both shift down into their blue positions by 2 percentage points. Regarding the *IS* curve, this is because investment spending depends on the real interest rate $r = i - \pi$. So the nominal interest rate needed to generate a given investment demand I_0 when inflation stands at −2% is 2 percentage points lower than in the zero-inflation equilibrium, namely $i_0 = r_0 - 2$. Regarding *LM*, the real money supply must have increased appropriately, because the economy wants to hold more liquidity L when the nominal interest rate is lower. There are no real macroeconomic effects, since income remains at Y^*.

The *LM* curve is nonlinear to accommodate possible liquidity traps that occur because at interest rates near zero the economy wants to hold all wealth as money (see Case study 3.1). In the current case this does not come into play because the deflation is modest enough not to call for negative interest rates in the deflation equilibrium. If a more severe deflation occurs, as shown in Figure 8.11, this is different.

In Figure 8.11, the same economy as postulated before experiences a more severe deflation of 4% annually. Ignoring the liquidity-trap argument, one might be tempted to identify the new equilibrium in B', where the new *IS* curve, shown in blue, intersects

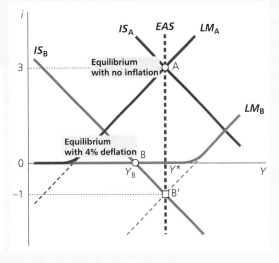

Figure 8.10

Figure 8.11

Case study 8.1 continued

the dashed section of the blue *LM* curve. This equilibrium is not feasible, however, since nominal interest rates cannot become negative and the dashed segment of the *LM* curve does not exist. So, instead, the new equilibrium obtains in B, where the new *IS* curve intersects the horizontal part of the *LM* curve. Compared to the initial equilibrium, where the real interest rate stood at 3%, the real interest rate has risen to $r = i - \pi = 0 - (-4) = 4\%$. As a consequence, investment demand and, hence, aggregate demand

are lower than before and fall short of potential income. Realizing that they cannot sell the output they would like to produce, firms cut their labour demand below potential employment to the level that suffices to produce income Y_B. As a consequence, involuntary unemployment increases and persists as long as the deflation continues. This illustrates that deflations, other than inflations, may seriously affect the real economy and carry a high risk of severe economic downturns and ballooning unemployment.

Inflation is an increase in the price level, expressed as a percentage rate of change.

Deflation is a fall in the price level.

Disinflation is a decrease in the rate of inflation.

Rational expectations

Under rational expectations individuals look beyond the history of the variable they want to forecast. Assume here that they know just as much as we know by now. Once they observe a shock or policy change, they use the *DAD-SAS* model to compute its effect on next period's inflation. They cannot foresee, however, when monetary policy changes its course. This comes as a surprise.

The starting point is the inflationary equilibrium A_0 in Figure 8.12. In period 1 monetary policy switches from the old money growth rate μ_{LO} to μ_{HI}. Since this had not been anticipated in period 0, wage contracts for period 1 are based on inflation expectations π_0. Thus the aggregate supply curve remains in $SAS_1 = SAS_0$. For the same reason as under adaptive expectations, equilibrium in period 1 obtains at point A_1, at higher income and higher inflation.

Events in and after period 2 differ from what happened under adaptive expectations. Individuals realize that the rate of money growth has changed. So no more surprises occur in the future. Individuals can employ their knowledge of the *DAD-SAS* model to compute correct inflation forecasts. What is

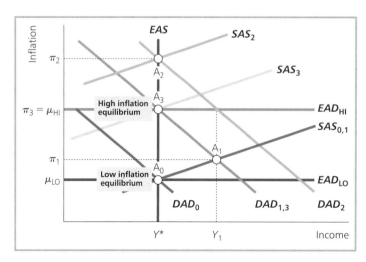

Figure 8.12 Starting from A_0, an unexpected acceleration of money growth moves the economy to A_1. If money growth remains high, DAD_2 obtains in period 2. Since high money growth and its consequence for inflation is anticipated, *SAS* is at SAS_2, and the economy is in A_2. In period 3 and after, A_3 obtains.

the correct, or rational inflation forecast for period 2? Two points must be noted here:

1 SAS_2 intersects *EAS* at the *expected* inflation rate.
2 *Actual* inflation is determined by the intersection between SAS_2 and DAD_2.

Combining points 1 and 2, actual and expected inflation can only be the same if SAS_2 and DAD_2 intersect on *EAS*. This holds in general:

> The rational expectation of next period's inflation is given by the point of intersection between the *EAS* curve and the *DAD* curve anticipated for next period.

So inflation is correctly anticipated to rise to $\pi_2 > \mu_{HI}$, bringing output back to its normal level, where it remains. This moves the *SAS* curve into SAS_3, and actual and expected inflation is at π_{HI} in period 3 and ever after.

To sum up: under rational expectations an unexpected, permanent increase in the rate of money growth stimulates output temporarily via surprise inflation. This effect evaporates one period later, leaving the economy with a permanently higher rate of inflation.

BOX 8.1   How to solve rational expectations models

The implications of the *DAD-SAS* model under rational expectations, discussed graphically and verbally in the main text, can be brought out more succinctly by solving the model formally. Numerous solution algorithms for rational expectations models exist. We settle for a particularly simple **recipe** that works well for the kind of model discussed in this chapter. What we are interested in is the rational expectations solution of the *DAD-SAS* model under flexible exchange rates, repeated here for convenience:

$$\pi = \mu - b(Y - Y_{-1}) \qquad \textbf{\textit{DAD}} \text{ curve} \qquad (1)$$
$$\pi = \pi^e + \lambda(Y - Y^*) \qquad \textbf{\textit{SAS}} \text{ curve} \qquad (2)$$

Our recipe involves the following three steps.

Step 1: Compute the reduced form for the endogenous variable you are interested in
A *reduced form* is an equation that features one of the endogenous variables, π or Y in our case, on the left-hand side of the equality sign, and only predetermined variables on the right. Predetermined variables are exogenous variables, such as μ and Y^*, or lagged endogenous variables, such as Y_{-1} whose value has already been determined in earlier periods. While taking step 1 we also consider any expected variables, such as π^e, as a predetermined variable.

Suppose we are interested in the determination of income Y. Then we need to eliminate the second endogenous variable, π, in which we are not interested right now, by substituting equation (2) into (1). Solving for Y yields the reduced form we were looking for:

$$Y = \frac{1}{b + \lambda}(\mu - \pi^e + \lambda Y^* + bY_{-1}) \quad \textbf{Reduced}$$

$$\textbf{form for } Y \quad (3)$$

The drawback with equation (3) is that its explanation of income rests on expected inflation, which is still unknown. So this is what we will have to clarify next.

Step 2: Compute the rational expectation of expected variables included in the reduced form
Remember what rational expectations imply: individuals are aware of the macroeconomic model, and they make use of this knowledge when forming expectations. So when labour unions and employers negotiated wage contracts at time $t - 1$, they were aware of equations (1) and (2). They expected these equations to hold at time t. But, since the relevant values of some variables were not known at time $t - 1$, when expectations had to be formed, expected values need to be substituted into the equations:

Box 8.1 continued

$$\pi^e = \mu^e - b(Y^e - Y_{-1}) \quad (1e)$$
$$\pi^e = \pi^e + \lambda(Y^e - Y^*) \quad (2e)$$

Equation (1e) says that the rate of inflation expected for next year is determined by the money growth rate expected for next year and the difference between the income that we expect for next year and the income we observe today. Equation (2) actually says that the labour market expects income to deviate from potential income only to the extent that they expect inflation to differ from expected inflation. Since, of course, they expect inflation to equal expected inflation, they must expect income to equal potential income: $Y^e = Y^*$. Substituting this into equation (1e) yields

$$\pi^e = \mu^e - b(Y^* - Y_{-1}) \text{ Rational inflation} \qquad \text{expectations} \quad (4)$$

So we found that in the context of our model rational inflation expectations depend on the expected money growth rate, which is exogenous to our model, and on how far income deviates from potential income. This brings us to the final step.

Step 3: Substitute the expectation computed in step 2 into the reduced form determined in step 1
Substitution of (4) into (3) and rearranging terms yields a mathematical equation describing income

determination in the *DAD-SAS* model under flexible exchange rates and rational expectations:

$$Y = Y^* + \frac{1}{b + \lambda}(\mu - \mu^e) \quad (5)$$

The equation says that income normally resembles potential income. It deviates from potential income only to the extent that money growth differs from expected money growth. So the central bank needs to surprise the market in order to generate an effect of monetary policy on real income.

Analogous insights obtain when we compute the rational expectations solution of the *DAD-SAS* model with a more fully specified *DAD* curve, or under fixed exchange rates.

Note. You may wonder why we did not eliminate expected money growth by subjecting it to the same treatment as expected inflation. The reason is that the behaviour of the central bank is not explained by our model. Monetary policy is exogenous, and so is the money growth rate. A rational expectation can only be computed for a variable that is explained by our model, one that is endogenous. Chapter 11 explains the behaviour of the government and the central bank. Then monetary policy will become an endogenous part of our macroeconomic model.

Perfect foresight

Individuals have perfect foresight if there are no surprises. They foresee everything: changes of endogenous variables, changes in the international environment and policy changes too.

In the current context this means that individuals foresee in period 0 that monetary policy will change in period 1. This could be either due to the central bank credibly *announcing* the policy change, or because individuals have learned to understand what makes central bankers tick. If the shift of the demand curve to DAD_1 is anticipated, rational expectations of next period's inflation rate are given by the point of intersection between DAD_1 and *EAS*. Incidentally, rational inflation expectations coincide with the new money growth rate. Hence, the real money supply remains unchanged and income remains at its equilibrium level (see Figure 8.13).

Figure 8.14 compares the time profiles of inflation and income, respectively, under the three expectations formation schemes. They restate and sum up what we already encountered in Figures 8.9, 8.12 and 8.13.

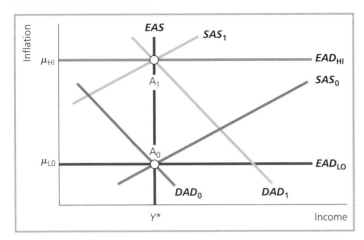

Figure 8.13 If the rise of the money growth rate is anticipated, the shift of *DAD* to DAD_1 is foreseen by the labour market. Anticipation of the correct inflation rate puts *SAS* into SAS_1 and the economy directly moves from A_0 into A_1 where it remains.

Note. This statement is an approximation. As the algebraic treatment in the first appendix to this chapter reveals, raising money growth raises the expected equilibrium rate of depreciation. Thus DAD_1 rises slightly higher than shown here, and the real money supply falls. For small or modest changes in money growth this effect is not important. We ignore it to keep things simple.

Fiscal policy

We now turn to an analysis of fiscal policy. Chapter 5 showed that governments may use tax and expenditure changes to affect income under an international arrangement of fixed exchange rates. For easy reference, a stripped-down version of the *DAD-SAS* model under fixed exchange rates is

$$\pi = \pi^{W} - bY + bY_{-1} + \delta\Delta G \qquad\qquad \text{\textit{DAD} curve}$$
$$\text{fixed exchange rates}$$

$$\pi = \pi^{e} + \lambda(Y - Y^*) \qquad\qquad \text{\textit{SAS} curve}$$

This compact version of the *DAD* curve assumes that world income remains constant, and that there are no realignments of the exchange rate.

Adaptive expectations
In Figure 8.15 the economy is in an initial equilibrium in which inflation is determined by the world inflation rate. This is because the commitment to

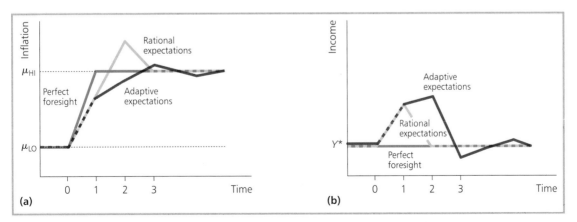

Figure 8.14 Panel (a) shows the response of inflation; panel (b) shows the response of income to a permanent increase of money growth. The responses are affected by how people form expectations.

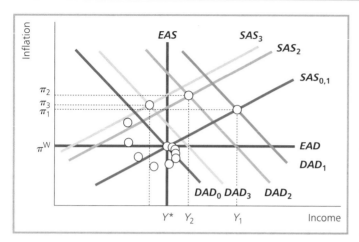

Figure 8.15 The exchange rate is fixed and the economy is in equilibrium with DAD_0 and SAS_0. A one-time increase in government spending shifts DAD into DAD_1, raising income along SAS_1 to Y_1 and inflation to π_1. Higher inflation expectations shift SAS into SAS_2 next period. DAD shifts down, however, since G does not rise any further. This process continues as sketched by the white circles until the economy is back in the initial equilibrium at $\pi = \pi^W$ and $Y = Y^*$.

a fixed exchange rate forces the central bank to let the home money supply grow at the rate of world inflation. Raising government expenditures by $\Delta G_1 = G_1 - G_0$ shifts the DAD curve to the right. Since this comes unexpectedly, the economy moves up an unchanged SAS curve, experiencing an income boost and some inflation.

The experienced inflation π_1 is expected to prevail next period, $\pi_2^e = \pi_1$. This shifts the aggregate supply curve up to SAS_2. At the same time, the aggregate demand curve shifts back down to DAD_2 because government expenditures do not rise any further and, hence, $\Delta G_2 = G_2 - G_1 = 0$. Here the joint effect is that inflation continues to rise while income falls. In period 3 inflation begins to recede and income falls further, below its normal level. In time, inflation eases back to its original level, and so does income.

Again, the details of the adjustment process depend on specific parameter constellations. For instance, if the DAD curve is very flat, inflation may already fall in period 2, driving income below Y^* earlier. The big picture, however, is not sensitive to parameter specifics. A one-time expenditure increase stimulates income and kindles inflation. Both these effects are short-lived, however, and are followed by falling inflation and even a temporary recession.

Rational expectations

If the income rise comes as a surprise but subsequent implications for inflation are correctly foreseen, the economy responds as shown in Figure 8.16. First-period results are the same as in the adaptive expectations scenario. The unexpected increase in government expenditures raises income to Y_1 and inflation to π_1. In period 2 DAD shifts down to DAD_2. Since this is expected, inflation expectations are rationally set to π_2, positioning SAS at SAS_2. Thus income is back to its normal level and remains there. In period 3 inflation is back to the level of world inflation as well.

Perfect foresight

Fully informed individuals already anticipate the first-period shift of aggregate demand to DAD_1. Hence, rational expectations move the aggregate supply

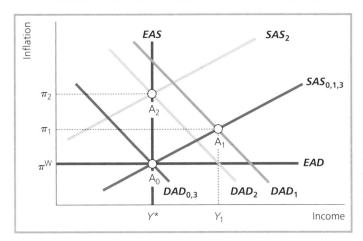

Figure 8.16 Starting from A_0, an unexpected increase in government purchases moves the economy to A_1. Since G does not rise any further, DAD_2 obtains in period 2. Since inflation expectations are formed rationally, SAS is at SAS_2, and the economy is at A_2. Finally, in period 3 and after, A_0 obtains.

curve up to SAS_1 (see Figure 8.17). The attempt to stimulate output evaporates, leaving only inflation at π_1. In period 2 things are back to what they were before the expenditure rise.

Again, Figure 8.18, panels (a) and (b), compares inflation and output, respectively, under the three expectations scenarios. The crucial point is that output effects become shorter as we move from adaptive via rational expectations to perfect foresight.

Policy effectiveness in the *DAD-SAS* model

Our look at monetary and fiscal policy has brought out one point quite clearly: the extent to which policy may influence income and output crucially hinges upon how individuals form inflation expectations. Only if there is a strong adaptive element in expectations formation will output gains last for some time. If expectations are rational, only the initial policy surprise may

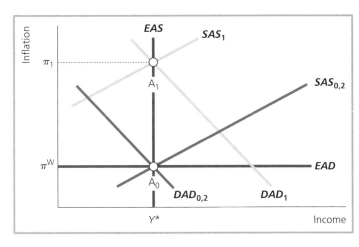

Figure 8.17 When the increase in government purchases is anticipated, the shift of *DAD* to DAD_1 is foreseen by the labour market. Anticipation of the correct inflation rate puts *SAS* into SAS_1 and the economy moves from A_0 into A_1. Similarly, the position of DAD_2 is anticipated by the labour market, which puts *SAS* into SAS_2 and the economy back into A_0. Here the economy remains.

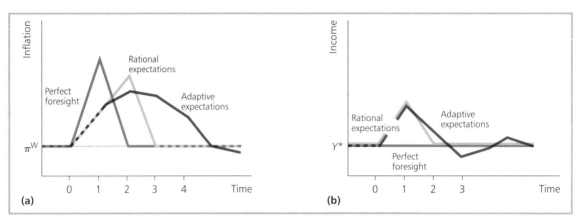

Figure 8.18 Panel (a) shows the response of inflation; panel (b) shows the response of income to a one-time increase in government purchases. The responses are affected by how people form expectations.

CASE STUDY 8.2 Quantity equation, Fisher equation and purchasing power parity: international evidence

Focusing on business cycles, Chapter 8 and the preceding chapters focused on the short-run relationships between monetary aggregates. While these relationships can be complicated in the short and medium run, long-run (or equilibrium) relationships are quite simple and serve as useful anchors from which variables may only deviate temporarily.

One way of identifying the key long-run relationships is by considering the Mundell–Fleming model (Figure 8.19), with an added long-run AS curve at Y^* (which we presume constant for convenience). The point of intersection marks the long-run equilibrium in which all markets clear. For the economy to remain in this equilibrium, the LM curve, the IS curve and the FE curve must stay put in the indicated positions. What does this imply?

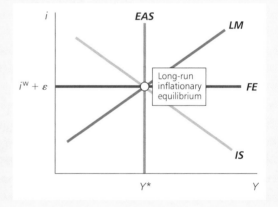

Figure 8.19

LM curve

The position of the LM curve is determined by the real money supply M/P. If LM must not shift, the real money supply must not change. Hence M and P must grow at the same rates. Inflation π must equal money growth μ, so the empirical implication is that in the long run

$$\pi = \mu \qquad \text{from **quantity equation**} \qquad (1)$$

Inflation equals money growth, not necessarily from year to year, but in the long run, over a span of decades.

IS curve

The position of the IS curve depends on the real exchange rate, government spending and world income. Keeping world income constant in line with domestic income, and noting that government spending cannot continuously change (relative to income) in the long run, then the real exchange rate must not change if IS must not shift. Thus $EP^W/P = $ constant. Thus foreign prices in domestic currency, EP^W must grow at the same rate as domestic prices P. Since the growth rate of foreign prices in domestic currency is approximated by the

Case study 8.1 continued

(a)

(b)

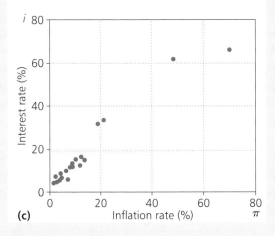

(c)

Figure 8.20

rate of depreciation ε plus world inflation π^W, this condition reads $\varepsilon + \pi^W = \pi$. Solving for ε yields

$$\varepsilon = \pi - \pi^W \qquad \text{from \textbf{purchasing power parity}} \qquad (2)$$

which says that in the long run the rate of depreciation equals the inflation differential between our country and the rest of the world.

FE curve

The position of the *FE* curve depends on the foreign interest rate and expected depreciation. Since expected and actual depreciation should be the same in equilibrium, the equilibrium *FE* curve reads $i = i^W + \varepsilon$. Substituting equation (2) for ε and noting that $i^W - \pi^W$ is the world real interest rate r^W, we obtain the so-called Fisher equation which states that the nominal interest rate is the sum of a constant (representing the real world interest rate) and inflation:

$$i = r^W + \pi \qquad \textbf{Fisher equation} \qquad (3)$$

The three long-run relationships behind equations (1)–(3) – the quantity equation, purchasing power parity, and the Fisher equation – are confronted with data from a sample of countries in Figure 8.20. Panel (a) looks at the *quantity equation* and shows that in the long run inflation always goes hand in hand with money growth. This relationship becomes particularly strong when inflation is very high, as during hyperinflations. Panel (a), of course, is only a slightly modified version of Figure 7.11 in Case study 7.1.

Purchasing power parity is being tested in panel (b). Being averages over some three decades, the data are well in line with equation (2). The more we inflate relative to the rest of the world, the faster the exchange rate depreciates.

Finally, panel (c) supports the Fisher equation which proposes a one-to-one relationship between the nominal interest rate and inflation.

Food for thought

■ Does the validity of these equilibrium relationships depend on the exchange rate regime? Why or why not?

■ To be more realistic, let potential income (at home and abroad) grow at a constant rate. Which of the equilibrium conditions is affected by this, and how?

create a short-lived income rise. Finally if the policy stimulus is anticipated, as is assumed under the hypothesis of perfect foresight, income does not respond at all.

The length of the output response to unexpected policy intervention depends on the structural characteristics of the economy. In particular, the longer wage contracts are, the longer output responses will last. This is because observation of the policy shock can only lead to renegotiated wage contracts after the old contracts expire.

The general lesson for policy-makers is ambiguous. It is in their power to influence output, but they can do so only via surprise implementation of monetary and fiscal policy. Surprises work at the cost of expectations errors of labour market participants, however. So the more often the government or the central bank resorts to surprises, the more frequent and the larger the committed expectations errors are, and the more likely individuals will feel compelled to sharpen their forecasting technique. Somewhere down the road they will be able to identify the situations in which policy-makers normally respond and anticipate (and thus nullify) all policy interventions. The lesson would be to use policy sparingly to retain its potency.

Note. Empirical research found that even anticipated policy affects output. The underlying transmission channel is not well understood. The implication is that the kind of temporary output effect derived above may also obtain if inflation expectations are not adaptive.

CHAPTER SUMMARY

- An economy's supply side can be represented in inflation–income space by means of a vertical long-run or equilibrium aggregate supply curve (*EAS*), and a positively sloped surprise aggregate supply curve (*SAS*).

- The demand side can be represented in inflation–income space by means of a negatively sloped dynamic aggregate demand curve (*DAD*).

- Under flexible exchange rates the aggregate demand curve has a negative slope for the following reason: a price increase reduces the real money supply. Since the domestic interest rate is fixed to the world interest rate, the demand for money must be reduced by a decline in income.

- Under fixed exchange rates the aggregate demand curve has a negative slope for the following reason: a price increase reduces the real exchange rate. This appreciation creates an excess supply of domestic goods at the old level of income. Since the interest rate is fixed to the world interest rate, supply can only equal demand at a lower level of income.

- The simplest version of adaptive expectations lets individuals expect last period's inflation to occur again next period. Forming expectations this way is simple and cheap. If inflation changes only infrequently, it may also be quite accurate.

- If simple expectations formation results in large and frequent errors, and if errors are costly, individuals are likely to move on to a more elaborate expectations formation. One such elaborate scheme is rational expectations.

- If individuals form rational expectations, we expect them to know as much as we do. That means, they are assumed to know our model.

- Under fixed exchange rates fiscal policy (that is, a government expenditure change or a tax change) may temporarily affect output and income if it comes as a surprise.

■ Monetary policy affects output when exchange rates are flexible, if it comes as a surprise.

■ Anticipated fiscal or monetary policy does not affect output. All it does is have an impact on inflation.

Key terms and concepts

adaptive expectations *226*
DAD curve *221*
DAD-SAS model *222*
deflation *234*
disinflation *234*
EAS curve *223*
economically rational
   expectations *227*
fiscal policy *237*
Fisher equation *232*

inflation *234*
inflation expectations *225*
market psychology *221*
monetary policy *228*
perfect foresight *227*
policy effectiveness *239*
rational expectations *227*
real interest rate *232*
SAS curve *220*

EXERCISES

8.1 In this chapter the *SAS* curve was written as $\pi = \pi^e + \lambda(Y - Y^*)$. Derive aggregate supply in the long run: that is, when inflation expectations equal actual inflation.

8.2 Under flexible exchange rates, domestic inflation is determined by the growth rate of domestic money supply, whereas inflation is determined by the foreign inflation rate if the exchange rate is fixed.
(a) Explain why.
(b) Suppose you govern a country whose economy is linked to other economies by fixed exchange rates. A reduction of inflation is overdue. Are you inclined to switch to a regime of flexible exchange rates?

8.3 Consider an economy with flexible exchange rates, which can be described by the following *DAD* and *SAS* curves:

$$\pi = \mu - 0.025(Y - Y_{-1}) \qquad \text{DAD curve}$$
$$\pi = \pi^e + 0.075(Y - Y^*) \qquad \text{SAS curve}$$

Assume that output in the preceding period was 150 units, which is 50 units below full employment output Y^*. The growth rate of money supply is 10% and agents expect an inflation rate of 5%.

(a) Draw the *DAD* and the *SAS* curves and compute current output and inflation.
(b) The central bank considers reducing the money growth rate from 10% to 5%. Assume that the inflation expectations of the agents remain unchanged and draw the new *DAD* and *SAS* curves to analyze the immediate effect on inflation and output of such a policy change.

8.4 It is often claimed that the government can permanently keep output above potential output, but at an ever 'accelerating' inflation rate. Explain this statement using the *DAD-SAS* model.

8.5 Trace the short-run and long-run effects of a surprising once-and-for-all increase in the foreign inflation rate for an economy with adaptive inflation expectations and
(a) a flexible exchange rate
(b) a fixed exchange rate.

8.6 Trace the short-run and long-run effect of an unexpected reduction of foreign inflation for an economy with a fixed exchange rate for the case of
(a) adaptive inflation expectations
(b) rational inflation expectations.

8.7 Consider an economy with a flexible exchange rate. Inflation expectations are formed rationally, but contracts extend over two periods. Every period, 50% of the contracts expire and are rewritten for the following two periods. Analyze the effect of a once-and-for-all increase in the money growth rate if
(a) the policy change comes as a surprise
(b) the policy change is announced one period ahead.

8.8 Suppose a country's economy is initially at point A (Figure 8.21). One year later it sits at point B.

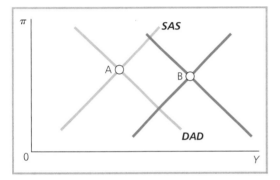

Figure 8.21

Indicate what has happened to the variables listed in the table under scenarios (a)–(e) by completing the table. Assume $Y*$ to be constant.

	(a)	(b)	(c)	(d)	(e)
Exchange rate system	flexible	flexible	flexible	fix	fix
Real money supply					down
Real wage					
Real exchange rate					
World interest rate	unchanged	down		unchanged	unchanged
World prices	unknown	up		unknown	down
Government spending	unchanged	unchanged	up		down

8.9 An open economy with fixed exchange rates is characterized by the following equations:

SAS curve: $\pi = \pi^e + \lambda(Y - Y*)$
DAD curve: $\pi = \pi^W - b(Y - Y_{-1}) + \delta\Delta G$

Find the rational expectation solution for income Y using the recipe explained in Box 8.1. Under what conditions does income Y exceed potential income $Y*$?

Recommended reading

A closed-economy version of the *DAD-SAS* model is developed in Rudiger Dornbusch and Stanley Fischer (1994) *Macroeconomics*, 6th edn, McGraw-Hill: New York. Unfortunately, this feature has been dropped from later editions of this text.

Bhaskara Rao (2007) 'The nature of the *ADAS* model based on the ISLM model', *Cambridge Journal of Economics* 31: 413–22, who calls the *DAD–SAS* the *ADAS* model, and provides a link between *IS-LM* and current research.

APPENDIX	The algebra of the *DAD* curve

The *DAD* curves under flexible and fixed exchange rates can easily be derived from the *AD* curves assembled in the appendix to Chapter 7.

Flexible exchange rates

Equation (A7.10) is the *AD* curve under flexible exchange rates. Taking first differences, denoting inflation by $\pi \equiv p - p_{-1}$ and money growth by $\mu \equiv m - m_{-1}$, letting the first fraction be b, and noting that potential income is fixed, so that $\Delta Y^* = \Delta \overline{Y} = 0$ gives the **DAD curve under flexible exchange rates** as

$$\pi = \mu - b(Y - Y_{-1}) + h(\Delta i^{\mathrm{W}} + \Delta \bar{\varepsilon}^{\mathrm{e}})$$

Fixed exchange rates

Equation (A7.11) is the *AD* curve under fixed exchange rates. Taking first differences yields the **DAD curve under fixed exchange rates**:

$$\pi = \varepsilon + \pi^{\mathrm{W}} - \frac{1 - c + m_1}{x_2 + m_2}(Y - Y_{-1}) + \frac{x_1}{x_2 + m_2}\Delta Y^{\mathrm{W}} + \frac{1}{x_2 + m_2}\Delta G$$

Again, the position variables of the *FE* curve, i^{W} and ε^{e} do not show here because we assumed the *IS* curve to be vertical: that is, investment is independent of the interest rate.

APPENDIX	The genesis of the *DAD-SAS* model

A common phrase cautions that you may not see the wood for the trees. Perhaps you feel a bit like this having worked through all this material. If so, the schematic representation of the genesis of the *DAD-SAS* model in Figure 8.22 asks you to step back and put each of the concepts introduced in place.

We started by looking at the economy's demand side, assuming that supply did not require special attention, since firms would supply whatever was demanded anyway. The first stepping stone was the **Keynesian cross**. There all categories of demand except consumption were exogenous or depended on variables like the interest rate or the exchange rate that were exogenous. In a second stage we refined the goods market, representing all possible equilibria by the **IS curve**. Since treating interest rates and exchange rates as exogenous variables was not satisfactory, we introduced the money market, which clears on the **LM curve**, and the foreign exchange market, which clears on the **FE curve**. Putting these three markets together yields the **Mundell–Fleming model**. This model simultaneously determines the interest rate, the exchange rate and aggregate income, and permits a first analysis of how fiscal and monetary policy or shocks from the rest of the world affect our economy. A weakness of the Mundell–Fleming model is the assumption of a fixed price level. Dropping this assumption, different current equilibrium income levels obtain at different inflation rates. These are summarized in the

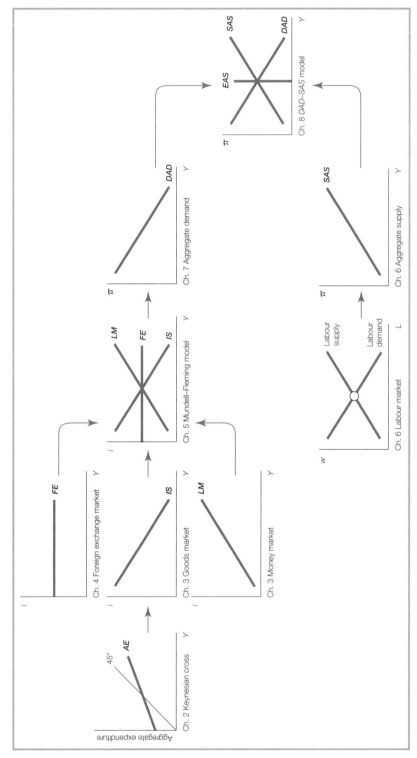

Figure 8.22 The genesis of the *DAD-SAS* model.

AD curve or, which is the same concept in different clothing, in the *DAD* **curve** shown here.

The analysis of aggregate supply started in the **labour market**. In an ideal setting, labour supply and demand would interact so as to produce a real wage at which nobody would be out of work involuntarily. Institutional features or imperfections may prevent the labour market from reaching this ideal. When inflation changes, in particular if it does so unexpectedly, employment moves away from its normal level, and so does output supplied. The levels supplied in aggregate at different inflation rates are combined in the *SAS* curve.

The *DAD-SAS* **model** or, alternatively, the *AD-AS* model we chose not to show here, draws the demand side (*DAD*) and the supply side (*SAS*) together. It permits the analysis of the effects of policy measures and external shocks on inflation and the deviation of income from potential income.

APPLIED PROBLEMS

EMPIRICAL RESEARCH

How does monetary policy affect output?

Under flexible exchange rates the *DAD-SAS* model discussed in this chapter reads

$$\pi = -bY + bY_{-1} + \mu \qquad (1)$$

$$Y = Y* + \frac{1}{\lambda}\pi - \frac{1}{\lambda}\pi_{-1} \qquad (2)$$

We had managed to keep its dynamic structure simple and transparent by assuming that most adjustments take place immediately and that inflation expectations are simply $\pi^e = \pi_{-1}$. Reality may be more complicated: consumption may not respond to income changes immediately; exports are likely to react to a new exchange rate only with a lag; and so on. Because of this, and particularly when they work with higher frequency data such as observed quarterly, economists often prefer not to restrict the model's dynamics by a priori assumptions, but *let the data speak*. For this purpose the above model is generalized to something like

$$\pi = a_0 + a_1\pi_{-1} + a_2\pi_{-2} + a_3Y_{-1}$$
$$\quad + a_4Y_{-2} + SHOCK1 \qquad (1')$$

$$Y = b_0 + b_1Y_{-1} + b_2Y_{-2} + b_3\pi_{-1}$$
$$\quad + b_4\pi_{-2} + SHOCK2 \qquad (2')$$

where SHOCK1 and SHOCK2 stand for all the exogenous influence on the two equations revealed by our analysis, such as monetary and fiscal policy, world variables or supply-side shocks. Economists call such a system of equations a *vector autogression* (VAR), because a vector of endogenous variables (here π and Y) is regressed on past values of this vector.

OLS estimation of the two equations yields numerical values for the *a*s and *b*s. We may then simulate, that is compute from period to period, how a shock of type 1 (in the first equation) or of type 2 (in the second equation) translates into a response of income and inflation over time.

In the above spirit, Stefan Gerlach and Frank Smets ('The monetary transmission mechanism: Evidence from the G-7 countries', Bank for International Settlements, Basle, Working Paper No. 26, April 1995) estimate a VAR model with three endogenous variables, inflation, output and the interest rate, allowing for a maximum lag of five periods (measured in quarters). After employing an advanced procedure (that is beyond our scope) to identify monetary shocks from other demand shocks and from supply shocks, their estimated model generates the following output responses to a standardized one-unit contraction of the money supply (see Figure 8.23).

The interesting aspect about this result is that the behaviour of output after a one-time reduction of the money supply is so similar in the four countries and matches quite well what the simple *DAD-SAS* model proposes. After the reduction of the money supply, output begins to fall (except for a small upwards blip in Germany), reaching its lowest point in the second year. Thereafter output rises again. It takes four to five years, however, until the shock has been absorbed and output is back to normal.

Table 8.1

	1983	1984	1985	1986	1987	1988	1989	1990	1991	1992	1993	1994	1995
OECD inflation forecasts (in %)	15.5	13	9	7.5	5.5	5.8	5.2	7.2	6.9	5.7	5.6	4.5	3.3
Actual inflation rates (in %)	14.9	12	9	6.3	5.3	5.7	6.3	6.2	6.8	5.4	4.8	4.7	4.9

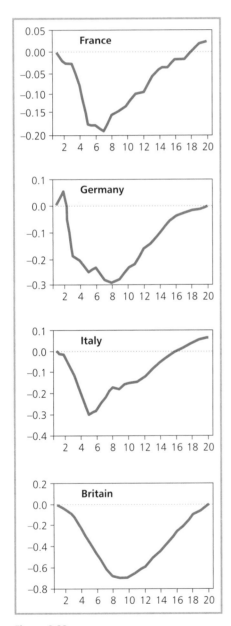

Figure 8.23

WORKED PROBLEM

Inflation forecasts for Italy

Forming an inflation expectation is like a forecast of next period's inflation. In this sense the OECD forecasts of macroeconomic variables are this organization's expectations of what these variables will be. (There is one fundamental difference between the OECD's expectations and mine. OECD forecasts may and probably do influence the market's expectations, and thus may feature a self-fulfilling element. We ignore this complication here.) Table 8.1 gives the OECD's annual inflation forecasts for Italy along with subsequent actual inflation rates. One question of interest is how the OECD computes forecasts. Are OECD inflation expectations formed adaptively, as proposed in most parts of the text, or by much more complicated and elaborate methods? One way to check this is by trying to explain OECD forecasts by the general form of adaptive expectations introduced in the first margin note of section 8.4, which reads $\pi^e = \pi^e_{-1} + a(\pi_{-1} - \pi^e_{-1})$. Rearranging gives $\pi^e = (1 - a)\pi^e_{-1} + a\pi_{-1}$. Estimating this equation with the above data gives

$$\pi^e = 1.15 + 1.05\pi_{-1} - 0.29\pi^e_{-1} \quad R^2_{adj} = 0.87$$
$$\quad\;\;(1.67)\;\;(2.20)\qquad\;(0.65)$$

Annual data 1984–95

The first result to note is that this simple equation explains 87% of the variation in OECD forecasts, which appears to be quite a lot. The constant term is 1.15 but not significantly different from zero. Last period's inflation goes almost one-to-one into the forecast, and the t-value of 2.20 meets our rule of thumb for significance. By contrast, with an absolute t-statistic of 0.65 the coefficient of −0.29 for last period's forecast is not significant. Summing this up, the hypothesis $\pi^e = \pi_{-1}$ employed to facilitate the graphical presentation in the text appears to describe OECD forecasts for Italy between 1984 and 1995 quite well.

YOUR TURN

The Economist and the law of one price

Purchasing power parity suggests that one unit of currency should have the same buying power in different countries (in terms of this chapter's variables: $EP^W = P$). When applied to a specific good, purchasing power parity turns into the law of one price: expressed in a common currency, a given good should have the same price in all countries.

Table 8.2 gives prices for *The Economist* as cited on the title page of 17 June 1996 and the same day's sterling/local currency exchange rates for seventeen European countries plus the United States.

Check whether prices set by *The Economist* obey the law of one price. You may want to start from the equation $P_i = R_i P_{UK}/E_i$, where P_i is the local currency price in country i, E is the sterling rate per currency unit of country i, and R_i measures how the price in country i relates to the price charged in Britain, $P_{UK} = 2.20$, transformed into local currency. If $R = 1$ the law of one price holds. To check this, take logarithms to obtain $\log P_i = \ln R_i + \ln 2.20 - \ln E_i$. Testing whether the data support the law of one price is done against the null hypotheses that the coefficient of $\ln E$ is 1 and that the constant term is $\ln 2.20$ (or $\ln R = 0$).

Table 8.2

Country	Price in local currency	Exchange rate
A	60	0.061
B	160	0.021
CH	7.7	0.517
D	7.9	0.426
FIN	24	0.139
F	27	0.126
DK	34	0.111
GR	1000	0.003
HU	600	0.004
IRE	2.3	1.027
I	8000	0.0004
NL	8.9	0.380
N	35	0.099
P	680	0.004
E	590	0.005
S	35	0.097
GB	2.2	1
US	3.5	0.648

Economic growth (I): basics

After working through this chapter, you will understand:

1 What determines the levels of income and consumption in the long run.

2 What growth accounting is and how it is used to measure technological progress.

3 Why and how a country ends up with the capital stock it has.

4 Why having a larger stock of capital may open more consumption possibilities, but may also require people to consume less.

5 Why some countries are rich and some are poor.

6 What makes income per head grow over time.

We now possess a model that permits us to understand what makes *actual* income fluctuate around *potential* income. This *DAD-SAS* model explains why the circular stream of income oscillates – that is, becomes wider and thinner within its natural bed. We have not yet discussed what shapes the bed of the stream, since we assumed that this shaping would proceed slowly and thus has different causes to the more short-run fluctuations of the stream. It is these longer-run trends in income to which we now turn.

9.1 Stylized facts of income and growth

The empirical motivation for turning our attention to the determinants of potential income and steady-state income derives most forcefully from international income comparisons. As we saw in Chapter 2, a person in the world's richest economies on average earns 50 times as much as a person in the poorest countries. Such differences, documented again for a different set of countries and data in Figure 9.1, can hardly be attributed to an asynchronous business cycle with one country being in a recession and the other enjoying a boom, though business cycles *are* important. In the course of a recession income may recede by 3–5%; by up to 10% if the recession is bad; or even more if it is a deep recession like the Great Depression of the 1930s. But this happens very seldom, and not even this would come close to accounting for income differences observed within Europe, let alone the rest of the world.

The bottom line is that while the models we added to our tool-box in the first eight chapters of this text are important and useful vehicles for understanding and dealing with business cycles, they do not help us to understand

Empirical note. In 2009, during the financial crisis, incomes dropped by 4.4% across Europe, but by 17.7% in Latvia. Greek incomes receded by some 19% within five years after 2007.

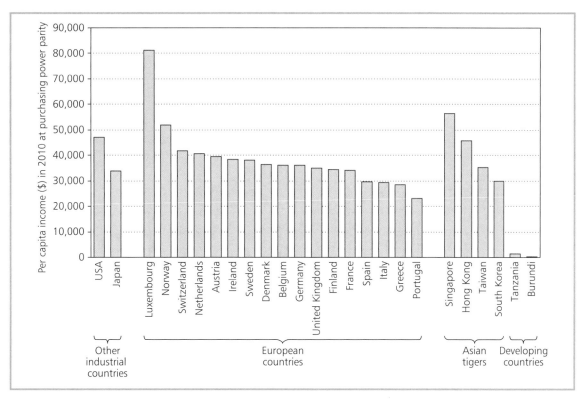

Figure 9.1 In Western Europe per capita incomes (adjusted for differences in purchasing power) in the richest countries remain about 30% higher than in the poorest countries. Worldwide, however, per capita incomes in the industrialized countries are some 50 times higher than in the poorest countries. For example, per capita incomes in Burundi and Tanzania are $411 and $1413, respectively, compared with $36,100 in Belgium and $52,013 in Norway.
Source: IMF, World Economic Outlook Database.

international differences in income. The reason for such huge income gaps can only be discrepancies in equilibrium income: that is, potential income.

The ultimate goal of this analysis is to develop an understanding of international patterns in income and income growth as depicted in Figures 9.1 and 9.2. Figure 9.2 focuses on income growth rates instead of income levels. To prevent the business cycle effects of a given year from blurring the picture, average growth rates for the longer period 1960–2009 are given. The first thing to note is that just as incomes differ substantially between countries, so does income growth. The Asian tigers grew almost three times as fast as some European countries and the US, and even within Europe some countries grew twice as fast as others.

Figure 9.2 also shows income levels. This time it is those observed in 1960, at the start of the recorded growth period. The group of European countries reveals a negative relationship between the initial level of income and income growth. Countries starting at lower income levels tend to grow faster. Thus incomes converge: lower incomes gain ground on higher incomes.

It appears, though, that this convergence property is not robust across continents and cultures. Many Asian economies, the tigers are examples, grew

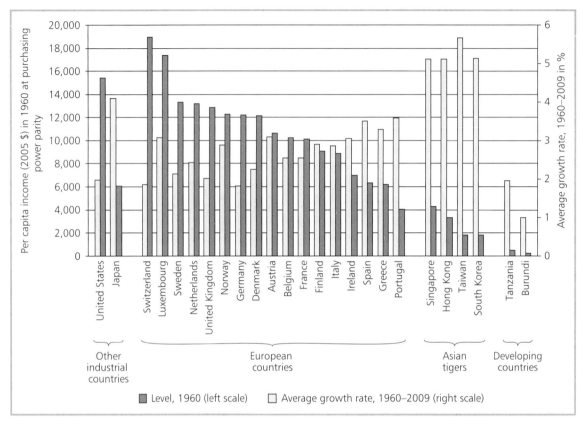

Figure 9.2 The graph compares average income growth between 1960 and 2009 with per capita incomes in 1960. There is a negative correlation for the European countries. Those with low incomes in 1960 enjoyed high growth after that date. Japan, the USA and the Asian tigers also fit this pattern. Burundi and Tanzania do not fit in. With their low 1960 income levels they should have experienced much higher income growth since then.

Source: Penn World Tables 7.0, Alan Heston, Robert Summers and Betina Aten; Penn World Tables version 7.0, Center for International Comparisons of Production, Income and Prices at the University of Pennsylvania.

much faster than European counterparts with similar incomes in 1960. Other countries, unfortunately (Burundi and Tanzania are the examples shown here), do not seem to catch up at all and appear trapped in poverty. These are some of the more important observations we will set out to understand in this and the next chapter.

9.2 The production function and growth accounting

Production function

At the core of any analysis of economic growth is the production function. We draw again on the production function we made use of when studying the labour market in Chapter 6. Real output Y is a function F of the capital stock K (in real terms) and employment L:

$$Y = F(K, L)$$ **Extensive form of production function**   (9.1)

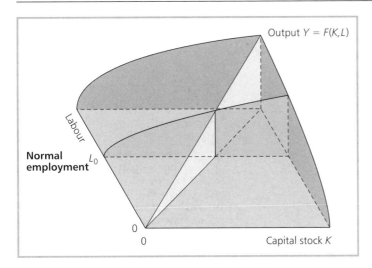

Output $Y = F(K,L)$

Labour

Normal employment L_0

0

0   Capital stock K

Figure 9.3 The 3D production function shows how, for a given production technology, output rises as greater and greater quantities of capital and/or labour are being employed. As a reminder, for first and second derivatives we assume F_K, $F_L > 0$ and F_{KK}, $F_{LL} < 0$.

Figure 9.3 displays this function again, which is called the **extensive form** of the production function. Note, however, that the axes have been relabelled. This is because we now shift our perspective. In Chapter 6, when deriving the labour demand curve, we asked how at any point in time, with a given capital stock that could not be changed in the short run, different amounts of labour employed by firms would affect output produced.

Here we want to know why a country has the capital stock it has. To obtain an unimpaired view on this issue, we now ignore the business cycle. For a start we assume that employment is fixed at normal employment L_0, at which the labour market clears. In order not to have to differentiate all the time between magnitudes per capita or per worker, we even suppose that all people work. So the number of workers equals the population. All our arguments remain valid, however, if workers are a fixed share of the population. If this share changes, the effects are analogous to what results from a changing population as will be discussed in section 9.6.

The assumptions that economists make about the production function shown in Figure 9.3 are (adding a third one) as follows:

■ Output increases as either factor or both factors increase.
■ If one factor remains fixed, increases of the other factor yield smaller and smaller output gains.
■ If both factors rise by the same percentage, output also rises by this percentage.

As we know from Chapter 6, the second assumption refers to partial production functions. For our current purposes we place a vertical cut through the production function parallel to the axis measuring the capital stock. Figure 9.4 shows the obtained partial production function that fixes labour at L_0.

What we said about the partial production function employed in Chapter 6 applies in a similar way to the one displayed in Figure 9.4. The output gain accomplished by a small increase in K (which is called the marginal product of capital) is measured by the slope of the production function. As the given labour input is being combined with more and more capital, one-unit increases of K

The marginal product of capital is the output added by adding one unit of capital.

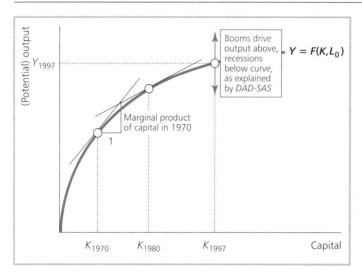

Figure 9.4 This partial production function shows how output increases as more capital is being used, while labour input remains fixed at L_0. The slope of $F(K, L_0)$ measures how much output is gained by a small increase of capital. The two tangent lines measure this marginal product of capital at K_{1970} and K_{1980} and indicate that it decreases as K rises.

Note. Equation (9.1) really should have been written $Y^* = F(K, L^*)$ to explain how potential output relates to the capital stock at potential employment. We drop the asterisk with the understanding that **Y and L denote potential output and potential employment in this and the next chapter.**

A production function has constant returns to scale if raising all inputs by a given factor raises output by the same factor.

yield smaller and smaller output increases. As the two tangents exemplify, there is decreasing marginal productivity of capital.

An important point to note is the following: this chapter's discussion of economic growth ignores the short-lived ups and downs of the business cycle by keeping employment at potential employment L^* at all times. Hence the partial production function given in Figure 9.4 measures how **potential output** Y^* varies with the capital stock. Consequently, throughout this chapter, whenever we talk about output or income, we really mean potential output or income! Having said this, we will refrain from characterizing potential employment and output by an asterisk in the remainder of this and the next chapter. Actual output in 1997, with the capital stock given at K_{1997}, may be above potential output Y_{1997} if there is a boom, or below Y_{1997} in a recession. Such deviations, due to temporary over- or underemployment of labour, are ignored here, but are exactly what the *DAD-SAS* model explained.

The third assumption refers to the level at which the economy operates. If we double all factor inputs, the volume of output produced also doubles (see Figure 9.5). This is assumed to hold generally, for all percentages by which we might increase inputs. The production function is then said to have constant returns to scale. Diminishing returns to scale can be ruled out on the grounds that it should always be possible to build a second production site next to the old factory and employ the same technology, number of workers and capital to produce the same output.

Growth accounting

Growth accounting is similar to national income accounting. The latter provides a numerical account of the factors that contribute to national income, without having the ambition to explain, say, why investment is as high as it is. Similarly, **growth accounting** tries to link observed income growth to the factors that enter the production function, without asking why those factors

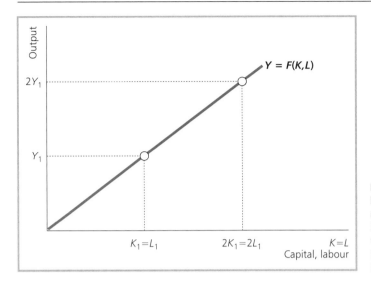

Figure 9.5 This production function shows how output increases as capital and labour rise in proportion. $F(K,L = K)$ is a straight line, indicating that we assume *constant returns to scale*: if capital and labour increase by a given percentage, output increases by the same percentage.

developed the way they did. This question is left to **growth theory**, to which we will turn below.

As the word 'accounting' implies, growth accounting wants to arrive at some hard numbers. A general function like equation (9.1) is not useful for this purpose. Economists therefore use more specific functional forms when turning to empirical work. The most frequently employed form is the **Cobb–Douglas production function**:

Note. The formulation of this particular functional form as a basis for empirical estimates is due to US economist turned politician Paul Douglas and mathematician Charles Cobb.

$$Y = AK^{\alpha}L^{1-\alpha} \qquad \text{Cobb–Douglas production function} \qquad (9.2)$$

As Box 9.1 shows, this function has the same properties assumed to hold for the general production function discussed above, plus a few other properties that come in handy during mathematical operations and appear to fit the data quite well.

Equation (9.2) states that income is related to the factor inputs K and L and to the production technology as measured by the leading variable A. This leaves two ways for economic growth to occur, as Figure 9.6 illustrates. In panel (a) we keep technology constant between 1950 and the year 2000. Income grows only because of an expanding capital stock and a growing labour force. In panel (b) technology has improved, tilting the production function upwards. As a consequence GDP rises at any given combination of capital and labour employed.

The two motors of economic growth featured in the two panels of Figure 9.6 operate simultaneously. Growth accounting tries to identify their qualitative contributions. This is tricky, since the three factors comprising the multiplicative term on the right-hand side of equation (9.2) interact, affecting each other's contribution. A first step towards disentangling this is to take natural logarithms. This yields

$$\ln Y = \ln A + \alpha\ln K + (1 - \alpha)\ln L \qquad (9.3)$$

meaning that the logarithm of income is a weighted sum of the logarithms of technology, capital and labour. Now take first differences on both sides

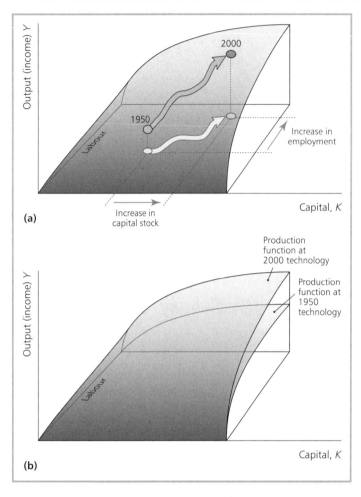

Figure 9.6 The two panels give a production function interpretation of income growth. Panel (a) assumes constant production technology. Then the production function graph does not change in this diagram. Income has nevertheless grown from 1950 to 2000 because the capital stock has risen and employment has gone up. Panel (b) illustrates the effect of technological progress on the production function graph. The upwards tilt of the production function would raise income even if input factors did not change. In reality all three indicated causes of income growth play a role: capital accumulation, labour force growth and technological progress.

Source: K. Case, R. Fair, M. Gärtner and K. Heather (1999) *Economics*, Harlow: Prentice Hall Europe.

Maths note. An alternative way to derive the growth-accounting equation starts by taking the total differential of the production function $Y = AK^\alpha L^{1-\alpha}$ which is $dY = K^\alpha L^{1-\alpha}dA + \alpha AK^{\alpha-1}L^{1-\alpha}dK + (1-\alpha)AK^\alpha L^{-\alpha}dL$. Now divide by Y on the left-hand side and by $AK^\alpha L^{1-\alpha}$ on the right-hand side to obtain (after cancelling terms) $\frac{dY}{Y} = \frac{dA}{A} + \alpha\frac{dK}{K} + (1-\alpha)\frac{dL}{L}$ which is the continuous-time analogue to equation (9.4).

(meaning that we deduct last period's values) to obtain $\ln Y - \ln Y_{-1} = \ln A - \ln A_{-1} + \alpha(\ln K - \ln K_{-1}) + (1-\alpha)(\ln L - \ln L_{-1})$. Finally, making use of the property (mentioned previously and derived in the appendix on logarithms in Chapter 1) that the first difference in the logarithm of a variable is a good approximation for this variable's growth rate, we arrive at

$$\frac{\Delta Y}{Y} = \frac{\Delta A}{A} + \alpha\frac{\Delta K}{K} + (1-\alpha)\frac{\Delta L}{L} \quad \text{Growth accounting equation} \quad (9.4)$$

stating that a country's income growth is a weighted sum of the rate of technological progress $\Delta A/A$, capital growth and employment growth. All we need to know now before we can do some calculations with this equation is the magnitude of α. This is not as hard as it may seem, at least not if we assume that our economy operates under perfect competition. Perfect competition ensures that each factor of production is paid the marginal product it generates. As we already saw in Chapter 6 in the context of the labour market, then the real wage w equals the marginal product of labour. Similarly, the marginal product of capital equals the (real) interest rate r.

Empirical note. In 2007, the European Union had a labour income share $wL/Y = 1 - \alpha$ of 59%. Greece had the lowest value at 31%, and Britain the highest at 74%.

Total labour income is wL, and total capital income rK. A very useful and convenient property of the Cobb–Douglas production function is that the exponents on the right-hand side indicate the income share this factor gets of total income. Hence $1 - \alpha = wL/Y$ is the labour income share and $\alpha = rK/Y$ is the capital income share (for a proof see Box 9.1 on the Cobb–Douglas function). The labour income share $1 - \alpha$ is around two-thirds for most industrial countries. It is relatively stable over time and can be computed from national income accounts by dividing total labour income by GDP.

Once we have a number for α, equation (9.3) can be used to sketch the graph of the contributions of technology, capital and labour to the development of (the logarithm of) income. Does it matter that technology cannot really be measured? Actually not; in fact, equation (9.4) is usually used to compute an estimate of the rate of technological progress. Solving it for $\Delta A/A$ yields

$$\frac{\Delta A}{A} = \frac{\Delta Y}{Y} - \alpha \frac{\Delta K}{K} - (1 - \alpha)\frac{\Delta L}{L} \qquad \text{Solow residual}$$

To plug in numbers, suppose income grew by 4.5%, the capital stock by 6%, employment by 1.5%, and $\alpha = 1/3$. Then

$$\frac{\Delta A}{A} = 0.045 - \tfrac{1}{3}0.06 - \tfrac{2}{3}0.015 = 0.015$$

BOX 9.1 The mathematics of the Cobb–Douglas production function

Instead of the general equation $Y = AF(K, L)$, economists often use the **Cobb–Douglas production function**

$$Y = AK^\alpha L^{1-\alpha} \qquad (1)$$

with α being a number between zero and one. It has the same properties given for equation (1), but can be used for substituting in numbers and is easier to manipulate mathematically.

Diminishing marginal products
We obtain the marginal product of labour by differentiating (1) with respect to L:

$$\frac{\delta Y}{\delta L} = (1 - \alpha)AK^\alpha L^{-\alpha} = (1 - \alpha)A\left(\frac{K}{L}\right)^\alpha \qquad (2)$$

This expression becomes smaller as we employ more labour L. Thus the marginal product of labour decreases. Similarly,

$$\frac{\delta Y}{\delta K} = \alpha AK^{\alpha-1}L^{1-\alpha} = \alpha A\left(\frac{L}{K}\right)^{1-\alpha} \qquad (3)$$

reveals that the marginal product of capital also falls as K rises.

Constant returns to scale
If we double the amount of capital and labour used, what is the new level of income Y'? On substituting $2K$ for K and $2L$ for L into the production function, we obtain

$$Y' = A(2K)^\alpha(2L)^{1-\alpha} = A2^{\alpha+1-\alpha}K^\alpha L^{1-\alpha}$$
$$= 2AK^\alpha L^{1-\alpha} = 2Y$$

Hence, income doubles as well. Generally, raising both inputs by a factor x raises output by that same factor x. Thus returns to scale are constant.

Constant income shares
If labour is paid its marginal product, say in a perfectly competitive labour market, then the wage rate equals (2), and total labour income wL as a share of income is written as

$$\frac{wL}{Y} = \frac{(1 - \alpha)AK^\alpha L^{-\alpha} L}{AK^\alpha L^{1-\alpha}} = 1 - \alpha$$

Labour income share

If $1 - \alpha$ is the labour income share, the remainder, α, must go to capital owners. To verify this, determine rK/Y, letting the interest rate r equal the marginal product of capital given in (3).

CASE STUDY 9.1 Growth accounting in Thailand

As Figure 9.7 shows, Thai GDP more than doubled between 1980 and 2003. If we plug Thailand's average labour income share of 60% during that period into a logarithmic Cobb–Douglas function we obtain

$$\ln Y = \ln A + 0.4 \ln K + 0.6 \ln L$$

To display the percentages that each of the right-hand side factors contributed to income growth since 1980, we may normalize Y, K and L to one for this year, so that their respective logarithms become zero.

The upper curve in Figure 9.7 shows the logarithm of income, which is the variable we set out to account for. The lowest curve depicts $0.6 \ln L$, the contribution of employment growth. It shows that population or employment growth explains but a moderate part of observed income growth. The second curve adds the contribution of capital-stock growth to the contribution of employment growth.

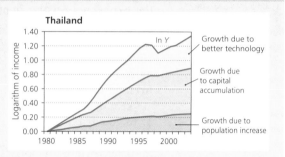

Figure 9.7

This effect is large. Almost half of Thailand's income gains result from a rising capital stock. The remaining gap between this second curve and the third curve, the income line, represents the Solow residual. It is supposed to measure the effect of better technology on income. This contribution is smaller than the contribution of capital stock growth, but larger than the contribution from employment growth.

The equation says that of the 4.5% observed growth in income 2 percentage points may be attributed to the growth in the capital stock and another 1 percentage point to employment growth. This leaves 1.5 percentage points of income growth unexplained. Since these cannot be attributed to input factor growth, they must represent improved technology. This number fills the gap in the growth accounting equation (9.4), the residual, and is generally referred to as the **Solow residual**. The Solow residual serves as an estimate of technological progress. Table 9.1 shows empirical results obtained in the fashion described above.

One interesting result is that the four included European economies had very similar growth experiences from the 1960s through the 1980s. Employment growth played no role at all. About one-third of the achieved increase in output is due to an increase of the capital stock. Almost two-thirds, however, resulted from improved production technology.

Table 9.1 Sources of economic growth in six OECD countries

	Percentage of income growth attributable to each source		
	Technological progress	Growth of capital stock	Employment growth
Britain	61	38	0
Germany	55	45	0
France	63	33	4
Italy	65	32	2
Japan	45	44	11
USA	20	37	42

Source: S. A. Englander and A. Gurney (1994) 'Medium-term determinants of OECD productivity growth', OECD Economic Studies, 22.

The experience of Japan and the United States was somewhat different. In both countries, technological progress played a much smaller role than in Europe. This is most striking in the United States, where improved technology contributed only 20%, while 42% of achieved output growth came from an increase in employment.

Growth accounting describes economic growth, but it does not explain it. Growth accounting does not ask why technology improved so much faster during one decade than during another, or why some countries employ a larger stock of capital than others. But it provides the basis for such important questions to be asked. We now begin to ask these questions by turning to **growth theory**.

9.3 Growth theory: the Solow model

The Solow growth model, sometimes called the **neoclassical growth model**, is the workhorse of research on economic growth, and often the basis of more recent refinements. We begin by considering its building blocks and how they interact.

We know from the circular flow model (or from the Keynesian cross) that, in equilibrium, planned spending equals income. Another way to state this is to say that leakages equal injections: $S - I + T - G + IM - EX = 0$. To retain the simplest possible framework for this chapter's introduction to the basics of economic growth, let us reactivate the global-economy model with no trade and no government ($IM = EX = T = G = 0$). (Growth in the open economy and the role of the government will be discussed in the next chapter.) Then net leakages are zero if

$$I = S \qquad\qquad (9.5)$$

(Planned) investment must make up for the amount of income funnelled out of the income circle by savings. If people consume the fraction c out of current income, as captured by the consumption function $C = cY$, they obviously save the rest. Thus the fraction they save (and invest) is $s = 1 - c$. Total savings are

$$S = sY \qquad\qquad (9.6)$$

Combining (9.5) and (9.6) gives

$$I = sY$$

Substitution of (9.1) for Y yields

$$I = sF(K, L) \qquad\qquad (9.7)$$

There is a second side to investment, however. It does not only constitute demand needed to compensate for savings trickling out of the income circle, but it also adds to the stock of capital: by definition it constitutes that part of demand which buys capital goods. Note, however, that in order to obtain the net change in the stock of capital, ΔK, we must subtract depreciation from current gross investment I. If capital depreciates at the rate δ, we obtain

$$\Delta K = I - \delta K \qquad\qquad (9.8)$$

Maths note. Equation (9.9) is a difference equation in K. Standard solution recipes fail because the equation is non-linear due to the F function. Therefore economists usually resort to qualitative graphical solution methods.

The requirement line shows the amount of investment required to keep the capital stock at the indicated level.

Substitution of (9.7) into (9.8) gives

$$\Delta K = sF(K, L) - \delta K \tag{9.9}$$

Equation (9.9) tells us that the capital stock grows when the first term on the right-hand side, private savings or gross investment, exceeds the amount of capital we lose through depreciation. A graph sheds light on when this is the case.

The first term on the right-hand side is the production function already shown above, multiplied with the savings rate. Figure 9.8 shows both the production function and the savings-and-investment function.

The second term on the right-hand side is a straight line with slope δ. Let us call this the requirement line, because it states the investment required to keep the capital stock at its current level. If the savings function is initially steeper than δ, there is one capital endowment K^* at which both lines intersect. It is only at this capital stock that required and actual investment are equal.

The reason that K^* stands out among all other possible values for K is because it marks some sort of gravity point. This is the level to which the capital stock tends to converge from any other initial value. To see this, assume that the capital stock falls short of K^*. Then actual investment as given by the savings function obviously exceeds required investment. So in the entire segment left of K^* net investment is positive and the capital stock grows. This process only comes to a halt as K reaches K^*.

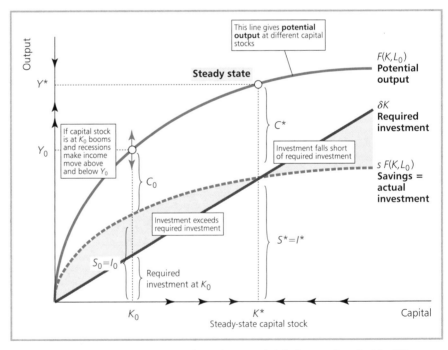

Figure 9.8 The solid curved blue line shows how much is being produced with different capital stocks. The broken blue line measures the fixed share of output being saved and invested. The difference between the curved lines is what is left for consumption δ. The grey straight line shows investment required to replace exactly capital lost through depreciation. If actual investment equals required investment, the capital stock and output do not change. The economy is in a *steady state*. If actual investment exceeds required investment, the capital stock and output grow. If actual investment falls short of required investment, the capital stock and output fall.

If K initially exceeds K^*, actual investment falls short of the investment level required to replace capital lost through depreciation. So to the right of K^* the capital stock must be falling, and it continues to do so until it eventually reaches K^*. Once we know K^*, the equilibrium or **steady-state** level of the capital stock, it is easy to read the steady-state level of income Y^* off the production function.

To avoid confusion, it is important to distinguish the two equilibrium concepts that we now have for income. **Potential income** is a short- or medium-run concept. It is the level around which the business cycle analyzed in the first eight chapters of this book fluctuates within a few years. During that time the capital stock cannot change much and may well be taken as given. In Figure 9.8 this capital stock may be at K^* or at any other point such as K_0. Booms and recessions occur as vertical fluctuations around the potential output level marked by the partial production function. **Steady-state income** is the one level of potential income that obtains once the capital stock has been built up to the desired level. Returning to this level after a displacement, say, during a war, may take decades.

9.4 Why incomes may differ

(Potential) income levels may differ between countries if the parameters of our model differ. For one thing, the labour force (which we simply set equal to the population) can differ hugely between countries. Remember that by postulating a fixed labour force L_0 we had sliced the neoclassical production function at this value. For a larger labour force we would simply have to place that vertical cut further out. This would result in a partial production function (with labour fixed at $L_1 > L_0$) which is steeper and higher for all capital stocks (see Figure 9.9). So an increase of the labour force (say, due to a higher population) turns the partial production function upwards.

For a given savings rate the upward shift of the production function pulls the savings function upwards too. If more is being produced at each level of the capital stock, more is being saved and invested. Since, on the other hand, depreciation remains unaffected by population levels, the new investment curve intersects the requirement line at a higher level of the capital stock. Not

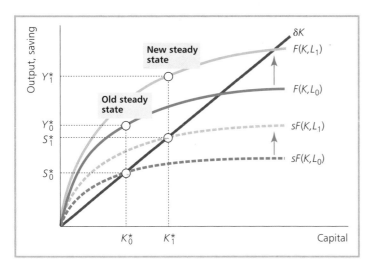

Figure 9.9 An increase of the workforce from L_0 to L_1 turns the partial production function upwards, while keeping it locked at the origin. The curve is higher and steeper for all capital stocks. The savings function moves upwards too. It now intersects the unchanged requirement line at higher levels of output and capital.

surprisingly, therefore, high population countries should also have high capital stocks and high aggregate output. Note that this result says nothing about per capita levels of capital and income, which may be the variables we are ultimately interested in.

An important catchphrase in discussions of international competitiveness and comparative growth is *productivity gains*. While in our model marginal and average factor productivity change during transition episodes, this is due to changing factor inputs. These effects are important and may be long-lasting. But they do peter out as we settle into the steady state. When we talk about productivity gains in the context of growth, however, we really mean the more efficient use of inputs. Such *technological progress* implies that given quantities of labour and capital now yield higher output levels.

Figure 9.10 illustrates the effects of a once-only improvement of the production technology. Any quantity of capital, combined with a given labour input, now yields more output than with the old technology. The production function turns upwards, just as it did when population increased. The investment function turns upwards too. With the requirement line remaining in place, both the equilibrium capital stock and equilibrium output rise. Despite the striking similarity between Figures 9.9 and 9.10 there is an important difference: although income rises in both cases, technological progress raises *income per capita* while population growth does not.

A third parameter that may differ substantially between countries is the savings rate. The effect of raising the savings rate is also easily read off the graph (Figure 9.11). While in this case the production function stays put in its original position, the higher share of output being saved and invested is now turning the savings function upwards. With depreciation being independent of the savings rate, the point of intersection between the new investment function and the new (= old) requirement line lies northeast of the old one. This result is important. It shows that for a given population and given technology, the steady-state level of income can be raised by saving more.

Figure 9.11 may also sharpen our understanding of the terms steady state as opposed to transition dynamics along the potential income curve: if the savings rate rises, a new steady state or long-run equilibrium obtains in which the

A steady state is an equilibrium in which variables do not change any more. The movement from one steady state to another is called transition dynamics.

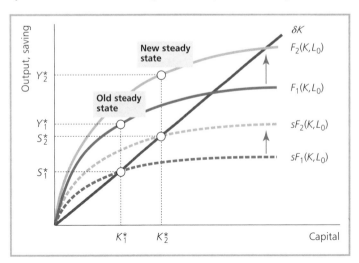

Figure 9.10 An improvement in production technology, which changes the production function from F_1 to F_2, turns the partial production function upwards, while keeping it locked at the origin. The curve is higher and steeper for all capital stocks. The savings function moves upwards too. It now intersects the unchanged requirement line at higher levels of output and capital.

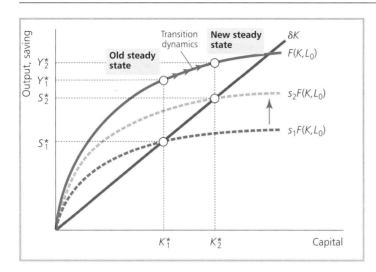

Figure 9.11 An increase of the savings rate from s_1 to s_2 turns the savings function upwards, while leaving the partial production function in place. The savings function now intersects the requirement line at higher levels of output and the capital stock. The movement from the old to the new steady state is called *transition dynamics*.

income is higher. Once the new steady state is reached, however, income does not grow any further. Income growth is zero in both steady states. To move from the old to the new steady state takes time, however, as higher savings only gradually build up the capital stock. During this period of transition we do observe a continuous growth of income.

CASE STUDY 9.2   Income in Eastern Europe during transition

Eastern European countries that made the transition from socialist planned economies to democratic market economies all experienced a very similar income response. Figure 9.12 shows GDP time paths for the Czech Republic, Estonia, Hungary, Poland, Russia and Slovenia, all indexed to 1989 = 100.

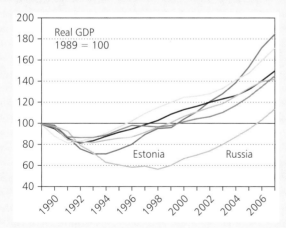

Figure 9.12

All countries observed an initial decline in income of more than 10% and often close to 20%. Exceptions are Russia and the former Soviet republic of Estonia, where the drop in income was noticeably larger. In Estonia it amounted to almost 30%, while the long and dramatic deterioration in the Russian Federation totalled almost 45%. For all countries except Russia it took about ten years to recover from their deterioration in incomes. In Russia, where 1989 levels of income were only reached in 2006, it took almost twice as long.

The magnitude and length of these economic downturns are well beyond what we call typical business cycles. While changes on the demand side contributed to these developments, supply-side developments as captured by the Solow model offer a more convincing explanation of what happened. Consider the familiar graphical representation of the Solow model in Figure 9.13, where the 'Socialist steady state' is shown in light grey.

When the transition from socialist planning to a free market economy started, two things happened that are relevant here:

Case study 9.2 continued

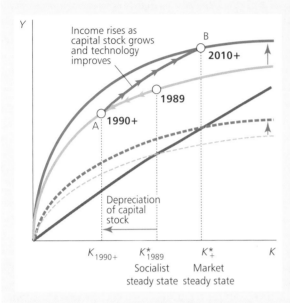

Figure 9.13

■ The value and prices of outputs were evaluated on the global market rather than set by government planning. In many cases this meant that factories were geared towards the production of goods that were produced more efficiently and, hence, more cheaply in other countries. For example, firms that had churned out Ladas, Moskvitchs, Skodas and Trabi cars on the orders of communist planning bureaus within the sheltered trading area of the communist bloc could not compete on world markets and had to be closed in many cases, or otherwise modernized with enormous investment. Assembly lines had to be shredded, and the

old and obsolete industrial sector shrank rapidly. In terms of the neoclassical growth model, a substantial part of the capital stock had to be written off and discarded because there was no market use for it.

■ Amplifying this effect, even machinery that could still be used wore out and depreciated much more quickly because producers that had previously been subsidized by the state went out of business and, therefore, professional maintenance service and replacement parts were no longer available. In terms of Figure 9.13, this turned the requirement line very steep for a few years (not shown), accelerating the rate at which the capital stock shrank.

From the perspective of the Solow model, the story behind the U-shaped income patterns in Eastern European transition economies is that the collapse of socialist regimes triggered a number of years during which the usable capital stock shrank. The economy moved along the production function from the socialist equilibrium to point A. When new investment, domestic and from abroad, began to rebuild the capital stock, two things happened. First, income grew again, along the same path along which it initially shrank, this time from A towards the initial equilibrium. Secondly, new capital and modernization brought better technology and more efficient production processes, turning the partial production function upwards. As this happened in steps, the economy moved along a path that connects A with the new market-economy steady state in B, surpassing the pre-transition income level within a few years.

9.5 What about consumption?

Before getting too excited about the detected positive impact of the savings rate on income, remember that to work and produce as much as possible is hardly a goal in itself. Rather, the ultimate goal is to *maximize consumption*. The complication with this is that it is not clear at all what a higher savings rate does to consumption. While we have seen above that a higher savings rate leads to higher income, a higher savings rate leaves a smaller share of this income available for consumption. Without closer scrutiny the net effect remains ambiguous.

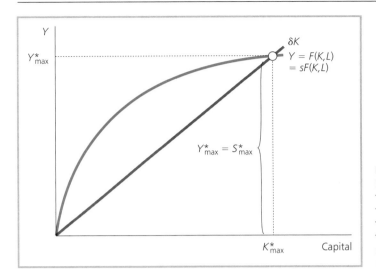

Figure 9.14 If individuals save all their income ($s = 1$) the savings-and-investment function coincides with the production function. Capital and income grow to their maximum levels. But since all of that maximum income must be saved to replace depreciating capital, nothing is left for consumption.

To clarify things, put the savings rate at its maximum, $s = 1$. Then the savings-and-investment function turns all the way up into a position that is identical to the production function. Whatever is being produced is being saved and invested. The good news is that this drives the capital stock up to its *maximal* steady-state level K^*_{max}, and also provides maximum steady-state income Y^*_{max}. The bad news is that not a penny of this income is left for consumption. Consumption is zero (see Figure 9.14).

At the other extreme, with a savings rate of zero, the investment function becomes a horizontal line on the abscissa. People consume all their income and save and invest nothing. Depreciation exceeds investment at all levels of the capital stock. So the capital stock shrinks and continues to do so until all capital is gone and no more output is produced and no more income can be generated. Thus, again, consumption is zero (see Figure 9.15).

The golden rule of capital accumulation

With these two corner results, and after having shown in Figure 9.8 above that positive consumption is possible for an interior value of the savings rate, a savings rate must exist somewhere between the two boundary values of zero and 1, checked above, which maximizes consumption. To identify this savings rate, remember that *in the steady state savings equals required investment*. Therefore consumption possibilities that can be maintained in the steady state are always given by the vertical distance between the production function and the requirement line. Initially, as long as the production function is steeper than the requirement line, this distance widens as the capital stock grows. The reason is that additional capital yields more output than it sucks up savings needed to maintain this increased capital stock. At higher levels of the capital stock we observe the opposite effect. The switch occurs at a threshold where the slopes of the production function and the requirement line are equal.

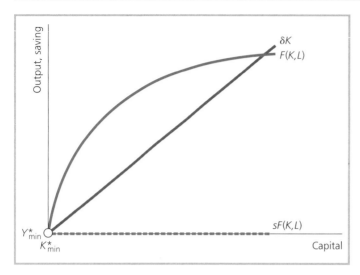

Figure 9.15 If individuals do not save at all ($s = 0$) the savings-and-investment function coincides with the abscissa. Capital and income fall to zero. Therefore, even though individuals are ready to spend everything they earn, no income leaves nothing for consumption.

The **golden rule of capital accumulation** defines the savings rate that maximizes consumption. At the resulting capital stock, additional capital exactly generates enough output gains to cover the incurred additional depreciation.

The golden rule of capital accumulation says that the savings rate should be set to s_{gold}, just so as to yield the capital stock K^*_{gold}, the output level Y^*_{gold} and the consumption level C^*_{gold}.

To pick out the *golden steady state* from all available steady states, proceed as follows (see Figure 9.16):

1 Draw in the production function. Ignore the savings function for now, as we do not know the golden savings rate yet.

2 Draw in the requirement line. In a steady state actual investment equals required investment. So the requirement line defines all possible steady states available at various savings rates.

3 Note that the vertical distance between the production function and the requirement line measures consumption available at different steady states.

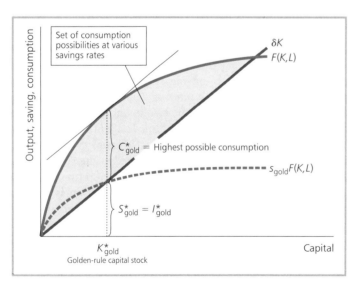

Figure 9.16 The vertical distance between the production function $F(K, L)$ and the requirement line δK measures consumption at various steady states. Consumption is maximized where a parallel to the requirement line is tangent to the production function. This point of tangency determines the consumption-maximizing capital stock and the golden-rule savings rate required to accumulate and maintain this capital stock.

4 Consumption is maximized where a line parallel to the requirement line just touches the production function. This point defines golden-rule output and the golden-rule capital stock.
5 Since the actual savings curve must intersect the requirement line at the golden-rule capital stock, this identifies the golden-rule savings rate.

Dynamic efficiency

If the actual savings rate does not correspond with the savings rate recommended by the golden rule, should the government try to move it towards s_{gold}, say by offering tax incentives? Well, that depends.

Assume first that the savings rate is too high, and that this led to the steady-state capital stock K_1^* and a level of consumption C_1^* that falls short of maximum steady-state consumption C_{gold}^* (see Figure 9.17). When citizens change their behaviour, lowering the savings rate from s_1 to s_{gold}, consumption rises immediately to C_1. Subsequently, consumption gradually falls as the capital stock begins to melt away, but it will always remain higher than C_1^*. The time path of consumption looks as displayed in the left panel of Figure 9.18. To reduce the savings rate from s_1 to s_{gold} would provide individuals with higher consumption today and during all future periods – at no cost. The sum of all consumption gains, compared to the initial steady state, is represented by the

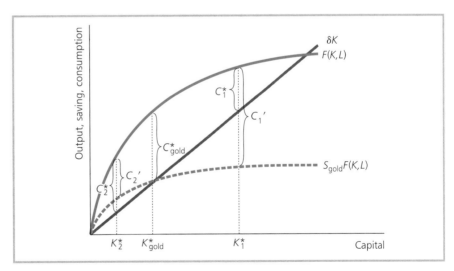

Figure 9.17 When the savings rate exceeds s_{gold}, a steady-state capital stock such as K_1^* results, and consumption is C_1^*. When lowering the savings rate to s_{gold}, the immediate effect on consumption is a drop to C_1'. While the capital stock subsequently shrinks towards K_{gold}^*, consumption is always given by the vertical distance between the production function and the savings function. It exeeds C_1^* at all points in time. When the savings rate falls short of s_{gold}, a steady-state capital stock such as K_2^* results, and consumption is C_2^*. After raising the savings rate to s_{gold}, consumption initially falls to C_2'. While the higher savings rate makes the capital stock grow towards K_{gold}^*, consumption remains as given by the vertical distance between the production function and the savings function. It is initially smaller than C_2^*, but later surpasses it and remains higher for good.

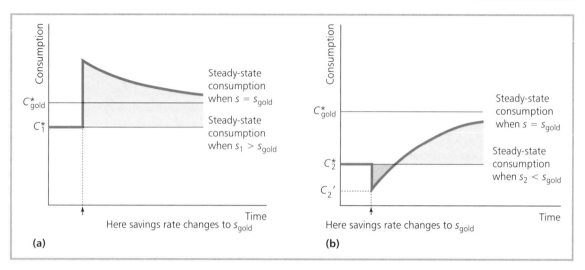

Figure 9.18 Savings rates smaller or larger than that required by the golden rule restrict the country to lower steady-state consumption. Paths of adjustment from the old, suboptimal steady state to the new, golden steady state differ in the two cases shown in Figure 9.18, panels (a) and (b). If $s > s_{gold}$, reducing the savings rate to s_{gold} improves consumption now and forever (panel (a)). The country would gain all the consumption indicated by the area tinted blue if it adopted s_{gold}. Sticking to s_1 is dynamically inefficient. If $s < s_{gold}$, the country faces a dilemma (panel (b)). Raising s to s_{gold} only pays off later in the form of consumption gains tinted blue. Before consumption improves, the country goes through a period of reduced consumption. These losses are tinted grey.

Empirical note. Most countries save less and, hence, accumulate less capital than the golden rule suggests. Thus, they do face the dilemma of whether to reduce today's consumption in order to raise tomorrow's.

area shaded blue. Not to jump at the opportunity to reap this costless gain would be foolish or irrational – or inefficient. This is why a steady state like K_1^*, or any other steady-state capital stock that exceeds the golden one, is called **dynamically inefficient**.

Things are different when the savings rate is too low, say, at s_2. Then the steady-state capital stock K_2^* obtains, and, again, the accompanying level of consumption C_2^* falls short of C_{gold}^* (Figure 9.17). To put the economy on a path towards the golden steady state, the savings rate needs to increase from s_2 to s_{gold}. While this will succeed in raising consumption in the long run, the price to pay is an immediate drop in consumption from C_2^* to C_2'. Only as the higher savings rate leads to capital accumulation and growing income does consumption recover and, at some point in time, surpass its initial level (Figure 9.18, panel (b)). Consumption in the more distant future can only be raised at the cost of reduced consumption in the short and medium run. The consumption loss incurred in the early periods (shaded grey) is the price for the longer-run consumption gains (shaded blue). So the question boils down to how much weight we want to put on today's (or *this* generation's) consumption as compared to tomorrow's (or *future* generation's) consumption. This is not for the economist to decide. His or her proper task is to set out the options. But when future benefits are being discounted heavily compared to current costs, it is not necessarily irrational not to raise the savings rate from s_2 to s_{gold}. This is why a steady state like K_2^*, or any other steady-state capital stock that falls short of the golden one, is called **dynamically efficient**.

9.6 | Population growth and technological progress

Populations grow continuously. So the partial production function shifts upwards all the time, making the capital stock and income rise and rise. Even after the economy has settled into a steady state, we are still required to draw new production and savings functions for each new period, but this is awkward. Also, the representation used so far puts countries like Germany and Luxembourg on quite different slices cut off our three-dimensional production function shown as Figure 9.3. That means that we have to use a different partial production function for each country.

To get around such problems, we now recast the Solow growth model into a form that is better suited for comparing economies of different sizes and for analyzing countries with growing populations. This version should measure *output per worker* on the ordinate and *capital per worker* on the abscissa. To obtain such a *new representation of the same model*, we first need to know what determines output per worker. This is not difficult. Recall our assumption that the production function $Y = F(K, L)$ has constant returns to scale. Then, say, doubling both inputs simply doubles output: $2Y = F(2K, 2L)$. Or multiplying all inputs by the fraction $1/L$ multiplies output by $1/L$ as well:

$$(1/L)Y = F[(1/L)K, (1/L)L]$$

Cancelling out, this is written as

$$Y/L = F(K/L, 1)$$

Now represent per capita (or, since we let employment equal the population, per worker) variables by their respective lower-case counterparts (that is, $k \equiv K/L$ and $y \equiv Y/L$). Denote the resulting function $F(k,1)$ more concisely as $f(k)$, without the redundant parameter of 1, and we have the desired simple function, called the **intensive form**,

$$y = f(k) \qquad \text{Intensive form of production function} \qquad (9.10)$$

Per capita income is a positive function of capital per worker only. As Figure 9.19 shows, y increases as k increases, but at a decreasing rate.

Next we need to know what makes k rise or fall. Capital per worker changes for three reasons:

1 Any investment per capita, i, directly adds to capital per worker.
2 Depreciation eats away a constant fraction of capital per worker.

These are the two factors influencing capital formation already considered above, although here we cast the argument in per capita terms. There is a third and new factor:

3 New entrants into the workforce require capital to be spread over more workers. Hence, capital per worker falls in proportion to the population growth rate n.

Combining these three effects yields

$$\Delta k = i - \delta k - nk \qquad (9.11)$$

The first term on the right-hand side states that investment per worker i directly adds to capital per worker. The second term states that depreciation

Maths note. The properties $f'(k) > 0$ and $f'' < 0$ can be shown to follow from what we assumed for $F(K, L)$.

Maths note. The total differential of $k \equiv K/L$ is $d(K/L) = (1/L)dK - (K/L^2)dL$ or $d(K/L) = dK/L - (K/L)(dL/L)$. Substituting the variables defined in the text gives $dk = i - (n + \delta)k$. The expression given in the text follows if we take discrete changes of k (Δk instead of dk).

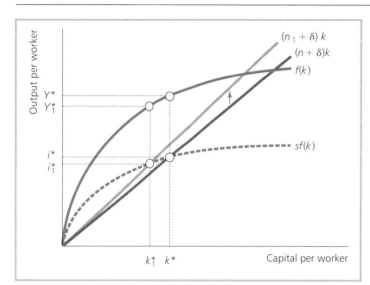

Figure 9.19 The solid curved line shows per capita output as a function of the per capita capital stock. Per capita savings and investment are a fraction of this output. The steady state obtains where per capita savings equal required investment per capita. If population growth increases, the requirement line becomes steeper. The new steady state features less capital and lower output per worker.

eats away a fraction δ of existing capital per worker. The third term states that an $n\%$ addition to the labour force makes the capital stock available for each worker fall by $n \times k$.

Investment per worker i equals savings per worker sy. So replacing i in equation (9.11) by sy and making use of equation (9.10), we obtain

$$\Delta k = sf(k) - (n + \delta)k$$

In the steady state the capital stock per worker does not change any more ($\Delta k = 0$). Hence, the two terms given on the right-hand side must be equal. To achieve this, investment not only needs to replace capital lost through depreciation, but must also endow new entrants into the workforce with capital. This is why the slope of the requirement line is now given by the sum of the depreciation rate and of population growth.

With the relabelling of the axes in per capita terms and the augmented requirement line, the graphical representation and analysis of the model proceeds along familiar lines.

The steady state obtains where the investment function and the requirement line intersect. If the capital stock per worker is smaller than its steady-state value k^*, actual investment exceeds required investment and income and capital per worker grow. In the region $k > k^*$ the opposite obtains and both k and y fall.

What happens if two countries are identical except for population growth? The only effect that higher population growth has is to turn the requirement line $(n + \delta)k$ upwards. Now each period a higher percentage of workers must be equipped with capital if the capital stock per worker is to stay at its current level. At the old steady state k^*, investment is too low and k begins to fall towards the lower steady-state level k_1^*. So the model yields the testable empirical implication that *countries with higher population growth tend to have lower capital stocks per worker and also lower per capita incomes*.

Another unrealistic assumption employed so far is that the economy in question operates with the same production technology all the time. In reality technology appears to improve continuously. One way to incorporate technology into the production function is by assuming that it determines the efficiency E of labour. The production function then reads

$$Y = F(K, E \times L)$$

where the product $E \times L$ is labour measured in efficiency units. Representing technology in this fashion is particularly convenient for our purposes. All we have to do is divide both sides of the production function not by L, as we had done above, but by $E \times L$. This yields a new production function

$$\hat{y} = f(\hat{k})$$

with $\hat{y} \equiv Y/(EL)$ and $\hat{k} \equiv K/(EL)$.

For a familiar graphical representation of this production function we simply write output *per efficiency unit of labour* $\hat{y}$ instead of output *per worker* on the ordinate. The abscissa now measures capital per efficiency unit $\hat{k}$. The production function shows how output per efficiency unit of labour depends on capital per efficiency unit (see Figure 9.20).

The requirement line now tells us how much investment per efficiency unit of labour we need to keep the capital stock per efficiency unit at the current level. In order to achieve this, investment must now

- replace capital lost through depreciation (as above),
- cater to new workers (as above), and
- equip new efficiency units of labour created by technological progress, which we assume to proceed at the rate ε (this is new):

$$\Delta \hat{k} = \hat{i} - (\delta + n + \varepsilon)\hat{k}$$

Maths note. The total differential of $\hat{k} \equiv K/(EL)$ is $d(K/(EL)) = (1/(EL))dK - (K/(EL^2))dL - (K/(E^2L))dE$ or $d[K/(EL)] = dK/(EL) - (K/(EL))(dL/L) - (K/(EL))(dE/E)$. Substituting the variables defined in the text gives $d\hat{k} = \hat{i} - (n + \delta + \varepsilon)\hat{k}$. The expression given in the text follows if we take discrete changes of $\hat{k}$.

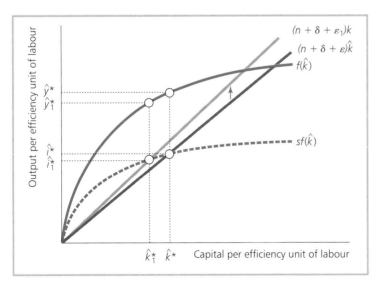

Output per efficiency unit of labour

$(n + \delta + \varepsilon_1)k$
$(n + \delta + \varepsilon)\hat{k}$
$f(\hat{k})$

$sf(\hat{k})$

Capital per efficiency unit of labour

Figure 9.20 The axes measure output and capital per efficiency unit of labour. With this qualification the production function, the savings function and the requirement line look as they did in previous diagrams. The steady-state and transition dynamics are determined along by-now familiar lines. If technology improves, making labour more efficient, the requirement line becomes steeper. The new steady state features less capital and lower output per efficiency unit, but more capital and higher output per worker.

CASE STUDY 9.3   Income and leisure choices in the OECD countries

When microeconomists analyze individual behaviour they usually assume that two things enhance a person's utility: first, consumption (which is limited by income); second, leisure time (the time we have to enjoy the things we consume). This makes it obvious that judging the well-being of a country's citizens by looking at income would be just as one-sided as judging their well-being by looking at leisure time.

Using data for the year 1996, Figures 9.21 and 9.22 show that a country's per capita income and its leisure time need not necessarily go hand in hand. Figure 9.21 shows per capita incomes relative to the OECD average normalized to 100. The richest country in the sample is the USA, with per capita income 35% above average. The poorest country is Portugal, whose income falls short of the OECD average by 33%. Figure 9.22 ranks countries according to leisure time per inhabitant. As we may have expected, there appears to be some trade-off: many countries with the world's highest per capita incomes are at the end of the leisure timescale. They appear to achieve their high incomes mostly by working a lot, and having much less time left for off-work activities than others. On the other hand some countries with very low per capita incomes are doing very well in the leisure time ranking. Spain is one such example.

Exceptions from this general trade-off appear to be Portugal, which fares poorly both in terms of income and leisure time, and Norway which (probably helped by North Sea oil revenues) generates

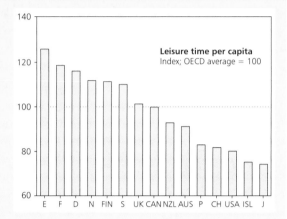

Figure 9.22

one of the highest per capita incomes while at the same time enjoying above average leisure time.

Figure 9.23 merges the data shown separately in Figures 9.21 and 9.22 into a scatter plot. This diagram illustrates the apparent trade-off situation from a somewhat different angle. Most countries that clearly perform above average in one category pay for this by dropping below average in the other category. As just mentioned, though, clear exceptions from this general rule are Norway and Portugal (and, to some extent, New Zealand).

Figure 9.21

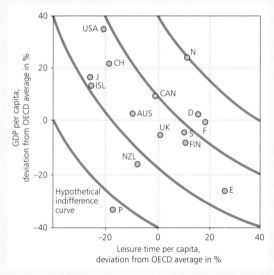

Figure 9.23

Case study 9.3 continued

So which country's citizens are better off? This is difficult to say. Strictly speaking, one country's citizens are only unequivocally better off than others, if they have both more income and more leisure time. For example, Norwegians are certainly better off than Canadians. Britons are better off than New Zealanders, and the Swiss are better off than the Japanese. However, whenever one country is better off in one category, but worse off in the other, we cannot really tell. This applies when comparing France with the USA, or Spain with Australia. Without a way of weighing 1% more leisure time against 1% less income, no judgment is possible.

As a crude attempt, however, note that in the OECD area a day contains about eight hours of work time and eight hours of leisure time. In equilibrium, one hour of leisure time may be worth about as much as we can produce in one hour of work time. If not, individuals would (try to) either work more and enjoy fewer hours of leisure, or work less to have more time off. So 1% more income is worth about the same as 1% more leisure time.

This means that indifference curves in leisure/income space would have a slope of about -1 when income and leisure time are at the OECD average, or exceed or fall short of it by the same percentage. This would be the case on a 45° line connecting the lower left and upper right corners of the diagram. If both income and leisure time yield decreasing marginal utility, indifference curves might look like those sketched in the diagram. A country's citizens' utility level would then be the higher the further to the right is the indifference curve reached by that country.

One might argue that countries need not all have the same preferences. So each country may optimize choices in the context of its own set of indifference curves, and its location in Figure 9.23 may simply be the best it can do. Then, of course, we have no generally accepted basis for making comparisons between countries.

Data source and further reading: J.-C. Lambelet and A. Mihailov (1999) 'A note on the Swiss economy: Did the Swiss economy really stagnate in the 1990s, and is Switzerland really all that rich?' *Analyses et prévisions*.

The steady-state and transition dynamics are obtained along reasoning analogous to the one employed above. In equilibrium, income per efficiency unit of labour remains constant. Since *efficiency units of labour* grow faster than labour, due to technological progress, output (and capital) per worker must be growing. To show this mathematically, we may start by noting that in the steady state income per efficiency units of labour does not change, $\Delta \hat{y} = 0$. From the definition $\hat{y} \equiv \frac{Y}{EL}$ we obtain per capita income y by multiplying by E:

$$y \equiv \frac{Y}{L} = \frac{Y}{EL} E = \hat{y} \times E$$

Finally, we recall that the growth rate of the product $\hat{y} \times E$ can be approximated by the sum of the growth rates of $\hat{y}$ and E:

$$\frac{\Delta y}{y} = \frac{\Delta \hat{y}}{\hat{y}} + \frac{\Delta E}{E} = \frac{\Delta \hat{y}}{\hat{y}} + \varepsilon = 0 + \varepsilon = \varepsilon$$

This shows that even though income per efficiency units of labour does not change in the steady state, $\Delta \hat{y} = 0$, income per capita nevertheless does. It grows at the rate of technological progress ε. So we finally have a model that explains *income growth* in the conventional meaning of the term.

As regards comparative statics, a faster rate of technological progress turns the requirement curve upwards, thus lowering capital and income *per efficiency unit*. Does this mean that faster technological progress is bad? With regard to per capita income, the answer is no. Remember that the one-off technology improvement analyzed in section 9.4 raised capital and output *per worker*. The same result must apply here, where the one-off technological improvement simply occurs period after period. Therefore, *faster technological progress raises the level and the growth rate of output per worker.*

9.7 Empirical merits and deficiencies of the Solow model

Empirical work based on the Solow growth model usually proceeds from the assumption that, in principle, the same production technologies are available to all countries. Thus all countries should operate on the same partial production function and experience the same rate of technological progress. This leaves only two factors that may account for differences in steady-state per capita incomes.

The first is the savings or investment rate. The higher a country's rate of investment, the larger the capital stock per worker, and the higher is per capita income. Figure 9.24 looks at whether this hypothesis stands up to the data by plotting per capita income at the vertical and the investment rate at the horizontal axis for a sample of 98 countries.

By and large, the data support this aspect of the Solow model, but not perfectly so, since the data points are not lined up like pearls on a string, but instead form a cloud. However, we should only have expected a perfect alignment if there were no other factors that influence per capita income. If two countries with the same investment rate differ in these other factors, they will have different per capita incomes.

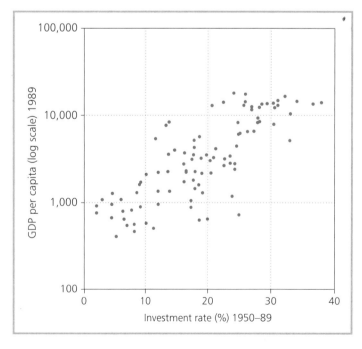

Figure 9.24 According to the Solow model, the higher a country's savings or investment rate (and, hence, capital accumulation), the higher its income (per capita). The graph underscores this prediction for a large number of the world's economies.

Source: R. Barro and J. Lee: http://growth.blogs.ilrt.org.

This chapter's basic version of the Solow model singles out one such factor: the population growth rate. The faster the population grows, the smaller is per capita income. The reason is that if the population grows fast, a lot of new workers enter employment every year. They arrive with no capital. Hence, a large part of what those who work save is needed to equip new entrants with capital. Only a relatively small part of saving can be used to replace depreciated capital. As a consequence, this country cannot afford a high capital stock per worker and must be content with a comparatively low per capita income.

Figure 9.25 checks whether this second hypothesis is supported by the data, and the answer is yes. Again, the relationship is not strict. In fact, the cloud of data points is fairly wide. But again, this does not come as a surprise, since different savings rates would give countries that have the same rate of population growth different per capita incomes.

Empirical note. Worldwide some 60% of the differences in national per capita incomes can be attributed to differences in the investment rate and in population growth.

When researchers use statistical methods to study the combined influence of investment rates and population on per capita incomes, they usually find that 60% of the income differences can be traced back to differences in investment rates and population growth. So the basic Solow model appears to be carrying us a long way towards explaining why some countries are rich and why some are poor. But it also leaves a sizeable chunk of income differences unexplained. While the above argument implicitly assumes that all countries have already settled into their respective steady states, other work explicitly acknowledges that adjustment may be slow and that most countries are on a transition path. Then incomes would differ, even if all countries had the same steady state. In this case, the Solow model yields an interesting proposition regarding the relationship between the level of income and income growth.

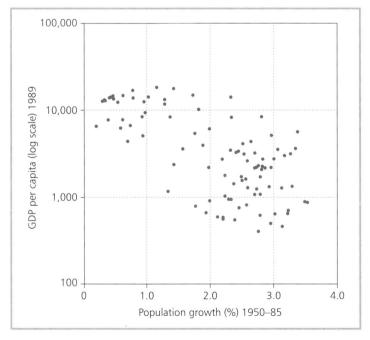

Figure 9.25 According to the Solow model, the higher a country's rate of population growth, the lower its income (per capita). This prediction also seems to hold for a large number of the world's economies, though less clearly so than the prediction checked in Figure 9.24.

Source: R. Barro and J. Lee: http://growth.blogs .ilrt.org.

Per capita incomes in countries that are in the steady state only grow at the rate of technological progress. If a country's capital stock is below its steady-state value, income growth is higher than the rate of technological progress, because the capital endowment per worker rises. If the capital stock exceeded its steady-state value, per capita income could not grow at the rate of techno-logical progress because capital endowment per worker falls. All this can be generalized into the so-called **absolute convergence hypothesis**, which states that there is a negative relationship between a country's initial level of income and subsequent income growth. Figure 9.26 checks whether empirical data feature income convergence.

Empirical note. In homogeneous groups of countries, lower income levels are typically related to higher growth rates. In more diverse samples this does not apply.

There are two messages in this data plot. First, there is no worldwide con-vergence of incomes. Many poor countries grow more slowly than the rich countries, thus widening the income gap. Second, within relatively homoge-neous groups of countries (the Western European countries have been singled out in blue), convergence does indeed occur.

Do these two observations and the Solow model match? Well, at least they do not contradict it. The Solow model only proposes absolute convergence for countries with the same steady states: that is, for countries with similar invest-ment rates and population growth. This holds reasonably well for Western Europe, and it is why incomes there do seem to converge. On the other hand, population growth and savings and investment rates differ dramatically be-tween different regions of the world. Thus across continents, religions and cul-tures sizeable differences in the steady states exist and the Solow model would only postulate convergence to those specific steady states. This is the **relative convergence hypothesis**.

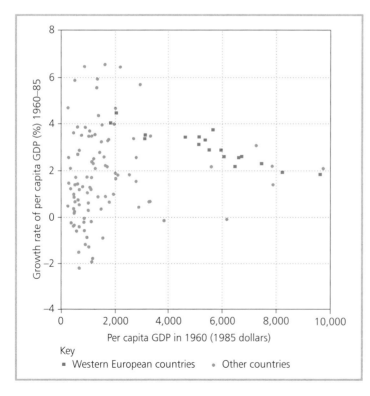

Key
■ Western European countries   • Other countries

Figure 9.26 The data for 122 countries visualize a key finding of empirical growth research: worldwide, there is no absolute convergence of incomes. While many low-income countries (say, in the $0–2,000 bracket) experienced faster in-come growth than high-income countries (say, in the $6,000–10,000 bracket), just as many experienced much slower growth. This picture changes if we focus on west-ern European countries only (highlighted in blue): there, basically all countries with low incomes in 1960 grew faster than those countries that had high incomes at that time. This finding generalizes as: within groups of homogeneous countries (with similar history, culture, political system, etc.) absolute incomes appear to converge.

Source: R. Barro and J. Lee: http://growth.blogs .ilrt.org.

Empirical note. Between 1900 and 1998 Burundi's population grew at an average of 2.6% per year and the average investment rate was 9%. By comparison Germany's population growth was 0.5% and the investment rate was 21%.

While the empirical evidence assembled above underscores why the Solow model is a useful first pass at long-run issues of income determination and growth, it also hints at some important questions that remain open, such as the following:

■ Some 40% of international differences in per capita incomes cannot be attributed to differences in population growth and investment rates, as our workhorse model indicated. This suggests that not all countries operate on the same partial production function. A possible reason for this might be that we have overlooked an important production factor.

■ From a global perspective there seems to be no convergence of income levels. While part of this can be attributed to differences in population growth and investment rates alone, this does not suffice. Again, does that mean that our view of the production function was too simple?

■ A more fundamental, conceptual defect of the Solow model is that it does not really explain economic *growth*. Rather, per capita income growth occurs driven by exogenous technological progress, as a residual which the model does not even attempt to understand.

These main points are illustrative of some of the deficits of the basic Solow model which have motivated refinements and a new wave of research efforts on issues of economic growth. The next chapter looks at some of these refinements and discusses some of the more recent achievements.

CHAPTER SUMMARY

■ The level of output produced in a country is determined by the stock of capital, the labour force and the state of production technology.

■ The rate of saving determines the capital stock and, hence, output. A rise in the savings rate increases output permanently, but has no permanent effect on the growth rate. It raises the growth rate during a (very long) transition period, however.

■ Higher savings always raise income, but may reduce consumption. The golden rule of capital accumulation determines the savings rate that maximizes consumption (per capita). At the capital stock resulting from this rule the addition of more capital would not generate the additional income needed to replace obsolete or worn-out capital that needs to be written off.

■ The only factor that, in the presence of constant returns to scale, can make living standards grow in the long run is technological progress.

Key terms and concepts

EXERCISES

9.1 A country's production function is given by $Y = AK^{0.5}L^{0.5}$. In the year 2001 we observed $K = 10,000$, $L = 100$ and $Y = 10,000$. Suppose that during the following year income grew by 2.5%, the capital stock by 3% and employment by 1%. What was the rate of technological progress?

(a) Address this question first by computing the Solow residual from the growth accounting equation.

(b) The text stated that the growth accounting formula is only an approximation. To quantify the involved imprecision, answer the above question next by proceeding directly from the production function. This yields the precise number. Compare the results obtained under (a) and (b).

9.2 Consider the Cobb–Douglas production function: $Y = K^{\alpha}L^{\beta}$.

(a) Under what conditions do marginal returns to capital diminish if labour stays constant?

(b) Under what conditions does the function display constant returns to scale?

(c) Suppose marginal returns to capital do not diminish. Is it still possible for the function to exhibit constant returns to scale?

9.3 The per capita production function of a country is given by

$$y = Ak^{0.5}$$

The parameters take the following values:

$$s = 0.2 \qquad n = 0.05 \qquad \delta = 0.2 \qquad A = 5$$

Calculate the per capita capital stock k^* and per capita output y^* in the steady state.

9.4 Suppose two countries have the same steady-state capital stock, but in country A this is due to a larger population, whereas in country B it is due to a more advanced technology and thus higher productivity. How does the steady-state income of country A differ from the steady-state income of country B? Does it make sense to say that country B is richer than country A?

9.5 Consider two countries (C and D) that are identical except for the savings rate, which is higher in country C than in country D. Which country is richer? Does this necessarily mean that welfare is higher in the richer country?

9.6 Suppose two countries, Hedonia and Austeria, are characterized by the following production function: $Y = K^{0.3}L^{0.7}$. In both countries the labour supply is constant at 1, there is no technological progress, and the depreciation rate is 30% (an unrealistically high portion, compared with empirical estimates).

(a) Compute the golden-rule level of the capital stock.

(b) What is the savings rate that leads to the golden-rule capital stock?

(c) Suppose you are in charge of the economy of Hedonia where the savings rate is 10%. Your goal is to lead Hedonia to eternal happiness by implementing the golden-rule steady state. To this end you impose the golden-rule savings rate. Compute the levels of income and consumption for the first five periods after the change of the savings rate, starting at the initial steady state. Draw the development of output and consumption and explain why you might run into trouble as a politician.

(d) Being kicked out of Hedonia, you are elected president of Austeria where people save 50% of their income. Do the same experiment as before and explain why, in the not too distant future, Austerians will build a monument in your honour.

9.7 Judge the prosperity of an economy where the growth rate of income is 8% due to a constant rate of population growth of 8%. Is this economy better or worse off than an economy with 4% growth and a population growth rate of 3%?

9.8 How does a change in the savings rate affect the steady-state growth rate of output and consumption? Does this result also hold for the transition period (i.e. until the new steady state is reached)?

9.9 Consider an economy where population growth amounts to 2% and the exogenous rate of technological progress to 4%. What are the steady state growth rates of

(a) $\hat{k}, \hat{y}, \hat{c}$ (where the hats denote 'per efficiency unit of labour')?

(b) k, y, c (that is, per capita capital, income and consumption)?

(c) K, Y, C?

9.10 The economy is in a steady state at $\hat{k}^* = 100$. The efficiency of labour grows at a rate of 0.025 (2.5%), population growth is 0.01, and depreciation is 0.05 annually.

(a) At what rate does K grow?

(b) At what rate does per capita income grow? If the production function is $\hat{y} = 10\hat{k}^{0.5}$, what is the steady-state output per efficiency unit of labour?

(c) What is the country's savings rate?

(d) What should the country save according to the golden rule?

9.11 Per capita income in the Netherlands was $25,270 in 1999 and grew by 3.8% during the following four years. Per capita income in China was only $780 in 1999, but it had risen by 24.43% by 2003.

(a) Show that, despite this large difference in income growth rates, absolute per capita incomes did not grow closer.

(b) Given the Dutch income growth rate between 1999 and 2003, how large would China's growth rate have to be in order to make the absolute income gap between the two countries shrink?

(c) Compute the ratio between Chinese and Dutch per capita incomes in 1999 and in 2003. Compare your results with the results obtained under (a). Discuss.

Online resources

Interactive applet on Solow growth model www.eurmacro.eu/tutor/solow.html
Interactive applet on Solow growth model (per capita version) www.eurmacro.eu/tutor/solowpc.html
Interactive applet on Cobb-Douglas production function www.eurmacro.eu/tutor/cobb-douglas.html
X-exercise revisiting the paradox of thrift www.eurmacro.eu/xercises/
    paradoxofthrift2.html
Interactive road map www.eurmacro.eu/tutor/map.html

Self quiz

www.eurmacro.eu/SelfQuiz/sq-ch09.html

Recommended reading

Robert M. Solow (1970) *Growth Theory: An Exposition*, Oxford: Oxford University Press. An extension, including human capital (to be addressed in Chapter 10) and empirical tests, is put forward in N. Gregory Mankiw, David Romer and David Weil (1992) 'A contribution to the empirics of economic growth', *Quarterly Journal of Economics* 107: 407–37.

Barry Bosworth and Susan Collins (2008) 'Accounting for growth: Comparing China and India', *Journal of Economic Perspectives* 22: 45–66, provides an interesting and non-technical application of growth accounting. David Cook (2002) 'World War II and convergence', *Review of Economics and Statistics* 84: 131–8, estimates how quickly potential income recovers after wartime destruction of the capital stock.

APPLIED PROBLEMS

EMPIRICAL RESEARCH

Does the distribution of income affect economic growth?

The Solow model proposes that, under certain conditions, countries converge to a common income level. Starting from this proposition, Torsten Persson and Guido Tabellini (1994, 'Is inequality harmful for growth?', *American Economic Review* 84: 600–21) study the question of whether economic growth, in addition to the initial level of income as proposed by the convergence hypothesis, is also affected by how income is distributed in a society. They measure the convergence potential of a country by GDPGAP, which is the ratio between the country's GDP and the highest current GDP of any country in the sample. The higher that ratio is, the smaller growth is expected to be. Income inequality is measured by INCSH, i.e. the share in personal income of the top 20% of the population. So the higher INCSH is, the more unevenly income is distributed. To eliminate short-run (business cycle) fluctuations, observations (data points) are measured as averages over subperiods of 20 years each, starting as far back as 1830. Including nine countries in the sample gives 38 such subperiods (or observations). The following regression obtains:

$$\text{GROWTH} = 7.206 - 2.695 \text{ GDPGAP} - 6.911 \text{ INCSH}$$
$$\phantom{\text{GROWTH} = } (5.72) \quad (2.70) \phantom{\text{ GDPGAP} - } (3.07)$$
$$R^2_{\text{adj}} = 0.30$$

The result suggests, first, that growth features convergence. The lower a country's income is relative to the leading country, that is the smaller GDPGAP, the faster income grows. Second, a more uneven distribution of income depresses growth. The coefficient of -6.911 (which is significantly different from zero, as the t-statistic of 3.07 indicates), suggests that if the income share of the top 20% of the population increases from, say, 0.50 to 0.65, income growth falls by a full percentage point ($-6.911 \times 0.15 = -1.03665$). The coefficient of determination of 0.298 reveals, however, that the two variables included in the regression explain only 30% of the variance of growth between countries and across time.

WORKED PROBLEM

Do European incomes converge?

Table 9.2 gives real per capita incomes in 1960 (in $1,000, purchasing-power adjusted) and average income growth between 1960 and 1994 in 18 Western European countries. Do these numbers support the convergence hypothesis of the Solow model? To obtain an answer to this question we may regress average income growth $\Delta Y/Y$ (in %) on 1960 income Y_{1960} (in $1,000). The estimation equation is

$$\Delta Y/Y = 4.35 - 0.273 Y_{1960} \quad R^2 = 0.85$$
$$ (26.09) \quad (9.61)$$

Table 9.2

	GDP/capita in $1,000 1960	Average growth 1960–94
Austria	5.152	2.9
Belgium	5.554	2.7
Denmark	6.748	2.4
Finland	5.384	2.7
France	5.981	2.7
Germany	6.660	2.6
Greece	2.066	3.6
Iceland	5.191	3.0
Ireland	3.147	3.9
Italy	4.660	3.0
Luxembourg	8.269	2.4
Netherlands	6.104	2.6
Norway	5.656	3.4
Portugal	1.864	3.8
Spain	3.165	3.4
Sweden	7.505	2.0
Switzerland	9.637	1.7
United Kingdom	6.509	2.3

The obtained coefficient of -0.273 is in line with the convergence hypothesis. $1,000 less income in 1960 gave rise to an additional 0.273 percentage points of annual income growth during the following 34 years. The t-statistic of 9.61 for this coefficient permits us to refute the null hypothesis of no convergence ($c_1 = 0$). The coefficient of determination of 0.85 tells us that 85% of the differences in average income growth between the 18 countries included in our sample may be attributed to income differences that existed back in 1960.

The constant term 4.35 indicates how fast a country would have grown, had its income in 1960 been zero, which does not make a lot of economic sense. Alternatively, we may measure 1960 income as deviation from the average income of all countries in that year. The regression equation then becomes

$$\Delta Y/Y = 2.90 - 0.273(Y_{1960} - Y_{average}) \quad R^2 = 0.85$$
$$\quad\quad (51.23) \quad (9.61)$$

Nothing has changed, except for the constant term. Its value of 2.90 says that a country that started with average income in 1960 grew at a rate of 2.9%.

YOUR TURN

Convergence plus distribution

Data on income inequality are provided by a number of sources. Try to find a measure of and data on the distribution of income in the countries included in the sample studies in the worked problem above. (In case you do not succeed, try 'Measuring income inequality: a new database', *World Bank Economic Review*, September 1996.) Now check whether you can replicate the Persson–Tabellini result, which says that a more uneven distribution of income depresses GDP growth. Do so by augmenting the growth equation used in the worked problem with your measure of income inequality.

Economic growth (II): advanced issues

What to expect	

After working through this chapter, you will understand:

1 How government spending and taxes fit into the Solow growth model.

2 How the globalization of capital markets affects a country's income and growth prospects.

3 What the difference is between physical capital and human capital, and how these affect income and growth.

4 What poverty traps are and what measures can get a country out of them.

5 The nature of and processes behind endogenous growth.

So far we employed a global-economy model without government to explain and understand national growth experiences. We saw that even such a deliberately simple model carries us a long way towards understanding international income and growth patterns. But we also saw that it leaves us with a number of loose ends. Also, this baseline model does not permit us to analyze the recent pronounced moves towards globalization in the form of more international trade and integrated, worldwide capital markets. And the model is rather subdued in the sense that things are the way they are and there was no discussion of what governments or other institutional bodies could do to improve a country's material fate.

This chapter tries to mend this by first asking how the government fits into the Solow model and how public spending and taxation decisions affect a country's long-run macroeconomic performance. It also looks at the emerging trend to not necessarily place our savings in a local bank's savings account, but to go farther afield and invest our money in Turkish government bonds, US blue chip stocks, or some start-up company in India or China. Another topic we have on our agenda since the beginning of the last chapter is what keeps some countries trapped in poverty, and what can be done about it. And finally, moving close to the frontier of current research on economic growth, we discuss the role of education and the quality of the workforce, and what other mechanisms besides technological improvements may make per capita incomes improve – endogenously.

10.1 The government in the Solow model

In Chapter 1 we summed up the leakages from and the injections into the circular flow of income in the equation $S - I + T - G + IM - EX = 0$. Rearranging this into

$$\underbrace{I + \underbrace{(EX - IM)}_{\substack{\text{Investment}\\\text{abroad}}}}_{\text{Total private investment}} = \underbrace{\underbrace{S}_{\substack{\text{Private}\\\text{saving}}} + \underbrace{(T - G)}_{\substack{\text{Public}\\\text{saving}}}}_{\text{National saving}}$$

(margin note) Arranged this way, the circular flow identity reveals that national saving is either invested at home or abroad.

reveals a more general correspondence than the simple $I = S$ equation used in the basic Solow model. The complete circular flow identity implies that *all national saving, both private and public, equals total private investment, at home and abroad.* When discussing economic growth in Chapter 9 we ignored the government sector and international trade (setting $T = G = IM = EX = 0$), thus ending up with the equality between private saving and investment $S = I$. Let us now keep the government in the equation while still leaving out the foreign sector (the role of foreign investment will be discussed in the next section). Investment is then determined by

$$I = S + T - G$$

So investment may be financed by private and public saving, since $T - G$ is the government budget surplus, or government saving. Assuming that individuals save a constant fraction s of disposable income, $S = s(Y - T)$, where $s = 1 - c$, we obtain

$$I = s(Y - T) + T - G \tag{10.1}$$

Now recall from the last chapter that the capital stock K changes if investment exceeds depreciation, $\Delta K = I - \delta K$. Substituting (10.1) into this equation, making use of the production function $Y = F(K, L)$, and rearranging terms gives

$$\Delta K = sF(K, L) + (1 - s)T - G - \delta K$$

The first three terms on the right-hand side represent national savings (which equals investment). The last term is depreciation. Following the line of argument employed in Chapter 9, we may determine the steady state (in which $\Delta K = 0$) graphically (see Figure 10.1). δK is a straight line through the origin. National savings is composed of $sF(K, L)$, the broken dark blue curve that is proportional to the production function, and the terms $(1 - s)T - G$, which bear on the vertical position of the national savings line.

Figure 10.1 reveals why high government spending is considered so harmful for the longer-run prospects of the economy. A rise in government spending shifts the savings line down, reducing national savings and investment at any level of K, reducing the steady-state capital stock and steady-state income.

The obvious reverse side of this is that taxes do exactly the opposite. As they rise, national savings and investment increases and steady-state income moves higher. But then why do economists not fervently recommend tax increases?

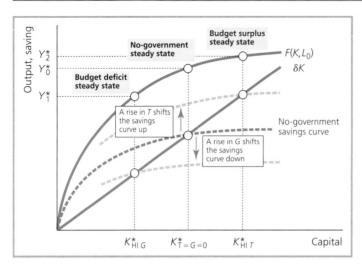

Figure 10.1 The no-government ($G = T = 0$) steady state features the capital stock $K^*_{T=G=0}$ and income Y^*_0. Raising government spending and driving the budget into deficit shifts the savings line down, lowering the steady-state levels of K and Y. Taxes operate as involuntary savings. As they rise, the savings line shifts up and the steady-state levels of both K and Y rise.

There are a number of reasons – some more of an economic nature, and some more political:

- Remember that the variable we would ultimately like to maximize is consumption. Just as the golden rule gave us an optimal private savings rate in the previous chapter's basic Solow model, similar reasoning yields an optimal, golden national savings rate in the current extended model with government. If national savings is already at the level suggested by the golden rule, tax rises would be detrimental to steady-state consumption.

- Even if conditions are such that a tax rise would raise steady-state consumption, its effect on *current* consumption is negative. This is because the current capital stock and current income are given, and higher taxes leave us with less income at our disposal. Consumption then develops according to the lower adjustment path outlined in Figure 9.18(b). A decision to raise taxes in order to spur national savings then involves a weighing of current consumption sacrifices against future gains. If we place less weight on future consumption compared with current consumption, it may well be rational not to raise taxes.

- A tax increase does not only lower current potential consumption at given current potential income, as proposed by the Solow model. As we learned from our discussion of business cycles in Chapters 2–8, raising taxes will also drive the economy into a recession, driving income and consumption temporarily below their respective potential levels. This aggravates the argument advanced in the previous paragraph.

- Governments exhibit a tendency to spend all their receipts, thus raising G whenever T rises. Raising G and T by the same amount, however, reduces investment and steady-state income. This is because a €10 billion increase in G shifts the savings line *down* by exactly €10 billion, while the matching €10 billion increase in T shifts the savings line *up* by only €8 billion (supposing $s = 1 - c = 0.2$). The attempt of the government to save by raising taxes leaves the private sector with less disposable income (€10 billion less). So individuals save €2 billion less. A rise in taxes – that is, an increase in public savings – *crowds out* some private savings.

■ It is very important to note, and often overlooked, that for the above results to hold we must assume that the government only consumes and never invests. This is obviously not true as a certain share of public investment goes into roads, railways, the legal system, and education. How does this affect our argument? Suppose, government spending is composed of government consumption G_C and government investment G_I, so that $G \equiv G_C + G_I$. Then the capital stock changes according to

$$\Delta K = I + G_I - \delta K \qquad (10.2)$$

The circular flow equation $I = S + T - G_C - G_I$ can be solved for total investment, private and public, $I + G_I = S + T - G_C$. Substituting this into equation (10.2) gives

$$\Delta K = S + T - G_C - \delta K$$

Suppose, further, that the government routinely invests a fraction a of all government spending, so that $G_I = aG$ and $G_C = (1 - a)G$. Substituting $G_C = (1 - a)G$ and $S = s[F(K, L) - T]$ into equation (10.2) gives

$$\Delta K = sF(K, L) + (1 - s)T - (1 - a)G - \delta K$$

Empirical note.
Governments typically spend a rather small share of outlays on investment projects. In Germany, for example, the government invests less than 4% of its spending. This falls way short of private savings rates, which run around 25%.

The question of whether an increase in government spending that is being financed by a tax rise of equal size boosts steady-state income or not, does not have a clear-cut answer. It obviously does boost income if $a > s$: that is, if the government invests a larger share of its spending than the private sector is prepared to save and invest out of disposable income. Then total investment, the steady-state capital stock and steady-state income all rise. A rise in G that was fully used for public investment would certainly push up steady-state income, even if accompanied by a tax increase of equal size. Note, however, that during the transition to this new, better steady state, individuals have to make do with lower disposable income and lower consumption. By contrast, matching reductions of G and T always bear short-run gains in consumption, even though the long-run, far-away options are worse.

The Ricardian equivalence theorem is named after British economist David Ricardo (1772–1823) who first advanced the underlying argument.

Some economists advocate an extreme view of the crowding out of private savings by taxes that we encountered above. The Ricardian equivalence theorem maintains that government deficit spending does not affect national savings at all. In terms of Figure 10.1, no matter whether G rises, or T rises, or both rise, the savings line does not change; the government does not do anything to the steady state. The reason, according to this view, is that households realize that running a deficit and adding to the public debt today will lead to higher interest payments and eventual repayment in the future. To provide for the higher taxes that will then be needed (to provide for interest payments or repayment), individuals start saving more today. They save exactly the same amount the government overspent. The essence of this argument is that it is irrelevant whether higher government spending is financed by higher taxes or by incurring debt. In no case will it reduce national savings, but only private consumption.

The main argument advanced against Ricardian equivalence is that lives are finite. Then people have no reason to save more if they expect future generations to repay the debt. The counter argument here is that since people typically leave bequests, they obviously care about the welfare of their off-spring. This should make them act as if lives would never end. If a smaller weight is placed on the utility of our children, grandchildren and so on as compared to our own utility, this weakens the Ricardian equivalence argument. Private savings may then be expected to respond to budget deficits in a Ricardian fashion, but not to the full extent of keeping national savings unchanged. This is also very much what the mixed empirical evidence on the issue seems to suggest.

But then if continuing deficit spending and growing debt is crowding out some private savings and investment, isn't this justification enough to oppose deficits and debt? Not generally – the point to emphasize is that deficit spending crowds out *private* investment. As we have already argued above, total investment, public and private, is only then guaranteed to fall if the deficit is caused by government consumption. If the government is running up the public debt by investing in education, infrastructure, basic research, national security, and so on, the call can be made only after comparing the returns of the government's projects with the returns of the private projects that are crowded out. Returns on the first category can be extremely high. Frequently cited examples are wars that typically make the national debt explode.

10.2 Economic growth and capital markets

So far economic growth has been discussed from the viewpoint of an isolated individual country. Economists call such an economy a closed economy. We had not even bothered to make use of this term since closed economies are on the verge of extinction. One of the few remaining examples that comes to mind is North Korea. As a rule though, modern economies are open economies. Since the closed economy model is nevertheless useful in helping us understand what happens globally, in a world that does not do business with any outside partners, we call it the global economy model. The alternative model that describes an individual nation which interacts with other countries is, therefore, called the national economy model.

What, then, is the justification for having spent more than one full chapter on the global economy model of economic growth when it is so unrealistic? There are three reasons:

■ It permitted us to introduce the idiosyncratic perspective of growth theory and its building blocks in the simplest possible, yet nevertheless demanding, framework.
■ The obtained baseline results are of interest from the perspective of world-wide development.
■ Many of the obtained results also apply to the national economy, though in a muffled form.

It is time now to move on and refine what we have learned by looking at how the obtained baseline results for the global economy are affected by international capital flows in the search for the highest yield. This new issue is discussed in terms of the standard graphical formulation of the Solow model.

CASE STUDY 10.1	National incomes during the Second World War, east and west of the Atlantic

Wars have dramatic impacts and leave scars on society and personal lives. Also, effects on macroeconomic aggregates, such as income and prices, are often drastic. Without implying, of course, that wars are properly considered a macroeconomic event, nevertheless they often provide a 'laboratory experiment' that reveals important macroeconomic insights.

Figure 10.2 shows real GNP in France and the USA between 1938 and 1949. What strikes the eye is the contrasting experience:

■ French income took a deep dive just after the beginning of the Second World War and did not recover fully until long after the war had ended.
■ In the United States income rose sharply after the country was drawn into the war in December 1941. It dropped back towards the country's long-run growth path after the war had ended.

Do the tools and models of macroeconomics at our disposal explain these differences?

GNP in France
Consider GNP: France's direct involvement in the war, with large parts of the country being invaded and occupied by German troops, led to a destruction of a substantial part of the capital stock – factories, roads, bridges, railway stations, ports and so on. It is estimated that by the end of the war about a third of France's capital stock had been destroyed. Demand-side considerations were dwarfed by these enormous adverse supply-side effects.

The macroeconomic consequences of changes in a country's production factors are best traced

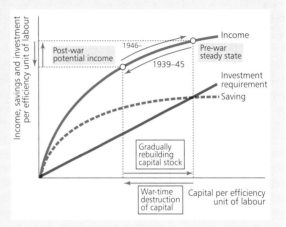

Figure 10.3

in the Solow growth model. A stylized account of France's experience is given in Figure 10.3. The point of intersection between the investment function and the investment requirement line identifies France's pre-war steady state. Wartime losses of productive capital drove the capital stock to the left and income down the production function accordingly. This is where France started at the end of the war. The data suggest that while the initial recovery was quick, it still took France decades to fully rebuild its capital stock to the level desired.

GNP in the USA
US involvement in the Second World War was very different from that of France. The US mainland was never a direct target for German or Japanese attacks, not to mention invasions. Thus the US capital stock stayed at or near its steady-state level throughout those years. What changed dramatically when the US government prepared for and fought the war, however, was the level of government spending and, thus, of aggregate demand. Figure 10.4 shows how the level of total government expenditure, expressed in 1992 prices, rose from $158 billion in 1938 to a peak level of $1,158 billion in 1944. In 1947 government spending was back down to $290 billion.

A proper model to analyze such huge changes of aggregate demand on aggregate income is the aggregate-supply/aggregate-demand model. Figure 10.5 depicts America's pre-war situation of 1940 and traces the stylized macroeconomic responses as they should have happened according to the *DAD-SAS* model. The position of the *DAD*

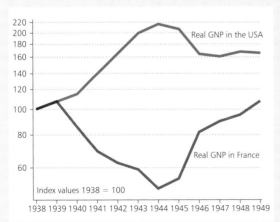

Figure 10.2

Case study 10.1 continued

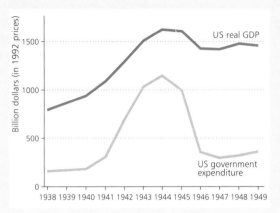

Figure 10.4

curve (the locus of demand-side equilibria) is determined by a number of factors. Ignoring all other influences in order to focus on the overwhelming surge of government spending, the *DAD* curve under fixed exchange rates (or for a large open economy) is written as $\pi = \pi^{w} - b(Y - Y_{-1}) + \delta\Delta G$. We complete this model by writing the *SAS* curve $\pi = \pi_{-1} - \lambda(Y - Y^{*})$ and then use real numbers for ΔG to simulate the development of inflation and income.

Table 10.1 shows actual data for ΔG. Substituting these values into the above equation, the *DAD-SAS* model predicts movements of income and inflation as shown by the dots in Figure 10.5.

The model's response is an increase in income in 1941 and 1942. Income remains well above potential income in 1943, but drops back below its potential

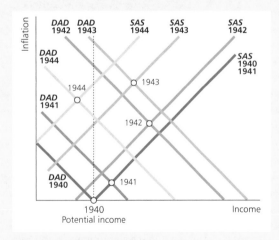

Figure 10.5

Table 10.1 Change in US government spending (in 1992 dollars, billions)

Year	1940	1941	1942	1943	1944	1945	1946
ΔG	2.5	114	404	340	126	−146	−650

Source: Survey of current business, May 1997.

level in 1944. Comparing this with Figure 10.4, the difference between theory and reality is that actual US income did not come down as quickly as the *DAD-SAS* model suggested. Factors that may have contributed to this are:

- Inflation expectations may not have increased as quickly as we assumed.
- Wage and price movements may have been restricted during the war, if only in some sectors of the economy.
- Other exogenous or policy variables, such as taxes, are likely to have changed as well.
- Behavioural parameters may have changed. For example, wars caution people to save higher shares of their incomes, which affects the dynamics of the model.

But while the graphs and our focus on government spending alone do not trace all details in US income movements during the Second World War, the big pattern is certainly there.

Bottom line
The main message of this case study is that the contrasting experiences of France and the United States during the Second World War are accounted for by France being subject to a destruction of its capital stock that dominated everything else, while the United States economy benefited from a surge in aggregate demand due to a dramatic increase in government spending. Two standard workhorses of macroeconomics, the aggregate-supply/aggregate-demand model and the Solow growth model, permit us to trace the macroeconomic consequences of these influences. In essence, the bilateral comparison shown in Figure 10.2 emphasizes that the development of income may at times be driven by demand-side factors and at other times by supply-side factors.

Food for thought
While *G* and *Y* did move closely together in the USA during the Second World War, the government spending multiplier turns out to be only 0.4, which is unusually small. What factors may be responsible for such a small multiplier?

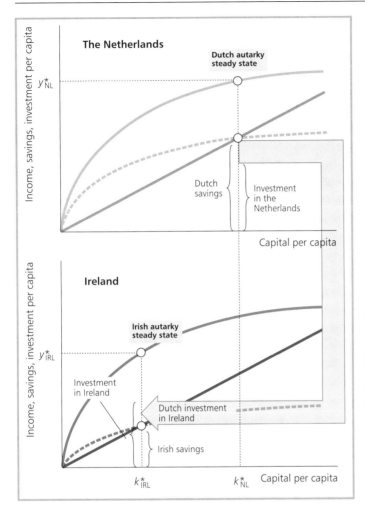

Figure 10.6 Here 'Ireland' and 'The Netherlands' have the same production functions and replacement lines. The Dutch save much more, however, so that capital and income per capita in the autarky steady state (with no capital flows across borders) is much higher. Due to the abundance of capital the marginal product of capital is much lower here than in Ireland. As soon as permitted, therefore, Dutch savings are invested in Ireland. The Dutch capital stock falls and the Irish capital stock grows. If the two countries were the same in all other aspects, the capital stock per capita would eventually be the same in both countries.

Figure 10.6 shows the familiar picture, only now we consider two countries instead of one. The two countries are linked by an integrated capital market like the one we considered to be the norm in the Mundell–Fleming and the *DAD-SAS* models. Let the two countries be 'The Netherlands' and 'Ireland'. The Netherlands is shown in the upper segment of the graph, Ireland in the lower one.

Both countries operate on the same production functions because they have access to the same technology. Also, capital depreciation proceeds at the same pace in both countries, so that the straight requirement lines are the same. The only difference between the two countries that matters at this level of aggregation is that the Irish savings rate is, and has been, much lower than the Dutch one. Thus, as we know from Chapter 9, the Dutch capital stock in the autonomous or closed-economy steady state is higher, making sure that Dutch steady-state income exceeds that of Ireland (all in per capita terms).

Enter cross-border capital flows. Remember that the slope of the partial production function measures the marginal product of capital. Under perfect competition this is the return investors can expect. Now, if both countries are

Maths note. The slope of the production function measures the marginal product of capital, independently of whether we use the *extensive form* $Y = K^{\alpha}L^{1-\alpha}$, holding L constant, or the *intensive form* $y = k^{\alpha}$. Differentiation yields $\delta Y/\delta K = \alpha(L/K)^{1-\alpha} = \alpha k^{\alpha-1} = dy/dk$.

initially in their respective 'autarky' steady states, which obtains when capital flows are controlled (as has been the case for many nations, including EU members, throughout the 1980s), abolishing controls opens new opportunities for investors. Due to a relative shortage of capital, investing in Ireland carries the promise of higher returns. This guides banks and portfolio managers to funnel Dutch savings out of the country and into Irish firms. Investment in the Netherlands is driven below savings. Investment in Ireland is driven above Irish savings. The Irish capital stock begins to grow. The Dutch one starts to fall. Both economies converge towards a new steady state in which the capital stock and investment are the same in both countries. Dutch capital exports equal Irish capital imports. What are the consequences of capital market integration?

Since the marginal product of capital is higher at Ireland's autarky point than at that of the Netherlands, the combined incomes of the two countries rise. The reason is that savings are taken out of the Netherlands, where capital is affluent and relatively unproductive at the margin, and funnelled into Ireland, where more income is generated than is lost in the Netherlands.

At a higher level of total income in both countries total savings and investment must be higher. This assertion may not be quite as obvious as this statement makes one believe, for reasons hidden in the following paragraph. Note, however, that since total income is higher, the combined capital stock must be higher. Since depreciation is the same in both countries, investment (and savings) must be higher in the free-capital-flows steady state than in the old capital-controls steady state.

Who benefits? Do the Netherlands suffer from abolishing capital controls? You may be inclined to think so, given that both the capital stock and income in this country fall. Note, however, that we are dealing here with one rare instance when a careful distinction between gross domestic product (GDP) and gross national product (GNP) as measures of income is crucial. Recall that GDP measures economic activity (or income) generated within the geographical boundaries of a country. GNP measures the incomes accruing to the inhabitants of a country independently of where these are generated. The partial production function given in the upper part of Figure 10.6 measures income generated within the boundaries of the Netherlands, that is Dutch GDP. This part of Dutch income does indeed fall, as is illustrated in the upper panel of Figure 10.6. But by investing part of their savings in Ireland, Dutch people can claim part of the income generated in Ireland. Again, since investments in Ireland outperform former investments in the Netherlands, the income gains accruing in Ireland more than make up for the drop in GDP experienced in the Netherlands. Thus Dutch GNP rises, as does Irish GNP.

So does the globalization of capital markets benefit everybody? In the aggregate, the answer is yes. All participating countries are likely to move up to higher (GNP) income levels. But beyond the aggregate, unfortunately the answer is no. Since the capital stock in the Netherlands falls (or grows at a slower pace than it would have otherwise), labour productivity falls (or lags behind). This exerts downward pressure on wages and total labour income in the Netherlands. The strain this puts on society is magnified by the fact that capital incomes rise even more than labour incomes fall. This is not only a problem that the rich countries of Europe face with regard to the poorer ones, but also a problem that Europe and other industrialized countries face with regard to the developing part of the world. (See Box 10.1 for a numerical look at this issue.)

BOX 10.1 An illustration of the income and distribution effects of globalization

Countries A and B are identical in size, $L_A = L_B = 100$, depreciation rates, $\delta = 0.1$, and production functions, $Y = K^{0.5}L^{0.5}$. Savings rates differ at $s_A = 0.2$ and $s_B = 0$. Each country's *autonomous steady state* results from the equality between saving and depreciation, $sK^{0.5}L^{0.5} = \delta K$ (see Table 10.2).

Autonomous steady states
Substituting numbers for s and δ we find that if country A operates autonomously, its steady-state capital stock is $K_A^* = 400$ and income is $Y_A^* = 200$. B does not save at all. It thus operates at the subsistence level with no income and capital (see Table 10.2). Note that the incomes computed here are GDPs.

Steady states with a global capital market
Since country B does not save and will never own any capital, all global saving must be done by country A. Since interest rates must be the same in this steady state, capital stocks must be the same: $K_A = K_B = K$. K_B belongs to country A and yields interest income. A alone must save enough to maintain the world capital stock:

$$0.2(10\,K^{0.5} + 0.5 \cdot 10\,K^{0.5}) = 0.1(K + K)$$

$$\underbrace{}_{\text{GDP}_A}\;\underbrace{\phantom{0.5 \cdot 10 K^{0.5}}}_{\substack{\text{Capital income} \\ \text{inhabitants of A} \\ \text{receive from B}}}\;\underbrace{}_{\substack{\text{World} \\ \text{capital stock}}}$$

$$\underbrace{\phantom{0.2(10K^{0.5} + 0.5 \cdot 10 K^{0.5})}}_{\text{GDP}_A}$$

$$\underbrace{\text{Country A's and world saving}}\quad\underbrace{\text{World depreciation}}$$

Solving this for the world capital stock yields $2K = 450$, of which half is in each country. Hence $K_A = 225$, $K_B = 225$, and $Y_A = Y_B = 150$.

Table 10.2

Country A	Country B
$0.2 \cdot K_A^{0.5} \cdot 10 = 0.1\,K_A$	$0 \cdot K_B^{0.5} \cdot 10 = 0.1\,K_B$
$20 = K_A^{0.5}$	$0 = K_B^{0.5}$
$K_A^* = 400$	$K_B^* = 0$
$Y_A^* = 200 = \text{GDP}_A$	$Y_B^* = 0 = \text{GDP}_B$

Income distribution
Country A's GDP falls from 200 to 150 because its capital stock shrank from 400 to 225. But: GNP = GDP + factor incomes from abroad. Hence, since A owns B's capital stock, it gets all capital income generated in B. In the production function $Y = K^{0.5}L^{0.5}$ the capital income share is 50%. Hence A gets half of B's GDP: that is, $150/2 = 75$. This gives the gross national products:

$$\text{GNP}_A = 150 + 75 = 225$$

$$\underbrace{75 + 75}$$

$$\underset{\substack{\text{Labour} \\ \text{income}}}{\nearrow}\quad\underset{\substack{\text{Capital} \\ \text{income} \\ \text{at home}}}{\nearrow}\quad\underset{\substack{\text{Capital} \\ \text{income from} \\ \text{abroad}}}{\nwarrow}$$

and

$$\text{GNP}_B = 150 - 75 = 75$$

$$\underbrace{}_{\substack{\text{Capital income} \\ \text{generated in B} \\ \text{to be paid to A}}}$$

In this numerical exercise the workers of the rich country A are the losers of globalization. Their income drops from 100 to 75, while capital incomes rise from 100 to 150.

The Feldstein–Horioka puzzle refers to a contradiction between real-world experience and theoretical reasoning. The data show that countries with higher savings rates have higher investment rates, while theory suggests that under perfect mobility of international capital this should not be the case.

Are there signs that in the real world capital does flow as proposed by the Solow growth model? An important caveat to the role of international capital flows central to the above arguments is the Feldstein–Horioka puzzle. It is posed by the empirical finding that gross domestic savings rates (comprising private and public savings) and domestic investment are highly correlated, very much as we would expect in a closed economy. This holds over time for individual countries, and across countries, as Figure 10.7 shows.

In **open economies** with perfectly free capital flows all countries' investment rates should be the same, independent of national savings rates. Data points should be positioned unsystematically around a horizontal line, but this is obviously not the case. In a **closed economy** investment and savings are identical, lined up on a line with slope one (with deviations caused by measurement

Figure 10.7 Open economies with free movement of capital should have investment rates that are independent of domestic savings rates (the horizontal line). In closed economies the correlation between the two should be 1 (the 45° line). Reality lies between these extremes. Investment goes up with savings, but high savers export capital while low savers import it. Data are averages for 1980–89.

Source: OECD, *Economic Outlook*.

errors). However, this is not the case either. Instead the data are scattered around a positively sloped line that is flatter than the 45° line, having a slope of 0.58. This means that if a country's savings rate increases, more than 40% of added savings are invested abroad. Despite some variance in the data points that suggest the influence of other factors, there is an evident pattern: countries with savings rates of 24% or above are net investors in other countries. Countries with savings rates below 22% are capital importers. Only in the narrow (grey) band between 22 and 24% do we find a few countries that do not fit the general pattern.

So the mechanisms proposed by the Solow growth model seem to be at work, though not with the intensity the model suggests. Note that the data are for the 1980s, however, when more capital controls were still operational than nowadays. The liberalization of capital markets in Europe and other parts of the world should continue to intensify capital migration and further weaken the correlation between national savings and investment.

To summarize then, the first major bonus that comes with integrated markets is that they provide for more flexibility to employ production factors where they are most productive. This section has elaborated on the effects that result from removing obstructions to free movement of capital. In terms of an aggregate EU (or world) production function, these efficiency gains turn the partial production function upwards, raising the EU capital stock and income per capita. Similar effects could result, in principle, from free movement of labour. In practical terms, however, labour mobility is not likely to be a quantitatively relevant source for efficiency gains.

Empirical note. In 2009 only 2.4% of people *living* in an EU country were *citizens* of other EU countries. By contrast, the share of foreign employment including workers from *outside* the EU was 6.4%.

Integrated goods markets

Efficiency gains that result from the integration of capital markets are likely to be reinforced by removing barriers to trade in the product markets. Many economies are not large enough to support many suppliers to operate at an efficient level. Therefore, monopolies, monopolistic and other imperfect competition are frequent phenomena. Examples are banks, chemical industries, car manufacturers, airlines, and so on. Providing free access to all national markets for all firms (as initiated in the Single Markets Act of the European Union) will increase competition, which puts firms under pressure to use factors of production more efficiently than before. This again must be expected to turn the EU production function upwards. Figure 10.8 shows this effect that other, less advanced integration efforts also strive at, such as the Free Trade Agreement of the Americas (FTAA).

Empirical note. The Cecchini Report estimated that 'one market' would lead to efficiency gains between 4.25 and 6.5% of GDP. Other studies argued that these numbers were too low: they ignored that the capital stock would rise and overlooked the possibility of permanently higher growth (as in the *AK* model to be discussed below). Taking this into account, the present value of EU income could eventually rise between 11 and 35% of 1992 GDP.

Let EU output possibilities before 1992 be represented by the dark blue production function. Suppose the EU was in the indicated pre-1992 steady state, determined by the intersection between the requirement line and the dark blue dashed savings schedule. After the unification of EU markets in 1992 the more efficient use of production factors and competitive pressures (and opportunities) in the goods markets turn the production function up into the light blue position. At the old capital endowment per worker, income per worker would rise from y_{old} to y_{92}. This is not the end of the story, however. At higher income people save more. So savings exceed required investment, and the capital stock begins to rise. In a slow and long process income per worker grows to its new steady state level y_{92+}.

The factors discussed here suggest that the single-market project of the European Union should ultimately lead to higher incomes in the union, and trigger several decades of higher growth while economies make the transition from the old to the new steady state.

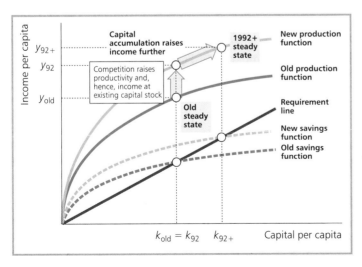

Figure 10.8 The single European market is thought to raise steady-state income in two stages. In a first stage, more competition raises productivity, turning the production function up. So even with the old capital stock more income will be generated. At this higher income people will save more. Thus the capital stock will grow, permitting income to grow further until y_{92+}.

10.3 Extending the Solow model and moving beyond

Last section's extension of the Solow model to a scenario of national economies linked by global capital markets has severe consequences for the international convergence of incomes. Remember that the global (or closed-economy) version of the Solow model proposes *conditional convergence* only: income convergence towards a country's specific steady state as determined by its own national savings and population growth rates. By contrast, the open-economy version of the Solow model tells us that in a globalized world a nation's savings and population growth rates do not really matter. International capital flows in search of the highest yields make all countries end up with the same capital stock per worker and, hence, more or less the same per capita income. To the extent that international investment not only comes out of current income, but may also reflect the movement of existing capital (machines or entire production facilities) across borders, the speed of income convergence may be much more rapid than before the current wave of globalization.

Another look at income convergence data

We already saw in Chapter 9, Figure 9.26, that there is no worldwide convergence of incomes. When we take a closer look at groups of countries (say, as defined by income levels, or geographic regions) convergence is often found. Figure 10.9 illustrates this.

Plotting per capita income data from the second half of the twentieth century on a logarithmic scale, panel (a) reveals income convergence among three of the world's richest countries, and panel (b) shows the same for the four largest EU member states. Incomes also converge among smaller European countries (panel (c)), though convergence may sometimes pause, as it did in Greece. And finally, as shown in panel (d), even when income convergence within a region may not have occurred, as in this group of South-east Asian countries, the region as a whole has generally moved closer towards the world's highest per capita incomes.

But if all these partial observations are reasonably well in line with the general message of the Solow model regarding convergence, what is it then that spoils the global picture? The answer to this question has a lot to do with the African experience which departs drastically from the general trend in the rest of the world that we exemplified in Figure 10.9. Figure 10.10 shows per capita incomes in Gabon, the Ivory Coast, Senegal and Zambia as typical examples for the large group of sub-Saharan African countries. In these countries per capita incomes not only did not converge towards those of the richer countries, but they stagnated or even fell, either as a general trend, or after some respectable growth had been achieved during the first one or two decades following independence. Overall, income growth in many countries in this region, but in others as well, appears disconnected from the global trend. It seems as if these countries were trapped in poverty. Is there a way to reconcile this sobering observation with the general approach of the Solow model?

One may be tempted to argue that the Solow model already provides for the possibility of some countries being poor and others rich, focusing on savings and population growth. While this is true, the model offers no plausible

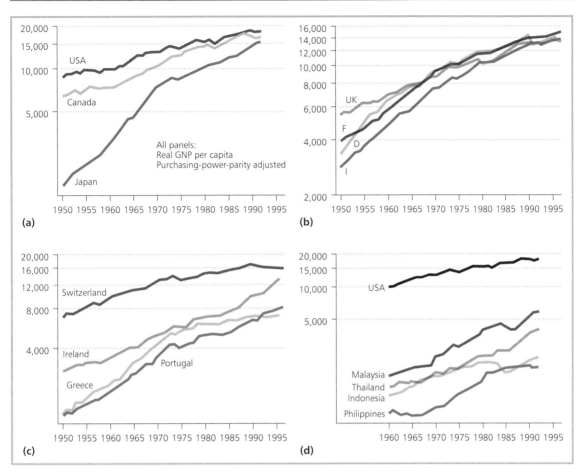

Figure 10.9 This figure presents evidence of income convergence within many of the world's regions and income brackets. Convergence appears particularly strong in panel (a) showing Canada, Japan and the USA, but also among the major European countries shown in panel (b). Convergence with Greece as an exception from the rule is documented in panel (c). Finally, panel (d) indicates hardly any convergence in South-east Asia, but at least the region as a whole converged towards US income.

Sources: Penn World Tables; World Bank, *World Development Indicators*; A. Maddison, *Monitoring the World Economy 1820–1992*, OECD.

explanation of the huge size of observed income differences. A simple *numerical exercise* may illustrate this.

As we know from the discussion following equation (9.11), the steady-state condition in the per capita Solow model is $\Delta k = 0 = sy - (n + \delta)k$. Let the per capita production function be $y = \sqrt{k}$. Substituting this into the steady-state condition for y and solving the resulting equation for $\sqrt{k} = y$ gives

$$y = \frac{s}{n + \delta}$$

Substituting some real numbers for s and n and a plausible magnitude of 0.1 for δ into this equation, we obtain $y = 0.08/(0.028 + 0.1) = 0.63$ for a hypothetical economy with the parameters of Sierra Leone and $y = 0.21/(0.004 + 0.1) = 2.02$ if we use the savings and population growth rates of Denmark. So, given the differences in s and n, Denmark's per capita

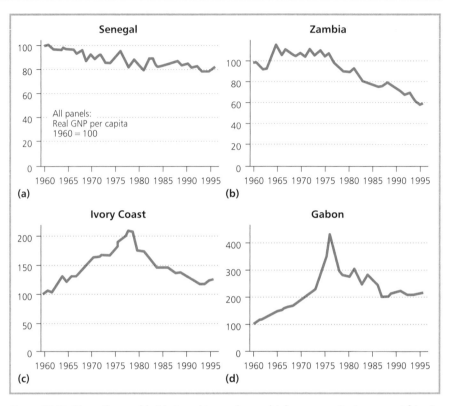

Figure 10.10 Given the worldwide trend towards ever higher per capita incomes, Africa is evidently a drastic exception. Many African countries, very often those among the world's poorest, have suffered falling per capita income for the past two decades or longer.

Sources: Penn World Tables; World Bank, *World Development Indicators*.

income should be about three times as high as Sierra Leone's. In 1998, however, Denmark's per capita income was more than 50 times as large as Sierra Leone's. So, realistically, while the Solow model may explain modest differences in incomes, it is not capable of providing a realistic account of the magnitudes of actual income gaps observed in today's world. We must, therefore, look for modifications and refinements of the Solow model that may provide such an account. The concepts we will encounter during this expedition are *poverty traps*, *human capital*, and *endogenous growth*.

10.4 Poverty traps in the Solow model

When a model has more than one stable steady state, the low-income steady state is often called a poverty trap. Once trapped in this steady state, the economy cannot escape without massive outside injections of capital.

Poverty traps may occur if one or more of the assumptions employed in the Solow model are violated. We look at the three building blocks of the model's graphical form to give examples of what may go wrong.

Poverty trap, type 1 The Solow model proposes a production function with constant returns to scale which implies decreasing marginal returns of the involved production factors. Now suppose that this does not hold

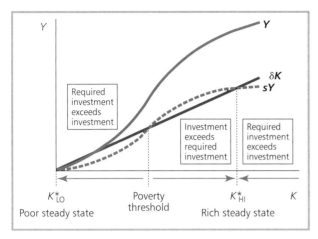

Figure 10.11 One type of poverty trap may occur when there are economies of scale at low levels of the capital stock. Then a second (positive) level of the capital stock exists at which the savings and required investment lines intersect. Since here the savings line cuts through the required investment line from below, it constitutes an unstable equilibrium which marks a threshold separating capital stocks that shrink towards the poor steady state from capital stocks that grow towards the rich steady state.

A production function features economies of scale if output more than doubles when all inputs double.

over the entire range of feasible capital stocks. Instead, let there be economies of scale when the capital stock is very small. If these economies of scale are strong enough, the partial production function could feature increasing marginal products of capital in this segment. Over the entire range the partial production function might look as shown in Figure 10.11.

If households still save a constant fraction of income, the saving and investment line mimics the production function, featuring an increasing slope at low values of K and a decreasing slope as we move further to the right. So what? The shape of the investment curve has changed slightly. Does this matter? As a result we now have three points of intersection between the investment curve and the requirement line – one more than before. We always had two points of intersection and, hence, two steady states. But we never even mentioned the one positioned in the origin. We will see in a minute why the current scenario makes this one more important.

Let us consider the stability properties of our three steady states. We learned previously that K grows when savings and investment exceed required investment, and that K falls in the opposite case. Applying this in the neighbourhood of the 'rich' steady state all the way on the right, we are led to conclude that it is stable. If the capital stock exceeds K^*_{HI}, it falls. If it is below K^*_{HI}, it rises. Or does it?

In the region below K^*_{HI} savings exceed depreciation only as long as the capital stock exceeds the marked poverty threshold. Once the capital stock falls below this threshold, it will fall further and further until all capital is gone. This has dramatic policy implications. Suppose a country is in the poor steady state and receives international aid to build up its capital stock and move out of poverty. Such aid may generate results in the form of rising income. But if aid is not sufficient to push the capital stock beyond the poverty threshold, the country descends back into poverty once aid flows less generously or even subsides. The lesson this seems to teach is that aid which comes in as a trickle is a waste. What is needed is a big push, an investment injection big enough to drive the capital stock beyond the poverty threshold. After that the country may be left to stand on its own feet and continue to grow into the rich steady state.

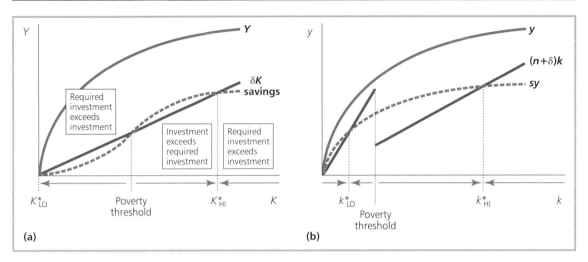

Figure 10.12 Two other kinds of poverty traps are shown here. Panel (a) depicts one similar to type 1 discussed in Figure 10.11. The only difference is that the cause is not economies of scale in the production function but non-linear savings behaviour. Panel (b) shows that non-linear population growth may also be the cause of a poverty trap.

Poverty traps may also derive from other causes. Figure 10.12 shows two more possibilities.

Poverty trap, type 2   Panel (a) in Figure 10.12 shows a scenario almost identical to the one discussed above, only this time the anomalous savings function is not due to economies of scale, but to a more sophisticated savings behaviour. Households (can) save only a small fraction of income when incomes are low (and the capital stock is small). The savings rate rises to some finite positive fraction s when income rises. Since the savings line is similar to the one we had in Figure 10.11, and its intersection with the requirement line determines steady states, we again have three steady states: two stable ones – a poor one at the subsistence level and a rich one; and an unstable one in between that functions as a poverty threshold. Only after this mark is crossed does endogenous capital accumulation make the country rich.

Poverty trap, type 3   Panel (b) of Figure 10.12 makes the requirement line be different from the way it looked in the usual scenario. Remember that required investment per capita is $(\delta + n)k$. So far we had assumed that for any given country the population growth rate n was just a constant number, 1% or 2.6%, that had to be added to the depreciation rate to obtain the slope of the requirement line. Suppose now that population growth is at n_{LO} up to a given capital stock, but drops to $n_{HI} < n_{LO}$ once it reaches this threshold. The result is a segmented requirement line that is steeper at low capital stocks.
    While the assumption employed here is definitely artificial and oversimplifying, it serves to make the point that once the requirement line is non-linear, there may be more than one stable steady state. The low-income steady state is the gravity point for all capital stocks at which population growth is still high. The per capita capital stock at which the population growth rate drops defines the poverty threshold. Only after the capital stock has moved beyond this critical value can the country accumulate enough capital per worker on its own to move towards the high-income steady state.

You may wonder whether we wasted space by detailing different versions of poverty traps, when it seems that the lesson to be learned is always the same: if rich countries' governments, or better still, pertinent international organizations such as the International Monetary Fund (IMF) or the World Bank, want to use money earmarked for development aid efficiently and achieve outcomes that are long lived, they should go for a *big push*. Doing this at least offers the promise of generating lasting results. Spreading the same amount over a longer period of time is not likely to achieve anything but transitory effects on income that soon vanish.

This policy prescription is not undisputed. Critics insist that the globalization of capital markets renders development aid by governments and international organizations obsolete. As we learned in section 10.2, global capital markets cut the old link between a country's (per capita) capital stock and its propensity to save and population growth. So all that the world's poor economies need to do is open up for foreign investors. Then international capital in search of high yields will flow in, and will continue to do so until the country's capital stock has reached world standards.

Is this argument sound? Well, as so often, the answer depends. It depends on the kind of poverty trap a country is stuck in. In poverty traps of type 2 and 3 it is not the production function that causes the problem. Throughout, the marginal product of capital falls. Hence, poor countries will indeed attract international capital. If allowed in, this will guide the country out of poverty, across the poverty threshold, towards the rich steady state.

However, this does not work if the country is caught in a type 1 trap. In Figure 10.11 capital remains unproductive at low levels. Only as we move towards the poverty threshold does the marginal productivity improve significantly, enough to attract foreign investment. So the initial policy recommendation remains very much valid: a big push in the form of development aid is initially needed to make the country attractive to global capital markets. Only then will private investment take over and finish the job.

There are other possible explanations as to why incomes may differ much more than the basic Solow model implies. As is often the case, a specific empirical deficiency of the basic model led researchers to reconsider and rethink. Consider the following observation.

Independent of whether a country is on a transition path or in a steady state, if all countries share a common production function, differences in per capita incomes should be perfectly explained by differences in the capital stock per worker. How does this hypothesis fare against real world data? Consider the 1988 data for per capita incomes and capital stocks in Japan, Korea and the USA, marked by the shaded squares in Figure 10.13. Income per capita is highest in the USA. Per capita income in Japan is only two-thirds of that value, that of Korea only two-sevenths. On the other hand, the capital stock per capita in Japan is estimated to be 50% higher than in the USA, and even Korean levels are already half as high as American ones. This seems to imply that the three countries are on *different* production functions after all.

A valid caveat might be that estimating the capital stock is very tricky and results are necessarily crude and unreliable. So perhaps actual capital stocks in Japan and Korea, which cannot be observed directly, are much lower than estimated and, in effect, do put them on a common production function with the United States? There is a problem with this interpretation, however. Remember that the

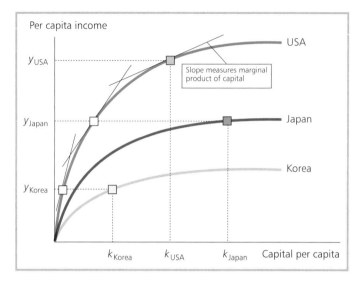

Figure 10.13 Data on the capital stock and income per capita (indicated by shaded squares) do not seem to put Japan, Korea and the United States on a common partial production function.

Source: Erich Gundlach (1993) 'Determinanten des Wirtschaftswachstums: Hypothesen und empirische Evidenz', *Die Weltwirtschaft*: 466–98.

slope of the production function measures the marginal productivity of capital, and, hence, also the returns of capital investments. Now if Japan and Korea are not really in the shaded positions indicated by the data, but in their respective white positions on the US production function, capital should be much more productive and pay much higher returns than in the US. In fact, compared with returns in the US, returns in Japan should be twice as high and in Korea even twelve times as high. This should attract foreign investment and make these countries capital *importers*. In reality, though, both Japan and Korea have *exported* net capital on a huge scale while the United States is the world's biggest importer of capital.

So while the Solow growth model seems to be a reasonable first look at the issues of economic growth, one more big issue remains open: *not all countries seem to operate on the same production function.*

This raises the question of whether we might have overlooked an important production factor. In trying to find an answer, one promising avenue of research starts by rethinking the definition of capital.

10.5 Human capital

Traditionally, capital was thought to comprise objects such as machines, buildings, roads, cars, software – items that can be bought and used in the production process in combination with labour. Recent research recognizes that capital can also have a non-material dimension – knowledge, experience, skills. Since all these elements are implanted in the production factor labour, they are collected under the term human capital. Output then is a function of capital K, human capital H and labour L:

The abilities, experience and skills which determine the production capacity of the labour force are called human capital.

$$Y = F(K, H, L) \tag{10.3}$$

Proceeding as we did when we rewrote the narrower production function used above in per capita terms, we divide both sides of equation (10.3) by L to obtain

$$y = f(k, h) \tag{10.4}$$

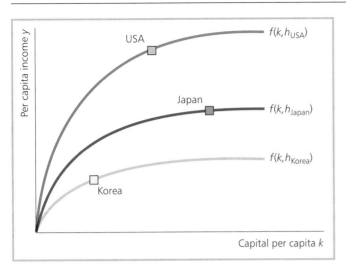

Figure 10.14 Korea, Japan and the United States are considered to be on the same human-capital-augmented production function as given by equation (10.4) if Japanese human capital was higher than Korean, but lower than American. Then different partial production functions would apply for the three countries as shown here.

Holding h, human capital per worker, constant, we may draw (10.4) in a y-k diagram. An increase in h turns this partial production function up. As illustrated in Figure 10.14, the comparative performance of Japan, Korea and the US in 1988 would fit our human-capital-augmented version of the Solow model if human capital in Japan were lower than in the US but higher than in Korea.

Empirical work has shown that incorporating human capital into the Solow model significantly improves the model's potential to explain international differences in income and growth. One problem with such studies is that human capital is very difficult to measure and empirical proxies are necessarily very crude. There are a few options, though, that let us cross-check whether the human capital rationalization proposed in Figure 10.14 makes sense.

Consider the United States and Japan. Here we still need to explain why the Japanese stock of capital (per capita) exceeds the American one. If we assume that both countries have roughly the same investment requirement line, the Japanese savings rate obviously needs to be much higher than the American one (see Figure 10.15). Looking at the data, this is indeed the case. Between 1980 and 1990 savings in Japan amounted to 32% of income, while in the US they were as low as 18%.

It should be obvious that the inclusion of human capital does not change the basic philosophy of our growth model. If we assume both technological progress and human-capital-augmented labour in the form $E \times H \times L$, then again everything remains the same if we look at capital per human-capital-augmented efficiency units:

$$\Delta \widetilde{k} = \widetilde{i} - (\delta + n + \varepsilon + \eta)\widetilde{k}$$

where η is the human capital growth rate. With the appropriate relabelling of the axes we can now draw another version of the familiar diagram to determine steady states and transition paths (see Figure 10.16). The difference from earlier versions is that now the investment curve $\widetilde{i} = f(\widetilde{k})$ interacts with the requirement line $(\delta + n + \varepsilon + \eta)\widetilde{k}$. To keep $\widetilde{k}$ unchanged, investment must not only replace capital lost due to depreciation, but also accommodate population, efficiency and human capital growth.

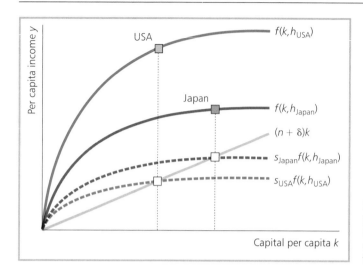

Figure 10.15 If Japan operates on a lower production function (say, due to lower human capital), the Japanese savings rate must be much higher in order to explain that the capital stock in Japan is higher.

Expanding the production function to include human capital has three noteworthy effects:

Empirical note. Some 80% of the differences in per capita incomes between countries can be attributed to differences in the investment rate, in population growth and in human capital.

- There is another, testable empirical implication: the higher a country's human capital stock (per person), the higher is per capita income. Figure 10.17 checks this, using the average years of schooling as a measure of a person's human capital stock. Based on this measure, the positive effect of human capital on income is clearly brought out by the global sample of data.
- The generalized Solow model, which attributes income differences to differences in investment rates, in population growth and in human capital, explains about 80% of the income differences observed between countries.
- The identified role of human capital in the production process gives expanded leverage for governments to influence a country's income. New emphasis is given to investment into education and training.

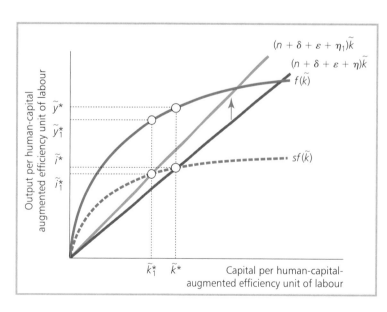

Figure 10.16 The axes measure output and capital per human-capital-augmented efficiency unit of labour. Apart from this, the production function, the savings function and the requirement line look as they did in previous diagrams. Steady-state and transition dynamics are determined along familiar lines. If human capital growth rises, the requirement line becomes steeper. The new steady state features less capital, lower output per human-capital-augmented efficiency unit, but more capital and higher output per worker.

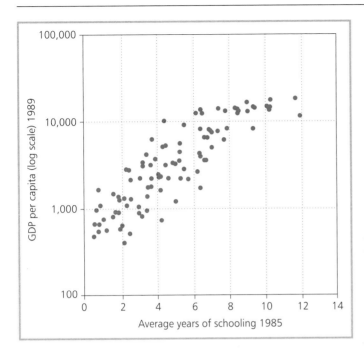

Figure 10.17 According to the extended Solow model that includes human capital in the production function, the higher a country's human capital per worker, the higher its per capita income. Using average years of schooling as a measure for human capital, the graph underscores this prediction for a large number of the world's economies.

Source: R. Barro and J. Lee: http://www.nuff.ox.ac.uk/economics/growth/barlee.htm

Maths recap. The logarithm of a variable which grows at a constant rate is a straight line. The rate of growth determines the slope of this line.

In a way, the version with human capital is the most general version of the Solow growth model. Since many previous, simpler versions may be considered special cases of this section's model, we will pause here to review the main results. As Figure 10.18 shows, the labour force grows at a slower rate than do output, capital and consumption, implying that output, consumption and the capital stock all grow on a per capita basis. The differences in the slopes of the logarithmic growth paths reflect technological progress plus human capital accumulation.

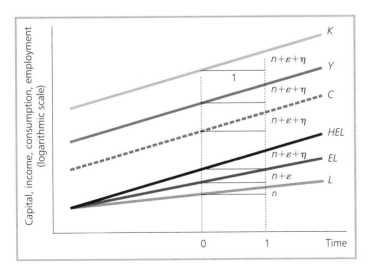

Figure 10.18 In the steady state, capital, output and consumption grow at the same rate. This rate exceeds population growth by the rate of technological progress plus the rate of human capital accumulation.

BOX 10.2 **Labour efficiency vs human capital: an example**

The general Cobb–Douglas production function $Y = AK^\alpha(HEL)^{1-\alpha}$ includes both labour efficiency E and human capital H. An example may demonstrate the necessity for drawing such a distinction:

- **Labour efficiency E** represents a form of technological progress. An example is the invention of the typewriter. Equipped with it, any secretary becomes more productive, independent of his or her typing skills.
- **Human capital H** is always attached to a specific person. In the context of our example, human capital could be the skill of ten-finger touch typing. While a typewriter makes even a person constrained to two-finger look-and-peck typing more productive, ten-finger touch typing boosts productivity to yet another level.

The important difference between labour efficiency and human capital is that, in principle, the first is technological and, thus, available to everybody – worldwide. A country with the required financial means can always buy this technology on the world markets and equip its workers with it. Human capital, on the other hand, cannot be detached from the worker who acquired it. The human capital stock of a country is necessarily the result of a lengthy process of formal learning and training on the job. If countries feature significant differences in the human capital of their workers, then even global capital markets could not make their incomes converge quickly. The speed of income convergence would be restricted by how quickly human capital converges.

We may ask whether there are any merits to distinguishing between labour-augmenting technological progress and human capital accumulation. Indeed there are, though formally both variables play identical roles in the model. The difference is that technology, while making labour more efficient, is not tied to labour. It can easily be transferred across borders and make labour more efficient in any country. By contrast, human capital cannot be separated from a particular workforce. It must be accumulated in this workforce over time. This distinction is of great importance when we think about possible policies designed to influence economic growth.

10.6 Endogenous growth

Despite its new merits, the human-capital-augmented Solow growth model still only explains income *levels*, and not why incomes *grow*. Growth in equilibrium is still due to exogenous improvements in production technology or human capital accumulation. Recently proposed new theories make a point of explaining how technological progress or human capital may be generated endogenously. We will look at one particularly simple example of such a model of endogenous growth.

Endogenous growth occurs when forces within the model, such as capital accumulation, make income grow, rather than outside influences such as unexplained technological progress.

The *AK* model

Suppose the production function includes human capital and has the form

$$Y = AK^\alpha(HL)^{1-\alpha} \tag{10.5}$$

where A reflects the production technology. Assume that human capital is positively related to the capital endowment per worker, say

$$H = K/L \tag{10.6}$$

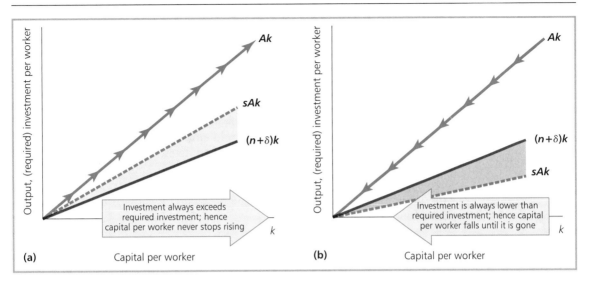

Figure 10.19 (a) When the marginal productivity of capital does not decrease, it is possible that actual investment always exceeds required investment. Then capital always continues to grow, making labour productivity grow, and causing permanent growth of output and consumption per capita. (b) In the *AK* model it is also possible that actual investment always falls short of required investment. Then the capital stock always continues to fall, and so do output and consumption per capita.

because workers who have the opportunity to work with advanced computers and sophisticated software can sharpen skills and accumulate useful experience faster than others. Substitution of (10.6) into (10.5) gives the production function $Y = AK$, or, after dividing both sides by L, in per capita terms

$$y = Ak \tag{10.7}$$

Models of this type are referred to as *AK* models. What separates this production function from previous ones is that *the marginal productivity of capital $\Delta Y/\Delta K = \Delta y/\Delta k = A$ does not decrease as the capital stock rises*. Since capital not only aids in production directly, through its role as an input, it also has the side effect of raising human capital, and so output (per capita) increases linearly with the capital stock (per capita). Figure 10.19 illustrates why this *can* explain endogenous growth.

The partial production function $y = Ak$ is now a straight line, and so is the savings–investment line sAk. There is a single steady state, positioned at the origin. Whether this is stable or not depends on whether the requirement line $(n + \delta)k$ is steeper than the investment line. Panel (a) depicts the second case. Here the investment line is steeper than the requirement line, $sA > n + \delta$. Hence, for positive capital stocks and incomes, investment is always higher than the investment required to keep the capital stock where it is currently. Hence, once the capital stock is greater than zero, the capital stock grows, and grows, and never stops. And with it income grows and grows, and never stops growing. We have endogenous income growth fuelled by permanent capital accumulation.

Panel (b) shows that the *AK* model scenario is no guarantee of eternal growth. If the savings rate is too low relative to depreciation and population growth rates, $sA < n + \delta$, the capital stock is destined to shrink and income will drop all the way back to the subsistence level. So the poverty trap is also looming in the AK model.

Globalization

Does globalization help? Will investment flows rescue a low-saving country from the poverty trap? One would not think so, since the marginal product of capital that marks the payoff to investors is constant in a linear production function of the form $Y = AK$. It is the same in both panels (or countries) of Figure 10.19, and the same at all capital stocks. Put formally, the marginal product of capital, which equals the slope of the production function, is equal to

$$\frac{\Delta Y}{\Delta K} = A \tag{10.8}$$

Upon closer scrutiny, however, matters are a little more complicated. Remember that the production function for the individual firm is $Y = AK^{\alpha}(HL)^{1-\alpha}$. Under perfect competition, when each firm is small relative to the size of the economy, the individual firm will ignore the consequences its own investments have on human capital – because this effect takes time and a fluctuating workforce will spread it over the entire economy. With H considered given, the marginal product of capital from the firms' perspective is

$$\frac{\Delta Y}{\Delta K} = \alpha A \left(\frac{HL}{K}\right)^{1-\alpha}$$

On the AK line, where $H = K/L$, this reduces to

$$\frac{\Delta Y}{\Delta K} = \alpha A \tag{10.9}$$

This has two interesting implications:

■ The marginal product of capital as seen by individual firms is also the same for all countries, and it is independent of the savings rate. This means that poor countries will not attract the foreign investment needed to reverse the downward drift of their incomes. Globalized capital markets are of no help.
■ The marginal product of capital is higher from the perspective of society than it is in the calculation of an individual firm, since $A > \alpha A$. This is because human capital formation is a positive externality to investment in physical capital, a public good. Since this is neglected by firms, they do not invest enough, which may justify subsidization of investment or savings by the government.

Empirical implications

The AK model has empirical implications that differ from those of the Solow model. Proceeding from the per capita version of the model, which allows for the fact that in reality populations do grow, this production function reads $y = Ak$. It implies the growth-accounting equation

$$\frac{\Delta y}{y} = \frac{\Delta A}{A} + \frac{\Delta k}{k} \tag{10.10}$$

meaning that per capita income growth is the direct sum of the rate of technological progress and per capita capital growth. The capital stock per worker changes according to $\Delta k = sAk - (\delta + n)k$. Dividing both sides by k we obtain the growth rate of k:

$$\frac{\Delta k}{k} = sA - (\delta + n) \tag{10.11}$$

Substituting (10.11) into (10.10) we finally obtain

$$\frac{\Delta y}{y} = \frac{\Delta A}{A} + sA - \delta - n \tag{10.12}$$

This equation has *two empirical implications*:

■ A country's per capita income *growth* is higher, the higher its savings rate s.
■ A country's per capita income *growth* is lower, the higher its population growth rate n.

Both hypotheses resemble implications of the Solow model. But now, in the *AK* model, s and n affect income *growth*, while in the Solow model they affected income *levels*.

Figure 10.20 looks at the first implication by plotting per capita income growth against the investment rate. The data are in line with the implications of the *AK* model, revealing that higher investment rates accompany or cause higher income growth.

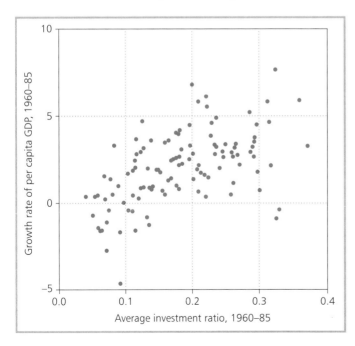

Figure 10.20 The *AK* model predicts that countries with higher savings or investment rates experience higher income growth per capita. The graph shows that this prediction is well in line with actual investment and per capita income growth rates in this global sample.

Source: R. Barro and J. Lee: http://www.nuff.ox.ac.uk/economics/growth/barlee.htm

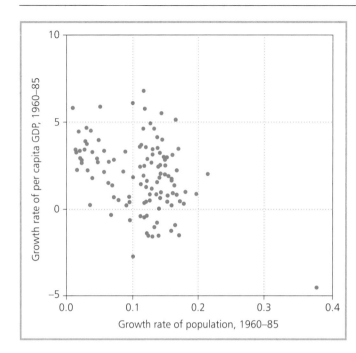

Figure 10.21 The *AK* model implies that those countries with higher population growth rates experience lower income growth per capita. The graph shows that there is some support for this prediction in the data for this global sample.

Source: R. Barro and J. Lee: http://www.nuff.ox.ac.uk/economics/growth/barlee.htm

The second implication is scrutinized in Figure 10.21. The support for the *AK* model is much weaker here. If there is a negative correlation between per capita income growth and population growth, a trace of visual support comes mostly from a single country (Kuwait on the lower right). However, a small negative correlation is not enough, since equation (10.12) claims that the correlation coefficient should be −1. This is clearly not the magnitude conveyed by the data.

Solow growth model vs endogenous growth models

The Solow model, and its offspring, focused on the role of savings and capital accumulation as determinants of income. Growth of income per worker can occur either endogenously during some period of transition to a higher-income steady state, or for technological progress which falls from the sky. Recently advanced endogenous growth models attempt to remedy or overcome these and other perceived weaknesses of the Solow model by looking at the processes which generate technological advancements, at human-based skills and how these are acquired and enter the production process, and at public investment into infrastructure. Much of this work is important and exciting, but it is too early to pass judgement on the ideas advanced.

For practical purposes the difference between the Solow model and certain endogenous growth models like the *AK* model may be less dramatic than their fundamentally different philosophies suggest. In the *AK* model an increase of the savings rate may raise output growth permanently. In the Solow model it would lead to higher growth during some period of transition to the new steady state only. Empirical work based on the Solow model suggests that this transition period may last anything between 20 and 40 years.

CHAPTER SUMMARY

- The only factors that, in the presence of constant returns to scale, can make living standards grow in the long run are technological progress or human capital accumulation.

- The globalization of capital markets should raise GNP in all participating countries. GDP and wage incomes may well fall (relative to trend) in those countries that until now had higher savings rates and income levels.

- The globalization of capital markets raises capital incomes relative to wage incomes in the initially rich countries. It may thus make the functional distribution of income (between capital and labour) more uneven.

- The integration of labour and product markets is well under way in Europe, and projected in other regions. This should raise income levels by raising productivity and boost growth rates for a number of decades through capital accumulation.

- There is nothing inherently wrong with public deficits and debt. Deficit spending and debt accumulation needs to be justified, however, either by the higher total investment that results from it, or by rates of return on public investments that exceed potential rates of return on private projects that are crowded out.

- If the production function, savings behaviour or other features differ from what is assumed in the standard Solow model, there may be more than one stable steady-state income. The low-income steady state may work like a poverty trap, and efforts to raise income above this level often fail.

- Ways out of poverty traps depend on the specific nature of the trap at hand. In some cases an opening of capital markets to international investors will do. In other cases a big push of development aid may be needed.

- A higher capital stock may boost the accumulation of human capital. This may cause capital productivity to fall more slowly than expected or not at all, as illustrated by the *AK* model. The result is endogenous growth through capital accumulation.

Key terms and concepts

AK model *304*

circular flow identity *283*

economies of scale *297*

endogenous growth *304*

Feldstein–Horioka puzzle *291*

foreign investment *289*

globalization *306*

human capital *300*

income distribution *291*

national savings *283*

poverty trap *296*

public saving *283*

Ricardian equivalence *285*

EXERCISES

10.1 Suppose we are looking at the global economy with a standard constant return to scale production function. Let us now introduce the public sector, where $T - G$ is public saving.
  (a) What happens to steady-state income if the government raises T (without increasing public spending)? What happens to per capita consumption in the long and in the short run? (Can you make a definite/unconditional statement?)
  (b) Suppose the government is not able to save the increase in tax revenue, but spends all of the surplus immediately for government consumption. What happens now to steady-state income?
  (c) Finally, suppose that not all the government spending is used for consumption goods, but a part of it is used for public investment. What share of the additional tax revenue must the government invest if steady-state income should increase in response to this policy change, and the private savings rate is 20%?

10.2 A country's goods and capital markets are isolated from the rest of the world. Consumption out of disposable income is given by $C = 0.8 (Y - T)$.
  (a) How does the steady-state capital stock respond if only government spending is raised while taxes remain unchanged? What happens if taxes are raised while government spending is unchanged? Show this formally.
  (b) Let the government raise spending and taxes by the same amount. How does this affect the steady-state capital stock? Explain.
  (c) How is the result obtained under (b) affected if 50% of government spending is public investment?

10.3 Consider an economy with the following production function: $Y = K^{0.5}L^{0.5}$. The labour force L is 100, the savings rate is 0.3, and the rate of depreciation is 0.1.
  (a) Determine the steady-state levels of per capita income and consumption.

  (b) Now suppose that the government wants to increase national savings by levying an income tax of 20%. Compute the new level of steady-state per capita consumption. Does it increase or decrease compared with the result obtained in (a)? What happens to per capita consumption in the short run?
  (c) Consider the steady state where $t = 0.5$. Is it dynamically inefficient? Proceed as in (b).

10.4 Consider two separate economies that are identical in the size of their labour force ($L_A = L_B = 100$) and the production function including technology, but differ in their savings rates. The production function for both economies is $Y = K^{0.5}L^{0.5}$. Let the rate of depreciation be 10%. Suppose the savings rate in country A is 25%, whereas people in country B do not save at all.
  (a) Determine the autonomous steady-state incomes and capital stocks in both countries. What is the level of per capita consumption in each country?
  Now suppose that a global capital market is introduced such that capital can be transferred from one country to another costlessly.
  (b) Determine the steady-state incomes and capital stocks in both countries in this new environment. What happens to income (GNP) and thus consumption, both in the long run and in the period when the capital market is opened?

10.5 Consider a world with two economies and a global capital market. The two countries are alike except for their savings rate (the savings rate in country B is smaller). Thus, in the initial steady state: $K_A = K_B$, $Y_A = Y_B$, but $GNP_A > GNP_B$ and, thus, $C_A > C_B$.
  (a) What will happen to investment flows (and thus Y, K, GNP and C) if technology in country B improves?
  (b) Suppose next that the depreciation rate of capital in country A increases (because of ecological reasons, e.g. in country A there are more floods, thunderstorms or fires).

Does this have any impact on the steady-state variables of Y, K, GNP or C?

(c) Finally, imagine that the population in country B doubles. What implications does this have on the two economies? (Consider again Y, K, GNP and C, but also per capita consumption.)

10.6 Start from the basic scenario supplied in Box 10.1. In a situation with a global capital market, how are GDP, GNP and factor income shares affected if

(a) the savings rate in country A falls to $s_A = 0.1$?

(b) country B's population is four times as large as country A's ($L_B = 4L_A$)?

10.7 Consider an economy with the Cobb–Douglas production function $Y = K^{0.5}L^{0.5}$. The savings rate is 0.3, the rate of depreciation 0.05 and the rate of population growth n depends on per capita income: if per capita income is low, population grows at a rate of 0.1, if per capita income is high, the population growth rate reduces to 0.05.

(a) Determine per capita output and consumption in both steady states.

Next suppose that the economy is initially in the steady state with $n = 0.1$. The population growth rate declines as soon as per capita income has reached 2.5 units. Now the World Bank decides on a development programme for this country.

(b) How big does the help package from the World Bank need to be in order to be effective in the long run? (Determine the required per capita capital transfer.)

(c) What happens if the per capita capital transfer is smaller than required? (Explain why the steady-state income cannot rise in this case.)

10.8 Consider an economy with the following production function: $Y = K^{0.5}(HL)^{0.5}$, where H is human capital which grows at the constant rate $\eta = 5\%$ and the population growth rate is $n = 1\%$.

(a) Determine the steady-state levels of $\tilde{y}$ and $\tilde{c}$ for $s = 0.2$ and $\delta = 0.1$.

(Hint: Start by determining the steady-state condition for capital per human-capital-augmented efficiency unit of labour.)

(b) What are the growth rates of income, consumption and capital in the steady state?

(c) What happens to per capita consumption, and why?

Suppose now that the government wants to raise welfare and, therefore, starts an education reform, which raises η from 5% to 10% at zero costs.

(d) What are the short- and the long-run effects on per capita production, on $\tilde{c}$, and on per capita consumption? What do you conclude about the success of the education reform (does it unambiguously increase welfare)?

10.9 Recall our numerical exercise with data for Denmark and Sierra Leone in section 10.3. This time suppose the production function reads $Y = \sqrt{K}\sqrt{HL}$ which, after dividing both sides by L, rewrites $Y/L \equiv y = \sqrt{k}\sqrt{H}$. Given the data for n, s and $\delta = 0.1$, how many times higher would human capital have to be in Denmark in order to account for a 50 times higher level of per capita income? Assume $\eta = 0$.

10.10 Consider an economy with the per capita production function $y = Ak$.

(a) How does the per capita capital stock evolve over time?

(b) What happens to this economy if $sA > n + \delta$?

(c) What happens if $sA < n + \delta$?

10.11 Again, let the production function be $y = Ak$. Suppose now that $A = 0.5$, $s = 0.2$, $n = 0.03$ and $\delta = 0.05$.

(a) Determine the per capita consumption growth rate in this economy.

(b) Where does growth in this model come from?

(c) What would happen if the depreciation rate changed from 0.05 to 0.1?

Interactive applet on 2-country Solow growth model www.eurmacro.eu/
   tutor/solow2country.html

Interactive road map www.eurmacro.eu/tutor/map.html

Self quiz

www.eurmacro.eu/SelfQuiz/sq-ch10.html

Recommended reading

The issues touched on in this chapter are the focus of much recent and current research. Examples of the many recent papers worth reading are:

■ Paul Collier and Jan W. Gunning (1999) 'Why has Africa grown slowly?', *Journal of Economic Perspectives* 13: 3–22, who distinguish between 'policy' and 'destiny' factors that caused slow growth in Africa over the past three decades.

■ Alan B. Krueger and Mikael Lindahl (2001) 'Education for growth: Why and for whom?', *Journal of Economic Literature* 39: 1101–36. This paper provides a discussion of and empirical evidence on the effects of schooling on individual income, on the one hand, and on GDP growth on the other hand.

The leading intermediate text on economic growth is Charles Jones (2001) *Introduction to Economic Growth*, 2nd edn, New York: Norton.

Probably the best non-technical book on growth and development is William Easterly (2002) *The Elusive Quest for Growth: Economists' Adventures and Misadventures in the Tropics*. Cambridge, MA: MIT Press. Both informative and amusing.

APPENDIX   A synthesis of the *DAD-SAS* and the Solow model

The tool-box assembled in the first ten chapters contains two major models:

■ the *AD-AS* or *DAD-SAS* model, which serves to explain the short-run fluctuations of income; and
■ the Solow model (plus extensions), our workhorse for understanding the long-run trends in income.

Figure 8.22 in the Chapter 8 appendix, 'The genesis of the *DAD-SAS* model', had already reviewed the building blocks of the *DAD-SAS* model and indicated how they fit together. Figure 10.22 picks up this information and shows where the Solow model and its foundations fit into this road map of macroeconomics.

The road map distinguishes between the economy's demand and supply side. The *DAD-SAS* model focused on the demand side, augmented by the short- and medium-run aspects of the supply side as represented by the labour market. Broadening our view of the supply side, the lower part of the graph starts from the production function in the lower left. The production function implies two partial production functions, one holding K fixed and one holding L fixed. The first leads to the firms' labour demand curve and, matched with the labour supply curve, determines the employment level at the current capital stock. The second partial production function is an integral part of the Solow growth model and helps determine the capital stock in the long run. The capital stock, in turn, impacts on how much income can be produced with a given level of employment and, hence, codetermines the position of the long-run aggregate supply curve (*EAS*) at potential income. Hence, by explaining slow movements of income occurring in the long run, the Solow model provides an anchor for the *DAD-SAS* model.

APPLIED PROBLEMS

EMPIRICAL RESEARCH

Human capital and income growth

This chapter augmented the Solow model with human capital. In this model an increase in human capital generates higher GDP growth for years, if not decades, until the new, higher steady-state income level is finally reached. What complicates the empirical testing of this model is that human capital is a complex variable for which no simple measure exists. Researchers very often use the level of education as a proxy for human capital. In this spirit, Robert Barro ('Human capital and growth' (2000), *American Economic Review Papers and Proceedings* 91: 12–17) regresses GDP growth on years of secondary and higher schooling of females and males, and on various other variables. Selected results drawn from different regressions are shown in Table 10.3.

A striking result is that better schooling (and, hence, human capital) of men seems to spur income growth while better schooling of women does not. According to the estimated coefficient of 0.0044, which due to the *t*-statistic of 2.44 is significantly different from 0, an additional year of male secondary or higher schooling raises income growth by almost half a percentage point. The coefficient for female years of schooling is even negative, though insignificant statistically. How can female education not matter for growth when our model says it should? Barro suggests that this may be due to ongoing discrimination of women in many countries which prevents an efficient use of well-educated females in the labour market.

Does this mean that while discrimination lasts it does not pay to invest in female education? Not at all.

Table 10.3 Effects on income growth

Independent variable	Coefficient	*t*-statistic
Male secondary and higher schooling	0.00440	2.44
Female secondary and higher schooling	−0.00110	−0.275
Fertility rate (logarithm)	−0.00275	5.50

Note that Barro's regressions also signal a negative effect of the fertility rate. Now the fertility rate and female education are not independent of each other, but move together, in opposite directions (there is a negative correlation in the data). Females with more school years have fewer children. So when a country invests in female education, discrimination may prevent direct effects on income growth. But since this drives down fertility and, hence, population growth, income growth is spurred nevertheless. If Barro's presumption is correct, this effect is strengthened if female discrimination in the labour market is reduced.

WORKED PROBLEM

Testing the *AK* model

This chapter showed that, according to the *AK* model, the *growth rate* of per capita income varies negatively with population growth and positively with the investment (or savings) ratio. We now want to check if these relationships as summarized in equation (10.12) hold for a group of 22 countries (representative of the larger sample of 135 countries

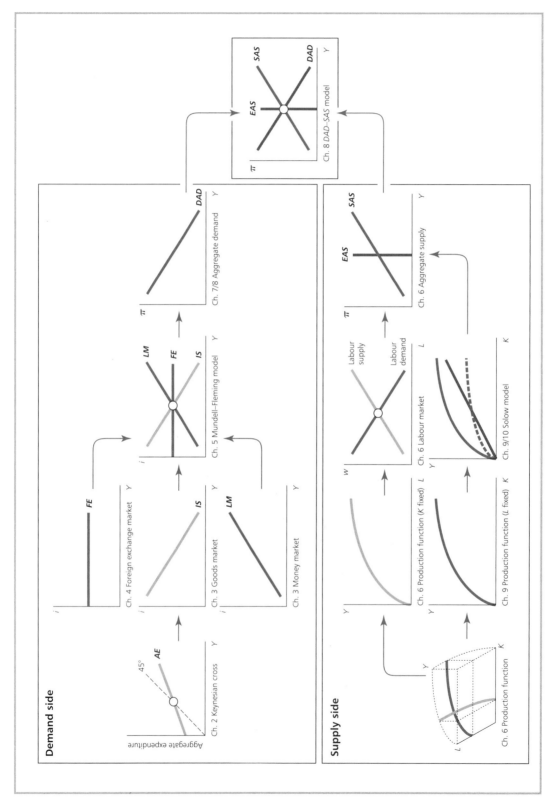

Figure 10.22 A synthesis of the *DAD-SAS* and Solow model.

Table 10.4

	Per capita income growth $\Delta y/y$ (in %)	Investment ratio I/Y (in %)	Population growth rate n (in %)
Algeria	2.01	24.04	2.85
Congo	3.52	29.19	2.73
Ethiopia	0.34	5.40	2.34
Ivory Coast	0.86	12.72	3.92
Kenya	0.97	17.64	3.58
Zimbabwe	1.75	21.28	3.16
Guatemala	0.95	8.93	2.83
Haiti	0.17	6.94	1.76
Honduras	0.79	13.89	3.32
Mexico	2.49	19.65	2.99
Nicaragua	0.90	14.10	3.19
Panama	3.42	26.62	2.60
Peru	0.83	12.29	2.72
India	1.38	16.83	2.24
Israel	3.22	28.96	2.82
Nepal	0.38	5.77	2.38
Austria	3.36	23.45	0.28
Belgium	3.24	23.66	0.30
Cyprus	4.68	31.47	0.60
Norway	3.77	29.35	0.59
Switzerland	1.79	29.80	0.75
Australia	2.16	31.67	1.71

All variables are averages for 1960–85.

shown in Figures 10.20 and 10.21) for which data are given in Table 10.4.

Regressing per capita income growth on the investment ratio gives us the following empirical relationship (absolute t-statistics in parentheses):

$$\frac{\Delta y}{y} = -0.60 + 0.13\frac{I}{Y} \qquad R^2_{adj} = 0.73$$
$$\quad\;\; (1.61)\;\;(7.52)$$

Hence, investing 1% more of output increases the income growth rate by 0.13%. This result fits well with the visual impression that we get from looking

at Figure 10.20 and is in line with what we expect from the *AK* model. The estimated coefficient is also highly significant due to its t-statistic of 7.52. Finally, in this sample 73% of the differences in income growth rates between countries can be attributed to differences in investment ratios.

The regression of income growth on population growth gives

$$\frac{\Delta y}{y} = 3.40 - 0.64n \qquad R^2_{adj} = 0.25$$
$$\quad\;\; (6.03)\;\;(2.84)$$

So, a 1% increase in the population growth rate decreases the income growth rate by about two-thirds of a percentage point. Again, this result is as expected from both the model and Figure 10.21. At 0.25 the coefficient of determination is much lower than it was in the preceding equation, however.

YOUR TURN

More on the *AK* model

This chapter's worked problem used statistical methods to gauge whether real-world data support the *AK* model. One may argue, though, that the obtained results did not tell us much beyond what we already had learned from inspecting Figures 10.20 and 10.21. (This is not quite true, however, since econometric analysis provides information on the reliability or significance of results, something that 'eyeball econometrics', visual inspection of graphs, cannot provide.) An obvious disadvantage of graphs is that they can only display the relationship between two variables. This does not do complete justice to equation (10.12) which says that both the investment ratio and population growth affect income growth at the same time. Econometrics can handle much more complicated relationships by performing *multiple regressions*.

Regress income growth on both the investment ratio and population growth at the same time. Compare the coefficients obtained from this multiple regression with those obtained from the simple regressions reported in the worked-problem section. Why might they differ? Which aspects of your results support the *AK* model? Which aspects do not?

CHAPTER 11

Endogenous economic policy

What to expect

After working through this chapter, you will know:

1 What makes governments tick.

2 Why government policies may *create* booms and recessions rather than fixing them.

3 What a political business cycle is, and what it looks like.

4 What time inconsistency means, and why it may lead democracies astray into equilibria with undesirably high inflation rates.

5 How to view monetary (and fiscal policy) in the context of a game between the government and the labour market, in which the labour market makes the first move.

6 That ways out of the time inconsistency trap include tying the hands of policy-makers, making them more susceptible to reputational considerations, and making them act more conservatively in terms of concern for price stability.

Policy-making is the control of macroeconomic instruments, say, the decision to raise taxes next year or to intervene in the foreign exchanges today. **Institutions** provide guidelines or restrictions for **policy-makers**. The European Monetary Union is an institution, as is the WTO, and the European Central Bank with its underlying laws.

The first ten chapters completed the tool-box for understanding how economies work on the aggregate level. And this is where conventional textbooks stop. But it falls short of what we need in order to understand many current macroeconomic events, including the experience of, the issues of, and further plans and prospects for European economic integration. The reason is that, yes, by now we appreciate how particular institutions or specific policy measures affect the economy. Therefore, it should also be clear that the European economies are where they are and face the problems they do *because* of the policies that were conducted and *because* of the institutions that were constructed or inherited. But since neither policy choices nor the design of institutions do regularly follow the recommendations of economists, we must next ask what determines the choices of policy-makers and the design of institutions. Conventional macroeconomics is not equipped to answer such questions. It is these questions and related issues that will be addressed in this chapter.

11.1 What do politicians want?

When economists set about explaining the decisions of consumers, firms, investors, households, workers and any other players in the economic arena, they follow an established standard procedure. Step 1 identifies the available

A constraint lists what people can get, given a budget or other limiting factors. Preferences indicate what people want.

options. For a household, these are given by the budget constraint, which reduces purchasing options to those that the household can afford. Step 2 picks the best option out of affordable options. This requires the specification of preferences: that is, what consumers like and how they rank their options.

Steps 1 and 2 are standard fare in *microeconomics*. The building blocks of *macroeconomic* models are also thought to reflect the optimal choices of individual decision-makers, sometimes in an explicit, non-compromising fashion, and sometimes in an indirect, simplifying, pragmatic way. One example in this book which followed standard microeconomic procedure was the discussion of monopolistic trade unions as a potential cause of unemployment in Chapter 6. We assumed that the options available to the trade union were restricted to points on the demand-for-labour curve of firms (step 1). Next we defined trade union preferences in terms of the wage sum (step 2). This permitted us to postulate that trade unions' wage bargaining will aim for that point on the labour demand curve that maximizes the wage sum. It never crossed our minds that simply telling the trade union to reduce the real wage in order to eliminate unemployment would actually make them do it. We were well aware that if our recommendation would lead to a reduction of the wage sum, the union would not follow.

Curiously, when economists talked about monetary and fiscal policy issues in the not too distant past, they naively assumed that all they had to do was confront the policy-maker with their recommendations, and he or she would implement them. Such a view of policy-making is obviously not consistent with how economists analyze the behaviour of other actors – and this is changing.

In order to understand why policy-makers conduct the policies they do, sometimes adopting, but frequently ignoring advice from economists, and why they shape institutions the way they do, we must also follow standard procedure.

Step 1: the constraint

The options of the government are restricted by the economy, by the interplay of goods prices, interest rates, wages, exchange rates, income and so on, as it results from the interaction of various markets. In the context of our current discussion the economy is condensed into the *DAD-SAS* model. In the very short run – that is, within the current period – demand-side (monetary and fiscal) policies geared towards shifting *DAD* are restricted in what they may achieve by the short-run *SAS* curve.

Step 2: the preferences

Like everybody else, politicians maximize utility. However, this assertion is trivial – in fact, useless. You cannot put it to use or prove it wrong unless you become more specific about the things that yield utility to politicians. Economists do that in other fields too: utility maximization of firms is often narrowed down to profit maximization. Trade union utility was represented by the wage sum. Individuals are often thought to maximize income.

Now what do politicians maximize? Things that they appear to be interested in include changing the course of their country according to what they think is good – such as a proper place in the history books, power, prestige, and much more. This makes for a rather complicated utility function, and it is hard to see how it fits into our *DAD-SAS* model. Fortunately, two arguments make politicians' preferences more transparent and more useful for our purposes. First, many of the above and other things that politicians are presumably interested in can only be pursued properly when in office. So politicians who need to be elected must pay close attention to *public support*. Second, public support for governments very much reflects how the economy is doing (a case in point is former US President Bill Clinton's 1992 War Room slogan, 'It's the economy, stupid!'). When making that judgement, the public measures the state of the economy by a digestible number of key indicators. The chief variables emerging from decades of empirical research are inflation and unemployment, both of which the public likes to be low. Since unemployment is low when income is high, and vice versa, we may also postulate that *the public likes low inflation and high income*. This way the public's preferences are expressed in terms of exactly those two macroeconomic variables measured along the axes in Chapter 8's graphical treatment of the *DAD-SAS* model. This will come in handy below.

Let public support for the government depend on inflation π and income Y according to

$$s = \bar{s} - 0.5\pi^2 + \beta Y \qquad \text{Public support function} \quad (11.1)$$

where s stands for the public support of the incumbent party or government, say, as measured by the vote share received at an election or in an opinion poll. We will give an alternative interpretation to this equation below. As displayed in Figure 11.1, public support or government utility, if public support is what the government is interested in, rises as income rises, and falls, at an accelerating pace, as inflation goes up.

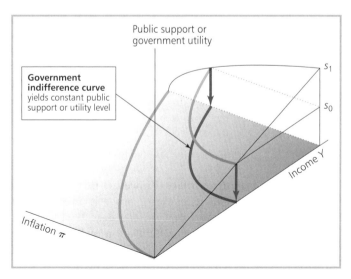

Figure 11.1 Public support for the government rises linearly as income rises. It falls faster and faster as inflation increases. A given level of support, s_0, determined by placing a horizontal cut at the appropriate height, can result from different combinations of inflation and income. The cut determines this curved line, which can be projected down onto the inflation–income surface. Placing the cut higher up at s_1 gives an indifference curve further to the right.

Government indifference curve yields constant public support or utility level

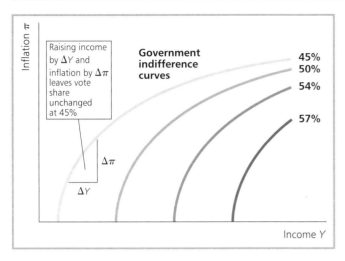

Figure 11.2 Government indifference curves or iso-support curves represent greater support by voters or the public if they are located further to the right.

A government indifference curve (which we also call an iso-support curve) in π-Y space lists all combinations of π and Y between which the government is indifferent (or that yield the same public support).

To represent government preferences in 2D on the inflation–income plane we may resort to the concept of indifference curves. Government indifference curves combine all macroeconomic outcomes that yield a given level of public support, say s_0. In order to obtain this indifference curve (which, in fact, is an iso-support curve), slice horizontally through the 3D vote function at a height s_0 indicating the vote share you want to maintain. The curved edge of this slice aligns all pairs of inflation and income that guarantee the government the support s_0. This curve can be projected down onto the π-Y surface. To identify macroeconomic situations that yield a higher support level s_1, just place the horizontal cut higher at s_1. Projected down onto the π-Y surface, this indifference curve (not shown here) is to the right of the previous one, reflecting, of course, that as we move right towards higher income levels, the government draws more votes. Figure 11.2 shows a set of government indifference curves.

11.2 Political business cycles

Support levels in Figure 11.2 are measured and ranked in terms of government vote shares achieved at (hypothetical) elections. Actual elections are not being held every period, however, but only at more or less regular intervals. If the government primarily cares about remaining in office, it need only worry about public support during years or quarters in which an election takes place. How does public support translate into an election result?

Being rational individuals, voters vote for the incumbent government if it is *expected* to produce a better performance than the challenging opposition parties during the forthcoming term. Since voters have little incentive to become very well informed, they are likely to settle for an economic forecast of this performance that simply extrapolates current (and, possibly, recent) achievements into the future.

CASE STUDY 11.1 Elections and the economy

This chapter's discussions of political business cycles and the inflation bias crucially depend on whether the state of the economy, as measured by a parsimonious set of macroeconomic variables, is a key determinant of public support for political parties and electoral success. Professor Ray Fair of Yale University has confronted this idea with real-world data in the context of US presidential elections.

He proposes that election outcomes as measured by *VOTES*, the percentage of the two-party vote received by the incumbent party, are being determined by two sets of variables. The first set is political or structural. It captures information like whether there is an incumbent president, or whether the country is at war. The second set adds economic variables to this equation. These are:

- *INFLATION* (since the last election)
- *GROWTH* (per capita income growth during the election year)
- *GOODNEWS* (the number of quarters since the last election, during which per capita income growth exceeded 3.2%).

Referring to the non-economic part of the equation as *OTHER,* Fair's 2008 estimate of his election equation reads

$$VOTE = OTHER - 0.657 \times INFLATION + 0.68 \\ \times GROWTH + 1.075 \times GOODNEWS$$

The numbers reported in this equation were derived from actual data on votes, inflation, and so on, by means of statistical methods (see the Appendix to this book: *A primer in econometrics,* for more on how this is done, and this chapter's *Recent research* for a closer look at the estimation equation). They state that when inflation rises by 1 percentage point on an annual basis, the incumbent party loses 0.657 percentage points of its votes. One more percentage point of per capita income growth during the election year adds 0.68 percentage points. And one more quarter during which per capita income growth exceeded 3.2% adds 1.075 percentage points to the incumbent party's share of votes.

In order to gauge how well Ray Fair's equation describes the real world, we may plug historical data into the right-hand side of the equation and then compute the vote shares proposed by this equation. The circles on the solid line in Figure 11.3 indicate the vote shares thus 'predicted' for the Democratic party. Does the equation do well in explaining *actual* election results, which are represented by unconnected dots? It appears that it does. Predicted and actual election outcomes, represented by blue squares, are close together for most of the time frame under consideration. Things deteriorated visibly since the 1990s, with the equation predicting election outcomes less accurately from 1992 to 2004. It still succeeded in identifying the winners correctly, however, with the exception of Bill Clinton's surprise win over George Bush in 1992. In 2008 the Fair equation's prediction was spot on again, predicting Barack Obama's victory.

The performance of Fair's US presidential election equation lends support to the hypothesis that a country's economic performance is a key determinant of election outcomes, as proposed by the public support function (11.1), which plays a key role in this chapter.

Links

More on Ray Fair's election equation, including regular updates, can be found on his homepage at fairmodel. econ.yale.edu/vote2012/index2.htm. Links to data for teaching purposes and to his book on the subject are provided at fairmodel.econ.yale.edu/rayfair/pdf/2011b.htm.

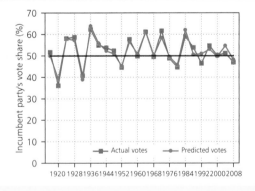

Figure 11.3

To construct the simplest conceivable case that can also be easily dealt with in a graph, let voters cast votes on the basis of election-year macroeconomic performance only. Anything that happened prior to the election year is completely ignored (or forgotten). Then the indifference curves depicted in Figure 11.2 may also be considered **iso-vote curves**. They directly translate election-year inflation and income into a government vote share. Assume, to keep things simple still, that election periods (two years long) and non-election periods (two years long) alternate. The interests (and behaviour) of the government in these two periods are quite different. During election periods the government tries to produce a state of the economy that yields the highest vote share according to equation (11.1). By contrast, states of the economy during non-election periods are not being judged by the government on the basis of the public support they spawn immediately, but on the basis of their effect on the public support that can be generated when the next election comes up.

What does all this mean for our understanding of economic policy? For a start, let the economy be in the no-inflation equilibrium given by point A in Figure 11.4. Assume that we are in an election year and the aggregate supply curve is in position SAS_E. The government knows that votes will be cast on the basis of this year's economic performance. Iso-vote curves indicate how the state of the economy translates into votes. The government's vote share rises as we move onto indifference curves positioned further to the right. What are the government's options?

One option is to keep inflation at zero. The economy stays put in the current non-inflationary equilibrium – and the government is voted out of office with a vote share of 45%. A second option is to switch to expansionary policy. This shifts DAD to the right, and, for given inflation expectations, the economy moves up SAS_E. As we move up SAS, election prospects look brighter and brighter. The reason is that, at very low inflation rates, voters rate the gain from an income increase achieved by moving up SAS_E higher than the

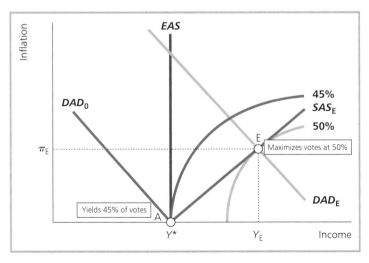

Figure 11.4 Let SAS_E be the aggregate supply curve during the election year. Then SAS_E describes all combinations of inflation and income that the government can generate by manipulating the DAD curve. The maximum vote share obtainable in our arbitrary numerical example is 50%. It results if DAD is moved into DAD_E, where SAS_E is tangent to an iso-vote curve.

loss resulting from the accompanying increase in inflation. But this does not go on for ever. At point E, where SAS_E just touches one of the indifference curves, these two effects balance exactly. If we moved beyond this crucial point, election prospects would begin to deteriorate. So the best thing a government with an eye on getting re-elected can do is to stimulate the economy just enough to bring it to point E. This situation maximizes the government's vote share. In the graph it just secures re-election with a vote share of 50%.

The policy instrument to be used depends on the exchange rate system. Increasing money growth shifts DAD up under flexible exchange rates. Under fixed exchange rates tax cuts or government expenditure increases will do the job.

A lesson we learned from Chapter 8 is that a situation as given by E cannot be sustained. If the government raises inflation to π_E in the election year in order to raise income and win the election, inflation expectations will be higher in the year *after* the election. In the simple case $\pi^e = \pi_{-1}$ this shifts SAS up to SAS_N for the non-election period, making for a much less favourable trade-off when the next election comes up (see Figure 11.5). How is the government going to respond to this? Is it going to regret that it started to meddle with the economy for re-election purposes in the first place?

That depends. Under two conditions it need not really have any regrets. Remember that public support during non-election periods does not matter to the government. If inflation expectations are formed adaptively and if voters forget or discount past states of the economy, the government can bring down inflation by generating a recession in the non-election period without costs in terms of future votes. Assume that it wants inflation expectations to be back to 0 for the next election period, so that SAS will be at SAS_E again. Then all the government has to do in the non-election period is shift down the DAD curve to DAD_N, thereby creating a recession and squeezing inflation out of the system. By the time the election arrives next period, this recession will already be forgotten. The government may again stimulate the economy, move up SAS_E to E, and win the election.

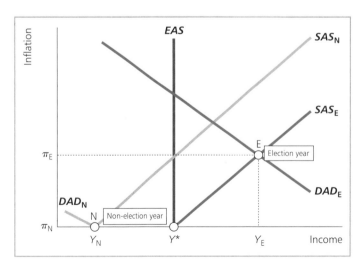

Figure 11.5 Instead of keeping the economy steady at the best point on *EAS*, which is $\pi = 0$ and $Y = Y^*$, a government that maximizes votes at periodic elections may deliberately want to make the economy fluctuate. Monetary expansion moves the economy to E in election years. Restrictive policy moves *DAD* down and the economy to N in non-election years. Note that oscillating between E and N is only *one* political business cycle, one that illustrates the logic. The government could drive votes still higher by creating an even worse recession during non-election years, with a negative inflation rate.

BOX 11.1   Political business cycle mathematics

Figure 11.5 shows *one* political business cycle that illustrates how the government can improve its re-election prospects by creating election-related ups and downs of the economy. But that does not mean that this is the best the government can do, that this is *the* political business cycle.

This box shows what *the vote-maximizing political business cycle* looks like. The economy is described by the *SAS* curve with simple adaptive inflation expectations $\pi^e = \pi_{-1}$:

$$Y = Y^* + \frac{1}{\lambda}(\pi - \pi_{-1}) \tag{1}$$

By manipulating the *DAD* curve the government can generate any inflation it wants. We therefore assume, as a short cut, that the government *controls* inflation. This makes π a policy instrument. Voter support derived from the state of the economy during a given period depends on inflation and income:

$$s = \bar{s} - 0.5\pi^2 + \beta Y \tag{2}$$

The use of mathematics permits us to drop the assumption that voters forget past economic performance completely, which we employ in the text to facilitate graphical analysis. Now votes are being affected by current and past economic performance,

$$V = s + \omega s_{-1} \tag{3}$$

where ω is a voter memory coefficient restricted to the range between 0 and 1.

By substituting equations (1) and (2) into (3) we make the government vote share V dependent on (current and past values of) the policy instrument alone, which the government controls.

$$V = -0.5\pi^2 + \frac{\beta}{\lambda}(\pi - \pi_{-1}) - 0.5\omega\pi^2_{-1}$$
$$+ \omega\frac{\beta}{\lambda}(\pi_{-1} - \pi_{-2}) \tag{4}$$

The constants Y^* and $\bar{s}$ have been set to zero to obtain a more compact equation. This will not affect our results.

The question we are asking now is what pattern of inflation maximizes the government vote share. If election and non-election periods alternate, then the government vote share received during an election, V, depends on inflation during this election period, π, on the inflation rate during the preceding non-election period, π_{-1}, and on inflation two periods ago, π_{-2}, when there also was an election.

If we are looking for a repeatable cycle, one that is optimal when it is repeated over and over again, π and π_2 must be identical because they both refer to election periods. Using the subscripts E and N to indicate whether a variable refers to an election or a non-election period, we may therefore write

$$V_E = -0.5\pi_E^2 + \frac{\beta}{\lambda}(\pi_E - \pi_N) - 0.5\omega\pi_N^2$$
$$+ \omega\frac{\beta}{\lambda}(\pi_N - \pi_E) \tag{4'}$$

Election-period inflation π_E is optimal if, by changing it, we cannot raise votes any further. Mathematically speaking, the derivative of V_E with respect to π_E must be zero. From this first-order optimality condition

$$\frac{\delta V_E}{\delta \pi_E} = -\pi_E + \frac{\beta}{\lambda} - \omega\frac{\beta}{\lambda} = 0$$

it follows that the vote-maximizing inflation rate during an election period is

$$\pi_E = (1 - \omega)\frac{\beta}{\lambda} \tag{5}$$

which is positive. By analogous reasoning, the first-order optimality condition

$$\frac{\delta V_E}{\delta \pi_N} = -\frac{\beta}{\lambda} - \omega\pi_N + \omega\frac{\beta}{\lambda} = 0$$

tells us what level the inflation rate needs to be set to during non-election periods if we want to maximize votes during elections:

$$\pi_N = -\frac{1 - \omega}{\omega} \times \frac{\beta}{\lambda} \tag{6}$$

Since $\pi_N < 0 < \pi_E$ the inflation rate fluctuates between positive and negative values in the rhythm of elections. The amplitude of these swings depends on three parameters. First it depends on β, which measures the weight of income in the public support function. The greater this weight, the more pronounced is the cycle. Second it depends on λ: the smaller λ, the flatter the *SAS* curve, the larger the cyclical swings. Finally, it depends on ω, the voter memory parameter. Equations (5) and (6) reveal that the political business cycle is crucially dependent on whether voters forget past events. If they forget past periods fully, political business cycle swings become infinitely large. If voters do not forget at all ($\omega = 1$), the political business cycle disappears and inflation is being kept constant at $\pi_N = \pi_E = 0$. Income then remains at Y^*.

In contrast to *normal* business cycles, **political business cycles** have their roots in the political system, usually in the motivation of politicians or parties.

Note the blasphemy in this result: the government, the principal addressee of economists' advice, the very institution that we expect to draw on our improved understanding of how the economy works to *smooth* the course of the economy, uses just this understanding to generate booms and recessions that would not be there otherwise. Since this business cycle is generated by politicians, for political reasons, it is called a political business cycle.

11.3 Rational expectations

As has just been indicated, the possibility of a political business cycle derives from the assumption that inflation expectations are being formed adaptively. Adaptive expectations are an economical forecasting scheme wherever they perform well, or if it is not easy to improve upon them. How well do adaptive expectations perform and how difficult is it to improve upon them in the context of the political business cycle?

Expectations are never correct during the political business cycle. The election year boom is created by inflating unexpectedly. The non-election year recession is due to a surprise disinflation. Hence, formation of adaptive inflation expectations commits systematic errors that follow the simple time pattern given in Figure 11.6. If the government were to exploit adaptive expectations formation repeatedly, individuals would soon see through the emerging pattern. Is it difficult to improve inflation forecasting? Not really – all that individuals need to realize is that demand expands during election periods and contracts when there is no election.

What complicates rational expectations formation in the context of the political business cycle is that where the government puts the *DAD* curve is not independent of the expected inflation rate. On the other hand, rational expectations formation is facilitated by the fact that, even though the position of the *DAD* curve that maximizes votes depends on π^e, the government

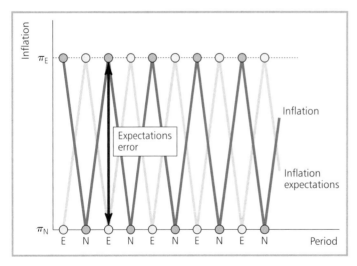

Figure 11.6 In the two-period example of a political business cycle, inflation is always π_E in election years and π_N in non-election years. Inflation expectations lag behind by one period, thus following just the opposite pattern. Expectations errors also follow a very easy-to-recognize two-period pattern.

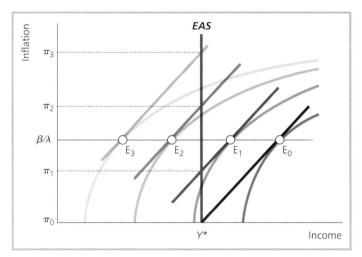

Figure 11.7 The public support function employed here has a special property. No matter what inflation rate is expected, i.e. no matter where the *SAS* curve is positioned, public support is always maximized by generating the same inflation rate $\pi = \beta/\lambda$. This may require different rates of money growth, however, depending on which inflation rate is expected.

Maths note. In Y-π space the *SAS* curve writes $Y = Y^* + \lambda^{-1}(\pi - \pi^e)$ with slope $dY/d\pi = 1/\lambda$. The vote function rearranges to $Y = \beta^{-1}(s - \bar{s} + 0.5\pi^2)$ with slope $dY/d\pi = \pi/\beta$. Votes are highest where both slopes are equal: that is, when $\pi = \beta/\lambda$.

always generates the same election period inflation rate. Given the vote function (11.1) above, this vote-maximizing inflation rate is β/λ. If this sounds a bit abstract, consider Figure 11.7.

Figure 11.7 contains a set of aggregate supply curves, each reflecting a different expected inflation rate. Once inflation expectations have been formed and wages have been negotiated, the *SAS* is fixed to a unique position. Given this position, and no matter where it is, the government stimulates demand so as to move up along *SAS* to the point where it is tangent to an indifference curve. In the diagram we end up at E_1 if expected inflation is π_1, at E_2 if expected inflation is π_2, and so on. With the particular vote function employed here, it turns out that all Es obtain at the same inflation rate β/λ. In other words, no matter what inflation the labour market expects, the government always spawns the same inflation rate β/λ.

So an economy that anticipated the election-related 'stop and go' policies of the government rationally expects inflation to be at β/λ during the next election period. The economy does not then end up at E as planned, but at E′ instead (Figure 11.8). The irony is that, in terms of votes, now the government is worse off than if it had never even considered manipulating the economy for election purposes and had stayed at A. Vote shares related to A are 45%, E yields 50%, and E′ yields 42% only.

The inflation bias derived here for the election period also obtains for non-election periods if income and inflation experienced then are still remembered by voters on election day. To see this, just assume that states of the economy during election and non-election periods influence voters' decisions with equal weight. Then the period length behind equation (11.1) is a full election term. But then elections are implicitly being held in every such period, and the rational expectations bias results in every period.

An alternative way of arriving at the results that the inflation bias obtains in every period, election or not, is by adopting a view entertained in a very influential line of research. It simply states that *politicians are also voters*, and thus have the same preferences as voters. They too like inflation to be low and

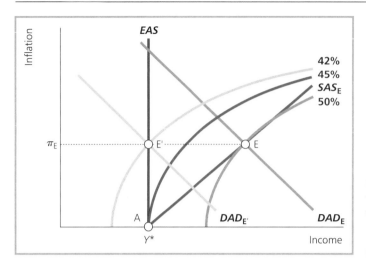

Figure 11.8 Once individuals anticipate that the government inflates to β/λ during election years, inflation expectations move up to β/λ and the economy ends up in E′ instead of E, the point at which the government was aiming.

income to be high, independent of re-election considerations. So they try to maximize a utility function such as equation (11.1) at all points in time.

Is there any way out of the rather unpleasant position in which the government has been put by people forming expectations rationally? Couldn't the government simply pledge that it will never again resort to election period stimulations? If individuals buy that, wouldn't it bring the economy at least back to point A? The big question is whether the government can succeed in persuading the economy that it will stick to the pledged new course.

11.4 Policy games

From a stylized perspective, the government has two options (to stimulate or not to stimulate), and so has the economy (to expect stimulation or not to expect stimulation). Given this, four stylized outcomes may result every time this *game* is played (see Figure 11.9):

1 The labour market does not expect an expansion and the government does not expand (point A).
2 The labour market does not expect an expansion but the government expands anyway (point E).
3 The labour market expects an expansion and the government really expands (point E′).
4 The labour market expects an expansion but the government refrains from expanding (point N).

Economists speak of a game if individual A's best choice depends on what individual B does, and B's best choice depends on what A does.

Ranking these points in terms of the vote shares they deliver gives E > A > E′ > N. You may substantiate this claim by adding the four relevant government indifference curves to Figure 11.9. Decision problems in which the ultimate outcome depends on the moves taken by more than one player are called games.

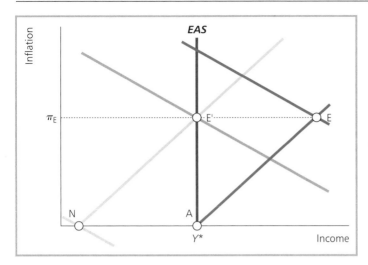

Figure 11.9 Inflation is determined in a 'game' between the labour market and the government. First the labour market fixes wages based on an expectation of whether the government will inflate or not, which results in the light or dark blue *SAS* curve, respectively. Then the government inflates to π_E or does not inflate. To inflate always yields higher support than the option not to inflate. Hence, inflation is expected and we end up in E'.

Let's make the current game a bit more specific. The two **players** are the government and a monopolistic trade union. The union represents labour in collective wage negotiations so as to maximize the wage sum. Assume that the vote-maximizing inflation rate stands at 10%. The options of the government are either to expand ($\pi = 10$) or not to expand ($\pi = 0$). The trade union can base wage claims either on an expected expansion ($\pi^e = 10$) or on the belief that the government will not expand ($\pi^e = 0$). Table 11.1 presents this game and the possible outcomes in the form of a matrix.

One feature that we have not mentioned yet is that the game is *sequential*. The trade union must move first. It cannot wait to observe what the

Table 11.1 The policy game between the trade union and the government. Here the inflation game is cast in terms of specific numbers and a labour market dominated by a monopolistic trade union which maximizes the wage sum. The trade union tries to anticipate inflation correctly, for if it errs, the wage sum falls. No matter what the union expects, votes for the government are always highest if it inflates. Hence $\pi = 10$ is the dominant strategy, and is expected. The economy ends up at E'.

		Government (maximizes votes; moves second)	
		Does not expand $\pi = 0$	Expands $\pi = 10$
Trade union (maximizes wage sum; moves first)	Expects no expansion $\pi^e = 0 \rightarrow w = 0$	A $Y = Y^*$; $\pi = 0$ Vote share: 45% Wage sum unchanged	E $Y > Y^*$; $\pi = 10$ Vote share: 50% Wage sum falls
	Expects expansion $\pi^e = 10 \rightarrow w = 10$	N $Y < Y^*$; $\pi = 0$ Vote share: 38% Wage sum falls	E' $Y = Y^*$; $\pi = 10$ Vote share: 42% Wage sum unchanged

government does, but has to form an inflation expectation and commit to a nominal wage for the length of the contract, typically a year. In a second step, after nominal wages are fixed, the government may decide to inflate or not, as it pleases.

The best thing that the trade union can do is anticipate the government's reaction. By making its first step the union effectively narrows the government's choices down to either the top row or the bottom row in the matrix. So the first question to be asked is: if we, the trade union, decide for the top row by not expecting inflation, what will the government do subsequently? The government can choose between inflation (which yields 50% of votes) and non-inflation (which yields 45% of votes). So it will certainly opt for inflation. The second question is: what will the government do if we expect it to inflate? This puts us in the second row. Again, the government's choices are to inflate (which gives 42% of votes) or not to inflate (which gives 38% of votes). And again, the obvious choice is to inflate. Since the government's optimal choice is always to inflate, no matter what the trade union expects, this is called a **dominant strategy**. But then this is also the action that the trade union must rationally expect. So under rational expectations the union expects the government to inflate, the government does inflate, and the economy ends up at point E′.

The importance of this result derives from the fact that the country is stuck in a suboptimal situation. Voters and the government, who share the same utility function, could both be made better off, without making anybody else worse off, by reducing inflation, moving down from E′ to A. But within the scenario postulated here, this does not seem to be feasible. As long as the short-run *temptation to inflate* exists, a pledge not to inflate is not credible. We may say that democracies, as institutions, have a built-in inflation bias.

An **inflation bias** exists if the inflation rate in equilibrium is higher than the optimal long-run inflation rate of zero.

When **time inconsistency** is at work, a policy that seems optimal from today's view is no longer considered optimal when it is time to act.

What gives rise to this inflation bias is a general problem called time inconsistency. It does not only plague monetary policy, as discussed here. It is at work whenever a policy that initially seemed ideal for today and the future is no longer considered to be so by the decision-maker when the time comes to act upon it. Generations of parents have experienced this problem, without knowing its name. Efforts to influence their offspring's behaviour often turn into a game in which parents vow stern consequences, but find it preferable not to follow through when it is time to act. And policy-making in other areas, from taxing imports to paying subsidies, is haunted by the apparent impossibility to follow through on a plan which, at the outset, looked perfectly reasonable.

Wait, though. Perhaps we only came up with such a worrisome result because we overlooked the fact that the government and the trade union play this type of game not only once, as we assume above, but again and again? Let's look into this by assuming that the government and the trade union play this game twice. Couldn't the government's pledge to low inflation during the first round of play become credible because keeping it might carry the added benefit of low inflation expectations (and, hence, a more favourable trade-off) when the game is played the second time? To understand this, let's get more specific again.

The government may consider that if it announced and implemented low inflation this period, it could coax trade unions into also believing a low inflation announcement next period. This would put next period's *SAS* curve into SAS_E and permit the government to renege on its announcement and maximize utility at E. So the added benefit from playing the low inflation card this period, to be reaped next period, is to achieve E instead of E'. The gain in terms of votes (or utility) is 8 percentage points. Next, look at how this affects the game played in the first round.

The 8 percentage points vote bonus next period accrues whenever the government does not expand this period. So the effect on next period's votes must be added to the direct benefits of the low inflation strategy, measured in current-period votes. Adding 8 percentage points to all entries in the left-hand column pushes the total benefit from the does-not-expand strategy to 53% and 46%, respectively (see Table 11.2).

No matter what the trade union does, the best response for the government now appears to be not to inflate. Doesn't this turn 'do not inflate' into the dominant strategy and remove the inflation bias? Unfortunately not – because our line of reasoning does not pass the test of rationality. The flaw is that the government *mistakenly* believes that its policy stance today influences next period's inflation expectations. When the game is played the second time, it is the *final play*. So the government need not worry about losing its reputation any more. It would not do any good one period later. Trade unions realize this and rationally expect high inflation in period 2, the final period, and the government does deliver. But when second-round behaviour and outcomes are already determined, efforts to influence second-round expectations are futile. The 8 percentage points of added benefits written into the does-not-expand column in Table 11.2 are not real. So the government will play the high inflation strategy in period 1. Since this is rationally expected, both period 1 and period 2 outcomes are E', the inflation bias position.

This line of reasoning can be generalized. Playing this game repeatedly, five times or fifty times, does not help to get rid of or reduce the inflation bias

Table 11.2 **The policy game with two-period horizon.** If the government not only cares about votes this period, but also about next period's votes, it may consider that playing the no-inflation card this period may make the no-inflation strategy credible next period, offering better options then. The value of this, if it did accrue, would be 8 percentage points difference between a vote share of 50% in E and one of 42% in E'. Adding this to the 'does-not-expand' column appears to make no-inflation the dominant strategy. But is this rational?

		Government	
		Does not expand	Expands
Trade union	Expects no expansion	A Vote share: 45 + 8 = 53% Wage sum: 100	E Vote share: 50% Wage sum: 95
	Expects expansion	N Vote share: 38 + 8 = 46% Wage sum: 93	E' Vote share: 42% Wage sum: 100

BOX 11.2 **From the political business cycle to the inflation bias**

There is a close link between the political business cycle and the inflation bias. This becomes evident if we drop the assumption that the labour market forms inflation expectations, somewhat naively, by adapting it to actually observed inflation. This leads to the model

$$Y = Y^* + \frac{1}{\lambda}(\pi - \pi^e) \qquad \textbf{SAS curve} \quad (1)$$

$$s = \bar{s} - 0.5\pi^2 + \beta Y \qquad \textbf{Period support} \quad (2)$$
$$\textbf{function}$$

$$V = s + \omega s_{-1} \qquad \textbf{Vote function} \quad (3)$$

which is the same as the model employed in box 11.1, except for the treatment of inflation expectations. We now assume that these are being formed *rationally*, based on knowledge of the model composed of equations (1)–(3), and thus cannot be influenced by manipulating actual inflation. As elsewhere in this chapter, we assume that π is the government's policy instrument.

Upon substitution of equations (1) and (2) into (3) and the use of subscripts E and N to identify election and non-election periods, we obtain the vote function

$$V_E = -0.5\pi_E^2 + \frac{\beta}{\lambda}(\pi_E - \pi_E^e) - 0.5\omega\pi_N^2$$
$$+ \omega\frac{\beta}{\lambda}(\pi_N - \pi_N^e) \qquad (4)$$

To determine the optimal (that is, vote maximizing) inflation rate during an election period, we need to note two things: first, inflation expectations have already been formed by the labour market and found their way into the negoti-

ated money wage; and second, the government cannot influence future inflation expectations by setting current inflation in a specific way. The labour market would look through this, because it knows what the government really wants. So when we maximize equation (4) with respect to π_E we treat π_E^e and π_N^e as constants. This yields

$$\frac{\delta V_E}{\delta \pi_E} = -\pi_E + \frac{\beta}{\lambda} = 0 \quad \rightarrow \quad \pi_E = \frac{\beta}{\lambda}$$

and

$$\frac{\delta V_E}{\delta \pi_N} = -\omega\pi_N + \omega\frac{\beta}{\lambda} = 0 \quad \rightarrow \quad \pi_N = \frac{\beta}{\lambda}$$

These results say that under rational expectations vote-maximizing governments always generate the same inflation rate, independently of whether it is an election or a non-election period. Since the labour market knows this, these inflation rates are expected:

$$\pi_E^e = \pi_E = \pi_N^e = \pi_N = \frac{\beta}{\lambda}$$

So there are no more inflation surprises. Therefore, income always remains at potential income:

$$Y_E = Y_N = Y^*$$

The essence of these calculations is that when inflation expectations become rational, the political business cycle disappears. The economy does not settle into its long-run optimum, however, which is where prices are stable and potential income is being generated. Instead, there is permanent inflation which does not raise income one bit above its potential level. This is why this useless level of inflation is called an **inflation bias**.

---

while there is a recognized final round of play. By backward induction we can always demonstrate that if the outcome in the final round must be E′, E′ also results in the second last round. But then E′ must also result in the third last round, and so on.

The only scenarios that may partly fix or alleviate the inflation bias problem are, first, if the game is being played an infinite number of times, or second, if the final round is determined stochastically, say, by throwing a die. In both cases there is no previously identifiable final round from which to trace back the inflation bias to the present. Reputational considerations may play a role in such a context, and may help to reduce the time inconsistency problem.

This innocent-looking result is not trivial. Popular thought holds that politicians can be prevented from drifting away from the preferences of their constituencies by limiting the number of terms they may serve in office. The foremost example of this is the US presidency. The results derived here point to the opposite effect. The only way to keep politicians in line with what is good for voters is by *avoiding* fixing a final term in office.

11.5 Ways out of the time inconsistency trap

Having identified the apparent inflationary bias in democracies, are there ways out of it? Any such remedy must tackle the very causes of the inflation bias. As Figure 11.10 highlights once again, the inflationary bias, or time inconsistency dilemma, if you wish, is made up of three ingredients:

1 The **constraint**, as represented by the *SAS* curve. Anything that would make the short-run or surprise aggregate supply curve steeper would reduce the inflation bias.
2 The **preferences**, as represented by iso-vote or indifference curves. Anything that makes monetary policy care less about income gains (or other gains from surprise inflation) makes indifference curves flatter. The result is a smaller inflation bias.
3 **Instrument potency**. This refers to the ability of the policy-maker to manipulate the money supply so as to maximize utility. If monetary policy was taken out of the control of the policy-maker, the *DAD* curve could not be shifted into the position shown in Figure 11.10. To the extent that *DAD* has to remain lower, reduced inflation expectations would keep *SAS* lower as well, removing or reducing the inflation bias.

Modifying the constraint

There is little established knowledge about how the government should make the *constraint* more favourable. More than anything else, making the *SAS*

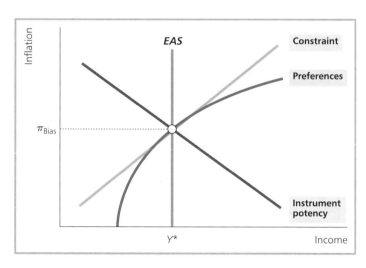

Figure 11.10 The inflationary bias results from the interplay of three factors: the constraint (as represented by *SAS*), restricting available states of the economy; the preferences of the government, implying a short-run temptation to stimulate; instrument potency, which refers to the power of the policy-maker to employ demand management discretionarily.

curve steeper would call for more flexible money wages – say, due to shorter wage contracts and automatic inflation adjustment clauses. Under most countries' laws, such things fall under the autonomy of employers and trade unions.

Changing preferences

A number of things can be done here. Most straightforwardly, if preferences play such a decisive role, why not simply appoint a person to the position of central bank governor who is known for his or her relentless commitment to price stability? Such people would have a rather flat, if not horizontal, set of indifference curves and could successfully maintain a high level of price stability. Figure 11.11 illustrates this effect.

Two problems are related to this remedy. First, its implementation may be painful in terms of income losses. Any new central bank governor may have to prove his or her commitment to price stability and build up such a reputation over time. During this time, monetary policy must be more restrictive than expected, which carries recessionary side effects. Second, other disturbances, supply shocks in particular, may hit the economy. In such situations a certain concern for income on behalf of the central bank may be desirable for society as a whole.

A second way to affect the preferences driving monetary policy is by making the **central bank** independent of the government. This only helps, of course, if the central bank has less to gain from surprise inflation than the government. This is quite likely to be the case. If the indifference curves represent public support or re-election prospects, a central bank (which does not have to seek re-election) is less likely to care than a government. If indifference curves represent politicians' utility, government officials have interests in surprise inflation that go beyond the temporary income gains discussed above, which central bank officials do not have. Most important among those effects,

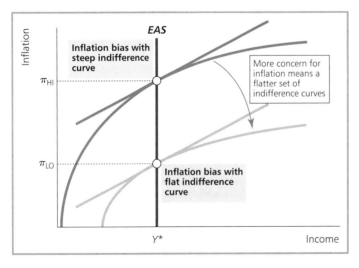

Figure 11.11 If the policy-maker does not care much about higher income, more income is needed as compensation for one more percentage point of inflation. This makes indifference curves flatter and the inflation bias smaller.

surprise inflation reduces the real value of government debt. This makes surprise inflation very tempting for the *government* of a country with large public debt, but much less so for the central bank.

Eliminating instrument potency

As mentioned before, if monetary policy cannot be employed for surprise-stimulations of aggregate demand, the labour market need not anticipate related inflationary consequences, and the inflationary bias is reduced or disappears altogether. Two options stand out in this context.

The Friedman rule, after US Nobel prize winner Milton Friedman, calls for the money supply to grow at a constant rate approximating long-run income growth.

1 **Adopting a money growth rule.** Specifying a money growth rule by explicit or implicit contract, by law, or even in the constitution, could be done in a number of ways: by specifying a fixed number, of which the Friedman rule would be an example; or by formulating an appropriate response to the general macroeconomic conditions, as stated in the Taylor rule. If this rule is properly designed to prevent the government or the central bank from using monetary policy to create surprise inflation, it can eliminate the inflationary bias (see Figure 11.12).

The Taylor rule, proposed by US economist John Taylor, says the interest rate should deviate from its long-run target if inflation differs from its target and/or income departs from potential income.

2 **Fixing the exchange rate.** A second way to take monetary policy out of the hands of domestic policy-makers is by fixing the exchange rate to some foreign currency or a basket of foreign currencies. Under such conditions money growth is taken out of domestic policy-makers' discretion. Instead, it must follow the path required to keep the exchange rate at the fixed level. While long-run inflation is a monetary phenomenon in the sense that it reflects the growth of our money supply, fixing exchange rates turns it into an *imported* monetary phenomenon. The pace of inflation is set by monetary policy in the country (or countries) to which our currency is pegged. This other country's inflation bias, which our model calls world inflation, becomes *our* inflation bias. An extreme case of fixing the exchange rate is a currency union. In the case of European Economic and Monetary

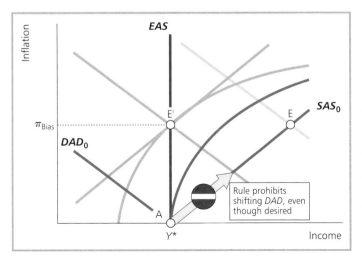

Figure 11.12 The policy-maker would *like* to move up along SAS_0 towards E. Under rational expectations this would lead into E'. The law ties the policy-maker's hands, freezing DAD in DAD_0. Aware of this, the labour market rationally expects zero inflation, which results in SAS_0. The economy stays at the superior point A with no inflation bias. A fixed exchange rate does the same trick. Then A reflects the inflation bias of the country to which we peg our currency.

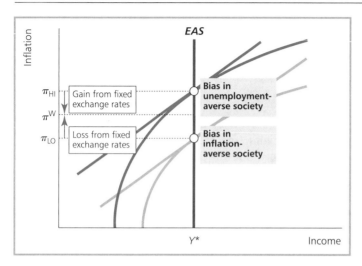

Figure 11.13 If a society or government is strongly averse to unemployment, thus valuing income gains highly, it has steep indifference curves and a high inflation bias. Such a country can reduce its inflation bias by fixing the exchange rate. An inflation-averse country has a low inflation bias. It may experience a deterioration of its inflation performance after fixing the exchange rate.

Union (EMU), monetary policy is delegated to a supranational authority, the European Central Bank (ECB). It is the preferences of the ECB and its independence from member governments that eventually determines the inflation bias of EMU and its individual members.

Figure 11.13 illustrates how committing to a fixed exchange rate can be a way of reducing inflationary bias. Government and society may benefit from doing so if the inherent domestic inflation bias exceeds the world inflation rate. If the domestic bias is lower than world inflation, joining a fixed rate system would aggravate the problem of inflation.

Note, however, that price stability can only be imported in the described fashion if the exchange rate is permanently fixed, and credibly so. Periodic devaluations would drive a wedge between world inflation and domestic inflation, causing inflation performance to deteriorate. We shall return to these issues in the context of the European Monetary System in Chapters 12 and 14.

CASE STUDY 11.2 Who wanted the euro? The role of past inflations

In the second half of the 1990s, during the advent of the euro, a single European currency was not equally welcome in all 15 member states of the European Union. At the high end of the spectrum, 70% of Italy's public welcomed a single European currency while only 15% rejected it. At the low end only 25% of Danes wanted the euro while a hefty 60% said 'nej'. Why this difference? If a country's public decides rationally, opinions should reflect the benefits that the euro is expected to bring for the country.

A key accomplishment expected from the introduction of the euro is that it would discipline monetary policy by transferring responsibility for it from the often quite government-dependent national central banks (that generated a high inflation bias) to the very independent European Central Bank (expected to guarantee a very low inflation bias). Who would benefit most from this rearrangement? It must obviously be those countries that, without the disciplining effect of the Maastricht convergence criteria and the common currency, suffered from the highest inflation rates (revealing the lowest discipline in national monetary policy) in the past. Figure 11.14 illustrates the essence of this argument, using Austria, Germany, Spain and Italy as examples. The indicated dots represent past performance. The dot for the European Central Bank marks expected future performance should the country adopt the euro. So Spain and Italy can expect a relatively large drop in their inflation rates and, if all these countries' citizens have the same preferences as indicated by the indifference curves shown, should benefit the most. Thus we should expect that *the*

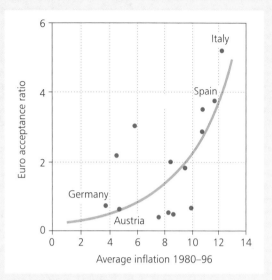

Figure 11.15

higher a country's inflation rate was in the past, the more its public should welcome the euro.

Figure 11.15 permits a detailed examination of this hypothesis. The horizontal axis measures average inflation between 1980 and 1996 (measuring the monetary discipline produced by national central banks) for each of the 15 member states. The vertical axis measures the euro acceptance ratio (yes percentage divided by no percentage).

The data support the above hypothesis. Countries like Italy and Spain, which had experienced very high average inflation of some 12% between 1980 and 1996, welcomed the euro the most. Acceptance ratios were 5 and 4, respectively. Austria and Germany, on the other hand, whose central banks had been able to keep inflation in check quite well even without the euro, bluntly rejected the euro. Acceptance ratios were only 0.9 and 0.7, respectively.

In terms of this chapter's discussion of the inflation bias and how it depends on the conservativeness and independence of the central bank from the government, the public in the EU member states seems to know quite well why it wants the euro – or why it doesn't.

Source and further reading: Manfred Gärtner (1997) 'Who wants the euro – and why? Economic explanations of public attitudes towards a single European currency', *Public Choice* 93: 487–510.

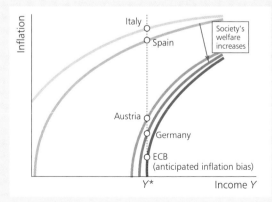

Figure 11.14

CHAPTER SUMMARY

- Governments favour certain states of the economy over others. While they dislike inflation, they usually welcome inflation surprises. The main reason is that this may generate temporary gains in income, which the government may want itself or expect to draw applause from voters. Another reason that the government may feel tempted to generate surprise inflation is that this may reduce the real value of government debt.

- If inflation expectations feature an adaptive element and if voters' memories are not perfect, re-election motives may tempt governments to create a political business cycle.

- A political business cycle typically features booming output and income during the time leading up to an election, and a recession soon after the election.

- If inflation expectations look through the election pattern, becoming rational, the political business cycle disappears.

- A policy geared towards price stability often lacks credibility. Rational inflation expectations anticipate that governments may be willing to trade higher inflation for temporarily higher income. As a consequence, democracies seem to suffer from an inflationary bias.

- The inflationary bias may be characterized as the outcome of a game played between the trade union and the central bank. Playing this game repeatedly does not change the outcome, as long as there is a pre-fixed final round of play.

- When the final round of play is not foreseen, say because it is determined by chance, reputational considerations may reduce the inflationary bias.

- Ways out of the inflationary-bias/time-inconsistency dilemma are as follows:
  - Appointing conservative (i.e. inflation-averse) central bankers and making the central bank independent of the government.
  - Establishing fixed rules for monetary policy which the central bank must obey.
  - Pegging one's currency to that of a country with a proven low inflation record.

Key terms and concepts

central bank independence *332*

constraint *317*

Friedman rule *333*

game *326*

government indifference curve *319*

inflation bias *328*

institutions *316*

instrument potency *331*

iso-support curve *319*

policy games *326*

policy-makers *316*

policy-making *316*

political business cycle *324*

preferences *317*

public support function *318*

Taylor rule *333*

time inconsistency dilemma *328*

vote maximization *323*

EXERCISES

11.1 Suppose that due to a shift in voters' preferences, fighting inflation yields less political support compared with increasing output. How is this reflected in the slopes of the government indifference curves? What do these indifference curves look like if the public is entirely indifferent towards inflation?

11.2 Let country A's *SAS* curve be $Y = 0.5 + (\pi - \pi^e)$, that is it has slope 1 and normal output is 0.5. The public support or vote function is $s = 49 - 0.5\pi^2 + Y$.
(a) What is the vote-maximizing inflation rate? (Hint: votes are maximized when the slope of the indifference curve equals the slope of *SAS*. The maths is much simpler if the indifference curve is solved for Y (and not for π) and its slope $dY/d\pi$ is derived as a function of π.)
(b) Suppose inflation expectations are $\pi^e = 0.5$. Can the government win this election?
(c) What are the government vote shares in the cases $\pi^e = 0$ and $\pi^e = 1$?

11.3 The Fair election equation discussed in Case study 11.1 proposes that votes depend on current income *growth* rather than the *level* of income. We may approximate this by postulating the support function $s = -0.5\pi^2 + \beta(Y - Y_{-1})$. Let votes still be cast according to $V = s + \omega s_{-1}$.
(a) What does the political business cycle look like algebraically under these conditions, when the economy's supply side is still standard *SAS*, i.e. $\pi = \pi_{-1} + \lambda(Y - Y^*)$?
(b) Compare your result with the result provided in Box 11.1. What are the reasons for any observed differences?

11.4 Let country B's *SAS* curve be $Y = 0.5 + (\pi - \pi^e)$, the same as country A's in exercise 11.2, while its vote function is $s = 95 - 0.5\pi^2 + 10Y$.
(a) By how much can B reduce its inflation bias by fixing the exchange rate between its currency and A's currency?
(b) What may keep B from entering such an exchange rate arrangement?

11.5 We understand why a political business cycle (PBC) may occur if elections are to be held every two years.

(a) What happens to the PBC if a coin is tossed each year and an election is called only if we have 'tails'?
(b) What happens to the PBC if a die is rolled and only a six results in an election?

11.6 Suppose the popularity of the government in an economy with flexible exchange rates not only depends on inflation and income but also on the 'strength' of the domestic currency. How does this affect the government's inclination to trigger off politically motivated monetary expansions? Do you think that putting 'currency strength' into the government's utility function is a reasonable approach?

11.7 It was shown in this chapter that with a specific objective function of the government, the inflation bias amounts to β/λ. Thus, the inflation bias increases with β and decreases with λ. Explain intuitively the effect of these two parameters. (Hint: for the influence of λ you have to go back to the derivation of the aggregate supply curve.)

11.8 In this chapter it was assumed that unions move first, choosing their expectations on inflation, and that the monetary authority decides on monetary policy afterwards. Assume a particular institutional framework that makes the government choose monetary policy first and unions move second. Would such a reversal eliminate the inflationary bias? Pay-offs are as given in Table 11.1.

11.9 Consider the development of inflation in the United States and Germany from 1960 to 1990. Until 1973 the Deutschmark was tied to the US dollar by fixed exchange rates. Remember that in a system of fixed exchange rates a small country's inflationary bias is dictated by the larger country to which its currency is tied. Does the graph you assembled support the hypothesis that Germany and the United States maintained such a relationship? Try to explain why the system of fixed exchange rates eventually broke down in 1973.

Online resources

Interactive applet on the political business cycle www.eurmacro.eu/tutor/politicalbusinesscycle
   .html

Self quiz

www.eurmacro.eu/SelfQuiz/sq-ch11.html

Recommended reading

Models of political business cycles are surveyed in Manfred Gärtner (2000) 'Political macroeconomics: A survey of recent developments', *Journal of Economic Surveys* 14(5): 527–61.

The empirical evidence is reviewed in Bruno S. Frey and Friedrich Schneider (1988) 'Politico-economic models of macroeconomic policy: A review of the empirical evidence', in Thomas D. Willett (ed.)

Political Business Cycles: The Political Economy of Money, Inflation, and Unemployment, Durham and London: Duke University Press: 239–75.

Applications to US presidential elections are discussed in Ray C. Fair (2009) 'Presidential and Congressional Vote-Share Equations', *American Political Science Review* 53(1): 55–72.

APPLIED PROBLEMS

EMPIRICAL RESEARCH

The economy and US presidential elections

Ray C. Fair (1996) 'Econometrics and presidential elections', *Journal of Economic Perspectives* 10(3): 89–102, offers a non-technical update of earlier

efforts to explain the Democratic Party's share by economic variables and what he calls incumbency variables. His new equation reads as follows:

Endogenous variables:
V Democratic Party's share of the two-party vote

Exogenous variables:

Variable	Coefficient	t-value	Explanation
cnst.	0.468	(90.62)	constant
I	−0.034	(1.26)	Democrats are in White House ($I = 1$); Republicans are in White House ($I = -1$)
$I \times d$	0.047	(2.09)	$d = 1$ if World War went on during last 15 quarters; else $d = 0$
$g3 \times I$	0.0065	(8.03)	**income growth** during last 3 quarters ($g3$)
$p15 \times I \times (1 - d)$	−0.0083	(3.40)	**inflation** during last 15 quarters ($p15$)
$n \times I \times (1 - d)$	0.0099	(4.46)	number of last 15 quarters with **good news** (meaning $g > 2.9$)
DPER	0.052	(4.58)	Democratic President is running (DPER = 1); Republican President is running (DPER = −1)
DUR	−0.024	(2.23)	number of consecutive terms in office by incumbent party (negative for Republicans)

$R^2 = 0.96$; 20 presidential elections 1916–92

The economic variables highlighted in the equation all have a significant influence on the incumbent's re-election prospects: if income growth speeds up by 1 percentage point, his vote share rises by 0.65

percentage points. If inflation moves up by 1 percentage point, his vote share falls by 0.83 percentage points. There is an added bonus to high income growth. For each quarter in which it exceeds 2.9%, which

Table 11.3

	A	B	D	DK	E	F	FIN	GB	GR	I	IRL	NL	P	S
EMUYES	0.90	2.73	0.71	0.46	3.93	2.54	0.75	1.06	3.22	5.08	3.47	1.70	1.63	0.52
AVINFL	4.72	5.89	3.70	7.52	11.96	8.50	8.61	9.86	10.79	12.13	10.15	4.49	9.51	8.3

represents good news, the vote share rises by 0.99 percentage points. The equation explains 96% of the variation in the Democratic Party's vote share. It predicts the winner in 17 out of the 20 presidential elections since 1916 correctly. The use of the *I dummy* variable serves to turn effects on the Democratic vote share around when a Republican holds the presidency. The *d dummy* variable serves to sever the link between inflation and good news, and the vote during the World Wars.

WORKED PROBLEM

Who wanted the euro? (part I)

Journalists and politicians closely monitored public attitudes towards the single European currency. Table 11.3 gives the result of one such opinion poll conducted in December 1995. Those in favour of the euro outnumber those opposing it 5 to 1 in Italy, but are in a 0.46 minority in Denmark.

These attitudes certainly reflect complex fears, hopes and historical experiences. Most of these have been ignored in this chapter's discussion. Instead, it was emphasized that from a macroeconomic perspective those countries that suffered from the highest inflation rates in the past may gain most from moving to a single currency. To look into how far this argument carries us, let us regress the measure of acceptance of European Monetary Union, EMUYES, on each country's average inflation rate since when the European Monetary System was put on track in 1980, AVINFL. This yields

$$\text{EMUYES} = -0.77 + 0.34 \text{ AVINFL} \qquad R^2_{adj} = 0.35$$
$$\phantom{\text{EMUYES} = } (0.74) \quad (2.85)$$

The equation says that in part the differences in euro acceptance in the EU countries can be attributed to different inflation experiences. Those who did well in the past see less necessity for the euro than those who did not. We may go further, pursuing the argument that inflation hurts people at an accelerating rate as inflation goes up. We may incorporate this by raising AVINFL to the power of 2. The result is

$$\text{EMUYES} = 0.27 + 0.024 \text{ AVINFL}^2 \qquad R^2_{adj} = 0.45$$
$$\phantom{\text{EMUYES} = } (0.45) \quad (3.40)$$

A non-linear relationship seems to explain public attitudes to the euro even better. In fact, if we make the non-linearity even more extreme, say, by raising AVINFL to the power of 6, this seems to fit the data even better, raising the coefficient of determination to 0.63.

$$\text{EMUYES} = 1.09 + 0.000001 \text{ AVINFL}^6 \qquad R^2_{adj} = 0.63$$
$$\phantom{\text{EMUYES} = } (3.56) \quad (4.85)$$

The implication is that the public does not seem to worry about inflation as long as it remains at low or moderate levels. But concern arises quickly and dramatically as inflation goes up further.

YOUR TURN

Inflation and central bank independence

This chapter suggests that central banks should be expected to have flatter indifference curves in inflation–income space than governments, making them less prone to resort to inflation. So the more independently of the government a central bank can pursue monetary policy, the lower inflation should be on average. Use the data in Table 11.4 on average inflation rates between 1980 and 1996 (AVINFL) and central bank independence (CBI) to investigate this hypothesis.

Table 11.4

Country	CBI index	AVINFL
A	9	4.72
AUS	9	8.91
B	7	5.89
CH	12	4.04
D	13	3.70
DK	8	7.52
E	5	11.96
F	7	8.50
GB	6	9.86
GR	4	10.79
I	5	12.13
IRL	7	10.15
JP	6	5.23
NL	10	4.49
NZ	3	10.87
P	3	9.51
USA	12	6.24

The European Monetary System and the Eurozone at work

What to expect This chapter puts the tools acquired earlier to work on some key European experiences and projects. We will see:

1 How the *IS-LM* and Mundell–Fleming models can be used to understand international spillover effects of economic policy.

2 How a monetary system works and what caused the 1992 crisis in the European Monetary System (EMS).

3 How EMS member states were affected by the 1992 crisis, what choices they had, and why some chose different options than others.

4 That the European exchange rate mechanisms (ERM and ERM II) are exchange rate target zones, and how the exchange rate behaves within such a zone.

5 What is meant by the credibility of a target zone and how market psychology may affect this credibility in a self-fulfilling fashion.

6 How monetary and fiscal policy works in a currency union in general, and in the Eurozone in particular.

7 What the roles of the European Union's **Stability Pact, no-bailout clause**, and the Fiscal Compact to be implemented soon are.

It is harvest time – time to show that the tools acquired so far in this book are not merely nice, shiny gimmicks, but serve to improve our understanding of what goes on in the real world in a significant way. And there is much to understand and address: wild swings in exchange rates; speculative attacks and currency and debt crises, and efforts to contain and prevent these by new institutional arrangements; inflation and hyperinflations that may erode a lifetime's nominal savings within months; government and private debt explosions threatening employment and growth.

This chapter looks at the issue of **international monetary arrangements,** of which the exchange rate system is a key building block. Regarding exchange rate systems, the models we have learned to work with have always been discussed under the polar cases of flexible and fixed exchange rates. As we have mentioned a number of times, however, while these extremes are useful theoretical benchmarks, they are rarely encountered in such purity in the real world, as the historical data on current and capital account balances given in Figure 4.3 underline. In practice, countries have invented and experimented with many shades in between and beyond these stylized benchmarks. Europe's history and immediate future is particularly rich and exciting in this respect, and there is much to be learned from past and ongoing issues and events.

In the current chapter we focus on two experiences and projects: one is the European Monetary System built around an exchange rate mechanism (ERM) that has been and continues to be instrumental in Europe's economic integration, with periods of success and episodes of crisis. The second is the introduction of Europe's single currency, the euro, completed on 1 January 2002, probably the boldest such effort in economic history. We will look at how this new arrangement affects policy-making and what risks it carries.

12.1 Preliminaries

As a background for the discussion to follow we need to provide some institutional information and some smaller concepts.

The European Monetary System and the exchange rate mechanism

The EMS came into operation in March 1979. Along with its key element, the exchange rate mechanism (ERM), it was introduced to reduce exchange rate variability caused by overshooting and speculative bubbles and promote monetary stability in Europe. In its later stage, the ERM embraced twelve countries that had pegged their exchange rates at an official parity between any pair of currencies. It served as the final stepping stone on the way to full monetary union, as laid out in the treaty of Maastricht, to replace national currencies by euro coins and bills on 1 January 2002.

The ERM differed from an *ideal* system of fixed exchange rates in two respects:

1 Official parities are understood to be central rates around which exchange rates may fluctuate within a margin. For most of the existence of the EMS the upper limit of this band was 2.25% above parity, the lower limit 2.25% below. As an exception, wider bands of ±6% were temporarily entertained for some currencies. In an effort to end the EMS crisis of 1993, all bands except for the guilder/Deutschmark exchange rate were widened to ±15%.
2 Central parity rates are considered fixed but adjustments may be negotiated. Realignments were implemented frequently for some currencies (eight times in the case of the Italian lira between 1979 and 1987), but only as an exception for most.

The original ERM ceased to exist when stage three of European Economic and Monetary Union (EMU) started on 1 January 1999 with the irrevocable fixing of exchange rates in connection with the introduction of the euro by initially eleven EU members and their transfer of monetary competence to the European Central Bank (ECB). In its place, ERM II provides a similar framework for exchange rate policy cooperation between those countries that adopted the euro and EU members that remain outside the euro area. Membership in ERM II is voluntary. However, prospective Eurozone entrants are obliged to participate in ERM II for at least two years before joining the euro area.

The Eurozone

The **Eurozone** denotes the group of EU members that have adopted the euro as their common currency.

As of 2013, 17 EU members have given up their national currencies in favour of a single European currency called the euro. This part of the EU is usually referred to as the **euro area** or Eurozone. The transition process began on 1 January 1999, when exchange rates between national currencies and the euro were irrevocably fixed, the European Central Bank (ECB) was founded and participants were determined. It ended on 1 January 2002 when euro bills and coins entered circulation and national currencies were withdrawn. The current list of members comprises Austria, Belgium, Cyprus, Estonia, Finland, France, Germany, Greece, Ireland, Italy, Luxembourg, the Netherlands, Malta, Portugal, Slovakia, Slovenia and Spain. The United Kingdom, Denmark and Sweden have opted not to participate.

For a more comprehensive account of European economic and monetary integration you may want to consult Figure 12.1.

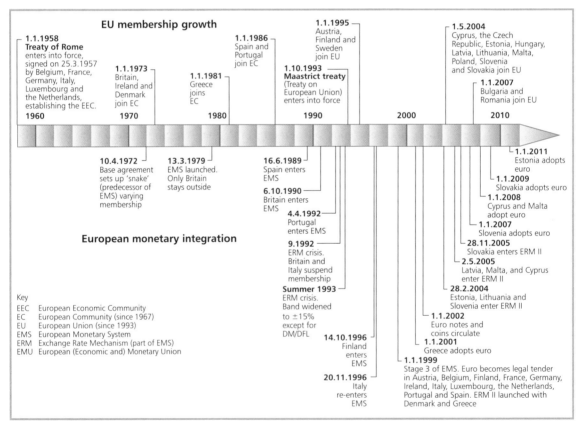

Figure 12.1 EU membership increased from the six countries that signed the Treaty of Rome on 25 March 1957 to 27 in 2007. The current name, the European Union was adopted in 1993 when the Treaty of Maastricht came into force. European monetary integration was spawned (or propelled) by the collapse of the Bretton Woods System of fixed exchange rates around 1971. Starting with the initiative of a handful of countries to stabilize their exchanges rates in the 1970s, monetary integration efforts peaked when 12 countries discarded their national currencies in favour of the euro on 1 January 2002. Under ERM II Denmark, Lithuania and Latvia are pegging their currencies to the euro as of 2012.

Source: K. Case, R. Fair, M. Gärtner and K. Heather (1999) *Economics*, Harlow: Prentice Hall Europe, with subsequent updates.

The national economy versus the global economy

When discussing business cycles we have taken either of two perspectives: that of the *global economy* that does not have an external sector; and that of the *national economy* which is too small to have a noticeable effect on the rest of the world and thus takes the world interest rate and world income as exogenous variables. This is often referred to as the *small open economy*.

Both models complement each other quite nicely. The global economy model can be used to represent the world around us – the world minus the national economy we are looking at. Since the national economy is too small to really affect the rest of the world, no great harm is done by ignoring the rest of the world's trade and financial relations with this national economy. So the global-economy model (which we also call the *IS-LM* model, because it has no foreign exchange market) explains how world income and the world interest rates are being determined (see Figure 12.2).

World income and the world interest rate then set the stage on which the national economy performs: i^W positions the *FE* curve for the national economy; Y^W codetermines the national economy's *IS* curve (Figure 12.2).

This is a very specific kind of interaction, of course, in which effects run in one direction only. It is useful for analyzing a small country's economy in its global environment. Analyzing the interaction between two similar-sized countries or between large economic blocs requires some adjustments, however, as we will see later in this chapter.

The *n*th currency

We argued earlier that fixing the exchange rate takes monetary policy out of the hands of the central bank. While this is generally true, it does not apply to all countries in the system. Basically, an exchange rate is simply the price of

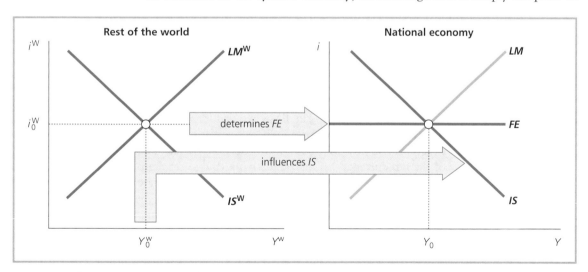

Figure 12.2 The *IS-LM* and the Mundell–Fleming model complement each other. The Mundell–Fleming model describes the working of the (small) national economy, which is affected by the (rest of the) world income and the (rest of the) world interest rate. The *IS-LM* model can be used to describe the rest of the world (the world minus our small national economy), and how income and the interest rate in this 'rest of the world' are determined. These then affect the national economy.

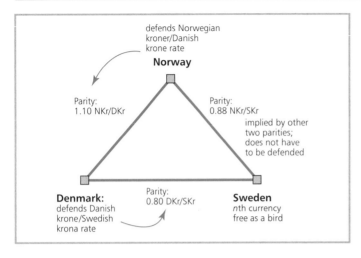

Figure 12.3 A Nordic Monetary System, with Sweden being the anchor. If three countries fix three bilateral exchange rates, one of them may conduct monetary policy as it pleases. If Denmark intervenes to keep the Danish krone/Swedish krona rate at parity, and Norway defends the Norwegian kroner/ Danish krone rate, at the same time they defend the Norwegian kroner/ Swedish krona rate. This frees Sweden from the obligation to intervene. In a system with n countries only $n - 1$ central banks must intervene. The nth country is free.

one currency in terms of another. In a way (and we have already looked at this in some detail) this price reflects the relative amounts of the two currencies in circulation. To keep this relative amount at a value that leaves the exchange rate unchanged, you do not need two central banks that cooperate and intervene. If two countries fix the exchange rate, one of the two central banks may move its money supply as it pleases, as long as the other one does exactly what is needed to keep the exchange rate at parity.

As Figure 12.3 illustrates, this also holds if three countries fix bilateral exchange rates. If, in a Nordic Monetary System, Denmark and Sweden were to set the rate of exchange between Danish krone and Swedish krona to 2, it suffices if Denmark intervenes to maintain that rate. If Norway and Denmark fix their kroner/krone rate to 2, then Norway alone can maintain that rate by intervention. But then these two rates implicitly guarantee a Norwegian kroner/Swedish krona rate of 4, without Sweden doing anything. So Sweden controls the nth currency.

The term 'nth currency' derives from the general insight that in a system involving n currencies only $n - 1$ central banks must intervene. The last one, issuing the nth currency, is free to determine its own course of monetary policy.

The Bretton Woods system was a system of fixed exchange rates operational until 1971. It was designed at an international conference held in 1944 in Bretton Woods, New Hampshire. Under the accord one fine ounce of gold was worth US$35. Other countries then defined the values of their own currencies in terms of US dollars.

Under the Bretton Woods system, operational during the twenty-five years following the Second World War, the role of the nth currency was explicitly assigned to the US dollar. The EMS avoided formally appointing an nth currency. It even required all countries involved to share the burden of intervention. Most experts agree, however, that in practice, the Deutschmark had adopted the role of the nth currency. So the Bundesbank (Buba) set the pace of monetary policy within the EMS, along with managing the exchange rate with regard to outside currencies like the dollar and the yen. The other $n - 1$ member countries had the responsibility for keeping exchange rates within the bands around parity values.

12.2 The 1992 EMS crisis

The relationship between the rest of the world and the individual country studied in Figure 12.2 bears an obvious analogy with the connection between the country with the nth currency in a fixed-exchange rate system and the other member countries. In the first case, the rest of the world sets the interest rate with which the individual small open economy must live. In an exchange rate system, such as the EMS or the Bretton Woods system, the *n*th currency controls monetary policy and generates an interest rate the other member countries have to live with in one way or another. The strains this can put on such a system made the Bretton Woods system collapse in 1971 and pushed the EMS to the brink of failure in 1992. We will use the *IS-LM* and Mundell–Fleming models to bring out the core issues of the 1992 EMS crisis.

The trigger of the crisis is usually seen as the peculiar mix of fiscal and monetary policy following German unification. A sharp increase in government spending was needed to start rebuilding the public infrastructure and provide financial incentives to attract private investment in the east of the country, and to cushion soaring unemployment. This would shift *IS* way to the right in an *IS-LM* diagram for the country with the *n*th currency. Concerned that this stimulation of aggregate demand may sooner or later trigger price increases, the Bundesbank switched to a restrictive monetary policy, shifting the *LM* curve to the left. The most striking result from this interplay between fiscal expansion and monetary contraction was a sharp rise in German interest rates, with the money market rate peaking at 9.72% in 1992 (for more details see Case study 12.1).

Repercussions and options

The high and rising interest rates in Germany were bound to have repercussions on other members of the European Monetary System of fixed exchange rates. Prior to the unification-related rise in German interest rates, a typical EMS member state's economy, say that of the Netherlands, may be represented by the lower of the three points in Figure 12.4. We can leave it open for now where this was relative to full employment, since, as we shall see below, different countries were in different phases of the business cycle.

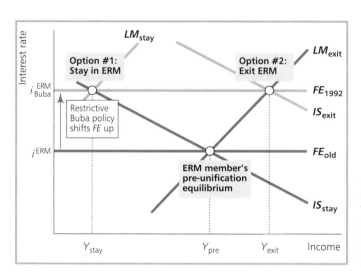

Figure 12.4 By driving up German interest rates, which determine interest rates in the EMS, the Bundesbank confronted other members with a difficult choice: remain in the ERM and suffer a fall in income, or leave the ERM and benefit from temporarily higher income.

CASE STUDY 12.1 German unification as a tug of war

German unification provided economists with a huge laboratory experiment. Here we look at this event first, because it provides an interesting application of the Mundell–Fleming model introduced in Chapter 5, and secondly, because many see it, or its mishandling, as the culprit responsible for derailing the EMS in 1992–93.

The issues

It became clear in early 1990 that East and West Germany were moving towards full economic and political integration. From a macroeconomic perspective this entailed merging the two countries' goods and labour markets and introducing a common currency. This confronted West Germany with the issues laid out in Figure 12.5(a) in the context of the Mundell–Fleming model.

The situation in West Germany prior to unification may be thought of as a long-run equilibrium.

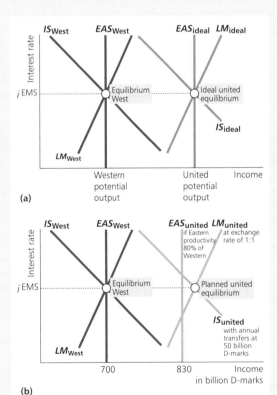

(a)

(b)

Figure 12.5

With the mark being the nth currency in the EMS, the Bundesbank (Buba) could conduct monetary policy at its discretion, determining German interest rates freely and thereby positioning the *FE* curve for the other EMS members.

Against this background, the question of immediate concern was how to merge the two economies without repercussions on the interest rate (which might strain the EMS) and without creating inflation (which would run counter to the legal responsibility of the Buba). A plan to achieve this would have to contain three components:

- An estimate of **potential output in East Germany**. Added to West German potential output this yields an estimate of unified potential output.
- A plan to position the **IS curve for united Germany** so as to intersect the potential output line at the EMS interest rate.
- A plan to position the **LM curve for united Germany** so as to intersect the potential output line at the EMS interest rate.

Kohl's master plan

Estimating productivity and income levels of centrally planned economies is difficult because their output is not valued by markets. With this caveat, East German per capita income was estimated at some 80% of the western level, yielding an East German GNP estimate of DM 130 billion. Adding this to West German GNP of DM 700 billion puts the united *EAS* curve at $Y^* = 830$.

A forecast of the position of the *IS* curve had to start with an assumption of investment and consumption behaviour and an estimate of additional government spending. The latter could not be obtained by extrapolating West German government spending levels, but needed to include sizeable transfers to the east, needed to lick the Eastern infrastructure into Western shape and cover social security and unemployment payments. The Kohl government claimed that **DM 50 billion of government transfers** annually would suffice. As this would require substantial deficit spending (public borrowing from the private sector) this would put the *IS* curve to the right of the ideal *IS* curve drawn into Figure 12.5(a).

Case study 12.1 continued

Finally, the position of the *LM* curve would be crucially affected by the rate at which East German currency would be converted into West German D-marks. A high price would mean that the Buba would have to supply little additional liquidity, shifting the *LM* curve moderately to the right, making the interest rate rise. A low price would force the Buba to pump a lot of liquidity into the new *Länder*. This would cause a large shift of *LM* to the right. Combined with the large shift of the *IS* curve to the right this would stimulate output way beyond full employment output, thus triggering inflation.

The Buba and the administration had conflicting preferences regarding the conversion rate. The Buba wanted to maintain or regain price stability and pleaded for a high conversion rate of 2:1, though this meant higher interest rates and lower income. The government, with an eye on the first general election in united Germany scheduled for late 1990 (and won by Kohl), wanted to avoid decisions that would depress income. Inflation could be expected to materialize with a lag long enough not to hurt re-election prospects. In a stunning revelation of the limitations of Buba independence, the government steamrolled the Buba and committed to a conversion rate of 1:1.

The light blue lines in Figure 12.5(b) sketch the macroeconomic constellation anticipated to result from the described decisions.

The Bundesbank strikes back

Instead of the ideal plan, the Buba found itself pushed into an uncomfortable position with a high inflation potential while the administration's unification plans took shape in 1990. Two developments aggravated fears of an inflation surge:

■ As in many formerly communist countries, capital stocks, productivity and capacity levels had been vastly overestimated for East Germany. New insights gained during 1990 and 1991 placed potential output much lower than our sketch of the Kohl plan assumed in Figure 12.5.

■ Partly due to the previous point, transfers to the east had to be revised upwards dramatically. Instead of the initially circulated DM 50 billion

annually, transfer requirements soon turned out to be around DM 150 billion. As a consequence of the upward revision of transfers by DM 100 billion annually, the *IS* curve sat much further to the right than planned.

Figure 12.6(a) compares Germany's actual situation after unification (dark blue lines) with the Kohl plan (light blue lines). Differences reflect the three developments listed above.

The Buba had already found the *Kohl plan* unacceptable. Unable to fend it off or strike a compromise, it had protested against the 1:1 conversion rate, considering the inflation potential intolerable and incompatible with its legal obligations. Rather than staying put and waiting for inflation to reduce the real money supply and eliminate excess demand, the Buba decided to follow the relentless disinflation course on which it had already embarked prior to unification, in the face

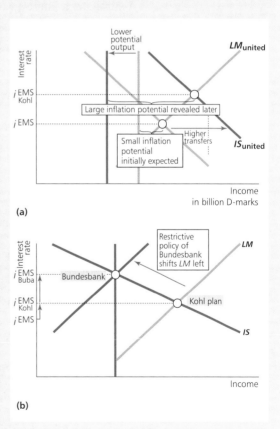

(a)

(b)

Figure 12.6

Case study 12.1 continued

of 5%-plus inflation rates in 1989. *LM* shifted up sharply into the full blue position (Figure 12.6(b)). The price to be paid was further increases in the already high interest rate, which peaked at 9.72% in August 1992 and set the stage for the 1992 EMS crisis discussed in the main text.

The foremost effect of the development in Germany (described in Case study 12.1) for the Netherlands is an upward shift of the *FE* curve. This leaves the Netherlands with two options:

- *Option #1*. Stay in the ERM. This amounts to defending the current exchange rate by buying guilders, thus reducing the money supply. The upward shift of the *LM* curve raises Dutch interest rates as well, thus driving down output and income.
- *Option #2*. Leave the ERM. This would bring the money supply back under Dutch control and fix *LM* in the old position. The adjustment to a new equilibrium takes place via a depreciation of the Dutch guilder, which stimulates exports and shifts the *IS* curve out into the light blue position. Again, Dutch interest rates are driven up, but this time income rises.

And equivalent to the second option, at least for the moment, the Netherlands could also realign the guilder against the Deutschmark and keep membership in the ERM active.

Choices

Governments tend to make choices on the basis of cost–benefit comparisons. The major *drawback* of staying in the ERM (option #1) compared with leaving it (option #2) are the negative effects on income and employment. This added burden may be more difficult to bear if the country is already in a recession. As our discussion in Chapter 11 suggests, public support (or re-election prospects) by and large reflect the state of the economy. So a government of a country already in a recession may not survive the further deterioration to be expected from option #1. It is therefore likely to do almost anything that promises quick improvement, such as resorting to option #2.

The major *advantage* of option #1 over option #2 is clearly that it keeps the country's option alive to be part of European Economic and Monetary Union (EMU). Countries that wished to take part needed to meet a series of **convergence criteria** evaluated in 1997. One of these, the exchange rate convergence criterion, required that the currency of each member state must have remained within the normal fluctuation margins of the ERM for at least two years prior to the evaluation. This excluded both exiting the ERM and realigning parities on its own initiative. While exiting in late 1992 would not have ruled out being back on track in 1997, it would have put membership prospects in rather serious jeopardy. In the light of this, a country was more likely to remain in the ERM and fight it out if it were seriously interested in taking part in economic monetary union and if its failure to meet other convergence criteria was not likely to rule out EMU membership anyway.

Table 12.1 **EMU aspirations and the business cycle.** In 1992, interest in being part of EMU was probably highest in France and lowest in the United Kingdom. Prospects to meet the convergence criteria were intact in France, but bleak in Italy. Having shrunk by 2.1% since 1990, Britain's economy was much less prepared to take further strain than the other two.

	Interest in and prospects for European Economic and Monetary Union	Income growth 1990–92	
France	Seriously interested in EMU; meets all five convergence criteria in 1991 and four in 1992.	Total: 1990: 1991: 1992:	4.5 2.5 0.8 1.2
Italy	Interested in EMU; does not meet any convergence criterion in 1991 or 1992.	Total 1990 1991 1992	4.1 2.1 1.2 0.8
United Kingdom	Modestly interested in EMU; meets two convergence criteria in 1992; signed Maastricht Treaty only after given right to opt out.	Total: 1990: 1991: 1992:	−2.1 0.4 −2.0 −0.5

Source: Swiss National Bank, *Monatsberichte*.

To see whether this framework explains actual choices made in 1992, consider the three largest EMS members besides Germany. Table 12.1 summarizes the shapes of these nations' economies and ranks their interests in and their prospects for an eventual participation in economic and monetary union and a common currency.

France

France had committed itself fully to EMU. Plans to make the Banque de France more independent of the government, as required by the Maastricht Treaty, were being finalized. It was also working with determination on the other Maastricht criteria, of which it met all five in 1991 and four in 1992. In 1992 the French economy was not booming, but was not stalling either. Growth was down from the very high rates experienced in the second half of the 1980s, but still amounted to 4.5% over the 1990–2 period. So the high interest rates brought about by the Bundesbank were certainly not welcome, but did not hit the French economy with a recession already under way. In this situation, with a lot at stake regarding EMU and a modestly comfortable state of the economy, France decided to remain in the ERM and fight it out.

Italy

Italy's economy looked very much the same as that of France, with possibly slightly more of a downward trend. EMU prospects were completely different, however. While Italy was also interested in participating in the common European currency to come, it had not been able yet to meet a single one of the five criteria spelled out in Maastricht. Prospects to change that soon looked dim. Leaving ERM, therefore, could not do much additional harm. Not surprisingly, Italy was one of the countries that decided to leave ERM.

BOX 12.1 Convergence criteria in the Maastricht Treaty

In 1988 European governments set up the Delors Committee to examine the issue of economic and monetary union and to develop a programme aimed at its implementation. The resulting Delors Report led to the Maastricht Treaty on European Union, which was negotiated in December 1991 and came into force in November 1993. While this treaty covers a wide range of integration issues, its most prominent feature is the formalization of how to bring about economic and monetary union and, in particular, a common currency (termed *euro* in 1995). In addition to other more general, softer criteria, the **Maastricht Treaty** spells out the following main **criteria for monetary and fiscal convergence** as a precondition for a country's participation in European Monetary Union:

- Government debt must not exceed 60% of GDP.
- The government budget deficit must not exceed 3% of GDP.
- Inflation must not exceed average inflation in the three EU countries with the lowest rates by more than 1.5 percentage points.
- Interest rates on government bonds must not exceed average rates in the three EU countries with lowest inflation by more than 2 percentage points.
- Membership in the ERM must have been maintained for no less than two years without having initiated a devaluation.

These criteria also have to be met by prospective future entrants into the euro area.

United Kingdom

The UK's position contrasted sharply with that of France. There was a very strong opposition to EMU, even within the government. Negotiations in Maastricht could only be kept from breaking down by granting Britain the right to opt out of monetary union. In this regard, therefore, little was to be lost by exiting ERM in 1992. More importantly, Britain was in an entirely different phase of the business cycle from France and Italy. Income had fallen by 2% in 1991 and was still falling in 1992. Additional negative effects from the high German interest rates appeared increasingly unbearable. Against this background, it is of little surprise that Britain was the first country to quit ERM during the crisis.

The Mundell–Fleming model and some arguments from political economy provide a good first grasp of the macroeconomic issues and choices surrounding the unification of the two Germanies and the EMS crisis of 1992. To obtain more detailed insights into the anatomy of currency crises, of which there were more before and after 1992, we need to take a closer look at how the EMS works. We begin by introducing the concept of exchange rate target zones and then proceed to discuss speculative attacks.

12.3 Exchange rate target zones

As noted at the beginning of this chapter, what sets the EMS's exchange rate mechanism apart from an ideal system of fixed exchange rates is that it allows exchange rates to fluctuate within a band around parity. Figure 12.7 shows central rates of exchange for the Deutschmark against the Danish krone, the French franc, the guilder, the lira, the peseta, and the pound, and, when applicable, bands of intervention. While bands have normally been ±2.25%

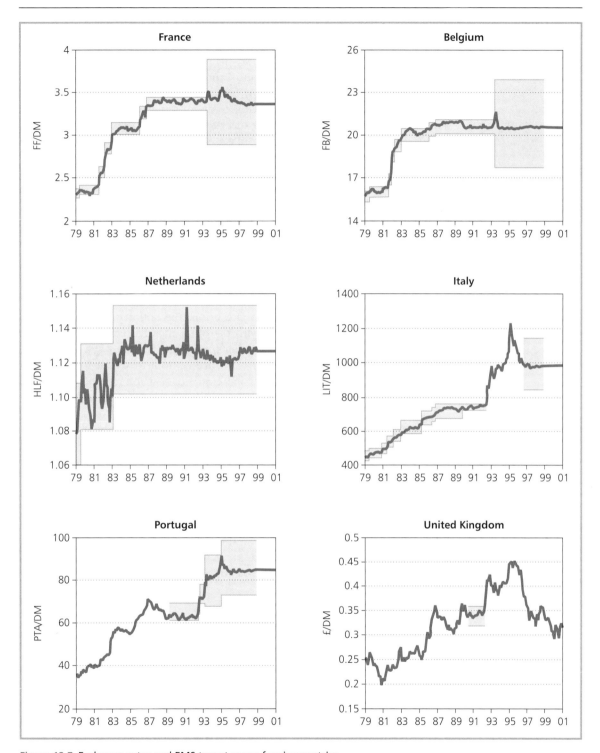

Figure 12.7 Exchange rates and EMS target zones for six countries.

Source: Eurostat.

around the central rate, occasionally countries have been granted wider bands of $\pm 6\%$. The 1993 EMS crisis even forced authorities to widen the band to $\pm 15\%$ for most currencies.

The graphs illustrate the evolution of the EMS until the irrevocable fixing of exchange rates for countries that adopted the euro on 1 January 1999, and offer samples of its diversity. After frequent realignments during its early stage the system settled into its most successful phase between 1987 and 1992, during which no realignments took place. It is interesting to note that wider bands, as in the case of Italy, may leave bands overlapping, so that the exchange rate may ease from one band into the next without dramatic jumps. This contrasts with the realignments of the French franc in the early years, which made the franc jump into the new band. Note also the dramatic and permanent depreciations of the pound and the lira after leaving the ERM, the undramatic effect of the widening of the bands to $\pm 15\%$ on exchange rates, and the near monetary union between the guilder and the Deutschmark.

As an exchange rate hits or threatens to hit one of the limits, the countries involved have the two options mentioned earlier. Normally, they are obliged to intervene by buying or selling foreign currency in order to keep the exchange rate in the band. Or, as an exception, the country may negotiate a realignment, a new central parity with the other member countries. At times this has been considered necessary rather frequently. Between 1987 and 1992 no such realignments were necessary. A third option, to which Italy and the United Kingdom resorted in October 1992, was to suspend membership of the ERM, letting the exchange rate be determined by market forces only.

Before we discuss how exchange rates behave within bands or target zones, as they are often called, we discuss the role of foreign exchange market intervention. Central banks, even in countries that are not part of some fixed exchange rate system, have been found to intervene in the foreign exchange market to reverse or stem movements of currency prices. What does that do?

> **Foreign exchange market intervention** is the purchase or sale of foreign currency by the central bank aimed at influencing the exchange rate.

To keep the argument simple, take an economy with perfectly flexible prices, so that potential output is produced all the time. As we have seen in Chapter 5, section 5.7, then the current exchange rate e is a weighted average of the exchange rate expected for tomorrow and the fundamental determinants of the exchange rate, such as the money supply. Consider only this one fundamental variable, m, and let the others be zero. Then the exchange rate equation is

$$e = \alpha m + (1 - \alpha)e^{e}_{+1} \tag{12.1}$$

This formulation again highlights the prime reason for the apparent volatility and instability of foreign exchange markets. Whatever the market believes, happens. If the exchange rate is expected to appreciate, it appreciates. We shall return to this below.

On a rational basis, if the market does not expect the fundamental determinants of the exchange rate, here represented by m, to change next period, then it will not expect the exchange rate to change – unless the exchange rate is on a bubble path, which we rule out for now. Then tomorrow's exchange rate is expected to be the same as today's. Inserting $e^{e}_{+1} = e$ into equation (12.1) and solving for e gives

$$e = m \tag{12.2}$$

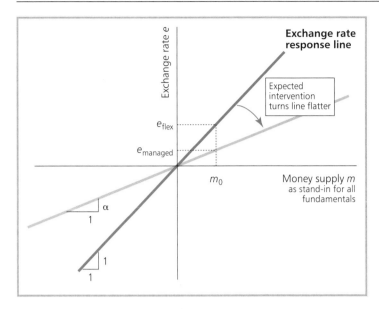

Figure 12.8 Under flexible exchange rates, if the money supply moves to m_0, and is expected to stay there, the exchange rate rises to e_{flex}. If central bank intervention is expected to reduce the money supply to its previous level in the next period, the exchange rate rises to $e_{managed}$ only. As this argument applies for all current levels of m, foreign exchange market intervention turns the exchange rate response line into the flatter, light blue position.

Movements of the money supply, which we use as a stand-in for all fundamentals, translate one-to-one into movements of the exchange rate. The blue line, drawn with a slope of 1, in Figure 12.8 illustrates this.

Our assumption that the money supply is not expected to change next period does not mean that it cannot do so. Recall from Chapter 3 (Box 3.1, 'Money and monetary policy') that the central bank only controls the monetary base M0. Broader monetary aggregates M are connected to the monetary base by means of a multiplier B, $M = B \times M_0$. Expressed in logarithms this is written as $m = b + m_0$. The multiplier is affected by many different things, some of which are little understood. To reflect this, let changes in b be random, $b = b_{-1} + v$, where v is a random variable with an expected value of zero. Substituting this into the above definition of money, we obtain what is called a random walk for m:

> A variable follows a random walk if it is just as likely to rise next period as to fall. The change of such a variable is not predictable. The expected change is zero.

$$m = m_{-1} + v \tag{12.3}$$

According to equation (12.3), in each period the likelihood that the money supply rises is just as high as the likelihood that it falls. Hence it is rational to expect that it does not change at all, and we obtain equation (12.2) again.

The scenario discussed is reminiscent of flexible exchange rates. The path of monetary policy is completely unaffected by observed movements of the exchange rate. This is different under a so-called managed float. Assume that the central bank has a target level for the exchange rate of $\hat{e} = 0$. With that aim it always adjusts the monetary base m0 so as to reverse previous random effects on the money supply and bring the money supply back to a target level of zero. While the actual money supply next period is $m_{+1} = v_{+1}$, the expected money supply is $m^e_{+1} = 0$. This sets the expected exchange rate to $e^e_{+1} = 0$. Substituting this into equation (12.1) gives

> Managed floating is a mixture between flexible and fixed exchange rates. Central banks intervene to influence the exchange rate (say, to keep it within some range), but do not defend a fixed rate.

$$e = \alpha m$$

The point to note here is that anticipated *foreign exchange market intervention makes the exchange rate response line flatter* (see the light blue line with slope α in Figure 12.8). Our specific example reveals that a given deviation of the money supply (or of a composite fundamental) from its target level leads to a smaller deviation of the exchange rate from its equilibrium level if the fundamental is expected to be driven back to its target level next period, than if this is not the case. From a more general perspective we have a continuum of slopes between α and 1: the more vigorous the intervention response of the central bank is expected to be, the flatter the exchange rate response line will be and the closer its slope will be driven down from 1 towards α. For example, if the central bank was known to reverse only half of an observed deviation of the fundamental from its target level next period, the slope of the exchange rate response line would be between that of the dark blue line and that of the light blue line in Figure 12.8.

Target zones are a combination of flexible exchange rates (near the centre of the band) and one with mandatory interventions (at the margins). It should be clear from the above discussion that if central banks intervene as soon as the exchange rate moves away from the central rate, this will flatten the exchange rate response line. A more surprising insight into the workings of a target zone system is obtained if we employ the following two stylized assumptions:

1 The target zone is only defended by intervention at the margins. Within the band the exchange rate is left to be determined by market forces alone.
2 Market participants are fully convinced that there will be no realignment of the central rate. In other words, the target zone is perfectly credible.

It can be shown by means of some fairly complicated mathematics that the exchange rate response line in such a target zone is S-shaped, as shown in Figure 12.9. Here the following reasoning will suffice.

Let the exchange rate be at parity and the money supply at the corresponding value of $m = 0$. Since the money supply can only change randomly, with an expected value of zero, it is equally likely that it will hit or exceed m_{UP}, where a

Maths note. The target zone literature casts equation (12.1) in continuous time. This prevents the exchange rate from actually moving out of bounds before intervention strikes back. We stick with the discrete-time view entertained throughout this book and downplay the above possibility by assuming that the time unit is very small, say, a minute.

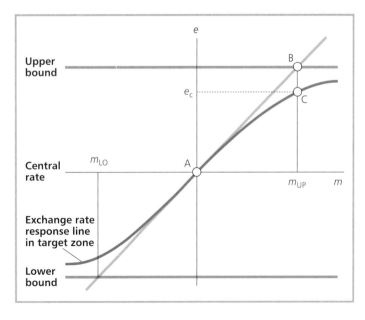

Figure 12.9 The straight line through A and B says which exchange rate obtains at a given money supply under flexible exchange rates; m_{UP} puts the exchange rate at the upper band. In a target zone this money supply moves the exchange rate only to e_C, since the central bank will probably be forced to reduce the money supply next period. Generally, the response line in a target zone is S-shaped.

flexible exchange rate would break through the upper bound, or that it will fall below m_{LO}, where a flexible exchange rate would fall below the lower limit. In other words, the probability of a positive intervention is exactly the same as the probability of a negative intervention. Hence the expected intervention is zero. The money supply is expected to remain where it is. The exchange rate response line has the same slope of 1 as under flexible exchange rates.

Next, let the money supply be at m_{UP}, which would place a flexible exchange rate right on the upper bound. The probability that the next random shock places the money supply above m_{UP} is 50%. In such cases the central bank would have to intervene and prevent m from actually rising. There is another 50% probability that a negative shock makes m fall. Combining these two possibilities results in an expectation that m (and e) will fall next period. As a consequence, the exchange rate does not rise as high this period as it would have without the expectation of intervention next period.

Figure 12.9 contrasts the behaviour of the exchange rate under flexible rates with that within a target zone. While m_{UP} would drive a flexible exchange rate up to the upper limit, in a credible target zone it will only move to e_{C}. Since the likelihood of future central bank intervention increases as we move closer to the upper bound, the exchange rate response line becomes flatter and flatter. Similar reasoning near the lower bound bends the target zone exchange rate response line into the shape of an S.

The most important property of an exchange rate target zone is that it dampens the fluctuations of the exchange rate. Reactions along the S curve to given fluctuations of fundamentals are smaller than under flexible exchange rates. If fundamentals that are beyond the control of the domestic policy-maker move out of bounds, the exchange rate still remains within. And even way inside the band, exchange rate responses are smaller due to the fact that the S curve has a slope smaller than 1. The effect is strengthened if interventions are not only undertaken at the margins but intra-marginal as well, as permitted, though not required, in the EMS. It is also one argument against the widely held view that widening the band to $\pm 15\%$ in 1993 had the same effect as suspending the EMS altogether and rendering exchange rates flexible. Then the exchange rate responses to movements in m would be described by the 45° line. If the wider bands have yielded *credible* bounds, however, they should dampen exchange rate fluctuations inside the band, even if exchange rates never hit the widest bounds.

Empirically, the S shape of the exchange rate response line has been found to be only a first approximation for the EMS. More realistic, though not radically different, properties obtain if the model concedes that bounds may be imperfectly credible and that the central bank may begin to intervene inside the band. The second modification has little significance for the following look at speculative attacks. However, the first one, credibility of the band, plays a key role.

Effects similar to what we have just described for target zones may be at work in less formal exchange rate arrangements. This could be a unilateral, temporary fixing of an upper or lower bound only. The Swiss National Bank's announcement of a minimum exchange rate of Swiss francs 1.20 per euro in September 2011, with the promise to enforce it with 'utmost determination', is such an example. Whether such efforts have the desired stabilizing effect depends on the credibility of the announcement. Therefore, rather strong wording is typically heard in such cases.

Figure 12.10 This shows a hypothetical line-up of EU members on the EMS exchange rate response line. Here the exchange rates of Britain and Italy only remain below the upper bound as long as the target zone is credible. If credibility deteriorates, the exchange rate response line begins to straighten and the exchange rates are pushed against the upper bound.

12.4   Speculative attacks

We are now ready to take a second look at the 1992 crises in the European Monetary System. Figure 12.10 presents a stylized sketch of a set of exchange rates in the EMS as we enter 1992.

To keep things simple and transparent, assume that after more than five years without realignments, and with the Maastricht Treaty's commitment to economic and monetary union and a common currency in place, all target zones were perfectly credible. Then the same S curve applies for all member states, and we may line up countries according to how central rates compare with current fundamentals.

In the judgement of many observers, Britain had entered the ERM in 1990 with a substantially overvalued central rate for sterling. In other words, fundamentals would place its free-market exchange rate against, say, the Deutschmark, way above the central rate, possibly even outside the zone's upper band. So Britain would have to be located way to the right on the S curve. Next to Britain we may want to position Italy and France, and then the Iberian countries and Greece. The Dutch guilder had been comfortable near central parity for quite some time.

Consider now Figure 12.11, which zooms in on the first quadrant of Figure 12.10 and focuses on Britain only. Sterling's pre-crisis position on the blue S curve was fine as long as the upper bound was credible. But, as the EMS began to lose credibility and EMU appeared doomed in the wake of the Maastricht Treaty's rejection by Danish voters, intensifying discussions in other countries, and of uncertain prospects for the French referendum, the S curve straightened somewhat to the slightly lighter blue position. Sterling hit the upper bound.

The EMS credibility crisis makes the British pound the first currency to hit the upper bound (step 1) and forces the Bank of England to intervene (step 2).

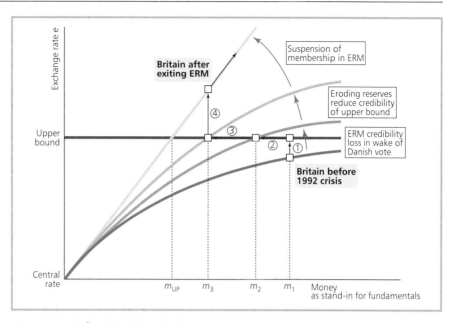

Figure 12.11 Before the 1992 crisis the British money supply was at m_1, and e was determined by the lowest, dark blue curve. When Denmark's 'no' undermined EMS credibility, the response line moved into the second, slightly lighter position, pressing e against the upper bound, forcing the Bank of England (BoE) to support the pound, reducing m to m_2. Eroding currency reserves reduced the target zone's credibility further, shifting the response line into the third position, forcing the BoE to reduce m to m_3. Leaving the ERM turned the response line straight, permitting sizeable depreciations of the pound out of previous bounds.

To keep the pound within bounds, the money supply needs to be lowered from m_1 to m_2 by selling foreign exchange reserves. This loss of foreign exchange reserves weakens the Bank of England's muscle for future defences of the upper bound. The market knows this quite well. Hence, the upper bound's credibility deteriorates further, straightening the S curve even more into the third position from bottom. Having started only weeks earlier, overwhelming foreign exchange market speculation forced Britain to suspend membership of the ERM on 16 September 1992. In line with the stylized path in Figure 12.11, sterling lost over 20% against the Deutschmark within days after leaving the ERM.

This graph should not imply that there is a set course of events once a speculative attack gets under way. Many such attacks have been fended off. Moving left, as characterized by steps 2 and 3, may eventually re-establish credibility, easing the exchange rate (and the S curve) back into the band.

Proof that the Bank of England did not accept defeat easily is given by a 5 percentage points jump of the interest rate within one day to fend off speculators. And Sweden, which was not a member of the ERM but had pegged the krona to the ECU in 1991, on 16 September raised its overnight lending rate to 500%!

The arguments given here augment the macroeconomic account of the 1992 crises given in the 'Choices' section earlier in this chapter. Here we looked at some details of currency crises which the previous story had not taken into account. There we focused on the cost–benefit ratios for some countries that were at the centre of speculation. In the context of the current target zone framework, these cost–benefit considerations suggest that, and explain why,

George Soros, known as *The man who broke the Bank* of *England* ever since, made over $1 billion profit by short selling sterling.

the band for the British pound lost credibility sooner and faster than others, straightening the UK's *S* curve out sooner and faster. The earlier view thus easily augments and supports the current argument.

Self-fulfilling prophecies

Our view of speculative attacks during currency crises does not rest on the presumption of some sinister plot by speculators. Uncoordinated reactions by competitive markets may well suffice.

On the other hand, it deserves to be emphasized that, in analogy to speculative bubbles, the process that we called a 'speculative attack' need not be triggered by a real reason. If *market psychology* alone and completely unfoundedly develops doubts about the credibility of the target zone, the *S* curve straightens and makes the exchange rate actually move towards one of the bounds. This forces monetary authorities to intervene to reduce the foreign exchange reserves, thus reducing the credibility of the band further. The result will look like what we sketched for the 1992 crises of the EMS. So the initially unwarranted reservation about the viability of the current central rate and its surrounding band of fluctuation may indeed prove self-fulfilling.

This insight holds generally. Whatever the market expects in the foreign exchange market happens in a self-fulfilling way. If such expectations lack a fundamental basis, however, these effects cannot last. In this light the data do not seem to support the view, at times widely held, that speculation drove the pound sterling out of the ERM, against fundamentals. Then the pound should have returned to previous EMS target zone levels once speculators had shifted attention to other currencies. As the UK panel in Figure 12.7 showed, this was not the case. Between September 1992 and September 1995 the pound on average remained 22% above its central parity rate versus the Deutschmark that applied while ERM membership was active. The same holds *a fortiori* for the lira.

12.5 Monetary and fiscal policy in the euro area

Our discussions have covered the global economy, the national economy, and the relationship between the two: that is, interdependence in a system of fixed exchange rates or a target zone. What we have not looked at yet is the case of a group of countries sharing a common currency, the experiment on which a large part of the European Union embarked at the turn of the millennium. Such an arrangement is called a **currency union** or a **monetary union**. We will first look at how fiscal and monetary policy works in a monetary union and then check whether our insights shed any light on why certain institutional arrangements and precautions were taken during the advent of the **European Economic and Monetary Union (EMU)**. Let us start by looking at monetary policy.

Monetary policy in a monetary union

Monetary policy in the euro area is conducted by the European Central Bank (ECB). True, technical operations are in the hands of national central banks, but these act only on ECB orders. Thus it is the ECB which controls the total supply of euros in the Eurozone. Note the wording, however. In a monetary union the central bank controls the overall money supply within the union. It has no control over the money supply in any individual member country. So if the total money supply in the Eurozone is M, and M_i denotes money supplied and held in country i, we have

$$M = M_A + M_B + M_{CY} + M_D + M_E + M_{EST} + M_F + M_{FIN} + M_{GR} + M_I$$
$$+ M_{IRE} + M_{LUX} + M_M + M_{NL} + M_P + M_{SK} + M_{SLO}$$

All that the ECB can control when conducting monetary policy is M, the aggregate. How much of it is being supplied and held in Austria, Belgium, Germany, Spain and so on, is up to the market. The ECB keeps a lid on the total, since the sum of national money supplies in all member countries equals M.

It does not matter which country's central bank actually conducts the expansion. To understand this, consider a stylized monetary union made up of two countries A and B only, Austria and Belgium. To make matters simple, suppose A and B do not trade in goods and services, though they do have integrated money and capital markets. Let us further ignore this monetary union's links with the rest of the world to focus on internal links only. The dark blue lines in Figure 12.12 depict an initial equilibrium (points C) in which both countries' interest rates are equal, of course.

Now suppose the ECB orders Austria's central bank to expand the money supply. The Österreichische Nationalbank complies, say, by purchasing Austrian government bonds from Austrian residents. This shifts LM_A to the right into

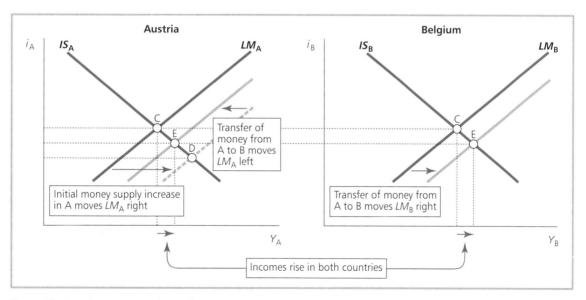

Figure 12.12 In a monetary union it does not matter in which country the money supply is actually increased, since it tends to spread evenly over all member states. One way to rationalize this is as follows: suppose the Austrian central bank increases the supply of euros, moving Austria's *LM* curve to the right. This tends to drive Austrian interest rates below Belgium's. This induces international investors to sell Austrian bonds and purchase Belgian bonds instead. This reduces the supply of euros in Austria and increases the supply of euros in Belgium. Thus, the Austrian *LM* curve moves to the left and Belgium's *LM* curve moves to the right. Movements come to a halt when both countries' *LM* curves intersect their respective *IS* curves at the same interest rate.

the dashed position because this action injects liquidity into the Austrian economy. This added liquidity exerts downward pressure on Austrian interest rates, moving the economy *towards* point D in the left-hand panel in Figure 12.12 (though not really *onto* D).

The downward pressure on interest rates makes Austrian bonds unattractive compared with Belgian bonds. So, Austrians will try to sell their bonds and purchase Belgian bonds. This moves euros across the border. The money supply falls in Austria but rises in Belgium. Technically, LM_B moves to the right from its original position, driving Belgian interest rates down, and LM_A moves left from its temporary dashed position, driving Austrian interest rates back up. This process cannot end before both countries' interest rates meet somewhere between their initial values and Austria's level associated with point D. In Figure 12.12 this is where the LM curves are at their light blue positions. In the end, the money supply has increased in both countries, independent of where the initial money supply increase took place. Interest rates in the monetary union have fallen and income has risen in all member countries.

To keep the argument reasonably transparent we assumed that Austria's central bank extended the money supply by purchasing Austrian bonds held in Austria. The same comparative static effect obtains, however, under more complicated assumptions. For example, if Austria's central bank extended the money supply by purchasing Austrian government bonds held in Belgium it would have increased Belgian money holdings with the same end result of the money supply increasing and interest rates falling in both countries. But the sequence of reactions would have been somewhat different. Reality is somewhere between these two extreme cases, though a bit closer to the first since individuals exhibit a clear home bias in their holding of financial assets: Austrians hold a much higher share of Austrian bonds (and stocks) in their portfolio than Belgians (or any other nationals) do.

How are results affected when there is trade? In this scenario, a monetary expansion has the same qualitative effect on i and Y. There is another stimulus channel, though. As Austria expands the money supply and its income rises, its demand for Belgian exports increases and IS_B shifts to the right. For the same reason, IS_A also moves to the right. In equilibrium, both incomes are higher and the interest rate is lower.

Fiscal policy in a monetary union

Discipline in fiscal policy was, and will continue to be, an important test for countries wanting to qualify for membership in the European Monetary Union. At the 1996 intergovernmental conference in Dublin heads of state agreed on a list of sanctions to come into operation if a member country resorted to excessive government spending after the start of EMU. And now for many the main lesson from the Eurozone's debt crisis that broke in 2010 is that criteria need to be stricter still and sanctions must be scarier, as summed up in the **Fiscal Compact** due to enter into force in 2013. Why this fear that governments might not be able to resist the temptation to spend excessively? While a full discussion of deficits and debt must wait until Chapter 14, the model employed here provides a first answer as to why governments dread the idea of other governments spending excessively in a monetary union.

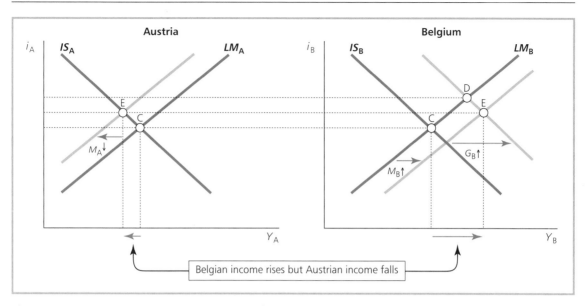

Figure 12.13 In a monetary union an expansionary fiscal policy move by one country can have negative repercussions on other countries' incomes. Suppose Belgium's government increases spending to stimulate Belgian incomes. While this succeeds, it drives up Belgian interest rates, attracting international investors. Since these sell their Austrian bonds, taking their euro proceeds out of Austria, the supply of euros in Austria falls. This shifts the Austrian *LM* curve left (and at the same time Belgium's to the right) and drives Austria's interest rate up (and at the same time Belgium's down) until both countries' interest rates match again. Since Austria ends up with a higher interest rate than before, it pays for Belgium's income gains by being driven into recession.

Short-run effects

Let Belgium and Austria again be in the equilibrium positions associated with the dark blue curves (Figure 12.13). Now Belgium unilaterally decides to boost income by raising government spending. The multiplier effect shifts Belgium's *IS* curve to the right into the light blue position. If Belgium was the world, income and the interest rate would rise and a new equilibrium would obtain at point D. Being in a monetary union with Austria, however, repercussions are felt in Austria as soon as the Belgian interest rate begins to rise.

Since the Austrian interest rate moves up with Belgium's, income falls, moving the economy northwest as shown in the left-hand panel in Figure 12.13. The result is an excess supply of money in Austria. In Belgium, while the interest rate is still above the value associated with point C, there is an excess demand for money. In this situation, as we have encountered before, excess liquidity flows out of Austria into Belgium. So the Belgian *LM* curve shifts to the right and Austria's *LM* curve moves to the left. The new equilibrium obtains on the light blue *LM* curves where interest rates are equal.

The long-run implications of fiscal policy excesses

Figure 12.13 describes the short- to medium-run effects of fiscal policy in a currency union. These income gains and recessionary effects on the rest of the currency union are temporary, however. So what is the longer-run legacy if individual members succumb to substantial deficit spending?

We may use the same diagram in Figure 12.14. This time, let the two countries be Germany and Greece. And suppose that incomes in both countries,

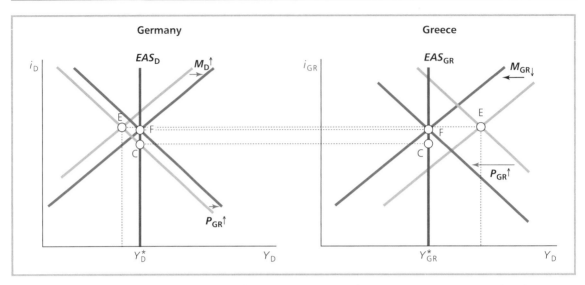

Figure 12.14 In a monetary union expansionary fiscal policy stimulates the acting country's economy, but depresses incomes in other member countries. See point E in both panels and the argument given in Figure 12.13. This effect will not last when both countries initially operated at capacity levels. Rising prices in Greece (possibly complemented by falling prices in Germany) impair Greece's competitiveness relative to Germany, moving its *IS* curve left and Germany's right. Accompanied by endogenous money flows across borders, the new long-run equilibrium obtains in point F.

before Greece set out on its public spending spree, were at their potential levels. Then the vertical equilibrium aggregate supply curve passes through the initial equilibrium points marked C. As before, the short-run response to the increase in Greek government spending is to bring the two countries into the temporary, demand-side equilibrium positions marked E, in which Greece enjoys a boom and Germany is in a recession. Since now production capacity is overused in Greece and underused in Germany, prices will eventually begin to move.

Prices in Greece start to rise. This harms the international competitiveness of the Greek economy. Exports fall and Greece imports more goods from abroad. There is reduced demand for goods produced in Greece in general, which manifests itself in a shift of Greece's *IS* curve to the left.

The opposite happens in Germany. There is downward pressure on prices. Prices are often not as flexible downwards as upwards. But even if German prices did not fall, Germany's *IS* curve would move to the right, because Greece's products have become more expensive and this channels additional demand towards German products. If prices in Germany actually fall, this only reinforces this process.

Now as soon as prices rise in Greece (and, maybe, fall in Germany) this drives Greek interest rates below Germany's, with the consequence that money flows from Greece to Germany. This shifts the German *LM* curve to the right and Greece's *LM* curve to the left. This may be a bit difficult to trace in our diagram. But we can state the properties of the new long-run equilibrium, where the described process comes to a halt.

1 The Greek *IS* curve is to the left of the *IS* curve that passes through point E. The German *IS* curve is to the right of the *IS* curve that passes through point E.

2 The Greek *LM* curve is to the left of the *LM* curve that passes through point E. The German *LM* curve is to the right of the *LM* curve that passes through point E.

3 *IS* and *LM* curves must intersect on the *EAS* curve, in both countries.

So, in qualitative terms, the new long-run equilibrium is at a point such as F. This new equilibrium has some interesting properties that cannot be read off the diagram. In order to see these, we return to the finger exercise we did with the circular flow identity in Case study 1.2. While it was a pure accounting exercise back then, we now know how the involved macroeconomic variables are determined and related.

Let us look at Greece first. We are interested in how the components related by the circular flow identity changed between the initial long-run equilibrium in C and the new long-run equilibrium in point F. Starting on the right: exports are lower because prices have increased. Hence the minus sign underneath the variable *EX*. For the same reason imports have risen (+). Government spending increased (+), which started the whole process. Taxes have not changed (0). They are a fraction of income, and income is unchanged at potential income at both D and F. Savings are also a fraction of disposable income, which has not changed. So savings have also remained the same (0). The question mark underneath investment means that we are not sure yet about its direction of change, although the graphs seem to indicate that the interest rate increased and, therefore, investment should be lower. We will return to this issue in a minute. The third line reports the change of the three major aggregates in this equation. Net imports increased, that is, the current account deteriorated. Public net savings, or the government budget, also got worse. Since we do not know which of the two changes dominates the other, this does not help us identify what happened to private net savings.

Greece $S - I + T - G + IM - EX = 0$ Circular flow identity

$\underbrace{0 \quad ?}_{?} \quad \underbrace{0 \quad +}_{-} \quad \underbrace{+ \quad -}_{+} = 0$ Direction of change between equilibrium points C and F

Let us now do the same exercise for Germany. Here also, all variables that only depend on income did not change. Exports, the mirror image of Greek imports, rose and imports fell, improving the current account. Since Germany's public spending has not changed and, therefore, its budget did not change, the improved current account must by matched by increased private net savings. At unchanged savings this is only accomplished if investment falls. So investment must be lower, which tells us that the interest rate must be higher. This proves what we already might have read off the diagram.

Germany $S - I + T - G + IM - EX = 0$ Circular flow identity

$\underbrace{0 \quad -}_{+} \quad \underbrace{0 \quad 0}_{0} \quad \underbrace{- \quad +}_{-} = 0$ Direction of change between equilibrium points C and F

We are now in a position to state the main, long-run implications of excessive public spending of a country in a currency union, on the country itself and on other countries. Some of these effects will mirror each other. Others will not.

First, and this is trivial, of course, an increase in government spending worsens the budget situation of the country and its public debt keeps growing. The question under what conditions debt may even increase faster than income will be addressed in Chapter 14. There is no direct effect on the government budgets of other countries in the currency zone.

Second, an increase in government spending has a negative effect on the current account. Thus, the country's external debt, debt *vis-à-vis* other countries, keeps growing. Other countries in the currency zone experience a positive effect on their current account.

Third, there is upward pressure on all country's interest rates in the currency zone, at least as long as the central bank does not respond. This may depress investment and income in the long-run. See also the alternative channel and the arguments we looked at in Chapter 10, section 10.1.

Finally, both higher prices, which are the very cause of a reduced real money supply and higher interest rates, and the tendency of the currency zone's exchange rate to appreciate have an at least temporary negative effect on currency zone members' competitiveness relative to outside countries.

Constraints on fiscal policy: stability pact and no-bailout clauses

The result shown in Figure 12.13 reveals why country A has no sympathy for country B's deficit spending: in a monetary union, one country can resort to expansionary fiscal policy to boost income at home. However, this will depress incomes in other member states. And the long-run perspective developed in Figure 12.14 indicates that eventually the monetary union at large pays a price in the form of higher interest rates, higher prices and structural imbalances that show in widening current account deficits and surpluses.

The prospect that in EMU individual countries may be tempted to discard fiscal discipline in pursuit of national income gains, for which the other members pay a price in the form of recessions and other costs that accrue in the longer run, has motivated the member states to sign a 'Stability and Growth Pact' (for details see Box 12.2). In a nutshell, this agreement permits Belgium (and other members) to resort to deficit spending in excess of 3% of GDP only if it slides into a severe recession of a 2% income contraction within 12 months. Deficit spending in less extreme times would give other members the right to levy a severe fine on Belgium.

Another precaution contained in the Treaty on European Union, signed in Maastricht in 1992, is the **no-bailout clause** which prohibits the European Union, governments, and the ECB from bailing out national governments in the case of default. The idea here is that, as government debt rises relative to GDP as a consequence of extended deficit spending, financial markets will realize that this country's risk of defaulting on its debt or interest payments is increasing and, therefore, attach a risk premium RP for loans to this country. Similar to our discussion of the Asia crisis in Case study 5.1, this modifies the equilibrium condition for the international capital market in our fictional two-country currency union to

$$i_B = i_A + RP_B$$

So, by provoking a higher **default risk**, rising Belgian government debt permits Austrian interest rates i_A to remain below Belgium's because of the Belgian risk premium RP_B. Therefore, the effect shown in Figure 12.13 will be muted. LM_B will not shift as much to the right and LM_A need not shift

BOX 12.2 The Stability and Growth Pact

The original pact

At the December 1996 Dublin summit and subsequent meetings, EU member states agreed on a Pact for Stability and Growth, aimed at ensuring a long-term orientation of fiscal policy. In essence, the pact is to prevent members from running excessive budget deficits. Extending the respective Maastricht criterion into phase 3 of European Monetary Union, the pact for stability and growth begins with the following judgement:

- Government budget deficit ratios smaller than 3% are not excessive.
- Government budget deficit ratios higher than 3% are normally considered excessive, unless the country suffered a serious economic setback.

Whether a serious economic setback has occurred is judged as follows:

- A decline in real GDP of at least 2% (in a year) is always a serious setback.
- A decline in real GDP of less than 0.75% is never a serious setback.
- A decline in real GDP of between 0.75 and 2% of GDP is evaluated for its seriousness on a case-by-case basis by the Council of Ministers (or ECOFIN, the supervisory body).

If a budget deficit is judged excessive, ECOFIN calls upon the member state to take effective measures within four months. Should the member fail to comply with the recommended measures, the Council of Ministers may apply sanctions with a two-thirds majority vote. These include:

- An interest-free deposit of 0.2% of GDP to be paid in the first year of excessive spending.
- In addition, 0.1% of GDP to be paid as a fine for each percentage point beyond the 3% limit.

The sum of both components is not to exceed 0.5% of GDP annually. If after two years the budget deficit is still excessive, the initial deposit of 0.2% of GDP becomes a fine.

The reforms of 2005

On 22–23 March 2005 the European Council agreed on a reform of the Stability and Growth Pact, reflecting recent experiences and changes demanded by a number of EU member states. Under the revision, member states must still keep their public deficits under a 3% deficit/GDP ratio and their debts under a 60% debt/GDP ratio. However, the pact's rules have been made more flexible. Most importantly:

- *Any decline* in real GDP is now considered a serious setback (under which no excessive deficit procedure will be launched), and even a prolonged period of low growth may be.
- When calculating deficits, 'other factors' may be taken into account. Leeway may be given when a country spends on efforts to 'foster international solidarity and to achieving European policy goals, notably the reunification of Europe if it has a detrimental effect on the growth and fiscal burden of a member state'. Such factors might include a country's contributions to the EU budget, certain military spending, or Germany's cost of reunification.
- When a budget deficit is judged excessive, a country has six instead of only four months to take corrective measures. Also, such measures will be judged on the basis of their medium- and long-run effects, even if the immediate consequences may be unfavourable in budgetary terms.

The reforms of 2011

In March 2011, as a response to the European sovereign debt crisis, the EU member states adopted another reform, sometimes referred to as the *Sixpack*, aimed at straightening the rules of the SGP.

Four of the six instruments are used to reform the EU Stability and Growth Pact: by strengthening budgetary surveillance; by providing for an effective enforcement of surveillance; by speeding up sanctions and making them more consistent; and by adjusting national account statistics and forecast practices to comply with EU standards.

The other two instruments address the prevention and correction of macroeconomic imbalances, and the enforcement of corrective measures.

BOX 12.3 **What does the Maastricht Treaty say on bailouts?**

The **Treaty on European Union**, known as the **Maastricht Treaty**, signed on 7 February 1992, contains a controversial **no-bailout clause**. Article 103 prohibits governments and Article 104 prohibits the European Central Bank from coming to the rescue of member states with budget or debt problems:

Article 103, section 1. → There is no bailout from the EU or governments.
The Community shall not be liable for or assume the commitments ... of any Member State.

Article 104, section 1. → There is no bailout from the European Central Bank.
Overdraft facilities ... with the ECB ... in favour of ... Member States shall be prohibited,

as shall the purchase directly from them by the ECB ... of debt instruments.

But then there is Article 100, which is often overlooked. It provides an escape clause that does permit financial assistance under exceptional circumstances.

Article 100, section 2. → There may be a bailout.
Where a Member State is in difficulties ... caused by exceptional occurrences beyond its control, the Council may ... grant ... Community financial assistance to the Member State concerned.

It might be difficult to argue that the real estate and financial crisis of 2007 had not created such exceptional circumstances.

---

as much to the left. This argument rests on the assumption that government bond yields, the interest rates for government bonds, and other interest rates move in step with each other, which very often is the case. We will look at the implications of discarding this assumption in Chapter 15.

The smaller shifts of both *LM* curves is beneficial on two counts: Belgium's income gain remains smaller, making it less tempting to engage in deficit spending in the first place. And Austria's income loss also remains smaller, dampening the repercussions on this country. But while the theoretical implications of a no-bailout clause are undisputed, criticism has emerged on two issues. The first is whether the effect is strong enough to really keep government spending in check. If the government runs a large deficit of 5% of GDP in a given year, raising the ratio of the public debt relative to income from 90% to 95%, is that really going to have a noteworthy impact on the risk premium? The second criticism or caveat concerns the credibility of the no-bailout clause. When push comes to shove, will governments really permit a member to slide into bankruptcy? It is because of such doubts that EU governments considered it wise to augment the already installed no-bailout clause by the Stability and Growth Pact. The wisdom behind this was revealed during the global financial crisis in the Fall of 2008, when, within weeks, huge rescue packages from the international community, including the International Monetary Fund, were needed to save Iceland, Hungary and the Ukraine from going bankrupt.

These packages are dwarfed, of course, by the bailout funds needed during the ensuing Eurozone sovereign debt crisis.

Bottom line

This chapter made the point that the Mundell–Fleming model is capable of sorting out the main policy issues and options in a variety of institutional environments. As an example of a major event that can be accessed by means of this model we looked at the merger of the two Germanies in 1990 and the ensuing crisis in the EMS. Augmented with the insight that policies are endogenous and that policy-makers have incentives of their own, observed policy decisions are easily rationalized. An even closer understanding of the 1992 climax is obtained by detailing the behaviour of exchange rates within target zones. The working of target zones gives credibility and speculation a prominent role and makes exchange rate systems such as the EMS vulnerable to warranted or unwarranted speculative attacks.

We further saw that the Mundell–Fleming model, extended into a two-country version, provides useful insights into the macroeconomics of a currency union such as EMU. In particular, it illustrates the risks of discretionary fiscal policy by individual countries that are created in the short and in the longer run, for other countries and the union as a whole, and the necessity for restrictions.

CHAPTER SUMMARY

- The issues and policy decisions surrounding German unification are clearly identified by means of the Mundell–Fleming model.
- Enjoying the freedom of the nth currency in the EMS, the Bundesbank decided to fight potential inflation, confronting other EMS members with high interest rates.
- High interest rates meant lower aggregate demand for other EMS members. This was least acceptable for those countries already in deep recession. In 1992 this made the United Kingdom the candidate most likely to be the first to suspend membership.
- Exchange rates respond in a less volatile manner to observed changes in economic fundamentals if the central bank is expected to intervene in the foreign exchange market in a stabilizing fashion.
- A target zone like the EMS obliges central banks to intervene when the bounds are hit.
- 'Market psychology', in the sense that speculators spot weaknesses detached from fundamentals, affects exchange rates that are flexible or operate within a band. Therefore irrational speculation may well start an EMS crisis. However, the widely held view that speculation against the pound and the lira during the 1992 crisis was not warranted by fundamentals is not supported by how these two currencies fared after membership in the ERM had been suspended.
- Policy issues in a currency union can be analyzed within a two-country version of the Mundell–Fleming model.
- The European Central Bank controls the money supply in the euro area. It cannot control the money supply in individual member countries – very much like the way the Bank of England cannot control the money supply in Essex, London or the Midlands. Therefore, monetary policy in a currency union affects all members in the same way.
- Expansionary fiscal policy by one member of a currency union has adverse effects on the other members in the short run, and on the entire union in the longer run.

■ Rules as set out in the Stability and Growth Pact, or no-bailout clauses may prevent such policies or dampen their negative effects on others to the extent that they are enforced and credible.

Key terms and concepts

Bretton Woods *344*

convergence criteria *348*

currency crisis *344*

currency (monetary) union *358*

default risk *364*

EMS crisis *344*

euro area *342*

European Economic and Monetary Union (EMU) *358*

European Monetary System (EMS) *341*

Eurozone *342*

exchange rate mechanism (ERM) *341*

foreign exchange market intervention *352*

Maastricht Treaty *350*

managed float *353*

no-bailout clause *364*

*n*th currency *343*

random walk *353*

self-fulfilling prophecy *358*

speculative attacks *356*

Stability and Growth Pact *365*

target zone *354*

EXERCISES

12.1 How would you check whether a country is in charge of the *n*th currency in a system of fixed exchange rates?

12.2 Suppose that a *small* open economy within the EMS went through a transformation similar to that following German unification. How would the course of events differ from that induced by German unification? (Hint: it is crucial to note at the outset what distinguishes a small open from a large economy.)

12.3 Recast the policy issues surrounding German unification and the 1992 EMS crisis in the *DAD-SAS* model. Recall that Germany controls the *n*th currency and thus determines the system's interest and inflation rates.

12.4 Consider the following EU members' exports to Germany as a share of GDP. In the context

of the Mundell–Fleming model, why does this suggest that option #1, to stay in the EMS, was less painful for the Netherlands than it was for Italy, France or the United Kingdom?

	Exports to Germany as share of GDP
NL	0.16
I	0.04
F	0.04
GB	0.03

12.5 In this chapter you were introduced to the concept of a 'random walk' (equation (12.3)). To make this concept less abstract, generate your own random walk over 20 periods. This may be done as follows. Toss a coin and write a '1' if heads occur and '−1' if tails occur. Repeat this and add the result of the second round to the previous outcome (remember that the equation characterizing a random walk was $m = m_{-1} + \nu$, where ν is a random disturbance, i.e. the outcome of tossing a coin, in our case). Toss the coin a third time and add the result, and so on. What specific properties do you observe? (Repeating this exercise may give you an even better idea about the properties of a 'typical' random walk.)

12.6 Recall that in equation (12.1) the exchange rate was described as a weighted average of the money supply and expectations: $e = \alpha m + (1 - \alpha)e_{+1}^e$. We learned that when the central bank is known to intervene in the foreign exchange market after a shock so as to return the exchange rate to target values of 0 in the next period, the exchange rate response line reads $e = \alpha m$. Now suppose the central bank considers $e = 0$ only a long-run target and gives itself more time to reach it.
   (a) What does the exchange rate response line look like graphically when the central bank intervenes less vigorously in the sense described?
   (b) To make it more precise, suppose the central bank always aims at the middle between the exchange rate observed in the last period and the long-run target. So the market always expects the exchange rate $e_{+1}^e = 0.5e$. Derive the exchange rate response line formally for this case.

12.7 Consider the stylized European Economic and Monetary Union comprising only two countries A and B. Suppose LM and IS are subject to occasional stochastic shocks (see our discussion in Box 3.4). Would you recommend the ECB to fix the money supply or to fix the interest rate if it wants to stabilize income? Discuss the issue

under different assumptions about the nature of the shocks, which can be either synchronized (the same in both countries) or country-specific. This yields four constellations you need to discuss as listed in the following matrix:

	LM curve stochastic	IS curve stochastic
Synchronized shocks	(a)	(b)
Country-specific shocks	(c)	(d)

Simplify by ignoring trade and the rest of the world.

12.8 Suppose the two-country currency union discussed in the text is small compared with the rest of the world. How, then, does an increase in Belgium's government spending affect incomes in Belgium and Austria (assume A and B do not trade with each other, but do trade with the rest of the world)
   (a) when the exchange rate versus the rest of the world is flexible?
   (b) when the exchange rate versus the rest of the world is fixed?

12.9 Look at Figure 12.8. Suppose the exchange rate is fully flexible. Draw on this digram the path the exchange rate follows when a bubble starts. Also show what happens when the bubble bursts. Now look at Figure 12.9 and let the current equilibrium be at point A. Under what conditions could an exchange rate bubble start?

12.10 Case study 5.2 discussed the decision of the Swiss National Bank to define a lower boundary of 1.20 for the Swiss franc/euro exchange rate on 6 September 2011. How did this affect the Swiss francs' exchange rate response line? Draw a diagram similar to Figure 12.9.

Online resources

Interactive applet on 2-country Mundell–Fleming model www.eurmacro.eu/tutor/2countrymundellfleming.html
Interactive learning module on macroeconomics of financial crises www.eurmacro.eu/xercises/crisis.html

Self quiz
www.eurmacro.eu/SelfQuiz/sq-ch12.html

Recommended reading

The authority on the early years of German unification is Gerlinde Sinn and Hans-Werner Sinn (1992) *Jumpstart: The Economic Unification of Germany*, Cambridge and London: MIT Press.

On European Monetary Union you may consult Charles Wyplosz (1997) 'EMU: why and how it might happen', *Journal of Economic Perspectives* 11: 3–22.

On target zones see Lars E. O. Svensson (1992) 'An interpretation of recent research on exchange rate target zones', *Journal of Economic Perspectives* 6: 119–44.

Finally, on currency crises and speculation, see Barry Eichengreen, Andrew K. Rose and Charles Wyplosz (1995) 'Exchange market mayhem: antecedents and aftermaths of speculative attacks', *Economic Policy: A European Forum* 21: 251–96.

APPENDIX   The two-country Mundell–Fleming model

The usual perspective taken in this book when analyzing an individual country, the national economy, is that this economy is too small in economic size to have a measurable influence on the rest of the world. Such a small open economy can be analyzed by means of the Mundell–Fleming model, letting the 'world' variables be exogenous. Effects run in one direction only, from the rest of the world to the national economy, but not in reverse.

We took a similar perspective when discussing German unification effects on other EU members, neglecting that developments in France or Britain would feed back on the German economy. This helps simplify the analysis but, while results usually point in the right direction, is not completely accurate. The discussion of fiscal and monetary policy in a monetary union (section 12.3) for the first time explicitly looks at the interaction between two countries of similar size, using a separate Mundell–Fleming model for each country. This type of model is called the **two-country Mundell–Fleming model**.

Because the algebra of the two-country Mundell–Fleming model is cumbersome, the text settles for a graphical analysis. This appendix supplies selected algebraic results for the two-country Mundell–Fleming model that may be used to refine your understanding of how open economies interact under different institutional arrangements. No effort is made to be comprehensive, however. Also, results are only stated rather than derived.

Flexible exchange rates

Model:

$$Y_A = cY_A - bi_A + G_A + x_1Y_B \qquad Y_B = cY_B - bi_B + G_B + m_1Y_A$$
$$+ x_2E - m_1Y_A + m_2E \qquad\qquad - m_2E - x_1Y_B - x_2E$$
$$M_A = kY_A - hi_A \qquad\qquad\qquad M_B = kY_B - hi_B$$

$$i_A = i_B$$

Endogenous: Y_A, Y_B, i_A, i_B, E
Exogenous: M_A, M_B, G_A, G_B

Selected results:

$$Y_A = \frac{h}{2a}(G_A + G_B) + \frac{(1-c)h}{2ak}(M_A - M_B) + \frac{b}{a}M_A$$

$$i_A = i_B = \frac{k}{2a}(G_A + G_B) - \frac{1-c}{2a}(M_A + M_B)$$

with $a \equiv (1-c)h + bk > 0$

Comments: What is new here, compared with the small-country Mundell–Fleming model, is that fiscal policy works: G_A affects Y_A. The reason is that A is now large enough to affect the two countries' common interest rate, so there is no complete crowding out. The effects here are symmetrical: it does not matter in which country government spending or the money supply changes.

Fixed exchange rates (*n*th currency supplied by country B)

Model: same as above
Endogenous: Y_A, Y_B, i_A, i_B, M_A
Exogenous: M_B, E, G_A, G_B

Selected results:

$$Y_A = \frac{bk + h(1 - c - x_1)}{a}G_A + \frac{hx_1 - bk}{a}G_B$$
$$+ \frac{b(1 - c + 2x_1)}{a}M_B + \frac{[h(1-c) + 2bk](x_2 + m_2)}{a}E$$

$$i_A = i_B = \frac{k(1 - c + m_1)}{a}G_B + \frac{km_1}{a}G_A$$
$$- \frac{(1-c)(1 - c + m_1 + x_1)}{a}M_B - \frac{(1-c)(x_2 m_2)k}{a}E$$

with $a \equiv (1-c)(bk + 1 - c + m_1 + x_1) + 2m_1 bk > 0$

Comments: Results are very much in line with what we saw for the small open economy: government spending works, as does monetary policy conducted abroad. The interest rate is dependent on fiscal policy, the money supply in the *n*th-currency-country B, and the exchange rate.

Currency union

Model:

$$Y_A = cY_A - bi_A + G_A + x_1 Y_B \qquad Y_B = cY_B - bi_B + G_B + m_1 Y_A$$
$$- m_1 Y_A \qquad\qquad\qquad - x_1 Y_B$$
$$M_A = kY_A - hi_A \qquad\qquad M_B = kY_B - hi_B$$
$$i_A = i_B$$
$$M = M_A + M_B$$

Endogenous: $Y_A, Y_B, i_A, i_B, M_A, M_B$

Exogenous: M, G_A, G_B

Selected results:

$$Y_A = \frac{bk + 2h(1 - c + x_1)}{a} G_A + \frac{2hx_1 - bk}{a} G_B + \frac{b(1 - c + 2x_1)}{a} M$$

with $\quad a \equiv 2[bk + (1 - c)h](1 - c + m_1 + x_1) > 0$

$$i_A = i_B = \frac{k}{2[bk + (1 - c)h]}(G_A + G_B) - \frac{1 - c}{2[bk + (1 - c)h]} M$$

Comments: Results may be compared with what we discussed in Figure 12.13. There when Belgium raises government spending, interest rates go up. This also shows in the equation. We also found that while Belgian fiscal policy can stimulate Belgian income, this goes at the expense of Austria's income. In the above equation whether an increase in G_B raises or reduces Austrian income depends on the sign of the numerator $2hx_1 - bk$. Note that when we developed the graph we assumed the two countries did not trade, that is we let $x_1 = 0$. Then the effect of an increase of G_B on Y_A is unequivocally negative. If we make x_1 larger, Austrian exports become more dependent on income in Belgium. They thus benefit from a rise in Y_B. Once x_1 is large enough, an increase in Belgian government spending may increase income at home and abroad.

APPLIED PROBLEMS

EMPIRICAL RESEARCH

Intervention in the foreign exchange market

When central banks buy or sell foreign currency they intervene in the foreign exchange market. While they are obliged to do so under fixed exchange rates or within target zones, such as the EMS, they have been found to intervene voluntarily when exchange rates are officially flexible. The question of whether they intervene just to smooth the path of the exchange rate or in order to drive the exchange rate towards some perceived target exchange rate interested researchers in the 1980s. My paper 'Intervention policy under floating exchange rates: An analysis of the Swiss case' (*Economica* 54, 1987, pp. 439–53) reports the estimation equation

$$I_t = -9.92 - 0.10(e_t - e_{Target})$$
$$\quad\quad (7.74) \quad (2.38)$$
$$R^2_{adj} = 0.75 \quad \text{Monthly data 1974.01–1984.06}$$

where I is intervention as measured by the change in foreign exchange reserves of the Swiss National Bank, e is the Swiss francs per dollar exchange rate and e_{Target} is a presumed exchange rate target assumed to be the average real exchange rate of 1973. The significant coefficient of -0.1 suggests that if the exchange rate was considered too low, the Swiss National Bank sold dollars.

The paper also reports the equation

$$I_t = -10.49 - 0.39\,\varepsilon_t \quad R^2_{adj} = 0.75$$
$$\quad\quad (8.24) \quad (2.17)$$

Monthly data 1974.01–1984.06

where ε is the rate of depreciation. The significant negative coefficient of 0.39 (with a t-statistic of 2.17) suggests that whenever the Swiss franc depreciated (appreciated), the central bank sold (bought) dollars.

So it appears that the Swiss central bank's foreign exchange market interventions reflect two motives, 'exchange rate targeting', as suggested by the first equation, and what is called 'leaning against the wind', as suggested by the second equation.

WORKED PROBLEM

Interest rates and inflation

It is sometimes argued that of the two Maastricht criteria on inflation and interest rates, one is redundant. This is because, according to the Fisher equation, nominal interest rates simply contain an inflation premium over a (presumably constant) real interest rate:

Interest rate = constant + inflation rate

We may use the data in Table 12.3 on government bond yields and inflation to check the validity of the Fisher equation. The resulting regression equation is:

$$\text{INTEREST} = 5.32 + 1.32 \text{ INFLATION } R^2_{adj} = 0.83$$
$$(8.96) \quad (8.45)$$

83% of the differences in long-term nominal interest rates are explained by differences in inflation. The equation contains two interesting messages about real interest rates. First, they are currently very high. If a country had zero inflation, nominal (which then equals real) interest rates would stand at 5.32. Nominal interest rates do not vary with inflation with a factor of 1. The estimated coefficient of 1.32 suggests that nominal

interest rates go up faster than inflation, which makes real interest rates higher at higher inflation. To test whether 1.32 is significantly larger than 1, we may test 1.32 against the null hypothesis that the true coefficient is 1. To obtain an appropriate t-statistic we compute $1.32 - 1 = 0.32$ and divide this by the standard error, which is $1.32/8.45 = 0.17$. So the t-statistic for 1.32 against the null of 1 is $0.32/0.17 = 2.1$.

YOUR TURN

Are business cycles out of sync?

The Fisher equation is a long-run or equilibrium relationship between i and π. At potential income (on *EAS*), when the business cycle is in 'neutral', the real interest rate is constant. During a boom inflation rises more than nominal interest rates, and real interest rates fall. During recessions real interest rates rise. Use this information and the data given in the worked problem above to check whether in 1995 your country was in the same phase of the business cycle as the others. The general idea is to find out whether your country's interest rate was significantly higher or lower than the interest rate proposed by the estimated Fisher equation. (Hint: To find out whether Sweden's interest rate is exceptionally high or low, construct a dummy variable that is 1 for Sweden and 0 for all other countries. Then check whether this dummy variable's coefficient is significant.)

Table 12.3

Country	A	B	DK	SF	F	D	GR	IRL	I	LUX	NL	P	E	S	GB
Interest rate (in %)	7.3	7.9	8.6	9.4	7.8	7.1	18.4	8.5	12.3	6.2	7.2	11.7	11.5	10.7	8.4
Inflation rate (in %)	2.5	1.6	2.2	1.3	1.7	2.2	9.9	2.6	4.7	2.1	2.2	4.2	4.7	2.6	3.3

Inflation and central bank independence

What to expect

After working through this chapter, you will understand:

1 What can be done in practical terms to reduce a country's inflation bias.

2 What role central bank independence plays (and the EMS played) in improving inflation performance.

3 Why having the most independent central bank, in a country or as the leader in a fixed rate system or currency union, may not be the best choice for a country that expects to be hit by occasional supply shocks.

4 Why Germany and Switzerland lost substantially more income during the 1974 oil price explosion than Britain and France.

5 That disinflation costs are measured by the sacrifice ratio, and how the latter is computed.

6 How much it typically costs to lower inflation by one percentage point, in euros, dollars, francs, pounds or other currencies.

7 The rationale behind the Maastricht criteria on interest rates and inflation that paved the way to European Monetary Union.

Inflation is a political phenomenon, much less an economic one. From an economic perspective we know how to avoid inflation and how to reduce it. In the short run, outside influences on inflation that escape the control of policy-makers may interfere. But beyond that, if inflation does not disappear in the medium and long run, it is not because we do not *know how* to get rid of it, but because we do not *want* to get rid of it. Well, even the last statement is not quite accurate: we may want to get rid of it, but short-run incentives prevent us from following through. Very much like an overweight person may want to shed weight, and know quite well how to. But the immediate though temporary gratification from nutrition sins may prevent the person from achieving his or her goal.

Key building blocks of the political economy of inflation have already been discussed in Chapter 11. They feature prominently in academic discussions of **European monetary integration**. Both the blueprint for the European Central Bank and the merits of the EMS are mostly evaluated in terms of how they affect **inflation performance**. This chapter picks up the tools provided in Chapter 11 and examines how the institutional setting in which central banks operate affects inflation performance. The interrelationship between *central bank independence*, the *exchange rate system* and inflation will be discussed from a refined theoretical perspective. This perspective will be put to use in a number of case studies and more general attempts to understand real-world experience with inflation and how to fight it.

13.1   Inflation, central bank independence and the EMS

A major insight developed in Chapter 11 was that a country's average level of inflation may be much higher than the level that society (and the policy-maker) would like. The size of this **inflation bias**, which is caused by the **time inconsistency** of monetary policy, is determined by three factors:

1 The policy-maker's **preferences**, as represented graphically by his or her indifference curves.
2 **Instrument potency**, the discretionary leeway that the policy-maker has in using monetary policy.
3 The **constraint** imposed by the macroeconomy on the policy-maker's choices, in the form of the slope of the *SAS* curve.

Chapter 11 has already discussed these factors. We now move on to look at them in more detail, one at a time, and then proceed to present some empirical implications and confront them with data.

Preferences

In Chapter 11, with regard to preferences, we noted that the *government* is likely to gain more from surprise inflation than the *central bank*. The reason is that, while both institutions may applaud the achieved income gains to the same extent, there are added bonuses that accrue only for the government. The most important one is that surprise inflation *reduces the government's real debt*. Since this reduces interest payments to service old debt, and provides an opening for incurring new debt, extra latitude is provided for government spending. Another bonus is that by making the central bank buy government bonds, thus creating money and inflation, the government can *finance part of its spending*. As a result, the government's indifference curve in inflation–income space is usually steeper than that of the central bank. Figure 13.1 illustrates this.

Whether actual monetary policy reflects the steep indifference curve of the government or the flat indifference curve of the central bank depends on how much independence the central bank enjoys from the government. This

> Central bank independence measures the extent to which the central bank may conduct monetary policy without having to respond to what the government wants.

central bank independence does not only come in black and white: it is observed along a continuum between the extremes. This means that the indifference curves that effectively drive monetary policy also have many different slopes. They turn flatter as the central bank's independence gradually increases. Hand in hand with this comes a reduction of the inflation bias. The bottom line is that *countries with more independent central banks should feature lower average inflation rates*. Figure 13.2 presents some data on this issue and underlines that the reality conforms quite well with this implication of our model.

It plots average inflation in eighteen countries against a measure of central bank independence. At one extreme, this measure assigns values of 13

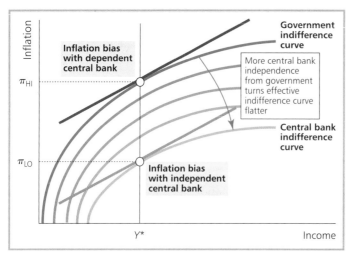

Figure 13.1 Governments benefit from surprise inflation not only because it boosts income, but also because it reduces real government debt. In addition, governments can raise income by creating inflation. This tends to make a government's indifference curve steeper than a central bank's, yielding a higher inflation bias. Making the central bank more independent flattens the effective indifference curve and lowers inflation.

Empirical note. Some 60% of the differences between the average inflation rates observed in industrial countries is explained by differences in the independence of their central banks.

and 12 to the highly independent central banks of Germany and Switzerland. On average these countries experienced inflation rates of about 4% between 1973 and the mid-1990s. At the other extreme, a value of 3 is assigned to the most government-dependent central bank of New Zealand (but see Case study 13.1!). New Zealand's and other only slightly more independent central banks, like Italy's and Spain's, before they adopted the euro generated average inflation rates between 10% and 12%. All the other countries with central bank independence between these extreme values also feature inflation rates between the extremes.

In support of our theoretical arguments, the lesson taught by real-world experience appears to be a simple one: in order to permanently enjoy a substantially improved inflation performance, all a country needs to do is rewrite its central bank law. So why do not all countries simply do this? The answer to this question consists of three parts and will occupy us throughout this chapter.

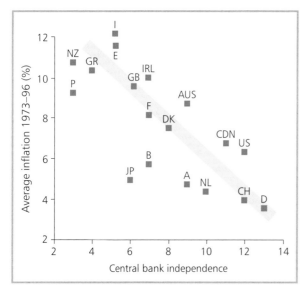

Figure 13.2 The figure shows average inflation between 1973 and 1996 to be negatively correlated with the independence of a country's central bank.

Sources: IMF, *IFS* – for inflation; and for CBI – V. Grilli, D. Masciandaro and G. Tabellini (1991) 'Political and monetary institutions and public finance policies in the industrial countries', *Economic Policy* 13: 341–92.

CASE STUDY 13.1   New Zealand's Reserve Bank Act: a case from down under

Being fed up with one of the worst inflation performances among industrial countries, in late 1984 New Zealand's incoming government directed the central bank to reduce inflation. After some success in the following years albeit at the cost of rising unemployment, this new objective was formalized in a new Reserve Bank Act in 1989. The Act directs the central bank to focus monetary policy exclusively on achieving and maintaining stability in the general level of prices. This goal is to be specified in a Policy Targets Agreement (PTA) to be negotiated between the minister of finance and the central bank governor who is to be appointed or reappointed.

The first PTA was signed on 2 March 1990. The agreement provided that an inflation rate between 0% and 2% was to be achieved by December 1992. Failure to achieve the goal formulated in the PTA could invoke the dismissal of the governor.

In terms of our standard graph this PTA made the central bank governor's indifference curves virtually horizontal at an inflation rate of 2%. As Figure 13.3 illustrates, an SAS curve now touches a kinked indifference curve on the EAS curve at $\pi = 2$. Assuming that control over inflation is not perfect, it is to be expected that the central bank will play it safe by keeping inflation well inside the target zone, around 1%.

Figure 13.4 illustrates the effect that the new Reserve Bank Act had on inflation. It shows that New Zealand had been on a disinflation path since the mid-1980s. The light blue zone indicates the inflation target range as laid down in the first PTA signed in 1990 and as confirmed or modified in subsequent

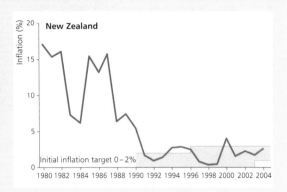

Figure 13.4
Source: IMF, *IFS*.

PTAs agreed upon in the Decembers of 1990, 1992, 1996, 1997 and 1999, and in September 2002. The initial target range for price stability of 0–2% was to be achieved by December 1992. When a new government was elected in October 1990, the PTA was renegotiated. And in the light of the Gulf crisis, the deadline for achievement of price stability was extended by twelve months until December 1993. The central bank achieved the target well ahead of this deadline – but missed it completely in 1994, 1995 and 1996. The answer to why Reserve Bank governor Donald T. Brash remained in office sheds some light on the practical problems with inflation targets, and reveals some rather amusing semantics.

From the beginning, the central bank questioned whether consumer price inflation (which is shown in Figure 13.4 and is called 'headline inflation') was really the appropriate measure of inflation performance. Instead, it eventually succeeded in having inflation performance gauged by a new rate called 'underlying inflation' which ignores inflation in certain sectors or categories and is typically lower than consumer price inflation. The Reserve Bank Act permits such loopholes. Others are that the price stability target may be renegotiated if indirect taxes change, if the terms of trade change significantly, or after a domestic crisis such as a natural disaster. What is more, the government may always order the central bank to change the inflation target, but must do so publicly and discuss reasons in parliament.

When even with this adjusted inflation rate the target was still missed in 1994, 1995 and 1996, the next PTA, signed in December 1996 featured a new definition of price stability including the 0–3% range

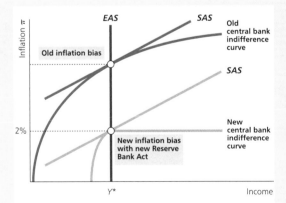

Figure 13.3

Case study 13.1 continued

of inflation. After some successful years this new target was missed again in 2000, when December prices were 4% higher than those in 1999. However, Dr Brash survived this as well.

Another interesting aspect is how not only the definition of price stability evolved through successive PTAs, but also its weight and relation to other macroeconomic goals. In the 1990 and 1992 contracts, price stability was the only goal the Reserve Bank had to pursue. Nothing else existed. The PTA said that it should 'implement monetary policy with the intention of achieving/maintaining a stable general level of prices'.

The 1996 and 1997 contracts recognized that other macroeconomic goals existed by speaking of 'maintaining a stable general level of prices, so that monetary policy can make its maximum contribution to sustainable economic growth, employment and development opportunities within the New Zealand economy'. The implication is that, yes, these other goals exist, but we serve them best by maintaining price stability.

The December 1999 PTA goes one step further by stipulating: 'In pursuing its price stability objective, the Bank . . . shall seek to avoid unnecessary instability in output, interest rates and the exchange rate.' This brings further macroeconomic variables into the picture and cautions the Reserve Bank to keep an active eye on the short-run side effects of monetary policy on these.

The most recent PTA was signed on 23 September 2002 by Donald Brash's successor, Dr Alan Bollard. It brought two more noteworthy changes. First, the inflation target zone was narrowed from 0–3% to 1–3%, conceding that very low inflation rates may actually harm economic growth. Second, the target now needs to be met 'on average over the medium term', and not on an annual basis any longer, thereby giving the Reserve Bank more flexibility to respond to shocks in the economy.

Further reading: The Reserve Bank of New Zealand home page at **www.rbnz.govt.nz** provides much more information on this experience including the full-length PTAs.

First, a number of countries have indeed taken pertinent steps in recent years. One example comprises EU member states, which were required by the Maastricht Treaty to make their central banks more independent as a move towards EMU. Other countries like Canada, Great Britain and New Zealand have adopted **inflation targets**. As Case study 13.1 illustrates, this also makes central bank indifference curves flatter at a defined threshold.

Second, a perfect inflation performance brought about by a completely independent central bank comes with a price tag that scares some governments away. We will look at this in section 13.2, where we permit the economy to be hit by occasional **shocks to aggregate supply**.

Third, the transition from a high-inflation equilibrium to a low-inflation equilibrium may be accompanied by income losses and thus be quite painful. Section 13.3 looks into these **disinflation costs**.

Instrument potency

Instrument potency, the policy-maker's control over the money supply, may be removed in one of two ways.

Monetary policy may be required by law (or, as some have demanded, by the constitution) to follow a specific rule that simply leaves no room for discretion. This rule may come in the form of a **fixed rule** that specifies, say, 3%

for annual money growth. We mentioned in Chapter 11 that Nobel laureate Milton Friedman had long advocated this type of rule. Alternatively, a **contingent rule** could make money growth dependent on the state of the economy. An example of such a contingent rule would be $\mu = Y^* - Y$, stating that if income Y falls short of equilibrium income Y^* by x units, money supply growth μ must equal $x\%$ also. While the optimal nature of such rules is discussed quite seriously in academic journals, and empirical studies often find that the Taylor rule seems to predict monetary policy quite well, no country seems to have taken any pertinent steps yet to implement such a rule formally.

A second way to deprive the domestic policy-maker of monetary instrument potency is by **pegging the currency** to some foreign currency, thus virtually handing monetary policy over to the foreign central bank. These days many countries endorse this option. It can, in fact, be done without the consent of the other country. According to the International Monetary Fund (IMF), in 2008 only 84 out of 188 countries covered had not pegged their currency in one form or other to one or more foreign currencies. And only 40 of those were committed to market-determined, flexible exchange rates. Out of those 40 countries (which include Albania, the Czech Republic, Hungary, Iceland, Norway, Poland, Sweden, Switzerland, the UK and Turkey from Europe) many still intervened in the foreign exchanges on occasion in order to prevent undue fluctuations (see Case study 5.2). The remaining 104 countries on which the IMF reports, seriously limited exchange rate movement by arrangements from a spectrum of possibilities that reach from the outright adoption of a foreign currency via a currency board to crawling pegs.

A prominent European example of pegging the exchange rate is the European Monetary System. It played a major role from 1979 onwards as a forerunner to EMU, and its successor, ERM II, is designed to facilitate the monetary integration of new entrants into the European Union and EMU. To learn from this experience, we will now take a closer look at how inflation is determined in such a multi-currency system and then bring together the obtained insights with the involved countries' inflation performance.

Travelling back in time to the pre-euro era, suppose two economies, Germany and Italy, are evaluating plans to form a currency union. The motivation is that, instead of making its own central bank more independent, Italy may hand monetary policy over to the very independent Bundesbank, and thus be rewarded with the lower German inflation bias. Germany would keep the same inflation as before and does not seem to gain anything. It is therefore hard to see Germany's motivation for getting involved in such a currency union and assuming the role of the nth country. This becomes even more puzzling if we look at how the exchange rate system affects the constraint, the *SAS* curve.

The constraint

When a country moves from flexible to fixed exchange rates, its *SAS* curve becomes flatter when drawn onto a $\pi = Y$ diagram. To acquire an intuitive understanding of this, we need to distinguish between consumer prices and producer prices.

The consumer price index measures how much a typical 'basket of consumption goods' costs in a particular country. This basket comprises goods

---

The Taylor rule reads $i = i^{\text{target}} + 0.5(\pi - \pi^{\text{target}}) + 0.5(Y - Y^*)$ with Y^* indexed to 100. Then the income gap $Y - Y^*$ is in per cent. Instead, the income gap can be written as $\ln Y - \ln Y^*$.

A currency board fixes a country's exchange rate and maintains total backing of its money supply with foreign exchange.

Under a crawling peg the exchange rate is adjusted periodically in small, preannounced steps.

The consumer price index measures the price of a fixed basket of consumption goods, part of which is produced domestically, and part of which is imported.

The producer price index measures the average price of goods and services produced domestically.

produced at home and goods produced abroad. Consumer price inflation affects the buying power of nominal income. It is therefore the relevant inflation rate in the public support function. The producer price index measures how much producers receive for the goods and services produced at home. Only as producer prices inflate unexpectedly will output and income rise. Producer price inflation is the relevant inflation rate in the *SAS* curve.

In a two-country world with Germany and Italy, consumer price inflation is a weighted average of the inflation of goods produced in Germany π_D and of goods produced in Italy π_I. The latter we must transfer into Deutschmarks, so we must add the rate of depreciation ε. This yields

$$\pi = \alpha\pi_D + (1 - \alpha)\varepsilon + (1 - \alpha)\pi_I \qquad \text{Index of consumer price inflation}$$

where α is the share of home-produced goods in the German consumption basket.

Under fixed exchange rates a surprise increase of German consumer price inflation π, say, from 0% to 10%, increases both the price of goods produced in Germany (which we assume to possess the nth currency) and of Italian goods by $\pi_D = \pi_I = 10\%$; $\varepsilon = 0$ by definition. If exchange rates are flexible, the same German consumer price inflation leads to a smaller change of German producer prices of, say, $\pi_D = 5\%$. The reason is the depreciation of the real exchange rate, which requires the nominal exchange rate to rise by 15%, if we suppose $\alpha = 0.5$. But since only the 5% increase of home-produced goods induces producers to raise output, the output increase will be smaller than under fixed exchange rates, when home goods prices rose by 10%. As a result, *the SAS curve is steeper under flexible exchange rates.* This effect is more pronounced if the economy is more open, that is if α is smaller. Then the share of foreign goods in the domestic price index becomes larger, and *exchange rate overshooting* drives an even larger wedge between π and π_D.

Figure 13.5 summarizes the effect of institutional factors on the slope of the *SAS* curve.

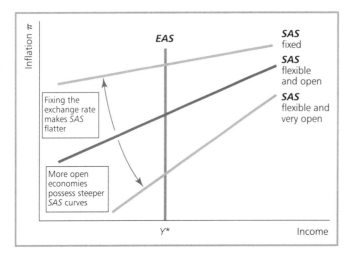

Figure 13.5 A country with flexible exchange rates has moderately sloped *SAS* curves, such as the dark blue one if it fixes the re-exchange rate, and assumes the role of the *n*th currency. *SAS* curves become flatter. If exchange rates are flexible and the economy becomes more open, the *SAS* curves become steeper.

Figure 13.6 *SAS* curves are steeper under flexible exchange rates (dark lines) than under fixed ones (lighter lines). Germany's (Italy's) inflation bias is π_D (π_I) when rates are flexible and π_{DEMS} (π_{IEMS}) when rates are fixed. If the lira becomes the *n*th currency in the EMS, both countries' inflation performance deteriorates to π_{IEMS}. If the mark becomes the *n*th currency, Germany's performance deteriorates, but Italy's improves.

We are now equipped to discuss the stylized choices facing Germany and Italy. These are sketched in Figure 13.6.

If Germany and Italy fix the exchange rate and Italy provides the currency anchor (the *n*th currency), the system's inflation bias is π_{IEMS}. This would make both countries worse off. If Germany provides the anchor, the systems bias is lower at π_{DEMS}. Now Italy gains in the form of a large reduction of its average rate of inflation. Germany's inflation performance deteriorates, though probably by much less than Italy's performance improves. In any case, Germany is probably only prepared to pay this price if Italy offers concessions in other areas.

Figure 13.6 displays only asymmetric solutions, in the sense that one country sets or dominates monetary policy in the system. Alternatively, and this is the vision that the founders of the EMS put on paper, a system could be symmetric. The member states were supposed to cooperate and share the burden of adjustment to a common policy. In terms of Figure 13.6, such a symmetric system would produce an inflation rate higher than that obtained under German leadership. As measured by average inflation, this would make both Germany and Italy worse off. It does not come as a surprise, therefore, that the member states eventually put their own spin on the EMS blueprint, implicitly agreeing on an asymmetric solution that, at least at that time, was considered beneficial to all participants.

A currency union between two countries is obviously only feasible if the inflation bias of the high inflation country under flexible exchange rates is higher than the inflation bias that the low inflation country is likely to produce under fixed exchange rates. For this to be the case, preferences must differ substantially. This provides a simple explanation for the fact that Switzerland had much less interest in entering the EMS than, say, Ireland or Italy.

A quick transition from the high inflation equilibrium of the country that abandons monetary autonomy to the *n*th currency's low inflation equilibrium can only be expected in the ideal case of an irrevocably fixed exchange rate. Target zones, as the $\pm 6\%$ band operational for the lira until 1990, provided some temporary leeway. Resorting to occasional realignments even provided a permanent one. Figure 13.7 may help to judge the EMS's success in bringing down inflation.

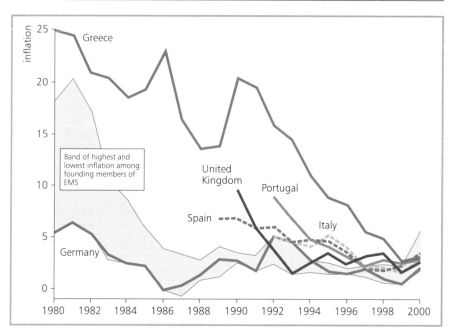

Figure 13.7 The graph shows that inflation rates of the EMS founding members that remained in the ERM have converged (blue band). The inflation rates of Portugal, Spain and the United Kingdom were also drawn onto or into the band after they joined the ERM. This took much longer for Greece, which did not join the ERM until March 1998. Italy and the United Kingdom drifted out of the band for a while after 1992.
Source: IMF, IFS.

The light blue band area shows the spread in the inflation rates in the founding members of the EMS between 1980 and 1995. This spread has systematically narrowed and moved closer to a virtually unchanged lower limit. In addition to the spread, inflation in six countries is highlighted. One is Germany, which has formed or been near the lower limit throughout. Three others are Portugal, Spain and the United Kingdom, which joined the ERM at a later stage. Their inflation performance is shown beginning with the year in which they joined. Another is Italy, which was a founding member. Its inflation rate is shown from 1992, the year in which it suspended membership in the ERM. Finally, Greek inflation is shown for contrast, to exemplify inflation outside the ERM.

The graph conveys these messages, all of which are in line with the theoretical propositions discussed above:

1 Inflation in the countries that launched the EMS in 1979 had converged toward its lower end. The lower end has mostly been provided by German inflation. This suggests that the Deutschmark was the *n*th currency, a role carved out by mutual consent among the partners.
2 Countries that joined the ERM at a later date saw their inflation rates, if not within the band already, being sucked into or onto the narrowing band of the initial members.
3 Countries that suspended membership in the ERM – Britain and Italy did so on 16 September 1992 – found their inflation rates drifting out of the EMS band, if only temporarily so.

A puzzling observation, though, was Ireland's inflation rate of 5.4% in 2000, quite visibly higher than those of other euro area members. It remained about twice as high as in the euro area for another three years. But, as our model suggests, this could not last. So Irish inflation was down to 2.3% in 2004 compared to 2.1% in the euro area.

Bottom line

From the perspective of price stability the best thing a country can do is one of the following:

1 bind its central bank by a zero inflation rule;
2 appoint the most conservative (that is, inflation-averse) central banker possible;
3 make its central banker as independent from the government as possible; or
4 peg the exchange rate to the currency of a country with one or more of the above features.

It appears that a central bank can never be too conservative, and is never independent enough. The next section puts this result in perspective. In a world in which unexpected things happen all the time, a central bank may indeed be too independent.

13.2 Supply shocks and central bank independence

So far we have discussed the political economy of inflation in an environment with no uncertainty. But what happens if outside events, beyond the direct control of the policy-maker, hit the economy unexpectedly? Due to their surprise nature, such events cannot be built into recent wage contracts. Thus they are bound to displace the labour market and the entire economy from equilibrium. In such a situation, might a country regret having a central bank committed (by a rule, by virtue of a fixed rate, or because of its preferences) to the goal of price stability only? Wouldn't it be nice, at least in such a situation, to have a central bank that strikes a balance between the income (and unemployment) consequences and the inflationary effects of such a shock? This section discusses these issues.

An archetypal example of an adverse supply shock is the oil price explosion that occurred in the wake of the 1973 Middle East crisis. By 1974 oil prices, which had been fairly stable for decades, were more than four times as high as in 1973. Since rising oil or other materials prices push up the production costs for each additional unit of output produced, firms will scale down production in order not to incur losses. At any given price level, and in a given period at any given rate of inflation, firms produce less than they did before the increase in oil prices. So the quadrupling of oil prices pushed the *SAS* curve to the left. (If the price increase is permanent, it might also shift the *EAS* curve. We need not consider this here since we are are only looking at the short-run effects and choices.) The post-shock aggregate supply curve displays the central bank's options (see Figure 13.8).

A neutral option is to keep money growth unchanged. This leaves *DAD* in its old position and moves the economy up *DAD* to point B, thus splitting the

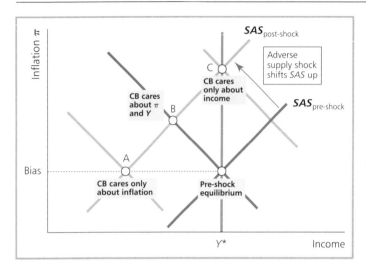

Figure 13.8 The economy starts from the indicated pre-shock equilibrium. An adverse shock to aggregate supply, such as an increase of oil prices, shifts the *SAS* curve left. If money growth remains unchanged, the economy moves to B. A central bank (CB) that only cares about inflation reduces money growth to obtain A. A central bank that does not want income to fall raises money growth to obtain C.

repercussions of the shock into an effect on income and an effect on inflation. Instead, a so-called *hard-nosed* central bank with extreme inflation aversion would permit no inflation. By topping the negative supply shock with a reduction of money growth *DAD* moves down, causing a large recession at point A. Finally, a so-called *wet* central bank would accept no decrease of income. It accommodates the negative supply shock with an acceleration of money growth. This moves *DAD* up, keeping income unchanged at the cost of substantial inflation at point C.

Figure 13.9 shows the income and inflation responses to the 1974 shock in six industrial countries. Response patterns are similar in many respects. In 1974 and 1975 all income growth rates were substantially below previous experience. This is what happens in a growing economy if we move to the left

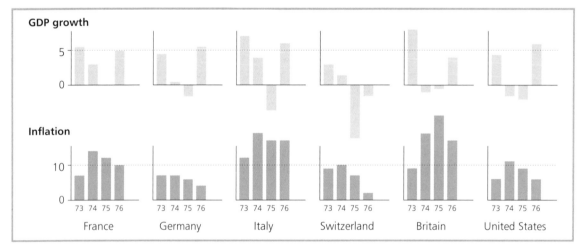

Figure 13.9 The figure shows income growth and inflation at the time of the 1974 oil price explosion in six countries. While France, Italy and Britain permitted inflation to rise substantially and permanently, the other three countries did not. (Germany and Switzerland even came out of the shock with lower inflation than they had before.) It appears as if the first three countries prevented growth from falling as much as it did in the other three.

Source: IMF, *IFS*.

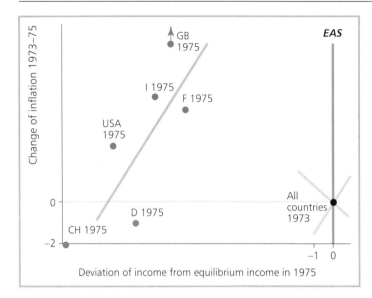

Figure 13.10 In a stylized interpretation, countries were on *EAS* in 1973, prior to the first oil price shock. In 1975 the countries were in the positions marked by blue dots. Shades of *SAS* and *DAD* curves insinuate an interpretation of the six countries' choices in the context of the theoretical framework given in Figure 13.8.

Source: IMF, *IFS*.

of Y^*. In most cases growth was even negative. Finally, with the exception of Switzerland, growth was back to normal by 1976. Inflation experience is a bit more diverse. While most countries apparently accommodated the oil price shock by allowing inflation to increase dramatically, Germany and Switzerland kept a lid on inflation and even ended up with lower inflation after the shock.

Figure 13.10 combines the six countries' income and inflation experiences into a standardized π-Y diagram. For easier comparability, all countries are given a common point of departure for 1973. The vertical axis then measures by how much inflation *changed* in each country from 1973 to 1975. The horizontal axis measures the difference between actual and potential income in 1975.

The countries' positions relative to their situations in 1973 indicate a positively sloped line. In accord with the *DAD-SAS* model, those countries that permitted the smallest increase in inflation experienced the most severe income losses. Even more interestingly from the perspective of this chapter, the six countries' choices are readily explained by reference to the degree of independence of their central banks. The most independent central banks of Germany and Switzerland drove inflation even further down during the crisis, accepting the largest recessions. A small inflation rise was tolerated by the US Federal Reserve System, which is considered slightly less independent than the Bundesbank and the Swiss National Bank. Higher inflation was generated by the decidedly more government-dependent central banks of France, Italy and Britain, thus achieving a much smaller recession.

It is quite possible that the Germans and the Swiss would have benefited from having a less hard-nosed central bank in this extraordinary situation, one that would have permitted some inflation just this once. But if you have such a government-dependent central bank when a shock hits, you also have it when there are no shocks. That means you also have a higher inflation bias generally. So one must balance these two effects. The choice is affected by how frequently shocks hit the economy. The more often they hit, the more we would like the central bank to take proper care of it. But if we expect shocks to hit frequently and the central bank to respond with inflation, this again affects the inflation bias and may render stimulation ineffective when a shock hits. So the choice is obviously a complicated one and we need to go back to the drawing board and work out the theoretical argument with proper care.

As a first step we need to consider the preferences of voters, governments and central banks. Until now we had assumed that higher income was *always* preferred to lower income. One might question the generality of this assertion for the following reason.

Let the economy be at full employment output $Y^*_{classical}$ as carved out by a competitive labour market. Then surprise inflation could make income rise still further along the *SAS* curve, but only by making people work at real wages at which they actually would have preferred not to work. This makes income increases beyond $Y^*_{classical}$ undesirable. So we may suppose the preference functions of the government, the public and the central bank to be of the general form (where Y^d stands for desirable income which is identical to $Y^*_{classical}$):

$$s = \bar{s} - 0.5\pi^2 - 0.5\beta(Y - Y^d)^2 \qquad \text{Society's preferences} \quad (13.1)$$

This new formulation stresses that public support for the government (or central bank utility) falls at an accelerating rate as either of two bads increases: inflation or the deviation of output from the desired full employment level. Indifference curves in this slightly more complex case are ellipse shaped around the most preferred point $\pi = 0$ and $Y = Y^d$ as shown in Figure 13.11. In the area to the left of desired income Y^d indifference curves look much the same as those employed in Chapter 11. Only as we move to the right of Y^d do things change. As long as the kind of real rigidities discussed in Chapter 6 keep potential income Y^* *below* desired income Y^d, all our insights obtained with the simpler preference function in Chapter 11 continue to apply.

Note a difference in the **government reaction function**, however. This function was horizontal in Chapter 11, meaning that the government would always respond with the same inflation rate once expectations had been formed. With our new refined preference function, the government reaction curve is negatively sloped, as Figure 13.11 illustrates. The economic rationale is that

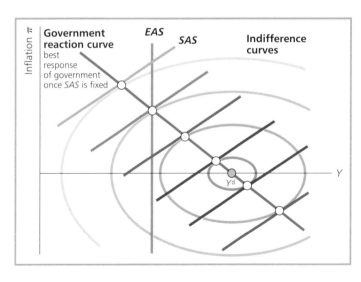

Figure 13.11 If the public prefers higher income only up to a point Y^d, iso-support curves are ellipse shaped, with $\pi = 0$ and $Y = Y^d$ at their centre. For any given *SAS* curve, optimal inflation is given by the point where *SAS* touches an indifference curve. Connecting these points gives a falling government reaction curve. Flatter ellipses, reflecting more concern for inflation, yield flatter reaction curves.

further income gains become successively less tempting as we move closer to desired income. Once desired income is reached, no further increases are desired, and no price in the form of inflation will be paid. As long as $Y^* < Y^d$, however, an inflation bias obtains in equilibrium (which is where the government reaction function intersects *EAS*).

Now suppose that the government's and the public's preferences are identical and may be represented by the ellipses in Figure 13.11. By handing monetary policy over to an *independent central banker with ultra-conservative preferences*, this country has eliminated inflation. Let the central banker's preferences be so flat that they permit no trade-off of inflation for more income. This central banker chooses zero inflation, which is the optimal equilibrium choice from society's viewpoint.

Now let the country be hit by a negative supply shock that shifts the *SAS* curve to the left (see Figure 13.12, which replicates the scenario of Figure 13.8). Since the central banker's overriding goal is to keep inflation at zero, his or her reaction is to reduce the money supply, shift down the aggregate demand curve, driving income down to point A. This is not society's preferred reaction, however. The public's preferences would have been served best by moving up along the *SAS* curve to B, the point of tangency with its own indifference curve. In this way the supply shock would have created a smaller recession at the cost of some inflation. So in this one instance the public would have been better off with a not-so-independent (or less conservative) central bank.

It would be premature to generalize from this example that central banks should not be too independent after all. If this kind of shock occurs frequently, the labour market would build the anticipated reaction of the not-so-independent central bank into inflation expectations, shifting the *SAS* curve upwards. The result would be a not-so-favourable trade-off.

To arrive at a more general result, we need to make some assumptions about how often supply shocks occur. Let the *SAS* curve have slope 1 and be affected by a shock σ:

$$\pi = \pi^e + Y - Y^* - \sigma \qquad \text{Stochastic } SAS \text{ curve} \quad (13.2)$$

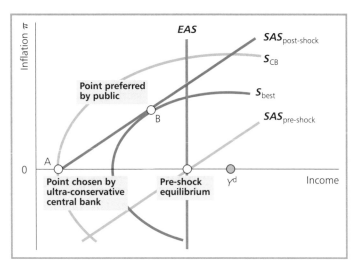

Figure 13.12 An adverse supply shock shifts *SAS* to the post-shock position. An ultra-conservative CB permits no inflation and steers the economy into point A. This gives the public the utility level s_{CB}. Less conservative choices further up on the post-shock *SAS* curve would have put society on higher utility levels. The best point would have been B.

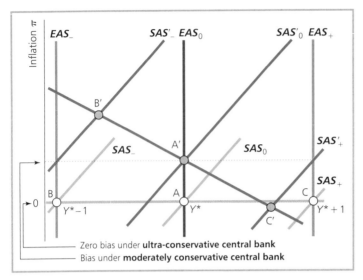

Figure 13.13 Shocks put potential income to Y^*, $Y^* + 1$ and $Y^* - 1$, each in one-third of all cases. The ultra-conservative CB never permits inflation, which puts the economy into points A, B or C. The moderately conservative CB's reaction function slopes down to the right (blue line). Its average inflation rate (or bias) puts SAS curves up (dark blue lines). Optimal responses in the three possible cases are A', B' and C', respectively.

Suppose σ has a value of 1 in one-third of the cases, a value of -1 in one-third of the cases, or else a value of 0. As Figure 13.13 shows, shocks move the equilibrium aggregate supply curve with equal probability of 1/3 into one of three positions: EAS_+ at $Y^* + 1$, EAS_0 at Y^*, or EAS_- at $Y^* - 1$. An ultra-conservative central bank with very flat indifference curves that approximate horizontal lines does not permit inflation in each of the three cases and steers the economy into one of the three white points given in the graph. Obviously, no inflation bias results. Supply shocks transmit into income shocks to their fullest extent.

Now let the government hire a slightly less conservative central banker who has some concern for income fluctuations. Let her reaction function be given by the negatively sloped blue line. This line is steeper than the horizontal reaction function of the ultra-conservative central bank (that coincides with the abscissa), but less steep than the government's own (or society's) reaction function. Since shocks have an expected value of zero $((1 + 0 - 1)/3 = 0)$, it is rational to expect no shock to occur. Then the rational expectation is given by the intersection between the EAS_0 curve and the central bank's reaction line. This is also the inflation bias of the new moderately conservative central banker. But then the SAS curves in the case of a positive or a negative shock also reflect this bias. Instead of being moved into SAS_-, SAS_0 and SAS_+ by a negative shock, no shock and a positive shock, respectively, supply curves are higher at SAS'_-, SAS'_0 or SAS'_+. In the case of a negative shock, inflation is driven along SAS'_- above expected inflation to reduce the recession (point B'). In the case of a positive shock, inflation is driven unexpectedly low along SAS'_+, to dampen the boom (point C').

How does the performance of the moderately conservative central bank compare with the performance of the ultra-conservative central bank? To see this we repeat the choices of both banks in Figure 13.14. This time we add the (steeper) indifference curves of the government (or the public), but move the underlying SAS curves into the background in order not to overcrowd the graph.

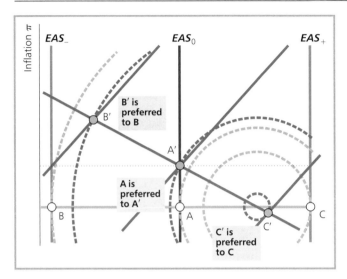

Figure 13.14 Gauged by the public's preferences, the ultra-conservative CB delivers the utility levels indicated by the light blue circles in one-third of the cases each. A moderate CB delivers utility indicated by the darker blue circles. B′ is much better than B. C′ is better than C. A′ is a little worse than A, but this occurs only in one-third of the cases. Adding everything up, the moderate CB outperforms the ultra-conservative CB.

The following results obtain:

1 If no shock occurs, the ultra-conservative central bank chooses A, the less conservative one chooses A′. In terms of society's preferences, A is slightly better than A′ from the perception of the government and the public.
2 If a negative shock occurs, the two central banks choose B and B′. Here the not-so-conservative central bank's choice is clearly superior.
3 In the case of a positive shock the points to compare are C and C′. Again, the less conservative choice is clearly superior.

Since all three situations occur with equal probability, the combined results produced by the less independent central bank are preferred to the no-inflation results produced by the ultra-conservative central bank.

Pegging the exchange rate

The above arguments also apply to the choice of an anchor currency in an exchange rate system. There also, a central bank may be too conservative as the issuer of the nth currency to perform optimally in a world with uncertainty.

A further complication arises here if member states are not exposed to the same kinds of shocks. If the anchor country is hit by a shock while the other countries are not, and its central bank responds as seems appropriate from a domestic perspective, the other countries are unnecessarily displaced from their current equilibrium situations. The German unification shock and its repercussions on the other EMS members, discussed in Chapter 12, offers one such example on a rather grand scale. Another big one is the effect of the Vietnam war on fiscal and monetary policy in the United States, and the consequences transmitted by the Bretton Woods system onto many other countries.

Alternatively, one or more other members of the fixed exchange rate system may be subjected to a shock while the anchor country is not. In this case the concerned countries are unlikely to get the response they wish from the anchor country's central bank.

13.3 Disinflations and the sacrifice ratio

So far we have been concerned with the average inflation performance of a country. This made us think about important issues. Now it is time to note that while average inflation rates can be readily understood in terms of the institutional factors discussed above, they are only one side of the coin. No country in the world has experienced an approximately steady level or path of inflation. Rather, inflation rates seem to exhibit systematic upward and downward movements that cannot be attributed to random shocks to the *DAD* and *SAS* curves of our model. Figure 13.15 shows a wide range of inflation experiences since 1960 that support this interpretation.

If the occasional surges in inflation documented in the graphs are not to give rise to higher and higher inflation, they must be reversed by means of restrictive monetary policy. It is an important issue how such **disinflations** are to be engineered in order to minimize the accompanying **disinflation costs**. We will now look at disinflations and disinflation costs: first from a theoretical perspective, in the context of the *DAD-SAS* model; then from an empirical perspective that draws on real-world data and a case study.

Disinflation and its costs in the *DAD-SAS* model

What do we mean by disinflation costs? Consider a country that decides to cut money growth, and thus eventually inflation, in half. From what we learned in Chapter 8 about inflation and income dynamics in the *DAD-SAS* model, the income losses accompanying this disinflation depend on two factors: the *speed at which inflation expectations are reduced*, as indicated by the downward shift of the *SAS* curve; and the *flexibility of nominal wages*, as indicated by the slope of the *SAS* curve. Figure 13.16 looks at the first factor.

Starting from point A, suppose that the central bank *announces* in period 0 that it plans to halve money growth in period 1. What happens to income (and inflation) in period 1 depends on the responsiveness of inflation expectations to (or the credibility of) this announcement. Consider three stylized cases:

- If the labour market does not believe the disinflation announcement, *SAS* stays in SAS_{AE} and the economy moves to point B. Some inflation reduction is achieved, but there is also a large fall in income. The income loss per achieved reduction in inflation is high.
- The labour market believes the disinflation announcement. It adjusts inflation expectations rationally, shifting *SAS* down to SAS_{RE}. The inflation rate falls to the new target rate at no cost in terms of income losses. Inflation has been reduced without any cost.
- An intermediate case is that the labour market assigns some, but not full, credibility to the disinflation announcement. Attributing a probability of 50% for the policy change to happen puts *SAS* in the intermediate dashed position. Inflation is lower than in the first case and higher than in the second. The income loss is higher than in the second and lower than in the first case.

Figure 13.17 deals with the second influence on disinflation costs. To isolate this argument from the effect on expectations discussed above, consider

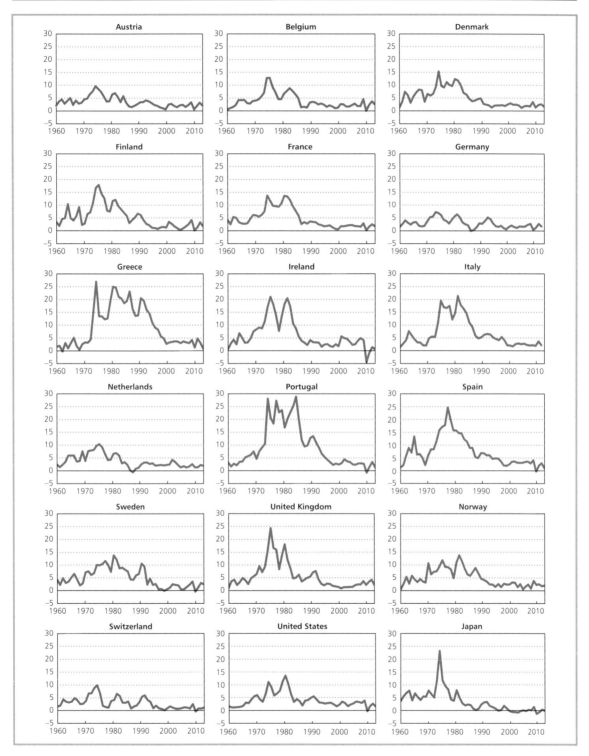

Figure 13.15 Inflation rates in Europe and the world, 1960–2013.
Sources: IMF, OECD.

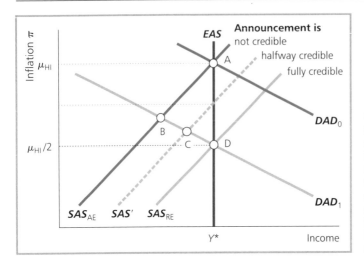

Figure 13.16 Being at A, the CB announces in period 0 that money growth will be reduced from μ_{HI} to 0.5 μ_{HI} next period. If this pledge is not credible, SAS stays in the dark blue position as under adaptive expectations. The economy ends up at B. If it is credible and its effects on inflation are foreseen, SAS_{RE} obtains and we move directly to D. If the announcement is half-heartedly believed, SAS moves to the dashed position and C obtains.

the case in which the disinflation begins unexpectedly. Again the goal is to halve inflation by halving money growth. If nominal wage growth responds slowly to labour market disequilibria and, hence, the SAS curve is rather flat, only a small part of the hoped-for reduction of inflation is achieved in period 1, at the cost of large income losses (point B). A more flexible labour market implies a steeper SAS curve and leads to point C. Finally, if wage growth is perfectly flexible, and hence the SAS curve is vertical, the inflation target is achieved immediately at no income-related cost.

The transition from a high inflation equilibrium to a low inflation equilibrium is costless in only two ideal scenarios: when the disinflation is announced prior to its implementation and this announcement is fully credible, or when the labour market is perfectly flexible, meaning that nominal wages move to balance supply and demand at all times. Whenever reality falls short of these ideal requirements, disinflations can only be engineered at the cost of income losses – and they take time.

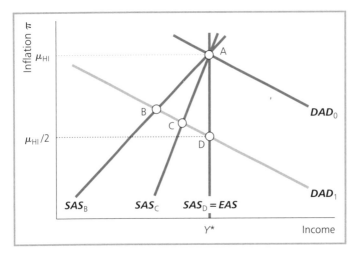

Figure 13.17 Beginning at A, money growth is cut in half unexpectedly in order to reduce inflation by 50%. If wages are very sticky, which makes SAS flat, inflation falls a little and income falls a lot. More flexible wages provide for a steeper SAS curve, giving more inflation reduction and lower income losses. Perfect wage flexibility makes SAS vertical. Inflation immediately falls to half its initial value at no sacrifice in income.

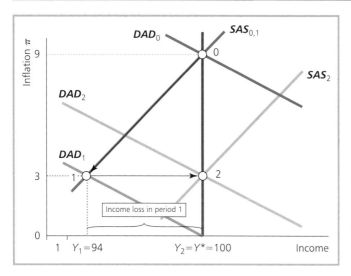

Figure 13.18 To reduce inflation from 9% to 3% in one step, as the big-leap approach recommends, *DAD* must shift to DAD_1. To this effect, money growth must be 0. The accompanying income loss, if *SAS* has slope 1, is 6. To keep inflation at 3% in period 2, money must grow again in period 2 to shift *DAD* up to DAD_2.

The sacrifice ratio is the loss of income (usually measured in percentage of potential income) caused by reducing inflation by one percentage point.

To see how the incurred costs relate to the obtained benefits, economists use a *standardized measure of disinflation costs*: the sacrifice ratio. This is computed by first adding up all income losses (or gains, if they occur) incurred during the disinflation (as a percentage of potential income) and then dividing this sum by the achieved reduction of inflation (in percentage points):

$$\text{Sacrifice ratio} = \frac{\text{Total income losses}}{\text{Inflation reduction}}$$

So the sacrifice ratio is the price of one percentage point less inflation in terms of percentages of potential income forgone. For an illustration of how the sacrifice ratio is computed, suppose that a central bank decides to reduce inflation from 9% to 3%. Assume that an announcement is not credible. Instead, inflation expectations are formed adaptively according to $\pi^e = \pi_{-1}$.

The big-leap approach attempts to produce a desired reduction of inflation in one giant step.

Figure 13.18 shows the big-leap approach to achieving the inflation target in period 1 immediately.

In Figure 13.18, money growth must come to a halt ($\mu_1 = 0$) in order to shift DAD_1 far enough down to bring inflation down to its target level immediately ($\pi = 3$). This is at the expense of an income drop by 6%, however $[(Y^* - Y_1)/Y^* = 6\%]$. The current inflation rate of 3 is the rate expected for period 2. This shifts *SAS* into the light blue position. Appropriate demand management holds inflation constant at $\pi_2 = 3$ and brings income back up to potential income Y^*.

Note two things. First, disinflation affects income only in period 1. Income is still in equilibrium in period 0, before the disinflation starts, and back in equilibrium in period 2, after the disinflation is over. So the sacrifice ratio is

$$SR = \frac{100(Y^* - Y_1)/Y^*}{\pi_0 - \pi_2} = \frac{100(100 - 94)/100}{9 - 3} = \frac{6}{9 - 3} = 1$$

Second, to achieve the inflation target quickly, money growth must follow a rather volatile pattern. (Recap: to identify this period's money growth in the graph, look for the point of intersection between this period's *DAD* curve and the vertical line over last period's income.) From a pre-disinflation rate of 9,

Figure 13.19 To bring inflation down from 9% to 3% in three steps, in line with the gradualist approach, *DAD* must first shift to DAD_1. Facing SAS_2, the next reduction to 5% in period 2 calls for another shift of *DAD* to DAD_2. When the inflation target of 3% is reached in period 3, income is still below Y^*. Only in period 4 is the new low inflation equilibrium reached.

money growth must fall to 0 in period 1, rise to 6 in period 2, and then fall back to 3 where it can stay. In particular, the acceleration in money growth from 0 to 6% in period 2, after the inflation target has already been reached, may create credibility problems for the central bank's new low inflation policy.

To avoid such wild swings in money growth, but particularly as a hedge against a severe recession, a gradualist approach to disinflation is often recommended. Figure 13.19 looks at such an example.

The gradualist approach attempts to achieve a desired reduction of inflation slowly, in a series of small steps.

Here the central bank reduces inflation from 9% to 3% in equal steps over a period of three years. In period 1 inflation is reduced to 7%. This surprise disinflation drives income down by two units to $Y_1 = 98$. Further disinflation steps, to 5% in period 2 and to 3% in period 3, keep income at 98, but do not drive it down any further. Once inflation is being kept stable at 3% in period 4, income rises back up into equilibrium and the disinflation is over.

Consider the sacrifice ratio for this gradual disinflation. Adding up the income losses for the disequilibrium periods 1, 2 and 3 we obtain

$$SR = \frac{100[(Y^* - Y_1) + (Y^* - Y_2) + (Y^* - Y_3)]/Y^*}{\pi_0 - \pi_4} = \frac{2 + 2 + 2}{9 - 3} = 1$$

Rather unexpectedly, the sacrifice ratio is exactly the same as with the big-leap approach. What is different, and what might be of concern, is the distribution of income losses over time. A deep recession (with an income drop of 6) in one year may not be the same as a minor recession (with an income deficit of 2) lasting three years.

The independence of the sacrifice ratio from the speed of the disinflation is a robust result as long as inflation expectations are being formed in a mechanical adaptive fashion. For markets that monitor monetary policy closely, it may be of interest in this context that the gradualist approach permits a more steady path of money growth. From periods 0 to 5, money growth rates are 9, 6, 5, 3, 4 and 3.

Disinflation and its costs in the real world – an alpine event

Computing the sacrifice ratio in a theoretical context is not difficult. But trying to do it in the real world poses problems. One major obstacle is how to identify disinflation episodes successfully. A disinflation episode is a time period during which the inflation rate is reduced deliberately, by purposeful policy action. This step is crucial, because we want to be sure that the change in inflation has caused the observed income response. A positive supply shock, for example, would shift *SAS* to the right, reduce inflation and raise output. It would obviously be a misinterpretation to conclude that the reduction in inflation has made income rise.

To eliminate such short-run or random fluctuations in inflation and focus on the bigger picture, we may smooth inflation data. Following a suggestion by Ball (1994), Figure 13.20 shows a moving average (over nine quarters, centred on the middle quarter) of Swiss inflation, in addition to the raw data. A fall of this smoothed inflation rate only qualifies as a disinflation if it exceeds a certain threshold, say, two percentage points. Application of this criterion to Switzerland identifies three disinflation episodes. Let us focus on the first one, which began in the second quarter of 1974 and ended in the fourth quarter of 1977. During this time the inflation rate was reduced from more than 9% to less than 2%.

Trying to compute the sacrifice ratio brings us to a second practical difficulty. In order to measure the effect of the disinflation on income, we need to guess what income would have done without the disinflation. In line with what we observed in Figure 13.18, it may be assumed that income is in equilibrium at peak inflation, just before the disinflation starts; that equilibrium obtains again one year (period) after the low inflation target is achieved; and that income would have moved linearly from the first to the second equilibrium level had there been no disinflation. Figure 13.20, panel (b), shows how this works for

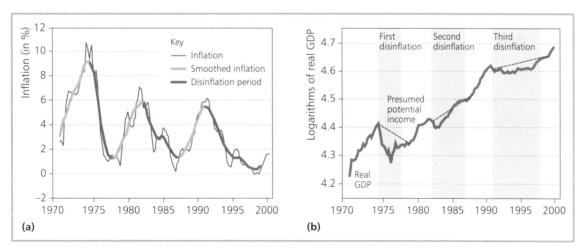

Figure 13.20 Panel (a) shows actual inflation and smoothed inflation in Switzerland. The bold segments highlight three disinflation episodes experienced since 1970. Panel (b) shows real GDP. Potential GDP is characterized by straight lines connecting incomes at the beginning and one year after the end of disinflation episodes. (Why? Check when *Y* is back at *Y** in Figure 13.18.)

Source: IMF, *IFS*.

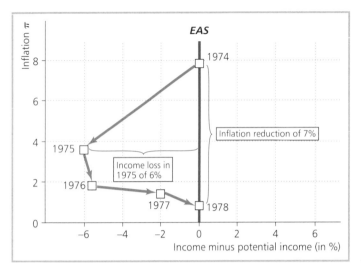

Figure 13.21 The graph traces the first Swiss disinflation in π-Y space. From about 8% in 1974 inflation is reduced via 4% in 1975, and 2% in 1976, to some 1% in 1977. Potential income is reached one year later. Income lost relative to falling potential income caused by quadrupling oil prices is 6% each in 1975 and 1976 and 2% in 1977.

Source: IMF, *IFS*.

the first Swiss disinflation. Note that potential income is presumed to have fallen even without the disinflation (probably due to the first oil price explosion). The income loss during each quarter of the disinflation is now simply measured as the vertical distance between actual income and our guess of potential income.

Figure 13.21 displays this episode in a π-Y diagram, to bring out the similarity to the display of theoretical disinflations in Figures 13.18 and 13.19. For improved transparency, the episode is documented with annual data. The horizontal axis measures income as deviation from potential income (in %), since in the real world the latter changes over time.

Assuming that income was in equilibrium in 1974, when the disinflation began, and in 1978, the year after it ended, the disinflation affected income in the displayed fashion. In 1975 income fell short of equilibrium income by 6%. In 1976 it remained 6% below equilibrium income. In 1977 it began to catch up, but was still some 2% lower than potential income. Looking at annual averages, this accompanied an inflation reduction from 8% to 1%. This gives the sacrifice ratio

$$ SR = \frac{6 + 6 + 2}{8 - 1} = \frac{14}{7} = 2 $$

The result is that one percentage point less inflation costs Switzerland 2% of a year's normal output during this disinflation. In 1995 prices this amounts to 7,000,000,000 Swiss francs. For each of Switzerland's 7 million inhabitants, one percentage point less inflation costs 1,000 francs. These numbers are corroborated by the other two disinflation episodes in Switzerland between 1982 and 1987, and between 1990 and 1996. The accumulated income losses from all three disinflations add up to about 70 billion Swiss francs.

The costs of inflation

According to what was said above, getting rid of a 10% inflation rate may well cost 20% of one year's income, or more. This is a high price, and the question is: why should we want to pay it? Because inflation is bad, of course. But why is 10% inflation worse than 5%, and 5% worse than 2%, and 2% worse than full price stability? This question must be kept apart from the question of why an increase of inflation, say from 5% to 10%, may be harmful.

The costs of increasing inflation

At first glance, this question appears to be ill-posed. Haven't we just seen that reducing inflation is costly? And don't we know that by symmetrical arguments an acceleration of inflation will spur temporary income *gains*? Yes, this is correct, even if such *gain ratios* (the income gain resulting from an increase in inflation by one percentage point) may not be exactly the same as the sacrifice ratios (say, if the *SAS* curves are curved rather than linear). But the fact that surprise inflation bears the promise of transitory income gains is exactly the reason that it is so tempting to inflate.

Then why should an acceleration of inflation be costly? To understand this, we must look behind income and see what happens to the distribution of wealth. Suppose an elderly man had saved during the earlier part of his life and now, via the banking system, lends his savings to young people (remember the lifetime consumption pattern discussed in Chapter 2?). Suppose he lends £10,000 to a young woman for one year. Both agree on a real interest rate of 3%. Since they expect 7% inflation, the nominal interest rate is 10%. So she expects to repay the loan plus interest after one year, which amounts to £11,000. Now assume that inflation surprisingly turns out to be 10% instead of the expected 7%. If both had foreseen this, they would have agreed on a nominal interest rate of 13%, and on repayment of £11,300. So the elderly man receives less than he wanted and the young woman pays less than she was prepared to. The unexpected acceleration of inflation redistributed £300 from the man to the woman.

This result can be generalized: *the main cost of unanticipated inflation is that it redistributes wealth from creditors (those with savings) to debtors*. In reality this often means redistribution from the old to the young, or from the public to the government.

The costs of steady inflation

To return to our initial question: after the acceleration of inflation has been completed, why is a permanently higher rate of inflation of, say, 10% worse than a lower steady rate? A first answer, given by the *DAD-SAS* model, says that it is not. Since the long-run *EAS* curve is vertical at potential income, income is independent of the level of steady inflation. And neither does inflation seem to have an impact on any other real variables, such as real wages, real interest rates, real exchange rates, consumption, taxes and so on. There is one real variable, however, that is affected. Remember that people determine their money holdings by comparing the return on money, which is zero, to the return on interest-bearing assets, which equals the nominal interest rate. Now if inflation is higher, the nominal interest rate must be higher to keep the real interest rate unchanged. Then people hold less money and spend more resources on replenishing their stock of money. What is the size of this effect? Empirical studies suggest that the real money supply falls by some 5% if nominal interest rates go up by one percentage point. So, as a rough guess, people would hold half the money at 10% inflation than what they would hold at 0%, meaning two instead of one or eight instead of four monthly trips to the cash machine. These so-called **shoe leather costs** are presumably not very high at moderate inflation rates, and are even partly offset by the fact that people now earn more interest since a larger part of wealth is kept in interest-bearing assets.

In a similar vein, higher inflation will use up the resources of firms that have to rewrite price lists and catalogues more frequently. We have already come across such **menu costs** in Chapter 8.

The image of presumably rather moderate costs of anticipated inflation derives from the assumption that institutions are designed to deal with an inflationary environment in a neutral way. However, an institution that hardly meets this ideal in the real world is the tax system. Taxes are usually levied on nominal wages, nominal wealth, nominal capital gains and nominal profits. If income taxes are not proportional, higher inflation gives rise to higher real taxes even though real income may not have changed. Similarly, real taxes on wealth and capital gains go up even if real wealth or real capital gains are unchanged. Such institutional deficiencies cause inflation to have distorting effects that are probably much higher than the shoe leather and menu costs discussed above.

The dependence of inflation costs on institutions adds a new dimension to the discussion of price stability. A country that does not want to live with 10% inflation may either lower inflation and make the accompanying sacrifices, or reform institutions so as to make the 10% inflation less painful. The latter option does not solve an apparent empirical problem, however, that remains little understood: high inflation rates seem to come with more variable inflation, which introduces uncertainty about future prices that may absorb substantial resources.

On the upside, there are scenarios under which a certain level of inflation, presumably in the lower half of the single digits, may even be beneficial. Liquidity traps, in which conventional monetary policy does not bite, are such a scenario. Since nominal interest rates sooner or later follow anticipated inflation, a country with zero inflation is more likely to fall into a liquidity trap when a crisis hits than a country with, say, an average inflation rate of 3%.

13.4 Lessons for European Monetary Union

The discussions of this chapter pose three questions regarding the shape and future of the Eurozone:

1 Does the European Central Bank possess an optimal degree of independence from government interference? 'Optimal' is used here in the sense that it combines a high degree of price level stability with a reasonable concern for income stabilization in times of exogenous shocks.
2 Are the current or prospective future member states similar enough to be hit by the same kinds of shocks in a similar fashion? Similarly, are their business cycles synchronized enough?
3 Had inflation converged sufficiently at an early stage to avoid costly and painful disinflation efforts during the politically sensitive final phase of transition to EMU?

EMU stands for European Economic and Monetary Union. However, it is often understood to refer to this union's more controversial second part, European Monetary Union, also called the Eurozone.

Regarding the first question, the statute of the European Central Bank makes it one of the most independent central banks in the world. If there is any risk, it is that the European Central Bank may be too independent.

On the second question, a lot of structural diversity still exists, as the sovereign debt crisis revealed. Much of this cannot be removed in the short run. For example, the EU will have to live with the fact that the United Kingdom is a net exporter of oil while the other members are net importers, and the particular conflict of interest this might generate should the UK decide to adopt the euro. Within the Eurozone, substantial productivity gaps have opened. The lesson is simply that it may be more risky for some countries to have a common currency than it is for others. Theories of optimum currency areas spell out criteria against which to judge whether adopting a common currency may be beneficial or not.

An optimum currency area is a region or group of countries for which it is beneficial to have a common currency.

The Maastricht criteria on inflation and interest rates address the third question and the last part of the second. The inflation criterion is supposed to ensure that the final convergence of inflation rates, demanded by the transition to the euro, is not accompanied by large employment sacrifices in certain countries. This would have given EMU a bad start and might even put EMU membership in jeopardy for some. Figure 13.22 shows that two-thirds of current EU members met the current inflation target of 2.4% in 1996. Note that most who did not were not current members of the EMS, or had major devaluations within the EMS since 1993.

Business cycle synchronization is achieved if two or more countries normally move into booms and recessions together.

The Maastricht criterion on interest rates may serve as an indicator of business cycle synchronization. Recall that nominal interest rates contain an inflation premium, at least in the long run. From the perspective of the Fisher equation the interest rate criterion is redundant, since what it does is secure inflation convergence. Figure 13.22 makes this point, showing that for only one out of the fifteen countries (Britain) did the interest rate criterion yield a different verdict than the inflation criterion in 1995. Note, however, that nominal interest rates are also subject to a liquidity effect. Due to sticky goods prices, nominal interest rates fall below normal levels during booms and rise during recessions. Therefore nominal interest rates may diverge even if two countries are on the same inflation trend, if business cycles are not synchronized. Deviation from a line with slope 1 through the data points in Figure 13.22 signals the extent to which a country's business cycle is out of synchronization compared with the others. This implies, however, that the interest rate criterion should be defined in terms of deviations from this line (above or below) instead of differences from the low inflation countries, and should use

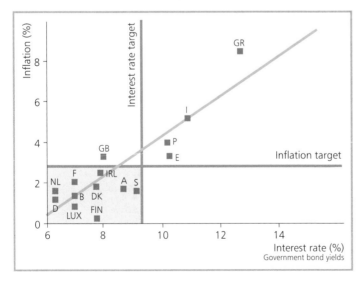

Figure 13.22 In equilibrium, on *EAS*, in the neutral phase of the business cycle, nominal interest rates are the sum of some fairly constant normal real interest rates and inflation. Data for the year 1995 illustrate this.

Source: SBC, *Economic and Financial Prospects*.

short-term interest rates instead of long-term rates as laid down in the Maastricht criterion.

CHAPTER SUMMARY

- A more independent central bank provides lower inflation. This proposition explains a large part of inflation differences between industrial countries.
- Countries that peg their exchange rate to some other currency see their inflation gradually converge with the other country's rate. Inflation experiences within the EMS support this proposition.
- Hard-nosed (conservative) central banks are likely to respond to a negative supply shock with restrictive monetary policy to keep inflation from rising. Wet (socialist) central banks, by contrast, are likely to respond with expansionary monetary policy to prevent a recession. The response of industrial countries to the oil price explosion of 1973/4 matches this pattern.
- If supply shocks are relatively frequent, the best central bank for society may not be the most independent one, but one that has some concern for income stabilization.
- If supply shocks are relatively frequent, it may not be optimal to peg the exchange rate to the country with the most independent central bank, but to one that has some concern for income stabilization.
- If two countries are being hit by supply shocks at different times or in opposing directions, pegging the exchange rate may not be beneficial.
- The sacrifice ratio measures the cost of reducing inflation by one percentage point in terms of lost income.
- The main cost of unanticipated inflation is that it redistributes wealth from creditors to debtors.
- Steady inflation causes shoe leather costs and menu costs. These costs are presumably small for moderate inflations. If institutions are not properly designed to deal with inflation, however, substantial distortions may add to these costs.
- A small amount of steady inflation may reduce a country's risk of falling into a liquidity trap when hit by a crisis.

Key terms and concepts

big-leap approach 393
business cycle synchronization 399
central bank independence 375
consumer price index 379
contingent rule 379
crawling peg 379
currency board 379
disinflation 390
disinflation costs 378
Economic and Monetary Union
  (EMU) 398

fixed rule 378
gradualist approach 394
inflation costs 396
inflation target 378
monetary policy rule 378
optimum currency area 399
pegging the currency 379
producer price index 380
sacrifice ratio 393
supply shock 383
Taylor rule 379

EXERCISES

13.1 Cukierman has provided another index of central bank independence. His values for the countries shown in Figure 13.2 are, where available, given in Table 13.1. Average inflation since 1973 is also given. Transfer the data onto a graph and judge visually whether the result obtained in the text also holds with this new index.

13.2 Let a country's stochastic *SAS* curve be given by $Y = Y^* + \pi - \pi^e + \sigma$, where σ equals 5 in 50% of the cases and -5 in the other 50%. The government's indifference curves are ellipse shaped, as postulated in the chapter. Whenever $\sigma = 5$, inflation is set to 2%; when $\sigma = -5$, inflation is 10%.
  (a) What is the rationally expected inflation rate?
  (b) Let $Y^* = 100$. What are the income levels in periods of positive supply shocks and in periods of negative supply shocks, respectively?
  (c) What do the observed inflation rates tell you about where the government's desired output is, relative to potential output?

13.3 Let a country's supply side be represented by the *SAS* curve

$$Y = Y^* + (\pi - \pi^e)$$

Inflation expectations are being formed adaptively ($\pi^e = \pi_{-1}$). Suppose the country's central bank decides to bring inflation down from 8%

to 1%. The disinflation process starts in period 1 and follows this pattern: 4% in period 1; 2% in period 2; 1% in period 3 and after.
  (a) Compute the aggregate income losses and the sacrifice ratio.
  (b) Display your results in a π-Y diagram. Compare your diagram with the Swiss disinflation engineered between 1974 and 1978 which is shown in the chapter.

13.4 One disinflation engineered by the Bank of England began in the second quarter of 1980 and ended in the third quarter of 1983. At the start of this period, trend inflation was at 16.6%; at the end it was 4.4%. Real GDP during this episode is given in Table 13.2.
  (a) Compute the aggregate income losses that may be attributed to this disinflation. (Assume that GDP was at its potential level in the second quarter of 1980 and again in the third quarter of 1984. Assume that potential income would have moved linearly from the first value to the second, had the disinflation not been implemented.)
  (b) Compute the sacrifice ratio for this disinflation episode.

13.5 Your country is stuck in an inflationary equilibrium with $\pi = 10\%$ and $Y^* = 100$. The economy is given by an *SAS* curve with adaptive expectations $\pi^e = \pi_{-1}$:

$$\pi = \pi_{-1} + (Y - Y^*) + 0.1\pi_{OIL}$$

Table 13.1

	A	AUS	B	DK	FIN	F	D	IRL	I	JP	NL	E	S	CH	GB	USA
CBI	0.31	0.58	0.19	0.47	0.27	0.28	0.66	0.39	0.22	0.16	0.42	0.21	0.27	0.68	0.31	0.51
Average inflation in %	8.91	4.72	5.89	7.52	8.61	8.5	3.7	10.15	12.13	5.23	4.49	11.96	8.3	4.04	9.86	6.24

Table 13.2

Quarter	80.2	80.3	80.4	81.1	81.2	81.3	81.4	82.1	82.2
UK real GDP	423.9	421.1	416.0	415.6	415.2	420.6	420.7	421.8	425.2
Quarter	82.3	82.4	83.1	83.2	83.3	83.4	84.1	84.2	84.3
UK real GDP*	425.8	428.2	436.7	438.0	442.2	446.7	451.6	449.4	449.2

*In billions of pounds sterling (at 1990 prices).

and the *DAD* curve

$$\pi = \mu - 0.5(Y - Y_{-1})$$

π_{OIL} denotes oil-price inflation. Although it would like to, your government does not dare to reduce inflation, since it does not want to bear the accompanying disinflation costs. Now in period 1, oil prices are cut in half permanently $(\pi_{OIL,1} = -50\%)$.

(a) By how much can inflation be reduced in period 1 without affecting income?

(b) What is the appropriate monetary policy that keeps income at 100? (Compute μ_1, μ_2 and μ_3.)

(c) What happens if the government uses the opportunity to reduce inflation, immediately and permanently, to 0? (Trace μ and Y.)

(d) Answer questions (a) to (c) assuming that the fall in oil prices lasted only one year.

13.6 Consider a *DAD-SAS* economy that is regularly hit by supply shocks. The distribution of these shocks is bell-shaped. Figure 13.23 shows the

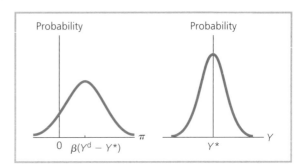

Figure 13.23

distribution of inflation and income that results when the preferences of the independent central bank and the public are identical.

(a) Now a new more conservative central bank president is appointed. How does this affect the shapes and positions of the above distributions?

(b) A more conservative central bank provides lower inflation. What may be the disadvantage of an ultra-conservative central bank?

Online resources

Interactive applet on monetary policy rules and central bank independence www.eurmacro .eu/tutor/centralbank.html

Self quiz

www.eurmacro.eu/SelfQuiz/sq-ch13.html

Recommended reading

The bible on issues of central bank independence is Alex Cukierman (1995) *Central Bank Strategy, Credibility, and Independence: Theory and Evidence*, Cambridge, MA and London: MIT Press.

The empirical evidence is gauged on a non-technical level in Alberto Alesina and Lawrence H. Summers (1992) 'Central bank independence and macroeconomic performance', *Journal of Money, Credit and Banking* 25: 151–62.

A survey of theoretical progress in political macroeconomics achieved in the 1990s is provided by Manfred Gärtner (2000) 'Political macroeconomics: a survey of recent developments', *Journal of Economic Surveys* 14: 527–61.

Sacrifice ratios are studied in Lawrence Ball (1994) 'What determines the sacrifice ratio?', in N. Gregory Mankiw (ed.) *Monetary Policy*, Chicago and London: University of Chicago Press.

A provoking view on inflation, central bank independence and monetary policy is offered in Paul Krugman (1996) 'Stable prices and fast growth: Just say no', *The Economist*, 31 August, pp. 17–20.

Several authors have forwarded proposals of how to integrate the kind of endogenous monetary policy discussed in this chapter into an *IS-LM* framework:

■ David Romer (2000) 'Keynesian macroeconomics without the *LM* curve', *Journal of Economic Perspectives* 14:149–69.
■ Carl Walsh (2002) 'Teaching inflation targeting: An analysis for intermediate macro', *Journal of Economic Education* 33: 333–46.

APPLIED PROBLEMS

EMPIRICAL RESEARCH

What explains sacrifice ratios?

Lawrence Ball ('What determines the sacrifice ratio?', in N. G. Mankiw (ed.) (1994) *Monetary Policy*, Chicago and London: University of Chicago Press) computes a sample of sacrifice ratios for different disinflation episodes in different countries. One question that he analyzes is whether the obtained sacrifice ratios depend on the SIZE of the disinflation (by how many percentage points is inflation reduced from the beginning to the end of the episode?) and by the LENGTH (how many quarters did the disinflation last?). The obtained estimation equation for twenty-eight episodes is (standard errors in parentheses):

$$\text{Sacrifice ratio} = 1.045 - 0.198 \text{ SIZE} + 0.120 \text{ LENGTH}$$
$$(0.325) \ (0.061) \qquad \quad (0.034)$$
$$R^2_{adj} = 0.30$$

Larger disinflations come at lower disinflation costs: the coefficient for SIZE is negative and significant (*t*-statistic $= 0.198/0.061 = 3.25$). On the other hand, spreading the disinflation over a longer time appears to make it more costly: the coefficient for LENGTH is positive, with a *t*-statistic of $0.120/0.034 = 3.53$). The coefficient of determination is only 0.30, however, meaning that only 30% of the differences of sacrifice ratios between disinflation episodes may be traced back to the size and the length of the disinflation.

WORKED PROBLEM

Does central bank independence ease disinflation pains?

Inflation can be reduced by moving down along the *SAS* curve. Then the slope of *SAS* determines the incurred sacrifices. Or the *SAS* curve may be shifted down by reducing inflation expectations. If this is accomplished, inflation may be reduced at no or at low cost. According to what we learned in this chapter, an independent central bank (which desires lower inflation than a dependent one) should be expected to be more successful in reducing inflation expectations. Hence, more CBI should come hand in hand with lower sacrifice ratios. Table 13.3 gives average sacrifice ratios for nine countries and CBI data.

To see whether there is a relationship we run a regression to obtain (standard errors in parentheses):

$$\text{Sacrifice ratio} = -0.441 + 0.206 \text{ CBI} \quad R^2_{adj} = 0.59$$
$$(0.553) \ (0.058)$$

The puzzling and unexpected result is that countries with more independent central banks have experienced higher sacrifice ratios. CBI explains some 59% of the differences in sacrifice ratios and the coefficient on CBI is highly significant (absolute *t*-statistic: $0.206/0.058 = 3.55$). Similarly puzzling results have been reported in a number of research papers. Convincing explanations have not been advanced yet.

Table 13.3

Country	AUS	CDN	F	D	I	J	CH	GB	USA
Sacrifice ratio	1.00	1.50	0.75	3.10	1.29	0.70	1.57	0.68	2.11
CBI	9	11	7	13	5	6	12	6	12

Table 13.4

Country	A	B	CH	D	DK	E	F	GB	GR	I	IRL	NL	P
Hourly wages in $	25.5	27	29	32.1	24.82	12	19	14	8	16.5	13	24	5.33
CBI	9	7	12	13	8	5	7	6	4	5	7	10	3
Overvaluation in %	1.23	1.12	1.52	1.29	1.35	0.95	1.18	1.01	0.68	1.04	0.94	1.22	0.76

YOUR TURN

Real wages and central bank independence

Wage costs are considered a key determinant of a country's international competitiveness. Table 13.4 gives hourly wages (converted into $) in thirteen European countries, ranging from $5.33 in Portugal to $32.1 in Germany. The second row gives the Grilli index of central bank independence. The last row gives the domestic currencies' overvaluation relative to the dollar as implied in the World Bank's *World Bank Atlas*. We had already used these data in Chapter 1.

If we compare wages in Britain with wages in Germany, we compare $WAGE_{UK \text{ in } £}$ to $E_{£/DM} \times WAGE_{D \text{ in } DM}$. Now German wages may exceed British wages for two reasons: because wages in Germany (expressed in DM) are pushed too high (by trade unions), or because the exchange rate is too high, that is, the mark is overvalued relative to the pound sterling. In the light of this, check whether international differences in wage costs may be attributed to currency overvaluation. Also look into the role played by CBI in this context.

Budget deficits and public debt

What to expect

After working through this chapter, you will understand:

1 How the government budget deficit affects the public debt, and how the public debt affects the budget deficit.

2 What structural changes in the industrialized countries brought the issue of the public debt into the headlines.

3 Why, when and for whom running a deficit and running up the public debt may be a burden.

4 For what reasons budget rules may be needed in a monetary union.

5 How the dynamics of the public debt are related to developments in the financial markets.

6 What kind of risks arise from the presence of multiple equilibria and self-fulfilling prophecy in government bond markets.

7 How to judge the potential of fiscal austerity, rescue funds, euro bonds or tighter regulation of financial markets to end and prevent future sovereign debt crises.

Until now the main thrust of the discussion has focused on monetary policy. Fiscal policy, the spending and revenue decisions of the government, has so far made only a brief appearance – as a means of influencing aggregate spending in the economy. It is time to take a closer look at the government budget – at spending and ways to finance spending, at budget surpluses and deficits and at the accumulation of such surpluses and deficits over time, which we call the public debt.

Understanding budget deficits and the public debt is particularly important in the context of current European developments. First, fixed exchange rates as offered by the European Monetary System (EMS in the past and ERM II at present and in the future), and even more so membership in the Eurozone, deprive countries of monetary policy as an instrument to influence the business cycle and to respond to shocks. This may make it tempting to use (or abuse) fiscal policy instead, as many countries did after 2008, when the recent real estate and financial crisis was at its worst.

Second, but related to the first reason, the convergence criteria agreed upon in the Maastricht Treaty, which current participants had to and prospective future members of the euro area will have to meet, comprise two on fiscal policy (which are also at the core of the Stability and Growth Pact): one restricts budget deficits to less than 3% of one year's aggregate income; the other requires the public debt to be below 60% of income. To obtain a clearer understanding of the rationale behind these and other convergence criteria we need to take a closer look at fiscal policy and how it relates to monetary policy as discussed so far.

The chapter will continue by discussing the argument that public deficits and debt place an unfair burden on future generations, and thus should be as low as possible, and that fiscal policy needs restrictions as spelled out in the European Union's *Stability and Growth Pact*.

The final section looks at how developments in the sovereign debt market may bear on the fate of a country's finances. Special attention will be given to the possibility of multiple equilibria and self-fulfilling prophecy, and why their presence constitutes a risk that countries fall victim to errors, moods and abuse in the financial markets.

14.1 The government budget

The government must balance expenditures and revenues, just as businesses and households do. It has some financing options, however, that are not available to individuals. Figure 14.1 displays the main sources of government revenues and uses of spending and defines some essential concepts.

On the expenditure side we have two categories. The first is regular government spending G, which we suppose here to comprise all public spending on consumption and investment, plus transfer payments. This differs from the narrower definition employed so far, where G denoted government consumption. The second, being made explicit in Figure 14.1 for the first time, is the government's interest payment on public debt B accumulated in the past, iB. Interest payments typically run at between 5% and 10% of government expenditures.

The prime source of revenue for the government are taxes T. We speak of a **budget deficit** if taxes fall short of expenditure:

$$\text{Deficit} = G + iB - T$$

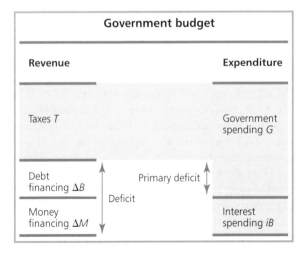

Figure 14.1 On the expenditure side there are government purchases G and interest payments on existing debt. Revenues comprise taxes and credit granted by the public (debt financing) or the central bank (money financing). If desired, G may be thought to include transfers. Then T must include items like social security contributions and unemployment insurance premiums. Unlike in previous chapters, G, T and B are nominal variables.

A better structural measure of the *current* government's budget policies is the **primary deficit**. This ignores government interest spending on the public debt, since the current government has little control over this expenditure category:

$$\text{Primary deficit} = G - T$$

The government enjoys *two options to finance a deficit*. It can go into debt by *issuing government bonds* to the public, or it can simply *create money* and use it to pay for the goods and services it buys and the interest on old government debt. There is actually a third possibility which we ignore here. This is to sell public assets. In recent years in particular, European governments have been selling their telecoms, railroads, public utilities companies, airlines and more on a grand scale. This makes things easier for now, but it must remain a temporary phenomenon, and to the extent that these companies have been profitable, selling them may put pressure on rather than help the government budget further down the road. Since even during the current privatization euphoria and resizing of the public sector, this source of revenue barely amounted to a very small fraction of government revenue, we may safely ignore it here.

Note that not the entire deficit adds to the public debt, but only that part financed by issuing debt to the public. *Money financing does not add to the public debt.* This is most straightforward in countries where the government can simply decide to print money in order to finance the deficit, with its treasury issuing currency to pay for goods, services and interest. In countries where the government does not have that option, the central bank may help to finance deficits by open market purchases of government bonds. This results in claims of one government agency on another, and interest is paid by one government agency to another. Entertaining a consolidated perspective of the government, or because even the world's most independent central banks forward profits to the treasury, government bonds held by the central bank (or other government agencies) are not considered part of the public debt.

14.2 The dynamics of budget deficits and the public debt

It is useful to consider the two ways of financing a budget deficit separately. We begin with the more important one and ignore money financing for now. Focusing on the financing of deficits by issuing new debt develops an understanding of the intrinsic dynamic interaction between **budget deficits** and the **public debt**. In a second step we then look into how the detected process links with monetary policy.

The public debt is the net amount that the government owes to the private sector at home and to foreigners.

No money financing and no inflation

Suppose an independent central bank refuses to finance budget deficits by issuing money. Then $\Delta M = 0$, and the **budget constraint**, the requirement that revenues must equal expenditures, as displayed in Figure 14.1, reads

$$T + \Delta B = G + iB \qquad \text{Budget constraint} \quad (14.1)$$

The equation indicates that the budget deficit ΔB, or the *change* in public debt, is related to the *level* of the public debt B. Stabilizing the debt – that is, letting $\Delta B = 0$ in equation (14.1) – requires $T - G = iB$. Only if the primary budget pays for interest payments on the debt does the debt remain unchanged.

Stabilizing the public debt in absolute terms does not appear to be a very reasonable goal to achieve. A country that grows and accumulates wealth may well find a growing debt acceptable, as long as the debt ratio, the ratio between debt and income, B/Y, does not grow. The Maastricht Treaty takes that view, specifying that in order to qualify for EMU a country's debt-to-income ratio must not exceed 60%. In addition, the deficit-to-income ratio, $\Delta B/Y$, must be below 3%, a criterion that continues to apply to EMU members according to the Stability and Growth Pact.

As a basis for discussing these criteria, but also if we want to compare countries of different sizes, or a country with growing income at different points in time, we need to express the budget constraint in terms of income shares. Suppose the price level is constant at $P = 1$. Then Y is both nominal and real income. Dividing both sides of equation (14.1) by Y and expressing variables as income shares by their respective lower-case letters ($b \equiv B/Y$, $g \equiv G/Y$ and $t \equiv T/Y$) yields

$$\frac{\Delta B}{Y} + t = g + ib \tag{14.2}$$

Be sure to note that $\Delta B/Y \neq \Delta(B/Y) \equiv \Delta b$. To the left of the inequality sign is the **deficit ratio**, i.e. the *budget deficit as a share of income*, as referred to in one of the Maastricht criteria. It gives current excess spending of the government as a share of aggregate income. To the right of $\neq$ is the change of the **debt ratio**, i.e. the *change of the public debt as a fraction of income*. It measures the change in the burden of all accumulated past deficits as a fraction of income. To see the relationship between $\Delta B/Y$ and $\Delta(B/Y)$, proceed from the definition $b \equiv B/Y$ which rewrites $B \equiv bY$. For small changes of b and Y we can make use of the approximation

Maths note. This approximation mimics the product rule in differential calculus, according to which the total differential of $B = bY$ is $dB = dbY + dYb$.

$$\Delta B = Y\Delta b + b\Delta Y$$

Dividing both sides by Y gives

$$\frac{\Delta B}{Y} = \Delta b + yb \tag{14.3}$$

where $y \equiv \Delta Y/Y$ denotes the growth rate of income. Substituting equation (14.3) into (14.2), noting that since inflation is 0 the nominal interest rate equals the real interest rate ($i = r$), and solving for Δb gives

$$\Delta b = g - t + (r - y)b \qquad \text{Debt ratio dynamics} \tag{14.4}$$

Mathematically minded people call equation (14.4) a first-order linear *difference equation*, as we learned in Chapter 5. A difference equation reveals how the change of a variable over last period's value, here $\Delta b \equiv b_{+1} - b$, is related to the previous level of this variable. In the current context, equation (14.4) thus describes how b, the public debt as a share of income, evolves over time.

Debt dynamics: scenarios		
	g > t Primary deficit	**g < t** Primary surplus
r < y High growth	Case A	Case B
r > y Low growth	Case C	Case D

Figure 14.2 The dynamics of the public debt depend on whether the government runs a primary deficit or a surplus, and on whether growth exceeds or falls short of the real interest rate. This yields four different cases to be discussed separately.

The debt ratio does not change any more if $\Delta b = 0$. Substituting this into equation (14.4) and solving for b yields the equilibrium debt ratio

$$b^* = \frac{g - t}{y - r} \qquad \text{Equilibrium debt ratio} \quad (14.5)$$

The sign of b^* is undetermined. Whether a country is required to be in debt or to be a creditor for equilibrium to obtain depends on whether or not the differences given in the denominator and in the numerator in equation (14.5) are of the same sign. If they are of the same sign, as in cases A and D in Figure 14.2, a constant debt ratio requires *debt*. In cases B and C the country needs to be a *creditor* in equilibrium. All this can be read off Figure 14.3. As the graphs, called phase diagrams, also reveal, however, the sign of $r - y$ not only has an impact on the nature of the equilibrium but also on *stability*.

A phase diagram is a geometric representation of a difference equation such as $\Delta b = g - t + (r - y)b$.

Plotting the values of Δb against b, as in Figure 14.3, yields a phase line. It is a straight line with a slope equal to $r - y$ and a vertical intercept equal to the primary deficit $g - t$.

A phase line is the path along which a variable moves in a dynamic model.

The movement of the economy along the phase line is easily determined: if $\Delta b > 0$, that is, north of the horizontal axis, b grows and movement is to the right. If $\Delta b < 0$, that is, south of the horizontal axis, b falls and movement is to the left. With these insights and the knowledge that we cannot move off the phase line, we may check the dynamic properties of the four cases.

■ *Case A.* In case A the government runs a primary deficit, and real income growth exceeds the real interest rate. Equation (14.4) may then be represented by a negatively sloped line that has a positive intercept. The top left-hand panel in Figure 14.3 shows such a line. This macroeconomic scenario is stable. No matter at what debt ratio b we start, as long as the primary deficit is as given, we always end up with a debt ratio of b^* in the long run. The reasoning for this is as follows. The interest rate determines how fast the debt grows due to interest payments alone, if these are being financed by issuing new debt. The income growth rate, of course, determines how quickly income grows. So with a balanced primary budget and income growth that exceeds the interest rate, the debt ratio converges to zero. Convergence also obtains with a primary budget deficit. But then equilibrium obtains at a debt level at which the reduction of the debt ratio due to income growth exceeding the interest rate is exactly balanced by what the primary deficit adds to the debt ratio.

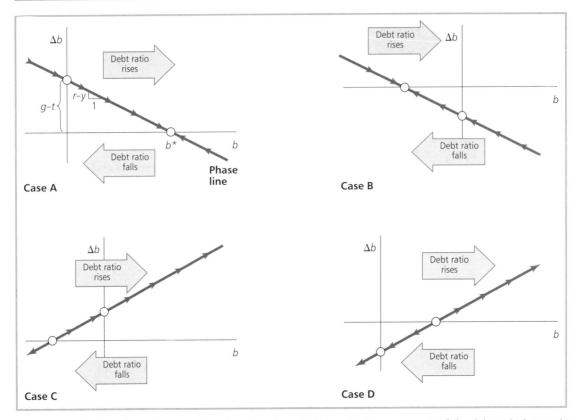

Figure 14.3 The four phase diagrams show the phase lines that describe the movement of the debt ratio b over time. If the slope of the phase line is negative (which is the case in A and B where $y > r$), the debt ratio converges to a steady state which is stable. If the slope is positive (as in cases C and D), a steady state exists, but it is unstable. After any small displacement the debt ratio moves away from it. Whether the steady-state debt ratio is positive or negative depends both on the sign of the primary deficit and on the slope of the phase line.

- *Case B*. Case B differs from case A with the countries now displaying a primary budget surplus. This makes the government a creditor in equilibrium. Due to $y > r$ this equilibrium is still stable.
- *Case C*. In this case the government runs a primary deficit as in case A. But now income growth falls short of the real interest rate. This has two important consequences. First, the government must be a creditor for the debt ratio to be in equilibrium. Second, this equilibrium is fragile. Any small displacements trigger endogenous processes that make the debt ratio explode in either direction. Stabilization is only possible by appropriate adjustments of the primary deficit ratio.
- *Case D*. The dynamics of the debt ratio are characterized by instability as in case C. Due to the government running a primary surplus, equilibrium requires the government to be in debt.

To develop a better grasp of what happens as we move along a phase line, let us take a closer look at the dynamics of case A. Figure 14.4 shows this case again, with the phase line depicted in the upper panel being flatter than in Figure 14.3 for added realism, so that we may plausibly assume that the horizontal and the vertical axes are using the same units of measurement.

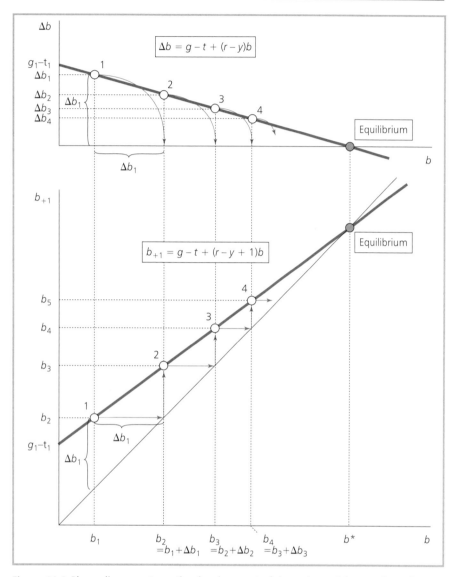

Figure 14.4 Phase diagrams trace the development of dynamic models over time. They come in two forms. The upper panel measures the variable of interest, here b, on the horizontal axis and the change of the variable, Δb, on the vertical axis. Δb must be added to b to obtain next period's value of b. The phase diagram in the lower panel also measures b on the horizontal axis, but next period's b, that is b_{+1}, on the vertical axis. When moving through time, next period's b must be transferred to the horizontal axis by means of the 45° line to become today's b as we enter the next period. This book uses the kind of phase diagram shown in the upper diagram. However, it may be useful to familiarize yourself with the type of diagram shown in the lower panel, as you may encounter it in other courses, textbooks or journal articles.

Now let the economy initially be at point 1 in the year 2009, running a primary deficit $(g_1 > t_1)$, a budget deficit $(\Delta b_1 > 0)$ and having a positive debt ratio $(b_1 > 0)$. We know from our previous discussion that the economy does not remain at point 1. Because of the budget deficit in 2009, the public debt will increase and be higher in 2010 than it was in 2009. How high will it be? To find out, the 2009 change in the debt ratio needs to be added to the 2009 debt ratio to yield the 2010 debt ratio ($b_2 = b_1 + \Delta b_1$). Graphically, therefore, the vertical distance of point 1 from the horizontal axis needs to be transferred to the horizontal axis and added to b_1. The rounded arrow depicts this transfer.

Having identified b_2, we can move up vertically until we hit the phase line in order to find out that the economy runs a deficit (ratio) of Δb_2 in 2010. This deficit again will add to the current debt next year, in 2011, and then we repeat the same procedure to find the 2012 debt ratio. Moving along the phase line step by step, driven by the described interaction between deficits and debt, this process continues under the parameter constellations presumed here until the debt ratio, with increments that get smaller and smaller, settles into its long-run equilibrium value of b^*.

There is another version of the phase diagram, which provides another way of depicting dynamic models in discrete time. Instead of writing debt-ratio dynamics as $\Delta b = g - t + (r - y)/b$, which stands behind the phase line shown in the upper panel of Figure 14.4, we may substitute $\Delta b \equiv b_{+1} - b$ and solve for b_{+1} to obtain

$$b_{+1} = g - t + (r - y + 1)b$$

This alternative phase line can be displayed in a diagram that measures b_{+1} and b on its two axes (see bottom panel of Figure 14.4). Note this line's properties:

■ It intersects the vertical line at $g - t$, just as the other phase line shown in the top panel.
■ The difference $r - y$ determines whether the line is steeper or flatter than the 45° line.
■ The line intersects the 45° line at b^*. Here $b_{+1} = b$: that is, the debt ratio does not change any more.

Now with the debt ratio being b_1 in the year 2009, the blue phase line tells us that the debt ratio increases to b_2 in 2010. Moving the dynamic equation one year ahead in time, we now use the 45° line to transfer b_2 from the vertical axis over to the horizontal axis. The phase line tells us that a debt ratio of b_2 in 2010 rises to b_3 in 2011. This continues under the current parameter constellations until the debt ratio, with increments that get smaller and smaller, eases into its long-run equilibrium at b^*.

The two approaches to phase-line analysis are shown in the two connected panels in Figure 14.4 in order to emphasize that they do lead to the same results. An advantage of displaying the models' dynamic behaviour as in the lower panel is that we can always read current and next period's values directly off the two axes. The advantage of using the version displayed in the upper panel, the version we prefer to use here, is that it shows budget deficits explicitly and thus facilitates the discussion of pertinent policy issues.

With such a rich menu of debt dynamics and equilibria available in theory, which is the relevant scenario in real life? The answer is that this depends on the country and on the year being considered. Table 14.1 shows how the primary surplus varies across countries and moves over time. There is no simple

Table 14.1 **Primary surpluses as a share of aggregate income: $t - g$.** Before the end of the millennium there was no clear trend in the development of primary balances. In each year shown here there are countries that run a primary deficit, and some that run a surplus. The new millennium started a rollercoaster ride, with the year 2000 being the best primary surplus year ever, except for the United States, and the year 2010 being the worst. Note that since tax receipts are susceptible to the business cycle, and also government outlays to some extent, so is the primary deficit.

	1975	1980	1985	1990	1995	2000	2005	2010
Austria	−1.6	0.1	0.1	0.9	−1.6	0.9	0.5	−3.4
Belgium	−2.0	−3.6	0.0	4.4	4.5	6.3	1.3	−2.3
Denmark	−2.1	−1.4	4.7	2.8	0.9	4.3	5.9	−3.5
Finland	4.2	2.9	2.6	3.7	−3.0	7.8	2.4	−3.6
France	−1.1	0.8	−0.9	0.3	−2.2	1.2	−0.5	−5.7
Germany	−4.7	−1.3	1.5	0.3	−0.1	4.0	−0.9	−4.0
Greece	−2.0	−0.7	−6.9	−5.9	2.0	3.0	−0.9	−2.3
Ireland	−8.5	−7.5	−3.5	3.4	1.9	6.3	2.5	−11.9
Italy	−9.9	−3.1	−4.6	−1.8	3.3	5.2	0.1	−0.4
Netherlands	−0.8	−1.7	1.1	−1.3	0.6	4.9	1.5	−4.7
Portugal	−4.0	−5.0	−2.2	2.0	0.8	0.1	−3.5	−3.4
Spain	−0.1	−2.6	−4.7	−0.8	−1.8	1.9	2.5	−8.5
Sweden	1.7	−4.4	−0.9	4.0	−5.5	5.9	3.0	−3.6
Switzerland	n.a.	n.a.	n.a.	1.0	−0.5	2.9	0.2	−1.7
United Kingdom	−2.4	0.0	0.7	1.0	−2.8	6.0	−1.5	−11.2
Japan	−1.9	−1.7	1.6	3.3	−3.4	4.1	−1.3	−9.5
United States	−3.7	−0.8	−2.1	−0.8	0.4	−6.2	−5.9	−7.4

Source: OECD, *Economic Outlook.*

pattern in the data that hits the eye. At all points in time there were countries with a decidedly positive primary balance and countries that ran a sizeable primary deficit. Some countries improved their primary balance over time, and some did not. In terms of the matrix given in Figure 14.2, countries were distributed fairly evenly in both columns and moved back and forth between them. If anything, more countries ran a primary surplus in 1995 than five, ten or fifteen years earlier. This 'trend' may not be quite realistic, however, since 1975 and 1980 were both recession years that followed major increases in oil prices. Recessions tend to make deficits larger than budgeted by depressing income and tax receipts.

Things changed dramatically in 2000, when all countries except the United States sported primary surpluses. This continued, with some qualifications, through most of the first decade of the new millennium. But in the aftermath of the global financial crisis and at the advent of Europe's sovereign debt crisis, the year 2010 classifies as the worst among all years presented in Table 14.1, showing even primary deficits in the double digits for Ireland and the United Kingdom.

Next, consider the difference between real income growth and the real interest rate, $y - r$, which determines the slope of the phase line. Table 14.2 reveals a clear pattern over time and easily explains why budget deficits and the public debt have moved to centre stage on the macroeconomic agenda. In the

Table 14.2 **Real income growth minus real interest rate:** $y - r$. There is a clear pattern in the difference between growth and the real interest rate. In the 1960s and 1970s (with the exception of Denmark), real interest rates fell short of income growth in all countries. Since the 1980s the opposite applies. This puts all countries in the second row of the matrix in Figure 14.2 above.

	1960–9	1970–9	1980–9	1990–9	2000–7	2008–9
Austria	3.86	1.69	−2.32	−1.79	−0.03	−3.14
Belgium	1.35	2.39	−3.71	−2.71	−0.21	−2.87
Denmark	3.01	−0.89	−4.95	−3.03	−0.59	−4.74
Finland	9.50	6.61	0.42	−4.83	0.82	−5.60
France	4.07	3.79	−2.14	−3.31	−0.49	−3.91
Germany	0.13	0.13	−2.78	−2.05	−0.93	−4.24
Greece	n.a.	n.a.	4.33	−4.38	2.96	−2.83
Ireland	1.86	4.71	−0.12	1.40	5.17	−10.07
Italy	3.62	5.46	−0.68	−4.43	−0.78	−5.70
Netherlands	4.59	2.20	−3.54	−1.05	0.08	−3.01
Portugal	n.a.	11.16	3.66	−0.75	0.03	−4.74
Spain	n.a.	6.20	−1.40	−2.48	2.44	−3.77
Sweden	2.28	2.49	−2.00	−3.59	0.17	−5.07
Switzerland	4.09	1.50	0.89	−1.03	0.35	−0.98
United Kingdom	0.07	3.09	−1.31	−2.52	−0.51	−3.70
Japan	10.16	6.03	−1.72	−2.52	−0.05	−5.11
United States	1.94	2.45	−2.57	−0.47	0.66	−3.64

Source: IMF, *International Financial Statistics.*

1960s all countries for which data are available had real income growth rates that were much higher than real interest rates. Thus deficit spending would not cause public debt to run out of bounds, and substantial leeway was provided for fiscal policy. Denmark, for example, whose growth rate exceeded the real interest rate by three percentage points, could have afforded a primary deficit of 2% to meet today's Maastricht convergence criterion of a 60% debt ratio in the long run.

In the 1970s the picture started to change. With growth rates falling worldwide, the difference between income growth and the real interest rate became smaller and was even negative for Denmark. This process continued and intensified into the 1980s. And in the 1990s a single country was left that exceeded the real interest rate. In terms of our case matrix in Figure 14.2, the industrialized countries, including Europe, had moved from the first row, representative of the 1960s, to the second row, representative of the 1980s and 1990s. The last two columns of our table show that the first decade of the common European currency had two faces. During the first eight years, until the real estate bubble collapsed in 2007, more than half of the countries experienced a favourable turn in macroeconomic conditions, with income growth rates that again exceeded the real interest rates that they paid on their debt. And for the other half the difference was small in absolute terms. But the financial crisis wreaked havoc again, this time on the economy. Severe recessions, on some occasions coupled with already rising interest rates, rendered the dynamics of government debt highly unstable in all countries. In terms of our case matrix

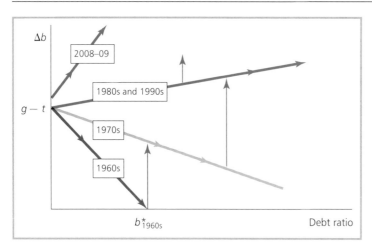

Figure 14.5 During the 1960s growth was much higher than the real interest rate, yielding a steep phase line and an equilibrium deficit ratio of b^*_{1960s}. In the 1970s the phase line becomes flatter, so that even with unchanged primary deficits the debt ratio would start to grow. Since the phase line became positively sloped in the 1980s, there is the danger of the debt ratio growing out of bounds. This intensified in 2008–09.

in Figure 14.2, the industrialized countries, including the European countries, had moved from the first line, representative of the 1960s, to the second line, representative of the 1980s and 1990s. In terms of phase lines, a stylized representation and explanation of the big picture in international debt dynamics is as shown in Figure 14.5.

For a country with a constant primary deficit ratio the 1960s can be represented by the steep negatively sloped line. High income growth caused debt ratios to converge towards b^*_{1960s}. Whether this equilibrium was already attained, or the country was still on the way, growth weakened in the second half of the 1970s, turning the phase line upwards. For the country pictured here it remained negatively sloped, but became much flatter. As a result the debt ratio began to grow again (or to grow faster), moving towards a new equilibrium much further out to the right. While this process was probably still under way, the determinant of the slope of the phase line, $y - r$, weakened even further and turned negative. Not only did this speed up the growth of the debt ratio again, it also made the whole process inherently unstable. There were no longer any internal forces at work that would prevent the public debt ratio from growing out of bounds. The financial crisis finally, by bringing the highest primary deficits and worst macroeconomic conditions yet, shifted the phase line into its highest and steepest position ever.

As Figure 14.6 shows, the development of debt ratios in current EU member states since 1970 reflects by and large the stylized interpretation proposed in Figure 14.5. With the exception of Great Britain (which entered the 1970s with the highest debt ratio of all), all countries saw their debt ratios rise dramatically from the mid- or late-1970s. Some stabilization efforts are visible in the mid- or late-1980s, with permanent success documented only in Ireland. In most countries there is a flattening of the path in the mid-1990s, often even a turnaround that may reflect efforts to meet the Maastricht criterion on public debt. After 2007 debt ratios surge again in almost all countries.

The diagrams shown so far have focused on this *debt(-to-income) ratio*. Since there is another Maastricht criterion that restricts the *deficit(-to-income) ratio* to less than 3%, we now take a look at this variable. Equation (14.2)

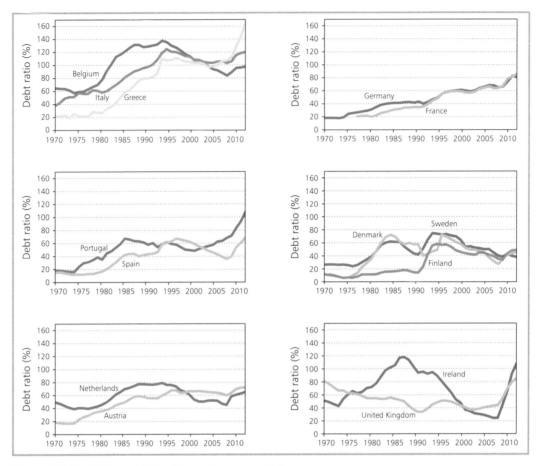

Figure 14.6 The history of debt ratios in EU member states.

Source: Eurostat.

Note. Since this section sets inflation to 0, we might also have written $(\Delta B/Y) = g - t + rb$ for the deficit ratio line. This would be misleading, however, as it is not correct when there is inflation. See equation (14.8).

directly shows how the deficit ratio fits into our graphs. Solving the equation for $\Delta B/Y$ gives

$$\frac{\Delta B}{Y} = g - t + ib \qquad\qquad \textbf{Deficit ratio} \quad (14.6)$$

How the deficit ratio $\Delta B/Y$ relates to the debt ratio b is determined by a positively sloped line in a diagram with the deficit-to-income ratio on the vertical axis and the debt-to-income ratio on the horizontal axis. The intercept with the vertical axis is given by the primary deficit again. So the line intersects the phase line on the vertical axis. The slope of the line is always positive (since $i > 0$) and equal to the interest rate. It is steeper than the phase line (which has slope $r - y$), unless $y < 0$ or $i < r$. Panels (a) and (b) in Figure 14.7 add the newly developed deficit ratio line to the phase line diagrams shown in panels (a) and (d) of Figure 14.3.

In case A, the debt ratio converges towards b^*. Movements along the phase line and into this equilibrium are being accompanied by synchronous movements along the deficit ratio line. Just vertically above b^* an equilibrium deficit ratio exists which happens to be stable in this scenario.

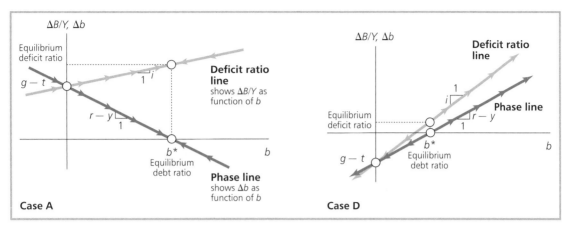

Figure 14.7 The dark blue *phase line* has slope $r - y$. It indicates the change of the debt ratio, Δb, that is associated with each level of the debt ratio b. The lighter *deficit ratio line* has slope i. It indicates the deficit ratio $\Delta B/Y$ that is associated with each level of the debt ratio.

Case D represents the case in which the primary budget is in surplus and income growth falls short of the real interest rate. Here the equilibrium debt ratio is unstable. And so is the equilibrium deficit ratio, which is obtained by moving up vertically to intersect the deficit ratio line.

In the light of the severe political and economic obstacles surrounding budget cuts, **money financing** of deficits may loom as a highly tempting alternative. We have ignored this option so far, for good reasons. Some countries prohibit their central banks from financing government deficit spending beyond certain very tight limits. And even in countries where central banks and governments have that option, monetizing the debt had rarely been used to a substantial extent. Here also, the financial crisis and the ensuing sovereign debt crisis caused many to change their views. Faced with the ultimate question 'to default or not to default', priorities have been reshuffled and the monetization of debt has become a viable option.

CASE STUDY 14.1 The rise and fall of Ireland's public debt

While most European countries (the exception being Britain) had witnessed a steep increase of debt ratios since the start of the 1970s, it is noteworthy that one country, Ireland, had managed to reverse this trend well before it was forced to do so by the 1992 Maastricht Treaty. Figure 14.8 documents the rise and fall of Ireland's debt ratio, with the turnaround showing before the turn of the decade. To develop an understanding of Ireland's remarkable achievement, a useful place to start is the debt-ratio dynamics equation

$$\Delta b = g - t + (r - y)b \qquad (1)$$

which states that two factors tend to make the debt ratio b grow: if the government runs a primary deficit, meaning that it spends more on goods and services, g, than it takes in as revenue, t; or if the real interest rate r exceeds real GDP growth y. Then an existing debt rises faster than GDP so that the debt ratio goes up even if the primary balance $g - t$ is zero. The graph of equation (1), the phase line, has a positive slope and describes an inherently unstable situation if $r > y$.

The lowest point in Figure 14.9 identifies Ireland's debt situation in 1980. The negatively sloped phase line passing through this point

Case study 14.1 continued

Figure 14.8

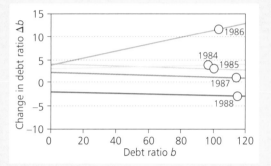

Figure 14.10

indicates that the government ran a primary deficit of nearly 10% of GDP. Since GDP growth obviously exceeded the real interest rate on government debt, the situation nevertheless was inherently stable. Even if the Irish government's structural spending behaviour had never changed, while GDP growth and the real interest rate had remained the same, the debt ratio would never have exceeded 85% of GDP.

The other three points shown in Figure 14.9 trace the development between 1981 and 1983. Two trends are visible: first, the macroeconomic environment deteriorated step by step. The real interest rate rose compared with real income growth, rendering the situation inherently unstable as early as 1983. Second, the primary deficit was reduced in small steps to just over 5% of GDP in 1983. This did not do much good, however, in face of the unstable macroeconomic environment (meaning r exceeding y). Both factors together made the debt ratio rise at an accelerating pace.

The situation changed in two respects after 1983, as Figure 14.10 documents. First, the Irish

government reduced the primary deficit ratio further. It was now driven below 5%. Also, the macroeconomic environment became more favourable again. With the exception of 1986, the phase lines were now more or less horizontal, indicating that the real interest rate and real GDP growth were about the same. Whether the debt ratio rises or falls then crucially depends on the sign of the primary balance. As long as there was still a primary deficit, the debt ratio continued to rise, though now at a slower pace. The decisive and lasting change came in 1988, when the government budget moved into surplus for the first time (where it has remained since). For the first time in more than a decade this made the debt ratio fall.

Figure 14.11 shows the period between 1989 and 1993 when Ireland's government managed to keep the primary balance in surplus. Together with a mostly favourable macroeconomic environment, this permitted the debt ratio to fall quickly. This process was only briefly interrupted in 1993 when the interest rate was so much higher than the rate of growth that despite the primary surplus an increase in the debt ratio resulted in the year 1994.

Figure 14.9

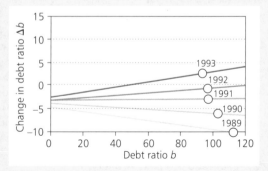

Figure 14.11

Case study 14.1 continued

Figure 14.12

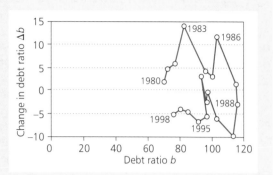

Figure 14.13

The most recent period from 1994 to 1998, shown in Figure 14.12, is one with little change in policy or the macroeconomic environment. Stable primary surpluses and favourable macroeconomic conditions accomplished a steady fall of the debt ratio.

What is the **bottom line** of this case study? The Irish experience between 1980 and 1998 (summarized in an almost circular, clockwise movement in Figure 14.13) reflects both trends in fiscal policy and changes in the macroeconomic environment. The increase in the debt ratio between 1980 and 1988 basically occurred because the macroeconomic environment became unfavourable. An increase in government spending was not at the root of this development. By contrast, the primary deficit ratio even became smaller and smaller during these years. But only when the deficit turned into a surplus *and* the macroeconomic environment became more favourable did the debt ratio begin to come down. Had the primary deficit remained as high as it was at the beginning of the 1980s the debt ratio would obviously have continued to rise in the 1990s. Also, had the macroeconomic environment remained as it was at the beginning of the 1980s, Ireland's debt ratio would never have exploded the way it did.

Afterthought: Ireland's relentless debt reduction continued and succeeded for another 10 years before, within three years, the repercussions of the financial crisis cast the country back to where it had started in the mid-1980s.

Further reading: Brendan Walsh (1996) 'Stabilization and adjustment in a small open economy: Ireland, 1979–95', *Oxford Review of Economic Policy* 12: 74–86.

With this motivation we next allow for money financing of deficits and for inflation, and then proceed to develop a wider perspective of fiscal and monetary policy.

Money financing and inflation

Drawing on Figure 14.1 once again, the budget constraint with money financing of the deficit is

$$T + \Delta B + \Delta M = G + iB \qquad \text{General budget constraint} \quad (14.7)$$

Here M is central bank money or high-powered money, denoted $M0$ in Chapter 3. Transmission into other monetary aggregates appropriate in the macroeconomic models discussed throughout the book obtains via the applicable multiplier. Ignoring this here does not detract from the essence of the argument. Note further that central bank money also changes for motives other than financing the deficit, and through other channels such as buying and selling foreign exchange. So equation (14.7) is not meant to imply that monetization of the deficit is the sole source of central bank money creation, but to show the added contribution that may result from monetizing parts of the budget deficit.

To allow for price changes all variables are nominal and now need to be expressed relative to nominal income PY:

$$\frac{\Delta B}{PY} + \frac{\Delta M}{PY} + t = g + ib \tag{14.8}$$

An approximation for $\Delta B/(PY)$ is obtained from solving the definition $b \equiv B/(PY)$ for B and forming the total differential (see maths note). After rearranging terms this yields

$$\frac{\Delta B}{PY} = \Delta b + (\pi + y)b \tag{14.9}$$

The money financing ratio $\Delta M/(PY)$ may be expanded by M to yield

$$\frac{\Delta M}{PY} = \frac{\Delta M}{M}\frac{M}{PY} = \mu m \tag{14.10}$$

where $m \equiv M/(PY)$ and, as a reminder, μ is the money growth rate. Substituting equations (14.9) and (14.10) into (14.8) and noting $r \equiv i - \pi$ yields our generalized description of debt ratio dynamics:

$$\Delta b = g - t - \mu m - (y - r)b \qquad \textbf{General debt ratio dynamics} \tag{14.11}$$

This generalization has provided two insights. First, the slope of the phase line, and hence the stability of the process, depends explicitly on the difference between income growth and the *real* interest rate. We had already presumed so above, by equating the nominal interest rate with the real interest rate at the absence of inflation. Now we have arrived at this result while explicitly allowing for inflation. Second, the position of the phase line depends not only on the primary deficit, but also on the amount of money financing relative to income. The government's revenue raised by money creation is known as **seignorage**, the flip side of which is the **inflation tax**.

Figure 14.14 illustrates that the required downward shift of the phase line into the lower, light blue position may be accomplished or ameliorated by printing money. If this appears as an easy loophole for governments that shy away from addressing structural budget problems, it is important to note that this option is not available to individual members of a currency union.

This chapter would not be complete if we ducked two crucial questions. The first, more basic one is: what is wrong with running deficits and accumulating debt? Is it really true that public debt places a burden on future generations, as is often claimed, and therefore is to be avoided? The second question is related to the first but is the more urgent one, given the modest growth performance in large parts of the euro area: does EMU, or a monetary union in general, need budget rules as spelled out in the convergence criteria and in the Stability and Growth Pact, and tightened in the Fiscal Compact? We begin with a brief discussion of the first, more general question.

Maths note. Rearranging $b = B/(PY)$ gives $B = bPY$. The total differential of a product of three variables is $dB = db PY + dPb Y + dYbP$, which can be proxied by $\Delta B = \Delta bPY + \Delta Pb Y + \Delta YbP$. Dividing by PY gives $\Delta B/(PY) = \Delta b + (\pi + y)b$, where $\pi = \Delta P/P$ and $y = \Delta Y/Y$.

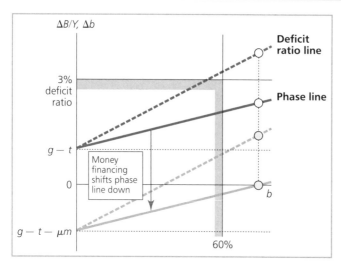

Figure 14.14 To stabilize the debt ratio of an economy (being in the white points) the phase line needs to be shifted down into the light blue position. This can also be achieved at an unchanged primary deficit by resorting to money financing of government spending.

BOX 14.1 Seignorage vs inflation tax revenue

When the government (via the central bank) prints money, two things happen:

■ The government endows itself with purchasing power, with a claim on the real output produced in the economy. This kind of government revenue is called **seignorage**.
■ To the extent that the increase in the money supply leads to inflation, the public loses part of its income. Real income lost due to inflation is sometimes referred to as **inflation tax**.

In equilibrium seignorage and the inflation tax are mirror images of each other (the part of real income claimed by the government is not available any more for purchase by the public), but outside equilibrium they are not.

Seignorage is defined as

$$\mu \frac{M}{P} \qquad \textbf{Seignorage}$$

The fraction measures the purchasing power of the nation's money supply which we have called the real money supply. If the government prints an additional 1% of the current money supply, its seignorage revenue equals 1% of the current money supply's purchasing power.

The inflation tax is defined as

$$\pi \frac{M}{P} \qquad \textbf{Inflation tax}$$

If inflation is 2%, the public's real money holdings shrink by 2%. To bring them back up to the desired

level, individuals need to add a part of their nominal income to their money holdings. This part of income, 2% of real money holdings, is not available for consumption. It is as if individuals were paying a tax.

It is useful to compare seignorage and the inflation tax in terms of the *DAD-SAS* model. If money growth is accompanied by inflation of the same magnitude, income remains unchanged at $Y = Y^*$. Then the cake (real income) did not increase and seignorage must equal the inflation tax. Government revenue goes up at the expense of reduced purchases of the public. If $\mu > \pi$, say as we move up the *SAS* curve, the cake (real income) increases. Seignorage may now exceed the inflation tax because part of the government's additional claim on real output can come from the additional income generated by the money supply increase. In the extreme Keynesian scenario with fixed prices, all seignorage revenue comes out of added output. Then the public pays no inflation tax in the short run.

There is a natural limit to how far seignorage may rise as inflation rises. The more inflation the government generates, the higher interest rates rise. But higher nominal interest rates make holding money more costly and, therefore, reduce real money holdings M/P. After some threshold people are likely to reduce real money holdings faster than inflation eats away at the existing real money supply. Further increases in inflation then reduce rather than increase seignorage.

CASE STUDY 14.2   Who wanted the euro? The role of government debt

In the mid-1990s not all 15 member states of the European Union welcomed the prospect of a single currency. At one extreme, 70% of Italians welcomed the euro while only 15% rejected it. At the other extreme only 25% of the Danish public wanted the euro while a hefty 60% did not. We saw in Case study 11.1 that part of this difference in attitudes can be attributed to different inflation experiences and, hence, different benefits from the price stability the ECB's monetary policy is expected to bring. We now ask whether fiscal policy experiences play a similar role in public attitudes.

A side effect of the adoption of the euro is that the Treaty of Maastricht disciplines *fiscal policy*. This will affect those countries most which revealed least discipline in government spending in the past. Why should the public care about government budgets? Well, we learned in Chapter 10 that if the government runs deficits, spending mostly on public consumption, there will be less investment, less capital formation and, hence, a steady state that is characterized by a lower capital stock and less income. Since the public debt roughly sums up all past deficits, it is a good indicator of fiscal discipline, or the lack thereof. We may thus postulate a negative relationship between the public debt ratio b and potential income Y^*, say in the form $Y^* = \bar{Y} - \alpha b$, where $\bar{Y}$ denotes maximum potential income to obtain when the government keeps its budget balanced on average. Of course, $\bar{Y}$ differs for each country depending on population size and other parameters.

Figure 14.15 illustrates the essence of this argument, using Belgium, Italy, Denmark and the UK as examples. The interpretation of the graph is as follows. The EMU dot denotes the hypothetical steady-state income each country can achieve once its spending is disciplined by EMU and the **Stability and Growth Pact**. The other dots reflect what each country may expect outside of EMU, based on past debt performance and on the assumption that potential income is negatively correlated with the debt ratio. Britain, for example, could expect to move from the Britain dot into the EMU dot and reap the associated utility gains. Generally, countries like Belgium and Italy (with debt ratios of 135% and 122%, respectively), can expect a relatively large increase in potential income and, if all countries' citizens have the same preferences as indicated by the indifference curves shown, should benefit a lot from adopting the euro. Denmark

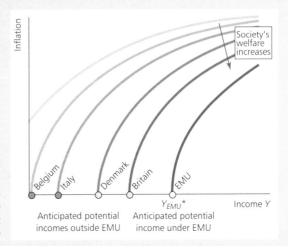

Figure 14.15

and Britain, with more moderate debt ratios of 70% and 57%, respectively, would have to settle for much lower benefits. Summing up: *The higher a country's government deficits (as summed up in the current public debt) were in the past, the more its public should welcome the euro.*

Figure 14.16 allows a detailed examination of this hypothesis. The horizontal axis measures the public debt in 1995 (reflecting the fiscal discipline mustered by independent national governments) for each of the 15 member states. The vertical axis

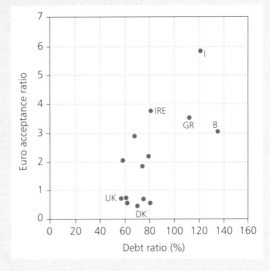

Figure 14.16

Case study 14.2 continued

measures the euro acceptance ratio (yes percentage divided by no percentage).

The data support the above hypothesis. Countries like Belgium, Italy and Greece, which had run up very high levels of debt, welcomed the euro a lot. Acceptance ratios ran between 3 and 6. Other countries such as the UK, Denmark and Finland, on the other hand, whose governments had succeeded in keeping the public debt in check even without the euro, bluntly rejected the euro with acceptance ratios around 0.5.

The correspondence between debt and the acceptance ratio suggested by the graph is not perfect. Italy, for example, has less debt than Belgium, but the acceptance ratio is twice as high. The explanation is that the acceptance ratio depends not only on debt but also on past inflation, and Italy had suffered from much higher inflation than Belgium, as we learned in Case study 11.2. For the same reason, because of pre-euro infla-

tion rates in double figures, Ireland has a rather high acceptance ratio despite a moderate debt ratio.

Tracing the acceptance ratio back to two explanatory variables, inflation and debt, reveals the limitations of graphical data analysis: it cannot properly handle and illustrate relationships between more than two variables. Adequate treatment of more complex relationships requires statistical methods, the kind you are encouraged to use in the 'Your turn' section in this chapter's applied problems. With this reservation, the empirical evidence on how the debt ratio influenced public attitudes towards the euro underscores our previous result (see Case study 11.2) that the public in the EU member states apparently knew quite well why it wanted the euro or why it didn't.

Source and further reading: M. Gärtner (1997) 'Who wants the euro – and why? Economic explanations of public attitudes towards a single European currency', *Public Choice* 93: 487–510.

14.3 What is wrong with having deficits and debt?

Though this question had not been specifically posed in Chapter 10, we had found the basic answer in section 10.1, where the influence of the government budget on economic growth is discussed in the context of the Solow model. It should suffice here to restate the main insights.

A government budget deficit needs to be financed by credit from the private sector (if we exclude money financing). That means it sucks up private savings, by domestic residents or from abroad, that are then no longer available for capital formation. This reduces the capital stock the country has in the steady state and, therefore, steady-state and potential income.

The insight that repeated budget deficits are bad for income in the long run comes with a few caveats:

- It only applies with full force when the government spends only on public consumption. When the government finances investment projects instead, budget deficits today may even be good for future income levels.
- It needs to be re-evaluated in the context of the golden rule of capital accumulation. If private savings were excessively high, a government budget deficit might be detrimental for steady-state income, but nevertheless raise present and future consumption.
- If the Ricardian equivalence theorem applied in strict form, the government would not be able to influence national (private plus public) savings. Private savings would simply respond so as to compensate for any changes in public savings. Then budget deficits would not impact on capital formation and steady-state income. While this is a theoretical possibility it appears that this is not the case in reality.

Structural budget deficits run by current generations accumulate debt on which future generations have to pay interest, meaning that this part of their income will not be available for consumption or capital formation. The extent to which this must be considered an unfair burden on future generations depends on whether future generations are compensated by appropriate returns. If today's deficits are due to excessive public consumption, then returns for future generations are zero and the verdict is clear: current generations do place an unfair burden on their offspring. If current deficits are due to investment spending, however, the verdict is open. As a general rule, the interest payment of future generations on government debt must be compared with the returns on investment projects conducted by previous generations before we can judge who is placing a burden on whom.

14.4 Does monetary union need budget rules?

You may have noted that the previous arguments were carefully put. Deficits *can* be in the best interest of society, present and future, and *may* be desirable to some extent. It would be naive, however, to downplay or ignore the temptation for governments in today's democracies to direct spending and deficit spending into areas chosen not according to prospective long-run returns for society, but on the basis of short-run political gains. Fiscal policy is driven by incentives similar to those we emphasized while discussing monetary policy in Chapter 11. Just as such incentives may lure monetary policy into generating an inflation bias, fiscal policy may suffer from a **spending bias** that leads to an excessive level of public debt. Having noted those tendencies, the crucial question is whether a monetary union increases the government's temptation to spend or puts a lid on it.

The main argument in support of budget rules in monetary unions focuses on the creation of externalities by one country for other countries. Just as individuals spend more on given products if they can put part of the costs onto the shoulders of others, so will governments. Due to its nth currency privileges the Bundesbank made other EU members bear part of the costs of its disinflation efforts after German unification, by raising their interest rates. After the transition to a single European currency, each member's fiscal policy action has a smaller effect on domestic interest rates than if the country had retained its own currency and flexible exchange rate. This is due to the open-interest-parity equilibrium condition for the international capital markets. If depreciation expectations are ruled out due to the adoption of a common currency, interest rates should remain the same in all member states at all times. This interest rate externality may undermine fiscal discipline, as we saw when discussing fiscal policy in a currency union in Chapter 12. Hence, budget rules as laid down in the Stability and Growth Pact need to be put in place to provide for appropriate guidelines.

The advanced argument for fiscal policy rules ignores the possibility that capital markets put a risk premium on countries that run up debt ratios. Since rising debt ratios raise default risk, such countries may only obtain additional loans at higher interest rates than other, more disciplined countries. This would permit interest rates to differ between countries, even though bonds are denominated in the same currency, and thus limit the interest rate externality.

The empirical evidence suggests that the risk premium may serve to caution fiscal policy. It can only do so if the risk is borne by the country whose policies generate it in the first place. If the market can be confident that some institution – this may be the International Monetary Fund on the world stage, or the other EU members in the case of the euro area – is committed to rescue individual countries that find themselves in financial trouble, there is no country-specific risk and, consequently, no risk premium that drives the domestic interest rate up. To prevent such bailouts, the Maastricht Treaty contains a no-bailout clause that ties the hands of governments and of the European Central Bank. Whether we are prepared to rely on financial markets and the risk premium to tame government spending depends on whether we consider such no-bailout clauses credible. If we do, no additional restrictions on fiscal policy are really needed and we could make do without the rules given in the Stability and Growth Pact.

Many observers did not consider the no-bailout clause very credible, and their mistrust already received support during the global economic crisis that started in 2007–08. This crisis had pushed several countries to the brink of bankruptcy. European countries that ran into difficulty were all rescued by multibillion bailouts: not from the ECB, but from other countries and institutions. In October 2008, Hungary received loans totalling €20 billion from the EU, the IMF and the World Bank. The Ukraine secured a $16.5 billion loan from the IMF. And Iceland, having run into serious trouble first, obtained a help package of around $6 billion from the IMF and its Nordic neighbours.

When a no-bailout clause is not credible and, therefore, interest rates cannot differ all that much between countries, additional constraints are needed. While fiscal policy criteria specified in the Maastricht Treaty must be considered arbitrary, they may have helped to make the launching of the euro less painful for some countries. Limiting fiscal policy by rules, as the Stability and Growth Pact does, has a price, however. It ties the hands of fiscal policy, which turns into a serious problem when monetary policy refuses to act, or has lost its bite, say when the economy is caught in a liquidity trap, as during the global financial crisis of 2008. The severity of the anticipated economic slowdown and the urgency for some sort of promising help from monetary policy encouraged the European Commission to put the Stability Pact temporarily on ice. But the problem returned with a vengeance when the debt crisis broke in 2010.

14.5 Government debt and the financial markets

The formalization of debt dynamics in equation (14.4) that provided the background for our discussion of public debt so far is kind of mechanical. It builds on a mechanism, though in a simplified fashion, that is true by definition. It is an accounting equation rather than an economic model. Key economic determinants of the fate of public finances are considered exogenous, and thus not an endogenous part of public debt dynamics. This could render the discussion of debt dynamics lopsided and may lead to a biased diagnosis and make governments reach for the wrong medicine in times of sovereign budget crises.

Letting inflation be zero, equation (14.4) rewrites

$$\Delta b = g - t + (i - y)b \qquad (14.12)$$

None of the determinants of debt dynamics in this equation are really exogenous from a macroeconomic perspective. Endogenizing all of them would require the integration of this equation into a complete macroeconomic model. We will take a step in this direction in the next chapter. For now we focus on the most volatile of these 'exogenous' variables, the interest rate, while still considering the other ones exogenous.

It is one of the key lessons taught by Europe's sovereign debt drama that unfolded since 2010 that the determinants of the stability and the level of public debt ratios are not slowly evolving, exogenous anchors. This lesson applies to interest rates in particular. They can respond nervously and massively to developments in other markets, and to mood swings in financial markets in particular. Figure 14.17 illustrates this impressively for the case of Greece. After a quiet first decade in the new millennium, during which even the real estate and financial crisis of 2007–09 only had a minor effect on the level and the volatility of Greek government bond yields, things changed dramatically in 2010. Within a year Greek government bond yields more than doubled. And within two years they were ten times as high as before the financial crisis. Only the 'haircut' decided on 9 March 2012, which made private lenders accept a **debt restructuring** by which they forfeited 'voluntarily' a substantial part of their claims against the Greek government, brought brief but temporary relief.

Government bond yields and sovereign debt rating

We will use a simple extension of our debt dynamics model to carve out some important implications of the integration of the market for government bonds into the global financial sector.

The interest rate in equation (14.12) is determined in the market for government bonds. We may look at this market in isolation because debt ratios move slowly compared to how quickly things can change in this market. The market for sovereign bonds is characterized by two equations:

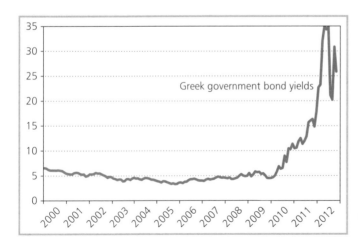

Figure 14.17 Greek government bond yields, as a measure of the interest rate the Greek government has to pay on its debt, experienced a quiet first decade in the new millennium. After 2010 yields virtually exploded and only dipped after a 'haircut' which forced most creditors to accept a loss of some 50% on their Greek government bonds.

The first one is an **equilibrium condition** that renders investors indifferent between a risk-free asset, which pays the interest rate i_0, and a government bond with an attached default probability of ω and an interest rate i. This relationship is not linear, as a simple example may illustrate: one euro invested in the risk-free asset grows to $1 + i_0$ within one period. One euro invested in the risky government bond may be expected to be worth $(1 - \omega)(1 + i)$ after one period. Risk-neutral investors are indifferent between these two assets only if expected returns are identical, that is, if $1 + i_0 = (1 - \omega)(1 + i)$. Solving this equation for i yields the equilibrium condition we are looking for:

Note. This model is based on David Romer, Advanced Macroeconomics, McGraw-Hill.

$$i = \frac{i_0 + \omega}{1 - \omega} \tag{14.13}$$

A second equation determines default risk. The idea is that each period the government decides on whether to service its debt or to default. This decision results from a cost-benefit analysis, from a look at the difference between the country's ability to pay and the size of the required payment.

The *ability to pay* is given by the country's tax revenue or, more precisely, by how much is left for interest payments after the deduction of non-interest spending. So we are looking at the determinants of the *primary deficit* ratio. These are government spending, the tax rate and income.

The *size of the required payment*, relative to income, equals the product $i \times b$. Therefore, the higher the interest rate, the higher government debt, and the lower the level of real income, the more tempting it is for the government to default, and the higher is, therefore, the country's default risk.

The result of this cost-benefit calculation may be summed up in the equation

$$\omega = \omega_0 + \beta i \tag{14.14}$$

where β is a positive parameter and ω_0 reflects all other influences, besides the interest rate, on the government's assessment of costs and benefits that we just discussed.

We may now solve the model of the government bonds market given by equations (14.13) and (14.14) by substituting the second into the former and rearranging terms to give the quadratic equation

$$\beta i^2 - (1 - \omega - \beta)i + i_0 + \omega_0 = 0$$

Maths note: A quadratic equation of the form $ax^2 + bx + c = 0$ has the solution

$$x_{1,2} = \frac{-b \pm \sqrt{b^2 - 4ac}}{2a}$$

This equation has the two solutions (see the recipe in the margin note)

$$i_1, i_2 = \frac{1 - \beta - \omega_0 \pm \sqrt{(1 - \beta - \omega_0)^2 - 4\beta(i_0 + \omega_0)}}{2\beta}$$

suggesting the presence of multiple equilibria. Before we turn to a graphical discussion of this model, let us spice it up by bringing credit rating agencies into the picture, which played key roles in recent debt crises.

Since default probabilities are not directly observed, financial markets rely heavily on credit ratings as indicators of risk. To keep things simple, let the sovereign debt rating R be a linear transformation of the default risk ω:

$$R = 21\omega \tag{14.15}$$

The coefficient of 21 assumes that ratings increase in 21 steps from AAA = 0 to D = 21. After substituting (14.16) into (14.13) and (14.14), equation (14.14) may be represented by a straight line in a diagram with the interest rate and the credit rating on the axes, as in Figure 14.18. When the rating is AAA = 0 this line meets the vertical axis at $i_{AAA} = -R_0/\beta$. There is also an upper limit i_D for the interest rate (which carries a rating of D = 21) at which the country is certain to default.

Equation (14.13) shows as a hyperbola which intersects the vertical axis at the risk-free interest rate i_0. As the rating deteriorates, the risk premium grows at an accelerating pace.

The points of intersections between the interest rate line and the rating line mark equilibria in the market for government bonds. In such an equilibrium the market charges the interest rate that reflects the credit rating, and the credit rating signals the correct default risk associated with this interest rate. How many such equilibria exist depends on the relative positions of the two lines. We will focus on the constellation with two points of intersection shown in Figure 14.18.

Points U and V in Figure 14.18 suggest that there is a good equilibrium with an excellent credit rating and a low interest rate, and another one that is not so good. This one carries significant default risk, and this shows in much higher interest payments. Which of these equilibria is relevant? In order to answer this question we need to go beyond statics and look at the *dynamics* of the market.

Suppose that there is a, however small, lag in the response of the interest rate to changes in credit ratings, and, possibly in the response of credit ratings to the determinants of default risk, which include the interest rate. Then an unjustified credit rating of, say, R_1 generates the interest rate i_1. This new interest rate lowers the rating to R_2, which lowers the interest rate to i_2. This process continues until the market has settled into the good equilibrium at U.

The leading credit rating agencies use similar rating scales and labels, but the number of steps between AAA and D may differ.

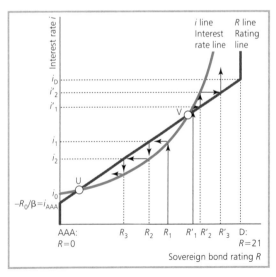

Figure 14.18 The *i* line indicates the interest rate that investors require at different default probabilities, as measured by the sovereign debt rating. The *R* line indicates how default becomes more likely when the interest rate goes up. Equilibria obtain where the two lines intersect. There is a third 'equilibrium', all the way to the right, where default is almost certain and interest rates grow very high. The equilibrium in the middle (point V) is unstable. It marks an insolvency threshold. Once it is crossed, markets drive the country towards insolvency. As long as the country remains to the left of the threshold, a return to the 'good' equilibrium (point U) is to be expected.

Since the same argument applies when the initial rating is too low, to the left of point U, the equilibrium U is *stable* – at least as long as we remain to the left of point V.

What happens when we move to the right of V? Suppose there is an unjustified rating downgrade to R_1'. Then the interest rate rises to i_1', which drives the rating further up to R_2', raising the interest rate still further, and this continues until default becomes unavoidable. This demonstrates that V is not a stable equilibrium. Instead it marks an **insolvency threshold**. Once it is crossed a process of **self-fulfilling prophecy** sets in, in which bad ratings generate the very interest rate that justifies them. The country moves towards a third, very bad equilibrium in which there is no way to avoid default. This third equilibrium is not identified by a point, because it constitutes some sort of trap. Default becomes virtually certain and the market basically refuses to extend loans to this country, at any interest rate.

Risks and policy options

Historically, most industrial countries have been positioned in their 'good' equilibrium with low interest rates. In this situation a country's solvency is protected by a buffer, the size of which is determined by the horizontal distance between points U and V. The further the insolvency threshold is away, the less likely any kind of disturbance, in the form of shocks to the rating or to the interest rate, may suffice as a trigger for a serious debt crisis. Two kinds of developments may make a country's situation more fragile, however.

First, any deterioration in the fundamental variables that determine the budget situation of the country. This could be due to unfavourable developments in any of the variables that determine the coefficient R_0 in the rating equation, as we noted above. In Figure 14.19, panel (a), this is shown as a downward shift of the rating line. If this shift is small, as shown by the dark blue line, it makes the good equilibrium worse and the threshold actually better by moving it to the left, thus shrinking the buffer and bringing the country much closer to falling into the abyss. If the shift is large, as shown by the black line, the good, stable equilibrium disappears and a crisis with ever-increasing interest rates and rating downgrades sets in, with inevitable default on the horizon.

Second, any changes in the form of errors, misperceptions, panics or even abuses in the government bond market. As illustrated in Figure 14.19, panel (b), such changes could mean that either the determination of interest rates deviates from previous patterns, say because the market fell into panic mode. Or it could mean that rating agencies commit errors, or, as has been argued or speculated, deliberately slap unwarranted rating downgrades on a country. In the first case, the interest rate that results from a given rating rises above what the interest line suggests. In the second case, the country is downgraded beyond the rating suggested by the rating line. Again, if the unexplained increase of the interest rate or of the credit rating is big enough to push the variable out of the neighbourhood within which the good equilibrium is stable, that is beyond the thresholds set by point V, a debt crisis is initiated that propels itself.

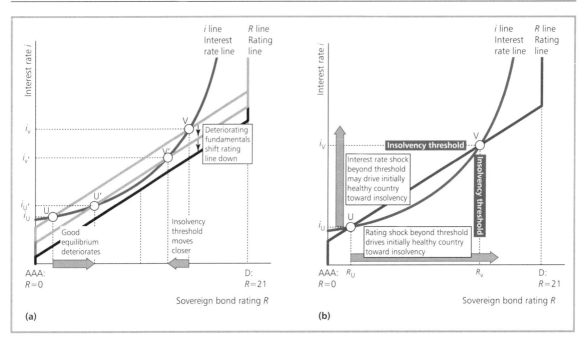

Figure 14.19 When fundamental determinants of public deficits and debt deteriorate – this could be an increase in government spending or a recession – the rating line shifts to the right. This indicates that default risk has increased at any given interest rate. As a consequence, the good equilibrium deteriorates and the insolvency threshold moves left (panel (a)). Panel (b) suggests that substantial shocks to the interest rate, or rating errors, may even push countries with healthy fundamentals onto a path towards insolvency.

This brings us to the question of what the policy options are when the government bonds market features multiple equilibria and a country finds itself at the risk of being pushed into a situation where market expectations or ratings become self-fulfilling. While this is not the place to go into the details of the many proposals that the recent sovereign debt crisis has generated, our model suggests three main categories into which this proposals fall.

Austerity and the fiscal compact

Austerity refers to cutting the budget deficit and reducing the debt by lowering government spending, sometimes coupled with raising taxes.

Budget measures aim at improving those fundamental variables that are believed to have generated the threat that the government can no longer honour its debt liabilities. These measures, summarized under the name austerity, target the position of the interest rate line. Reducing the deficit and subsequently lowering the debt should shift the rating line up, should improve or re-establish the good equilibrium if it was lost, and shift the insolvency threshold further out again, towards higher interest rates and worse ratings.

Fiscal austerity was the main medicine that the European Union, in coordination with the IMF, offered to its crisis members. Austerity is also considered the main line of defence against future debt crises. This is documented by the

The Fiscal Compact is a treaty to enter into force in 2013. It requires members' budgets to balance or be in surplus.

so-called Fiscal Compact to come into force in 2013 which, in its core, requires countries to keep their budgets balanced or in surplus.

Judgement on the advisability of austerity packages depends crucially on one's time horizon. For a country that anticipates medium- to *longer-run* budgetary and debt issues, improving its budget in order to render long-run debt ratios sustainable is certainly a necessity. A precondition for its success is, however, that budgetary consolidation is not achieved at the cost of sacrificing essential public investment into a country's infrastructure or human capital. This is a lesson we learned in Chapter 10.

If a country faces an *acute* debt crisis, however, with the threat of insolvency just around the corner, there are trade-offs involved that render the issue more complex. Yes, a reduction of the primary deficit via spending cuts has a positive effect on a country's solvency and should move the interest line up as intended. But this effect is partial, because, in all likelihood, this will come at the cost of receding incomes. This affects a country's solvency negatively. First, because it leads to lower tax revenues. And second, this is simple arithmetic, because deficit and debt *ratios* increase, even if deficit and debt *levels* remained constant. These two adverse effects leave it open whether the net effect of austerity on the interest line is an upward or a downward shift.

Eurobonds and rescue packages

A second group of measures calls for outside help. This could imply the purchase of government bonds by the European Central Bank, or direct loans to the country in trouble at preferred interest rates. The latter played a key role in 2010–12 when the Eurozone, in cooperation with the IMF and other countries, set up the **EFSF** (European Financial Stability Facility), a bailout fund to provide help for countries with acute solvency problems at affordable interest rates. This temporary solution is to be transformed into a permanent one called the **ESM** (European Stability Mechanism) after 2012. Other proposals intended to spread a crisis country's default risk on more shoulders are **Eurobonds**. These call for a joint issue of debt by all Eurozone members, which then pass these funds on to individual countries. All these measures essentially aim at severing the link between a country's presumably unfavourable essentials (meaning primary budget deficit, deficit ration, economic growth, and so on) and the interest rate it pays for its debt. If such measures succeed and the country effectively pays a lower interest rate than warranted by its budgetary and macroeconomic situation, thus technically experiencing a positive interest rate shock, this may indeed help it escape from the maelstrom that lies beyond the insolvency threshold U.

Speculation/bonds

The measures discussed above proceed from the diagnosis that it is the deterioration of fundamentals that has shifted either or both of the two lines in the government bonds market unfavourably and thus caused the country's fiscal and solvency problems. An alternative view concludes that these

CASE STUDY 14.3   Moody and Poor: rating sovereign debt

The major credit rating agencies, Fitch Rating, Moody's, and Standard & Poor's Ratings Services, played a controversial role in the financial crisis and are under criticism again in the Eurozone's sovereign debt crisis. Some argue that rating agencies are simply innocent messengers of bad news. Others question their competence, their integrity or even think they have an agenda. We leave it to the readers to surf the internet for arguments in support of and against these views. Here we look at two empirical points made in the context of this discussion.

Rating bias against governments

Figure 14.20 looks at two financial assets: government bonds and collateralized debt obligations (CDOs). It reports for a set of initial rating classes the percentages in each asset category that defaulted within five years after being put on the market.

The results are striking. While no country with a rating of A or better ever defaulted within the following five years, between 20 and 30% of CDOs in this asset class did so. The authors of the underlying study generalize this by saying that governments typically receive a rating that is four notches worse than for a commercial debtor or asset with the same risk.

Rating bias against PIGS

Table 14.3 looks at how the sovereign ratings of Portugal, Ireland, Greece and Spain (at some point called the PIGS) developed after the financial crisis. The middle column reports estimates of how many rating categories these countries should have been downgraded, based on their deteriorating financial and economic situation, if they had been

treated like other OECD members. The numbers are modest in all cases and never reach two rating categories. Compare this with the column on the right, which shows the actual downgrades of these countries by Fitch Ratings. These range from three notches for Spain to a whopping twelve notches for Greece. So for this group of countries some 2–12 notches of rating downgrades between 2009 and 2011 are left unexplained when the rating algorithm estimated for other countries are applied.

These obvious and well-documented biases against governments in general and a hand-picked group of Eurozone members in particular puts a serious question mark behind the claim that rating agencies are competent, unbiased and passive participants in the financial markets. The evidence is strong that rating errors or biases may have played a key role in the gestation of the Eurozone debt crisis, as sketched in Figure 14.19.

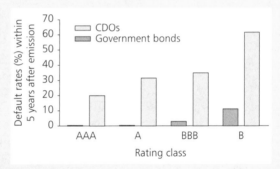

Figure 14.20 Default rates within five years after emission

CDOs means Collateralized Debt Obligations;
Source: Based on J. Cornaggia, K. Cornaggia and J. Hund (2012) *Credit Ratings across Asset Classes: A ≡ A?*, Mimeo, March, Table III. http://papers.ssrn.com/sol3/papers.cfm?abstract_id=1909091

Table 14.3 Justified and actual downgrades of PIGS countries, 2009–11

Country	Downgrade	
	justified by deterioration of fundamentals	actual, by Fitch Ratings
Spain	0.46 notches	3 notches (AA+ to AA−)
Ireland	1.32 notches	7 notches (AAA to BBB+)
Portugal	0.62 notches	8 notches (AA to BB+)
Greece	0.15 notches	12 notches (A to CCC)

Sources: Numbers are computed from M. Gärtner and B. Griesbach (2012) *Rating agencies, self-fulfilling prophecy and multiple equilibria: An empirical model of the European sovereign debt crisis 2009–2011*. University of St. Gallen, SEPS, Economics Working Paper No. 2012–15. http://ideas.repec.org/p/usg/econwp/201215.html

CASE STUDY 14.4   Culprit or victim: European debt and the financial crisis

The leading narrative on the causes of the Eurozone sovereign debt crisis is that this happened (i) because countries were 'living beyond their means', (ii) because governments were irresponsible in their spending behaviour, and (iii) because of blunders in the design of Europe's common currency project. This diagnosis is entertained by part of academia, by most of the media, and, interestingly and particularly, by the Eurozone's politicians themselves. A minority in all those camps contends, however, that this is a serious distortion of reality. Their claim is that what is really at the roots of the sovereign debt crisis is the financial crisis that followed from the collapse of the real estate bubble in 2007. What do the data say?

Figure 14.21 looks at those Eurozone members that were the first to come under fire from financial markets and rating agencies. The panel on the left shows the development of debt ratios in Greece, Ireland, Italy, Portugal and Spain from the introduction of the euro in 2000 until the beginning of the financial crisis in 2007. There is no evidence whatsoever that the introduction of the euro encouraged countries to overspend. Ireland's and Spain's debt ratios show a clear downward trend. Those of Greece and Italy remained constant, more or less. The only country with a visible upward trend is Portugal, though the level its

debt ratio reached even in 2007 would hardly be a cause for alarm.

The panel on the right shows the years after the start of the financial crisis. Without exception, this is when public finances really started to deteriorate. Not only in Greece or in Ireland, where the accomplishments of two decades of debt reduction were swept away within four years, not only in Eurozone countries, but virtually in all industrial countries in Europe and beyond. The reasons are the recessions into which the financial crisis drove most countries. At any level of public debt, the debt ratio rises by 5% when income drops by 5%, even when the budget is balanced. But budget deficits also exploded, because tax revenues fell, which are related to income, and because the government had to pick up the pieces after the crash in the financial markets: bail out banks; rescue car manufacturers and their suppliers; increase social security spending in the face of receding employment; and stimulate aggregate demand.

So the least that Figure 14.21 says is that we cannot look at the debt crisis as an isolated affair. Its linkages with the real estate and financial crisis need to be analyzed when we recommend policies and think about the prevention of future crises.

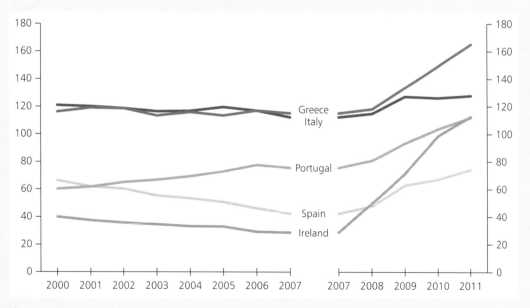

Figure 14.21

effects were minor. Economic and budget conditions had become not nearly as bad as the sovereign debt ratings that were dished out to a number of Eurozone countries or the exorbitant interest rates demanded by investors would make you believe. Instead, it is argued, market panic and schizophrenia in the wake of the financial crisis, the virtual impossibility to quantify sovereign default risk in historically unique situations and to assess its accuracy, and the excessive volume of derivative markets, paired with serious conflicts of interest, may have led to inflated ratings and interest rates and positioned these way to the right of the rating line and/or far above the interest rate line. If this alternative diagnosis is correct, fiscal austerity and rescue packages may be as promising as Don Quixote's battle against windmills. Measures to take in such a case would be tighter regulation and downsizing of financial markets, including a thorough investigation of the role of rating agencies. Small steps have been taken in this direction. These include a ban on so-called naked credit default swaps (CDSs) and the plan for a financial transaction tax in Europe. At present it looks like much of this may be symbolic rather than substantial.

> **Credit default swap (CDS)** A credit insurance against the default of a country. If traders own such bonds the CDS hedges against this risk. A CDS is 'naked' if traders do not own such bonds and merely bet on this risk.

Bottom line

The basic mechanics of debt dynamics are straightforward and more reminiscent of financial accounting than of economics. In quiet times the macroeconomic variables that enter these accounting exercises evolve in a rather controlled fashion. This permitted us to trace the bigger changes in Europe's debt dynamics over several decades with some success. Recent developments remind us, however, that in times of turmoil and panic in financial markets, when multiple equilibria and self-fulfilling prophecy loom, developments may become quite unpredictable. While the basic mechanics still work fine, interest rates can become so volatile and move so erratically and excessively that conventional measures fail as remedies. Ignoring this and focusing on fiscal austerity or even economic growth alone, without thorough scrutiny of financial markets and the regulation they need, may not produce adequate safeguards from such crises that stand the test of time.

CHAPTER SUMMARY

- Ways of financing a government budget deficit, the difference between expenditures and tax receipts, are to obtain a loan from the public or for the central bank to print money.

- To allow for meaningful comparisons between countries and across time, a country's deficit spending and debt position must be expressed relative to income, in terms of deficit-to-income and debt-to-income ratios.

- Whether a country is a net borrower or a net lender in equilibrium depends on whether the difference between income and the real interest rate and the primary deficit are of the same sign. If they are, equilibrium implies debt. If they are not, equilibrium implies a net lender position.

- Data on income growth and real interest rates suggest that during the last two decades of the twentieth century the dynamic interaction between deficits and debt was inherently unstable. In this situation, stabilizing the debt ratio requires appropriate adjustments of non-interest spending by the government.

■ The Maastricht Treaty's convergence criteria on deficits and debt force governments to adjust government budgets. The inflation criterion augments these and ensures that governments have little leeway in solving budget problems by recourse to money financing.

■ Monetary unions may undermine budgetary discipline unless the members can commit to a credible no-bailout clause. If that is not feasible, budget rules as laid down in the EU's Stability and Growth Pact may be needed.

■ The market for government bonds may feature multiple equilibria. One equilibrium is stable and sustainable. Another one is unstable and constitutes an insolvency threshold.

■ Once a country is pushed beyond its insolvency threshold, a process of self-fulfilling prophecy sets in. Credit rating downgrades raise interest rates to an extent that justifies further downgrades. This process continues until the country is forced to default. Default may be considered a third equilibrium.

Key terms and concepts

austerity *430*	government debt *422*
budget deficit *406*	inflation tax *420*
credit default swap (CDS) *434*	insolvency threshold *429*
credit rating agency *427*	money financing *417*
debt ratio (debt-to-income ratio) *408*	multiple equilibria *428*
	phase diagram *409*
deficit financing *406*	phase line *409*
deficit ratio (deficit-to-income ratio) *408*	primary deficit *407*
	public debt *407*
Eurozone debt crisis *433*	seignorage *420*
Fiscal compact *431*	self-fulfilling prophecy *429*
government budget constraint *407*	Stability and Growth Pact *422*
	spending bias *424*

EXERCISES

14.1 Table 14.4 presents data on debt and GDP for a number of European countries in 1992. Compute the debt ratios and determine the level of debt that would just meet the Maastricht criterion of 60% of GDP.

14.2 Consider a country with a primary deficit ratio of 2%, an income growth rate of 5% and a real interest rate of 3%.

(a) What is the equilibrium debt ratio b^*? Is the equilibrium stable?

Table 14.4

	D	F	i^b	GB	B	DK	FIN	GR
Nominal GDP[a]	3076.6	6776.2	1504.0	597.2	7098.4	851.3	476.8	18,238.1
Government debt[c]	1402.5	3076.1	1755.2	284.9	9306.0	627.4	220.3	16,140.7

Notes: [a]generally: in billions of domestic currency; [b]in trillion lire; [c]general government gross financial liabilities.
Source: OECD, *Economic Outlook.*

(b) What is the deficit ratio in the long-run equilibrium?

(c) The government wants to increase the primary deficit to 3.5% of national income. What is the debt ratio in the new equilibrium? What is the deficit ratio?

(d) Suppose the country wants to meet the Maastricht criterion of a maximum debt ratio of 60%. What would be the primary deficit that would just meet this criterion?

(e) The interest rate rises to 4%, whereas the growth rate decreases to 2%. What is the new equilibrium debt ratio $b*$ if $g - t$ remains at 2%? Starting from a debt ratio of 20%, does the country have a chance of reaching that equilibrium?

14.3 In this chapter, both the interest rate and the growth rate were taken as exogenously given. However, the Solow growth model presented in Chapter 9 provides us with the tools to determine whether, for a given country, the growth rate of income will be higher or lower than the interest rate in the steady state. (Recall that the interest rate equals the marginal product of capital and the net interest rate is the interest rate minus the rate of depreciation.) Determine the relation between the growth rate of output and the interest rate for the following:

(a) Country A, where the production function is $\hat{y} = \hat{k}^{0.3}$ (where $\hat{y}$ is output per efficiency unit), the savings rate is 20%, the exogenous rate of technological progress is 0.04, the population growth rate is 0.02 and the annual depreciation rate is 10%.

(b) Country B, where the production is $\hat{y} = \hat{k}^{0.1}$ (where $\hat{y}$ is output per efficiency unit), the savings rate is 30%, the exogenous rate of technological progress is 0.05, the population growth rate is 0.01 and the annual depreciation rate is 10%.

(c) Are both countries dynamically efficient?

14.4 In 1994 British interest rates were $i = 7.83$, inflation was $\pi = 2.67$ and real GDP growth stood at $y = 4$. The primary deficit ratio was 4.3. What is the equilibrium debt ratio, assuming that i, π, y and $(g - t)$ remain unchanged? Is the equilibrium stable?

14.5 Let debt dynamics follow the familiar equation

$$\Delta b = g - t + (r - y)b$$

The interest rate includes a risk premium RP,

$$r = \bar{r} + RP$$

and the RP increases linearly with the debt ratio:

$$RP = \alpha b$$

(a) Derive the phase line and discuss this country's debt dynamics. Do your results and insights differ from those obtained for the simpler model discussed in the text? Suppose income growth exceeds the risk-free real interest rate $\bar{r}$, which leads to the phase line shown in Figure 14.22. Our country is currently at point A.

(b) Where will your country's debt ratio move in the near future and eventually come to rest? Are there other equilibria?

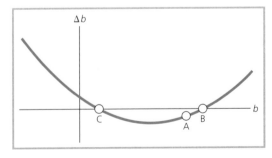

Figure 14.22

(c) While we are still at A, will it lower or raise the debt ratio if the government increases spending? Distinguish between the short run and the long run.

14.6 In Chapter 9 the dynamics of the Solow model were described by the nonlinear difference equation $\Delta K = sF(K, L) - \delta K$. Discuss the dynamic behaviour of the Solow model in a phase diagram by drawing the phase line and discussing its properties.

14.7 Consider a country with a primary deficit ratio of 25%, an income growth rate of 4%, a real interest rate of 6% and a debt ratio of 75%. Suppose that in preparation for entry into European Monetary Union, the government wants to stabilize the debt ratio by means of money creation, assuming an initial level of the real money supply of 41% of GDP.

   (a) By how many percentage points does the government have to reduce the primary deficit ratio in order to stabilize its debt ratio? Notice that to qualify for EMU this country also has to fulfil the criterion of not exceeding the EMU target inflation rate of 2% by more than 1.5 percentage points.

(b) Is the reduction of a country's deficit ratio always a reasonable course of action? What arguments speak against a reduction in government spending?

14.8 In a version of the Mundell–Fleming model with flexible prices, rational exchange rate bubbles may emerge, as we saw in Chapter 5. Draw the phase diagram for the relevant equation $e = \alpha m + (1 - \alpha) e_{+1}$ and discuss its properties. Use the type of phase diagram supplied in the bottom panel of Figure 14.4.

14.9 Let the market for a country's government bonds be represented by the interest rate equation $i = 2 + 0.1R^2$ and the rating equation $R = 0.8i$.
   (a) What interest rate does the country pay when it is in the 'good' equilibrium?
   (b) Being in this good equilibrium initially, what happens to the country's finances if its credit rating is lowered to A− = 7? Support your argument with a diagram.
   (c) Being in the good equilibrium initially, what happens to the country's finances if it is downgraded to BB = 12? Again, use a diagram to support your result.

Online resources

Interactive applet on debt dynamics www.eurmacro.eu/tutor/debtdynamics.html

Interactive applet on debt dynamics with risk premium www.eurmacro.eu/tutor/debtdynamics-rp.html

Interactive applet on government bonds market www.eurmacro.eu/tutor/sovereignbonds.html

Self quiz

www.eurmacro.eu/SelfQuiz/sq-ch14.html

Recommended reading

A well-written guide to the facts and issues of fiscal (and monetary) policy in EMU is Paul De Grauwe (2012) *Economics of Monetary Union*, 9th edn. Oxford: Oxford University Press. The model of sovereign debt crises discussed in section 14.5 is an adaption of the model developed in David Romer (2011) *Advanced Macroeconomics*, 4th edn, New York: McGraw-Hill.

APPLIED PROBLEMS

EMPIRICAL RESEARCH

Some political economy of government sector size

Nouriel Roubini and Jeffrey Sachs (1989, 'Government spending and budget deficits in the industrial countries', *Economic Policy: A European Forum* 8: 99–132) look at why different countries appear to aim for different levels of government spending. One of their regressions gives the result

$$(G/Y)_{Target} = 0.26 + 0.0018 \text{ LEFT} + 0.047 \text{ POL}$$
$$(4.90) \quad (2.89) \quad \quad (2.28)$$
$$R^2 = 0.49; \text{ cross-section data for 13 countries}$$

where $(G/Y)_{Target}$ is the long-run target ratio of government spending to output derived from another estimate, LEFT is the share of leftist parties in parliament (in%), and POL is an index that goes up if there are more parties in the ruling coalition.

The results suggest that left-wing parties desire a larger government sector. In fact, if the left-wing share in parliament increases from 0 to 100%, $(G/Y)_{Target}$ goes up by 0.18. The positive coefficient of POL indicates that $(G/Y)_{Target}$ rises if more parties stake their claims in a government coalition. The two variables explain 49% of the variation in targeted government spending ratios across countries.

WORKED PROBLEM

Interest rates, inflation and the risk premium

A credible no-bailout clause might render fiscal policy rules in a monetary union superfluous. The strength of this argument depends on whether markets do respond to risk strongly enough for risk differences to materialize in interest rate differences. To study this issue econometrically, consider the data in Table 14.5 for interest and inflation rates taken from *The Economist* for a sample of emerging-market economies and the accompanying default risk classification according to the Standard & Poor's credit rating.

We begin by regressing the interest rate on inflation to check for support of the Fisher equation (standard errors in parentheses):

$$i = 3.56 + 1.065\pi \quad R^2_{adj} = 0.92$$
$$(0.89) \quad (0.065)$$

The result is strong. With a *t*-statistic of $1.065/0.065 = 16.38$ the estimated coefficient is highly significant. Differences in inflation rates explain 92% of observed differences in interest rates. At 1.065 the coefficient of π slightly exceeds the value of 1 which the Fisher equation suggests. To find out if this contradicts the Fisher equation, we can calculate the respective *t*-statistic as $(1.065 - 1)/0.65 = 1$. So the *t*-statistic says that in this sample 1.065 is not significantly different from 1.

Before we can address the influence of risk on interest rates we need to transform the qualitative Standard & Poor's ratings into numbers. Why? Well, we cannot type ratings such as A–2 or B into our econometrics program. While other possibilities do exist, and you may want to experiment with some, we assume here that an A rating means no risk so that the RISK dummy variable would be 0. Then B is represented by a RISK value of 1, and C by a RISK value of 2. The subdivisions in the A category carry us in equal steps towards 1, the value for B, so that A–1 = 0.25, A–2 = 0.5 and A–3 = 0.75. A–1+ is assumed to be between A and A–1, that is A–1+ = 0.125. Adding the risk dummy variable to the Fisher equation gives

$$i = 1.74 + 0.9497\pi + 4.09 \text{RISK} \quad R^2_{adj} = 0.94$$
$$(0.94) \quad (0.065) \quad \quad (1.28)$$

The key result here is that increased sovereign risk drives up the interest rate. Downgrading a country's credit standing into the next main category – that is, from A to B or from B to C – raises the interest rate by 4.09 percentage points. Russia, for example, pays a risk premium of $4.09 \times 1 = 4.09\%$. Turkey's risk premium is even higher at $4.09 \times 2 = 8.18\%$.

A country with no inflation and an A rating would have a (nominal and real) interest rate of 1.74. If this country slips into risk catagory C, its real interest rate increases to almost 10% ($1.74 + 2 \times 4.09 = 9.92$).

YOUR TURN

Who wanted the euro? (part II)

One purpose of moving to a common European currency is to discipline *monetary policy* and get inflation under control. In line with this, the worked

Table 14.5

	Inflation rate π (in %)	Interest rate i (in %)	Sovereign credit rating	Risk dummy RISK
Hong Kong	−1.1	3.55	A−1+	0.125
India	2.5	7.08	A−3	0.750
Indonesia	13.0	17.35	C	2.000
Malaysia	1.5	3.30	A−1	0.250
Philippines	6.8	11.38	A−2	0.500
Singapore	1.2	2.40	A−1+	0.125
South Korea	5.0	5.10	A−1	0.250
Taiwan	0.1	3.90	A−1+	0.125
Thailand	2.2	3.00	A−2	0.500
Argentina	−1.0	12.09	C	2.000
Brazil	8.1	18.89	B	1.000
Chile	3.2	4.46	A−1+	0.125
Colombia	8.1	12.66	A−3	0.750
Mexico	6.6	7.24	A−2	0.500
Peru	2.2	7.90	B	1.000
Venezuela	13.0	13.07	B	1.000
Egypt	2.2	9.00	A−2	0.500
Israel	0.7	4.05	A−1	0.250
South Africa	6.3	9.66	A−2	0.500
Turkey	56.3	66.00	C	2.000
Czech Republic	5.9	5.58	A−1+	0.125
Hungary	10.5	11.00	A−1	0.250
Poland	6.2	15.35	A−1	0.250
Russia	22.2	25.00	B	1.000

Sources: Inflation and interest rates from *The Economist*, 11 August 2001.
Sovereign credit ratings from the Standard & Poor's homepage at www.standardandpoors.com.

problem in Chapter 11 showed that those countries whose citizens want the euro most are those that suffered from the highest inflation rates in the past.

A second purpose, or side effect, of moving to a common European currency is to discipline *fiscal policy*. This is spelled out by the Maastricht Treaty's fiscal policy criteria, and is to be made permanent by appropriate disciplinary mechanisms that are currently discussed. These would fine governments whose fiscal policy became too loose as measured against criteria similar to those of the Maastricht Treaty. A natural measure of loose fiscal policy in the past is the accumulated debt. So just as we expected high inflation in the past to pave the way to EMU acceptance, so should a high debt ratio. Use the debt ratio forecasts for 1996 given in Table 14.6, and check whether these are related to the EMUYES variable given in the worked problem in Chapter 8. Check also whether DEBT and AVINFL both determine public attitudes. Look at linear and non-linear influences.

Table 14.6

	A	B	D	DK	E	F	FIN	GB	GR	I	IRL	NL	P	S
DEBT	75	135	61	70	68	58	62	57	112	122	81	79	74	81

A closer look at economic crises

What to expect

After working through this chapter, you will understand:

1 How income growth and unemployment are linked via Okun's law.

2 How raw materials used in production, such as oil, interact with the labour market, and how the two oil price explosions of the 1970s affected unemployment.

3 How temporary shocks to equilibrium unemployment may give rise to long spells of unemployment due to persistence.

4 How persistence affects income dynamics and policy options in the DAD-SAS model.

5 How the bursting of a price bubble in the US housing market grew into a large-scale financial crisis and triggered a severe global recession after 2007.

6 That financial crises may come in many different forms.

7 How quantitative easing works and why it can be a powerful tool when economies are in a liquidity trap.

8 How debt brakes and austerity fit into our short-run models, and what their effects are.

Economies are always in a flux, responding to and digesting small shocks that reflect a constantly changing environment. These shocks cause and contribute to booms and recessions; the irregular but familiar ups and downs of market economies. What we learned so far focused on such scenarios.

But every so often shocks occur that are of a kind and magnitude that poses a much more serious, almost existential challenge to the self-healing forces of markets. The macroeconomic repercussions of such shocks cut deep and are often felt for a long time, and they have the potential to throw entire countries, regions or even the world economy into depression and turmoil. We did not sidestep such events in previous chapters, but relegated much of what we had to say to boxes and case studies.

In this chapter *crises* take centre stage. The main message will be that the time-proven tools of intermediate macroeconomics are only a starting point, albeit an important and robust one. When such workhorse models are applied flexibly and creatively, even apprentices of macroeconomics have tools at their disposal that enable them to be active and constructive participants in discussions of the current and future crises.

The chapter sets out with a brief introduction of two concepts, *Okun's law* and the *Phillips curve*, that somehow did not fit into earlier chapters, but are indispensable additions to any applied macroeconomist's tool box. The rest of the chapter is reserved for discussions of the two main triggers of large-scale crises: oil price explosions and financial crises. Regarding oil prices, an important question will be why these had such a lasting effect on unemployment. This leads us to the topic of persistence, which we will also discuss in the context of the *DAD-SAS* model. Regarding financial crises, we will first give a macroeconomic narrative of how the sub-prime crisis in the US evolved into a global recession. After that we will bring a new monetary policy tool, labelled quantitative easing, into our workhorse model. The chapter concludes with a discussion of the short-run effects of debt brakes and austerity.

15.1 Linking unemployment and growth

Before we move on to the topic of unemployment we need to note that unemployment and growth are closely related. To establish a link between unemployment and growth we proceed from a linearized production function in which output Y is proportional by a factor a to employed labour L:

$$Y = aL \qquad \text{Linearized production function} \quad (15.1)$$

Defining unemployment U as labour force N minus employment, $U \equiv N - L$, equation (15.1) turns into $Y = aN - aU$. Expanding (that is, multiplying and dividing) the last term by N gives $Y = aN - aNU/N = aN - aNu$, where $u \equiv U/N$ is the unemployment rate. This equation holds when the economy is in equilibrium. Then

$$Y^* = aN - aNu^* \qquad (15.2)$$

where Y^* is potential output and u^* is the equilibrium rate of unemployment. It also holds at other times, when Y and u deviate from equilibrium. Then

$$Y = aN - aNu \qquad (15.3)$$

Subtracting equation (15.2) from equation (15.3) and letting $a' \equiv aN$ gives

$$Y - Y^* = a'(u^* - u) \qquad \text{Okun's law (version 1)} \quad (15.4)$$

an equation known as **Okun's law**. It states that deviations of income from its potential level are proportional to the difference between the actual and the equilibrium unemployment rate. Now recall the surprise or short-run aggregate supply curve:

$$\pi = \pi^e + \lambda(Y - Y^*) \qquad \text{SAS curve}$$

The Phillips curve postulates a negative relationship between inflation and unemployment. This relationship is also affected by expected inflation.

Substituting Okun's law into the SAS curve and letting $\lambda' \equiv a'\lambda$ gives the famous Phillips curve

$$\pi = \pi^e + \lambda'(u^* - u) \qquad \text{Phillips curve}$$

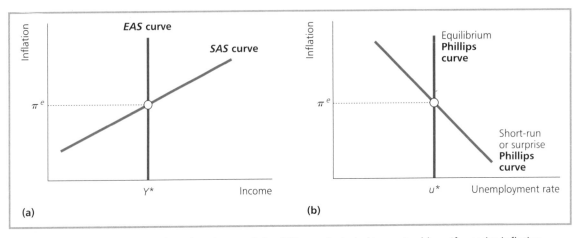

Figure 15.1 The Phillips curve is the mirror image of the *SAS* curve included in our tool-box. If surprise inflation raises income, it reduces unemployment at the same time. Just as the aggregate supply curve comes in a short-run (or surprise) version and in a long-run (or equilibrium) version, so does the Phillips curve.

which proposes a negative relationship between inflation and the rate of unemployment, the two foremost economic challenges of modern times.

Figure 15.1 shows the familiar *SAS* curve and the Phillips curve next to each other. The point to note is that the Phillips curve is simply a mirror image of the *SAS* curve. If inflation is as expected, income is at its potential level and the unemployment rate is at its equilibrium or, as it is sometimes called, its 'natural' level – natural in the sense that it reflects the current institutional environment, including such things as taxes or trade union power. As this environment changes, the natural unemployment rate changes. Unexpected inflation drives income beyond potential income and the unemployment rate below its natural level.

One version of Okun's law states that income growth is negatively related to the change in the rate of unemployment.

A second version of Okun's law results after taking first differences on both sides of equation (15.3), letting $a' \equiv aN$ again. This yields $Y - Y_{-1} = -a'(u - u_{-1})$. This formulation is fine in a theoretical context, in which production technology is kept unchanged. However, in empirical work we need to take into account that income growth only drives down unemployment when it exceeds the growth rate of potential income. Denoting potential income growth by b, the second version of Okun's law used in empirical work is $\Delta Y/Y_{-1} - b = -\hat{a}\Delta u$, or, after rearranging,

Note. Since $\hat{a} \equiv aN/Y_{-1}$, treating $\hat{a}$ as a constant is only a first approximation.

$$\Delta Y/Y_{-1} = b - \hat{a}\Delta u \qquad \text{Okun's law (version 2)} \quad (15.5)$$

Figure 15.2 documents Okun's law for Germany. The graph illustrates an important point: equation (15.5) may be rewritten as $\Delta u = (b - \Delta Y/Y_{-1})/\hat{a}$, which shows that unemployment only changes if the economy grows at a rate different from b. In an economy that grows along its potential output path, which assumes the labour market to be in permanent equilibrium, we would not expect the unemployment rate to change. So b is the economy's equilibrium growth rate, or the growth rate of potential output. As in most other countries, German growth slowed down considerably after 1973, meaning that b became smaller. We would expect this to shift 'Okun's law' line down. As can be seen from the graph this is indeed what happened. The pre-1973

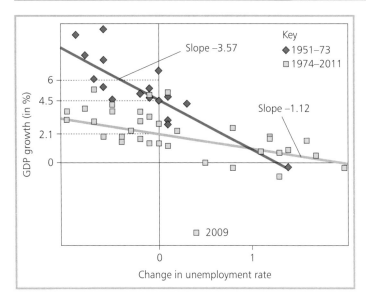

Figure 15.2 These data illustrate Okun's law for Germany. While the line shifted down after 1973, it also turned flatter. This means that a given change in GDP growth leads to larger changes in unemployment than before.

Source: OECD, *Economic Outlook*.

data marked by blue squares and the post-1973 data identified by grey squares obviously need to be described by two different lines, as statistical techniques reveal.

Three observations are important, and hold for most European countries:

1 The 'Okun's law' line for Germany has also shifted down since 1973. Now unemployment is left unchanged by a GDP growth rate of 2.1% instead of the 4.5% growth required before 1974.
2 The fluctuation of the data points about the line is more pronounced since 1974. So Okun's law holds with less precision. There is more interference from other influences.
3 The line not only moved down after 1973; it also became much flatter. This changes the link between growth and unemployment. Now a given negative shock to income growth pushes up unemployment much more than before 1973. During a recession unemployment deteriorates much more than it did before. Note, though, that this does not apply to the income drop of 5.1% in 2009, which is an obvious outlier.

15.2 The price of oil (and other raw materials)

Major shocks that classify as tidal waves in terms of what they do to unemployment and economic growth are rare. Prior to the financial crises that have kept us occupied since 2007, the only shocks in this class were the oil price explosions – the near-quadrupling of oil prices in 1974 and 1979–81. Figure 15.3 puts these into historical perspective. We already looked at some of the effects and policy responses in Chapter 13, section 13.2. Given that in the wake of these oil price shocks unemployment rates doubled in many industrialized countries, we need to take a closer look at how the price of oil (and other raw materials) affects the labour market. The straightforward explanation for the observed jump in unemployment is that when oil prices rise

Figure 15.3 While the price of crude oil, shown here in 2011 US dollars to correct for inflation, has always been quite volatile, the oil price explosions of 1974 and 1979–81 stand out. The new millennium brought a new surge in oil prices. Whether these will have similar effects to the earlier oil price explosions remains to be seen.

Source: http://www.wtrg.com/prices.htm

(in real terms) the labour demand curve shifts down. Employment falls, and unemployment increases. If wages are flexible downwards, the entire increase in unemployment will be voluntary. In the presence of downward rigidity of nominal wages, however, involuntary unemployment results, which only goes away as inflation erodes real wages.

There are two problems with this explanation:

1 The two oil price shocks were large, but temporary. In the second half of the 1980s real oil prices were back at their pre-1974 levels. So unemployment should also have returned to previous rates.
2 The oil price shocks not only hit the European economies, but Japan, the United States and others as well. US unemployment gives proof of this in the form of a slightly lagged upward jump after each oil price rise. The difference is that in each case this is reversed even before oil prices fell again.

So while the upward effects of rising oil prices on unemployment are almost universally observed, the two features to be explained are why European countries did not digest these shocks as quickly as others, and why they did not even enjoy falling unemployment when oil prices fell back to their old levels.

To obtain answers to these questions, let us discuss the connection between labour demand and oil prices in more detail and then hone the above argument by adding key institutional features to the labour market.

The labour demand curve and the price of oil

The macroeconomic models discussed so far do not really have a channel through which the price of oil or other raw materials could influence the economy. The reason is that we wrote the production function in a highly parsimonious fashion, focusing on two factors of production only, capital and labour. This view is sufficiently general for many purposes. But if we want to analyze the macroeconomic effects of dramatic changes in raw material prices, we need to recognize that raw materials are important inputs in the production of many goods. Highlighting oil as a production input, we may write a Cobb–Douglas production function as

$$Y = K^\alpha \, OIL^\beta L^{1-\alpha-\beta} \tag{15.6}$$

where OIL denotes the quantity of crude oil devoured in generating aggregate output, and technology is normalized to $A = 1$. For the same reasons advanced in our treatment of the labour market in Chapter 6, this production function implies a downward-sloping labour demand curve as sketched in panel (a) of Figure 15.4.

What is new here is that this labour-demand schedule is not only determined by the economy's capital stock, but also by the amount of oil put into production. The capital stock is a slow variable, as discussed in the 'growth' chapters (9 and 10). It is fairly constant in the short and medium run. However, firms are much more flexible in their use of oil. How much they use at any point in time is determined by an oil-demand schedule that is also implied in equation (15.6) and this is shown in panel (b) of Figure 15.4. In analogy to our discussion of the labour market, firms employ additional barrels of oil until the marginal product of oil equals the price of oil, p^{OIL}, on the world market. Worldwide this price reflects supply and demand, with a strong influence from OPEC, however. For the individual country the price of oil is more or less an exogenous variable to which it can adjust but which it cannot influence to a relevant extent.

Empirical fact. OPEC, the Organization of Petroleum Exporting Countries, the cartel of oil producing countries, controls 40% of the world's current oil production and holds more than 77% of known oil reserves.

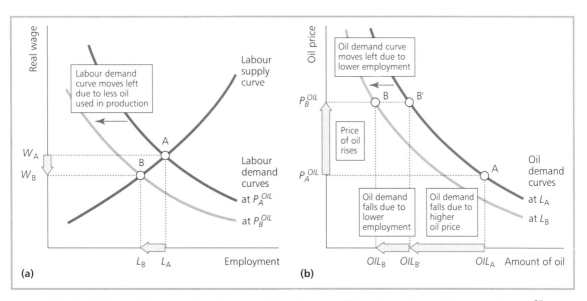

Figure 15.4 The initial equilibrium is given by point A in both panels. When the price of oil increases from P_A^{OIL} to P_B^{OIL} the initial response in panel (b) is a movement up the oil demand curve into B'. This is only a partial, incomplete response, however. With less oil being used, the labour demand curve moves left in panel (a), driving down employment. Since less employment makes oil less productive, this moves the oil demand curve left which in turn moves the labour demand curve further left, and so on. When all this comes to a halt, the labour and oil demand curves are in their respective light blue positions and the real wage and employment have fallen. Points B in both panels denote the new equilibria.

When OPEC uses its monopoly power to drive up the price of oil, the following happens. Firms realize that the marginal product of oil is now below its cost. They respond by reducing the amount of oil used until its marginal product equals the price of oil again. This is not the end of the story, however, as this has consequences for the labour market. Combined with the same amount of capital but less oil the marginal productivity of labour falls at all employment levels. This constitutes a downward shift of the labour demand curve and, as long as we are not operating in the vertical section of the labour supply curve, a drop in employment. This is still not the end of the story, however, since this change feeds back into the domestic demand for oil. With less labour to be combined with, the oil demand curve moves down even further, reducing the use of oil, which drives down the labour demand curve still further, and so on. Of course, these effects eventually peter out and the labour demand curve settles into its new position, drawn in light blue.

The algebra of oil prices and labour demand

Given the production function $Y = K^\alpha OIL^\beta L^{1-\alpha-\beta}$ the labour demand curve is obtained by differentiation with respect to L to obtain the marginal product of labour and requires this to equal the real wage:

$$\frac{dY}{dL} = (1 - \alpha - \beta)\frac{K^\alpha OIL^\beta}{L^{\alpha+\beta}} = w \qquad (15.7)$$

In the same way, the national economy's oil demand curve is obtained by differentiation with respect to OIL to obtain the marginal product of oil and setting this equal to the oil price:

$$\frac{dY}{dOIL} = \beta\frac{K^\alpha L^{1-\alpha-\beta}}{OIL^{1-\beta}} = p^{OIL} \qquad (15.8)$$

Both demand curves are interdependent, since each is influenced by the quantity employed in the other market. To carve out the dependence of labour demand on the price of oil, we solve equation (15.8) for OIL and substitute the result into equation (15.7). This yields the short- and medium-run labour demand curve (in the long run the adjustment of the capital stock would still have to be taken into account):

$$w = (1 - \alpha - \beta)\left(\frac{K}{L}\right)^{\frac{\alpha}{1-\beta}}\left(\frac{\beta}{p^{OIL}}\right)^{\frac{\beta}{1-\beta}} \qquad \text{Labour demand curve} \quad (15.9)$$

According to this equation, which is curved rather than linear as in our graphical simplification, the labour demand curve moves down and flattens if the price of oil increases. The response of employment and unemployment then depends both on the slope of the labour supply curve and on the stickiness of money wages.

Oil price shocks and unemployment: two stylized scenarios

Returning to our attempt to explain the international experience with unemployment and oil prices, consider the effects of two cumulative oil price increases and their reversal on unemployment in a stylized context. First,

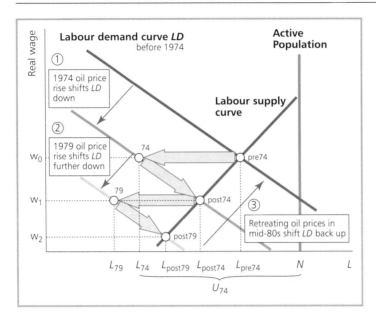

Figure 15.5 The oil price increases of 1974 and 1979 shifted *LD* down in two steps. Each time employment fell sharply (while wages were fixed in contracts negotiated before the shock) but recovered as wages fell. As oil prices dropped and *LD* shifted back up, wages and employment rose back to their initial values.

assume an 'American scenario', in which nominal wages are flexible except for the length of one-period wage contracts (Figure 15.5).

Labour market equilibrium before 1974 is marked by the intersection between the full demand and supply curves. The vertical line over N measures the active population. The difference between N and L_{pre74} gives unemployment as presumably measured by statistics. Some of this is involuntary (if real-wage rigidities exist) and some of it may be voluntary.

The quadrupling of oil prices in 1974 shifts the labour demand curve down to the medium blue position. Initially, as long as nominal wages are stuck in old contracts, employment falls to L_{74}, raising unemployment to U_{74}. After contracts expire, real wages fall to w_1, and employment rises to L_{post74}. This process is repeated in 1979–81, when the price of oil quadruples again. After a temporary large increase of unemployment, falling wages drive it back down to $U_{post79} \equiv N - L_{post79}$. Finally, around the mid-1980s, oil prices fall back to their initial level. This shifts the labour demand curve up into its original position, moving wages and unemployment back to their original values as well. The spell of increased unemployment is over.

Unemployment persistence

Next we try to understand what may have made Europe's unemployment so much more persistent than US unemployment. To this effect, consider a 'European scenario', in which we suppose wages to be negotiated by **labour unions with insider power** (as described in Chapter 6) – see Figure 15.6.

The point of departure, the pre-1974 equilibrium, is the same as in Figure 15.5, and so are the shifts in the labour demand curve. When the first oil price shock shifts labour demand down, employment falls to $L_{post74} = L_{74}$ (raising unemployment to U_{74}). Catering to employed members (the insiders) only, trade unions prevent the real wage from falling below its current level, despite

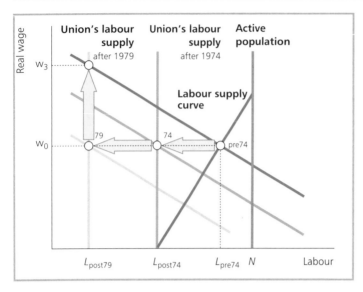

Figure 15.6 Again the oil price rises shift *LD* down twice. Two things differ from the 'American scenario'. First, employment does not recover from the initial drop, since unions do not permit wages to fall. Second, as *LD* shifts up again when oil prices drop, unions seize the occasion by pushing up wages. The employment reduction persists.

involuntary unemployment. The second oil price shock replicates the first one, raising unemployment further to $U_{79} = N - L_{post79}$ at an unchanged real wage. Finally, when the oil price eases back to where it started and the labour demand curve shifts back up into the full blue position, unions jump at the occasion by bargaining the real wage up to w_3 for their employed members, leaving a large number of mostly involuntarily unemployed people.

Figure 15.7 shows how unemployment, as measured by the horizontal distance between the active population N and actual employment L, is driven by two oil price shocks and their subsequent reversal in the two stylized scenarios proposed in Figures 15.5 and 15.6. Under the 'American scenario' the two oil price increases give rise to brief bouts of involuntary unemployment. Unemployment may remain somewhat higher after each bout, but only due to voluntary unemployment. Even this effect disappears after oil prices are back to normal.

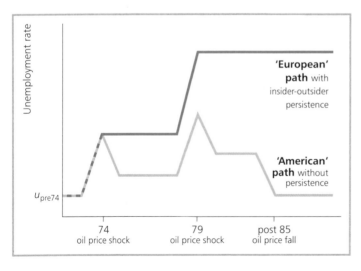

Figure 15.7 In the 'American scenario' the two oil price shocks of 1974 and 1979 cause temporary spells of unemployment. These disappear rather quickly. After oil prices drop to their initial levels, unemployment returns to its initial level. In the 'European scenario' the initial effect of oil price increases is the same as in the 'American scenario'. In Europe the effects persist, however. The eventual fall in oil prices has no effect on unemployment.

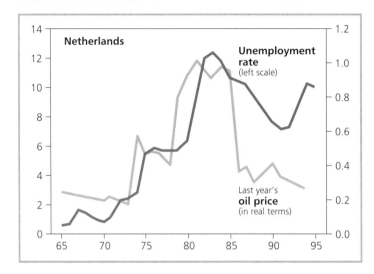

Figure 15.8 The Dutch experience closely matches the behaviour of unemployment in the wake of oil price changes derived above. The two oil price explosions shift unemployment to higher levels in two stages. When oil prices fall, unemployment seems to respond, but very slowly.

Source: IMF, *IFS*.

Under the 'European scenario' the two oil price increases ratchet unemployment up. After each rise, unions keep unemployment where it is. Even after oil prices fall again, there is no tendency for unemployment to fall. This general phenomenon whereby a rise in unemployment may also drag equilibrium unemployment up, and thus may not be reversed even after the initial cause for rising unemployment has disappeared, is known as **persistence**.

Do these stylized stories agree with the data? Not perfectly, but they can explain some essential differences between Europe and the United States. A look at the US unemployment rate in Figure 6.9 in Chapter 6 shows the bouts in unemployment after the two shocks in the 'American scenario'. The bouts last a bit longer than in our stylized analysis. But this is easily explained by noting that the majority of wage contracts in the United States are for two and three years.

In contrast, Figure 15.8 shows data from the Netherlands to represent the European scenario. The Dutch unemployment rate is plotted against the Dutch real oil price from the previous year.

From 1973 to 1986 the correspondence between the two series is very close. Each increase in the price of oil pushes unemployment up, and it stays there, just as the stylized analysis suggested. When the oil price falls again, the correlation between the two series breaks down. The unemployment rate does not follow. There is a downward trend, however, but it is a slow one. This suggests that the insider argument points in the right direction, although it overemphasizes the influence of insiders. Nevertheless, even with the presence of falling oil prices substantial persistence is there and this prevents the unemployment rate from falling as quickly as oil prices actually would permit.

15.3 Persistence in the *DAD-SAS* model

Persistence slows down the dynamics of the economy. In the extreme case labelled the European scenario, the economy would never return to its initial equilibrium, even after the shock has disappeared. This extreme form of persistence is often referred to as hysteresis. Hysteresis is probably rare in reality. But milder forms of persistence seem to be the rule rather than an exception. Persistence can have a variety of causes:

- **Trade union monopoly and insider power**, as discussed in the previous sections, is one possible source.
- **Adjustment costs of firms** could cause persistence as employment changes are not costless. It may then be preferable to adjust to a new employment level desired in the longer run in small steps rather than in one big leap.
- **Accumulation of work-specific skills takes time.** If workers become unemployed, their skills fall behind what their previous workplace requires in a dynamic economy with constant innovations and technological progress. When goods demand returns as the economy recovers after a recession, firms might not find the same work-specific and general skills among formerly unemployed that they had before the recession.

All these persistence effects operate on the supply side of the economy and affect the aggregate supply curve. While under the assumption of no persistence used throughout most of this book, surprise inflation influences aggregate output via $Y = Y^* + \frac{1}{\lambda}(\pi - \pi^e)$ and leads to the *SAS* curve

$$\pi = \pi^e + \lambda(Y - Y^*) \qquad (15.10)$$

Persistence means that past deviations of income from potential income continue to influence current income. Aggregate output then follows $Y = Y^{**} + \alpha(Y_{-1} - Y^{**}) + \frac{1}{\lambda}(\pi - \pi^e)$, where $0 \leq \alpha \leq 1$ is the persistence parameter, which may be solved for π to yield the generalized *SAS* curve

$$\pi = \pi^e + \lambda[Y - \underbrace{(Y^{**} + \alpha(Y_{-1} - Y^{**}))}_{\text{Potential income } Y^*}] \quad \textit{SAS } \textbf{curve with persistence} \ (15.11)$$

In this formulation Y^{**} is long-run potential income – some super equilibrium income. It only obtains after all persistence effects have petered out. Current potential income Y^*, the income that obtains if there is no surprise inflation, is given by the indicated sum in parentheses. *Current* potential income is determined by *long-run* potential income Y^{**} plus a fraction of last period's deviation of income from Y^{**}. The driving force behind this is that current movements of Y affect either the labour supply or the labour demand curve. In our discussion of oil prices, for example, the trade union labour supply curve was affected because of the union's preference for insiders. Or, to the extent that adjustment costs cause persistence, the labour demand curve follows movements of Y with a lag.

Equation (15.11) comprises two benchmark cases. When $\alpha = 0$ we are back in our normal scenario with no persistence and the *SAS* curve as given by equation (15.10). We discussed this case at length in Chapter 8. When $\alpha = 1$ we have *perfect* persistence or *hysteresis*. Then equation (15.11) simplifies to

$$\pi = \pi^e + \lambda(Y - Y_{-1}) \qquad (15.12)$$

This equation implies that when there is no surprise inflation, aggregate output remains where it was last period. In other words, last period's output becomes current potential income. Potential income wanders about without a long-run centre of gravity to which it converges, driven by demand-side shocks via surprise inflation, or by supply-side shocks such as price increases of raw materials. To some extent this corresponds to the 'European scenario' proposed in our discussion of oil prices above.

Hysteresis

Let us discuss the benchmark case of hysteresis first. Consider a reduction in money growth under flexible exchange rates. The *DAD-SAS* model then reads

$$\pi = \mu - b(Y - Y_{-1}) \qquad\qquad \text{\emph{DAD} curve} \quad (15.13)$$

$$\pi = \pi^e + \lambda(Y - Y_{-1}) \qquad \text{\textbf{SAS curve with hysteresis}} \quad (15.12)$$

In Figure 15.9 the economy is in the initial equilibrium at μ_{HI} and Y^*_{HI}. In period 1 the central bank reduces the money supply growth rate to μ_{LO}. Since inflation exceeds money growth, the real money supply falls, shifting the *DAD* curve to the left into position DAD_1. We find the exact position of DAD_1 by following the recipe given in Chapter 8: draw a horizontal line at the current money growth rate μ_{LO}. Draw a vertical line at last period's income, which is Y^*_{HI}. The intersection between the two lines constitutes a construction point through which DAD_1 passes with negative slope.

Unless the labour market had perfect foresight and anticipated the reduction in money growth, inflation does not follow the reduction of money growth instantaneously. When the policy change comes as a surprise, money wages for period 1 were fixed at the end of period 0 based on inflation expectations $\pi^e_1 = \pi_0 = \mu_{HI}$. SAS_0 says how firms respond to a reduction in goods demand, given the current nominal wage. In this case they move down SAS_0, reducing both output and inflation. Equilibrium in period 1 obtains where DAD_1 and SAS_1 (which is identical to SAS_0) intersect. Inflation has fallen to π_1 and income to Y_1.

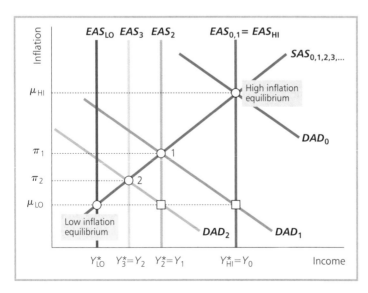

Figure 15.9 Under hysteresis and the specific kind of adaptive inflation expectations assumed here, the *SAS* curve never moves. This is because the effects on potential income (which falls and draws *SAS* to the left) and inflation expectations (which fall and draw *SAS* down) exactly offset each other. Hence the economy moves down *SAS* at a speed determined by the downward shifting *DAD* curve. Under hysteresis a change of monetary policy towards smaller money growth rates causes inflation and income to fall permanently.

Having observed this, labour market participants revise their plans. Assume inflation expectations are formed adaptively. Then the first revision is a reduction of inflation expectations to $\pi_2^e = \pi_1$. The second revision concerns potential employment and income. Under hysteresis potential income equals last period's income, that is $Y_2^* = Y_1$. This shifts the vertical *EAS* curve left to Y_1. Having noted this, we can use Chapter 8's construction recipe to identify the position of SAS_2: draw a horizontal line at expected inflation and draw a vertical line at (current) potential income. SAS_2 passes through the intersection of these two lines. Under hysteresis and the kind of adaptive expectations assumed here, this new position coincides with the old one. The *SAS* curve does not shift! The *DAD* curve, on the other hand, does not remain in its previous position. If the real money supply remained unchanged, income could remain at Y_1. This puts the curve into position DAD_2. Equilibrium in period 2 obtains at inflation π_2 and Y_2.

Moving on to period 3, for the same reasons given in the previous paragraph, the *SAS* curve does not change: the leftward shift due to a further reduction in potential income and the downward shift due to the reduction in inflation expectations exactly cancel out. The *DAD* curve moves still further down into DAD_3 (not shown) and income and inflation are π_3 and Y_3, respectively. This process continues in periods 4, 5 and so on, until the economy, in ever decreasing steps, settles into its new long-run equilibrium at $\pi = \mu_{LO}$ and $Y = Y_{LO}^*$.

The important and novel insight arrived at here is that under hysteresis monetary policy affects income permanently. Inflation is still a monetary phenomenon and equals money growth in the long run, but monetary policy exerts a lasting effect on real income. This also applies under rational inflation expectations, though the effect on income would be smaller, as you may easily convince yourself. Only under perfect foresight would monetary policy have no effect on income whatsoever.

Persistence

When persistence is not perfect, effects cannot last for ever, as under hysteresis. But income effects last longer than in the no-persistence scenarios discussed in Chapter 6. As a rule of thumb, we may say that the *DAD-SAS* model with persistence behaves very much like the model of Chapter 6 when the persistence parameter α is small, say 0.2 or 0.3. When α is 0.8 or 0.9, the model behaves very much as if there was hysteresis for a while until income eventually eases back into its original level. Let us now look at an intermediate case assuming $\alpha = 0.5$.

$$\pi = \mu - b(Y - Y_{-1}) \hspace{3cm} \text{*DAD* curve} \quad (15.14)$$

$$\pi = \pi^e + \lambda\big[Y - (Y^{**} + 0.5(Y_{-1} - Y^{**}))\big]$$
$$\text{*SAS* curve with persistence} \quad (15.15)$$

Again, the money supply growth rate is reduced unexpectedly in period 1, bringing the economy into the same period-1-equilibrium experienced under hysteresis. The difference from the hysteresis-scenario is that potential income does not follow the drop in actual income fully, but only half way: potential income is Y^{**} plus half of last period's deviation of income from Y^{**}. So

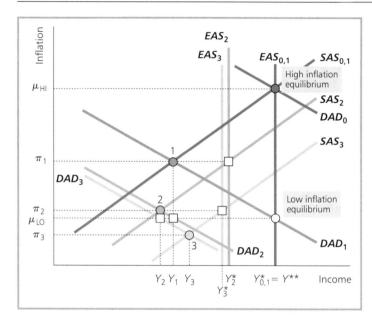

Figure 15.10 Under persistence inflation and income behave in a qualitatively similar way to the way they do in the *DAD-SAS* model without persistence, as discussed in Chapter 8. The important difference is that effects of monetary policy on income may last substantially longer. The reason is that when income falls, such as during disinflation as depicted here, temporary drops in income lead to temporary reductions in potential income. This is a drag when income is ready to rise back up towards its long-run potential income Y^{**}.

EAS_2 and current potential income are in the middle between Y^{**} and Y_1. The positions of SAS_2 and DAD_2 are again determined using our recipes. A horizontal line at expected inflation intersects EAS_2 at a construction point for SAS_2. And a horizontal line at μ_{LO} and a vertical line at Y_1 gives a construction point for DAD_2. So income continues to fall in period 2. Period 3 brings the turnaround, beginning to lead income slowly back towards Y^{**}. See Figure 15.10. You may want to compare this path with the path without persistence to see that persistence makes the recession more pronounced and longer lasting.

Less than full persistence does not dramatically change what we learned from the discussion of the *DAD-SAS* model in Chapter 8. There are still the same short-run and the same long-run effects. What does change, though, is the borderline that separates the short from the long run. Short-run effects now may last much longer and can be a lot more pronounced. In general, the implied behaviour fits empirical patterns of booms and recessions much better since policy surprises can affect income for several years even under rational inflation expectations.

15.4 Financial crises and risk premiums: a closer look

We have already looked at economic crises and risk premiums a number of times. You are also familiar with liquidity traps and speculative bubbles. This section develops a more coherent and detailed view of these concepts. And it builds on these concepts to provide a macroeconomic narrative of the sub-prime and financial crisis of 2007–09, and to develop some important insights into the nature, risks and policy options during financial crises in general.

The *IS-LM* model with risk premiums in the money and capital market

While the sub-prime and financial crisis started in the US housing market and hit the banks and other financial institutions first, it soon spread to and threatened the real economy. To accommodate this, we need a version of the *IS-LM* model that permits interest rates to differ between the money market and the goods market, and to be affected by different levels of risk.

We ignore international repercussions for now and start by modelling a closed economy. So we simply copy the *LM* and *IS* curves from Chapter 3, with two modifications: each financial market has its own interest rate; and each one carries its default risk.

As we already noted in Case study 3.1, the demand for money depends on the risk-adjusted interest rate. This is the money market interest rate i_{MM} minus the risk premium RP_{MM} which reflects the probability that your bank goes bankrupt. Then the equilibrium condition in the money market is $L = kY - h(i_{MM} - RP_{MM}) = M$, which may be solved for i_{MM} to give the *LM* curve

$$i_{MM} = RP_{MM} + \tfrac{k}{h}Y - \tfrac{1}{h}M \qquad \text{LM curve} \quad (15.16)$$

This *LM* curve moves upwards when trust in banks deteriorates. In times of banking crises households require compensation, a risk premium, for keeping money in savings or checking accounts.

The *IS* curve is straightforward, with investment demand now depending explicitly on the interest rate i_{CM} (for long-term loans) that is determined in the capital market:

$$i_{CM} = -\frac{1-c}{b}Y + \frac{\bar{I} + G}{b} \qquad \text{IS curve} \quad (15.17)$$

To complete the model we need a link between the two interest rates. This can be obtained by assuming that the money market interest rate reflects the capital costs for banks: that is what it costs banks to obtain liquidity from customers or other banks. Banks repackage this liquidity into long-term loans to firms, at a price that includes a markup. This markup may contain a constant term, which we set to zero for simplicity, and a term that reflects the risk attributed to this kind of loan. Then the capital market interest rate is determined by

$$i_{CM} = i_{MM} + RP_{CM} \qquad (15.18)$$

where RP_{CM} is the risk premium that banks request when they extend loans to the corporate sector. After substituting this equation into (15.17) and solving for the money market interest rate we obtain

$$i_{MM} = -RP_{CM} - \frac{1-c}{b}Y + \frac{\bar{I} + G}{b} \qquad \text{IS \emph{curve} with risk premium} \quad (15.17')$$

In this form the *IS* curve may still be displayed in the same diagram as the *LM* curve, even though the capital market features its own interest rate (see Figure 15.12 later). This *IS* curve moves down when loans to firms become more risky. Then each money market interest rate, the one measured along the vertical axis, maps onto a higher capital market interest rate and, hence, lower investment demand and income than before.

Before we develop a macroeconomic narrative of the financial crisis, we need to add the liquidity trap to our crisis version of the *IS-LM* model. We do so by requiring the *LM* curve to turn horizontal when the risk-adjusted interest rate becomes zero. Formally, this may be represented by the kinked *LM* curve

$$i_{MM} = RP_{MM} + \begin{cases} \frac{k}{h}Y - \frac{1}{h}M & \text{if } kY > M \\ 0 & \text{if } kY \leq M \end{cases}$$

kinked *LM* curve with horizontal segment   (15.19)

This *LM* curve combines two segments. The first is the familiar positively sloped line that is valid at positive risk-adjusted interest rates. This is the case when the demand for money derived from the income term alone, kY, exceeds the supply of money, M. Then we need a positive interest rate to bring money demand down to equal supply. In the opposite case, when $kY \leq M$, this would tend to drive the risk-adjusted interest rate into sub-zero territory, and the *LM* curve becomes horizontal. This is an interesting property. Since the horizontal segment is positioned at $i_{MM} - RP_{MM} = 0$, a liquidity trap may occur at positive interest rates in the money market. If I see a 5% chance that my bank goes bankrupt this month, then a 5% interest rate will not convince me to keep money in my accounts. My response will be the same as if the interest rate was zero in a risk-free environment.

The real estate and financial crisis 2007–09: a macroeconomic narrative

Few will dispute that the US housing market took centre stage in the first act of this crisis.

The bubble

Figure 15.11 shows the development of house prices in the United States, both in real and nominal terms. While real house prices had been more or less flat for almost half a century, they took off at an accelerating pace just before the turn of the millennium. At least in hindsight, a vast majority of experts agree that the doubling of real home prices within less than a decade (in nominal terms the increase is almost 150%) constituted a price bubble (see also section 5.8).

Along such a bubble path the expectation of future price movements becomes a key determinant of demand. Now houses were not purchased by and credit was not extended only to those who had the income to finance the required mortgage, but to almost anybody, with the assurance that interest could be paid out of another mortgage that would be added in a year after the price of the house had risen. This new and steadily increasing market segment for sub-prime mortgages expanded the demand for new homes to an extent that was thoroughly detached from fundamentals. While this game could continue as long as the bubble kept growing, homeowners and creditors became increasingly vulnerable, and the involved risk rose with the size of a bubble. Because, as we know from section 5.8, once a bubble slows or even stops

Sub-prime mortgages are loans to persons who do not have the income, wealth or credit history in general to qualify for a prime mortgage. Difficulty in maintaining the repayment schedule has to be expected.

Figure 15.11 In real terms US house prices remained more or less flat during the last two decades of the twentieth century. Then they almost doubled within less than ten years. Their collapse after 2006 played a central role in the real estate and financial crisis of 2007–09.

growing, prices have a tendency to descend quickly towards their fundamental equilibrium level. And this drop becomes steeper and steeper as the bubble grows.

The bubble bursts

Sure enough, in 2007 the bubble started to collapse. Now the housing market is certainly an important sector in any economy. But nevertheless the question must be asked as to why the collapse of a price bubble in the US housing market could trigger a global downturn that threatened to take on the dimensions of the Great Depression of the 1930s. After all, to put the collapse of this bubble in perspective: in 2007 outstanding loans on sub-prime mortgages amounted to about $1.3 trillion, which fell just short of 10% of US GDP. Some 20% of these mortgages were in default. So the sums that were at stake added up to about 2% of GDP. To push this further: between 2006 and 2008 house prices only fell by 10%. So the banks could still hope to recover close to 90% of their loans, even on houses that were fully mortgaged. This reduces potential losses to about 0.2% of GDP. How could this shake the world economy? For this to make sense, we need to look at a process called securitization, and at the role of derivatives, leverage and moral hazard.

Securitization

The process of securitization takes an illiquid asset and packages it into a security that is easily traded. In the case of mortgage-backed securities (MBSs) a large number of individual mortgages are bundled together into a mortgage pool. This pool is used as collateral for the MBS which can be sold to and traded among interested investors. Ideally, securitization should spread risk across more shoulders and thus make loans more available and cheaper. In reality, however, risk did not spread in a very transparent fashion. Since banks knew that after securitization the true credit risk might be difficult to detect for potential buyers of MBSs, and would cease to be their problem anyway, they had limited incentive to make an adequate assessment when a mortgage originated. This was helped by what, at least in hindsight, were

Moral hazard is a situation where agents take excessive risks because someone else bears the cost of their actions.

untenably good ratings of MBSs and other derivatives by credit rating agencies (see also Figure 15.20). While this explains the excessive risks taken by many players in this market deliberately, because of moral hazard, or because they were misled, it does not explain how the modest numbers mentioned in the previous paragraph could put the global economy into such jeopardy. Here leverage and derivatives come into play.

Leverage

This refers to the use of borrowed funds to acquire assets. It can increase the profitability of a bank to its investors. This is easily demonstrated by numerical examples:

Case 1: Suppose the bank's net worth or equity is €100 (million). It does not have any borrowed funds from customers. So it is *not leveraged*. If it extends all its net worth of €100 to prospective homeowners at an interest rate of 6%, the rate of return on equity is 6%.

Case 2: Now let the bank also manage €1,000 in deposits for which it pays its customers an interest rate of 2% and is required by law to keep 10% as reserves. Then it can extend €1,000 (€900 in deposits plus €100 in equity) in mortgages for which it receives €60 in interest payments. After deducting €20 in interest payments to its customers, profits amount to €40, a whopping 40% return on equity. This was made possible by a *leverage ratio*, the ratio of a bank's assets (reserves plus mortgages) to equity, of 11-to-1.

But now suppose that outstanding mortgages suffer a loss of 5%, because of foreclosures and price drops.

Case 1: The bank records a loss of €5 million. So the rate of return on equity is −5%. Equity is reduced, but still stands at €95 million.

Case 2: The banks loss on mortgages is €50 million. Its interest payment to customers is €20 million. The rate of return on equity is −70%. Most of the bank's equity is wiped out.

What these examples illustrate is the magnifying effect of leverage. While it boosts profits during good times, it also amplifies losses during bad times. High leverage ratios of banks that exceeded 30-to-1 in many cases are a main reason why the financial industry appeared so vulnerable when the air went out of the real estate bubble. Another factor contributing to the crisis was derivatives.

Derivatives

These are financial instruments that are only indirectly related to some underlying asset such as a mortgage or a security. Examples are credit default swaps (CDSs), which are insurance contracts that can be used by issuers of mortgages to transfer credit risk to a third party. But CDSs can also be 'naked', meaning that two parties essentially exchange bets on an event in which they have no direct stake. The existence of this kind of derivative, and of much more complex ones that no one really seemed to understand, the size of this market which some experts estimate to be around 50 times of world GDP, the lack of serious oversight and regulation, and the widespread lack of transparency regarding the exposure of financial institutions to this kind of activity, all contributed to a complete erosion of trust in the financial markets. Nobody

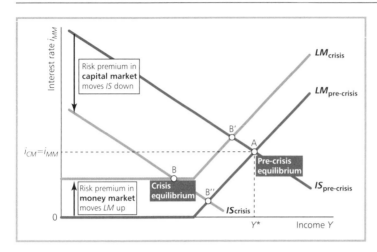

Figure 15.12 Suppose an economy operated at potential output Y^* before the financial crisis. When households lost trust and required a risk premium for putting money into banks, this shifted *LM* up, including its horizontal segment. This alone would have moved the economy into B'. In addition, banks lost trust in the corporate sector, causing them to request a significant risk premium for their loans to firms. This shifted *IS* down and the macroeconomic equilibrium during the crisis into point B.

felt able to gauge the exposure of counterparties, in finance or industry, to the risks and losses that resulted from the plummeting US housing market.

From the sub-prime and financial crisis to recession

The developments and features described above turned out to be a poisonous mix. It generated an atmosphere of panic and mistrust that had not been experienced for more than half a century, with consequences that Figure 15.12 traces in a stylized fashion based on the model described by equations (15.17') and (15.19). The economy's equilibrium before the crisis is at point A.

Only a minority of investors really understood what they owned, and nobody seemed able to put a price on the complex and opaque derivatives in their own and others' portfolios. Customers lost trust in their banks, which led to visible bank runs, as in the case of Northern Rock in the United Kingdom, or covert ones, as when BNP Paribas in France halted withdrawals. In the United States bank after bank collapsed or asked for government support, and when on 15 September 2008 Lehman Brothers, one of Wall Street's most prestigious players, declared bankruptcy it looked like the financial system might implode. Credit in the money market dried up as banks obtained liquidity from households or other banks only at outrageous risk premiums. The resulting upward shift of the *LM* curve would have driven money market rates up and the economy into a recession at point B'. Once it was clear that a major downturn was on its way, banks were unable to tell which firms would weather the storm. They thus felt compelled to attach a sizable risk premium to the interest rates they offered firms that were seeking loans. This drove capital market rates way above money market rates, causing a downward shift of the *IS* curve in a diagram with money market rates on the vertical axis. As a partial effect, such a confidence crisis in the capital market would have driven the economy into a recession at point B''. Both confidence crises together, in the banking sector and in the corporate sector, reinforced each other and led into a major recession at point B.

And indeed, for many industrial countries there was no escaping. While income growth only stalled in the European Union in 2008, incomes fell by 4.3% union wide in 2009. This included not only the biggest economies like Germany and the United Kingdom, where income receded by 5.1% and 4.0%, respectively, but also the small Baltic countries where income dropped by between 14.3% and 17.7%. What made this recession special and particularly scary was that it caught or put many countries in a liquidity trap with near zero interest rates. Traditional monetary policy, which could not be directed toward special needs of individual countries in the Eurozone anyway, is of no help in this situation. As a first resort, therefore, many governments implemented stimulus packages, either with the general aim of boosting aggregate demand or targeted towards specific sectors of the economy, such as the automobile industry. While this did not keep incomes from dropping, it probably prevented the recession from developing into a depression, making it less deep and shorter in many countries than it might have been otherwise.

Unfortunately, fiscal stimulus does not come without costs and without risk, as many European countries learned the hard way when they woke up to another crisis not much more than a year later. We will return to this in sections 15.5 and 15.6. Before we do so, let us develop a more general macroeconomic perspective of financial crises and, in particular, of how they may spread from one country to another.

The nature of financial crises and crisis contagion

Our first glimpse at financial crises kept things simple by postulating a closed economy. From the perspective of a relatively small country things look a lot more complex. Not only because the exchange rate system and issues of crisis *contagion* across borders come into play. Most importantly, there is no such thing as *a* financial crisis. There are different types of financial crises with different consequences, depending on whether the country has fixed or flexible exchange rates, and on whether the crisis is global in the sense that financial markets worldwide are affected, including the home country, or a domestic affair in the sense that financial markets abroad remain healthy. These criteria provide us with the six scenarios defined in Table 15.1, with each scenario carrying two sub-scenarios, labelled MM and CM, depending on whether the crisis erupts in the money market or in the capital market.

There is no need to go through all twelve scenarios. Most of them are relatively straightforward finger exercises with familiar-looking results. We look at two cases here that are less straightforward.

We start with a global crisis that affects the capital markets in all countries at the same time. Let the world be composed of a small open economy, represented in the left panel in Figure 15.13 by means of the Mundell–Fleming model, and the rest of the world which the individual country is too small to affect, represented by the *IS-LM* model in the panel on the right.

Table 15.1 **A classification of financial crises.** There is no such thing as a financial crisis. Crises differ according to whether they erupt at home or abroad, in the money market or in the capital market, under fixed or flexible exchange rates. Each scenario poses specific challenges and calls for policy responses that are tailored to this particular type of crisis.

		Flexible exchange rates		Fixed exchange rates	
		Crisis in money market	Crisis in capital market	Crisis in money market	Crisis in capital market
A global crisis that	includes the small open economy	1MM	1CM	2MM	2CM
	does not include the small open economy	3MM	3CM	4MM	4CM
A domestic crisis		5MM	5CM	6MM	6CM

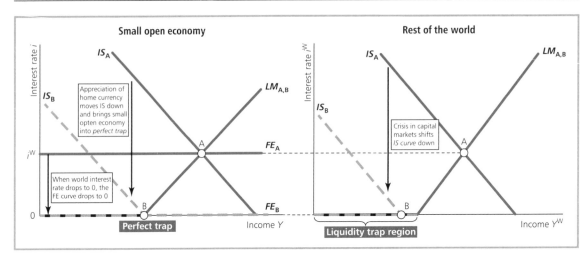

Figure 15.13 Exchange rates are flexible and a major crisis erupts in the rest of the world's capital market, driving the world interest rate towards zero. This shifts the small open economy's *FE* curve down to zero. As long as the home interest rate is still positive, there is excess demand for the home currency, and it appreciates. This shifts the *IS* curve down. The small country is driven into a recession in point B.

Before we start to discuss crises, we must re-examine the equilibrium condition in the international capital market. Under perfect mobility of capital, equilibrium in the international capital market requires risk-adjusted returns at home to match risk-adjusted returns abroad:

$$i_{CM} - RP_{CM} = i_{CM}^W - RP_{CM}^W \tag{15.20}$$

Substituting equation (15.18) and its rest-of-world version on both sides simplifies this into the familiar form

$$i_{MM} = i_{MM}^W \tag{15.21}$$

This says the money market rates must be equal across borders in order to generate an equilibrium in the international capital market. The reason is that the money market rate, which represents the credit cost to banks, equals the risk-adjusted interest rate in the capital market. Since our diagram measures the money market rate along the vertical axis, the *FE* curve is positioned at the interest rate in the rest of the world's money market.

Let us now look at scenario 3CM. Exchange rates are flexible and a crisis erupts in the rest of the world's capital market. A deterioration of trust infirms with increasing risk premiums becomes self-fulfilling by shifting the *IS* curve down (as shown in Figure 15.13), driving the economy into a recession, accompanied by a wave of bankruptcies in the corporate sector. Assume the crisis is so severe that the money market interest rate drops towards zero, casting the rest of the world into a liquidity trap at point B, the equilibrium determined by the solid lines.

The interest rate in the domestic money market, which is identical to the risk-adjusted interest rate in the domestic corporate sector, is initially higher than in the rest of the world. Therefore the home currency appreciates, shifting the small country's *IS* curve to the left and dragging it into recession as well. The new equilibrium at B has peculiar properties and poses a challenge to policymakers:

First, and this does not come as a surprise, the country is in a liquidity trap too, rendering monetary policy useless. But second, fiscal policy does not work either. Any attempt to shift *IS* to the right again by means of spending increases or tax cuts are being nullified immediately by a matching crowding out of net exports. Since the equilibrium sits exactly where the slope of *LM* turns positive, any attempted shift of *IS* to the right raises the interest, attracts capital inflows and, thus, makes the home currency appreciate. We may call this situation, in which neither monetary nor fiscal policy work, a *perfect trap*. Are there any options for this country to fight the recession?

In principle, there are two, though we will look at another one in the next section:

■ The reason why fiscal policy does not produce the intended results is because the country sits at the edge of the liquidity trap, at the end of the horizontal segment, where *LM* starts to rise. Now if the central bank increases the money supply, shifting *LM* to the right and, thus, extending the horizontal segment, it generates leeway for fiscal policy. Increased government spending can now shift *IS* to the right, until it is in the new point where *LM* begins to rise. So while neither monetary policy nor fiscal policy work in a perfect trap when used in isolation, a coordinated effort can do the trick. First, the money supply is increased to provide leeway; then fiscal policy uses this leeway to stimulate aggregate demand, enjoying a full multiplier effect.

■ The second option for the small economy is to fix the exchange rate at an appropriate level. If it fixes it at the initial level, the crisis in the world's capital market could even trigger a domestic boom, moving the equilibrium down the initial *IS* curve. Fixing it at a somewhat stronger currency value might at least prevent the recession.

Now look at scenario 5MM. The exchange rate is still flexible. But here we have a banking crisis at home - alone. This shifts *LM* up, putting upward pressure on i_{MM}. This tends to make loans to the domestic corporate sector more expensive, attracting financial investors from abroad. The currency appreciates and drives the economy into recession at point B in Figure 15.14.

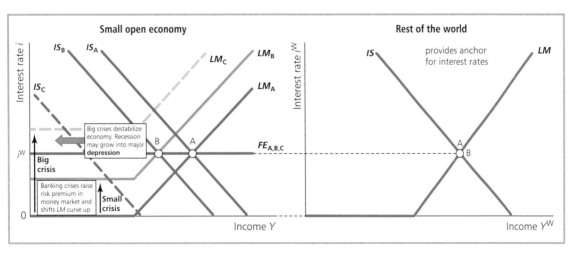

Figure 15.14 Exchange rates are flexible and a banking crisis gets under way in the home country. A minor crisis, which shifts the *LM* curve up into position *LM*$_B$, only triggers a minor recession by moving the economy into point B. A major crisis that generates a risk premium so large that the *LM* curve loses contact with the *FE* curve by moving into a position such as *LM*$_C$ may cast the country into an outright depression. This is because the money market interest rate remains stuck above the world interest rate and the home currency does not stop appreciating.

The magnitude of this recession reflects the magnitude of the domestic banking crisis. If the crisis is strong enough, it may even destabilize the domestic economy. Suppose the *LM* curve shifted up into the black position. Now its horizontal segment, indicating a risk-adjusted money market rate of zero, sits higher than the FE curve. The initial dynamics are the same as before, driven by an appreciating home currency. But now there is no end to it. Without intervention the recession grows deeper and deeper and could eventually develop into a full-blown depression. While the government could try to fight this type of recession by means of government spending increases, it will sooner or later run out of ammunition, and have to resort to more drastic intervention. These could include fixing the exchange rate or the implementation of capital controls.

Let these examples suffice for now. You will have the option to look at additional scenarios in the exercise section and in the online material recommended at the end of the chapter.

15.5 Quantitative easing: unorthodox monetary policy

When a country is caught in a liquidity trap or even in what we called a 'perfect trap', monetary policy is ineffective. In the first case monetary policy has to be replaced by fiscal policy. In the second case monetary policy needs to be implemented in a coordinated effort with fiscal policy which, used alone, would be ineffective as well. Unfortunatly, as Europe's debt crisis has shown, expansionary fiscal policy can be risky and may backfire quickly and unexpectedly at times when financial markets are itchy. This is why many countries have decided to or are planning to implement debt brakes that force fiscal policy into some sort of straight jacket. The intention is to keep the country's debt and financial speculators at bay. But it also restricts the use of government spending as means to stimulate the economy during or in anticipation of economic downturns. This has forced monetary policymakers to turn to a more creative, less orthodox use of monetary policy that runs under the label of **quantitative easing**. While operational details may be tricky and differ between countries, the basic idea behind quantitative easing, the idea that is relevant from a macroeconomic perspective, is not all that complex.

In order to understand what quantitative easing is about, we need a macroeconomic model in which the monetary sector is split into a money market and a capital market. The last section used versions of the *IS-LM* and Mundell–Fleming models with this property. The money market determines the short-run interest rate. This is the one that conventional monetary policy addresses and steers. The capital market determines the long-run interest rate. This is the one that firms need to deal with when they decide about investment projects.

Of course, the assumption that there are merely two interest rates is still an abstraction. In reality there is a host of time horizons, each with its own interest rate attached. The graphical display of how these interest rates (or yields) relate to the time horizon is called the yield curve. Yield curves are drawn for given categories of debt contracts, such as government bonds or commercial bonds. Figure 15.15 shows two yield curves for AAA-rated government bonds

The yield curve shows the *term structure of the interest rate* as a curve displaying yields or interest rates across different maturities.

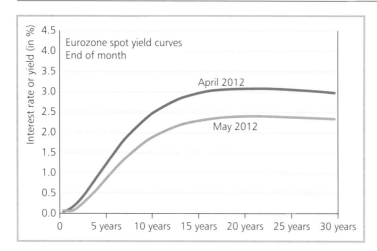

Figure 15.15 These yield curves show that while short-term interest rates remained stuck near zero and, thus, could not be lowered, longer-term interest rates, those that are most relevant for investment projects, fell by some 700 basis points between April and May 2012.

Source: European Central Bank

in the Eurozone for the months of April and May 2012. These provide some interesting insights:

- *Longer-run interest rates are usually higher than short-run rates.* The main reason for this is the *term premium.* Since the distant future is usually more difficult to predict than the near future, the term premium rewards investors for the additional risk of having their funds tied up for a longer period of time. Departures from this normal shape of the yield curve occur under exceptional circumstances, such as when markets believe inflation and, therefore, nominal interest rates, will rise or fall noticeably in the future. Then the yield curve may either become very steep or even negatively-sloped. Such an inverted yield curve has been the norm during times of deflation in the nineteenth century. Oftentimes, inverted yield curves also herald recessions.
- *Short-run and long-run interest rates need not be separated by a constant mark up.* For instance, the yield on 15-year AAA-rated government bonds fell by a full percentage point (that is, 100 basis points) between the end of April and the end of May 2012 while the interest rate on 3-month bonds in the same class remained virtually unchanged. For reasons given in the previous paragraph this may reflect a change in the expectations about inflation or income ten years from now. More generally, though, such a change simply reflects a change in the supply of and/or the demand for such debt instruments. This is where quantitative easing enters the picture.

How quantitative easing works and how it differs from conventional monetary policy may be demonstrated best in the context of an *IS-LM* model in which a liquidity trap looms. We made use of such a model in section 15.4. We start from the equations used there and add modifications as needed.

The money market equilibrium condition is of the kinked variety with a dormant liquidity trap, as shown in equation (15.19). The capital market features its own interest rate, as described by equation (15.17). As a generalization of equation (15.18) the interest rates determined in these two markets are linked by a markup μ_{CM} which we assume to be a positive function of the risk premium RP_{CM} and a negative function of D_{CM}, the purchase of long-term bonds exercised by the central bank during a given period.

$$i_{CM} = i_{MM} + \mu_{CM}(RP_{CM}, D_{CM}) \tag{15.18'}$$

After substituting this equation into (15.17) and solving for the money market interest rate we obtain

$$i_{MM} = -\mu_{CM}(RP_{CM}, D_{CM}) - \frac{1-c}{b}Y + \frac{\bar{I} + G}{b}$$

IS curve with risk premium (15.17')

The new feature of this *IS* curve is that purchases of long-term bonds by the central bank reduce the markup and thus shift the *IS* curve *up*.

Our second modification notes that the money supply during a given period is given by a conventional part $\bar{M}$ and an added part that the central bank spent on the purchase of long-term bonds:

$$M = \bar{M} + D_{CM} \tag{15.22}$$

Substituting this into equation 15.18 gives the modified kinked *LM* curve.

$$i_{MM} = RP_{MM} + \begin{cases} \frac{k}{b}Y - \frac{1}{b}(\bar{M} + D_{CM}) & \text{if } kY > \bar{M} + D_{CM} \\ 0, & \text{if } kY \le \bar{M} + D_{CM} \end{cases}$$

kinked **LM curve** with horizontal segment (15.19)

What we see here is that, because the acquisition of long-term bonds increases the money supply, it causes a downward shift of the *LM* curve.

We are now set to provide a graphical illustration of how quantitative easing works, and how it differs from conventional monetary policy.

Suppose the economy is represented by the dark blue yield curve shown in the left panel of Figure 15.16, which indicates that the money market interest

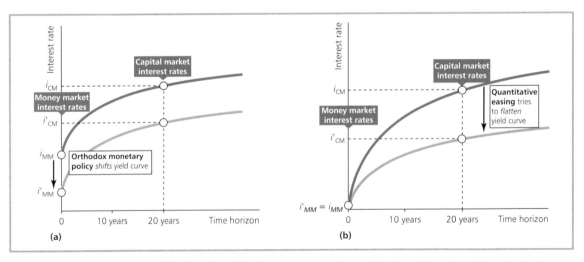

Figure 15.16 When monetary policy is used to stimulate aggregate demand, it aims at lowering interest rates in the capital market, the interest rate that corporations pay when they take out loans to finance investment projects. Conventional monetary policy achieves this by lowering the money market interest rate, which links to capital market interest rates via the yield curve (panel (a)). When this is not possible, because money market interest rates are near zero already, quantitative easing attempts to bring down capital market interest rates by flattening the yield curve (panel (b)).

rate is i_{MM} and the capital market interest rate is i_{CM}. If the central bank considers it necessary to stimulate aggregate demand, it may drive the money market interest rate down, either by pouring liquidity into the money market or by directly reducing those short-run interest rates over which it has control. When the money market interest rate falls, the yield curve shifts downward, pulling the capital market interest rate down too. Mission accomplished. Investment demand should begin to rise now. This is how conventional monetary policy works.

But this obviously does not work when there is no margin for further reductions of the money market interest rate, that is, when the country is in a liquidity trap. Then the yield curve looks like the dark blue line shown in, Figure 15.16, panel (b). In this situation the only remaining option is to try to *flatten the yield curve*. This requires the reduction of the markup. The central bank may achieve this by purchasing long-term debt titles, such as corporate or governments bonds. This brings the interest rate in the capital market down without affecting the money market interest rate. In crisis situations as described in Figures 15.12 to 15.14 above this shifts the *IS* curve back up, just as expansionary fiscal policy would. It, thus, exercises a dampening effect on the recession.

The downside of this kind of unconventional monetary policy is that the money supply increases substantially. This constitutes a looming potential for inflation. As long as the country is in a recession and in a liquidity trap, this does not matter much. The unlimited appetite for liquidity sucks up all money the central bank uses for its purchases. But once the recession ends and interest rates start to rise, the central bank must be quick to drain excess liquidity from the market.

But as long as the crisis lasts, the fact that quantitative easing shifts both the *IS* and the *LM* curve may come handy. Suppose the economy is in a perfect trap at point A in Figure 15.17. Then the upward shift of *IS* accomplished through the reduction of the markup would be crowded out entirely through currency appreciation. We learned previously that this is why fiscal policy,

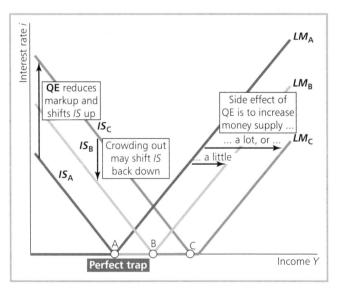

Figure 15.17 In A the economy is caught in a perfect trap. Orthodox monetary policy does not work because it cannot lower the interest rate below zero. Fiscal policy does not work because any increase in government spending triggers an appreciation and, thus, crowds out net exports. Using both instruments together may do the trick, however. Expanding the money supply widens the horizontal segment of *LM*. Along this segment a fiscal expansion does not raise the interest rate and is, therefore, not nullified by crowding out. Unorthodox monetary policy works as well. Because quantitative easing shifts both *IS* and *LM* to the right, it may even stimulate an economy that is caught in a perfect trap. When QE shifts *LM* a lot (to LM_c), income rises from A to C. When *LM* shifts only a little, there is some crowding out and point B obtains.

when used in isolation, does not work in a perfect trap, but must be implemented in a coordinated effort with monetary policy. The advantage of quantitative easing is that it constitutes such a coordinated effort in one package. Simultaneously with the upward shift of the *IS* curve the *LM* curve shifts to the right, providing the leeway for the upward shift of *IS* to work. The magnitude of this second shift determines whether there is no crowding out at all or some crowding out kicks in.

Quantitative easing is an important addition to the toolbox of central banks. But it must be used wisely – and it has limitations. We already mentioned the risk of inflation that derives from the money supply growth that is part of the package when a dose of quantitative easing is administered. More directly, this may also put a limit to what quantitative easing can achieve. After all, part of the markup that sits between short-run and long-run interest rates may not respond to quantitative easing. While the risk premium may indeed fall when the central bank convinces commercial banks that it will do whatever it takes to prevent a recession, this may be difficult to accomplish in the face of rising inflation expectations. Typically, the yield curve flattens when inflation expectations fall. How this should happen when the central bank is busy purchasing long-term bonds and expanding the money supply is difficult to imagine.

So, realistically, there is a lower limit to how far even aggressive quantitative easing may reduce long-term interest rates and, therefore, to how much it can stimulate aggregate demand. Therefore, it cannot replace fiscal policy entirely. Fiscal policy continues to play an important role in stabilizing economies in times of shocks and crises. But used unwisely, it can also have negative consequences in the longer run, as we learned in Chapters 10 and 14. These longer-run risks and the traumatic experiences with recent sovereign debt crises have convinced policymakers and many experts that rules are needed as guidelines for fiscal policy. We conclude this chapter by taking a closer look at the short-run implications of public finance imbalances and the implications of debt brakes.

15.6 From financial crises to debt crises and austerity

A debt brake, or balanced-budget amendment, is a constitutional rule that limits the deficits or debt levels which the government may generate.

We will look at these issues in two steps. In a first step, we add a third financial market to our model, the *market for government bonds*, and look at the effect of debt crises in this context, and at the pros and cons of different policy options. In a second step, we close the model by adding a debt brake. This is a constraint on fiscal policy that makes government spending and taxes to some extent an endogenous part of the economy.

Adding a market for government bonds to an *IS-LM* model has no direct effect on the behaviour of the economy. The *LM* curve continues to be

$$i_{MM} = RP_{MM} + \frac{k}{b}Y - \frac{1}{b}M \qquad \text{LM curve} \quad (15.16)$$

and the *IS* curve, to be drawn in the familiar diagram, still is

$$i_{MM} = -RP_{CM} - \frac{1-c}{b}Y + \frac{\bar{I}+G}{b} \qquad \text{IS curve} \quad (15.17')$$

We now have three interest rates. The interest rates in the two capital markets, the market for corporate bonds and the market for **governments bonds**, are linked to the money market interest rate via the respective risk premiums. This yields the no-arbitrage condition

$$i_{MM} = i_{CM} - RP_{CM} = i_{GB} - RP_{GB} \qquad \text{No-arbitrage condition} \quad (15.23)$$

where i_{GB} is the interest rate on government bonds. A sovereign debt crisis that makes the risk premium required for government bonds rise, increases the government's interest payments $i_{GB}B$ and tends to raise the budget deficit D.

$$D = G + i_{GB}B - T$$

There are no immediate effects on the economy as represented by the LM and IS curves. But we need to keep in mind that, as a matter of accounting mechanics, deficits today add to the level of debt and thus increase interest payments by the government tomorrow. So it is important to keep an eye on whether current deficits are compatible with long-term sustainability.

In addition, risky government finances usually cast doubt on the solvency of the economy at large. Just as the sub-prime crisis in the US housing market spread to the entire financial industry and the private economy in general, so may emerging doubts about the solvency of the government. Not only may the risk premiums in the money and the corporate bonds market be pulled up when the risk premium for government bonds increases. Government investment projects may be postponed. There may be fears of layoffs and pay reductions in the public sector, all with negative effects on aggregate demand.

Because of this overwhelming importance of sound public finances for the stability of the entire economy many countries have decided to put limits on the spending manners of their governments. The Stability and Growth Pact had been one such, not particularly successful, attempt by the Eurozone. We conclude this chapter by looking at the benefits and costs of such debt brakes.

The direct effect of debt brakes is felt in the real economy, represented by the IS curve. In standard form the goods market comprises the equations

$$Y = C + I + G \qquad\qquad \text{Goods market equilibrium} \quad (15.24)$$

$$C = c(Y - T) \qquad\qquad \text{Consumption function} \quad (15.25)$$

$$T = tY \qquad\qquad \text{Tax equation} \quad (15.26)$$

$$I = \bar{I} - bi_{CM} \qquad\qquad \text{Investment function} \quad (15.27)$$

To this we now add a debt brake. Suppose this requires the government to keep the budget deficit at α billion euros at all times:

$$G + i_{GB}B - T = \alpha \qquad\qquad \text{Debt brake} \quad (15.28)$$

As in the last section, the two interest rates in the markets for long-term bonds are linked to the money market interest rate via the no arbitrage condition given in (15.23).

Substituting (15.25), (15.26), (15.27), (15.28) and (15.23) into (15.24) and solving for i_{MM} gives the most comprehensive equation for the IS curve yet:

$$i_{MM} = \frac{1}{b + B[\bar{I} + \alpha - (1 - c)(1 - t)Y - (b \cdot RP_{CM} + B - RP_{GB})]}$$

$$\textbf{IS curve} \text{ with risk premium and debt brake} \quad (15.17'')$$

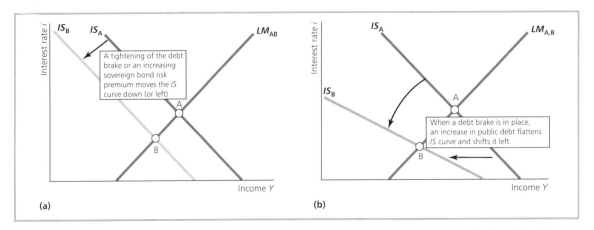

Figure 15.18 A tighter debt brake moves *IS* left. This is because the government must reduce the budget deficit by cutting public spending G. This lowers demand via the multiplier. The same effect obtains if the government pays higher interest rates because of a hike in the risk premium on sovereign bonds (panel (a)). An increase in the public debt B raises interest payments and leaves smaller amounts available for other public spending. Since this effect is stronger at higher interest rates, the *IS* curve flattens. It also shifts left when the government pays a positive risk premium.

The macroeconomic consequence can be traced after combining this equation with an *LM* curve, as in Figure 15.18.

Since the debt brake makes government spending G endogenous, the goods market responds to changes in all variables that enter equation (15.28). These include the result of structural policy decisions, such as the deficit ceiling α. It also includes the state of public finances inherited from previous governments. And it includes developments in the financial markets that affect the interest rate i_{GB}.

The deficit ceiling affects the position of *IS*. As shown in the left panel, reducing the latitude for fiscal policy by lowering α shifts *IS* down and thus affects income negatively in the short run. Similarly, if a crisis erupts in the sovereign bond market, *IS* shifts down, with recessionary effects. This is because an increase in RP_{GB} raises i_{GB} at all money market rates, which increases interest payments on accumulated debt, and thus forces the government to reduce spending G. Finally, an increase in government debt makes the *IS* curve flatter and shifts it to the left (panel (b)). As with an increase in the risk premium, when B rises, interest payments on government debt increase and the government is forced to cut spending, with immediate negative effects on aggregate demand and income.

So the effect of a rigid debt brake on an economy's short-run performance is clearly undesirable. In order to avoid this and tilt the balance in favour of benefits that accrue further down the road, a certain leeway must be built into such an arrangement that equips fiscal policy with the necessary leeway during times of crisis.

15.7 Lessons learned

This chapter took a deeper look at economic crises. The recent financial and sovereign debt crises, in particular, have consequences for how we do macroeconomics – as regards future research, how we conduct economic policy and what we teach. No consensus has emerged yet. But there are first lessons that a majority of macroeconomists are likely to derive from this experience. Some of them bear directly on the models we teach and use in policy discussions. Others are more generally directed at the attitude and emphasis in macroeconomics instruction.

There is increased interest in short-run fluctuations. As regards economic booms and recessions, recent decades were a period of calm, by historical standards. This led to a pronounced shift of emphasis from short-run issues towards long-run issues surrounding economic growth. Recent experience reminds us that the business cycle is not dead yet, and that recessions may raise their ugly heads any time, big time. And in ways never seen before.

Macroeconomics must take financial markets seriously, even in models taught at the undergraduate level. A famous Einstein quote demands that 'A scientific theory should be as simple as possible, but no simpler.' Recent crises have raised the bar in macroeconomics. In their pre-crisis guise our workhorse models are too simple to be of much use when the economy drifts out of tranquil waters. We have seen that it is not that difficult to add features like multiple interest rates, risk premiums, liquidity traps or debt brakes to the *IS-LM*, Mundell–Fleming and *AD-AS* models' baseline versions. But these need to find a more prominent place in curricula and tool boxes.

Financial markets are not always rational and efficient. Rationality and efficiency will continue to be important benchmarks when analyzing financial markets. But we need to keep in mind that deviations from this ideal may occur more often and more pronouncedly than previously thought. The IMF's Olivier Blanchard, one of the world's leading macroeconomists, has even diagnosed *schizophrenia* in how financial markets behaved in 2011. What is anything but easy to overlook – fear and panic, ignorance and abuse in financial markets – may drive economies to places where fundamentals alone would never have taken them.

The self-healing, equilibrating forces of markets appear weaker than we thought, or became weaker than they used to be. What happened since 2007 is hard to explain without conceding the existence of speculative bubbles, self-fulfilling prophecies and multiple equilibria in certain markets. These concepts may not lend themselves to an easy formal integration into undergraduate models. But they must definitely be attached and discussed in a narrative fashion or in the form of examples when we discuss crisis experiences. The cases we looked at are illustrative examples. In reality, self-fulfilling prophecies and multiple equilibria probably occur in many more forms and markets.

Financial markets may benefit from downsizing and better regulation. Insufficient or ill-designed regulation permitted run-of-the mill disturbances of manageable magnitude to grow into global beasts. The poisonous mix that triggered these disastrous developments included excessive leverage, the risk-camouflaging properties of securitization and derivatives, and their uncontrolled growth in very much unregulated segments of the financial industry. The question must be asked: do such products still serve the key purpose of financial markets and banking, namely to channel savings towards their most efficient use? Or do they essentially add a touch of gambling in which the casino always wins? The risks from overboarding financial markets reach new dimensions when combined with panic, herd behaviour and self-fulfilling prophecy, operating in a world where multiple equilibria appear to be widespread.

Regulation must also address issues of systemic risk and moral hazard in the banking sector, where the bills from risky investments gone sour are picked up too often by governments and taxpayers rather than those who own the bank and collect profits during good times.

Economic policy needs a bigger arsenal of weapons to fight major crises once they have started. While crisis *prevention* must and can be improved, it will never be perfect. When crises hit, policymakers need to be prepared. Monetary policy has been creative and flexible, replacing previous policy rules by unorthodox measures as needed. Fiscal policy has made a comeback. There are situations in which it is indispensable as an addition to or as a substitute for monetary policy. It is important that fiscal policy retains the leeway and flexibility to deviate from deficit and debt targets in times of crisis.

CASE STUDY 15.1 **US vs European job growth: cutting the 'miracle' to size**

A recurring theme in the business press, in political debates, in textbooks and in scientific work, is that rigid labour markets with powerful trade unions in most of Europe have not only driven up wages, but in the process virtually killed job growth. In stark contrast, US wages have stayed flat, while job growth is the envy of most other industrial countries. This argument is convincingly underscored by graphs like those shown in the four panels of Figure 15.19, where Britain, Germany and Italy represent the European experience.

The role of real wages and employment appears to be exactly reversed when we compare these (and other) European countries with the United States. Whereas wages remained flat while employment virtually exploded in the United States, just the opposite is observed in Europe. (Note that the dividing line really does appear to be the Atlantic, and not whether we compare Anglo-Saxon with non-Anglo-Saxon countries. At least, in the long-run perspective Britain's labour market experience does not differ very much from that of other European countries.)

The standard interpretation of the observed stylized facts is given in Figure 15.20, which uses the standard labour market diagram. In 1965 the labour demand curve was in the lower position on both sides of the Atlantic. Over time productivity growth raised the demand for labour, gradually moving the labour demand curve up.

In most European economies, strong labour unions and insider power kept their labour supply curves virtually vertical. Thus the upward shift of the labour demand curve drove up real wages

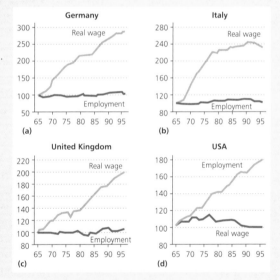

Figure 15.19

while employment remained more or less unchanged. In the United States, unobstructed competition in the labour market made the labour supply curve horizontal. Therefore, as the demand for labour increased, this produced a large increase in employment at unchanged real wages.

The 1996 labour demand curve demonstrates the trade-off the economies seem to face. While exact numbers differ between countries (see Figure 15.19), we may say that a country's real wage may (at least) have doubled during these three decades (as it did in Britain, Germany and Italy), or employment may

Case study 15.1 continued

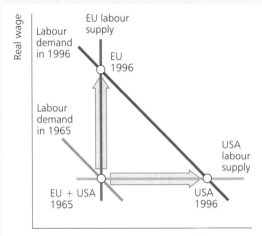

Figure 15.20

have (almost) doubled (as in the United States). Under either choice (or under intermediate choices), the wage sum about doubles.

Now one has to be careful. Without closer scrutiny, the argument presented here would have about the same validity as the recommendation that the United States should follow China's lead, where wages are but a fraction of US wages, while employment is several times US employment. Obviously, employment is only meaningful relative to the size of the population, because the size of the population determines the size of the labour market. How far employment can grow is obviously limited by the size of the active population (those aged 15 to 64). So perhaps another

factor behind America's job miracle is population growth.

Figure 15.21(a) repeats Figure 15.19(d), but adds the active population as an indicator for the development of the labour supply. Figure 15.21(b) shows the respective time series for France. The graphs reveal two interesting points. First, the active population grew much more in the United States than in Europe. US growth is some 50%, twice as much as in France. And France is not even representative of the rest of Europe, since in most of Europe the active population stagnated (see Table 15.2). And second, the active population goes a long way towards explaining employment growth in the United States (and in France). Of the 78.2% increase in employment between 1965 and 1996 almost two-thirds are due to population growth. The rise in net employment (employment relative to the active population) is still impressive, but much less of a miracle than the gross figure suggests.

The graphs suggest an entirely different interpretation why so many more jobs were created in the

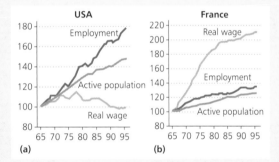

Figure 15.21

Table 15.2 Real wages and employment in Europe and the USA (changes between 1965 and 1996 in percentages)

	Britain	France	Germany	Italy	USA
Real wage	100.40	112.40	191.90	135.10	−1.70
Employment	4.30	34.00	4.80	3.00	78.20
Wage sum	109.00	184.60	205.90	139.20	75.20
GDP	94.69	143.37	142.24	159.76	109.90
Active population	8.40	25.70	14.90	14.90	48.60
Net employment	4.10	8.30	10.10	11.90	29.60
Net wage sum	92.20	130.00	162.40	107.10	27.40
Per capita GDP	79.46	103.30	119.24	135.36	53.64

Sources: OECD, *Economic Report of the President*, and IMF.

Case study 15.1 continued

United States compared with Europe, with much less of a role for trade unions and insider power. Consider Figure 15.22, where we suppose that in 1965 both Europe and the United States operated on the vertical part of the labour supply curve. In Europe the labour supply curve stayed close to its original position during the three decades that followed (France is the only European country with a noticeable increase in the active population). Hence, employment could not change very much, and all of the upward shift in the labour demand curve due to productivity gains went into wages. In the United States the vertical part of the labour supply curve moved to the right by almost 50% due to population growth. Note that this should have shifted the labour demand curve right as well. Why? Well, from the per capita version of the Solow model we know that similar economies should have a similar capital stock per worker in steady state. So when the active population grows the capital stock grows, shifting the labour demand curve to the right just as far as the labour supply curve moved to the right.

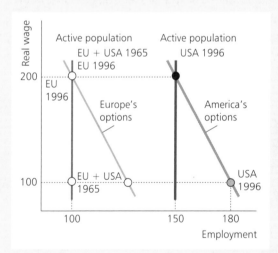

Figure 15.22

Now if this was the whole story, the United States should have ended in the black circle, with wages just as high as Europe's and employment 50% higher. The country, however, ended up in the blue dot instead, at a real wage rate only half as high as Europe's and employment 20% higher than it should be according to its active population. The line passing through the blue dot and the black circle appears to mark the true trade-off between wages and employment. In fact, it is the US labour demand curve. By the same token, the light blue line is Europe's labour demand curve and reveals Europe's options.

Table 15.2 casts a final glance at changes in the European and US labour markets between 1965 and 1996. East of the Atlantic we observe large real wage growth and small changes in net employment; west of the Atlantic real wages even fell, but net employment rose by as much as 20%. So the trade-off is much less favourable than we had concluded from Figure 15.19. According to the net wage sum (the change in the wage sum net of changes in the active population) all European countries clearly outperformed the US economy. In Europe net wage sums increased by between 162% in Germany and 92% in Britain, while the US net wage sum only rose by 27%.

Bottom line

Looking at real wages and employment the way we did in Figure 15.20 gives a wrong impression of how much more employment may be bought by exercising wage restraint. When we correct for changes in the active population, the trade-off becomes much less favourable, as Figure 15.22 shows. Looking at a summary measure: the net wage sum more than doubled in most European countries, while it grew by a meagre 27% in the United States. So the job growth achieved in the United States beyond population growth does carry a hefty price tag.

CHAPTER SUMMARY

- Empirically, income growth and unemployment dynamics are linked by Okun's law. The law states that the difference between growth and trend growth is linked to a given change in unemployment.

- Adverse supply shocks in the form of large oil price increases had visible direct effects on unemployment in most industrial countries. Why these effects have not disappeared even after oil prices receded again can only be explained by reference to persistence, which may be caused by insider–outsider mechanisms.

- Introducing persistence makes the *DAD-SAS* model's behaviour more realistic. Income needs more time to digest shocks, even when expectations are rational.

- Financial crises cannot be analyzed by means of models that feature one interest rate only. When serious problems arise in the money and capital markets we must permit interest rates in one market of the economy's monetary sector to differ from those in others.

- In flexible and creative hands, it is straightforward to augment our workhorse models, *IS-LM*, Mundell–Fleming and *DAD-SAS* with features that gained prominence during the recent crisis years. Examples are risk premiums and multiple interest rates, liquidity traps, quantitative easing and debt brakes.

- Essential ingredients in a macroeconomic narrative of why plummeting house prices in the US, after the collapse of the real estate bubble, pushed the global economy to the brink of collapse are excesses in securitization, derivatives and leveraging as a consequence of poor oversight and regulation.

- There is no such thing as *a* financial crisis. Financial crises come in many different shapes, depending on the financial market in which they hatch, their international dimension, and the governing exchange rate system.

- When liquidity traps rendered conventional monetary policy ineffective, central banks came up with new, unorthodox policy instruments under the heading *quantitative easing*. These essentially bypass the money market and target lending conditions to firms more directly.

- Debt brakes can also be discussed in *IS-LM* and related frameworks. Such rules carry risks. Without proper flexibility and leeway in times of crisis austerity can be self-defeating, working as an automatic *de*stabilizer during recessions.

Key terms and concepts

austerity *466*	moral hazard *457*
bubble *455*	Okun's law *442*
contagion *459*	persistence *452*
debt brake *466*	Phillips curve *441*
derivative *457*	quantitative easing *462*
financial crisis *455*	securitization *456*
government bonds *466*	sub-prime mortgage *455*
hysteresis *450*	yield curve *462*
leverage *457*	

EXERCISES

15.1 From statistical data, a country's Phillips curve is found to be $\pi = 9 + \pi^e - 0.5u$, where inflation and unemployment rates are in percentages.
   (a) What is the equilibrium rate of unemployment?
   (b) By how much does a surprising rise of inflation from 2(%) to 4(%) reduce unemployment?
   (c) If Okun's law for this country reads $\Delta Y/Y = 0.03 - 0.02\Delta u$, by how much does income grow (given your result obtained in (b))?

15.2 The estimate of Okun's law for the years 1974–2011 shown in Figure 15.2 reads: GDP growth $= 2.11 - 1.12\Delta u$, where u is the rate of unemployment. In 2009 GDP fell by 5.1%. The rate of unemployment increased by 0.4 percentage points. Is this what the estimated equation would have suggested? Or should unemployment have increased more, or less? Is the result different when you use the equation estimated for the years 1951–2011, which reads: GDP growth $= 4.11 - 2.89\Delta u$? Please compute the relevant numbers.

15.3 Consider the *DAD-SAS* model from Chapter 8. The economy's supply side is governed by the production function $Y = K^\alpha OIL^\beta L^{1-\alpha-\beta}$, which includes raw materials as a factor of production. The capital stock K is constant, but the demand for crude oil OIL and labour L depends on the prices of these inputs *in domestic currency*.
   (a) Suppose the exchange rate is fixed. How does the economy respond when the government devalues the domestic currency unexpectedly?
   (b) Suppose the exchange rate is flexible. How does the economy respond to a surprise expansion of the money supply?

Look at both questions under the assumptions of adaptive and rational inflation expectations.

15.4 In empirical work the movement of macroeconomic variables over time is often found to follow what statisticians call an autoregressive process. Taking unemployment as an example, such a process may read

$$u_t = \rho \cdot u_{t-1} + \varepsilon_t$$

where ε_t is a random disturbance and the equation is an AR(1) – a first-order autoregressive process. To get a better feel of the economic implications of the parameter ρ, do the following exercise. Suppose that u initially is at its long-run equilibrium level, which is 0. In period 1 the series is hit by a shock of size 5 (i.e. $\varepsilon_t = 5$). There are no further shocks, subsequently. Compute the values of u for periods 1 to 6, letting $\rho = 0.2$, $\rho = 0.9$ and $\rho = 1$, respectively. How does ρ affect the evolution of the time series? Considering Figure 15.7, what estimates of ρ would you expect for unemployment series in the United States and in European countries?

15.5 Suppose that the trade union's insider power is not perfect. By and by, some temporary outsiders regain employment and bid wages down. For concreteness, assume that in the medium run unions only manage to keep real wages in the middle, between where they would want to keep it if they had complete insider power and where wages would go if unions had no insider power at all.
   (a) Trace the effects of the two oil price explosions under these new assumptions. Start by modifying Figure 15.6. Then modify the time path given in Figure 15.7.
   (b) Does the result provide a better explanation of Dutch unemployment than the assumption of complete insider power? (Consult Figure 15.8.)

15.6 Suppose a country with fixed exchange rates reduces government spending G in order to meet the Maastricht convergence criteria. Use the graphical *DAD-SAS* model with persistence ($\alpha = 0.5$) to find out how this affects income
   (a) under adaptive expectations ($\pi^e = \pi_{-1}$)
   (b) under rational expectations
   (c) under perfect foresight.

15.7 An economy can be represented by

$$\pi = \mu - 0.5(Y - Y_{-1})$$

$$\pi = \pi^e + 2(Y - Y_{-1})$$

Initial income is $Y_0 = 500$. Inflation is 10%. In period 1 the money supply growth rate is reduced from 10% to 5%. What is the new level of income in the long run
(a) under adaptive expectations ($\pi^e = \pi_{-1}$)
(b) under rational expectations
(c) under perfect foresight?

15.8 Equation (15.17″) is an *IS* curve that features a goods market in which government spending is constrained by a debt brake. As a consequence a number of different variables such as the deficit limit, the risk premium that affect government bond yields and the level of public debt come into play. This debt level B both shifts the *IS* curve and affects its slope.

Examine whether these two effects reinforce each other, or whether one may neutralize the other. In other words, in which direction does the curve shift when B increases and by how much? In which direction does the slope change and by how much?

15.9 Table 15.1 offers an overview of how many different financial crises may occur, even if we split the economy's monetary sector into two financial markets only: the money market and the capital market.
(a) Check by means of a diagram what happens under scenario 2MM?
(b) What happens under scenario 4CM?

15.10 Suppose the economy may be described by the *IS* model proposed in the second part of section 15.6. What happens in this economy after a rating downgrade that pushes the country beyond the insolvency threshold? Develop your answer by merging this model with the debt crisis model described in section 14.5 and the debt dynamics equation discussed extensively in Chapter 14. There is no need to try to do this formally; a verbal discussion suffices.

Online resources

Interactive learning module on macroeconomics of financial crises www.eurmacro.eu/xercises/crisis.html

Self quiz
www.eurmacro.eu/SelfQuiz/sq-ch15.html

Recommended reading

A substantial part of this chapter's discussion of the nature and contagion risks of financial crises is based on Manfred Gärtner and Florian Jung (2011) 'Clothes for the emperor or Can research learn from undergraduate macroeconomics', *Kyklos* 64: 75–86.

One of the most interesting and comprehensive out of many volumes on policy lessons from the financial crisis is Olivier J. Blanchard, David Romer, A. Michael Spence and Joseph E. Stiglitz (eds) (2012) *In the Wake of the Crisis. Leading Economists Reassess Economic Policy*. Cambridge, Mass: MIT Press.

EMPIRICAL RESEARCH

Is unemployment persistent?

The simplest way to allow for a shock to the unemployment rate to persist is by writing an equation of the form

u_t becomes u_{t-1}
one year later

$$u_t = a + b\,u_{t-1} + \text{SHOCK}_t$$

Effect that remains
one year later

Immediate effect from shock

A one-time shock that occurs in period 1 affects u in the same period by the full amount. If $b = 0$ there is no persistence. Since no further shock hits next period, the rate of unemployment falls back to its normal level a. If $b > 0$, a higher unemployment due to a one-time shock in period 1 means a higher u_{t-1} one period later. Part of this, measured by $b u_{t-1}$, survives as unemployment next period. If $b = 1$ the effects of a one-time shock on u even persist indefinitely.

George S. Alogoskoufis and Alan Manning (1988, 'Unemployment persistence', *Economic Policy* 7: 427–69) try to determine the amount of unemployment persistence in different countries empirically. Remaining more general than in the above equation, they even include up to two lags in the unemployment rate, estimating

$$u_t = a + b_1 u_{t-1} + b_2 u_{t-2} + \text{random variable}$$

where the shocks to unemployment are assumed to be captured by the random variable.

Estimation results for a few selected countries, based on annual data for 1952–95, are given in Table 15.3 (the constant term is not shown).

Persistence can be measured by the sum of b_1 and b_2. It is strikingly high, ranging from 0.48 in the United States to 1.04 in France. Given in parentheses below, coefficients are not t-statistics in this example, but standard errors. For Germany, for example, the t-statistic of the estimate for b_1 against the null that $b_1 = 0$ is $1.29/0.17 = 7.59$. We may also test whether 1.29 is significantly larger than 1 by computing $(1.29 - 1)/0.17 = 1.71$. Applying usual significance standards, the answer is no.

WORKED PROBLEM

Okun's law and the Eurozone

International monetary arrangements evolve over time. After the collapse of the Bretton Woods system Germany had control over its own currency, the Deutsche mark, for more than 25 years. Around 2000 it introduced, in steps, the euro as a union-wide currency. We may wonder whether such institutional changes affect macroeconomic relationships such as Okun's law. We may, therefore, split the regression reported in Figure 15.2 into two periods. Data are provided in Table 15.4.

The first regression is for Deutsche mark period 1974–99. An ordinary least squares regression gives the result

$$\text{GDP growth} = 2.74 - 1.39\Delta U$$
$$(10.87)\ (5.36) \qquad R^2 = 0.53$$

1974–99

Table 15.3

	D	F	I	GB	J	USA
b_1	1.29	0.79	1.03	1.29	1.05	0.68
	(0.17)	(0.18)	(0.18)	(0.17)	(0.18)	(0.18)
b_2	−0.35	0.25	−0.08	−0.38	−0.14	−0.20
	(0.17)	(0.19)	(0.19)	(0.18)	(0.19)	(0.17)
$b_1 + b_2$ (persistence)	0.94	1.04	0.95	0.91	0.91	0.48
R^2_{adj}	0.94	0.98	0.95	0.96	0.82	0.64

Table 15.4

Year	Change in unemployment rate	GDP growth rate (in %)
1974	1.4	0.9
1975	2.1	-0.9
1976	-0.1	4.9
1977	-0.1	3.3
1978	-0.2	3.0
1979	-0.5	4.2
1980	0.0	1.4
1981	1.7	0.5
1982	2.0	-0.4
1983	1.6	1.6
1984	0.0	2.8
1985	0.2	2.3
1986	-0.3	2.3
1987	-0.1	1.4
1988	-0.2	3.7
1989	-0.8	3.9
1990	-0.7	5.3
1991	0.1	5.1
1992	1.2	1.9
1993	1.3	-1.0
1994	0.8	2.5
1995	-0.2	1.7
1996	1.1	0.8
1997	1.2	1.7
1998	-0.4	1.9
1999	-0.6	1.9
2000	-1.0	3.1
2001	-0.4	1.5
2002	0.5	0.0
2003	0.8	-0.4
2004	0.1	1.2
2005	1.3	0.7
2006	-1.0	3.7
2007	-1.9	3.3
2008	-1.4	1.1
2009	0.4	-5.1
2010	-0.5	3.7
2011	-0.7	3.0

Source: Statistisches Bundesamt

Parentheses contain absolute *t*-statistics. R^2 is the adjusted coefficient of determination.

GDP growth must exceed 2.74% in order to bring the unemployment rate down. One per cent more growth reduces the unemployment rate by $1/1.39 = 0.72$ percentage points. With a *t*-value of 5.36 this coefficient is highly significant. The equation 'explains' 53% of the variation in GDP growth.

Turning to Germany's experience after the euro was introduced, we estimate

$$\text{GDP growth} = 0.83 - 1.55\Delta U$$
$$(1.30) \quad (2.34) \quad R^2 = 0.29$$

2000–11

Now it seems GDP growth only had to exceed 0.83% in order to affect unemployment positively. The regression coefficient is 1.55, not all that different from the one we estimated before. However, the adjusted coefficient of determination, standing at 0.29, is much lower than before. This means that the relationship has been much weaker. One reason could be that a series of labour market reforms had an independent effect on unemployment throughout the decade. Also, the dip in GDP of more than 5% in 2009 had no effect on the unemployment rate. Maybe you could try to neutralize this year as a unique outlier by means of a dummy variable in order to check if the relationship is then closer to what it was before the euro was introduced.

YOUR TURN

The Phillips curve

The Phillips curve proposes that inflation and unemployment are negatively related: $\pi = \pi^e + a(u^* - u)$. Thus the Phillips curve combines the combinations of unemployment rates and inflation available for short-run policy choices. Table 15.5 gives unemployment and inflation rates in Switzerland between 1981 and

Table 15.5

Year	u	π
1980	0.2	4.0
1981	0.2	6.6
1982	0.4	5.7
1983	0.9	2.9
1984	1.1	2.9
1985	1.0	3.4
1986	0.8	0.8
1987	0.8	1.4
1988	0.7	1.9
1989	0.6	3.2
1990	0.5	5.4
1991	1.1	5.9
1992	2.5	4.0
1993	4.5	3.3
1994	4.7	0.9
1995	4.2	1.8
1996	4.2	1.8

1996. Use these data to estimate a Phillips curve and evaluate the result.

(Hints: Treat $u*$ as a constant to be estimated. You may want to experiment with different functional forms, supposing that inflation depends on u, or on $1Nu$, or on $\ln u$. For lack of data on inflation expectations we need to resort to adaptive expectations formation such as $\pi^e = \pi_{-1}$. Recall that the constant term in the Phillips curve includes the natural rate of unemployment. You may want to take into account the effect of the improvement of Swiss unemployment insurance in 1984 on equilibrium unemployment by allowing the constant term to be different after 1984. This can be done by including a so-called dummy variable which is zero before 1984 and 1 in 1984 and after.)

Sticky prices and sticky information: new perspectives on booms and recessions (I)

What to expect

After working through this chapter, you will know:

1 What the stylized behaviour and interplay of macroeconomic variables during business cycles looks like.

2 Which parts of observed stylized behaviour of macroeconomic variables conform with the *DAD-SAS* model, and where *DAD-SAS* fails.

3 Why and how the dynamic interaction of macroeconomic variables depends on the nature of shocks.

4 That the *SAS* curve may also be derived from the assumption of sticky prices, and how this version compares with the standard *SAS* curve based on sticky wages.

5 That a third cause of nominal stickiness that motivates a positively sloped *SAS* curve may be sticky information.

6 That in order to mimic the current behaviour of many central banks, the *DAD* curve may be replaced by a monetary policy rule.

Through most of the preceding 15 chapters we bragged about how well our macroeconomic workhorse models explain real-world experiences on macroeconomic issues related to business cycles and economic growth. And they really do, as underlined by many case studies and other empirical references. But scientists are much like devil's advocates, asking whether there weren't any challenges a particular model could not meet. By constantly putting their fingers on the weaknesses of established models, they generate new ideas and come up with new models and theories or refinements of existing ones. So, being students in the science of macroeconomics, we need to ask such critical questions here.

We had already done so in an almost relentless fashion in our discussion of economic growth, and thus motivated many less orthodox and recent developments such as poverty traps or endogenous growth theory, and the movement of human capital and technology to centre stage. In our analysis of economic fluctuations we have also covered a lot of ground, but nevertheless remained a bit further away from the current frontier of research than in our discussion of growth.

We will start with a reality check that distils some stylized business cycle patterns from real-world data, using methods as they are being employed in modern business cycle research. Measured against these stylized regularities we then ask: What are the virtues of the *DAD-SAS* model, and of its cousin, the *AD-AS* model? And where do these models' predictions clash with real-world findings? The virtues uncovered by this exercise will repeat and reinforce the message that the *DAD-SAS* model is a formidable tool for short- and medium-run macroeconomics, when used expertly and with care. Then, however, it will be the weaknesses uncovered by this exercise that will grab our attention and start this chapter off. These weak spots motivate why and how business cycle research has moved beyond or away from the *DAD-SAS* workhorse that featured so prominently in this book. This and the next chapter set out to fill this gap, at least partly so. Chapter 16 will focus on recent research that attempts to refine and advance the *DAD-SAS* model. Chapter 17 introduces an influential new, and quite different, approach to understanding macroeconomic fluctuations.

16.1 Reality check: business cycle patterns and the *DAD-SAS* model

Stylized properties of real-world business cycles

Figure 16.1 takes a look at four macroeconomic variables for the UK for the time period 1960–2004. These comprise real income (GDP) Y, private consumption C, investment I, and the real wage w. If we showed the raw data to be found at the indicated statistical sources, all variables would exhibit a strong upward trend that would dwarf the fluctuations we call business cycles and would make them difficult to see. Since we are interested in the behaviour of these variables during booms and recessions, we have removed trends from all four series and focus on the temporary fluctuations around these trend paths only.

Each of the three panels on the left plots real income along the time axis and compares its development, one by one, with each of the other three variables.

The upper panel looks at **income and consumption**. The ups and downs in consumption appear to follow the ups and downs in income quite closely. When income rises, consumption rises, very often with a similar percentage. The top panel on the right displays the same information, albeit in the form of a scatter plot. It plots each year's percentage deviation of consumption from trend against each year's deviation of income from trend. The regression line, which represents the average relationship between the two variables, has a slope close to 1. This indicates that whenever the deviation of income from its trend line increases by 1%, consumption deviation increases by about 1% as well. The cloud of data points hugs the regression line rather closely, so little deviation from this rule is to be expected. This is reflected in a high coefficient of correlation between the two series of 0.90. Consumption is said to be procyclical because it moves in the same direction as income during the business cycle. The scatter plot of a procyclical variable has a positive slope.

A variable is called procyclical if it moves in the same direction as income during the ups and downs of the business cycle.

The second row looks at the interaction between **income and investment**. Obviously, these two variables are procyclical as well. As can be seen from the display along the time axis, however, investment fluctuates much more wildly than income. A measure for this is given by the slope of the regression line in the scatter diagram, which exceeds 3. So when income falls by 1%, investment usually drops by more than 3%.

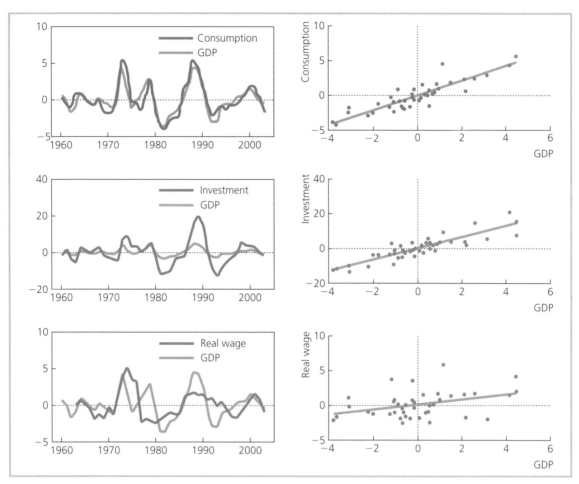

Figure 16.1 Using data from the UK to show how to distil stylized facts on business cycle fluctuations, the panels on the left plot the deviations of four macroeconomic time series from their respective trends. Such deviations may be interpreted as business cycle swings. On the basis of pairwise comparisons with income (GDP), we observe that consumption is procyclical. When income rises during a boom, consumption does so too. When income falls during a recession, so does consumption. Investment is procyclical also. However, while consumption fluctuates to about the same extent as income (measured by percentage deviations from trend), investment fluctuates much more. It is much more volatile. Finally, as seen in the bottom panel on the left, UK real wages are also procyclical. The panels on the right display the same information in the format of scatter diagrams. This makes it easier to see the nature and strength of the comovement of two variables.

How **income and real wages** move together is a bit less obvious in the bottom left diagram. So here the scatter diagram really helps. If doubts remain, the regression line confirms that the real wage is procyclical. Visual inspection shows, however, that this relationship is a bit wobbly, and this is being confirmed by the statistics. The correlation coefficient is low at 0.49. And the slope of the line is 0.48, meaning that you need a 2% boost in income (relative to trend) to see a real wage increase of 1%.

The relationships discussed here are part of the stylized facts on business cycles in industrial countries. While we distilled them from UK data, very much the same patterns are found in macroeconomic data for other industrial countries.

Stylized properties of *DAD-SAS* business cycles: Do they succeed?

We use a stochastic version of the *DAD-SAS* model with persistence and rational inflation expectations, as discussed in Chapter 15, to generate synthetic macroeconomic time series. The model is stochastic in the sense that it permits random shocks to the demand for money and to the demand for goods and services. Via the structural equations of the model, shocks translate into movements of income, consumption, investment and real wages. Figure 16.2 presents

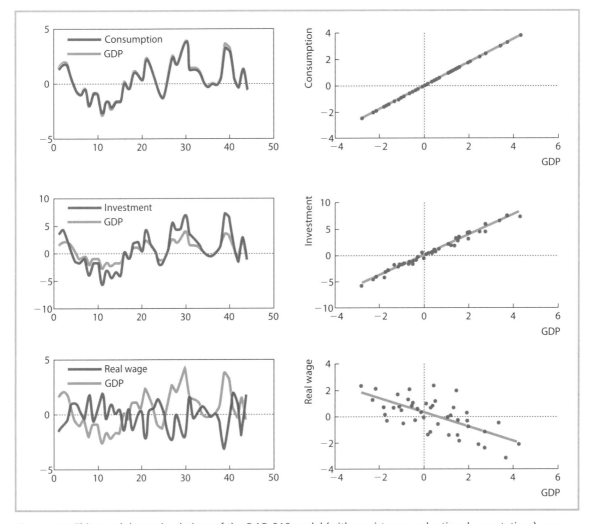

Figure 16.2 This panel shows simulations of the *DAD-SAS* model (with persistence and rational expectations) over 45 periods. The model is driven by a series of random shocks to the demand side (random shocks hit autonomous consumption, autonomous investment, and the money growth rate). Income (GDP) fluctuates in an irregular fashion, with recessions lasting several periods and occurring about once in a decade. Consumption is procyclical and about as volatile as income. Investment is also procyclical, but much more volatile than income. These two features of the *DAD-SAS* model fit stylized facts well. What is at odds with real-world experience is the countercyclical behaviour of the real wage. According to the model, the real wage rises when income falls during a recession, while empirically the opposite is observed much more often than not.

Note: Details of the simulations can be found at www.fgn.unisg.ch/eurmacro/tutor/dad-sas-sim.html

CASE STUDY 16.1	The Canadian business cycle

In macroeconomics, a stylized fact is a structural observation that is believed to hold for a majority of classified countries or time periods. Any useful macroeconomic model must be able to explain such observations. But the qualifier 'stylized' alerts us that there are exceptions. Often, there is much to be learned from studying such exceptions.

In terms of the comovement of income and the real wage, the Canadian experience is exceptional (see Figure 16.3). While in a majority of industrial nations the real wage is procyclical or at least neutral, Canada's real wage is clearly countercyclical. The slope coefficient is about −0.5, meaning that when income drops by 1% during a recession, the real wage rises by 0.5%.

While the good news is that Canadian real wages move as proposed by the *DAD-SAS* model, macroeconomists would have to come up with a good explanation of why the Canadian experience differs from that of many other countries. Such an explanation might include differences in the nature of shocks that hit Canada's economy as

opposed to other economies, or institutional idiosyncrasies that set Canada's labour market apart from the international standard.

When exploring the empirical virtues of a specific macroeconomic model, researchers look at many other macroeconomic variables in addition to consumption, investment and the real wage. Of particular interest is the real interest rate. Its comovement with income in a small open economy should be neutral according to the basic Mundell–Fleming framework in which the home interest rate is strictly fixed to the foreign one. When the economy is not so small and the *IS-LM* model of the economy's demand side comes into play, or when depreciation expectations permit a wedge between domestic and foreign interest rates, the real interest rate could also be anticyclical. There are no signs of this in the Canadian data, which does not come as a surprise given the moderate size and openness of the economy (Figure 16.4). In general, there seem to be fewer stylized facts that challenge the *DAD-SAS* model in the Canadian data than found for other industrial countries.

Figure 16.3

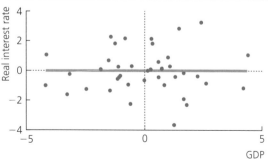

Figure 16.4

the results generated by one particular series of such random shocks in a fashion that permits direct comparison with the UK experience reported in Figure 16.1. The points to note are:

There is comovement in two macroeconomic variables if they fluctuate together.

- Income fluctuates in a fashion reminiscent of the fluctuations of real-world incomes. The cyclical swings are irregular, but, on average, recessions occur every 8–9 years on average.
- Consumption is procyclical. The slope coefficient of 1 says that movement in income is being followed by a comovement in consumption by the same relative magnitude.
- Investment is procyclical as well. But it is much more volatile than income. Mimicking UK experience, investment moves about three times as much as income.

So the good news is that the *DAD-SAS* model generates realistically looking movements in income as well as consumption and investment that match real-world experience quite well. Then what is the bad news? The bad news is in the bottom panels. In the *DAD-SAS* model firms facing an observed increase in the demand for their goods extend output only if labour becomes cheaper, that is, if the real wage falls. So the real wage is strictly countercyclical. Real wages fall during a boom, and they rise in a recession. Unfortunately, this is not what we observe in reality, at least not in the UK. The bottom panels of Figure 16.1 showed a procyclical movement of the real wage. This is not observed in all industrial countries. Sometimes the real wage is neutral. But it is rarely countercyclical. So in this aspect the *DAD-SAS* model is in conflict with what we find in reality.

A variable is called countercyclical if it moves in the opposite direction to income during the business cycle.

When relevant empirical defects of an economic model are being encountered, researchers typically respond in one of two ways: they either augment or refine the model under consideration – here the *DAD-SAS* model – in a way that mends the observed defect, or devise a new model with superior properties. Regarding business cycle modelling, macroeconomic research has gone down both avenues, with fruitful results. We now discuss both in some detail. This chapter focuses on research efforts that refine the *DAD-SAS* model but preserve its Keynesian foundation. Chapter 17 introduces real business cycles, which look at the ups and downs of real activity from an entirely different angle.

16.2 New Keynesian responses

Keynesian models are characterized by sluggish wages or prices, which prevent their respective markets from clearing quickly.

The label Keynesian is stuck on models in which one or more markets do not clear because the respective price is slow to respond. The Keynesian cross (of course!), *IS-LM* and the Mundell–Fleming model are Keynesian, because we assumed goods prices to be fixed. The *AD-AS* model is Keynesian as well. Recall, however, that prices in the *AD-AS* model are perfectly flexible. Thus the goods market always clears. It is the inflexibility of nominal wages, which are caught in long-term contracts, that prevents the economy from digesting shocks instantaneously. At the same time, the inflexibility of nominal wages makes the real wage countercyclical. In the presence of involuntary unemployment in equilibrium, any change in income involves a slide up or down

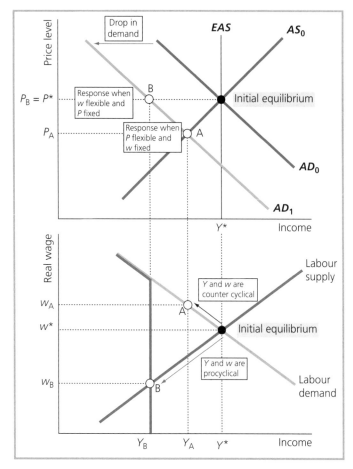

Figure 16.5 The two panels show how the economy responds to a drop in aggregate demand. Two scenarios are considered. In scenario A, prices are flexible and the nominal wage is fixed in one-period contracts. When the drop in demand moves AD to the left, there would be an excess supply in the goods market at the initial price level P^* in the amount $Y^* - Y_B$. As this drives down goods prices, demand rises and supply falls due to the rising real wage. The goods market clears at a price P_A. The real wage rises to w_A. The new, temporary equilibrium is at point A. Since the drop in income from Y^* to Y_A was accompanied by a real wage increase from w^* to w_A, the real wage is countercyclical. In scenario B, prices are fixed and the nominal wage is flexible. Now goods prices cannot respond when the shift of the AD curve drives down demand to Y_B at the initial price level. Since firms realize that there is no way to increase sales beyond Y_B, they restrict their demand for labour to the level of employment needed to produce Y_B. Thus their labour demand schedule now turns vertical at Y_B. The nominal wage falls until the real wage is low enough at w_B to clear the labour market.

the labour demand curve. And since firms only raise employment if labour gets cheaper, the real wage falls when the economy booms and rises in a recession.

Figure 16.5 illustrates this point graphically. To facilitate the mapping of points and movements from the AD-AS diagram shown in the upper panel onto the labour market diagram shown in the lower panel, the labour market diagram measures income rather than employment (the two are linked via the production function) on the horizontal axis. We start from an initial long-run equilibrium marked by black dots. Now let there be a sudden drop in demand, which shifts the aggregate demand curve left to AD_1. Since the demand for goods would fall short of supply at the initial price level P^*, prices, which we assume to be flexible, fall until the goods market clears in A. Since the nominal wage W is fixed, this price reduction raises the real wage from w^* to w_A, which, in turn, reduces employment and income. The economy ends up in point A in the lower panel as well. The point to note is that the real wage is countercyclical, since it rises when income falls.

Sticky prices

Since in reality real wages do not seem to behave countercyclically, macro-economists came up with the idea that it might be the stickiness in goods prices rather than in money wages that makes the economy respond to shocks in the observed way. Reasons why firms might want to reset prices only occasionally, even when demand-side and supply-side conditions change constantly, are related to the costs involved. These include such things as the writing or printing of new menus in restaurants (hence the term **menu costs**), new price lists and catalogues, or the renegotiation of longer-term contracts between firms and customers. Less directly, costs may also come in the form of lost market share, when one firm did raise prices while competing firms decided to postpone that decision.

The labour market when prices are fixed

In order not to mix the effects from sticky wages with those from sticky prices, suppose prices are fixed for one period ahead while the nominal wage is now fully flexible. Let us return to Figure 16.5 and see how such an economy responds to the presumed drop in aggregate demand.

When AD moves to the left this creates an excess supply of goods at the initial price level P^*. Since prices cannot change, all that firms can do in the face of this drop in demand is scale down production as well, to Y_B. Now, at the current real wage firms would like to produce much more, as signalled by the labour demand curve. But remember that this labour demand curve was derived on the premise that firms can sell all their production at a given current unit price, which we may call P^*. Now they realize that they can't. So it does not make any sense to produce more than Y_B. And it does not make any sense to demand and employ more workers than are needed to produce Y_B. In terms of the labour market diagram, this makes the labour demand curve turn vertical at Y_B. The real wage which firms would be prepared to pay for any additional work-hour has dropped to zero.

But now something important happens. Firms realize that they can get the employment needed to produce only Y_B units of output much cheaper. Put differently, with the new kinked labour demand curve there is excess supply in the labour market at the old real wage w^*. And because the nominal wage is flexible, it falls, until the labour market clears again at a lower real wage w_B. The important implication is that this constitutes a procyclical movement of the real wage. The real wage drops in a recession because the supply of labour needs to fall in line with the drop in demand.

The arguments advanced show that price stickiness may add a procyclical touch to the cyclical movement of the real wage. They do not yet really show how sticky prices fit into the AD-AS model and how they affect the rest of the model. In fact, we have not even had to talk about the shape of the aggregate supply curve yet. We will do this now, based on a more realistic set of assumptions.

The AS curve with sticky prices

Throughout our previous discussions of the AD-AS and DAD-SAS models, where prices were flexible, we assumed that firms sell their goods and services in perfectly competitive markets. In such an environment there is no leeway for discretionary price setting. All that a firm can do is accept the market price

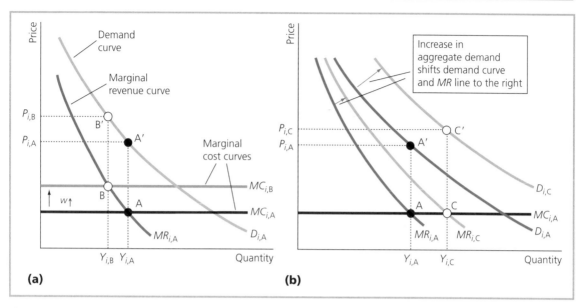

Figure 16.6 Under imperfect competition the firm faces a downward-sloping demand curve ($D_{i,A}$). Marginal revenues are downward-sloping as well ($MR_{i,A}$). Marginal costs are constant and, thus, depicted as a horizontal line ($MC_{i,A}$). Initial equilibria are at points A and A'. Panel (a) shows the firm's response to an increase in nominal wages. This shifts the marginal cost line up to $MC_{i,B}$. The firm responds by raising the price. The new equilibrium corresponds to B and B'. Panel (b) traces the response to an increase in demand. Now the demand line moves out right (into $D_{i,C}$), dragging the marginal revenue line along (into $MR_{i,C}$). The firm responds by selling more and raising the price. The new equilibrium points are C and C'.

A firm has a **monopoly** if it is the only firm to produce a good for which there are no (close) substitutes.

A firm operates under **monopolistic competition** if it is the only firm to produce a good for which there are close substitutes.

Marginal revenue is the change in revenue generated by selling one more unit of output.

as given and produce the quantity derived from the level of employment determined in the labour market. Any attempt to raise the price above the current market price would drive the demand for this firm's product to zero. Since other firms' products are perfect substitutes for this firm's product, raising the price above what other firms charge would drive all customers away. So when we talk about sticky prices, which makes prices a parameter that firms can manipulate deliberately, we assume at the same time that other firms' goods are not perfect substitutes, that there is less than perfect competition in the goods market. Thus each firm possesses some monopoly power and discretion for independent price setting. How do firms set prices in such an environment?

We start with a graphical discussion. You may remember Figure 16.6 from discussions of monopoly and monopolistic competition in your microeconomics lectures. Each panel features a downward-sloping demand curve for the featured firm's product depicted in light blue. The negative slope indicates that this firm, labelled i, has some monopolistic control over its price P_i, but that any price hike reduces demand. Under these conditions it is not guaranteed that a price increase is good for the firm's revenue P_iY_i, and profits, $P_iY_i -$ cost, because when the price goes up the firm gets more for the products it still sells, but it sells a smaller number of these products. P_i rises and Y_i falls, which leaves it open what happens to P_iY_i. The second, steeper negatively sloped line, drawn in full blue, aids in making the obviously complex decision of how to set the price. It is the marginal revenue curve MR. The marginal revenue is the change in a firm's revenue generated by selling one additional unit of output. Marginal revenue falls as output increases, and it may even become negative beyond a certain threshold. As a final element, both panels feature a horizontal line which denotes marginal costs MC_i. We let these be constant here for simplicity, but marginal costs that increase with output would not affect the argument. Equipped with these concepts, let us now turn to the question of what price this firm is going to charge for its product.

To maximize profits, the firm increases production until the marginal revenue no longer exceeds marginal costs. This is the case at point A, where the MC and MR curves intersect. According to the demand curve, this volume of output $Y_{i,A}$ can be sold at a price $P_{i,A}$. Since this price exceeds marginal costs, the firm makes a profit, and the difference between price and marginal cost is called a **mark-up**.

The two panels of Figure 16.6 reveal which factors are crucial for the firm's pricing decision:

- First, it is marginal costs. If marginal costs go up, say, because wages increase, the firm increases the price from $P_{i,A}$ to $P_{i,B}$ (panel (a)).
- Second, if the firm experiences an increase in demand for its product, say because real income has risen, the firm responds by a price hike as well. This is illustrated in panel (b), where both the demand and marginal revenue curves have shifted to the right, raising the quantity sold to $Y_{i,C}$ and the price to $P_{i,C}$.

We may put these insights into the form of an equation by making the (logarithm of the) firm's optimal (or desired) price, which we call $\hat{p}$ for convenience dependent on the (logarithm of) the aggregate price level p, and on aggregate income Y (relative to potential income):

$$\hat{p} = p + \lambda(Y - Y^*) \qquad \text{Firm's desired price} \quad (16.1)$$

The first term postulates that marginal costs vary with the aggregate price level. This accommodates the effect of wage costs, which immediately rise when the aggregate price level rises (due to the flexibility of the nominal wage rate), but also of the price of other firms' output which our firm may use as input. The second term proposes that the firm's demand curve moves with the business cycle. Since nominal wages are flexible, the labour market always clears at a constant real wage.

We are now set to derive the *AS* curve for sticky prices. To make things more realistic than our discussion in Figure 16.5, suppose the economy is heterogeneous. Half of the firms have sticky prices laid down in one-year contracts agreed upon before the start of the year. The other half has flexible prices which they can adjust at any time.

Firms with flexible prices set prices to their desired price, as discussed in Figure 16.6 and summed up in equation (16.1):

$$p_{\text{flex}} = p + \lambda(Y - Y^*) \qquad \text{Price set by firm with flexible price} \quad (16.2)$$

Firms with sticky prices have the same plan, but they must base pricing decisions on expectations. So prices that are fixed before the beginning of the current period are given by $p_{\text{fixed}} = p^e + \lambda(Y^e - Y^*)$. Since shocks cannot be anticipated and income may be expected to equal potential income in the absence of shocks, we drop the second term and write

$$p_{\text{fixed}} = p^e \qquad \text{Price set by firm with fixed price} \quad (16.3)$$

Since half of the firms have sticky prices and half of the firms have flexible prices, the aggregate price level is a mixture of fixed and flexible prices:

$$p = 0.5p_{\text{fixed}} + 0.5p_{\text{flex}} = 0.5p^e + 0.5[p + \lambda(Y - Y^*)] \tag{16.4}$$

Upon solving for p we obtain the AS curve

$$p = p^e + \lambda(Y - Y^*) \qquad \text{AS curve with sticky prices} \tag{16.5}$$

which transforms into the familiar SAS curve by following the procedure shown in Chapter 6:

$$\pi = \pi^e + \lambda(Y - Y^*) \qquad \text{SAS curve with sticky prices} \tag{16.6}$$

The message is that on the aggregate level, it does not matter whether it is the stickiness of nominal wages or the stickiness of certain firms' prices that causes the slow adjustment of the aggregate price level to shocks. We are now familiar with two stylized, extreme cases: one where prices are fully flexible while nominal wages are sticky (as postulated through most of this text), and one where nominal wages are fully flexible while prices are sticky (which we look at just now). Both scenarios led to very much the same SAS curve, which says that income can only exceed potential income to the extent that prices rise unexpectedly. The two scenarios differ, however, with respect to what goes on in the labour market, with the first one postulating countercyclical and the second one postulating procyclical behaviour of wages. In reality sticky wages and sticky prices probably do exist side by side. The relative importance of the two explanations probably differs between countries and reflects an economy's institutions and market structures.

16.3 The Phillips curves and monetary policy rules of current research

These days macroeconomists call all dynamic aggregate supply curves Phillips curves, no matter whether the output gap $Y - Y^*$ or the unemployment rate measures real activity.

We learned that the inability of the conventional, sticky-wage SAS curve to explain procyclical movement of real wages triggered researchers to explore alternative explanations of nominal stickiness in the macroeconomy. These efforts have produced two serious proposals. One is the New Keynesian Phillips Curve (NKPC). It became a serious contender in the 1990s, and we just dealt with it in the form of the SAS curve with sticky prices, focusing on economic intuition rather than formal rigour. Another one is the Sticky Information Phillips Curve (SIPC), which was proposed after the turn of the millennium. The remainder of this chapter looks at these two successful proposals in some detail.

This section also replaces the DAD curve used so far by a **monetary policy rule** that makes monetary policy an endogenous part of the economy, in the spirit of the discussions of Chapters 3 and 13, in particular. This facilitates our graphical analysis, and links our discussion to a line of modern research that explores the optimality and property of such rules.

From government reaction functions to monetary policy rules

As we discussed in Chapter 3, today's monetary policy is often discussed in the context of monetary policy rules. Combining an aggregate supply or Phillips curve with a monetary policy rule instead of a *DAD* curve is very much like studying the behaviour of an aeroplane flying on autopilot instead of asking how to use the flaps and rudders of a plane during normal flight and in bad weather. The first is probably a better description of how airplanes actually fly today. The second is essential to understanding how an airplane actually works and prepares the pilots for situations when they may have to interfere and override the autopilot.

Monetary policy rules are often derived from proposed utility functions, and are thus related to our discussions of endogenous policy and the informal derivation of government reaction functions in Chapters 11 and 13. In the spirit of our discussions and the public support functions used in Chapter 13, let the utility function of the central bank be

$$U = -0.5(\pi - \pi^{\text{target}})^2 - 0.5\beta(Y - Y^*)^2$$

Central bank utility function (16.7)

The central bank's utility U drops when either the rate of inflation or income deviate from respective target values, which are π^{target} for inflation and Y^* for income. Differentiating (16.7) with respect to inflation while using the *SAS* curve $Y = Y^* + \pi - \pi^e$ and setting the result equal to zero gives the first-order condition for an optimum, $dU/d\pi = -(\pi - \pi^{\text{target}}) - \beta(Y - Y^*) = 0$. This can be solved for π to obtain the monetary policy rule

$$\pi = \pi^{\text{target}} - \beta(Y - Y^*)$$

Monetary policy rule (MPR) (16.8)

The rule says that monetary policy attempts to move inflation to a targeted value but permits deviations if there is a gap between income and potential income. Just as the *DAD* curve, the monetary policy rule can be displayed in the π-Y diagram as a straight line, called the *MPR* line. It has slope $-\beta$ and intersects the EAS curve at $\pi = \pi^{\text{target}}$. As a shortcut, we assume that the central bank controls inflation directly. The *MPR* line has the advantage that it always stays in the same position, determined by potential income and the inflation target, and does not move about as the *DAD* curve does, the position of which also depends on lagged income Y_{-1}. The price to pay is that the obtained results only hold for this policy rule, but not necessarily for other rules or even for discretionary conduct of monetary policy.

The New Keynesian Phillips Curve

The New Keynesian Phillips Curve (NKPC) is a refined version of the *SAS curve under sticky prices* (equation (16.6)) that we developed above. While we cut some corners and took a somewhat static approach when we developed the latter, in order to facilitate access to the underlying ideas and implications, the NKPC places price stickiness in a fully intertemporal context.

Assume that only a fraction α of all firms may adjust prices each period. Firms that may change prices are determined by chance. Each period all firms have the same probability α of being selected, independently of whether their prices were adjusted for the last time one or several years ago. As a result, $1 - \alpha$ per cent of all firms have not adjusted prices for at least one period. $(1 - \alpha)^2$ per cent have not modified prices for at least two periods. Or $(1 - \alpha)^5$ per cent have prices they adjusted five or more years back for the last time. The aggregate supply curve that obtains under these assumptions has been given the name New Keynesian Phillips Curve and it takes the form:

$$\pi = \pi^e_{+1} + \lambda(Y - Y^*) \qquad \text{New Keynesian Phillips Curve (NKPC)} \quad (16.9)$$

The NKPC differs from (16.6) in the small time-subscript +1 only. Today's inflation, and thus the position of the curve in π-Y space, depends on the rate of inflation expected for the next period rather than on the rate of inflation that had been expected for today. This may appear a minor technicality, but it endows the NKPC with new properties compared to the conventional *SAS* curve, as we will see below. The intuition behind the appearance of expected *future* inflation in the NKPC is that if a firm adjusts prices today, it cannot be certain whether it will have an opportunity to readjust tomorrow. Therefore, it sets today's prices also in anticipation of price movements to come in the future. The mathematical derivation of the NKPC is not complex. But in order not to interrupt the line of argument here, it has been relegated to Box 16.1.

BOX 16.1 **The mathematics of the New Keynesian Phillips Curve**

To derive the New Keynesian Phillips Curve (NKPC) we note that current aggregate prices *p* reflect both the past and what firms expect of the future:

The future: Equation (16.1) gives the desired price of a firm that can set its price today and expects to reset its price again tomorrow. Such a firm does not have to look into the future. In the NKPC framework, when a firm has the opportunity to change its price it knows that it may not be able to do so again tomorrow, or even for a longer period of time. Therefore, its sets its price to a level that does not only take today's conditions into account, but expected future developments as well. This adjustment price *q* is a weighted average of today's desired price $\hat{p}$ and all future desired prices. The weights given to future desired prices decline. They reflect the probability that any firm will not have had the opportunity yet to reset its price at the indicated point in time. Thus the adjustment price of those firms that may adjust this period is

$$q = \alpha\hat{p} + \alpha(1 - \alpha)\hat{p}^e_{+1} + \alpha(1 - \alpha)^2\hat{p}^e_{+2}$$
$$+ \alpha(1 - \alpha)^3\hat{p}^e_{+3} + \cdots$$
$$= \alpha\sum_{j=0}^{\infty}(1 - \alpha)^j\hat{p}^e_{+j}$$

By noting that the terms in the last line add up to $(1 - \alpha)q^e_{+1}$, we may rewrite this equation more compactly as

$$q = \alpha\hat{p} + (1 - \alpha)q^e_{+1} \qquad (1)$$

The past: Equation (1) tells us how firms set prices when able to do so. Today's aggregate price level is made up of prices set this period, but also of prices set a while ago. Technically, at any point in time the aggregate price level is a weighted average of all adjustment prices set this year, last year, and in the more distant past. Here the weights decline as we move further back in time. They indicate the percentage of firms that have not had the opportunity to reset prices since the indicated time period. Thus the current aggregate price level is

$$p = \alpha q + \alpha(1 - \alpha)q_{-1} + \alpha(1 - \alpha)^2 q_{-2}$$
$$+ \alpha(1 - \alpha)^3 q_{-3} + \cdots$$
$$= \alpha\sum_{j=0}^{\infty}(1 - \alpha)^j q_{-j}$$

The sum of the terms in the last line equals $(1 - \alpha)p_{-1}$. So we can rewrite this equation as

$$p = \alpha q + (1 - \alpha)p_{-1} \qquad (2)$$

Now solve (2) for *q*, insert the result into (1), insert equation (16.1) for all $\hat{p}$ and collect like terms to obtain

$$2(1 - \alpha)p = (1 - \alpha)p_{-1} + \alpha^2 y + (1 - \alpha)p^e_{+1}$$

Finally, deduct $(1 - \alpha)p_{-1}$ and $(1 - \alpha)p$ from both sides and you obtain equation (16.9), the NKPC.

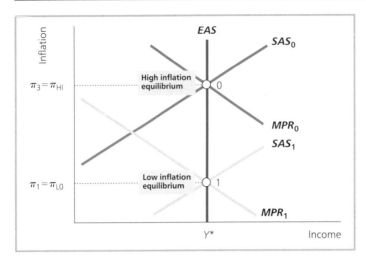

Figure 16.7 When the central bank lowers the inflation target unexpectedly in period 1, those firms that may adjust prices must ponder the possibility that they may not be able to do so again in period 2. These firms' inflation expectation for period 2 determines the position of the NKPC in period 1. Expecting that the *MPR* curve will remain at MPR_1, the rational inflation expectation is $\pi_2^e = \pi_{LO}$. This moves *SAS* into the position SAS_1 immediately, bringing the economy into its new long-run equilibrium in point 1 without delay and without any negative side-effects in terms of income losses.

Despite the attention the NKPC received in an avalanche of research during the past two decades, criticism is rising. By pointing to some serious dents in the empirical performance of the NKPC, a growing number of researchers challenges the once dominating role of the sticky-price based modelling of aggregate supply and proposes remedies or alternatives. Major drawbacks of the NKPC pointed out during this discussion are:

- **Surprise disinflations or inflations generate no income response** This is illustrated in Figure 16.7, where the economy had been in the high-inflation equilibrium π_{HI} up to period 0. Now the central bank unexpectedly lowers its inflation target to π_{LO}, moving the *MPR* line from MPR_0 to MPR_1. Believing that the central bank will stick to its new inflation target, *rational expectations* formation causes firms to lower the inflation rate they expect for period 2 to π_{LO}, which moves the *SAS* curve down into SAS_1. As a consequence, the economy jumps directly from the old high-inflation into the new low-inflation equilibrium. This disinflation is costless, as it does not generate any repercussions on income or unemployment.

  Incidentally, the same result obtains when inflation expectations are of the quick *adaptive* mould $\pi_{+1}^e = \pi$ rather than *rational*. Then the NKPC turns into $\pi = \pi + \lambda(Y - Y^*)$. This implies a vertical *SAS* curve at $Y = Y^*$, which leaves no room for income responses after any shocks to aggregate demand.

- **Anticipated disinflations generate booms** Now let the central bank announce in period 1 that it will lower its inflation target from π_{HI} to π_{LO} in periods 2 and after. The difference to the case discussed above is that there is no change in monetary policy yet in period 1, which leaves the *MPR* line put in $MPR_{0,1}$ (Figure 16.8). Still firms anticipate that the *MPR* line will move down into MPR_2 in period 2. The only rational response to this is to expect a drop in inflation to $\pi_2^e = \pi_{LO}$, which shifts the supply curve to SAS_1. Equilibrium in period 1 obtains in point 1, where SAS_1 and $MPR_{0,1}$ intersect. The economy booms because, due to inflation now falling short of money growth, the real money supply increases, which puts pressure on the interest rate and makes the home currency depreciate. Income returns

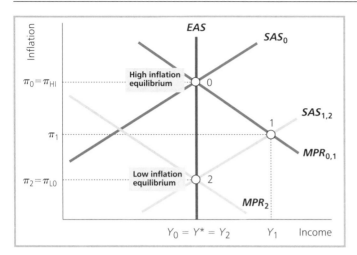

Figure 16.8 When the central bank announces in period 1 that it will lower the inflation target in period 2 from π_{HI} to π_{LO}, firms that may adjust prices know that they may not be able to do so again in period 2. These firms' inflation expectation for period 2 determines the position of the NKPC in period 1. Expecting that the MPR curve will move to MPR_2, the rational inflation expectation is $\pi_2^e = \pi_{LO}$. This moves SAS into the position $SAS_{1,2}$ immediately. Since the MPR curve still remains in MPR_1, the economy experiences a boom, moving into point 1. In period 2 the economy settles into its new, low inflation equilibrium in point 2.

to potential income when the policy-rule change is actually implemented and the new low-inflation equilibrium is reached in period 2.

The above result for adaptive inflation expectations $\pi_{+1}^e = \pi$ still holds, of course. There is no income response to the disinflation announcement. But now the economy remains in the old high-inflation equilibrium during periods 0 and 1, and drops into the new equilibrium in period 2.

■ **Monetary policy may keep income permanently above potential income, despite rational expectations** One of the things an overwhelming majority of macroeconomists agree on is that money is neutral in the long run. This means that there should not be any systematic monetary policy, any path of money creation, that keeps income above or below potential income permanently. The NKPC fails this test because a policy that leads to permanently falling inflation will keep output permanently above potential income. This holds even when inflation expectations are rational, as can be seen after rearranging the NKPC to yield $\pi - \pi_{+1}^e = \lambda(Y - Y^*)$.

■ **The NKPC does not account for real-world inflation inertia** Another stylized empirical fact in macroeconomics that we have not mentioned yet is that there is considerable inertia (or persistence) in inflation rates. To illustrate this: when researchers take annual inflation rates for the UK and use statistical methods to find out how current inflation is linked to past inflation, they obtain something like

$$\pi = 1 + 0.9\pi_{-1} - 0.1\pi_{-2} + \text{SHOCK}$$

This quantitative equation, estimated from real-world data, suggests that 90 per cent of any year's inflation will show up again in next year's inflation. To illustrate this with numbers: note that the equation implies a long-run inflation rate of 5 per cent. This is obtained by noting that in equilibrium the inflation rate does not change any more. The equation then becomes $\overline{\pi} = 1 + 0.9\overline{\pi} - 0.1\overline{\pi}$. Solving this for $\overline{\pi}$ we obtain $\overline{\pi} = 5$. Now let there be a one-time shock to inflation of 5 per cent in 2010, which raises inflation above equilibrium to 10 per cent. In 2011 the shock has disappeared, but inflation is still at $1 + 0.9 \times 10 - 0.1 \times 5 = 9.5(\%)$. By 2012 inflation has eased down to $1 + 0.9 \times 9.5 - 0.1 \times 10 = 8.55$ and in 2013 it is $1 + 0.9 \times 8.55 - 0.1 \times 9.5 = 7.745$. So three years after the inflation shock hit, less than half the shock has been digested. This is what is meant by **inflation inertia**. And since inflation adjusted rather quickly in the NKPC model under rational inflation expectations, inflation inertia is not a feature the NKPC is prepared to explain.

The Sticky Information Phillips Curve

Once again, it was the failure of the ruling aggregate supply or Phillips curve, in this case of the NKPC, to explain accepted stylized facts that sent researchers back to the drawing board and explore new ways to model aggregate supply. The most promising proposal as of 2009 is the Sticky Information Phillips Curve (SIPC). This approach assumes both nominal wages and prices to be flexible. Nominal stickiness comes from the assumption that firms find it costly to update and process information. So, while all firms may adjust prices whenever they like, some do so on the basis of current information, while many others use information that is dated.

Suppose that only a fraction α of all firms updates information each period. Which firms update is determined by chance. Each period all firms have the same probability α of being selected, independently of how much time has passed since they updated their information for the last time. As a result, $1 - \alpha$ per cent of all firms have not updated information for at least one period, $(1 - \alpha)^2$ per cent have not updated information for at least two periods, and so on. The aggregate supply curve that obtains under these assumptions has been given the name Sticky Information Phillips Curve. It looks less elegant than the Phillips curves we looked at so far (see margin note), and becomes even bulkier, but more transparent, if we write out the sums:

$$\pi = \lambda\pi^e_{[-1]} + \lambda(1 - \lambda)\pi^e_{[-2]} + \lambda(1 - \lambda)^2\pi^e_{[-3]} + \cdots$$

$$+ \frac{\alpha\lambda}{1-\lambda}(Y - Y^*)$$

$$+ \alpha\lambda\Delta Y^e_{[-1]} + \alpha\lambda(1 - \lambda)\Delta Y^e_{[-2]} + \alpha\lambda(1 - \lambda)^2\Delta Y^e_{[-3]} + \cdots$$

Sticky Information Phillips Curve (16.10)

The first two lines reveal that the SIPC has a lot in common with the sticky wage *SAS* curve on which this textbook has focused.

All terms in the first line are expected inflation rates for the current period, as in the conventional *SAS* curve. As a new feature, however, it is not only inflation expected on the basis of last period's information that matters, but on the basis of information available in previous period's as well, though with declining weights. These weights add up to a sum of one.

The second term brings the income gap into play. It is identical to the respective term in the *SAS* curve.

The third term is completely new. It is similar to the first line, because it lists expectations based on information available at different points in time. In this case, however, these expectations refer to the change in income $\Delta Y \equiv Y - Y_{-1}$ that firms anticipated for the current period.

Margin notes:

Making use of the sum operator, the Sticky Information Phillips Curve writes more compactly as

$$\pi = \lambda\sum_{j=0}^{\infty}(1 - \lambda)^j\pi^e_{[-1-j]}$$

$$+ \frac{\alpha\lambda}{1-\lambda}(Y - Y^*)$$

$$+ \alpha\lambda\sum_{i=0}^{\infty}(1-\lambda)^j\Delta Y^e_{[-1-j]}$$

Making use of the rule noted in the maths note on page 50, we obtain

$$\lambda\sum_{j=0}^{\infty}(1 - \lambda)^j$$
$$= \lambda \times 1/[1 - (1 - \lambda)]$$
$$= 1$$

The formal derivation of the SIPC is quite cumbersome and beyond an intermediate textbook. Also, the dynamic behaviour of an economy with a SIPC cannot be readily tracked in our familiar π-Y graph. Therefore, we settle for a *simplified version* of the sticky information model that retains the flavour and key properties of the SIPC. We call it the **truncated Sticky Information Phillips Curve.**

The simplified scenario proposes that one third of all firms update information every period. As a consequence, the current price level p is a weighted average of the prices set by firms with current information, q, with last period's information, $q_{[-1]}$, and with information already two periods old, $q_{[-2]}$:

$$p = \frac{1}{3}q + \frac{1}{3}q_{[-1]} + \frac{1}{3}q_{[-2]} \tag{16.11}$$

Firms with current information set prices to the desired price: $q = \hat{p} = p + \lambda(Y - Y^*)$. Firms with older information set prices to the price they expect to desire this period on the basis of this old information, i.e. $q_{[-1]} = \hat{p}^e_{[-1]} = p^e_{[-1]} + \lambda(Y^e_{[-1]} - Y^*)$ and $q_{[-2]} = \hat{p}^e_{[-2]} = p_{[-2]} + \lambda(Y^e_{[-2]} - Y^*)$. These equations introduce new notation, using the brackets $[-1]$ and $[-2]$ as subscripts. Up to now, when we wrote the expectation of a variable, say p^e or π^e, we always assumed that expectations were formed one period back. In the SIPC model this does not suffice. We need to be more flexible. Now the number the subscript reports in brackets says how many periods ago the expectation was formed. For example, $\pi^e_{[-1]}$ is today's inflation expected one period ago. $Y^e_{[-2]}$ is current income expected two periods ago. We could not express this with our previous notation.

After substituting the prices set by the three groups of firms into equation (16.11) and subtracting p_{-1} from both sides we obtain the truncated SIPC

$$\pi = 0.5\pi^e_{[-1]} + 0.5\pi^e_{[-2]} + 0.5\lambda(Y - Y^*) + 0.5\lambda(Y^e_{[-1]} - Y^*)$$
$$+ 0.5\lambda(Y^e_{[-2]} - Y^*) \qquad \text{Truncated SIPC} \quad (16.12)$$

It contains all the ingredients of the SIPC, expected inflation, the income gap, and expected movements in income, except that we cut off the stickiness of information after two lags.

It is instructive to compare the performance of the SIPC with that of the NKPC by re-examining the deficits of the NKPC discussed above.

- **Surprise disinflations or inflations generate income responses** Consider Figure 16.9, where the economy is initially in a high-inflation equilibrium again, and the central bank implements an unexpected reduction of its inflation target to π_{LO} in period 1. Since this had not been expected in period 0 or any prior period, the SIPC stays put and the economy moves into a recession in point 1.

    When looking at period 2, and at dynamic behavior of this model in general, it helps to note that the position of the *SAS* curve is always determined by the average of the expectations held by firms with last period's information and by firms with information that is already two periods old. We may, therefore, draw the (hypothetical) *SAS* curve that would obtain

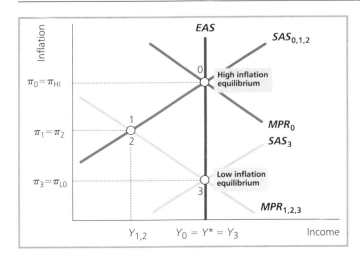

Figure 16.9 When the central bank surprises firms by lowering the inflation target in period 1, *SAS* stays where it was in period 0. Its position is determined by the expectations of firms that updated information one or two periods ago. The economy falls into a recession in point 1. In period 1, one third of all firms may update information in period 1 and form new inflation and income expectations for period 2. These firms know that some firms still operate on expectations that were formed before the surprise policy change and expect $\pi^e_{2[1]} = \pi_{1,2}$ and $Y^e_{2[1]} = Y_{1,2}$. The recession continues. In period 3 all expectations reflect the knowledge of the policy change and the economy settles into the low-inflation equilibrium in point 3.

from each group's expectations alone, and then position the actual *SAS* curve right in the middle between these two curves.

Now, in period 2 the group with the oldest information has not realized yet that the inflation target has changed. Hence, the *SAS* curve resulting from their (pre-shock) expectations would remain in the initial position, at SAS_0. The middle group notes the shock, but it also knows that some firms have not. So it has to form inflation and income expectations that includes both this knowledge. If they expected inflation to drop to π_{LO} and income to return to Y^* in this period already, their *SAS* curve would pass through the new long-run equilibrium. But then the aggregate *SAS* curve would be higher, and inflation would exceed and income would fall short of expectations. So this group must expect more inflation and less income. After some experimenting, we find that the only rational expectation, the one that will not fail, is to expect both income and inflation to remain at their period 1 values. Then the *SAS* curve of the middle group is the same as of the third group and, thus, also the actual *SAS* curve. And the economy actually remains where it was in period 1.

In period 3 all groups have observed the policy change and anticipate income to return to Y^* and inflation to drop to π_{LO}. Thus the *SAS* curve is at SAS_3 and the new, low-inflation equilibrium has been reached.

What makes the response of our model with an SIPC different from what we encountered previously is the amount of persistence in income and of inertia in inflation that we observe, even though we postulated inflation expectations to be rational.

■ **Anticipated disinflations generate smaller income responses than surprise disinflations** This case is shown in Figure 16.10. Starting from an initial high-inflation equilibrium, the central bank announces a reduction of its inflation target in period 1. There is no immediate reaction to this news, since the two relevant curves remain at $SAS_{0,1}$ and $MPR_{0,1}$. In period 2, one third of the firms has formed expectations in period 0, before the announcement was made. Their *SAS* curve remains in the initial position, passing through the high-inflation equilibrium. As discussed in the previous section, the only rational expectation of the middle group of firms,

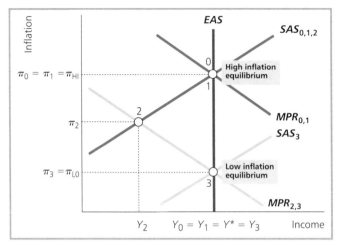

Figure 16.10 When the central bank announces in period 1 that it will lower the inflation target in period 2, this has no immediate effect on the economy. The *SAS* and *MPR* lines stay where they were in period 0, and so does the economy (point 1). When the inflation target is actually lowered in period 2 and *MPR* moves into $MPR_{2,3}$, this is still not included in the expectations of one third of firms that were formed back in period 0. Those firms who do update information are aware of that and rationally expect $\pi^e_{2[1]} = \pi_2$ and $Y^e_{2[1]} = Y_2$, which leaves *SAS* in the same position again. The economy falls into a recession in point 2. In period 3 all expectations reflect the knowledge of the policy change and the economy moves into the low-inflation equilibrium in point 3.

who know that the *MPR* will be at MPR_2 and the third group's *SAS* will remain unchanged, is to expect inflation π_2 and income Y_2, which leaves their *SAS* curve in the old position also. As we enter period 3, the central bank's policy announcement has entered the information set of all firms. So the *SAS* curve is in position SAS_3 and the economy settles into the low-inflation equilibrium.

In qualitative terms, the economy's reaction to an announced change in monetary policy is the same as to a surprise change. Both scenarios trigger a recession. But a policy announcement has merits nevertheless because it makes the recession shorter.

■ **No monetary policy may keep income permanently above potential income** Only unexpected changes in inflation and/or income drive income away from potential income. Thus, in order to keep income above potential income permanently, monetary policy would have to create the same surprises period after period, which can be ruled out when inflation and income expectations are rational.

■ **The SIPC accounts for realistic inflation inertia** Even in our truncated version that restricts the maximum lag in the collection of information to two periods, a one-time shock may affect inflation (and income) for two periods. In the full SIPC given in equation (16.10) a (decreasing) number of firms sets prices based on much older information. This obviously adds to the inflation inertia detected in our simplified graphical approach. Thus the SIPC is better prepared to explain empirically observed inflation inertia than any of the other theories employed in this book.

16.4 Supply shocks in the *DAD-SAS* model

We now turn to another explanation of why wages may move procyclically in the *DAD-SAS* model. This one is even more straightforward and orthodox than the one just discussed, because it reinstates the assumption of sticky wages and flexible prices that has been standard in this book.

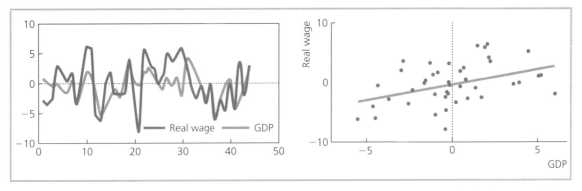

Figure 16.11 When the *DAD-SAS* model is driven by supply shocks, the real wage turns procyclical. The reason is that the core movement in labour (which means the effect that remains after contracts have been renegotiated after a shock to the labour demand curve) is up and down the labour supply curve, which has a positive slope and, hence, makes employment and the real wage move in the same direction.

In the simulation of the *DAD-SAS* model shown in Figure 16.2 we permitted shocks on the economy's demand side only. This reflects the basic philosophy of the model that it is the demand side where the music plays. On the other hand, however, we had conceded many times throughout this book that a host of real-world experiences, including the rise in European unemployment, cannot be properly understood without incorporating supply shocks into *DAD-SAS*. Our key reference there was oil price shocks. But economists have found that many other sorts of shocks occur on the economy's supply side. Most notably, productivity, widely understood, develops in irregular bursts rather than smoothly. Or preferences regarding leisure or the discounting of the future may change, which has supply-side effects as well. So we may ask how the *DAD-SAS* model behaves if it is hit by productivity shocks rather than demand shocks. The simulation results say: not very differently, except for the result shown in Figure 16.11.

In Figure 16.11 the real wage is procyclical. The cause of this is that now there is a different motor behind business cycle movements. Now a boom is triggered by a sudden boost in productivity. Labour becomes more productive, and firms demand more labour at any given real wage. The labour demand curve shifts to the right. But, at least beyond a certain threshold determined by current unemployment, more labour only becomes available when the real wage increases. So the real wage, employment and output all move in the same direction. They move procyclically. This also applies during a recession. Then real wages, employment and income all drop. This means that the procyclical nature of many empirical real wages does not necessarily contradict the *DAD-SAS* model when macroeconomic shocks happen mostly on the supply side. This is good news, but it also raises the following important question.

The *DAD-SAS* model describes economic fluctuations as deviations of income from potential income, which, in turn, is assumed to develop slowly and smoothly. It goes to great lengths in modelling the economy's demand side, which drives these deviations, splitting it into as many as three markets and modelling the behavioural characteristics of at least half a dozen different actors. The supply side, condensed into a single market, does not receive nearly as much attention. Now, after we learned that *DAD-SAS* only fits stylized empirical facts if supply shocks (shocks to potential income) are permitted a prominent role, one may wonder whether priorities have been set right. Should we not model the short- and medium-run movements in potential income in greater detail to obtain a better picture of how supply shocks find their way into the economy?

A group of macroeconomists attempted just that: to model the determination of equilibrium income, of potential income, in detail and with explicit microfoundations. They even propose that wages and prices are fully flexible, so that the economy never really deviates from potential income. According to their model, called the real business cycle model, economic fluctuations are actually movements in potential income. The model derives its name from the fact that when wages and prices are fully flexible, money is neutral. It does not affect real variables. In this case the classical dichotomy holds. The monetary sector of the economy and the real sector lead independent lives. There is no interaction. Money only affects nominal variables such as prices, nominal wages, nominal interest rates or the nominal exchange rate. It has no effect on the economy's real variables such as income, consumption or employment. Therefore, if our goal is to understand the fluctuations of real variables, we ignore nominal variables when money is neutral and focus on the real ones. Hence the name real business cycle model.

> According to the classical dichotomy, real variables (such as real income) are determined by real factors (such as technology), while nominal variables (such as prices or nominal wages) are determined by nominal factors (such as the money supply). Real and nominal variables are unrelated.

> Real business cycle models claim that economic fluctuations can be attributed to technology shocks and shocks to preferences. They have explicit microfoundations and no role for nominal variables such as money.

CHAPTER SUMMARY

- An alternative way of checking the empirical usefulness of macroeconomic models is by comparing their implications with the stylized behaviour of macroeconomic variables during real-world business cycles.

- Two very robust stylized facts from real-world business cycles are that consumption and investment are procyclical, meaning that they fall below their trend paths during recessions, when income falls below its trend path, and they rise during booms. The *DAD-SAS* model reproduces this stylized fact.

- Another, somewhat less robust stylized fact is that real wages are also procyclical. This stylized fact is at odds with the *DAD-SAS* model – when the business cycle is driven by shocks to aggregate demand. Then the model proposes countercyclical real wages.

- The *DAD-SAS* model can generate procyclical real wages once we include supply shocks as a major force driving the business cycle.

- The *DAD-SAS* model can also generate procyclical real wages, even in the absence of supply shocks, if it is the stickiness of prices rather than the stickiness of wages that is the cause of slow adjustment to nominal shocks.

- Recent refinements of the aggregate supply curve include the New Keynesian Phillips Curve, which is based on sticky prices, and the Sticky Information Phillips Curve, which assumes that firms are slow to update information on which they base decisions.

■ Some properties of the New Keynesian Phillips Curve are not in line with real world experience. In particular, money does not seem to be neutral, there is little inertia in inflation, and announced disinflations generate booms. The Sticky Information Phillips Curve does not appear to have such weaknesses.

■ Assuming that the central bank conducts monetary policy according to a rule rather than in a discretionary fashion, leads to the representation of the economy's demand side by means of a monetary policy rule line rather than a *DAD* curve. Obtained results are in line with what we learned from using the *DAD* curve.

Key terms and concepts

classical dichotomy *499*	New Keynesian economics *484*
comovement *484*	New Keynesian Phillips Curve *489*
countercyclical movement *484*	procyclical movement *480*
inflation inertia *494*	real business cycle model *499*
Keynesian *484*	Sticky Information Phillips Curve *494*
marginal revenue *487*	sticky prices *486*
monetary policy rule *490*	stylized facts *480*
monopolistic competition *487*	Truncated SIPC *495*
monopoly *487*	

EXERCISES

16.1 For the United States and various other industrial countries nominal interest rates are procyclical. They fall during recessions and rise when the economy booms. Is this observation in line with the *DAD-SAS* model?

16.2 When simulating the *DAD-SAS* model, *I/Y* and *C/Y* scatter plots result that line up the data on a straight line. By contrast, empirical scatter plots are more dispersed, like a cloud. Does this mean that the *DAD-SAS* model is at odds with real-world observations? Are there straightforward modifications under which the *DAD-SAS* model might also generate more 'cloudy' scatter plots rather than 'pearls on a string'?

16.3 Redraw Figure 16.5, this time assuming that not all prices are fixed, but only half of all firms' prices.

16.4 Suppose the economy's supply side is characterized by the New Keynesian Phillips Curve, while aggregated demand is driven by the monetary policy rule $\pi = \pi^{\text{target}} - (Y - Y^*)$.
(a) Following the procedure described in Box 8.1, derive an equation describing the behaviour of inflation under rational inflation expectations.
(b) Derive an equation describing the level of income generated by this model under rational expectations.

16.5 Take the equation $\pi = 1 + 0.9\pi_{-1} - 0.1\pi_{-2} +$ shock (with inflation rates measured in per cent) that represents an empirical estimate we obtained for the United Kingdom.
(a) What is the equilibrium inflation rate in the United Kingdom (the rate at which inflation would cease to move if no more shocks occurred)?

(b) Suppose inflation is at its equilibrium rate. Now an inflation shock pushes inflation up by 4 percentage points. How many periods does it take until inflation has receded to 6%?

16.6 Suppose 50% of all firms update information each period. The other half updates information one period later. Let the economy's demand-side be described by the *DAD* curve $\pi = \mu - \beta(Y - Y_{-1})$.
  (a) What does the truncated *SIPC* look like under these conditions?
  (b) Use the recipe provided in Box 8.1 to derive the behaviour of income under rational expectations. Compare your result with those obtained on the basis of the sticky-wage *SAS* curve in Box 8.1.

(c) Derive an equation for inflation under rational inflation expectations.

16.7 Figures 16.7–16.10 show how an economy characterized by a New Keynesian or a truncated Sticky Information Phillips Curve responds to unexpected and expected reductions in the central bank's inflation target when the central bank follows a monetary policy rule. Now let the demand side be characterized by a conventional *DAD* curve.
  (a) Let aggregate supply be characterized by the *NKPC*. How does the economy respond to a surprise reduction in the money growth rate?
  (b) Let aggregate supply be characterized by the *SIPC*. How does the economy respond to a surprise reduction in the money growth rate, and how to an announced reduction?

Recommended reading

An excellent, more technical treatment of recent research developments in macroeconomics is found in Wendy Carlin and David Soskice (2006) *Imperfections, Institutions and Policies Macroeconomics*, Oxford: Oxford University Press. A more advanced text recommended for more on the microeconomics behind sticky prices, sticky wages and sticky information is David Romer (2011) *Advanced Macroeconomics*, 4th edn, New York: McGraw-Hill Higher Education. The Sticky Information Phillips Curve was proposed by Gregory Mankiw and Ricardo Reis (2002) 'Sticky Information Versus Sticky Prices: A Proposal To Replace The New Keynesian Phillips Curve', *Quarterly Journal of Economics* 117(4), pp. 1295–328. While this paper may be a bit technical from an undergraduate perspective, it contains many simulations that permit graphical comparisons of how the New Keynesian and the Sticky Information Phillips Curve respond to a variety of shocks.

Real business cycles: new perspectives on booms and recessions (II)

What to expect

After working through this chapter, you will know:

1 What it means to underpin a macroeconomic model with microfoundations.

2 How utility-maximizing households decide on how much to work and how much to consume.

3 Why households may decide to work or save more (or less) today as compared to tomorrow.

4 That models of real business cycles offer an alternative explanation of an economy's ups and downs by describing fluctuations as movements of potential income, and not as deviations from potential income.

5 What intertemporal substitution is, and how it extends the effects of one-time shocks to productivity or preferences on income, employment and other macroeconomic variables, giving them patterns that look like orthodox business cycles.

In the 1980s a group of economists proposed the so-called real business cycle model. Their approach was radically different from the views and models that existed at that time, both in terms of the *economic focus* it employed, and in terms of the employed *methodology*, as summarized in Table 17.1 and spelled out in more detail below.

The mathematical analysis of such models is quite demanding and beyond the scope of an intermediate textbook. And it often yields few insights of economic substance. We therefore settle for a graphical analysis that cuts some corners, but permits us to focus on developing the intuition behind the real business cycle approach. We will proceed in three steps:

■ After laying out the basic philosophy of the real business cycle approach, we first present the **building blocks** of a textbook version of such a model.

■ Next we consider **how choices are being made** within this framework, while still entertaining a partial perspective, however.

Table 17.1 Comparing the *DAD-SAS* to the real business cycle model

	DAD-SAS and related models	Real business cycle model
Economic focus	Focus is on demand side of economy. Potential income assumed to move slowly. So business cycles are mainly understood as deviations of income from potential income.	Focus is on supply side of economy. Income never deviates from potential income. Potential income is assumed to move in a fashion that resembles recessions and booms of business cycles.
Methodology	Postulates relationships in a pragmatic fashion, taking into account economic theory, empirical support and tractability.	Builds model on first principles, so called **microfoundations**. Households maximize utility. Firms maximize profits.
Key assumptions	Nominal stickiness – either prices or nominal wages adjust or information is collected slowly.	No nominal stickiness. Agents employ perfectly rational intertemporal view.

■ In a final step, we merge those partial perspectives to find out how the different parts of the model interact, and how this interaction provides a **novel explanation of business cycle dynamics**.

17.1 Real business cycle philosophy

The real business cycle approach aspires to **reunite macroeconomics with microeconomics**. All behaviour, be it savings, investment or employment decisions, is derived from first principles rather than being postulated on the basis of plausibility arguments or observed empirical regularities. For example, rather than postulating a consumption function of the form $C = cY$ it is proposed that households maximize some utility function that includes consumption as a central argument. It turns out that income is a key determinant of consumption all the same, but that the two variables are linked in a more complex, less rigid fashion.

Real business cycle models typically feature two kinds of agents only, firms and households. The task is to analyze how the behaviour of these agents affects the properties of the business cycle. For this purpose one analyzes the behaviour of one firm that maximizes profits, and the behaviour of one household that maximizes utility. In order to derive the macroeconomic implications of the results obtained, it is then postulated that all firms are alike, so that the behaviour of the one firm analyzed is representative of the behaviour of all firms. In the same way, all households are assumed to be alike and behaving in the same way as the one representative household that was singled out for study. This is why this kind of model is called a **representative agents model**. In addition to assuming that the decisions of one firm and of one household are matched by all other firms and households, macroeconomic constraints need to be brought into play when proceeding from the microeconomic to the macroeconomic level. An example of such a macroeconomic constraint is the circular flow identity. The purely microeconomic analysis of the behaviour of an isolated household – as conducted in microeconomic textbooks – may safely ignore this constraint. The macroeconomic study of the behaviour of all households may not.

17.2 A real business cycle model

Since our goal is to develop an intuitive understanding of the sources of *real* business cycles, we keep the environment as simple as possible. We ignore international aspects and the public sector, and consider a **closed economy with no government**. Firms operate in a perfectly competitive environment in which factors are paid their marginal product. Households are rational, forward-looking agents that maximize utility.

The model

We start with those parts of the model that are already familiar from previous chapters. This emphasizes what the real business cycle approach has in common with the more traditional approach used in this textbook. We then move on to study the differences.

The first building block is the neoclassical production function

$$Y^s = A \times F(K, L) \qquad \text{Firms' output; aggregate supply} \quad (17.1)$$

already used extensively in our study of labour markets and economic growth in Chapters 6, 9 and 10. Firms generate output, or we may say, aggregate supply Y^s, by employing capital K and labour L, drawing on current technology A. Marginal products are positive and decreasing. We assume that technology is stochastic, changing in an unpredictable way from one period to the next.

The dynamics of the capital stock is given by

$$K_{+1} = K + I \qquad \text{Capital formation} \quad (17.2)$$

The fact that there is no capital depreciation in this equation means that we are talking about net variables: I is *net* investment, which is gross investment minus depreciation. Thus income Y is *net* domestic product, which is gross domestic product less depreciation. These modifications substantially facilitate the graphical display of real business cycle dynamics discussed below. Note further that there is a time lag between investment on the one hand and the capital stock and income on the other: this period's investment only adds to the next period's capital stock and output.

In a closed economy without government, aggregate expenditure comprises only consumption C and investment I:

$$Y^d = C + I \qquad \text{Aggregate expenditure} \quad (17.3)$$

With prices being flexible, the goods market clears at all times, and the equilibrium condition

$$Y^s = Y^d = Y \qquad \text{Goods market equilibrium} \quad (17.4)$$

holds permanently.

An innovative feature of the real business cycle model is that utility-maximizing households decide on the level of consumption and the labour supply. These decisions are based on maximization of the forward-looking utility function

$$U = u(C, 1 - L) + \frac{1}{1 + \beta}\, u(C_{+1}, 1 - L_{+1})$$

Household utility function   (17.5)

where L is the fraction of total time devoted to work. Hence, the remainder, $1 - L$, denotes leisure time as a share of total time. Utility depends positively on consumption and leisure time. A reduced value is being placed on utility that accrues in the future. This is measured by the subjective discount rate (or rate of time preference) β. If, say, the discount rate is 10%, that is $\beta = 0.1$, then the next period's utility carries only $1/(1 + 0.1) \approx 90\%$ of utility that accrues today. In full-scale real business cycle models, as studied in macroeconomic research, the horizon of households is infinite. Our model simplifies things by limiting the horizon of households to two periods only. This keeps the model tractable in graphical terms. The price we pay is that this leaves some irrationality in household behaviour when we study how business cycle movements in income and other macroeconomic variables may result from this model.

The behaviour of households

Households maximize utility by deciding on the following:

■ How much to work (and how much leisure to enjoy), today and in the future. This is tantamount to deciding on a lifetime pattern of income.
■ How much to consume (and save) out of current and future income. This lifetime pattern of consumption need not coincide with the lifetime pattern of income, but it must be financed by it.

It needs to be emphasized that households at the same time decide how much to work, which affects the economy's supply side, and how much to consume, which is a determinant of aggregate expenditure. The fact that these two decisions are interrelated and are even taken by the same agents renders the traditional distinction between supply and demand a bit artificial. In fact, real business cycle studies often do not even use these terms. We nevertheless stick with them to highlight the link to the more conventional models analyzed in previous chapters.

The decisions over how much time to work or enjoy leisure, how much to consume or save, and how to allocate one's consumption and work over one's lifetime, are all interrelated. You cannot really take one of these decisions rationally without being aware of the others. In order to cut through this Gordian knot, which in a full-scale model only complex mathematical solution algorithms run on computers can disentangle, we will look at the decisions to be made within the current period and at intertemporal choices separately.

Household behaviour: current-period choices

Applying standard procedures of economic analysis to the study of household behaviour involves, as a first step, the identification of the constraint under which households operate. This lays out the available options. The second

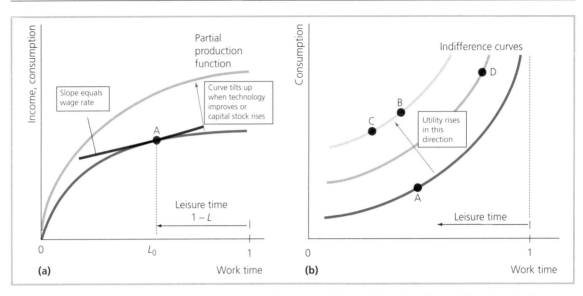

Figure 17.1 Panel (a) shows the macroeconomic constraint households are facing. It is the partial production function familiar from the study of the labour market in Chapter 6. It shows how income rises at a decreasing speed when work time increases. In long-run equilibria there is no net investment, so income equals consumption. The constraint tilts upwards when the capital stock rises or technology improves. Panel (b) represents preferences by means of indifference curves. Both consumption and leisure time (measured from right to left) generate decreasing marginal utility. This makes the indifference curve convex to the point where consumption and leisure time are both zero.

step adds preferences to the picture. This determines which is best among all available options.

Step 1: the constraint The options of households are determined by the production function. Since this period's capital stock and technology are given, income only changes when employment changes. So the relevant constraint is the familiar partial production function, with the capital stock fixed (see Figure 17.1, panel (a)).

The constraint tells us in what combinations income and leisure time are available economy-wide, and it shows the trade-off involved. Note, though, that actually we would have liked to know in what combinations the two utility-generating variables consumption and leisure time are available. This does not pose a problem regarding leisure time, since this is simply time *not* spent working. If we measure work time from left to right, leisure time can be measured from right to left. But beyond that, the partial production function serves as a useful constraint only if consumption and income are the same. This will not always be the case. But under what conditions will it be so?

The answer is in a long-run equilibrium, in a steady state. Consumption equals net income, which is the very definition of income we are looking at here. Since the capital stock does not change in a steady state, *net* investment is zero. All gross investment is absorbed by the need to replace capital that wears out. And since net income equals the sum of consumption and net investment, as stated in equation (17.3), net income must equal consumption when net investment is zero. So the partial production function is a valid constraint in long-run equilibrium, from which the economy may deviate temporarily while it moves from one equilibrium to another.

The constraint is perceived differently from the perspective of an individual household than it appears from the viewpoint of the entire economy. Starting from a point such as A, an individual household looks at a linear constraint as indicated by the straight line. This is because it faces a real wage given by the slope of the production function which, it may reasonably assume, will not respond to this one household's work decisions. This is because any change of one individual household's work-hours will not even be visible in our macro-economic diagram. But since all households are identical and make the same decision, the sum of all small changes in all households' work-hours will be visible. Therefore, the aggregate economy cannot move along the linear constraint. Instead it moves along the partial production function, which is non-linear due to decreasing marginal productivity. While this happens, the real wage changes, always adjusting to the slope of the production function at the respective level of employment.

Step 2: the preferences   We assume that the utility function $u(\cdot)$ is normal in the sense that marginal utilities from consumption and leisure are positive and decreasing. Then preferences can be represented in a consumption–leisure diagram by means of indifference curves that are convex to the point where consumption and leisure time are zero. The shape of these indifference curves, shown in Figure 17.1, panel (b), tells us that as we move to the right and leisure time becomes smaller and more precious, further losses in leisure time need to be compensated by larger and larger consumption increases. Household utility increases when consumption or leisure time rises. Thus utility always increases when, starting from a point such as A, we move north, west, or northwest into points like B, C or even D. As a consequence, indifference curves positioned further up mark higher utility levels. So when households decide on how much to work, they aim for the highest indifference curve possible.

Step 3: the optimal choice   By merging the constraint and preferences onto a single diagram, we may identify the optimal choice of the representative household (Figure 17.2). Households maximize utility by aiming for the point of tangency between the constraint and one of their indifference curves. This is the case where employment equals L^* and income is Y_A^*. Extending work hours beyond that mark would raise income and consumption. But the loss of leisure time incurred would hurt households even more, and thus utility would drop. Moving in the opposite direction a reduction of work-hours would raise leisure time, but the incurred drop in income and consumption would dominate, and utility would be reduced.

Comparative static effects   The point of optimality moves whenever preferences change and/or the constraint shifts. Real business cycle research focuses on the latter, though the preference channel is recognized as well, as another theoretical though empirically less relevant or less accessible possibility.

In the context of our model the constraint, the production function, can turn upwards for two reasons: first, when technology improves, and second, when the capital stock rises. In both cases the new point of tangency between the new partial production function and an indifference curve carries a higher level of income (see Figure 17.2). The effect on employment is ambiguous, however.

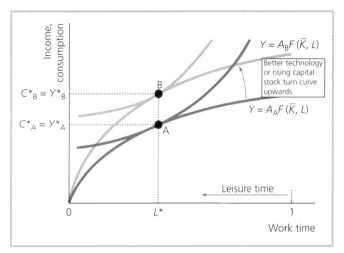

Figure 17.2 Households maximize utility by setting work time so as to reach the highest indifference curve possible. When technology is A_A, this point of optimum is A. Optimal employment is L^*, which generates income Y^*_A and, in long-run equilibrium, consumption C^*_A. When the production function turns upward due to better technology or more capital, a new point of optimum such as B obtains. B always has higher income. Employment could rise or fall, depending on the specifics of the production and utility functions. Here employment is unchanged, mimicking empirical experience.

Depending on the specific form of the production and utility functions, employment may rise or drop when A or K goes up. Taking clues from the real world, where annual work-hours have remained more or less the same for decades in many industrial countries (except where reductions have been negotiated in an effort to combat excessive unemployment), we may assume that the long-run effect on employment is more or less neutral. As technology improves and the capital stock rises over time, there is no noticeable effect on employment. So we move up roughly vertically, from point A to a point such as B.

Remember our caveat that the point of optimality just derived describes a *long-run* equilibrium only, a point of gravity. From this the economy may deviate for extended periods of time. Such deviations occur after the economy is hit by shocks. The nature of such deviations, and the subsequent paths of return to the old equilibrium or adjustment to any new long-run equilibrium, is determined by intertemporal optimization. This refers to optimizing decisions that span more than one period of time. Intertemporal elements are being introduced into our analysis by the fact that household utility is being affected by both current and future consumption and leisure, and by the fact that there are macroeconomic relationships linking the present and the future. We now turn to an analysis of such intertemporal considerations.

Intertemporal optimization denotes optimization decisions that comprise variables that stem from more than one period of time.

Household behaviour: intertemporal choices

Households have to decide not only how to allocate time between work and leisure, and split income between consumption and saving today (or this year). They also have to make a plan for these same decisions tomorrow (or next year). Of course, today's decisions cannot be made independently of tomorrow's. This is most obvious in the case of consumption: if I consume less (and save more) today, I will be able to consume more tomorrow. But it also applies to leisure time: by working more today I may be able to enjoy more leisure time tomorrow.

We now analyze the intertemporal decisions of households: how they plan to spread consumption over their two-period horizon, and how to allocate their work time over the two periods. These two decisions are interdependent.

Maths note. The two-period budget constraint states that since today's income is either consumed or saved, $Y_1 = C_1 + S_1$, and consumption next period is limited by the sum of period-2 income and period-1 saving plus interest, $C_2 = Y_2 + (1 + r)S_1$, the **present value** of consumption must equal the present value of income:
$$C_1 + \frac{C_2}{1 + r} = Y_1 + \frac{Y_2}{1 + r}$$
This is rewritten $C_2 = (1 + r)Y_1 + Y_2 - (1 + r)C_1$, which defines a straight line with slope $(1 + r)$. The **concept of present values** makes payments comparable that accrue at different points in time. For example, when the interest rate is 4% annually, €100,000 becomes €104,000 in a year. Then we may say that at an interest rate of 4% the present value of €104,000 next year is €100,000. Formally: present value = €100,000 = €104,000/(1 + 0.04).

To obtain an unobstructed view of each decision, however, we will pretend that each can be taken in isolation, while the other has already been taken.

The consumption constraint   Intertemporal consumption choices can be analyzed in a diagram that measures current consumption on the horizontal axis and future consumption on the vertical axis. Here we assume that households have already decided on how much to work today and tomorrow. If the incomes that are thus being earned today and tomorrow were being consumed immediately, in the period in which they accrue, this would generate a specific point in the intertemporal consumption diagram, which we call the **endowment point**. In a long-run equilibrium current and (expected) future income are identical. Then the endowment point sits on the 45° line. When the economy has been thrown off its long-run equilibrium, current income will differ from future income, and endowment points off the 45° line result.

In Figure 17.3 the household has decided to work equally in both periods. Thus the endowment point A sits right on the 45° line. Does this point also indicate the household's consumption pattern? Only in a barter economy that produces nothing but perishable goods which cannot be stored and thus need to be consumed right away. Then all income would be consumed in the period in which it was earned. Once non-perishable goods are being produced, households have the option of consuming each unit of income either today or tomorrow. All their consumption options would now be lined up along a constraint that passes through the endowment point and has slope −1. To make things even more realistic, enter credit markets, where households can lend or

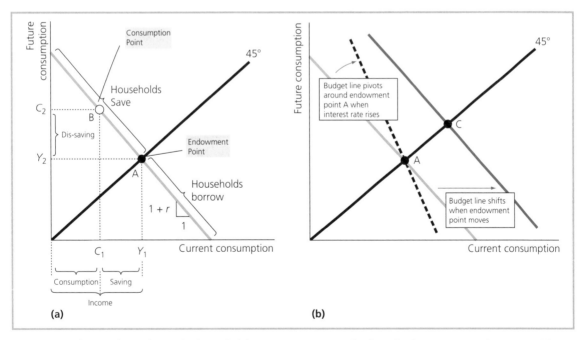

Figure 17.3 When credit markets exist, households may move consumption into the future or up to the present. The endowment point A in panel (a) shows the consumption pattern that results when all income is consumed during the period in which it accrues. Then period consumption equals period income. By borrowing or lending, households may enjoy any consumption pattern that lies on a straight line passing through A and having slope $-(1 + r)$. To consume the pattern indicated by B, households must save $Y_1 - C_1$ in period 1 and spend $(1 + r)(Y_1 - C_1) = C_2 - Y_2$ in period 2.

borrow at the real interest rate r. This improves the household's options of transforming today's income into future consumption further. After forsaking 1 euro's worth of consumption in period 1 and putting it in the bank, the household can withdraw 1 euro plus interest payment next period. Period-2 consumption thus increases by $(1 + r)$ euros. So the constraint along which households may select their intertemporal consumption pattern is a straight line which passes through the endowment point and has slope $-(1 + r)$. By saving in period 1 they can achieve consumption patterns such as the one characterized by point B that are related to but can be quite different from the income pattern. Or they may borrow to raise period-1 consumption above period-1 income. The intertemporal budget constraint shifts when the endowment point moves to a point such as C, and it pivots around the endowment point when the interest rate changes (see panel (b)). The latter effect will play an important role later on.

The consumption preferences   Let us now return to household preferences as formalized by equation (17.5). Preferences have an intertemporal component as well. Suppose for now that leisure in periods 1 and 2 is given, and let us characterize preferences by means of indifference curves in a $C_2 - C_1$ diagram (Figure 17.4). These have the familiar shape. The slope is negative, which means that if you take away some of tomorrow's consumption, households need to be compensated with more current consumption in order to keep them at the same level of utility. Further, indifference curves are convex to the origin. That means they bend away from the point where nothing is being consumed. This is because marginal utility decreases. Therefore, if we start at point D (where period-2 consumption is high and not valued all that highly at the margin) and reduce period-2 consumption by one unit, we need smaller compensation in terms of additional period-1 consumption than if we had

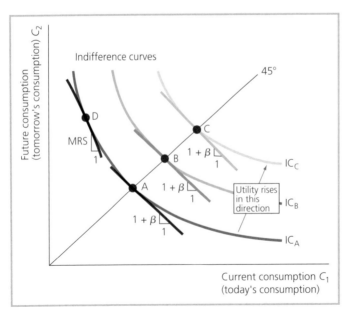

Figure 17.4 With decreasing marginal utility of consumption, intertemporal indifference curves are convex. Households maximize utility by selecting the consumption point that is associated with the highest possible indifference curve. This is where the linear intertemporal constraint just touches an indifference curve. At such a point the marginal rate of substitution (representing the slope of the indifference curve) equals 1 plus the interest rate r. In any long-run equilibrium, in which household consumption is constant, on the 45° line, the marginal rate of substitution equals 1 plus the time discount rate β. Since this must be equal to 1 plus the interest rate, such an equilibrium is characterized by $r = \beta$ (the interest rate equals the time discount rate).

started from point A (where period-2 consumption is relatively low and one additional unit of it raises utility a lot).

The rate at which households are willing to give up future consumption in exchange for one more unit of current consumption is called the marginal rate of substitution (MRS). Graphically, if we think in infinitesimally small units, the marginal rate of substitution equals the absolute value of the slope of the indifference curve. It is being affected by two things: first, by the marginal utilities which period-1 and period-2 consumption levels generate in a given point; and second, by the household's rate of time preference β, which states how impatient they are, how much they prefer consumption today over consumption tomorrow. As we slide along an indifference curve, the MRS changes. There is one point on each indifference curve, however, where the MRS has a very specific value and a straightforward interpretation. This is where indifference curves intersect the 45° line. At any such point, today's and tomorrow's consumption are the same. So the marginal utilities of today's and tomorrow's consumption are also the same. Therefore, if there were no discounting of the future, households would be prepared to trade current for future consumption at a rate of one to one. The indifference curve would have a slope of -1. The MRS would equal 1. But since, according to the utility function, one unit of period-2 consumption is worth only $1/(1 + \beta)$ units of period-1 consumption, households require $(1 + \beta)$ units of consumption in period 2 in exchange for one unit of consumption in period 1. This means that the slope of all indifference curves equals $-(1 + \beta)$ at their respective points of intersection with the 45° line. Almost trivially, utility increases as we move onto indifference curves positioned further up and to the right, as they feature higher current and/or future consumption.

The intertemporal consumption optimum The household's optimal intertemporal consumption pattern can be identified after merging indifference curves (preferences) and the budget constraint (options) onto a single diagram (Figure 17.5, panel (a)). As before, let the economy be in a long-run equilibrium. This positions the endowment point A, the intertemporal income pattern, on the 45° line. Since households maximize utility, they want to reach the highest indifference curve available. With this determining their choice from the options offered by the budget constraint, they pick the point of tangency between the budget line and an indifference curve as their preferred choice. So the slope of the budget line running through the endowment point is the key determinant of this choice.

Panel (a) reveals an interesting property of long-run equilibria (or steady states) in the real business cycle model: if the economy is in a long-run equilibrium, the budget constraint touches an indifference curve right on the 45° line. We previously found that on the 45° line the slope of any indifference curve is $-(1 + \beta)$. We also know that the slope of the budget line is $-(1 + r)$. And since in a long-run equilibrium these two slopes are equal, that is $-(1 + r) = -(1 + \beta)$, the time discount rate equals the interest rate:

$$r = \beta \qquad \text{Long-run equilibrium condition} \quad (17.6)$$

This holds in any long-run equilibrium on the 45° line and should thus be noted as a long-run equilibrium condition.

The marginal rate of substitution states at what ratio households are willing to exchange small amounts of current consumption for future consumption.

Maths note. To obtain the marginal rate of substitution (MRS), let work time be constant in equation (17.5). Taking the total differential and solving this for $\frac{dC_2}{dC_1} = -(1 + \beta)\frac{\partial u/\partial C_1}{\partial u/\partial C_2}$ yields a general equation for the MRS (i.e. the slope of the indifference curve). On the 45° line we have $C_1 = C_2$ and, hence, $\partial u/\partial C_1 = \partial u/\partial C_2$. Substituting this into the general equation yields $\frac{dC_2}{dC_1} = -(1 + \beta)$ as the MRS at the point of intersection of indifference curves with the 45° line.

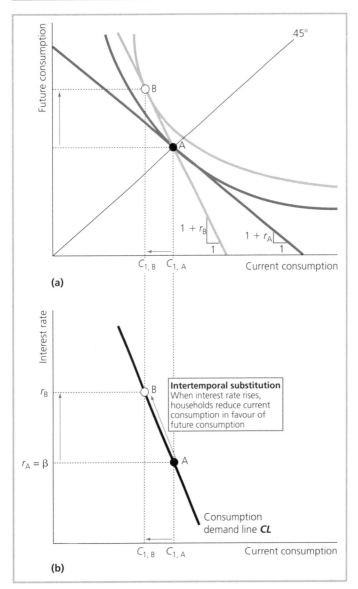

(a)

(b)

Figure 17.5 Initially the economy is in a long-run optimum on the 45° line. Here the consumption point equals the endowment point A, and the interest rate equals the time discount rate. When the interest rate rises above the rate of time preference, from r_A to r_B, the constraint pivots around the endowment point A. Now households maximize utility at B, which implies shifting some of the current consumption into the future. The act of saving today to enjoy spending tomorrow is called intertemporal substitution of consumption. Panel (b) shows that current consumption and, hence, the magnitude of intertemporal substitution of consumption depend negatively on the interest rate.

Temporary deviations of the interest rate from its long-run equilibrium value occur in the aftermath of shocks. If r is driven up, the constraint turns steeper. This signals that saving a certain amount today buys more added consumption in period 2 than it did previously. Other than in the initial optimum at the endowment point, people now save part of current income. As a reward, period-2 consumption exceeds period-2 income by period-1 saving plus interests earned. The optimal response is to move up to the point of tangency between the new budget line and an indifference curve (point B).

The effect just described can be generalized: the higher the interest rate on current savings, the more households save out of current income, and the lower is current consumption. So the mechanism exemplified in Figure 17.5, panel (a), by means of two optimal points A and B suggests a negative relationship between current consumption and the interest rate. This can be displayed by a negatively sloped consumption demand line CL in an r/Y diagram (Figure 17.5, panel (b)).

The intertemporal pattern of employment The postponing of consumption to future periods when interest rates are high, or the spending of income to be earned in the future on current consumption when interest rates are low, is referred to as intertemporal substitution. This phenomenon also drives the second decision variable of households, the supply of work time, or labour. The line of argument is analogous to our discussion of intertemporal substitution in consumption. In this discussion we assumed that the work time decision with the resulting income pattern had been made, and asked how households would allocate their incomes in the form of consumption spending over time. Now we switch our perspective. We now assume that the consumption decisions for periods 1 and 2 have been made and ask how households allocate work-hours over time in order to finance their *consumption plan*. This question can be analyzed in a diagram with current leisure time and future leisure time on the two axes (Figure 17.6).

Indifference curves do not require any further discussion. They are convex-shaped as shown in panel (a) for familiar reasons. The rationale behind the constraint shown in panel (b) may be less straightforward than in our discussion

> Intertemporal substitution is the allocation of things like consumption spending or work-hours over time in an effort to increase utility.

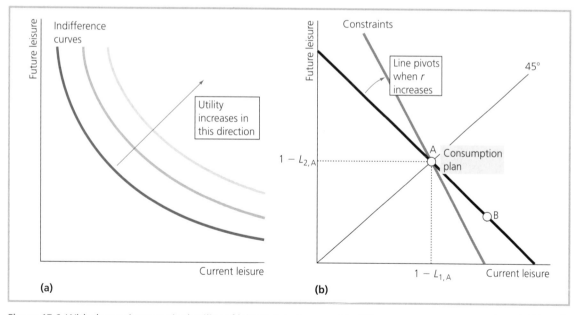

Figure 17.6 With decreasing marginal utility of leisure, intertemporal indifference curves are convex (panel (a)). Utility rises as we move northeast. Panel (b) shows the intertemporal constraint. Assume that we are in a long-run optimum where household consumption does not change over time. If households work just enough to pay for planned consumption each period, work times are $L_{1,A} = L_{2,A}$. The consumption plan translates to point A with leisure times $1 - L_{1,A} = 1 - L_{2,A}$. The very same consumption pattern can be financed by other allocations of work and leisure across time. For instance, they may work more today and save some of this income for tomorrow, when they can afford to work less (point B). All combinations of current and future leisure that pay for the consumption plan behind A sit on a straight line passing through A. This line turns steeper when the interest rate goes up. Then one hour less leisure today buys us more added leisure tomorrow than when the interest rate is low.

of intertemporal consumption decisions, however. Now the intertemporal consumption plan plays the same role the endowment point played in Figure 17.5. Suppose again that the economy is in a steady state. Then today's and tomorrow's consumption are the same. And if the income needed for each period's consumption was to be earned in the very same period, without lending or borrowing in the credit market, this would translate into a given amount of required work time. In a steady state this point that relates work-hours to intended consumption spending sits on the 45° line. We call this point the **consumption plan**. One way to realize the consumption plan associated with point A is by working the fraction $L_{1,A}$ of one's time in period 1, and $L_{2,A}$ in period 2.

Credit markets offer other options as well. Households may wish to enjoy some more leisure time today in exchange for work in period 2 (point C). The options are endless, and all are lined up on a string whose slope reflects the interest rate and, possibly, anticipated changes in the wage rate. When the interest rate is high, giving up some leisure time today to work more and save the additional income provides households with more additional leisure time tomorrow than when the interest rate is low. Also, when today's wage rate exceeds tomorrow's wage rate, today's leisure time is more expensive than tomorrow's. So it is better to enjoy leisure tomorrow than it is to enjoy it today. The constraint thus turns steeper.

Figure 17.7 identifies the intertemporal allocation of leisure and work time. As in our discussion of optimal consumption patterns, utility is maximized where the constraint is tangent to one of the indifference curves. Panel (a) shows a long-run optimum at point A. Since in a long-run equilibrium neither income nor wages change, the slope of the constraint equals $-(1 + r)$, the marginal rate of substitution is $(1 + \beta)$, and, therefore, $r = \beta$. If the interest rate now rises, the constraint pivots around the consumption plan, and households reduce current leisure time more and more. The resulting increase in work time is accompanied by an increase in output. So, all other things being held constant, output increases when the interest rate increases. The mechanism behind this is the **intertemporal substitution of labour**.

Our analysis of household behaviour has generated two important macroeconomic implications. First, the volume of current output produced by firms rises at times when the interest rate rises. Second, current consumption demand falls when the interest rate goes up. Before we can compare economy-wide supply and demand in one diagram and analyze their interaction, we need to specify the demand for the second component of economy-wide demand, investment, exercised by firms.

The behaviour of the firm

The representative firm maximizes profits under perfect competition. This implies employing the two factors of production, capital and labour, up to the level where their marginal products equal marginal costs. We already studied one part of this behaviour in our discussion of the labour market in Chapter 6. There Figure 6.4 showed how a marginal-product-of-labour schedule can be derived from the partial production function with K fixed, and that this marginal-product-of-labour schedule at the same time represented the firm's labour demand curve. This labour demand curve is also in operation

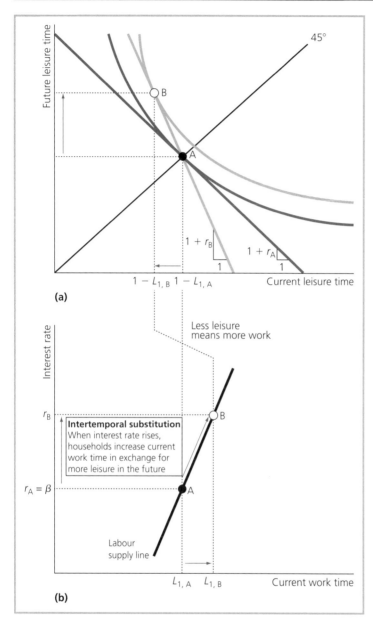

(a)

(b)

Intertemporal substitution
When interest rate rises, households increase current work time in exchange for more leisure in the future

Labour supply line

Less leisure means more work

Figure 17.7 Initially the economy is in a long-run optimum on the 45° line. Here the choice of leisure directly corresponds to consumption plan A (without recourse to the credit market), and the interest rate equals the time discount rate. When the interest rate rises above the rate of time preference, from r_A to r_B, the constraint pivots around the endowment point A. Now households maximize utility at B, which implies shifting some of the current leisure into the future. The act of working more today to enjoy more leisure tomorrow is called intertemporal substitution of labour. Panel (b) shows that current work time (employment) and, hence, the magnitude of intertemporal substitution of labour depend positively on the interest rate.

Maths note. Let the production function be $Y = AK^\alpha L^{1-\alpha}$. Setting the interest rate equal to the marginal product of capital, obtained by differentiating the production function with respect to K, yields the capital demand curve $r = \alpha A (L/K)^{1-\alpha}$. This curve moves up and to the right when A or L increases.

in the current model. It plays a subdued role in the background, though, determining the real wage as demand interacts with the supply of work time by households.

The firm's demand for capital is more decisive for real business cycle dynamics, for reasons to be discussed in a moment. We start by graphing the firm's desired capital stock, their *demand for capital*, as a function of the interest rate in Figure 17.8, panel (a). The reasoning is identical to the one behind the labour demand curve in Figure 6.4, except that we are now looking at the second factor of production. There are some differences between labour and capital, however.

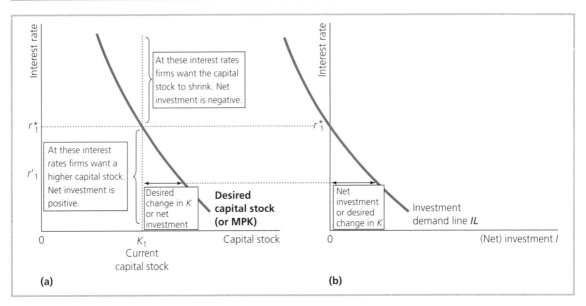

Figure 17.8 Panel (a) depicts the marginal product of capital (MPK) as a function of the capital stock employed. This marginal product of capital falls when the amount of capital already used increases. The marginal product of capital measures how much one more unit of capital is worth to the firm. Hence, at a real interest rate such as r_1^* the firm keeps demanding more and more capital until the capital stock is K_1, where the marginal product of capital equals the real interest rate. Assuming that the current capital stock is K_1, panel (b) shows the desired change in the capital stock, which is the firm's investment. This investment demand schedule is always drawn for a given current capital stock.

First, when firms want to change the capital stock, they need to invest. Since we are talking about net income and net investment, which means that the part of income needed to replace worn-out capital has already been set aside, (net) investment is positive if firms want to raise the capital stock because the interest rate is lower than the marginal product of capital, and (net) investment is negative if firms want to reduce the capital stock. This (net) demand for investment is shown in Figure 17.8, panel (b). It is simply the demand for capital minus the current capital stock. Investment is zero at r_1^*, where the interest rate equals the marginal product of capital.

A second difference between the demand for labour and the demand for capital and investment derives from the fact that when firms decide to hire more workers, they can put these to productive use immediately. When they decide to increase the capital stock and invest, however, they can use their newly acquired capital only with a lag. The consequence of this is that firms need to be forward-looking when they make investment decisions. So it is not the *current* marginal productivity of capital that determines the position of the investment schedule and, hence, investment demand, but the marginal productivity of capital *expected* for the next period. We need to keep this in mind when we look at the dynamic properties of the real business cycle model shortly.

The macroeconomic equilibrium

We have developed all the building blocks of our graphical real business cycle model. Let us look at how these pieces fit together to determine a macroeconomic equilibrium.

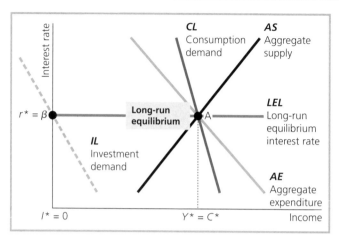

Figure 17.9 This graph shows the long-run equilibrium of the real business cycle model. The firms' supply of goods slopes upwards due to intertemporal substitution of labour. Households work more today when the interest rate is high. The two components of aggregate expenditure are downward-sloping. For a given capital stock and, thus, a given marginal productivity of capital, investment demand increases when the interest rate goes down. The consumption demand line slopes down due to intertemporal substitution of consumption. Households save less today when the interest rate is low. Adding investment and consumption horizontally gives the aggregate expenditure line. In long-run equilibrium, AS and AE intersect at the long-run equilibrium interest rate, which equals the time discount rate ($r^* = \beta$).

Figure 17.9 lays out the demand- and supply-side decisions of firms and households as they appear when the economy is in a long-run equilibrium. Remember that, while the diagram may appear deceivingly similar to a Mundell–Fleming diagram, the economic reasoning behind it is completely different.

We start with a horizontal line positioned at where the interest rate equals the subjective discount rate of households. This reflects our previous insight that in any long-run equilibrium, when in the absence of shocks all variables have come to rest, the economy sits on the 45° lines in our intertemporal diagrams where the interest rate equals the discount rate. So the bold horizontal line labelled *LEL* (long-run equilibrium line) is the locus of long-run equilibria, from which the economy may deviate temporarily.

Next, enter the aggregate supply curve *AS*, which is positively sloped. At the point of intersection with *LEL* there is no intertemporal substitution. Households supply the same amount of labour today and in the future. In the segment above the equilibrium line, the interest rate exceeds the time discount rate. There households increase their current supply of labour, with the expectation to work less in the future. The opposite effect occurs in the segment below the equilibrium line.

From Figure 17.5 we know that the consumption demand line *CL* is negatively sloped. But where do we put it? Here our previous insight helps that in a long-run equilibrium the capital stock does not change. So net investment is zero, and consumption equals (net) income. This means that if we want to depict a long-run equilibrium, the supply curve and the consumption line need to intersect on *LEL*, where $r = \beta$.

In order to complete our picture of aggregate expenditure, we need to add the investment line to the diagram. We just noted that net investment is zero when the economy is in a long-run equilibrium. Therefore the investment line intersects *LEL* exactly on the vertical axis. When $r > \beta$, firms want to reduce the capital stock. So investment is negative. At an interest rate below β investment is positive.

Aggregate expenditure AE is simply the horizontal addition of the investment and consumption demand lines. The point of intersection between the lines of total demand and supply determines the current macroeconomic equilibrium. By construction this point is on the LEL in this example, saying that the current equilibrium is a long-run equilibrium.

17.3   A graphical real business cycle

Our final task in this chapter is to show how one-time shocks in the real business cycle model may generate drawn-out responses of major macroeconomic variables that match stylized empirical observations. Let this shock be an unexpected, permanent improvement in production technology – a so-called technology shock. At the time of the shock the economy had settled into a long-run equilibrium depicted as point 0 in Figure 17.10. The sudden improvement in technology occurs in period 1 and triggers a quite complex sequence of effects that we now develop step by step.

A technology shock is a one-time change in production technology.

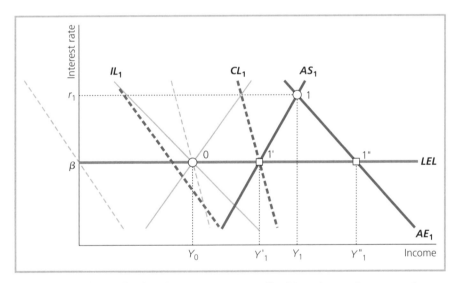

Figure 17.10 When technology improves unexpectedly, this makes work more productive, shifting AS to the right into AS_1. Households raise consumption by as much as their income would rise if the income hike were considered permanent. The new consumption line is CL_1. Because the marginal productivity of capital has increased as well, the investment demand line moves right to IL_1. Adding the new investment and consumption lines horizontally reveals that the AE line moves further than the AS line. Thus there would be excess demand at the initial (long-run equilibrium) interest rate. This excess demand is eliminated by an interest rate increase to r_1. This triggers intertemporal substitution of labour, which increases supply, and of consumption, which decreases demand. The latter is augmented by the negative effect on investment demand. Current-period equilibrium is at point 1.

The period of the shock

It is obvious that technological progress moves the aggregate supply line to the right. At all interest rates and, hence, all associated levels of employment, workers are more productive. So more output is being produced. This shifts the aggregate supply line from AS_0 to AS_1. But how can we tell exactly how far the AS line shifts? Here it helps to go back to the current-period optimization and comparative statics of household behaviour discussed in Figure 17.2. The change in income shown there is the rise in income which would occur if – hypothetically – the economy settled directly into a new long-run equilibrium. We are not saying that it does. But if it did – we can always carry out thought experiments – then we could read the size of the income change off the graph shown in Figure 17.2. And where would such a new long-run equilibrium point have to be? Yes, on the horizontal long-run equilibrium line. So this new long-run equilibrium would be at the point of intersection between AS_1 and the horizontal long-run equilibrium line at $r = \beta$ (point 1'), with output supplied being Y_1'.

Fortunately, Figure 17.2 provides even more information. In the long-run equilibrium consumption equals income. Therefore, if the now long-run equilibrium was actually at 1', consumption would have to equal income. This can be so only if the consumption demand line had shifted just as far as the AS line, into the position CL_1.

This leaves us with the task of determining what happened to the investment line. The position of this line reflects the marginal productivity of capital expected for next period (and beyond). Since firms know that the observed shock to productivity is a permanent one, they foresee that the marginal productivity will be higher next period than it was in the old period-0 equilibrium. In anticipation of this, they desire a higher capital stock. To achieve this, they plan to invest more than before at any given interest rate. The investment demand line moves to the right into position IL_1.

After adding now the consumption and investment lines horizontally to obtain the aggregate expenditure line AE_1, it becomes obvious that no new long-run equilibrium results in period 1. At the equilibrium interest rate $r = \beta$ output supplied falls way short of aggregate expenditure. Firms would want to produce output Y_1', while consumption and investment demand would total Y_1''. So the interest rate in period 1 cannot equal the time discount rate β. In fact, since the temporary equilibrium in period 1 obtains at the point of intersection between AS_1 and AE_1, at point B, way above LEL, the interest rate rises to $r_1 > \beta$. This rise in the interest rate closes the gap between total supply and demand by triggering intertemporal substitution of households. Intertemporal substitution works its way on both the supply side and the demand side:

- On the supply side, a rising interest rate gives rise to **intertemporal substitution of labour.** Households jump at the opportunity provided by the exceptionally favourable interest rate by expanding work time. Thus, as the interest rate rises, employment increases and output grows as we move up AS_1 from point 1' to point 1.

- On the demand side two things happen: first, a rising interest rate gives rise to **intertemporal substitution of consumption**. The attractiveness of high interest rates induces increased saving and postponement of some consumption until tomorrow. Therefore, as the interest rate goes up, consumption falls as we move up CL_1 from point 1'. Second, firms reduce investment as the interest rate goes up and makes investment projects more costly. Together with the intertemporal substitution of consumption, this makes aggregate expenditure fall as we slide up AE_1 from point 1" to point 1. Once the interest rate has risen to r_1 supply equals demand and the period-1 equilibrium has been reached at income Y_1.

The period after the shock

No new shocks occur in period 2 (see Figure 17.11). Macroeconomic variables nevertheless continue to move, since point 1 is not a long-run equilibrium. The motor behind these ongoing changes is the time-to-build assumption. The investment goods purchases in period 1 turn into productive capital in period 2, raising the capital stock with a lag. This makes labour still more productive, even though technology does not change, and thus moves the aggregate supply line still further to the right. For the reasons discussed above, the consumption demand line follows this movement and moves to position CL_2. In terms of the graph shown in Figure 17.2, the rising capital stock tilts up the partial production function. If the new equilibrium was a long-run equilibrium, consumption would equal income. Since such a (hypothetical) equilibrium would require $r_2 = \beta$ in order to avoid intertemporal substitution, CL_2 intersects AS_2 on the LEL line.

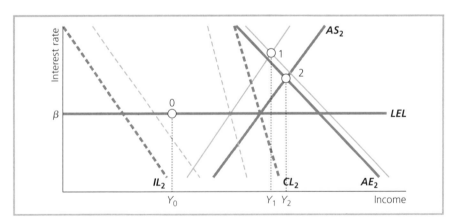

Figure 17.11 In period 2, one period after the surprise improvement of production technology, income continues to grow because firms are now producing with more capital (generated by positive net investment in period 1). This shifts the aggregate supply line to AS_2 and pulls along the consumption line to CL_2. Since a higher capital stock means a lower marginal productivity of capital, the investment demand line moves left. As a consequence the aggregate expenditure line moves slightly left as well (AE_2), shifting the current-period equilibrium to point 2.

As the capital stock increases, the marginal productivity of capital declines. Investment declines at all interest rates. The investment demand line moves slightly to the left. This puts the aggregate expenditure line into position AE_2 and identifies a new temporary equilibrium for period 2 at point 2. Compared to period 1, income continues to rise, but the interest rate begins to fall again. Since it remains above its normal (or long-run) level, however, there is still intertemporal substitution of consumption and work time, though at a reduced magnitude.

From the medium to the long run

The process just described continues in period 3 and drives the economy to point 3, though we refrain from tracing the shifting lines in an already crowded diagram: the capital stock rises again, accompanied by decreasing marginal productivity (Figure 17.12). This adds an, albeit smaller, amount to income, and permits a further reduction of the interest rate. In periods 4 and beyond the same effects are at work. But the additions to income and the reductions of the interest rate become smaller and smaller until the process finally peters out as the economy settles into a new long-run equilibrium at point ∞. After this has happened, the investment demand line is back in its original position and the interest rate equals the time discount rate again. Consumption equals income, net investment is zero. The capital stock is at the desired level.

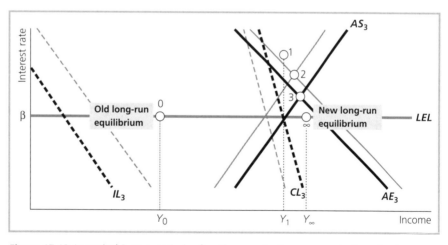

Figure 17.12 In period 3, two periods after the surprise improvement of production technology, income is still growing because the capital stock continues to grow. This shifts the aggregate supply line to AS_3 and pulls along the consumption line to CL_3. The marginal productivity of capital continues to fall, moving the investment demand line still further left to IL_3. As a consequence the aggregate expenditure line drifts slightly left again to AE_3, moving the economy to point 3. This process continues as long as net investment is positive, which is the case as long as the interest rate exceeds the time discount rate β. Income growth becomes smaller and smaller, however, and eventually peters out. The economy comes to rest in a new long-run equilibrium at a point marked ∞, where income and capital are higher and there is no more intertemporal substitution.

CASE STUDY 17.1   Technology change in Malaysia: the return of the Solow residual

Real business cycle (RBC) models propose that the main driving force behind macroeconomic fluctuations is technology shocks. Before arguing that such shocks are impossible to measure, making the RBC model virtually immune to empirical testing, remember Chapter 9 on the basics of economic growth. There we had used the growth accounting equation to obtain an estimate of technological change, which we called the Solow residual:

$$\frac{\Delta A}{A} = \frac{\Delta Y}{Y} - \alpha\frac{\Delta K}{K} - (1-\alpha)\frac{\Delta L}{L}$$

Figure 17.13

The equation states that the part of income growth that cannot be attributed to increases in the two factors of production, weighted by the respective factor income shares, must be attributed to technological change (or the change in total factor productivity, as A is also called). Having identified technology shocks this way, RBC researchers proceed as follows.

First, the data series for K and L are discarded. Then the computed technology data are plugged into a numerical version of an RBC model. The model then generates income responses, both as they result *directly* from technological change, and as they result *indirectly* from the effect of technological change on capital formation and employment. The movements and comovements of all three endogenous variables, income, capital and employment, and of other variables included in the model, such as consumption, investment, the real wage or the real interest rate, may then be compared with stylized macroeconomic facts to gauge the potential of the RBC model under consideration.

Figure 17.13 shows the Solow residual for Malaysia, along with income growth rates. The graph gives an impression of the challenges an RBC model faces. At the same time it points to some of the reservations held against the interpretation of the Solow residual as a measure of technological change.

As to the challenges, the graph shows that income growth rates are always higher than the increase in total factor productivity. At times this difference is small. Often it is substantial.

Between 1988 and 1997 the difference was about 6 percentage points on average, and not far from 10 percentage points occasionally. The task of an RBC model is to explain these differences, in particular their variations, as a consequence of technological change.

Many economists do distrust the Solow residual as a good measure of true changes in technology. For one thing, questions arise from the fact that, typically, the Solow residual is negative during recessions. In the case of Malaysia, the computed Solow residual suggests that the Asian crisis of 1998 was the consequence of technological regress in double digits. Since this seems implausible, and the meaning of technological regress is difficult to understand anyway, it has been argued that the Solow residual picks up many other effects that drive a wedge between it and true technology. Examples of such effects are the hoarding of labour: during recessions, firms may not fire all workers not needed for current production if they anticipate that they have to re-hire them within a short time. The accompanying drop in average productivity may give the wrong impression of technological regress. Similar arguments apply to the utilization of the capital stock, which varies during business cycles. These reservations, that the Solow residual measures much more than technology alone, are underscored by findings that the Solow residual can be forecasted from military spending, or even on the basis of monetary policy, which suggests that demand-side effects are included.

Our graphical analysis shows that one-time changes in technology (or other parameters) can generate drawn-out responses in income, consumption, investment, the interest rate, employment, and other macroeconomic variables, that resemble the pattern which these variables follow in many countries during typical business cycles. This is a new insight, which macroeconomic models featuring nominal rigidities as a cause of business cycle movements had overlooked. In the *DAD-SAS* model, for example, a one-time improvement in technology would shift the long-run aggregate supply curve to the right. But this would be a one-time event. And if prices and wages were flexible, the economy would jump into its new long-run equilibrium immediately. If adjustment takes time in the *DAD-SAS* model as well, it is because sticky wages slow the adjustment process down.

I had initially warned that the graphical approach to real business cycle models employed here cuts some corners in order to make the core ideas more accessible. In addition to the fact that we considered many decisions in isolation that are actually interdependent, one defect of our real business cycle story stands out most visibly and should be noted: in our graph, when households make plans in period 1, they expect the world to end in period 3. After one period has passed – we have entered period 2 – they learn that the world will not end in period 3. They now expect it to end in period 4. And this repeats itself again and again. The horizon of households never extends further than one period into the future, though the world never really ends. This is obviously not rational, for households would not have taken the exact same decisions if they had known. This irrationality is the price we pay for keeping the model on a level that can be dealt with in diagrams, rather than going through the complicated mathematics of a model in which households have infinite horizons. The good news is that such a fully rational real business cycle model exhibits the same qualitative behaviour and propelling mechanisms as our simplifying graphical model (see the recommended readings at the end of this chapter). All variables move in the same direction, and intertemporal substitution occurs just as described here. Thus whatever we learned here about the economic substance and processes behind the graphical real business cycle model is also at work in the more refined and perfectly rational models employed in research.

The last two chapters have moved beyond the workhorse model(s) of short- and medium-run macroeconomics that served us well through most of this text. They provided a sneak preview of the methodological approaches and theories you may encounter in academic journals or in graduate school. Many macroeconomists these days agree that much more is happening on the economy's supply side than the *DAD-SAS* model concedes. It also has become clear, however, that only a small part of economic fluctuations can be understood on the basis of the real business cycle model alone. Current models in macroeconomics thus feature elements from both models: a better explanation of the short- and medium-run dynamics of potential income, as provided by the real business cycle model; and an explanation of the deviations of income from potential income, as provided by the *DAD-SAS* model. Modern successors of *DAD-SAS* seek to provide microeconomic foundations for nominal stickiness and part of New Keynesian economics.

New Keynesian economics strives to provide microeconomic foundations for sticky wages and prices.

BOX 17.1 **A pocket guide to the history of macroeconomic thought**

Many bright minds have contributed to what macroeconomics is today. This box does not even try to do justice to the richness of ideas found in their writings. Instead, it settles for the modest goal of projecting the major **schools of macroeconomic thought** onto the AD-AS diagram and highlighting selected key contributions.

Classical economics
Long before the term macroeconomics had even been invented, classical economists (like Adam Smith, David Ricardo, David Hume and John Stuart Mill) believed that the flexibility of wages and prices ensured that markets very much cleared all the time. In the view of **classical macroeconomics** income remained so close to potential output that no policy intervention was warranted. Translated into the AD-AS diagram (which also had not been devised yet), the AS curve is vertical, and it moves slowly and smoothly as the labour force grows, the capital stock increases and technology improves. Shifts in the AD curve cannot affect income. When nominal variables, such as the money supply, change, this affects only the price level but none of the real variables. This phenomenon is called the **classical dichotomy**. We actually have two separate, independent parts of the economy: one where real variables like the capital stock or productivity determine other real variables like income, employment or the real wage, and the other where nominal variables like the money supply or

foreign prices determine other nominal variables like prices or the exchange rate.

Keynesianism
After a long reign well into the twentieth century, the experience of the Great Depression (1929–32) left the classical view in shambles. There was no way to rationalize a drop in industrial production of 47% within little more than three years, as had happened in the United States, or of 42%, as experienced in Germany, as a movement in potential income. British economist John Maynard Keynes came up with a new way to look at the economy. He argued that when there were high levels of unemployment, even at unchanged prices firms would produce any volume of output that was demanded. Under such circumstances AS is flat and the classical dichotomy breaks down. If an increase in government spending shifts AD to the right, this has real consequences in the form of a rise in income. While Keynes did not contest the possibility of a return of income to potential income in the long run, this was not the focus of his analysis. In fact, he shrugged it off with the famous remark: 'In the long run we are all dead.' With market forces considered too slow, Keynesians believed that during periods of lack of demand the government had to step in by means of fiscal and monetary policy.

In the orthodox Keynesian scenario prices remain fairly constant, as postulated in our IS-LM and Mundell–Fleming models. Later, faced by the

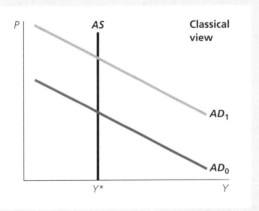

Figure 17.14 Demand fluctuations do not affect income. Potential income evolves slowly. Classical dichotomy holds at all times.

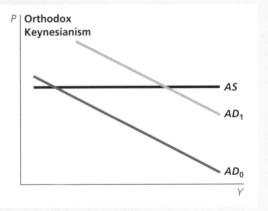

Figure 17.15a Demand fluctuations affect income only. Classical dichotomy does not hold.

Box 17.1 continued

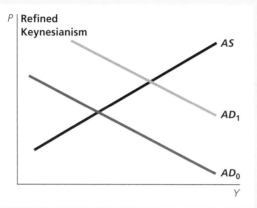

Figure 17.15b Demand fluctuations affect income and prices. Classical dichotomy does not hold.

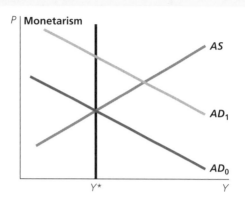

Figure 17.16 Demand fluctuations have a lasting affect on prices, but no lasting effect on income. Classical dichotomy holds only in the long run.

challenge to explain increasing inflation and encouraged by the Phillips curve that was discovered in the late 1950s, refined Keynesian views proposed a positively sloped *AS* curve. One rationalization for the underlying stickiness of money wages focused on money illusion: when workers were offered, say, a 10% higher money wage, they believed they were better off even if prices rose by the same or an even higher percentage. Thus as we move up this Keynesian *AS* curve the nominal wage rises and makes workers suffering from money illusion supply more labour. But prices rise faster than nominal wages. So the real wage falls, and firms demand more labour. This makes employment and income increase. Fluctuations in the *AD* curve generate movements along the *AS* curve. So increases in income always go hand in hand with inflation.

Monetarism

Again, the failure of the ruling model to offer a satisfactory explanation of a new empirical phenomenon set the stage for the success of a new kid on the block. The phenomenon was stagflation, and it occurred in the early 1970s. Stagflation is the occurrence of rising inflation and falling income at the same time. This cannot happen when the economy is bound to move up and down a given, positively sloped *AS* curve, as the Keynesian approach postulated. It can happen, though, if the economy moves up a given *AD* curve. For this to occur,

however, the *AS* curve needs to move. The first one to argue on these lines and to investigate why this may happen was Nobel Laureate Milton Friedman, the father of **monetarism**.

Monetarists had been challenging the Keynesian view for a while. One area of disagreement was whether monetary or fiscal policy was more effective in influencing aggregate demand. Monetarists believed it was monetary policy, with the rationalization that the *LM* curve was very steep and shifts in *IS* would generate only small responses in income. Keynesians favoured fiscal policy, believing that the *IS* curve was steep, so that shifts in *LM* would hardly have any real bearing on income.

A second line of criticism attacked money illusion. Monetarists insisted that money illusion was not compatible with rational behaviour. They maintained that workers looked at the buying power of their wage. So when prices rose, this would raise nominal wage demands by the same percentage. Thus, as actual prices rose, or expected prices in the presence of long-term wage contracts, *AS* would shift upwards. Since monetarists believed that price or inflation expectations were formed adaptively, this process would take time.

Figure 17.16 shows how the economy digests a money-supply increase which shifts *AD* to the right. After the initial jump in income and the price level, the economy moves gradually up the new *AD* curve, until it settles into a new long-run equilibrium on

Box 17.1 continued

the vertical long-run *AS* curve. During this adjustment we observe stagflation: falling income and rising prices.

While it had been a formidable challenger for more than a decade and its effects were lasting, the monetarist reign in macroeconomics was short-lived. At the time of victory it had already lost its bite. First, because its best parts had already found their way into a modern Keynesian approach represented by Nobel Laureates Paul Samuelson and Robert Solow, which had dropped money illusion, accepted the distinction between short- and long-run aggregate supply, with potential income as an anchor, and adopted adaptive inflation expectations to link the short with the long run, to form what some called a **neoclassical synthesis**. Second, because it came under attack itself from new classical macroeconomics for its use of adaptive expectations formation, which was considered irrational by a growing group of new classical macroeconomists led by US Nobel Laureate Robert Lucas and his compatriot Thomas Sargent.

New classical macroeconomics
New classical macroeconomics has a lot in common with monetarism. When displayed in an *AD-AS* diagram it looks deceivingly similar to the monetarist diagram with its distinction between a positively sloped short-run *AS* curve and a vertical long-run *AS* curve. But it goes one step further. It criticizes the assumption of adaptive expectations as too mechanical and, in fact, irrational. Adaptive expec-

tations can give rise to systematic forecast errors, which rational individuals seek to avoid, and its backward-looking nature cannot deal properly with future events, even when these are announced. A major innovation of new classical macroeconomics is to replace adaptive expectations formation with the concept of **rational expectations**, originally developed by John Muth.

Rational expectations propose that the labour market knows the model, which enables firms and trade unions to correctly work out the inflationary effects of any changes in aggregate demand. Whether, faced by a shift of the *AD* curve, the economy moves up the positively sloped *AS* curve or the vertical one depends on whether the shift was anticipated or not. Only when the shift comes as a surprise does the positivly sloped *AS* curve come into play and income rises along with prices, as in the monetarist model. When the shift is anticipated, the movement is up the vertical *AS* curve, and there is no income response.

In this scenario monetary or fiscal policy works only if it surprises the labour market and thus cannot be used systematically. In any case, deviations of income from potential income occur randomly and are very short-lived. This does not describe real-world business cycles correctly. Economists with a classical orientation therefore soon set out to mend this. They did so by means of a complete change of perspective: economic fluctuations no longer were considered deviations of income from potential income, but movements of potential income itself.

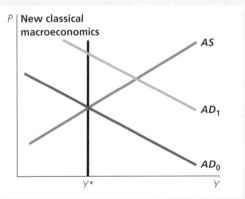

Figure 17.17 Demand and fluctuations have a surprise effect on income, but a lasting effect on prices. Classical dichotomy is violated only by surprises.

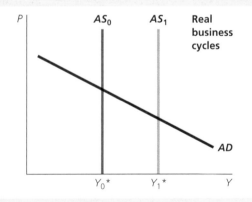

Figure 17.18 Demand fluctuations do not affect income. Potential income grows in cycles. Classical dichotomy holds at all times.

Box 17.1 continued

Real business cycles

This new perspective is known as **real business cycle theory.** Spearheaded by Edward Prescott and Finn Kydland from the United States and Norway, respectively, it discards the segmentation of macroeconomics into explanations of short-run fluctuations, caused by fluctuations in employment, and of long-run growth, caused by evolving capital stocks and technological progress, as artificial. Instead it proposes a coherent view in which technological change and capital stock dynamics affect short- to medium-run fluctuations in a significant way. The propagation mechanism, the process by which shocks to technology or preferences trigger drawn-out responses in income and other real variables, rests on intertemporal substitution of labour and consumption.

Real business cycle theory also discards the methodological differences that used to separate microeconomics from macroeconomics by analyzing the behaviour of optimizing agents which are considered representative for the entire economy. This behaviour makes the *AS* curve move about in ways that resemble the macroeconomic fluctuations known as business cycles. With prices and wages considered fully flexible, *AS* is vertical, and the classical dichotomy strikes again. Nominal variables and, hence, the position of *AD* do not bear on income.

While the methodological innovations of real business cycle theory are widely acknowledged, one of its key implications, that nominal variables do not affect real income, seems to be at odds with empirical observations. Current research seeks to tackle this, within the real business cycle framework, but also under the heading of New Keynesian macroeconomics.

New Keynesian macroeconomics

In the advent of what might turn out to be another synthesis, New Keynesian macroeconomics adopts the methodology and rationality postulates of real business cycle theorists, but rejects the paradigm of perfect markets and flexible wages and prices. Their agenda is to explore market imperfections that lead to involuntary unemployment (examples are efficiency wage theory or insider–outsider models) and to rationalize the stickiness of wages and prices observed in reality. Their models behave similarly to the *DAD-SAS* model in many respects, but their implications are richer due to a more prominent and complex role of expectations.

Literature
For a much deeper discussion see B. Snowdon and H.R. Vane (2005) *Modern Macroeconomics: Its Origins, Development and Current State.* Aldershot: Edward Elgar.

CHAPTER SUMMARY

- An alternative way to build macroeconomic models is by deriving the decisions of how much to save and how much to work explicitly from the utility maximization of households. Since such models consist of building blocks known from microeconomics, they are said to possess microfoundations.

- One pair of decisions households need to make concerns the presence: how to split a day's time between work and leisure, and how to divide current (disposable) income between consumption and saving.

- Another pair of decisions households make looks into the future: how much to work and consume today as compared to tomorrow. Such dynamic decisions may result in intertemporal substitution.

- Intertemporal substitution refers to the decision of households to work more (less) today in exchange for less (more) work in the future, or to consume less (more) today in exchange for more (less) consumption in the future, in order to increase utility.

- The first generation of macroeconomic models with microfoundations assumed fully flexible prices and wages. This makes the real economy independent of monetary developments, and business cycles result from disturbances in the real economy. Therefore, these models were labelled real business cycle models.

- Intertemporal substitution is the key propagation mechanism in real business cycle models. It causes one time shocks to productivity or preferences to generate income and employment responses that look like conventional business cycle patterns.

- Current research in macroeconomics typically employs the methodology developed in real business cycle research and adopts these model's explanation of short- and medium-term movements in potential income. New Keynesian models of the macroeconomy add nominal stickiness caused by slow wages, prices or information in order to explain deviations from potential income.

Key terms and concepts

classical dichotomy *524*
intertemporal optimization *508*
intertemporal substitution
  of consumption *513*
intertemporal substitution
  of labour *514*

marginal rate of substitution *511*
microfoundations *503*
New Keynesian economics *523*
real business cycles *504*
technology shock *518*

EXERCISES

17.1 Consider the current-period optimum derived in Figure 17.2.
  (a) What is the effect on income and employment if household preferences change in the sense that more utility is being derived from leisure time than was previously the case?
  (b) A country decides to limit the working week to 35 hours by law. How does this affect the current-period choice?

17.2 Figure 17.1 illustrates the labour-supply decision from a macroeconomic perspective. While it looks at one individual (or household), it assumes this to be a representative individual in the sense that its decisions are imitated by all other individuals. In what respect does the graphical treatment of the labour supply decision of a single individual who assumes to act

independently of others differ from what is shown in Figure 17.1?

17.3 Households are in a long-run equilibrium in the intertemporal consumption diagram.
  (a) Now this country obtains a sizable one-time grant from the World Bank, which it will not have to repay. How will this affect intertemporal consumption choices?
  (b) How will intertemporal consumption choices be affected if the World Bank only extended a loan this period that has to be repaid next period?

17.4 Suppose a country has implemented a 35-hour maximum working week, as postulated in Exercise 17.1(b). Suppose this restriction is binding in the sense that in equilibrium households actually would like to work more.

(a) How does this country respond to a positive, permanent technology shock?
(b) How does this country respond to a permanent deterioration of its production technology?
(c) Are the effects derived under (a) and (b) symmetrical?

17.5 Suppose there was no time to build. That means, investment would add to the productive capital immediately, without any lag. What kind of income response would a positive, permanent shock to technology trigger under these circumstances? Compare with the behaviour of the real business cycle model.

17.6 Suppose the time discount rate rises permanently. How does the economy respond to this according to the real business cycle model?

17.7 A hurricane destroys about 20% of a country's capital stock and infrastructure. According to the real business cycle model:

(a) How does this affect employment in the short, medium and long run?
(b) Is there intertemporal substitution in the supply of labour?
(c) Is there intertemporal substitution in consumption?

17.8 The following table shows correlations between income and other macroeconomic variables, as they are typically encountered in empirical studies of macroeconomic time series.

Variable	Consumption	Investment	Real interest rate	Employment
Coefficient of correlation (with income)	0.7	1.3	−0.3	0.7

Which of these coefficients fit the basic real business cycle model developed in this chapter, and which don't? Explain why.

Online resources

Interactive applet on real business cycle analysis www.eurmacro.eu/tutor/realbusinesscycles.html
Interactive applet permitting real business cycle simulations www.eurmacro.eu/tutor/realbusinesscycles2.html

Self quiz
www.eurmacro.eu/SelfQuiz/sq-ch17.html

Recommended reading

Intermediate macroeconomics textbooks that emphasize microfoundations a lot more than this text does are Stephen D. Williamson (2005) *Macroeconomics*. Boston, MA: Pearson Addison Wesley; and Robert J. Barro (2007) *Macroeconomics: A Modern Approach*. New York, NY: South-Western.

Our paper, Frode Brevik and Manfred Gärtner (2007) 'Teaching real business cycles to undergraduates', *Journal of Economic Education* 27, pp. 229–48, shows that the shortcuts taken by the graphical approach described in this chapter do not differ to a

relevant extent from the results obtained from an exact mathematical solution of the model.

A very readable assessment of real business cycle research is Sergio Rebelo (2005) 'Real Business Cycles: Past, Present, and Future', *Scandinavian Journal of Economics* 107, pp. 217–38.

More on recent developments in macroeconomics, including the microeconomics behind the real business cycle approach, can be found in David Romer (2011) *Advanced Macroeconomics*, 4th edn. New York: McGraw-Hill/Irwin.

A primer in econometrics

What to expect

Economists relentlessly confront their models, or parts thereof, with real-world data. A soft way to do this is by doing case studies. This book makes extensive use of this approach. A harder way makes use of the laws of statistics, and has developed into a discipline of its own, known as econometrics.

This appendix tries to introduce you in an informal way to what econometrics is all about. After working through this appendix you should be able to do the following:

1 Read statistical results.

2 Ask informed questions about statistical results.

3 Start doing statistical work on matters of interest to you (not just constrained to macroeconomics).

More specifically, you will understand:

4 How econometric methods allow you to quantify the parameters of models from real-world data.

5 How you can tell whether a model or equation fits the data well or not.

6 When you have to discard a model or a hypothesis because of insufficient support from real-world data.

Empirical research links economic theory with the real world. It prevents theory and reality from drifting apart and leading separate lives, by forcing both areas to communicate on a scientific level. Central to empirical research in economics is the methodological discipline called **econometrics**. The two **key tasks of econometrics** are as follows:

1 To **quantify parameters** present in theoretical models. (What is the marginal rate of consumption? What is the interest elasticity of the demand for money? How high is the natural rate of unemployment?)

2 To **test hypotheses** derived from theoretical models. (Does consumption really grow when income grows? Is it true that anticipated increases in the money supply do not affect output? Are exports affected by the real exchange rate?)

This appendix provides a basic understanding of how econometrics approaches these two tasks.

A.1 First task: estimating unknown parameters

Suppose you have been elected chairman of Paris Saint-Germain (PSG), and you are planning the budget for next season. A good **estimate** of your football club's expected receipts is crucial, since it tells you how much leeway you have for buying new players. Of course, you may simply anticipate the same receipts you had last season, or the average of the annual receipts from the last five years. But your manager insists that by investing in better players you may expect a higher ranking in Division 1, which draws more spectators into the home stadium and lets you expect higher receipts in general. While this sounds interesting, it is only useful if you know by how much an improvement of one league table position raises the number of spectators per game. Statistical methods allow us to estimate such a relationship from data on ranking and spectator crowds collected in the past.

Example

You have a red die and a blue one. In each round you first throw the red die, then the blue die. Somebody claims that the number of dots on the blue die follows the number of dots just observed on the red die. The proposed 'model' reads

$$dots_{blue} = constant + coefficient \times dots_{red}$$

or, put more formally,

$$b = \alpha + \beta r \tag{A.1}$$

where b represents the number of dots tossed with the blue die

r represents the number of dots tossed with the red die

α is a constant term (unknown, and needs to be determined empirically)

β is the regression coefficient (unknown, and needs to be determined empirically)

Equation (A.1) postulates a linear relationship between b and r that can be represented by a straight line; α says where the line cuts the vertical axis, and β indicates the slope. Together α and β identify the unique position of the line, as Figure A.1 shows.

In our artificial example we know, of course, that b and r are not really related, that is, β actually equals zero. Let us pretend that you do not know this true value of β (just as we do not know the true marginal propensity to consume). Therefore, all you can do is throw your dice and check whether the results comply with equation (A.1). After two rounds you may have obtained the results given in Table A.1.

Table A.1 Results from two rounds of dice

		Colour of die	
		Red	Blue
Round #	1	4	5
	2	2	3

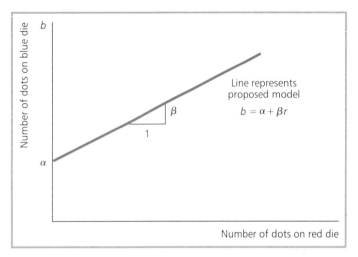

Figure A.1 The model proposed by equation (A.1) has a constant term (or intercept) α and slope β.

Note. If the die is not 'loaded' the true 'model' is $b = 3.5 + 0 \times r + \varepsilon$, where ε is an unforeseeable (random) impact with expectation zero. ε may take the values 2.5, 1.5, 0.5, −1.5 and −2.5, each with probability 1/6. For example, if we throw a 6, then according to the true model $6 = 3.5 + 2.5$ with $\varepsilon = 2.5$.

Each round's results can be represented by a point in a diagram with b measured along the vertical axis and r along the horizontal axis (Figure A.2). The line passing through both points has a positive slope, apparently indicating that b is indeed higher if r is higher.

The problem becomes more complicated as we add more rounds of dice throws. Suppose we obtain $b_3 = 3$ and $r_3 = 4$. As panel (a) in Figure A.3 reveals, we cannot draw a straight line that passes through all three data points at the same time. The line drawn through points 1 and 2 is off target in round #3. The error committed in explaining b_3 is ε_3. Similarly, any other straight line would have to miss at least one of the three points. And adding yet more data points only compounds the problem. What we need is a new criterion for positioning the straight line (or for determining α and β, which is the same thing).

The most frequently used method in economics is **ordinary least squares estimation**, or OLS. It is based on the following criterion for positioning the straight line:

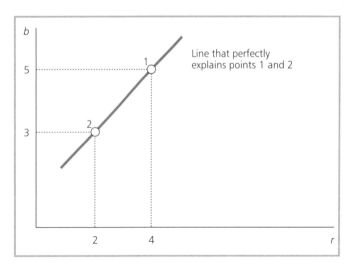

Figure A.2 If we have two observations only, a line drawn through these two points 'explains' both points perfectly.

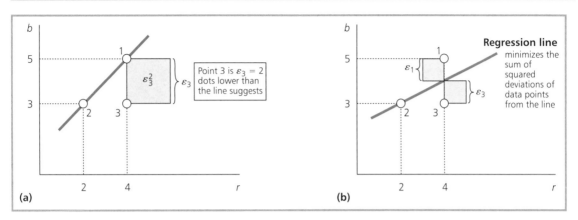

Figure A.3 With three observations, no straight line can pass through all points. The method of ordinary least squares positions the regression line so as to minimize the sum of squared deviations of all points from the line.

Position the straight line so as to make the sum of the squared deviations of all observation points from the line as small as possible.

Note. In panel (a) of Figure A.3 the sum of squared errors is $2^2 = 4$. If the proposed line divides the distance between points 1 and 3 in half, as in panel (b), the sum of squared errors is $1^2 + 1^2 = 2$.

According to this criterion it is better to have two of our three data points *a little bit* off the line than to have two points on the line but the third one *way* off. Figure A.3 illustrates this: clearly the sum of the squared residuals (or errors) is smaller in the case shown in panel (b) than in the case shown in panel (a).

By squaring the errors we increase the weight of large errors disproportionately. This makes sense if we consider large errors less likely than small ones. In general, OLS has a number of helpful statistical properties.

The fact that our example produced a positively sloped line even though the true line is known to be horizontal highlights one problem clearly: it is possible for statistical methods (OLS or some other method) to indicate a relationship between two variables that does not really exist. Such a relationship obtained in a limited sample of data points could be taken as evidence in support of a false model, or as falsification of a correct model. To prevent economists from doing this and as safeguards against other blunders, estimation results need to be subjected to statistical tests. The following sections elaborate on this.

A.2 Second task: testing hypotheses

Referring again to our Paris Saint-Germain example, after some number crunching with the help of their PCs and a good software package, your staff reports that gaining one place in the league table rankings draws an additional 1,453 people into the Stade de France. That sounds good for a start. But you know very well that this estimate is also influenced by other, random factors that influence the size of the crowd drawn on a given day, such as the weather. Therefore, to be able to gauge the risk you take, you would like to know how reliable the reported result is. Is it possible that it was obtained purely by chance, and that league positions and spectator turnout are not really related? Or what is the probability that each step up the league ladder draws at least 1,000 more spectators? To answer such questions statisticians have developed a whole battery of tests.

Example

It is 1812 and you are living in the Grindelwald Saloon in Yuma, Arizona. You play 'heads or tails' with Bonnie's grandfather, BG. The rules are as follows: BG holds a coin, tosses it up in the air, catches it and smacks it on the back of his other hand. If the coin lands 'tails up' he pays you $5; and if it is 'heads up', you pay him $5. Asking BG to let you have a look at both sides of the coin is considered a direct accusation of cheating. If you are proved right, you get your money back. If you are proved wrong, he will follow local custom and shoot you. For a similar reason you cannot simply stop playing and walk out.

Since you are a reasonable, but not completely risk averse person, you follow the rule to call an opponent a cheat only if you are 95% sure. In other words, you discard your initial guess (or hypothesis) that BG plays with an untampered coin only if an observed winning streak of BG's could result from an untampered coin with a probability of less than 5%.

The game starts:

- *Round #1.* BG flips tails. While this does annoy you, it can obviously happen with a probability of 50% even if the coin is clean. There is no reason to question BG's integrity.
- *Round #2.* The coin shows tails. Two tails in a row can happen with a probability of 25%. You obviously have bad luck, and $10 less.
- *Round #3.* Tails again. Clean coins can produce three tails in a row with a probability of 12.5%. Your anger is rising, and so are your doubts. But you continue to stick to your interpretation that BG is basically an honest fellow and simply in luck.
- *Round #4.* Almost expectedly, BG flips tails again and asks for five more dollars. By now you feel like kicking his shin bone. But since a clean coin could produce five tails in a row with a probability of 6.25%, you are only 93.75% confident that your initial guess that BG is honest is wrong. According to your own limit you do not yet discard your initial presumption.
- *Round #5.* Tails! That's enough. The probability of tossing tails five times in a row with a clean coin is 3.125%. You now feel confident that BG is a crook, and ask him to show you the coin.

The rest of the story contains some more advanced concepts that we do not really need – but you might be curious to know about them.

Version A

BG shoots you in cold blood because you called him a crook without foundation. In statistical terms you committed a **Type I error**: you rejected a hypothesis ('he is honest') although it was correct. You always run this risk when you subject a hypothesis to a statistical test, since perfect confidence cannot be achieved. The risk of committing a Type I error increases if you raise the limit that needs to be reached before you reject your initial hypothesis. With the benefit of hindsight you were right in not rejecting the initial hypothesis (technical term: the **null hypothesis**) after rounds #1, #2, #3 and #4 because the risk of error had not yet fallen below the significance level of 5%. Had we chosen a significance level of 10%, below which we would have discarded the null hypothesis that BG is honest, we would already have committed a Type I error in round #4.

Version B

You get your $20 back, buy yourself a younger horse, and BG goes to jail. You were right in rejecting the null hypothesis in round #5. However, we now know that you committed a **Type II error** after each of the first four rounds. You did not discard the 'he is honest' hypothesis although it was wrong. Type II errors also can never be excluded. The risk of committing one increases if we reduce the required level of significance. A significance level of 1% would have caused you to commit another Type II error in round #5.

Tampering with the significance level always reduces the risk of committing one type of error at the cost of increasing the risk of committing the other type of error. Thus you cannot reduce both risks together. In the face of this trade-off, the selection of a significance level is a compromise that reflects the costs incurred by either type of error. In our example, committing a Type II error costs you another $5. A Type I error costs you your life. So it certainly makes sense to set the significance level very, very low, to reduce the risk of committing a Type I error towards zero. When economists test their theories they routinely choose 5% significance levels. Occasionally, significance levels of 10% or 1% are also applied.

A.3 A closer look at OLS estimation

Simple and multiple regression

Models are always incomplete. This is because, by definition, models draw simplifying pictures of the real world by omitting factors considered inessential for the problem at hand. Our model for explaining crowds at Paris Saint-Germain home games should therefore correctly read

$$n_i = \alpha + \beta p_i + \varepsilon_i \tag{A.2}$$

where n_i is the size of the crowd at home game #i, the endogenous variable that we want to explain; α is the constant term; β the slope of the regression line; p the current rank of PSG in France's Ligue 1; and ε combines all the other factors affecting the crowd, such as the weather or the reputation of the visiting team.

According to the artificial data given in Figure A.4 the proposed negative relationship between league table ranking and crowd appears to exist. The negative estimate for β tells us how many spectators we lose if we slide down one place in the rankings. The constant term α simply helps to determine the position of the regression line. Its obviously purely hypothetical interpretation here is how large the crowd would be if PSG held rank 0.

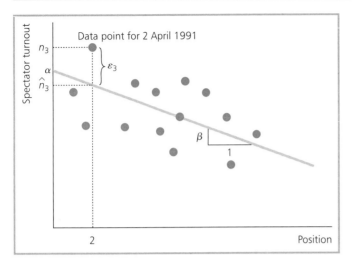

Figure A.4 The hypothetical cloud of data points implies a negative relationship between league position and spectator turnout. Rank 2 gives rise to an expected crowd $\hat{n}_3$.

Note. A hat over a variable indicates that we are dealing with the value suggested by the model, and not with the actual value. We will only use a hat when it is necessary to avoid confusion.

If we want to know the expected turnout when PSG is in second place in the league, we compute $\hat{n} = \alpha - \beta \times 2$ ($\hat{n}$ only gives an average number, an expected value). On 2 April 1991, when PSG was indeed in second place, they actually drew n_3 spectators instead of the $\hat{n}_3$ proposed by the empirical estimate, possibly because of a particularly interesting visiting team.

Up to now we have only tried to quantify relationships between two variables. Such regressions are called **simple regressions**. By contrast, **multiple regressions** involve the relationship between an endogenous variable and two or more exogenous (or explanatory) variables.

Extending what we have learned about simple regressions to multiple regressions is quite straightforward. Suppose we believe that turnout not only depends on the ranking of the home team p_i^{PSG} but on the ranking of the visiting team p_i^{Guest} as well. Then the true model becomes

$$n_i = \alpha + \beta_1 p_i^{\text{PSG}} + \beta_2 p_i^{\text{Guest}} + \varepsilon_i \qquad (A.3)$$

Now each game is characterized by three numbers and needs to be represented in three-dimensional space. Marking all observations in such a diagram, we obtain a cloud of data points. Equation (A.3) suggests that this cloud of points may be represented by a plane (or surface) (see Figure A.5).

Again α is the estimated constant term (or intersection with the vertical axis), β_1 measures the detrimental effect of PSG losing one position in the ranking, and β_2 how much it costs in terms of crowd turnout if the visiting team's ranking is also down by one position.

Again, the plane postulated by the model and estimated from the data will not give a perfect account of the data points. Actual numbers will be ε spectators above or below the estimated plane. In comparison to how we proceeded with simple regressions, multiple OLS positions the plane in the cloud of points so as to minimize the sum of squared estimation errors.

This procedure straightforwardly generalizes to more than two exogenous variables, but obviously cannot be illustrated graphically. Because of the direct comparison between simple and multiple regressions, we may illustrate the following concepts by means of easier-to-draw simple regressions.

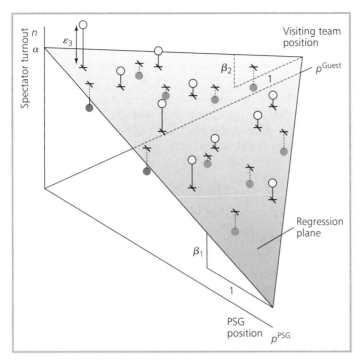

Figure A.5 Multiple regressions do not estimate a line, but a regression plane (or surface). Random influences may put actual observations above or below this plane.

How well does the model explain the data?

Whether we are happy with equation (A.3) depends on how well it explains the variations in turnout. This explanatory power of the equation is measured by the **coefficient of determination**. Figure A.6 provides a hypothetical illustration of what the coefficient of determination does.

The coefficient of determination, denoted by R^2, measures the share of the variation in the variable you want to explain that is actually being explained by your estimation equation. The variation of your endogenous variable is measured as the sum of the squared deviations of the observations from the average value of all observations. Returning to the game of dice,

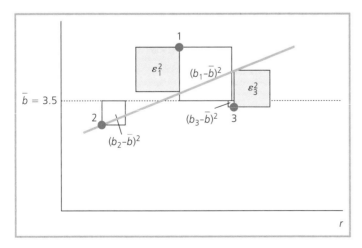

Figure A.6 The coefficient of determination (R^2) is a measure of how close observed data points are to the regression line. Graphically, (R^2) first sums up all white squares, then takes away the sum of all blue squares, and finally divides this difference by the sum of all white squares.

in Figure A.6 we have three observations averaging $\bar{b}$. The squared deviations of b_1, b_2 and b_3 from $\bar{b}$ are represented by white squares. Their sum, $(b_1 - \bar{b})^2 + (b_2 - \bar{b})^2 + (b_3 - \bar{b})^2 = \Sigma_1^3 (b_i - \bar{b})^2$, is the **variation** of b. The squared regression residuals, the sum of which the OLS method minimizes, are shown as blue squares. The sum of squares residuals, $\varepsilon_1^2 + \varepsilon_2^2 + \varepsilon_3^2 = \Sigma_1^3 \varepsilon_i^2$, is the variation of b left unexplained by the estimated line. Consequently, the difference between actual variation and unexplained variation, $\Sigma(b_i - \bar{b})^2 - \Sigma \varepsilon_i^2$, is the explained variation of b. Hence, the coefficient of determination is simply the explained variation as a fraction of the total variation of b:

$$R^2 = \frac{\text{explained variation}}{\text{variation}} = \frac{\Sigma(b_i - \bar{b})^2 - \Sigma \varepsilon_i^2}{\Sigma(b_i - \bar{b})^2}$$

$$R^2 = \frac{\text{sum of white squares} - \text{sum of blue squares}}{\text{sum of white squares}}$$

This fraction is limited to the interval between 0 and 1. If all observed data points are exactly on the estimated line (such as point 2 in Figure A.6), there are no estimation errors and, hence, no unexplained variation ($\Sigma_1^3 \varepsilon_i^2 = 0$). Thus the coefficient of determination equals 1, indicating a perfect 'fit' of the model. At the opposite extreme the model does not explain anything. The

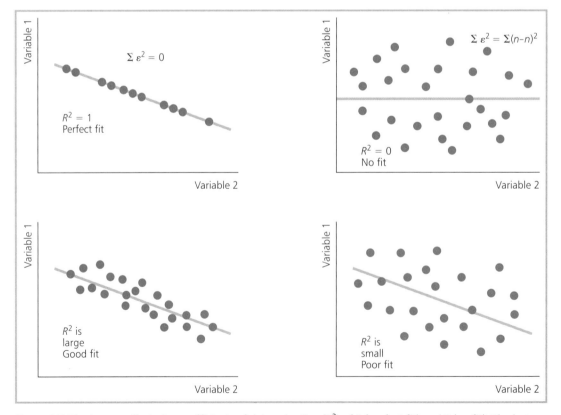

Figure A.7 The top row illustrates coefficients of determination (R^2) of 1 (perfect fit) and 0 (no fit). The bottom row illustrates intermediate cases of a good and a poor fit.

estimate of β is zero and the estimate of α equals $\overline{b}$. Now the explained variation is zero, and so is the coefficient of determination. The top two panels in Figure A.7 illustrate the two extreme cases.

Quite dissimilar clouds of data points may yield the same regression line. If, on average, points are close to the line, the coefficient of determination is high, that is close to 1 (see Figure A.7, bottom left-hand panel). If the points are far from the regression line, a low coefficient of determination results (see bottom right-hand panel in Figure A.7).

BOX A.1 | **The coefficient of determination: R^2**

The coefficient of determination, called R^2, takes values between 0 and 1. It reports the share of the variation of the endogenous variable that is explained by the estimation equation:

$R^2 = 0$ indicates that the estimation equation does not explain anything.
$R^2 = 1$ indicates that the explanation is perfect.

How reliable are the parameter estimates?

We know by now that econometric estimates of parameters are products of chance. If the average height of Italian women over the age of 21 is 165 cm, then the average height of a sample of ten women will usually not match the true value of 165. Similarly, estimates of parameters in a regression equation are influenced by random factors. This calls for the questioning of the reliability and implications of the obtained result. Suppose the true relationship between spectator turnout and league division standing was

$$n_i = 12{,}500 - 500p_i + \varepsilon_i$$

where ε = (number of dots showing when a die is thrown -3.5) $\times$ 1,000. Figure A.8 shows the values that ε can assume and the attached probabilities.

The 3D sketch in Figure A.9 shows how this random variable affects the model. The blue line on the base plane shows the true relationship between n

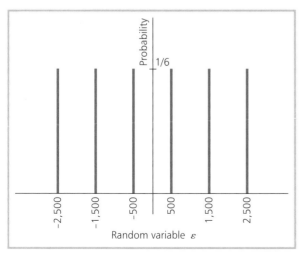

Figure A.8 Here the values of $-2{,}500$, $-1{,}500$, -500, 500, 1,500 and 2,500 occur with probability 1/6 each. The sum of these probabilities is 1. So no other values may occur.

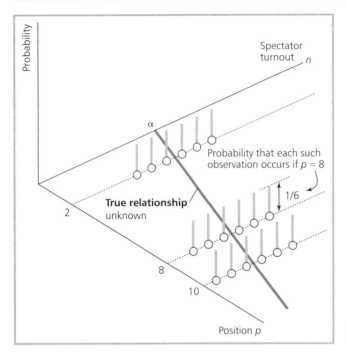

Figure A.9 Due to random influences, if $p = 2$ (or 8, or 10) any of the six white points may result with probability 1/6, making observations scatter around the true relationship given by the blue line.

and p. If PSG is in second place, we may expect a turnout crowd of 11,500, but the actual turnout will be $11,500 - 2,500$, $11,500 - 1,500$, $11,500 - 500$, $11,500 + 500$, $11,500 + 1,500$ or $11,500 + 2,500$, each with probability 1/6. Similar random effects on turnout are at work when PSG is in eighth or tenth place, or in any other position.

Panels (a) and (b) in Figure A.10 transfer the true relationship marked by the straight line and the possible data points onto a plane. Suppose now that

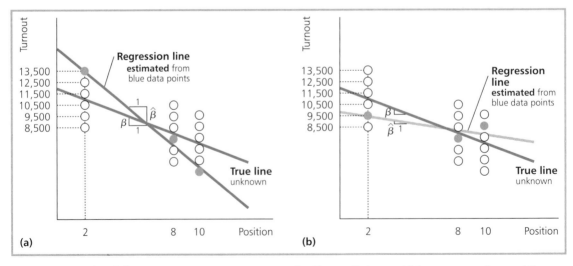

Figure A.10 Random influences on spectator turnout may give the results in panel (a) on one occasion, and those in panel (b) on another. The resulting regression line is steeper than the true line in the first case and flatter in the second. Thus the slope estimate $\hat{\beta}$ is subject to random influences.

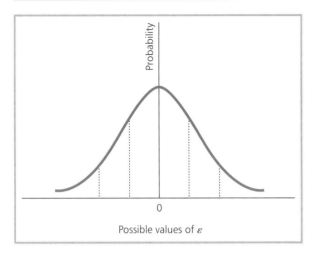

Figure A.11 Econometricians usually assume that random influences ε have a bell-shaped distribution. This means that most frequently disturbances are around 0 or small. Large positive or negative disturbances have a small probability of occurring. One important bell-shaped distribution is the normal distribution.

Note. What is being said *here* about the slope coefficient β and how to test it applies one-to-one to the constant term α.

in this situation two random **samples** of data are drawn, meaning that we are given two series of three observations of rounds in which PSG was in second, eighth and tenth place. The blue points in panel (a) mark the observations in the first sample and the blue points in panel (b) mark the observations in the second sample.

If a relationship between n and p is estimated from the first sample, the light blue line given in panel (a) of Figure A.10 results. The second sample gives the light blue line in panel (b). The first sample gives a regression coefficient that is larger than its true value of $500(\hat{\beta} > \beta = 500)$. From the second sample we obtain a regression coefficient that is too small. Although OLS estimation allows us to expect to obtain the true coefficient, this will normally not be the case in a given sample.

Note. It can be shown that if the error is normally distributed, so is the true distribution of the estimated coefficient. The estimated distribution of the estimated coefficient has a *t*-distribution. If we work with many observations (thirty or more) the *t*-distribution gets close to the normal distribution.

Econometricians assume that the random effects that influence the endogenous variable, here on turnout, are not determined by throwing a die, but are drawn from a **normal distribution** with expectation zero. A normal distribution is a bell-shaped distribution that is uniquely determined by its median (or average value), which determines where the bell sits on a horizontal axis, and by its variance, which determines how wide the bell is. Figure A.11 shows a normal distribution. The bell shape implies that small values (in the region of $\varepsilon = 0$) are much more frequent than large positive or negative values of ε. Now if ε is normally distributed around 0, then the crowd attendance when PSG is in second place in the league is normally distributed around the true value. Figure A.12 illustrates this.

We now come to the important conclusion of the current line of argument: if the crowd attendance figures that result from the true model are superimposed on random disturbances drawn from a bell-shaped distribution, then the regression coefficients estimated from many repeated random samples of observed data will have a bell-shaped distribution around the true coefficient. Figure A.13 illustrates this for the regression coefficient β. Of course, we do not know β, otherwise we would not have to estimate it. We also do not know the true distribution of the estimates around β. What we have is an estimated parameter $\hat{\beta}$ and an estimate of the bell-shaped distribution. For lack of better

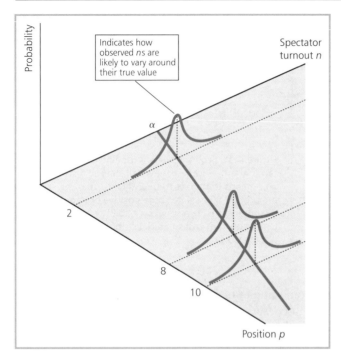

Figure A.12 When disturbances are normally distributed, the endogenous variable is also normally distributed. The graph illustrates this for three different values of the exogenous variable.

information we are persuaded that $\hat{\beta}$ is the true parameter and that the estimated distribution is the true distribution.

Two sets of questions are typically raised with the obtained estimates of the parameter and of its distribution. The first set constitutes a refinement of the first task of econometrics discussed in Section A.1. It augments the parameter estimate $\hat{\beta}$ with a confidence interval, a range within which the true parameter

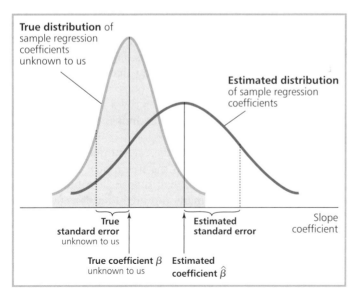

Figure A.13 Neither the true coefficient β nor the standard error of its distribution (left bell curve) is known to us. Instead, from the processed data we obtain a coefficient estimate $\hat{\beta}$ and an estimated standard error (right bell curve).

can be expected to be when having a certain probability. The second set of questions addresses the second task of econometrics, namely that of testing models or hypotheses, which is the theme of this section.

As we will see, both sets of questions are intimately related, but are being asked in different contexts.

Confidence intervals

While the estimate has produced a precise parameter value of 453, we may want to describe the result more cautiously; for instance, the coefficient is approximately 450. While this signals the stochastic or random nature of the result, it is rather vague. Fortunately, despite the uncertainty involved, the results allow us to be more specific. All we need to do is make use of the fact that a specific area underneath the bell-shaped distribution tells us the probability with which parameters in the underlying segment may occur. (The total area below the distribution must equal 1, by definition!)

Let us now mark a symmetric interval around the coefficient estimate that excludes 95% of the entire area beneath the distribution curve. In Figure A.14 this is the segment between 253 and 653. The interpretation is as follows. Whenever we draw a new data sample – and the next football season is like a new sample – then the new data will exhibit a relationship between n and p that is between 253 and 653 with a probability of 95%. Since such an OLS estimate is always an unbiased estimate of the true parameter, we may expect that the estimated interval from 253 to 653 includes the true parameter β with a probability of 95%.

It is easy to determine this 95% confidence interval. It stretches from two standard errors below the parameter estimate to two standard errors above the parameter estimate. Computer programs routinely give the standard error of each regression coefficient. The standard error of β is the square root of the variance of β which, as we know, measures the width of the bell-shaped distribution.

Note. Similar questions can be answered by applying the same principles. For example, what is the probability that the true parameter exceeds 200?

Note. The standard error is the square root of the variance. The two standard errors mentioned here are not exact, but good enough as a rule of thumb.

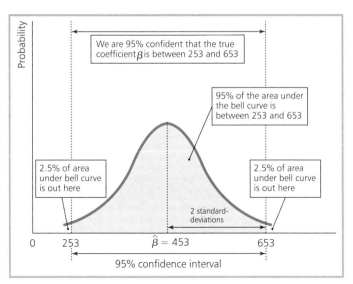

Figure A.14 The estimated distribution of the coefficient provides information as to the probabilities with which the true β is in a certain range. An important rule of thumb is that the true coefficient is between two standard errors left and two standard errors right of $\hat{\beta}$ with a probability of 95%. This range is called the 95% confidence interval.

Note. the relationship
confidence level =
1 − significance level.

Significance tests

Following the line of reasoning used when we played 'heads or tails' in Yuma (in the example above) we may phrase the test as follows. Suppose n and p are not really related, so that $\beta = 0$. What is the probability that we still obtain an estimate $\hat{\beta}$ from a random sample of data points? To answer this question, take the estimated distribution bell and slide it to the left so that its peak is directly over the presumed true value $\beta = 0$. Next we fix a significance level, usually of 5%, and then mark the sector within which we expect 95% of the coefficient estimates to be. In this case, this interval reaches from two standard errors below zero to two standard errors above zero. If the estimated parameter is outside this interval (shaded blue in Figure A.15), the probability that it was obtained in spite of the true parameter being zero is less than 5%. In this case we reject the null hypothesis $\beta = 0$. By analogy we could test other initial presumptions (or null hypotheses) such as $\beta = 1$. All we need to do then is check whether the parameter estimate is more than two standard errors away from the presumed value of 1.

Expressed more formally, significance tests are usually performed using the so-called **t-statistic**:

$$t = \frac{\text{parameter estimate} - \text{null hypothesis}}{\text{standard error}} = \frac{\hat{\beta} - \beta_0}{\sigma_\beta}$$

If my null hypothesis reads H_0: $\beta_0 = 0$, the t-statistic simplifies to

$$t = \frac{\text{parameter estimate}}{\text{standard error}} = \frac{\hat{\beta}}{\sigma_\beta}$$

If the t-statistic is greater than 2 or less than −2 (or if the *absolute* t-statistic is greater than 2), then the estimated coefficient is said to be significantly different from 0, i.e. from the null hypothesis. This renders the null hypothesis implausible and recommends that it be dropped. Unless stated otherwise, whenever this book's 'Applied problem' sections report t-statistics, these are absolute t-statistics, and they test against the null hypothesis that the true coefficient is zero.

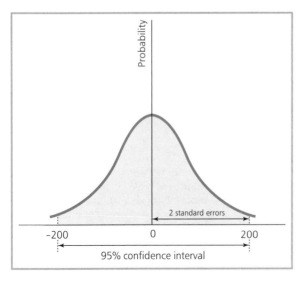

Figure A.15 If the true coefficient were 0, an estimate of $\hat{\beta}$ would be in the range of two standard errors left of 0 and two standard errors right of 0 with a probability of 95%. If we obtain an estimate outside that range, this could have happened with probability smaller than 5% only. In this case we discard our initial hypothesis that $\beta = 0$. The estimate $\hat{\beta}$ is said to be different from 0 at the 5% level of significance.

The above arguments may be condensed into the following formula:

Recipe for parameter tests

Step	What to do	Example
1	Read off the parameter estimate from the computer printout	-469
2	Read off the standard error of this parameter estimate from the computer printout	193
3	Specify a null hypothesis	$H_0{:}\beta_0 = 0$
4	Determine the interval that reaches from two standard errors below the null hypothesis to two standard errors above	-386 to 386
5	(a) Parameter estimates obtained from random samples fall within the interval identified in step 3 with a probability of 95% if the true coefficient is $\beta = 0$. The probability of obtaining a value outside this interval is only 5% (b) If the estimated parameter lies outside the ± 2 standard-error interval it is said to be significant (or significantly different from zero)	The parameter estimate of -469 is significant

APPENDIX SUMMARY

- Econometrics tries to quantify the relationship between the variables of economic models. It also tests whether presumptions (or hypotheses) about such variables are compatible with the data.

- The method of ordinary least squares (OLS) quantifies the relationship between variables by fitting a (usually linear) model, that is a straight line (or plane), in such a way into the cloud of data points that the sum of squared deviations of the data points from this line is as small as possible.

- The coefficient of determination R^2 indicates how well the model fits the data, that is how closely the data points are positioned to the estimated line. Being defined as the interval between 0 and 1, the larger the coefficient of determination, the better the model explains the data.

- The t-statistic usually addresses the question of whether the estimated coefficient is significantly different from zero (or, for short, is significant), that is, whether we may have obtained it by chance, despite the true coefficient being zero. The initial presumption (the null hypothesis) that the true coefficient is zero (that is, the two variables are unrelated) is usually rejected if the absolute t-value is larger than 2. Then the null hypothesis is false with a probability of more than 95%.

Key terms and concepts

coefficient of determination *539*

confidence interval *543*

estimate *531*

null hypothesis *535*

ordinary least squares (OLS) *532*

regression *536*

sample *541*

significance level *544*

t-statistic *544*

EXERCISES

A.1 The following data have been observed for variables x and y:

$$x \quad 1 \quad 8 \quad 8 \quad 3 \quad 5 \quad 5 \quad 2 \quad 4 \quad 7 \quad 6$$
$$y \quad 2 \quad 4 \quad 6 \quad 2 \quad 3 \quad 4 \quad 1 \quad 3 \quad 5 \quad 5$$

Show these points in a scatter diagram with y on the vertical and x on the horizontal axis.

Draw a regression line $y = \alpha + \beta x$ through the data points using your hand and your head (do not use formulas). Read α and β off your graph.

A.2 Discuss the O. J. Simpson trial in statistical terms. What is the null hypothesis from which jurors are requested to start? Translate the requirement 'beyond reasonable doubt' into statistical concepts. Do you believe that the jurors committed an error? If yes, was it an error of Type I or of Type II? In the civil law suit subsequently filed against O. J. Simpson the issue is not whether he is guilty 'beyond reasonable doubt' but with a probability of more than 50%. Does this increase the risk of committing an error of Type I or an error of Type II?

A.3 You are engaged in a game of dice. Your opponent throws only fives and sixes. After how many rounds do you discard your initial presumption (your null hypothesis) that the die is not loaded:
(a) at the 10% level?
(b) at the 5% level?
(c) at the 1% level?

A.4 You would like to check:
(a) whether the quantity theory of money holds. You therefore estimate the equation (in logarithms)

$$\text{Money supply} = a + b \times \text{Price level} + c \times \text{GDP}$$

(b) whether the exchange rate forecasts published biannually in *The Economist* are rational in the sense that they are not systematically wrong. To look into this you estimate

$$\text{Depreciation in period } t = \alpha + \beta \times \text{Depreciation forecast for period } t$$

(c) whether the rate of return in your country's stock market does not really possess any forecasting potential for the rate of return in the next quarter. You estimate

$$\text{Rate of return in period } t = c_0 + c_1 \times \text{Rate of return in period } t-1$$

(d) that the business cycle in the United States does not affect the business cycle in your country. The estimation equation reads

$$\text{Unemployment rate (your country)} = c + d \times \text{Unemployment rate (USA)}$$

Formulate one or more appropriate null hypotheses for all of the above questions.

Recommended reading

There are more than a dozen very good econometrics texts on the market. One outstanding example is Robert S. Pyndick and Daniel L. Rubinfeld (1998) *Econometric Models and Economic Forecasts*, 4th edn. New York: McGraw-Hill. However, this book does include more mathematics than we needed here. If you are looking for a book that makes the most of intuitive reasoning and graphical illustrations, here are three very good choices that you may want to look at:

■ Dougherty, Christopher (2011) *Introduction to Econometrics*, 4th edn. New York and Oxford: Oxford University Press.

■ Gujarati, Damodar N. and Dawn C. Porter (2008) *Basic Econometrics*, 5th edn. New York: McGraw-Hill.
■ Kennedy, Peter E. (2008) *A Guide to Econometrics*, 6th edn. Oxford: Wiley-Blackwell.

If you do not really want to get into econometrics, but would like to learn more about concepts introduced here while enjoying yourself at the same time, pick up a copy of Larry Gonick and Woolcott Smith (1993) *The Cartoon Guide to Statistics*, 4th edn. New York: Harper Perennial.

APPENDIX B

Glossary

Absolute convergence hypothesis See *convergence hypothesis*.

Active population Obtained by subtracting from the population those who are too young or too old to work.

Actual expenditure The sum of all planned and unplanned expenditure, including unplanned investment.

AD **(aggregate demand) curve** Downward-sloping curve in the price–income space of the AD-AS model. It shows the equilibrium incomes of the *Mundell–Fleming model* that obtain at different price levels.

AD-AS **(aggregate demand–aggregate supply) model** A macroeconomic model that explains the prevailing output and price levels through the interaction between aggregate demand and aggregate supply.

Adaptive expectations A simple way of forming expectations by looking only at the recent history of a variable. Example of adaptive price expectations: $p^e = p^e_{-1} + a(p_{-1} - p^e_{-1})$. Cf. *economically rational expectations*, *perfect foresight*, *rational expectations*.

Aggregate demand The total demand for domestically produced goods and services at given prices that obtains when firms are willing to produce any desired amount.

Aggregate expenditure The sum of all planned or voluntary spending on domestically produced goods and services.

Aggregate supply The sum of all goods and services produced at a given price level.

AK **model** A simple endogenous growth model following from an extension of the neoclassical growth model. It assumes that a higher capital stock boosts the accumulation of human capital. This causes capital productivity to grow, which results in endogenous growth through capital accumulation.

Appreciation A rise in the value (and, hence, in the price) of a currency relative to other currencies under flexible exchange rates. Cf. *depreciation*, *revaluation*.

AS **(aggregate supply) curve** Shows the quantity of goods and services supplied by all firms at different price levels. Cf. *classical aggregate supply curve*, *extreme Keynesian aggregate supply curve*, *Keynesian aggregate supply curve*, *long-run aggregate supply curve*, *SAS (surprise aggregate supply) curve*.

Austerity A term that refers to a policy of cutting the deficit by lowering government spending, sometimes coupled with raising taxes.

Average tax rate The ratio of total taxes to the tax base (say, income).

Balance of payments The balance of payments records a country's trade in goods, services and financial assets with other countries. In traditional terminology, the balance of payments comprises the current account, the capital account and the official reserve account. In new terminology, the balance of payment accounts are the current account, the capital account and the financial account. Cf. *current account*, *capital account*, *official reserve account*, *financial account*.

Bank of England The central bank of Great Britain. Cf. *central bank*.

Barter economy An economy without money. Households and firms must exchange goods and services for other goods and services.

Beveridge curve A negatively sloped line, depicting an inverse relationship between the vacancy rate and the unemployment rate. During business cycles the economy moves up and down this line.

Boom A rise in income relative to and above the path of potential income which culminates in a peak. Cf. *business cycle*, *recession*.

Bretton Woods system A system of fixed exchange rates operational until 1971. Conceived in 1944 at an international conference held in Bretton Woods, USA, it tied the value of the US dollar to the price of gold, and other countries had fixed exchange rates versus the dollar.

Bubble See *speculative bubble*.

Budget See *government budget*.

Budget deficit See *deficit*.

Bundesbank The central bank of Germany. Now part of the European System of Central Banks (ESCB). Cf. *central bank*.

Business cycle Refers to recurring medium-run fluctuations of income relative to potential income. Cf. *boom, depression, recession*.

Capital account Records the flow of financial assets into and out of the country in traditional balance of payments terminology. In new terminology, it records transfers not made out of current income, so-called wealth transfers, which are included in the current account in old balance of payments terminology. Cf. *balance of payments, current account, official reserve account*.

Central bank An institution primarily responsible for the conduct of *monetary policy* and supervision of the banking system.

Central bank independence A measure of how well protected a central bank's monetary policy decisions are from the political pressures and interventions of the government.

Circular flow identity Sums up leakages out of and injections into the *circular flow of income and spending*. The sum is always zero: $(S - I) + (T - G) + (IM - EX) = 0$.

Circular flow of income and spending (circular flow model) Shows the real and monetary flows between households and firms. It can be refined to include interactions with the government sector and other countries. Cf. *circular flow identity*.

Classical aggregate supply curve A vertical line in price–income space, stating that firms produce only one level of output Y^*, no matter how high prices are. Cf. *AS (aggregate supply) curve, Keynesian aggregate supply curve*.

Classical dichotomy Refers to the independence of real variables (such as real income) from nominal variables (such as the nominal money supply) in the classical model. Cf. *neutrality of money*.

Classical labour market In the classical view, perfectly flexible real wages keep the labour market in permanent equilibrium. No involuntary unemployment occurs.

Classical macroeconomics A view of the economy developed in the 19th century, before the term *macroeconomics* had been coined, originating with

the work of Adam Smith and David Ricardo. Due to flexible prices and wages and the interaction of supply and demand, all markets clear at all times, leading to a full-employment equilibrium. Cf. *classical dichotomy*.

Closed economy An economy that does not trade or interact financially with other countries. The global economy is a closed economy.

Cobb–Douglas production function A production function of the form $Y = F(K, L) = AK^\alpha L^{1-\alpha}$. Output Y is linked to capital (K), labour (L) and technology (A). Exponents denote the income shares of capital (α) and labour ($1 - \alpha$). Proposed by US economist Paul Douglas and mathematician Charles Cobb.

Coefficient of determination (R^2) A goodness-of-fit statistic used in econometrics, indicating how good an estimated equation fits the data, ranging from 0 (no fit) to 1 (perfect fit).

Comovement The tendency of two variables to move in parallel (procyclical) or in opposite directions (countercyclical) during business cycles. *Stylized facts* often refer to comovements.

Comparative static analysis Looks at how a model's equilibrium is affected by a shock or policy measure. It says nothing about whether and how the economy gets there. Cf. *dynamic analysis*.

Constant returns to scale See *returns to scale*.

Consumption Goods and services purchased by consumers.

Consumer price index Measures the price of a representative basket of consumption goods and services, part of which is produced domestically, and part of which may be imported. Cf. *producer price index*.

Consumption function A mathematical relationship between consumption and its determinants. A simple example relates consumption to disposable income: $C = c(Y - T)$.

Contagion A process that drives initially healthy industries or countries into trouble because of problems or crises that arose in other industries or countries.

Convergence hypothesis Claims that per capita incomes converge world-wide, implying that poor countries grow faster than rich ones (absolute convergence). The relative convergence hypothesis cautions that this holds only within groups of countries with similar investment and population growth rates.

Countercyclical variable Moves down (up) when income moves up (down) during the business cycle. Example: real wage in the *DAD-SAS* model. Cf. *procyclical variable*.

Covered interest parity See *interest parity*.

Crawling peg The crawling peg is an exchange rate system where the exchange rate is adjusted periodically in small, preannounced steps.

Credit rating An evaluation, typically made by a credit rating agency, of the risk that a debtor may default on his or her debt.

Credit rating agency A company that rates financial instruments or issuers of debt obligations. Issuers that are rated include governments.

Crowding out Occurs when expansionary fiscal policy reduces private spending (via net exports or investment). This may happen via effects on the interest rate, the exchange rate or prices.

Currency The sum of paper money and coins in circulation. Most of the time, the government of a country controls the supply of its own currency. A well-known exception to this rule is the euro, the currency of the *European Economic and Monetary Union (EMU)*.

Currency union A group of countries sharing a common *currency*. Cf. *European Economic and Monetary Union (EMU)*.

Current account In traditional balance of payments terminology, the current account records trade in goods and services and transfers. New balance of payments terminology excludes transfers from the current account.

Cyclical unemployment *Unemployment* that is added during recessions; the deviation of the unemployment from structural unemployment.

DAD **(dynamic aggregate demand) curve** The dynamic version of the *AD (aggregate demand) curve*. It is downward-sloping in inflation–income space.

DAD-SAS **(dynamic aggregate demand–surprise aggregate supply) model** The *DAD-SAS* model is a variant of the *AD-AS* model, explaining the dynamics of output and inflation through the interaction of *dynamic aggregate demand (DAD)* and *surprise aggregate supply (SAS)*.

Debt The public debt or government debt is the net amount that the government owes to the private sector at home and to foreigners.

Decreasing returns to scale See *returns to scale*.

Default risk The possibility that a borrower will not pay interest or repay outstanding debt on time.

Deficit A budget deficit occurs if tax revenue falls short of government expenditure (including public consumption and investment, transfers, and interest payments on public debt). The primary deficit ignores government interest payments.

Deflation A reduction of the price level. Deflation can be described as negative inflation.

Demand The volume of goods, services or assets that households, firms, the government or the rest of the world wish to purchase.

Depreciation (capital) The part of the capital stock lost over time because it wears out or becomes obsolete.

Depreciation (exchange rate) A fall in the value (and, hence, in the price) of a currency relative to other currencies under flexible exchange rates.

Depression An extreme *recession*.

Derivative A financial instrument that is only indirectly related to some underlying asset.

Deutsche Bundesbank See *Bundesbank*.

Devaluation A reduction in the value (and, hence, in the price) of a currency relative to other currencies officially implemented by the government under fixed exchange rates. Cf. *appreciation*, *depreciation*, *revaluation*.

Difference equation A mathematical equation in which the current value of a variable depends on past values of the same variable.

Diminishing marginal product A property of production functions, implying that the *marginal product* of a production factor falls as more of that factor is being used.

Discount rate The interest rate that central banks charge on loans they extend to commercial banks.

Disinflation A reduction of the inflation rate.

Disinflation costs Income losses caused by *disinflation*.

Disposable income The part of income left to households after the deduction of income taxes.

Dynamic analysis Looks at whether an equilibrium is stable, and traces the transition from one equilibrium to another. Cf. *comparative static analysis*.

Dynamic efficiency and dynamic inefficiency In models of economic growth a steady state is dynamically inefficient when a change in the saving rate would increase consumption today and in the future. It is dynamically efficient when future consumption could only be increased at the expense of lower consumption today. Cf. *golden rule of capital accumulation*.

Dynamic optimization See *intertemporal optimization*.

EAS **(equilibrium aggregate supply) curve** Shows the quantity of goods and services supplied by all firms at different price levels when the labour market is in equilibrium. It is vertical (at potential income) in a price–income or inflation–income diagram.

Econometrics Confronts economic theory with real-world data, employing statistical methods. Key tasks are the estimation of parameters and the testing of hypotheses.

Economic growth Long-run (or *secular*) increases in a country or region's level of income.

Economically rational expectations Suggest that individuals collect information to improve forecasts only until additional information costs more than it benefits.

Economies of scale Obtain if output produced more than doubles when all inputs double. Such a production function is also said to feature increasing returns to scale. Cf. *returns to scale.*

Efficiency See *labour productivity.*

Efficiency wage theory Rests on the assumption that workers are more efficient (productive) when they receive higher wages. When this relationship is strong enough, *real-wage rigidity* and *involuntary unemployment* obtain.

Efficiency units of labour A measure of labour input that multiplies the number of workers by their efficiency (as a measure of quality).

Effort See *labour productivity.*

EFSF (European Financial Stability Facility) The Eurozone's *temporary* bailout fund created in May 2010 when the European sovereign debt crisis started.

Elasticity Measures by how many percentage points one variable responds if some other variable changes by 1%.

Empirical tests Confrontations of hypotheses (predictions) derived from models (or theories) with real-world data or events. They serve to gauge whether a model (or concept) is useful or not.

Endogenous growth Occurs when forces within the model, such as human capital accumulation, make income grow, rather than outside influences such as unexplained technological progress.

Endogenous variable A variable that is explained within a particular economic model.

Equilibrium In a model, equilibrium obtains when there is no more inherent tendency of the endogenous variables to change. If the equilibrium is stable, the economy moves toward it from all disequilibria.

Equilibrium aggregate supply curve See *long-run aggregate supply curve.*

Equilibrium income The level of income that obtains in *equilibrium.*

Equilibrium unemployment Occurs after all adjustments have taken place in the economy.

ESM (European Stability Mechanism) The Eurozone's *permanent* rescue fund launched in the summer of 2012.

Euro Common European currency introduced parallel to national currencies in non-physical form on 1 January 1999. It replaced national currencies as legal tender on 1 January 2002.

Euro area Denotes the group of EU members that adopted the euro as their common currency. Members as of 2013 are: Austria, Belgium, Cyprus, Estonia, Finland, France, Germany, Greece, Ireland, Italy, Luxembourg, Malta, the Netherlands, Portugal, Slovakia, Slovenia and Spain.

Eurozone An official name for *euro area.*

Euroland Informal name for *euro area.*

European Central Bank (ECB) Supranational monetary authority of the *European Economic and Monetary Union (EMU)* established in 1998. It conducts monetary policy for the euro *area.* Cf. *European System of Central Banks, Eurosystem.*

European Economic and Monetary Union (EMU) Internal market with free trade, free movement of capital and labour, and a common currency. Its creation involved three stages. I (1 July 1990–31 December 1993): abolition of exchange controls. II (1 January 1994–31 December 1998): establishment of European Monetary Institute followed by European Central Bank. III (1 January 1999 and continuing): adoption of common currency. As of 2013, EMU has seventeen members. Denmark, Sweden and the UK have not accepted stage III. Other countries have not qualified (yet).

European Monetary System (EMS) Exchange rate regime established in 1979 under which members of the European Economic Community (EEC; predecessor of EU) linked currencies to make exchange rates less volatile. The main components were the ECU (a basket of member currencies) and the exchange rate mechanism (ERM). The EMS was replaced by ERM II at the start of Stage III of Economic and Monetary Union (EMU) on 1 January 1999.

European System of Central Banks (ESCB) Comprises the European Central Bank (ECB) and the national central banks of all 27 European Union member states. Cf. *European Central Bank (ECB), Eurosystem.*

European Union (EU) An economic and political partnership between 27 European democracies (as of 2008) laid out in the Maastricht Treaty in 1992. Its predecessor was the European Economic Community (EEC), created by Belgium, France, Germany, Italy, Luxembourg and the Netherlands in the Treaty of

Rome in 1958. The main bodies of the EU are the European Parliament, the Council of the European Union and the European Commission.

Eurosystem The central banking system of the euro area. It is a subset of the European System of Central Banks (ESCB) and comprises the European Central Bank (ECB) and the national central banks of countries that have adopted the euro. The Eurosystem and the ESCB will co-exist as long as there are EU member states outside the euro area. Monetary policy decisions are made by the ECB and executed by national central banks. Cf. *European Central Bank (ECB)*, *European System of Central Banks (ESCB)*.

Exchange rate The price of one unit of foreign currency in terms of domestic currency. Cf. *real exchange rate*.

Exchange Rate Mechanism (ERM) System of bilateral exchange rate target zones as part of the EMS, designed to smooth exchange rate fluctuations, launched in 1979. Exchange rates where flexible within a band of (usually) $\pm 2.25\%$ around a fixed parity, but had to be kept within that band by intervention of the central banks involved. ERM II replaced the original ERM after the introduction of the euro on 1 January 1999. It permits fluctuations within $\pm 15\%$ around parity and is often considered a waiting room for countries wishing to adopt the euro.

Exchange rate overshooting See *overshooting*.

Exogenous variable A variable that is determined outside a particular economic model.

Expansion See *boom*.

Expectations See *adaptive expectations*, *economically rational expectations*, *perfect foresight*, *rational expectations*.

Export function A mathematical relationship between exports and their determinants. A simple example relates exports to foreign income and the real exchange rate: $EX = x_1 Y^{\text{World}} + x_2 R$.

Exports Domestically produced goods and services sold to other countries.

Extensive form of the production function Relates real output to the factors of production (usually capital and labour) and technology. Example: $Y = AF(K, L)$. Cf. *intensive form of the production function*.

Externalities Side effects of a person's actions on other parties not directly involved.

Extreme Keynesian aggregate supply curve A horizontal line in a price–income diagram stating that, at the indicated price, firms are willing to produce any level of output that is demanded. Cf. *AS (aggregate supply) curve*.

Factor income share The percentage of total income paid to a factor of production.

Factors of production Resources used in the production of goods and services. In macroeconomics these are grouped into broad categories such as labour, capital and raw materials.

FE curve The foreign-exchange-market equilibrium line, usually drawn in an interest rate–income diagram; it shows all combinations of income and the interest rate for which the foreign exchange market is in equilibrium.

Fed The central bank of the United States of America. Short for Federal Reserve System. Cf. *central bank*.

Feldstein–Horioka puzzle In theory, a country's investment rate is independent of its saving rate when capital is perfectly mobile. The puzzle is that in reality the two are correlated nevertheless.

Financial account Name for the current account in new balance of payments terminology. It records the flow of financial assets across borders. Cf. *balance of payments*.

Fiscal policy Uses government spending and taxes to dampen the ups and downs of the business cycle.

Fisher effect See *Fisher equation*.

Fisher equation Due to US economist Irving Fisher (1867–1947), the equation $i = r + \pi$ makes the nominal interest rate the sum of the real interest and the inflation rate. It exemplifies the *classical dichotomy*, since the real interest rate is thought to be exogenous and thus remains unaffected by inflation. The inflation premium that raises the nominal interest rate over the real interest rate is called the Fisher effect. Empirically, the equation only holds in the longer run.

Fixed exchange rates International monetary arrangement in which governments announce exchange rates at which central banks buy or sell domestic currency. Cf. *foreign exchange market intervention*.

Flexible exchange rates An international monetary arrangement in which the determination of the exchange rate is left to the market, without interference from the central bank.

Flow variable A variable measured over a period of time. Examples are income or taxes. Cf. *stock variable*.

Foreign direct investment See *foreign investment*.

Foreign exchange market The market in which currencies are bought and sold.

Foreign exchange market intervention Any actions by central banks aimed at influencing the exchange rate, usually the purchase or sale of foreign currency, but sometimes also announcements purported to affect market expectations. Cf. *fixed exchange rates.*

Foreign investment Investment by citizens and governments of one country in industries of another.

Frictional unemployment Exists because it takes time to find existing jobs, to relocate or to retrain. Part of *equilibrium unemployment.*

Friedman rule US Nobel prize winner Milton Friedman called for the money supply to grow at a constant rate approximating long-run income growth. Cf. *monetary policy rule, Taylor rule.*

Fundamentals or fundamental variables. These are exogenous variables that determine the equilibrium price in an economy or in a specific market.

GDP (gross domestic product) A measure of total income (or output) generated within the borders of a country, no matter by whom. Cf. *GNI (gross national income), GNP (gross national product).*

GDP deflator A price index for all goods and services included in a country's GDP. It links nominal GDP (in current prices) to real GDP (at constant prices).

Global economy The world economy as a whole.

Globalization The integration of national economies into the global economy through elimination of barriers to trade and the free movement of the factors of production, including capital, labour and technology.

GNI (gross national income) A measure of output or income similar to GNP. Cf. *GDP (gross domestic product), GNP (gross national product).*

GNP (gross national product) A measure of total income (or output) generated by a country's inhabitants, no matter whether it accrues at home or abroad. Cf. *GDP (gross domestic product), GNI (gross national income).*

Golden rule of capital accumulation Identifies the saving rate that maximizes consumption in economic growth models. Cf. *golden steady state.*

Golden steady state Obtains when the saving rate is as suggested by the *golden rule of capital accumulation.*

Government budget Primarily a planning instrument listing expected revenues and expenses. In hindsight it breaks down actual government receipts and expenditures, and shows how deficits are being financed. Cf. *deficit.*

Government debt See *debt.*

Government purchases The sum of government consumption and government investment.

Government spending The sum of *government purchases* and *government transfers.*

Government transfers Payments from the government to individuals for which no goods or services are required in return. Example: social security and unemployment benefits.

Growth See *economic growth.*

Growth accounting Links observed income growth to changes in the observable factors of production. Income growth that cannot be attributed to observable factors of production is interpreted as technological change and usually referred to as the *Solow residual.*

Growth theory Develops theoretical models purported to explain international differences in income and economic growth.

Human capital Refers to the abilities, experience and skills that affect the productivity of workers.

Hyperinflation Very high inflation, usually in excess of 50% per month.

Hysteresis The extreme form of *persistence* that occurs when temporary shocks affect income permanently.

Identity An equation that holds by definition. Example: $w \equiv W/P$.

Import function A mathematical relationship between imports and their determinants. A simple example relates imports to income and the real exchange rate: $IM = m_1 Y - m_2 R$.

Imports Goods and services bought from other countries.

Income distribution The division of total income among households. Governments often try to reduce observed inequality by redistributing income from the rich to the poor.

Income gap Deviation of actual income from potential income.

Increasing returns to scale See *returns to scale.*

Index The compilation of measurements of different items into a single number. Example: the consumer price index combines the prices for goods included in the consumption basket into a single number.

Indexation Serves to maintain the real value of a contract's provisions by tying its nominal values (such as wages, rent or interest rates) to some price *index.*

Indifference curves A graphical representation of preferences that shows all combinations of economic variables that generate the same level of utility.

Inflation The percentage rate at which prices increase.

Inflation bias Exists if the inflation rate in equilibrium keeps above the optimal long-run inflation rate of zero.

Inflation target The rate of inflation that the central bank or the government aims at.

Inflation targeting A monetary policy rule that includes an inflation target, but possibly targets for other variables such as income, the interest rate or the exchange rate as well.

Inflation tax Describes the loss of real income suffered by households due to inflation. Defined as $\pi \frac{M}{P}$, it is the flip side of *seignorage* when the economy is in equilibrium.

Insider–outsider theory A model of the labour market in which the supply of labour is primarily determined by insiders as opposed to outsiders. Insiders are typically workers who are already employed and therefore have a strong influence on wage bargaining. Outsiders are unemployed and have no influence on wage bargaining. Insider–outsider behaviour generates real rigidities and explains involuntary unemployment.

Insiders See *insider–outsider theory*.

Insolvency The inability of debtors to service or repay their debt.

Institutions Economic, political or legal structures within which individuals operate. Examples are formal organizations, written law, and informal customs and norms.

Intensive form of the production function Relates real output per worker to the per-worker endowment with other factors of production (usually capital per worker) and technology. Example: $y = Af(k)$.

Interest parity An equilibrium condition for the international capital market, requiring returns at home to equal (expected) returns abroad. The equation $i = i^{\text{World}} + \frac{E_{+1}^e - E}{E}$ is called uncovered or open interest parity because the return on the right-hand side is an expectation. It is called covered interest parity when the expected exchange rate is replaced with the appropriate forward rate.

Interest rate The price at which funds may be borrowed today and paid back tomorrow. It reflects the cost of borrowing or the return on saving (lending). The real interest rate is the nominal interest rate minus inflation. It deducts from nominal interest payments the purchasing power lost due to price increases. Cf. *Fisher equation*.

Internal rate of return See *rate of return*.

International Monetary Fund (IMF) An organization created in 1944 that oversees the global financial system by following the macroeconomic policies of member countries, and offers financial and technical assistance to members facing balance of payments problems.

International Monetary System Explicit and implicit arrangements that govern monetary relations between countries. A key feature is whether the exchange rate is flexible or fixed.

Intertemporal budget constraint An equation relating spending at different points in time to income accruing at different points in time.

Intertemporal optimization Denotes optimization decisions that include variables observed at different periods of time. Also called dynamic optimization.

Intertemporal substitution The reallocation of consumption or work-hours across time in an effort to increase utility.

Investment The purchase of machines and other equipment to be added to the capital stock and used in production later on.

Involuntary unemployment Members of the *labour force* who would like to work at the current (real) wage rate but cannot find work.

IS curve A goods equilibrium line, usually drawn in an interest rate–income diagram; it combines all combinations of income and the interest rate for which supply equals demand in the goods market.

IS-LM model A macroeconomic model that emphasizes the economy's demand side by focusing on the interaction between the goods market and the money market. Firms are assumed to supply whatever is demanded. The model is useful for the short run and for the global economy or relatively closed national economies.

IS-LM-FE model See *Mundell–Fleming model*.

Keynes, John Maynard British economist (1883–1946) whose ideas had a major and lasting impact on macroeconomics. Taken aback by the Great Depression starting in 1929, he considered drops in aggregate demand a main cause of economic downturns and, therefore, advocated the use of monetary and, especially, fiscal policy to avoid or take the edge off recessions. One of the most influential economists of all time. Cf. *Keynesian cross, Keynesianism.*

Keynesian aggregate supply curve In the extreme case, a horizontal line in a price–income diagram, indicating that firms are prepared to produce whatever is demanded at the current price level. In a more moderate interpretation it has a positive slope, indicating that if prices rise, firms increase output. Cf. *AS (aggregate supply) curve, classical aggregate supply curve, extreme Keynesian aggregate supply curve.*

Keynesian cross A simple model of income determination, cast as a diagram which plots planned expenditure and actual expenditure against income. Equilibrium income obtains where both lines intersect. It shows that a given *exogenous* increase in spending can generate a much larger increase in income. Cf. *multiplier.*

Keynesian macroeconomics See *Keynesianism.*

Keynesianism A macroeconomic school of thought rooted in the ideas of *John Maynard Keynes.* Keynesians believe that stickiness of nominal wages and prices as well as other imperfections prevent markets from clearing quickly or at all. Thus government intervention on the economy's demand side by means of fiscal and monetary policy is called for during economic downturns.

Labour A factor of production, usually measured in hours worked.

Labour demand curve The aggregate labour demand curve shows the (aggregate) quantity of labour demanded by firms at different real wage rates.

Labour force The total number of men and women who are either working or actively looking for a job. Obtained by deducting *voluntary unemployment* from the *active population.*

Labour market The market in which employment (measured in work-hours) and the wage rate are determined through an interaction of labour supply and demand.

Labour productivity Labour productivity (or efficiency or effort) x is defined as output per work-hour, $x \equiv Y/L$. Cf. *unit labour costs, efficiency wage theory.*

Labour supply curve The labour supply curve shows the aggregate quantity of labour supplied by workers (or trade unions) at different real wage rates.

Labour union See *trade union.*

Large open economy An open economy with enough weight to affect the world interest rate and world income. Cf. *small open economy.*

Leakages Those parts of the circular flow of income and spending that disappear from the circle: that is, taxes, saving and imports.

Leverage This refers to the use of borrowed funds instead of one's own funds to acquire assets.

Liquidity trap A situation in which the interest rate is close to zero, so that individuals are prepared to hold

any amount of money that is being supplied. Then a money supply increase cannot lower the interest rate to stimulate investment demand.

LM **curve** The money equilibrium line, usually drawn on an interest rate–income diagram. It identifies combinations of income and the interest rate for which the demand for money equals a given money supply.

Long-run aggregate supply curve A vertical line in a price–income diagram, indicating that in the long run, when prices are as expected, the quantity of goods and services supplied by firms is independent of the price level. Cf. *AS (aggregate supply) curve, classical aggregate supply curve, extreme Keynesian aggregate supply curve, Keynesian aggregate supply curve.*

Long-run equilibrium Obtains after all variables have had time to adjust. Example: potential income in the *AD-AS* model. Cf. *long-run aggregate supply curve, short-run equilibrium.*

Maastricht Treaty Treaty on European Union signed in the Dutch town of Maastricht in 1992. Adding justice and home affairs as well as a common foreign and security policy to existing tasks, it developed the EC into the EU. European citizenship was established, with rights to live, work and vote in other member countries. Integration in employment and social issues was put on the agenda, and the blueprint for EMU and the eventual implementation of the euro was introduced.

Macroeconomics Studies the entire economy from a bird's-eye perspective. Cf. *microeconomics.*

Managed float A mixture between flexible and fixed exchange rates. Central banks intervene to influence the exchange rate, but do not defend a declared fixed rate.

Marginal In strict mathematical definition, 'marginal' means an infinitesimally small change. In less strict practical use, 'marginal' means an increase of a variable by one unit.

Marginal product The extra output produced by increasing a production factor by one unit while holding other factors of production constant. Mathematically speaking, it is the partial derivative of the production function with respect to a production factor.

Marginal propensity to consume Says by how much consumption rises if income increases by one unit.

Marginal rate of substitution (MRS) The rate at which less of one good must be accompanied by more of another to leave utility unchanged. In static analysis we look at two different goods at one point in time. In intertemporal analysis we look at one good at different points in time. Mathematically speaking, the MRS is the slope of an indifference curve.

Marginal tax rate The increase in taxes due to an increase in the tax base by one unit.

Mark-up The difference between the price and the marginal cost of a product.

Market psychology Refers to predictions or expectations that have no adequate foundation in the employed model. It affects financial markets, with eventual macroeconomic consequences, and carries the danger of self-fulfilling prophecy, meaning an initially unfounded prediction causes itself to become true.

Mathematical model A simplified, logically coherent story expressed by means of equations.

Menu costs The costs of changing a price or a wage rate.

Microeconomics Studies individual markets and entities, such as consumers or firms. Cf. *macroeconomics*.

Microfoundations A macroeconomic model possesses microfoundations when it is strictly based on explicit optimizing decisions of households and firms, as applied in microeconomics.

Minimum wage The lowest wage rate set by law or by collective negotiations.

Mismatch unemployment Occurs when the skills or geographic location of workers looking for jobs do not fit the respective pattern of available vacancies. Mismatch unemployment is part of *structural unemployment*.

Model A simplified, logically coherent story that links and explains economic variables like income, consumption and taxes. Cf. *mathematical model*.

Monetarism A school of thought led by Nobel prize laureate Milton Friedman that considers changes in the money supply the primary cause of economic fluctuations, therefore recommending stable money supply growth as suggested by the *Friedman rule* and rejecting activist policies to influence aggregate demand. Cf. *Friedman rule, monetary policy rule*.

Monetary policy Actions taken by the central bank targeting the demand side of the economy, using the money supply or the interest rate as instruments.

Monetary policy rule Makes the use of monetary policy instruments, such as the money supply and the interest rate, dependent on macroeconomic variables such as inflation and the income gap. Cf. *Friedman rule, Taylor rule*.

Monetary union See *currency union*.

Money Anything that sellers generally accept as payment for goods and services.

Money demand function A mathematical relationship between the demand for real money balances and its determinants. Example $L = kY - hi$.

Money illusion Exists when changes in nominal income are mistaken for changes in real income. A person suffers from money illusion if he thinks an increase in his wage rate from €10 to €20 has made him better off even though consumer prices have doubled as well.

Money market Market in which the supply of money provided by the central bank and the economy's demand for money meet and interact.

Money supply The central bank controlled quantity of money in circulation in an economy.

Monopolistic competition Exists if a firm produces a unique good for which there are close substitutes. As a result, the demand for its product increases when the price falls.

Monopoly A firm has a monopoly if it is the only firm to produce a good for which there are no (close) substitutes.

Moral hazard A situation in which agents take excessive risks because someone else bears the cost of their actions.

Multiplier Measures the rise in income resulting from a one-unit increase in autonomous expenditure.

Mundell–Fleming model Open-economy version of the *IS-LM* by Robert Mundell and Marcus Fleming, adding the foreign exchange (FE) market to the goods and money markets behind *IS-LM* to accommodate links of open economies to the rest of the world (hence also *IS-LM-FE* model). It continues to be a workhorse model used by applied economists and policy advisers.

National economy The economy of an individual country.

National income accounts Report data for GDP, its components and other related concepts.

National saving The sum of a country's private saving S and *public saving T − G*.

Natural unemployment See *equilibrium unemployment*.

Neoclassical aggregate supply curve Comprises the classical and the Keynesian aggregate supply curve by permitting price changes to affect aggregate supply in the short run, but not in the long run.

Neoclassical growth model A macroeconomic model for the long run that ignores business cycles. Proposed by *Robert Solow*, it shows saving and population growth rates to determine capital accumulation and per capita income. It explains global income patterns, but attributes economic growth to *exogenous* improvements in *technology*.

Neoclassical synthesis A label for mainstream economics during much of the second half of the 20th century, attributed to Paul Samuelson. It combines a Keynesian emphasis on aggregate demand to model the short run with a classical emphasis on aggregate supply for the long run.

Net taxes The difference between the government's tax revenue and its transfer payments.

Neutrality of money The claim that the money supply does not affect real variables such as income or unemployment.

New classical aggregate supply curve See *neoclassical aggregate supply curve*.

New classical macroeconomics A school of thought that focuses on the interaction of supply and demand decisions made by rational households and firms, and attributes a key role to supply even in the short run. Government intervention is only accepted if 'market failure' can be identified and policies can be shown to be welfare improving. The theory of *real business cycles* falls into this category.

New Keynesian macroeconomics School of thought emphasizing the key role of sticky wages and prices as well as other imperfections for understanding business cycles. It adopts the methodology introduced by the theory of *real business cycles*, while rejecting the paradigm of perfect markets.

No-bailout clause Part of the *Maastricht Treaty*, this is a safeguard against imprudent fiscal policy of EU members, prohibiting the *European Central Bank* from bailing out national governments in case of default.

Nominal Expressed in current currency such as euros or pounds, without looking at prices and thus correcting for changes in buying power. Cf. *real*.

Null hypothesis An initial hypothesis in empirical work. Its name derives from the fact that we check whether it is rejected (or nullified) by the employed data. An example of a null hypothesis is the statement 'The marginal rate of consumption in the equation $C = cY$ is zero.'

Official reserve account In traditional terminology, a balance of payments account that records foreign-currency transactions of the central bank. Cf. *balance of payments*.

Okun's law One version states that income growth is negatively related to the change in the rate of

unemployment. Another version states that the *income gap* is proportional to the difference between the actual and the equilibrium rate of unemployment.

Open economy An economy that trades goods, services and financial assets with other countries.

Open interest parity See *interest parity*.

Open-market operations The central bank's purchases or sales of bonds (or other financial instruments) in order to change the money supply.

Optimum currency area A region or group of countries that benefits from having a common currency.

Ordinary least squares (OLS) estimation A method used in econometrics for estimating unknown coefficients of a model from empirical data. The success is gauged by statistics like the coefficient of determination or the *t*-value. Cf. *regression analysis*.

Organization for Economic Cooperation and Development (OECD) A group of thirty developed countries committed to democracy and free markets. Founded in 1961, it publishes economic and social data, analyzes and forecasts economic developments, and researches changes and evolving patterns in areas such as trade, environment, agriculture and technology.

Organization of Petroleum Exporting Countries (OPEC) A group of thirteen oil-producing countries from the Middle East, Africa and South America that collaborates in managing oil exports to the rest of the world. Founded in 1960, OPEC accounts for two-thirds of global oil reserves and one-third of production. It gained prominence during the first oil price explosion of 1973.

Output gap See *income gap*.

Outsiders See *insider–outsider theory*.

Overshooting Occurs if the immediate, temporary response of the exchange rate to a disturbance (such as a money supply increase) exceeds the response observed in the long run.

Overvaluation (of a currency) Exists when the purchase of goods abroad is cheaper than at home.

Pact for Stability and Growth This pact was agreed on by the EU member states in 1996. It aims at ensuring a long-term orientation of fiscal policy. In essence, the pact is to prevent members from running excessive budget deficits. In a 2005 reform, the pact's rules have been made more flexible.

Partial production function Graphical display of how output varies with changes in one factor of production, while holding all other inputs and technology constant.

Peak See *boom*.

Perfect foresight As a theoretical concept, this assumes that individuals know and foresee everything, taking the concept of rational expectations to the extreme. Cf. *adaptive expectations*, *economically rational expectations*, *rational expectations*.

Persistence The tendency of income and other variables to digest temporary shocks only slowly.

Phillips curve A negative empirical relationship between nominal wage growth and the rate of unemployment discovered by A. W. Phillips in 1958. It was later modified and expanded into a theory explaining inflation using the *income gap* instead of unemployment, and including inflation expectations. Today it is also understood as a theoretical building block of macroeconomic models.

Planned investment That part of investment spending undertaken voluntarily, according to plan. Cf. *unplanned investment*.

Policy effectiveness Refers to whether monetary and fiscal policy influence real variables such as income.

Political business cycles Refer to booms and recessions deliberately generated by governments in order to improve re-election prospects.

Potential income The income that could be generated with the current capital stock if the labour market were in equilibrium.

Poverty trap A stable low-income equilibrium in a macroeconomic model with multiple equilibria. Escape from poverty traps requires exogenous intervention such as foreign aid or the opening of capital markets.

Preferences Indicate what people want, and how badly they want it. They are often expressed as a utility function or indifference curves.

Present value States how much a payment at a future date is worth today. Computed by deducting interest payments expected to accrue between dates.

Primary deficit See *deficit*.

Procyclical variable Moves down (up) when income moves down (up) during the business cycle. Example: employment in the *DAD-SAS* model. Cf. *countercyclical variable*.

Producer price index Measures the average price of goods and services produced in a country. Cf. *consumer price index (CPI)*.

Production function A mathematical relationship, specifying how output depends on the factors of production and technology. Example: $Y = A \times F(K, L)$.

Public debt See *debt*.

Public saving The excess of (net) tax revenue, i.e. taxes minus transfers, over government expenditure. Cf. *national saving*.

Purchasing power parity (PPP) Denotes the exchange rate E^{PPP} that equates prices abroad and at home in domestic currency: $E^{PPP} \times P^{World} = P$.

Quantitative easing The purchase of long-term government or commercial bonds in order to reduce the difference between long-term and short-term interest rates. Typically used when short-term interest rates are already near zero.

Quantity equation An identity stating that the money supply times the velocity of money circulation equals nominal income: $M \times V = P \times Y$.

Quantity theory of money A theory based on the *quantity equation*. Assuming that the velocity of money circulation is constant, it asserts that changes in the money supply lead to changes in nominal income.

R^2 See *coefficient of determination*.

Random walk Time path of a variable that is just as likely to rise next period as to fall. The change in such a variable is not predictable. The expected change is zero.

Rate of return The revenue generated by a project as a percentage of the invested funds, converted to an annualized rate.

Rating See *credit rating*.

Rating agency See *credit rating agency*.

Rational expectations Expectations formed by drawing on all available information. This may include a wide set of variables, or even knowledge of a macroeconomic model such as *DAD-SAS*. Cf. *adaptive expectations*, *economically rational expectations*, *perfect foresight*.

Real Expressed in constant prices; corrected for inflation. Real variables are obtained by dividing the respective nominal variable by the price level: Example: $w \equiv W/P$.

Real business cycles Macroeconomic models based on explicit microfoundations, assuming that all markets clear at all times and that economic fluctuations can be attributed to shocks to technology and preferences. There is no role for nominal variables such as money.

Real exchange rate The ratio between the price of a bundle of goods abroad and at home in domestic currency: $R = E \times \frac{P^{\text{World}}}{P}$. Cf. *exchange rate, purchasing power parity* (*PPP*).

Real interest rate See *interest rate*.

Real-wage rigidity Exists if wage rates do not fall despite unemployment.

Recession Decline of income relative to and below the path of *potential income* which bottoms out in a trough. Cf. *business cycle, boom, depression*.

Regression analysis A statistical method used in econometrics that models a dependent (explained) variable as a function of one or more independent (explanatory) variables and a random error term. Example: $C = c_0 + c_1 Y + \varepsilon$. Parameters are estimated so as to give the 'best fit' to the data, which is often evaluated by using the method of *ordinary least squares*. Regressions help quantify relationships, make forecasts or test hypotheses.

Relative convergence hypothesis See *convergence hypothesis*.

Representative agents models Assume all individuals to be alike regarding preferences and other features that determine behaviour. Hence, one representative individual can be singled out for the study of an entire economy.

Requirement line Shows the level of investment required to keep the capital stock at the indicated level. It is a key building block of the *neoclassical growth model*.

Reserve ratio A commercial bank's *reserves* as a fraction of all demand deposits it has issued. Regulations specifying respective details are called reserve requirements.

Reserve requirements See *reserve ratio*.

Reserves Money that banks have received from depositors but which they have not used to extend, because of reserve requirements or voluntarily.

Returns to scale Production functions have constant returns to scale if raising all inputs by a given factor increases output by the same factor, or proportionally. If output increases more than proportionally, there are increasing returns to scale (or economies of scale). If it increases less than proportionally, there are decreasing returns to scale (or diseconomies of scale). Cf. *economies of scale*.

Revaluation An increase in the value (and, hence, in the price) of a currency relative to other currencies induced by the government under a regime of fixed exchange rates. Cf. *devaluation*.

Ricardian equivalence theorem Proposition advanced by British classical economist David Ricardo (1772–1823) postulating that government deficit spending does not affect national saving, because households realize that running a deficit and adding to the public debt today will lead to higher interest payments and eventual repayment via higher taxes in the future.

Risk aversion An individual is risk averse if she prefers a guaranteed payment of less than €500 to playing a free lottery in which she can win either €0 or €1,000 with a probability of 50% each. Cf. *risk premium*.

Risk neutrality An individual is risk neutral if she is indifferent between a guaranteed payment of €500, and playing a free lottery in which she can win either €0 or €1,000 with a probability of 50% each.

Risk premium The additional payment (added to an interest rate or other return) required for engaging in a deal with an uncertain outcome.

Sacrifice ratio The loss of income as a percentage of potential income caused by reducing inflation by one percentage point.

SAS (surprise aggregate supply) curve The dynamic version of the *AS (aggregate supply) curve*. It indicates how much output firms are willing to produce at various levels of inflation.

Saving The part of *disposable income* not spend on consumption. Cf. *national saving, public saving*.

Secular trend The general direction in which a variable moves over a century or longer.

Securitization The process of taking an illiquid asset, such as a house or a mortgage, and packaging it into a security, that is, a paper, which is easily traded.

Seignorage The purchasing power the government endows itself with when printing money. Defined as $\mu M/P$, it is the flip side of the *inflation tax* when the economy is in equilibrium.

Shock An unexpected change in a parameter or exogenous variable of an economic relationship.

Shoe leather costs The costs incurred by reduced money holdings: say, by having to take more frequent trips to the bank.

Short-run equilibrium Obtains within a time horizon during which some slow or sticky variables may not have adjusted. Example: the *AD (aggregate demand) curve* and *AS (aggregate supply) curve* intersect in a short-run equilibrium where inflation expectations may be wrong. Cf. *long-run equilibrium*.

Significance test Asks whether the deviation of one or more estimated coefficients from the values proposed by the *null hypothesis* may have occurred by chance. A coefficient is considered significant, and the null hypothesis is rejected, when the probability that it occurred by chance is below a given threshold. The significance of a coefficient is often evaluated using the *t-statistic*.

Small open economy An open national economy too small to have a noticeable effect on the rest of the world, thus considering the world interest rate and world income exogenous variables. Cf. *global economy, large open economy, open economy, national economy*.

Solow, Robert M. A US economist (born 1924) particularly known for his work on the theory of economic growth. He was awarded the Nobel Prize in Economic Sciences in 1987.

Solow growth model, Solow model See *neoclassical growth model*.

Solow residual An estimate of the rate of change in total factor productivity. Computed as the part of income growth that *growth accounting* cannot attribute to changes in observable factors of production.

Sovereign debt crisis A situation in which a government (a sovereign) has difficulty servicing and/or repaying its debt.

Speculative attacks Occur when investors sell a currency because they expect a devaluation under fixed exchange rates, often spurred by balance of payments imbalances and a drop in foreign exchange reserves (needed to intervene in defence of the current exchange rate). The danger in such attacks is that they may constitute self-fulfilling prophecies. Cf. *market psychology*.

Speculative bubble A situation in which investors pay a price that exceeds the fundamental value of an asset or good in anticipation of even higher prices in the future.

Stability and Growth Pact See *Pact for Stability and Growth*.

Stable equilibrium See *equilibrium*.

Stagflation A combination of stagnation and inflation. Unemployment rises (income falls) and inflation increases, at the same time. Often caused by a negative (adverse) supply shock.

Standing facility An open credit or deposit line maintained by central banks available to commercial banks as needed to manage short-run fluctuations in liquidity. Examples: the Eurosystem's marginal lending and credit facilities.

Steady state A very long-run equilibrium that is relevant in growth models, requiring the capital stock to be at its equilibrium level.

Stickiness A variable is sticky if it temporarily resists change. Sticky prices and wages play key roles in modern macroeconomics. Causes include long-term contracts, *menu costs*, *money illusion* and imperfect information.

Sticky prices Prices that need time to adjust and thus do not always equilibrate supply and demand.

Sticky wages Wages that adjust slowly and thus do not always equilibrate supply and demand in the labour market.

Stock variable A stock variable is measured at a point in time. Examples: the money supply, employment and the exchange rate. Cf. *flow variable*.

Structural unemployment Structural unemployment is unemployment that does not go away in equilibrium. It is similar to and often used interchangeably with *equilibrium unemployment*.

Stylized fact A simplified presentation of empirical findings. While holding in general, deviations may be detected under scrutiny.

Supply shock A change in a parameter or exogenous variable involved in the economy's supply side. Example: Oil price explosion. Cf. *shock*.

Swiss National Bank The central bank of Switzerland.

Systemic risk The risk that the collapse of an individual entity or component of an economy may bring down the entire financial system or even the economy.

Target zone A hybrid exchange rate system, with elements of fixed and flexible exchange rate regimes. The exchange rate is flexible within a band around a fixed parity, but central banks must intervene when the rate approaches the upper or lower bound.

Tax rate The percentage of the tax base (income or sales) paid to the government.

Tax wedge The difference between the labour costs of firms and the wage that workers take home.

Taylor rule US economist John Taylor suggested that the *Fed* lets the interest rate deviate from its target if inflation differs from its target and/or there is an *income gap*. Cf. *Friedman rule, policy rule*.

Technology Method that transforms the factors of production into output. Often used interchangeably with *total factor productivity*.

Technology shock A one-time change in production.

Time inconsistency When time inconsistency is at work, a policy that seems optimal today is no longer considered optimal when it is time to act.

Total factor productivity A measure of technology that affects the productivity of all factors of production. Empirically, it is approximated via the *Solow residual*.

Trade union An alliance of workers to bargain collectively with firms over wages, hours, and working conditions, and to promote the welfare of workers in general.

Transfers See *government transfers*.

Trend The general direction in which a variable moves over time, ignoring short- to medium-run fluctuations.

Trough See *recession*.

t-statistic In *regression analysis*, the *t*-statistic is used to gauge the *significance* of a parameter estimate. Example and rule of thumb: if the absolute *t*-statistic exceeds 2, the estimated coefficient is said to be significantly different from 0.

Twin deficits Said to exist if an economy shows both a deficit on the current account and a government budget deficit.

Uncovered interest parity See *interest parity*.

Undervaluation (of a currency) Exists when the purchase of goods at home is cheaper than abroad.

Unemployment That part of the *active population* which is currently out of work. Composed of *voluntary* and *involuntary unemployment*. Cf. *cyclical unemployment*, *frictional unemployment*, *involuntary unemployment*, *structural unemployment*, *voluntary unemployment*.

Unemployment rate In theory, *involuntary unemployment* as a percentage of the *labour force*. In empirical data, some *voluntary unemployment* may have sneaked in.

Unit labour costs The wage costs per unit of output.

Unplanned investment Involuntary inventory changes by firms because they have misjudged demand and produced too much or too little.

Velocity of money A measure of the speed at which money changes hands, defined as the ratio of nominal income to the money supply.

Voluntary unemployment That part of the active population which is out of work but would not want to work at the current wage rate anyway. Cf. *involuntary unemployment, unemployment*.

Wage share The proportion of income paid out to workers.

Wealth The sum of an individual's or household's financial and physical assets.

World Bank A potent international organization with 185 member countries, set up after the Second World War, with the mission of eliminating global poverty by giving loans and offering advice and training in both the private and public sectors of developing countries. Critics accuse it of a neo-liberal agenda and promotion of Western interests.

World Trade Organization (WTO) An international organization with the prime objective of removing barriers to trade in goods and services, and intellectual property. It also administers global trade agreements and resolves disputes.

Online resources

A smart phone version of the glossary is available at www.eurmacro.eu/mobile/glossary.html

Economics Nobel prize winners and earlier giants

The brightest minds in the field of economics have paved the way for and contributed to the consolidated body of knowledge presented in this textbook. Many of those have been awarded **The Sveriges Riksbank Prize in Economic Sciences in Memory of Alfred Nobel.** Of the 69 laureates who have been honoured since the prize was established in 1969, we highlight those with the most direct bearing on the concepts and models taught and the general approach taken in this textbook.

Nobel prize laureates – with direct bearing on intermediate macroeconomics

George Akerlof Efficiency wages
Nobel prize in 2001 together with A. Michael Spence and Joseph E. Stiglitz, 'for their analyses of markets with asymmetric information'.

James Buchanan Political economy
Nobel prize in 1986, 'for his development of the contractual and constitutional bases for the theory of economic and political decision-making'.

Milton Friedman Expectations and monetary theory
Nobel prize in 1976, 'for his achievement in the fields of consumption analysis, monetary history and theory and for his demonstration of the complexity of stabilization policy'.

John Hicks *IS-LM* model
Nobel prize in 1972 together with Kenneth J. Arrow, 'for their pioneering contributions to general economic equilibrium theory and welfare theory'.

Paul Krugman Liquidity traps, crashes, crises
Nobel prize in 2008, 'for his analysis of trade patterns and location of economic activity'.

Finn Kydland Time inconsistency, real business cycles
Nobel prize in 2004 together with Edward S. Prescott, 'for their contributions to dynamic macroeconomics:

the time consistency of economic policy and the driving forces behind business cycles'.

Robert E. Lucas Rational expectations
Nobel prize in 1995, 'for having developed and applied the hypothesis of rational expectations, and thereby having transformed macroeconomic analysis and deepened our understanding of economic policy'.

Franco Modigliani Consumption behaviour
Nobel prize in 1985, 'for his pioneering analyses of saving and of financial markets'.

Robert Mundell *IS-LM-FE* or Mundell–Fleming model
Nobel prize in 1999, 'for his analysis of monetary and fiscal policy under different exchange rate regimes and his analysis of optimum currency areas'.

John Nash Game theory
Nobel prize in 1994, together with John C. Harsanyi and Reinhard Selten, 'for their pioneering analysis of equilibria in the theory of non-cooperative games'.

Edmund S. Phelps Golden rule of capital accumulation; natural rate of unemployment Nobel prize in 2006, 'for his analysis of intertemporal tradeoffs in macroeconomic policy'.

Edward S. Prescott Time inconsistency; real business cycles
Nobel prize in 2004 together with Finn E. Kydland, 'for their contributions to dynamic macroeconomics: the time consistency of economic policy and the driving forces behind business cycles'.

Paul A. Samuelson Consumer theory; comparative statics; neoclassical synthesis
Nobel prize in 1970, 'for the scientific work through which he has developed static and dynamic economic theory and actively contributed to raising the level of analysis in economic science'.

Thomas J. Sargent   Rational expectations
Nobel prize in 2011 together with Christopher A. Sims, 'for their empirical research on cause and effect in the macroeconomy'.

Reinhard Selten   Game theory
Nobel prize in 1994 together with John Nash, 'for their pioneering analysis of equilibria in the theory of non-cooperative games'.

Christopher A. Sims   Rational expectations
Nobel prize in 2011 together with Thomas J. Sargent, 'for their empirical research on cause and effect in the macroeconomy'.

Robert M. Solow   Neoclassical or Solow growth model, Solow residual
Nobel prize in 1987, 'for his contributions to the theory of economic growth'.

Joseph E. Stiglitz   Efficiency wages
Nobel prize in 2001 together with George A. Akerlof and Michael Spence, 'for their analyses of markets with asymmetric information'.

James Tobin   Money demand (Baumol–Tobin model)
Nobel prize in 1981, 'for his analysis of financial markets and their relations to expenditure decisions, employment, production and prices'.

Earlier giants

Modern macroeconomics has its roots in the works of so-called *classical* economists. While their work lacked the mathematical tools, the statistical methods as well as the data available to current generations, many ideas that characterize contemporary thinking can be found in their work.

Reflecting the superior stage of industrial development and material wealth of their time, most classical economists were of British origin. **Adam Smith** (1723–91) and other classical economists, including **Thomas Malthus** (1766–1834), **David Ricardo** (1772–1823) and **John Stuart Mill** (1806–73), focused on the economy's supply side.

Formidable classical or preclassical economists from other countries include **François Quesnay** (1694–1774) of France, who introduced the circular flow of income and, thus, the first macroeconomic model on record, and **Heinrich von Thünen** (1783–1850) of Germany.

Subsequent generations produced a steady flow of new ideas, spurred by the events and experiences of their times, bringing us to what we know and how we perceive the economy today. Those who contributed massively include the following:

Leon Walras (France, 1834–1910) was the first mathematical economist. He revolutionized economics with his rigorous formal analysis of the price system.

Alfred Marshall (England, 1842–1924) introduced demand and supply curves as theoretical concepts, as well as the critical distinction between the short run and the long run.

Irving Fisher (United States, 1867–1947) was one of the first to employ sophisticated statistical techniques. His work on money and prices provided the basis for later theoretical work in economics. It lives on in various versions of the Fisher equation.

John Maynard Keynes (England, 1883–1946) introduced emphasis on the demand side. By many he was considered the most influential macroeconomist of all time, and certainly also one of the most controversial. Keynesianism is a school of thought that attributes a key role to the demand side of the economy, as opposed to classical and new classical economics which focus on the supply side.

Online resources

A smart phone version of this appendix with video clips from the Lindau Nobel Laureate Meetings is available at www.eurmacro.eu/mobile/nobelprizemain.html

INDEX

Note: Page numbers in **bold** refer to definitions of terms